GREEN GOVERNANCE

The vast majority of the world's scientists agree: we have reached a point in history where we are in grave danger of destroying Earth's life-sustaining capacity. But our attempts to protect natural ecosystems are increasingly ineffective because our very conception of the problem is limited; we treat "the environment" as its own separate realm, taking for granted prevailing but outmoded conceptions of economics, national sovereignty, and international law. *Green Governance* is a direct response to the mounting calls for a paradigm shift in the way humans relate to the natural environment. It opens the door to a new set of solutions by proposing a compelling new synthesis of environmental protection based on broader notions of economics and human rights and on commons-based governance. Going beyond speculative abstractions, the book proposes a new architecture of environmental law and public policy that is as practical as it is theoretically sound.

Burns H. Weston is the Bessie Dutton Murray Distinguished Professor of Law Emeritus and Senior Scholar of the Center for Human Rights at The University of Iowa. A longtime – now honorary – member of the Board of Editors of the *American Journal of International Law* and a Fellow of the World Academy of Art and Science, he has authored, co-authored, and co-edited many books and articles, especially in international human rights and related international law fields. He also is known as an "engaged scholar," and for his activism and scholarship bridging human rights and environmental law he was awarded the honorary degree of Doctor of Laws (LL.D.) by Vermont Law School in 2009.

David Bollier is an author, activist, and independent scholar of the commons. He is the author or editor of twelve books, including four on various aspects of the commons. He is co-founder of the Commons Strategies Group, an international consulting project, and co-founder of Public Knowledge, a Washington advocacy group for the public's stake in copyright and Internet policies. Bollier is also Senior Fellow at the Norman Lear Center at the USC Annenberg School for Communication and Journalism, winner of the Bosch Prize in Public Policy at the American Academy in Berlin (Fall 2012), and a longtime rapporteur for the Aspen Institute.

Green Governance

ECOLOGICAL SURVIVAL, HUMAN RIGHTS, AND THE LAW OF THE COMMONS

BURNS H. WESTON
The University of Iowa College of Law

DAVID BOLLIER
Commons Strategies Group

For Mark.
with appreciation
for what you do.
Burns Weston
4/21/15

CAMBRIDGE
UNIVERSITY PRESS

CAMBRIDGE
UNIVERSITY PRESS

32 Avenue of the Americas, New York NY 10013-2473, USA

Cambridge University Press is part of the University of Cambridge.

It furthers the University's mission by disseminating knowledge in the pursuit of education, learning and research at the highest international levels of excellence.

www.cambridge.org
Information on this title: www.cambridge.org/9781107415447

First published 2013
First paperback edition 2014

A catalogue record for this publication is available from the British Library

Library of Congress Cataloguing in Publication data

Weston, Burns H., 1933–
Green governance : ecological survival, human rights, and the law of the commons / Burns H.
Weston, David Bollier.
  p.   cm.
Includes bibliographical references (p.) and index.
ISBN 978-1-107-03436-5 (hardback)
1. Environmental law – Philosophy.   2. Human rights – Environmental aspects.
3. Commons.   4. Global commons.   5. Environmental law, International – Philosophy.
6. Environmental protection – International cooperation.   7. Environmental justice.
I. Bollier, David.   II. Title.
k3585 .w476
344.04'6–dc23   2012029091

ISBN 978-1-107-03436-5 Hardback
ISBN 978-1-107-41544-7 Paperback

To our children and their families
Timothy, Leah, and Emma
Rebecca, Eduardo, Elijah, and Isabella
Malin and John
Martin, Linda, Olivia, and Cecilia
Johannes, Cathrine, Sima, and Joar

Samuel and Thomas

and all other children and grandchildren
who will have to contend
with the Anthropocene Age

Contents

Acknowledgments

Upon completing books, authors come to realize how, along the way, many helping hands make the entire journey possible. This was certainly the case with *Green Governance*. What began as a series of informed hunches, an essay then too long to meet standard law review page limitations, was allowed to expand and mature through the support of many generous and insightful people of varied talents.

Our first debt of gratitude must go to Harriet Barlow and the Harold K. Hochschild Foundation for having had sufficient faith in our vision to give us an indispensable seed grant. In the same spirit, University of Iowa College of Law Dean Gail Agrawal and Director of Financial Aid and Research Assistantships Susan Palmer provided much-needed research assistant support in both the early and late stages of our endeavor; and the staff of The University of Iowa Center for Human Rights assured us essential logistical and moral support throughout. Further, as our work germinated, we were fortunate to encounter Burns Weston's longtime friend Victor Arango who, as if on cue, introduced us to the Arsenault Family Foundation, which, thanks to Marcel Arsenault, provided significant, vital support toward the completion of our Book. Particularly helpful – and ever gracious, too – was Meadow Didier, former Program Director of the Arsenault Family Foundation, who clearly saw the value of our ideas and helped shepherd them forward.

We are similarly indebted to John Berger, Senior Editor at Cambridge University Press, who saw immediately the potential of our project and cheered us onward well before our manuscript was completed and ready for copy editors' eyes. Such publisher faith and encouragement is by no means commonplace, and it emboldened us to work more speedily and effectively than otherwise we might have done.

The preparation of a book of complexity such as ours entails much research, fact-checking, editorial intervention, and administrative assistance. For these tasks, we are especially grateful to Samuel M. DeGree, first as a law student research assistant at The University of Iowa College of Law, later as our full-time research associate. Early on, former Iowa law students Scott O. McKenzie, Suzan M. Pritchett, and Wan-chun (Dora) Wang graced us with insightful imaginations and research skills; in the closing months, Charles Michael Judd, newly elected *Iowa Law Review* Editor-in-Chief, gave adroitly and generously of his empathetic proofreading and source-checking expertise. We thank also Iowa law student Courtney L. Burks who helped us ever so graciously with our bibliography.

Words alone, however, cannot express adequately our profound gratitude to our friend (and early "co-conspirator") Anne Mackinnon, who selflessly shared her wise counsel and acute eye in editing, greatly improving our final manuscript preceding its submission to Cambridge University Press. For a book that pushes the boundaries of conventional wisdom, it is important to have smart, trustworthy friends who are willing to share their expertise and speak insightful – sometimes hard – truths. Anne is and was such a friend.

Much the same can be said of numerous others from whom we benefited greatly. We are especially grateful to those who, in a late October 2011 workshop, gave generously of their busy schedules to spend several days with us providing invaluable critiques of an earlier version of our manuscript and suggestions for how to improve it: Peter Barnes, Michel Bauwens, Jonathan C. Carlson, John Clippinger, Samuel Degree, Meadow Didier, Silke Helfrich, Stephen Humphreys, Anne Mackinnon, Bryan Norton, James Quilligan, Dinah Shelton, and Jack Tuholske.

We thank also Norman Lear for his generous hospitality in allowing us and our October 2011 workshop colleagues to meet at The Gulley, his inspiring retreat in southern Vermont. It is surely among the finest settings anywhere for serious yet informal conversation on chilly autumn days.

Along the way, we received invaluable substantive and tactical advice and encouragement from Richard Falk, Hermann Hatzfeld, Bill McKibben, David Orr, Sir Geoffrey Palmer, Francesca Rheannon, Geoffrey Shields, James Gustave Speth, Mary Christina Wood, and Blaikie and Robert Worth. We are deeply appreciative of their support.

Burns Weston wishes to recall, in addition, a tribute to his longtime colleague and friend Michael Reisman of Yale Law School, made at the outset of the original essay from which this book evolved. The tribute was written to make amends for an intent and circumstance that did not rhyme soon enough to contribute to a much-deserved festschrift honoring Professor Reisman and his fecund career: *Looking to the Future: Essays on International Law in Honor of W. Michael Reisman* (2010). Yet, as our essay, though posted for viewing at *www.commonslawproject.org*, never was officially published, this tribute is, therefore, formally – and happily – reaffirmed here. Anyone familiar with Reisman's brilliant *Law in Brief Encounters* (1999) will understand why – and why in our prior essay and this book in particular.

Finally, Burns Weston thanks Marta Cullberg Weston whose acute insight, personal sacrifice, and amazing patience proved to be a treasured asset from beginning to end, always willing was she to bend a new idea or pursue a daring line of thought. With her: book. Without her: no book.

David Bollier is grateful once again to Ellen Bollier for her love, good cheer, and encouragement throughout the odyssey of another book.

Prologue

At least since Rachel Carson's *Silent Spring*,[1] we have known about humankind's squandering of nonrenewable resources, its careless disregard of precious life species, and its overall contamination and degradation of delicate ecosystems.[2] In the last decade or so, these defilements have assumed a systemic dimension. Buoyed by capital surpluses not easily reinvested in ordinary production streams, business enterprises, commonly with the blessings if not the active partnership of government, are fiercely commercializing countless resources that were once beyond the reach of technology and markets – genetic material, nanoscale matter, large swaths of the ocean, major aquifers, the orbital paths of space, and much else. David Bollier has called this great, unacknowledged scandal of our time a "silent theft" and "the private plunder of our common wealth."[3]

The consequences visited on our natural environment, compounded by those sustained by our economy, communities, social fabric, and culture,

---

[1] Rachel Carson, *Silent Spring* (1962). Note also the publication in the same year of Paul Brooks & Joseph Foote, "The Disturbing Story of Project Chariot," *Harper's*, Apr. 19, 1962, at 60, exposing and ultimately hastening the demise of theoretical physicist Edward Teller's geo-engineering plans to detonate nuclear devices with 160 times the explosive power dropped on Hiroshima to create a deep water harbor on Cape Thompson on Alaska's Chukchi Sea coast 30 miles southeast of the Inupiat Eskimo village of Point Hope. "Our ability to alter the earth we live on is . . . appalling," the authors wrote. *Id.*

[2] In the United States at least, we in fact have known about the ecological damage that humans have wrought on our planet ever since George Perkins Marsh's *Man and Nature*, originally published in 1864, later republished in 1965 by The Belknap Press of Harvard University Press and again in 2003 by the University of Washington Press. Marsh, a diplomat and conservationist born in Woodstock, Vermont, whose work against clearcut foresting played a role in the creation of the Adirondack Park, is considered by many to have been America's first environmentalist.

[3] *See* David Bollier, *Silent Theft: The Private Plunder of Our Common Wealth* (2003).

have been ruinous. Briefly put, the State and Market, in pursuit of commercial development and profit, have failed to internalize the environmental and social costs of their pursuits and, in so doing, have neglected to take measures to preserve or reproduce the preconditions of capitalist production. The results include pollution and waste in the form of acid rain, hydrocarbon emissions, poisoned waterways, and toxic waste dumps; short-term overuse and destruction of natural resources such as forests, waterways, and fisheries, along with the roads, bridges, harbors, and other material infrastructure needed for their exploitation; and the devaluation of urban and other human settlements, exemplified by "brownfields" and suburban sprawl, which especially affect the poor and racial and other minorities. The policies and practices responsible for this state of affairs are morally and economically unacceptable; they are also environmentally unsustainable.

But the grim story does not end here. Lately, we have come to realize the extent to which atmospheric emission of carbon dioxide and other greenhouse gases – and consequent global warming and climate change – exacerbate the impact of those practices, imperil human rights, and threaten Planet Earth to an arguably unprecedented degree.[4]

The details are well documented, thanks to the United Nations Intergovernmental Panel on Climate Change (IPCC) and other authoritative sources.[5] In

---

[4] Bill McKibben, early to sound the alarm about global warming, titled his recent book *Earth: Making a Life on a Tough New Planet* (2010) to signify that already we have created a planet fundamentally different from the one into which most readers of this book were born. *See also* James Lovelock, *The Revenge of Gaia: Why the Earth Is Fighting Back – and How We Can Still Save Humanity* (2006); ——, *The Vanishing Face of Gaia: A Final Warning* (2009).

[5] Most of what follows is based on the findings of the IPCC. Although recently subject to political attack from those who would deny or diminish its core findings, it is widely and justifiably considered to be the primary source of scientifically based information on climate change. Established in 1988 by the World Meteorological Organization (WMO), a specialized agency of the United Nations (UN), and the UN Environment Programme (UNEP) to address the trends and risks of climate change, its assessment reports are based on peer-reviewed, published scientific findings. Its Fourth Assessment Report, published in 2007, was derived from more than 2,500 scientific experts, 800 contributing authors, and 450 lead authors from more than 130 countries. Co-winner (with former US Vice President Al Gore) of the Nobel Peace Prize in 2007, the IPCC is currently working on its Fifth Assessment Report, to be finalized in 2014. Its website provides abundant further information. *See* Intergovernmental Panel on Climate Change, *http://www.ipcc.ch* (accessed May 23, 2012).

Other authoritative sources on which we have relied include the US Global Change Research Program, which, begun in 1989 and, as stated on its website, "coordinates and integrates federal research on changes in the global environment and their implications for society" [US Global Change Research Program, *www.globalchange.gov* (accessed Apr. 12, 2012)]; the Millennium Ecosystem Assessment, called for by former UN Secretary-General Kofi Annan in 2000, initiated in 2001, and involving, as announced on its website, "the work of more than 1,360 experts worldwide . . . [in] state-of-the-art scientific appraisal of the condition

just the next two decades or less, without significant mitigation of greenhouse gas emissions we face a *minimum* 0.64°C—0.69°C (1.17°F—1.242°F) increase in Earth's mean surface air temperature (currently approximately 15°C, 59°F) and a "*likely*... 2°C—4.5°C" (2.6°F—8.1°F) increase "with a *most likely* value of about 3°C" (5.4°F) within the same time frame.[6] These predicted temperature increases are believed to be irreversible within the next five to ten years and therefore potentially catastrophic in future years, within the lifetimes of the majority of the world's population. Already they play a major role in the present-day loss of land, forests, freshwater systems, and biodiversity, and are projected to cause significant sea level rises;[7] a greater incidence of extreme weather; intensified flooding and soil erosion; expanded heat waves, droughts, and fires; the disappearance of life-sustaining glacial flows to major cities; aggravated desertification and crop failures (including Amazonian rain forest depletion and wheat crop losses in northern latitudes); famine in more than half the fifty-four countries of Africa; swelling populations of refugees in search

and trends in the world's ecosystems and the services they provide..." [Millenium Ecosystem Assessment, *http://www.maweb.org/en/Index.aspx* (accessed Apr. 12, 2012)]; and UNEP's February 2012 Working Paper focusing on the continent arguably most vulnerable to climate change in the world. United Nations Development Programme, *Demographic Projections: The Environment and Food Security in Sub-Saharan Africa* (Working Paper 2012–001, Feb. 2012), *http://web.undp.org/africa/knowledge/working-afhdr-demography-environment.pdf* (accessed May 1, 2012). See also Kirstin Dow & Thomas E. Downing, *The Atlas of Climate Change: Mapping the World's Greatest Challenge* (3d ed. 2011); Al Gore, *An Inconvenient Truth: The Planetary Emergency of Global Warming and What We Can Do About It* (2006); James Hansen, *Storms of My Grandchildren: The Truth About the Coming Climate Catastrophe* (2009); Lovelock, *supra* note 4; Mark Lynas, *Six Degrees: Our Future on a Hotter Planet* (2008); National Research Council, *Abrupt Climate Change: Inevitable Surprises* (National Academy of Sciences, 2002); Sir Nicholas Stern, *The Economics of Climate Change: The Stern Review* (2007) [hereinafter "Stern Review"].

[6] G.A. Meehl et al. "Global Climate Projections," in *Climate Change 2007: The Physical Science Basis Contribution of Working Group I to the Fourth Assessment Report of the Intergovernmental Panel on Climate Change* 749 (S. Solomon et al. eds., 2007) (emphasis added), available at *http://www.ipcc.ch/pdf/assessment-report/ar4-wg1-wg1-chapter10.pdf* (accessed May 1, 2012). True, we do not know precisely how much and how fast our planet will heat up during this century. It is difficult to make exact predictions about how long greenhouse gas emissions will continue to increase and how exactly Earth's interdependent ecosystems will react to warmer temperatures. But we do know that Earth's temperature has increased by 6°C in the last 100 years and that, without major human intervention, it is destined to get dangerously warmer – from 2°C to 6°C – within the coming 50–100 years. The authors of *The Atlas of Climate Change*, *supra* note 6, put it this way: "The pre-industrial concentration of carbon dioxide (CO_2) was 280 parts per million in the atmosphere. Most emissions scenarios expect a concentration of over 520 parts per million by 2100 in the absence of concerned climate policy." *Id.* at 40.

[7] The Greenland ice sheet is estimated to tip into irreversible melt when global warming rises to a range of only 1.9°C to 4.6°C (3.42°F–8.28°F) relative to preindustrial temperatures. *Id.* at 752.

of food and water (increasingly in the face of armed resistance); wider spreading of water- and vector-borne diseases; and the likely extinction of one-third
of all species.

More specifically, observe the IPCC, the United Nations Development
Programme, and other leading authorities,[8] Africa is threatened by projected
severe heat and consequent water stress to lose up to 247 million acres of
cropland by 2050, equal to the size of all US commodity cropland. The loss
of glaciers in the Tibetan Plateau will jeopardize the water supply of 1.5
billion Asians. Entire island nations will confront probable extinction, their
sovereignty swallowed by rising seas – imagine 75 million Pacific Islanders
swept from their homes into refugee status. Indigenous cultures – the Arctic
Inuit and Amazonian Kamayurá, for example – will likely wither away for
lack of food caused by overheated and receding habitats. Desperate people
in search of food, water, and safe shelter – like the "environmental refugees"
already fleeing Kenya's drought-stricken Rift Valley – are projected to number
as many as 250 million by 2020, dwarfing the number of political refugees that
traditionally has strained the world's caring capacities.

Renowned NASA climatologist James Hansen, among the first to sound
the climate change alarm three decades ago, puts it bluntly: "The crystallizing
scientific story reveals an imminent planetary emergency. We are at a planetary
tipping point [that is] incompatible with the planet on which civilization
developed . . . and to which life is adapted."[9] Prize-winning British scientist
James Lovelock, once a global warming skeptic, puts it this way: "Our future
is like that of the passengers on a small pleasure boat sailing quietly above the
Niagara Falls, not knowing that the engines are about to fail."[10] In his book
How to Cool the Planet, Jeff Goodell elaborates:

> In Lovelock's view, it doesn't matter how many rooftop solar panels we
> install or how tight we make the cap on greenhouse gas emissions – it's

---

[8] *See Fourth Assessment Report, Climate Change: 2007 Synthesis Report Summary for Policy-
makers 7–14 (2007). See also* the other leading authorities cited in note 5, *supra.*

[9] This quotation is a composite of several distinctive but almost identical statements from
Hansen's reports, lectures, and testimonies repeatedly cited on numerous reliable websites. *See,*
e.g., Jim Hansen, *State of the Wild: Perspective of a Climatologist, davidkabraham.com* (Apr.
10, 2007), *http://www.davidkabraham.com/Gaia/Hansen%20State%20of%20the%20Wild.pdf*
(accessed June 25, 2011); Bill McKibben, "The Carbon Addicts on Capitol Hill," *Wash.*
Post (Mar. 1, 2009), *http://www.washingtonpost.com/wp-dyncontent/article/2009/02/28/AR2009*
022801667.html (quoting James Hansen) (accessed June 25, 2011); James Hansen et al.,
Target Atmospheric CO$_2$: Where Should Humanity Aim?, http://www.columbia.edu/~jehl/
2008/TargetCO220080407.pdf (accessed June 25, 2011).

[10] Lovelock, *supra* note 4, at 6.

too late to stop the climate changes that are already under way. And those changes will be far more dramatic than people now suspect. By the end of the century, Lovelock believes, temperate zones such as North America and Europe could heat up by 17 degrees Fahrenheit, nearly double the high-end predictions of most climate scientists. Lovelock believes that this sudden heat and drought will set loose the Four Horseman of the Apocalypse: war, famine, pestilence, and death. By 2100, he told me, the earth's population could be culled from today's seven billion to less than one billion, with most of the survivors living in the far latitudes – Canada, Iceland, Norway, and the Arctic basin.[11]

If Hansen and Lovelock are even only half right, the ecological (and social) future bodes ill almost everywhere, evoking "discomfiting images of a non-future."[12]

How should we respond to these brute facts and projections? Since the early 1970s and especially since the landmark 1972 Stockholm Conference on the Human Environment, scores of multilateral treaties designed to protect the environment have been adopted,[13] including at least forty that deal specifically with resources affected by climate change.[14] Still, the environment is everywhere under siege, and the worst polluters – China and the United States leading the pack – remain unable to reach agreement on the curbing of greenhouse gas emissions. In climate change policy circles today, the call to action is no longer framed in the language of "prevention"; the focus has shifted, instead, to "mitigation" and, increasingly, "adaptation."[15]

---

[11] Jeff Goodell, *How to Cool the Planet: Geoengineering and the Audacious Quest to Fix Earth's Climate* 89–90 (2010).

[12] Burns H. Weston & Tracy Bach, *Recalibrating the Law of Humans with the Laws of Nature: Climate Change, Human Rights, and Intergenerational Justice* 60 (2009) (published by the Climate Legacy Initiative, Vermont Law School and The University of Iowa), available at *http://www.vermontlaw.edu/Academics/Environmental_Law_Center/Institutes_and_Initiatives/Climate_Legacy_Initiative/Publications.htm* (accessed Aug. 3, 2011).

[13] Judging from a 1998 UNESCO publication, there exist today more than 300 multilateral treaties and 900 bilateral treaties dealing with the biosphere alone. *See* Antonio Augusto Cançado Trindade, "Human Rights and the Environment," in *Human Rights: New Dimensions and Challenges* 118 (UNESCO: Janusz Symonides ed., 1998). For many of the multilateral treaties, global and regional, *see International Law and World Order: Basic Documents*, Titles I–V, especially Title V ("Earth-Space Environment") (Burns H. Weston & Jonathan C. Carlson eds., 1994–) (hereinafter "Basic Documents" for all five titles), available at *http://nijhoffonline.nl/subject?id=ILWO* (accessed May 1, 2012).

[14] *See, e.g.*, List of International Environmental Agreements, WIKIPEDIA.ORG, *http://en.wikipedia.org/wiki/List_of_international_environmental_agreements#Alphabetical_order* (accessed June 25, 2011).

[15] *See, e.g.*, McKibben, *supra* note 4.

Yet, even in this alarming setting we have options – economic, political, scientific, technological, cultural, and, not least, legal.[16] It is important that we explore and evaluate each, and as soon as possible if we are to guarantee against catastrophe – recognizing, however, that no option is likely to succeed over the long run if it bespeaks, fundamentally, a business-as-usual approach. Warns Øystein Dahle, chairman of the board of the Worldwatch Institute and former vice president of Exxon Norway, said:

> A great change in our stewardship of the Earth and the life on it is required if vast human misery is to be avoided and our global home on this planet is not to be irretrievably mutilated. . . . The challenge will . . . require a complete redesign of the working relationship between the political system and the corporate sector.[17]

James Gustave Speth, former dean of the Yale School of Forestry and Environmental Studies, now at Vermont Law School, asserts:

> The main body of environmental action is carried out within the system as currently designed, but working within the system puts off-limits [on] major efforts to correct many underlying drivers of deterioration, including most of the avenues of change. . . . Working only within the system will, in the end, not succeed when what is needed is transformative change in the system itself. . . . [Needed is] a revitalization of politics through direct citizen participation in governance, through decentralization of decision making, and through a powerful sense of global citizenship, interdependence, and shared responsibility.[18]

And David Orr, the Paul Sears Distinguished Professor of Environmental Studies and Politics at Oberlin College, comments:

---

[16] See, e.g., Lester R. Brown, *Plan B 3.0: Mobilizing to Save Civilization* (2008); Charles Derber, *Greed to Green: Solving Climate Change and Remaking the Economy* (2010); Goodell, *supra* note 11; Al Gore, *Our Choice: A Plan to Solve the Climate Crisis* (2009); Bert Metz, *Intergovernmental Panel on Climate Change, Working Group III, Climate Change 2001: Mitigation* (2001); Auden Shendler, *Getting Green Done: Hard Truths from the Front Lines of the Sustainability Revolution*, at ch. 7 (2010).

[17] Øystein Dahle, Board Chairman, Worldwatch Institute, From Cowboy Economy to Spaceship Economy, Remarks at Alliance for Global Sustainability Annual Meeting 2004 at Chalmers University of Technology, Göteborg, Sweden (Mar. 2004), in *Alliance for Global Sustainability, Proceedings: Research Partnerships Towards Sustainability* 15 (Richard St. Clair ed., 2004), available at *http://www.globalsustainability.org/data/AGSAM2004 Proceedings.pdf* (accessed June 25, 2011).

[18] James Gustave Speth, *The Bridge at the Edge of the World: Capitalism, the Environment, and Crossing from Crisis to Sustainability* 86, 225 (2008).

Like the [US] founding generation, we need a substantial rethinking and reordering of systems of governance that increase public engagement and create the capacities for foresight to avoid future crises and rapid response.... In the duress ahead, accountability, coordination, fairness, and transparency will be more important than ever.[19]

These and many other astute observers are coming to a shared conclusion: free-market economics (in both its classical and neoliberal guises) has given rise to a legal apparatus and political system that elevates territorial sovereignty and material accumulation over shared stewardship of the natural environment.[20] This is impeding our search for systemic, durable change.

At the same time, however, a variety of civil resistance movements around the world, new sorts of Internet-based collaboration and governance, and dissenting schools of thought in economics, environmental stewardship, and human rights are asserting themselves and gaining both credibility and adherents. This moment in history therefore presents an unusual opening in our legal and political culture for advancing new ideas for effective and just environmental protection – locally, nationally, regionally, globally, and points in between.

This book proposes a new template of effective and just environmental protection based on the new/old paradigm of the commons and an enlarged understanding of human rights.[21] We call it "green governance." It is based on a reconceptualization of the human right to a clean and healthy environment

---

[19] David Orr, *Down to the Wire: Confronting Climate Collapse* 40 (2009).

[20] *See, e.g.*, Gar Alperovitz, *America Beyond Capitalism: Reclaiming Our Wealth, Our Liberty, and Our Democracy* (2d ed. 2011) (featuring a new introduction by James Gustave Speth); Peter Barnes, *Capitalism 3.0: A Guide to Reclaiming the Commons* (2006); Brown, *supra* note 16; Cormac Cullinan, *Wild Law: A Manifesto for Earth Justice* (2d ed. 2011); Jared Diamond, *Collapse: How Societies Choose to Fail or Succeed* (2005); Gore, *supra* note 16; William Greider, *The Soul of Capitalism: Opening Paths to a Moral Economy* (2003); Hansen, *supra* note 5; Michael Hardt & Antonio Negri, *Commonwealth* (2009); Elizabeth Kolbert, Field Notes from a Catastrophe: Man, Nature, and Climate Change (2006); David C. Korten, *The Great Turning: From Empire to Earth Community* (2006); Bill McKibben, *Deep Economy: The Wealth of Communities and the Durable Future* (2007); Elinor Ostrom, *Governing the Commons: The Evolution of Institutions for Collective Action* (1990); Curt Stager, *Deep Future: The Next 100,000 Years of Life on Earth* (2011); Laura Westra, *Human Rights: The Commons and the Collective* (2011). *See also* David M. Nonini, "Introduction," in *The Global Idea of the Commons* 1, 13 (David M. Nonini ed., 2007).

[21] By "commons" (as in "commons-based") we mean, in a broad sense, collectively managed, shared resources – a kind of social and moral economy or governance system of a participatory community of "commoners" (sometimes the general public or civil society, sometimes a distinct group) that uses and directly or indirectly stewards designated natural resources or societal creations in trust for future generations. For definitional details, *see* Ch. 5, § A ("The Characteristics of the Commons"), *infra* at 124. *(cont.)*

and the modern rediscovery of the age-old paradigm of the commons, whose value can be seen in arrangements for governing emerging arenas such as the Internet and traditional ones such as rural forests and fisheries, town squares, universities, and community life.

The Commons is a regime for managing common-pool resources that eschews individual property rights and State control. It relies instead on common property arrangements that tend to be self-organized and enforced in complex and sometimes idiosyncratic ways (which distinguish it from *commu-nism*, a top-down, State-directed mode of governance whose historical record has been unimpressive). A commons is generally governed by what we call *Vernacular Law*, the "unofficial" norms, institutions, and procedures that a peer community devises to manage its resources on its own, and typically democratically. State law and action may set the parameters within which Vernacular Law operates, but the State does not directly control how a given commons is organized and managed. (For now, especially for global geo-physical common-pool resources such as the oceans and atmosphere, Vernacular Law takes a backseat to the State and the existing, inadequate system of multilateral institutional governance.)

In its classic form, a commons operates in a quasi-sovereign way, similar to the Market but largely escaping the centralized mandates of the State and the logic of Market exchange while mobilizing decentralized participation on the ground. In its broadest sense, commons could become important vehicles of green governance for assuring a right to environment at local, regional, national, and global levels. This will require, however, innovative legal and policy norms, institutions, and procedures to recognize and support commons as a matter of law.

The term "commons," we concede, can be confusing because it may not be immediately clear if the term is being used in a singular or plural sense – or as a "collective noun" which typically takes a singular verb tense. Thus, just as we speak of "the market" as a general entity taking a singular verb tense – as in "The market is up today" – so "the commons" can be construed as a general entity and take a singular verb tense, as in "The commons is a form of resource management." Confusion often results because "commons" ends with an "s," which suggests that it is a plural noun. We prefer, however, to avoid such dubious locutions as "commonses."

Beyond its collective-noun usage, it is customary to use the term "commons" to refer to discrete, particular regimes for managing common-pool resources, which should therefore take a singular verb tense, as in "That forest commons in Nepal is doing a fine job of conservation." Finally, the term "commons" often is used to speak about multiple, discrete commons, a usage that should properly use a plural verb tense, as in "The hundreds of digital commons on the Internet represent a new mode of production." Usage rules are muddled by the habit of some scholars to use the term "common" (without the "s") to denote both singular and collective-noun forms of "commons." Because this is a minority usage, however, we have adopted the standard usage of "commons," as just explained.

It is our premise that human societies will not succeed in overcoming our myriad eco-crises through better green technology or economic reforms alone. We must pioneer new types of governance that allow and encourage people to move from anthropocentrism to biocentrism and to develop qualitatively different types of relationships with nature itself and, indeed, with each other. An economics and supporting civic polity that valorizes growth and material development as the precondition for virtually everything else is ultimately a dead-end – literally.

We must therefore cultivate a practical governance paradigm based on, first, a respect for nature, sufficiency, interdependence, shared responsibility, and fairness among all human beings; and, second, an ethic of integrated global and local citizenship that insists on transparency and accountability in all activities that affect the integrity of the environment.

We believe that commons- and rights-based ecological governance – green governance – can fulfill this logic and ethic. Properly done, it can move us beyond the neoliberal State and Market alliance (what we call the "State/Market"[22]), an intimate collaboration that is chiefly responsible for the current, failed paradigm of ecological governance. A new Commons Sector, operating as a complement to the State and Market, could reinvent some of the fundamental ways that we orient ourselves to, and manage, natural ecosystems. It could give rise to new institutional forms, legal principles, socioecological management practices, economic thinking, and cultural values.

We realize that this is a daunting proposition. It entails a reconsideration of some basic premises of our cultural, economic, legal, and political orders. But demands for innovation in each of these areas – if not bold new break-throughs – are growing louder by the day. In their different ways, the Arab Spring, the Spanish Indignados, and thousands of Occupy encampments all testify to the deficiencies of conventional political structures and processes. As the economic crisis of 2008 has dragged on and gone global, the fissures that have fractured neoclassical economics have spread to other fields. Insurgent factions in ecological economics, environmental stewardship, human rights advocacy, commons scholarship, and Internet-based governance are proposing attractive, more compelling alternatives. The edifice of conventional wisdom and official pieties is visibly crumbling. What shall take its place?

Like it or not, we have embarked on a profound transition in our political economy and culture. This transition is difficult to navigate not just because the intellectual alternatives are still being worked out, but because environmental protection is not only about science; it is also about cultural identity

---

[22] For explication, *see infra* Ch. 1 note 1.

and politics. As sociopolitical analyst and critic Naomi Klein has argued, the political right, in the United States at least, sees environmentalism as a stalking horse intent on transforming the existing State/Market system into some kind of eco-socialism.[23] Indeed, there is little question that the State/Market in its current incarnations must change if the planet's ecosystems are to survive and thrive, but our vision of green governance does not call us back to communism or socialism, nor rally us to utopian eco-anarchism.

We believe that the pursuit of a clean and healthy environment through commons- and rights-based ecological governance is a feasible extension of existing models and trends – but one that will require some challenging transformations. We will need to liberate ourselves from the continuing tyranny of State-centric models of legal process and enlarge our understanding of "value" in economic thought to take account of natural capital and social well-being. In addition, we will need to expand our sense of human rights and how they can serve strategic as well as moral purposes and honor the power of nonmarket participation, local context, and social diversity in structuring economic activity and addressing environmental problems.

The more searching question is whether contemporary civilization can be persuaded to disrupt the status quo to save our "lonely planet." Can we as a society and individually surrender certain deep cultural commitments and evolve in new directions? At the moment, transformation is essentially blocked because any serious agenda for change must genuflect before the sacrosanct dogmas that law is exclusively a function of the State; that markets and corporations are the primary engines of value creation and human progress; that government involvement generally impedes innovation and efficiency; that the private accumulation of capital must not be constrained; and that ordinary people have few constructive roles to play in the political economy except as consumers and voters. These structural premises limit the scope of what is perceived as possible, and they are backed by powerful economic and political interests, Big Oil and Big Coal perhaps most prominent among them.

But we see practical reasons for hope. Insurgent schools of thought in economics and human rights are expanding our sense of the possible. At the same time, a worldwide commons movement is arising in diverse arenas to assert new definitions of value that challenge the contemporary neoliberal

---

[23] *See* Naomi Klein, "Capitalism vs. the Climate," *The Nation*, Nov. 28, 2011, at 11: "As . . . Larry Bell succinctly puts it in his new book, *Climate of Corruption*, climate change 'has little to do with the state of the environment and much to do with shackling capitalism and transforming the American way of life in the interests of global wealth redistribution.'"

economic and political order. Commons notions are enabling the expansion of human rights to embrace communitarian as well as individualistic values and the creation of self-organized, nonmarket, nongovernmental systems for managing agricultural seeds, groundwater, urban spaces, creative works, and a wide variety of natural ecosystem resources. In addition, diverse Internet communities and fledgling grassroots movements are demonstrating new modes of commons-based governance.

Taken together, these trends suggest the broad outlines of a way forward – a way to bring ecological sustainability, economic well-being, and stable social governance into a new and highly constructive alignment. If one attends to many robust trends now on the periphery of the mainstream political economy, one can begin to glimpse a coherent and compelling new paradigm that addresses many serious deficiencies of centralized governments (corruption, lack of transparency, rigidity, a marginalized citizenry) and concentrated markets (externalized costs, fraud, the bigger-better-faster ethos of material progress).

These trends are not only congruent; they are also convergent, together serving as complementary building blocks for a new paradigm of principled and effective ecological governance. As such, they speak to Dahle, Speth, Orr, and others who call for a fundamental rethinking and reordering of the ways in which we go about the world's environmental and related business (including even the business of war and peace, where climate change is likely to provoke nations and peoples to compete for dwindling natural resources). Indeed, given that "[b]usiness-as-usual now appears as an irreversible experiment with the only atmosphere humans have,"[24] it is impossible to think that responses to our "planetary emergency" can be successful without innovative, transformative action – legal, political, economic, and otherwise. New forms of commons- and rights-based ecological governance reflect a new worldview of thinking and doing, rooted deeply in human history and propelled, in this era of increasing environmental threats, by "the fierce urgency of now."

We begin our consideration of this new cosmology in Part I, first by reviewing the trends that are converging to support a new paradigm of green governance (Chapter 1). We proceed by assessing the strategically essential human right to environment as presently understood (Chapter 2). Next, we note and assess the emergence of alternative rights-based approaches (Chapter 3) and then we explore how human rights can help make the conceptual and functional transition to the new paradigm (Chapter 4).

---

[24] Weston & Bach, *supra* note 12, at 60.

Thereafter, we explicate the commons as a model for green governance (Chapters 5 and 6), imagine an architecture of law and policy that could support its successful operation in both small- and large-scale settings (Chapters 7 and 8), and speculate on the way forward "from here to there" – a human rights pathway by which interested parties might actualize the new policy frameworks needed (Epilogue).

We are mindful, certainly, that fundamental social change is typically slow when not marked by violence. We therefore do not denigrate ongoing efforts to advance the right to environment within the existing, traditional system.

Nor do we reject the search for other options, such as potentially complementary advances in science and technology relative to climate change. For example, given the laggard response to warnings of global ecological collapse by this century's end, we recognize that growing numbers of ethicists, scientists, and others have argued thoughtfully that we must begin to research geoengineering now so that it is available as a tool to protect the planet if and when global warming and climate change trends begin to reach irreversibly critical tipping points.[25] It is surely unwise, however, to rely on geoengineering – for example, "stratosphere doping" (injecting large quantities of nonreactive metal or sulfate nanoparticles into the atmosphere and stratosphere), which some say *may* prove necessary for at least temporary risk reduction in the relatively near future – as a first defense against climate change, particularly when tampering with ecosystems we do not fully understand. Geoengineering has the potential to lure us away from the essential task of reducing greenhouse gas emissions by tempting us with dubious technological fixes. Moreover, precisely because such fixes could cause unintended but nonetheless severely adverse weather consequences worldwide, geoengineering cannot escape the need for some

---

[25] *See, e.g.*, Dale Jamieson, "Ethics and Intentional Climate Change," 33 *Climatic Change* 323 (1996) (adapted in Dale Jamieson, "The Ethics of Geoengineering," *People and Place* (May 13, 2009), *http://www.peopleandplace.net/perspectives/2009/5/13/the_ethics_of_geoengineering*), available at http://www.springerlink.com/content/w673766t 3316r474 (accessed May 13, 2011); Michael Specter, "The Climate Fixers," *The New Yorker*, p. 1, May 14, 2012, available at *http://www.newyorker.com/reporting/2012/05/14/120514fa_fact_specter* (accessed Sept. 8, 2012); *see also* Goodell, *supra* note 11; David G. Victor et al., "The Geoengineering Option: A Last Resort against Global Warming?," *Foreign Aff.*, Mar./Apr. 2009, at 64. *But see* Jonathan C. Carlson, Sir Geoffrey W.R. Palmer, & Burns H. Weston, *International Environmental Law and World Order: A Problem-Oriented Coursebook* (3d ed. 2012) (readings in Problem 7–2); Eli Kintisch, *Hack the Planet: Science's Best Hope – or Worst Nightmare – for Averting Climate Catastrophe* (2010); "Organization for Economic Cooperation and Development (OECD)," *Climate Mitigation: What Do We Do?* (2008); Stephen Pacala & Robert H. Socolow, "Stabilization Wedges: Solving the Climate Problem for the Next 50 Years with Current Technologies," 305 *Science* 968 (2001); Sir Nicholas Stern, "Executive Summary," in *Stern Review, supra* note 5, at x–xxi.

form of global governance. Regrettably, many (if not most) geoengineering proposals engage the same kind of Industrial Age thinking that brought us global warming in the first place.

Climate change poses challenges that go far beyond reducing greenhouse gas emissions, and even these challenges do not define the entirety of the worldwide environmental *problématique* that begs for a solution. To pursue geoengineering as a solution represents a dangerous, myopic fantasy, especially when a practical, compelling alternative is at hand and offers the best promise for an environment fit for human beings and other living things. In our view, commons- and rights-based ecological governance is free of those dangers and limitations, and draws on a rich history of commons efficacy, versatility, and social appeal in many specific domains – water, land, fisheries, and forests – not to mention a variety of digital realms. It constitutes a "new/old" class of socioecological collaboration that, in the course of providing for human needs, can regenerate the human right to a clean and healthy environment and, more broadly, the fundamental, organic interconnections between humankind and Earth.

To be sure, much of the success of commons, ecological and otherwise, has stemmed from their character historically as decentralized, participatory, self-organized systems. It is fair, therefore, to wonder whether commons can be the basis for a larger, macro-solution without some new legal and policy architecture that can recognize and support the skillful nesting of different types of authority and control at different levels of governance ("subsidiarity"). At the same time, one might plausibly turn the question around: can any macro-solution succeed without genuine engagement with decentralized, participatory, self-organized systems?

Not to be overlooked, either, are the difficulties of recognizing indivisible collective interests in democratic polities that revolve around individual rights and entitlements. There is also the arguably larger challenge of devising new multilateral governance structures acceptable to the world's states while still empowering commoners and leveraging their innovations and energy as stewards of specific ecosystem resources. These and related issues we consider in the pages following, especially in Chapters 5–8.

We thus are embarked on a large intellectual task, one we cannot hope to fulfill in just one book; and it is for this reason that, in 2010, we launched an independent research initiative, the Commons Law Project.[26] The ensuing

---

[26] The Commons Law Project (CLP) is an outgrowth of the Climate Legacy Initiative (CLI), a now-concluded collaboration of the Environmental Law Center of Vermont Law School and the UI Center for Human Rights of The University of Iowa. In its concluding policy paper,

pages should be understood as an introduction to the project, whose work is ongoing. We take on this limited probe with humble acknowledgment that the challenges are enormous and that others bring greater ecological expertise to some important areas of investigation. At the same time, we believe that commons- and rights-based ecological governance has an essential role to play in forging a future for humanity through the practical assertion of our collective right to a clean and healthy environment. Reclaiming the commons must therefore rank as a preeminent societal priority.

the CLI recommended the development of "a law of the ecological commons." *See* Carolyn Raffensperger, Burns H. Weston, & David Bollier, *Recommendation 1 ("Define and Develop a Law of the Ecological Commons for Present and Future Generations,")*, in Weston & Bach, *supra* note 12, at 63.

PART I

1

Trends That Point Toward a New Synthesis

The future of a commons- and rights-based approach to a clean and healthy environment – green governance – cannot be considered in isolation from the larger realities of domestic and international markets and public policies, but neither can it be held hostage to a discourse that limits our sense of the possible. To actualize a flourishing ecological governance paradigm that respects all life on Earth now and in the future, we must upgrade our mental operating system from Neolithic to Anthropocene and strive for a worldview that accommodates qualitatively different relationships with Nature itself and with each other. We must cultivate a practical governance paradigm driven simultaneously by a *logic* of respect for nature, sufficiency, interdependence, shared responsibility, and fairness; and an *ethic* of integrated global and local citizenship that insists on transparency and accountability in all environmental dealings. Our willingness to perpetuate an economics and supporting civic polity that valorizes growth and material development as the preconditions for virtually everything else is, over the not-so-long run, a dead end – literally.

Reframing the goals of contemporary economics and public policy is a good way to begin opening new vistas of possibility. Properly done, it can move us beyond the neoliberal State and Market alliance[1] that has shown itself, despite impressive success in boosting material output, incapable of meeting human needs in ecologically responsible, socially equitable ways. It is now clear that the present-day regulatory State cannot be reliably counted

---

[1] For syntactical convenience, we oftentimes use the term "State/Market" to refer to the close symbiotic relationship between the State and Market in contemporary global governance. Each serves different roles and is formally separate from the other, but both are deeply committed to a shared political and economic agenda and to collaborating intimately to advance it. We do not mean to suggest that there are not significant variations in how the State and Market interact from one nation to another, but the general alliance between the two in promoting economic growth as an overriding goal is unmistakable.

on to halt the abuse of natural resources by markets.[2] It is an open secret that various industry lobbies have corrupted if not captured the legislative process. The regulatory apparatus, for all its necessary functions, has shown itself to be essentially incapable of fulfilling its statutory mandates, let alone pioneering new standards of environmental stewardship.[3] Furthermore, regulation has become ever more insulated from citizen influence and accountability as scientific expertise and technical proceduralism have come to be more and more the exclusive determinants of who may credibly participate in the process.[4] Given the parameters of the administrative State and the neoliberal policy consensus, we have reached the limits of leadership and innovation.

This book seeks to imagine new paradigms of ecological governance that might improve the management of natural systems while simultaneously advancing human rights. We do so in full recognition that many entrenched, unexamined premises about the future must be brought to light and challenged and that the vision we are proposing is fragile and evolving. In introducing his once-novel economic ideas, John Maynard Keynes warned: "The difficulty lies, not in the new ideas, but in escaping from the old ones, which ramify, for those brought up as most of us have been, into every corner of our minds."[5] This is precisely the problem we face in overcoming some old and deeply ingrained habits of thought and action to entertain a new, unfamiliar paradigm that conjoins a new economics, participatory/networked commons, and human rights. The logic, vocabulary, and inventory of relevant examples of this new worldview, while still embryonic, are rapidly expanding.

---

[2] *See, e.g.*, Earth Justice, *History of Regulatory Failure*, available at http://www.ucsusa.org/assets/documents/clean_vehicles/historyofdelayupdated_jano5.pdf (accessed May 17, 2011) (documenting the history of regulatory failures under the Clean Air Act since 1990).

[3] *See, e.g.*, D. J. Fiorino, *The New Environmental Regulation* (2006); Lynda L. Butler, *State Environmental Programs: A Study in Political Influence and Regulatory Failure*, 31 Wm. & Mary L. Rev. 823 (1990); Howard Latin, *Overview and Critique: Regulatory Failure, Administrative Incentives, and the New Clean Air Act*, 21 Envtl. Law 1647 (1991).

[4] The regulatory process in this way discriminates against localism because local communities and citizen groups are likely to have few scientific or legal resources at their command. *See, e.g.*, Frank Fischer, *Citizens, Experts and the Environment: The Politics of Local Knowledge* (2000) (calling for "meaningful nonexpert involvement in policymaking" because it "can help solve complex social and environmental problems by contributing local contextual knowledge to the professionals' expertise"). Among the examples Fischer cites are "popular epidemiology" in the United States, a process in which lay persons gather statistics and other information and curate the knowledge, *id.* at 151–57; the Danish consensus conference, a "citizen's tribunal" process that invites direct public participation on policy debates involving technological and environmental risk, *id.* at 234–41; and "participatory resource mapping" in Kerala, India, which actively enlisted citizens to become involved in local infrastructure planning. *Id.* at 163–66.

[5] John Maynard Keynes, *The General Theory of Employment, Interest and Money*, at vii (1936).

As it happens, a number of powerful trends – in economics, digital technology, and human rights – are converging in ways that can help us address this challenge. They are: (a) a search for new holistic economic frameworks resulting from the failure of neoliberal economics policy and practice to name and manage "value" in its broadest sense, especially ecologically; (b) new types of commons-based governance that are proliferating, on the Internet and in civic and ecological contexts; and (c) a new surge of worldwide protests against top-down autocratic rule and a corresponding assertion of basic human rights. These acts of resistance to both public and private autocracy – playing out first in the Seattle counter-globalization protests of 1999, and in the Arab Spring, Spanish Indignados, and Occupy movements more recently – have built new sociopolitical spaces in which to reimagine human rights as a key dimension of, and pathway to, socioecological governance and justice.

We believe that a new paradigm of *commons- and rights-based ecological governance* can build on the momentum of these secular trends. The separate strands of discourse that we now designate "the State," "the economy," "the environment," and "human rights," usually in isolation from one another, beg to be reconstituted – remixed and reframed – into a new synthesis. Such a synthesis is not just a new political and policy approach to old problems, but an integrated worldview and cultural ethic. A new paradigm of ecological governance – commons- and rights-based green governance – could do just that: help reconstitute people's relations with Nature, introduce new types of property rights, and contribute to the rise of a new Commons Sector, a confederation of commons in various realms that shares governance with the State and Market.[6]

The rationale for State support of individual commons and the Commons Sector is easily understood. Commons perform qualitatively different functions than do either the State or Market, generating and managing value in different and important ways. As we elaborate in Chapters 4 and 5, they have special advantages in advancing ecological sustainability. They typically limit exploitation of finite natural resources, leverage local knowledge in managing them, and honor the intrinsic value and intergenerational sanctity of natural resources. Additionally, commons foster democratic participation, temper inequality, and, by reducing overdependence on markets, help to meet basic

---

[6] As we explain in Chapters 5 and 6, *infra*, such a confederation, functioning in mutually supportive ways, could organize human energies and governance to serve different ends and check the excesses of both the State and Market. We call this the "Commons Sector," operating alongside the Public (State) and Private (Market) sectors. Social entrepreneur/businessman Peter Barnes was an early proponent of this concept. *See* Peter Barnes, *Who Owns the Sky?* 125–32 (2002).

human needs – core goals of any human rights agenda. By establishing the right infrastructure of policy and support, the State could act as a constructive partner with individual commons – much as it already does with markets. For its part, the Commons Sector could elicit considerable bottom-up creativity and energy at the local or "cellular" level while fostering greater moral and social legitimacy in governance.

Our basic argument is, thus, that commons governance (i.e., governance that seeks to actualize commons principles) can do more for the well-being of ecosystems and the natural resources within them than can the State and Market alone. Sometimes the Commons Sector would complement the State and Market, and sometimes it would constructively displace them. Individually or as part of a new Commons Sector, commons or commons-styled governance, can, with proper design and support, empower commoners (the general public or distinct communities) to manage ecological systems and resources. Such decentralized governance, working within specified parameters, could assure ecological stability and sustainability better than could the regulatory State alone, and it could assure also that fundamental human rights and needs are fulfilled more reliably than by the Market alone.

Critically, commons-based governance could also help to sidestep the growth imperatives of capital- and debt-driven markets that fuel so much ecological destruction. Because commons typically function at a more appropriate scale and location than does centralized government, and therefore draw on local knowledge, participation, and innovation, they offer a more credible platform for advancing a clean, healthy, biodiverse, and sustainable environment and its attendant human rights than does the dominant neoliberal consensus.

The burden of this chapter is to outline this paradigm-shifting journey, first by clarifying the backstory of emerging trends in economics, digital technologies, and human rights. The convergence of these trends makes a new commons- rights-based framework logically compelling and its timing propitious. To these emerging trends and the new synthesis to which they point we now turn.

A. THE TRAGEDY OF THE MARKET

Neoliberal economics policy merits our attention because this outlook, dedicated to the private capture of commodified value, is largely indifferent to nonmarket value except insofar as it may "blow back" to affect markets. Toxic spills become serious when they ruin someone else's market, such as fisheries or tourism, or when a company's negligent environmental performance spurs the public to criticize the corporate identity and brand, leading to lower sales and stock prices. Companies and markets, focused as they are on *exchange value*, have trouble recognizing *intrinsic value*, a fact that had a lot to do with the financial crisis of 2008 and that persists to this day.[7]

It is a truism in our market-oriented society that price is the best indicator of value and that the free play of the Market provides the fairest way to maximize societal wealth and efficiently allocate it. Because the Market is presumed to be more efficient and fair than government, the default strategy for managing natural resources is to privatize and marketize them. Price, moreover, is said to result from individuals, not governments or other collective institutions, freely determining what is valuable. As Margaret Thatcher famously declared, "There is no such thing as society."[8] People are said to maximize their individual, rational self-interests through the price system and market exchange; the collective good then naturally manifests itself through the Invisible Hand.

Guardians of the dominant economic order – politicians, policy elites, corporate leaders, bankers, investors – concede the periodic shortcomings of this governance template as executive misjudgments, scandals, scientific failures, and other shortcomings occur. Generally, however, they aver that the prevailing neoliberal system is, if not the best achievable system, nevertheless "good enough," particularly when compared with the alternatives of communism, socialism, or authoritarian rule.

Yet this system of market-based governance has proven catastrophic and is unsustainable in an ecological sense.[9] Neither unfettered markets nor the regulatory State has been effective in abating or preventing major ecological disasters and deterioration over the past several generations.[10] The structural

---

[7] Economic observer Yves Smith describes the fallacies of free-market theory; the embedded deceptions in "risk/return tradeoffs" used in assembling "efficient portfolios" of stocks; the investor predation caused by deregulation of financial markets; and the inevitable bubbles caused by willful miscalculations of risk. *See* Yves Smith, *ECONned: How Unenlightened Self Interest Undermined Democracy and Corrupted Capitalism* (2010); *see also* Gretchen Mortensen & Joshua Rosner, *Reckless Endangerment: How Outsized Ambition, Greed and Corruption Led to Economic Armageddon* (2011) (offering an authoritative account of the financial crisis).

[8] Interview by Douglas Keay with Margaret Thatcher, former Prime Minister of the United Kingdom, in London, U.K. (Sept. 23, 1987), available at http://www.margaretthatcher.org/document/106689 (accessed May 27, 2011).

[9] Notable critiques include Gérard Duménil & Dominique Lévy, *The Crisis of Neoliberalism* (2011); David Harvey, *A Brief History of Neoliberalism* (2005); Smith, *supra* note 7; Speth, *supra* Prologue note 18; *see also* Roberto Peccei, *Rethinking Growth: The Need for a New Economics*, I Cadmus, Oct. 11, 2011, at 9.

[10] Accord Orr, *supra* Prologue note 21; Speth, *supra* Prologue note 18; *see also* Mary Christina Wood, *Advancing the Sovereign Trust of Government to Safeguard the Environment for Present and Future Generations (Part I): Ecological Realism and the Need for a Paradigm Shift*, 39 Envtl. Law 43, at § III ("The Failed Paradigm of Environmental Law") (2009). Writes Wood:

imperatives of economic growth are, in the meantime, testing the ecological limits of the planet's ecosystems, as seen most vividly in the intensifying
global warming crisis. The environmental transformations now occurring on
Earth are unprecedented in geological history.[11] The pervasive, systemic environmental harms will not be solved remedied over the long term through
green technologies and similar palliatives, if only because the socioeconomic
imperatives that are driving economic growth and the aggressive exploitation
of nature will remain unchecked.[12]

To enhance the prospects for a truly viable right to environment, our challenge is to develop a worldview and governance system with a richer conception of value than that afforded by the neoliberal market narrative. The
foundational idea that private property rights, technological innovation, and
market activity are the inexorable engines of progress and human development
needs to be reexamined and recontextualized. John Ruskin famously called
the unmeasured, unintended harms caused by markets "illth."[13] In our times,
markets are producing as much illth as wealth; the governance systems for
anticipating and minimizing the creation of illth are clearly deficient.

One can analyze this problem from many perspectives, but at the most
basic level the price system is inadequate as an indicator of value. Although
crudely functional in indicating scarcity value, price as a numerical information signal cannot communicate situational, qualitative knowledge that
may be significant to human and ecological well-being.[14] Price may not

---

"The Modern environmental administrative state is geared almost entirely to the legalization of
natural resource damage. In nearly every statutory scheme, the implementing agency has the
authority – or discretion – to permit the very pollution or land destruction that the statutes were
designed to prevent. Rather than using their delegated authority to protect crucial resources,
nearly all agencies use their statutes as tools to affirmatively sanction destruction of resources
by private interests. For example, two-thirds of the greenhouse gas pollution emitted in this
country is pursuant to government-issued permits." *Id.* at 55.

[11] McKibben, *supra* Prologue note 5; J. R. McNeill, *Something New Under the Sun: An Environmental History of the Twentieth-Century World* (2000).

[12] *See* Tadzion Mueller & Freider Otto Wolf, *Green New Deal: Dead End or Pathway Beyond
Capitalism?*, 5 Turbulence 12, 12 (2010), available at http://turbulence.org.uk/turbulence-5/
green-new-deal/ (observing that "the point about any kind of 'green capitalism,' Green New
Deal or not, is that it does not resolve th[e] antagonism" between capitalism's need for infinite
growth and the planet's finite resources).

[13] John Ruskin, *Unto This Last: Four Essays on the First Principles of Political Economy* 105
(1862). We are grateful to Peter Barnes who brought this coinage to our attention.

[14] Ecological economist Joshua Farley writes: "The classic example of this phenomenon is the
diamond-water paradox – diamonds contribute little to human welfare, but are very expensive,
whereas water is essential to life but is generally very inexpensive." Joshua Farley, *The Role of
Prices in Conserving Critical Natural Capital*, 22 Conservation Biology 1399 (2008). For example, industrial agriculture has promoted vast monocultures of crops in near-disregard of the
local ecosystem, thanks to the generous use of synthetic fertilizers, pesticides, herbicides, and

represent actual scarcity in instances where it is applied to "natural capital" because ecosystems behave in highly complex, dynamic, and nonlinear ways that are not fully understood. Price is an inadequate guide to scarcity also because it may be applied to ecosystem structures that behave over time spans that exceed normal human perception (not to mention that of public policy institutions!) and from which people cannot be easily excluded (such as the atmosphere or oceans). "If people cannot be prevented from using a resource," writes ecological economist Joshua Farley, "they are unlikely to pay for its use, and the market will fail to produce or preserve appropriate amounts ... Markets systematically favor the conversion of ecosystem structure to economic production rather than its conservation for the provision of ecosystem services, even when the nonmonetary benefits of conservation outweigh the monetary benefits of conversion. Those who convert gain all the benefits of conversion but share the costs with the rest of the world."[15] This might be called the "tragedy of the market." The price of honey does not reflect the value of complex interdependencies in ecosystems that support honeybees, for example, nor do prices communicate the actual value of lower-order organisms and natural dynamics that are essential to the vitality of a fishery or forest.

Price has trouble representing notions of value that are subtle, qualitative, long-term, and complicated – precisely the attributes of natural systems. It has trouble taking account of *qualitatively different types of value on their own terms*, most notably the carrying capacity of natural systems and their inherent usage limits. Exchange value is the primary if not exclusive concern. This, in fact, is the grand narrative of conventional economics. Gross Domestic Product represents the total of all market activity, whether that activity is truly beneficial to society or not.[16] In terms of "the economy," the disasters of the

genetically modified seeds, often made possible by governmental subsidy. The transformation of farming practices to suit investment objectives, however, has degraded the long-term natural abundance of ecosystems and boosted the prevalence of pests, weeds, and pathogens.

[15] *Id.* at 1402.

[16] Clifford Cobb et al., *If the GDP Is Up, Why Is America So Down?*, Atlantic Monthly, Oct. 1995, at 59, available at http://www.theatlantic.com/past/politics/ecbig/gdp.htm (accessed May 23, 2011). In recent years, a growing recognition of the inadequacies of GNP as an index of "progress" has stimulated such initiatives as Bhutan's Gross National Happiness (GNH) Index, *Centre for Bhutan Studies*, available at http://www.grossnationalhappiness .com (accessed July 22, 2011); the German Bundestag Commission on "Growth, Prosperity, Quality of Life," *German Bundestag*, available at http://bundestag.de/bundestag/ausschuesse17/gremien/enquete/wachstum/index.jsp (accessed May 23, 2012); and French President Nicolas Sarkozy's Commission on the Measurement of Economic Performance and Social Progress. *Comm'n on the Measurement of Econ. Performance and Soc. Progress*, available at http://www.stiglitz-sen-fitoussi.fr/en/index.htm (accessed May 23, 2012). For details, *see* Eyal Press, *Beyond GDP*, The Nation, May 2, 2011, at 24–6.

Gulf of Mexico oil spill and the Fukushima nuclear disaster may actually turn out to be "good" because they end up stimulating economic activity.

Conversely, anything that does not have a price and exists "outside" the market is regarded as without value. In copyright law, for example, anything in the public domain is seen by copyright lawyers as essentially worthless. If a work in the public domain were so valuable, it would have a price, after all.[17] To imperial nations, lands occupied by natives traditionally have been seen as *res nullius* – ownerless spaces that remain barren until the alchemy of the Market and "development" create value.[18] By this same reasoning, an ecological resource such as the earth's atmosphere, wetlands in their original state, and even human and nonhuman genes (i.e., without assigned property rights or market price) are regarded as "not valuable" or "free for the taking."[19]

It should not be surprising, then, that normal Market activity frequently rides roughshod over ecological values. The resulting harm usually is presumed to be modest or tolerable, or at least not the direct concern of business. Indeed, economists consider the unintended by-products of Market activity to be "externalities," as if they were a peripheral concern or afterthought. In truth, it is easy to overlook externalities because they tend to be diffused among many people and large geographic areas and to lurk on the frontiers of scientific knowledge.

Externalities are marginalized, as well, because there is a cultural consensus that the mission of government is, in any case, to promote development through constant economic growth. Conscientious and aggressive government efforts to minimize externalities are seen as interfering with this goal.[20] Nature,

---

[17] *See* David Bollier, *Viral Spiral: How the Commoners Built a Digital Republic of Their Own* 42–68 (2009) (Ch. 2: "The Discovery of the Public Domain"); *see also* David Lange, *Recognizing the Public Domain*, L. & Contemp. Probs. 44 (1981).

[18] *See, e.g.,* John Locke, Second Treatise of Government, *reprinted in* The Selected Political Writings of John Locke 32 (Paul E. Sigmund ed., 2005) ("[L]et [man] plant in some inland, vacant places of America, we shall find that the possessions he could make himself, upon the measures we have given, would not . . . prejudice the rest of mankind.").

[19] The lack of formal property rights, and the failure to recognize customary lands as commons, is a major reason why "people's common lands are frequently deemed to be unowned or unownable, vacant, or unutilized, and therefore available for reallocation," writes Liz Alden Wily, a specialist in land tenure policies and author of the report. Liz Alden Wily, *Int'l Land Coalition, The Tragedy of Public Lands: The Fate of the Commons Under Global Commercial Pressure*, at viii (2011). Wiley also notes: "While all 8.54 billion hectares of commons around the world may be presumed to be the property of rural communities under customary norms, this is not endorsed in national statutory laws." *Id.* at vii.

[20] *See, e.g.,* Milton Friedman & Rose Friedman, *Free to Choose* 54–55 (1980) ("Wherever the state undertakes to control in detail the economic activities of its citizens, wherever, that is, detailed central economic planning reigns, there ordinary citizens are in political fetters, have a low standard of living, and have little power to control their own destiny."). Keeping externalities to some minimally acceptable level is necessary also to assure trust and stability in markets

labor, knowledge, and time are not accorded independent, intrinsic value but, rather, are regarded as raw inputs for the vast societal apparatus known as "the economy," whose primary engine today is the corporation. This is the essence of conventional governance, a system oriented toward fostering private property rights, technological innovation, and market exchange as the bases for solving myriad societal issues while enriching investors.

In the pantheon of economics and public policy, then, nonmarket value tends to recede into the shadows. Realms such as ecosystems, community, and culture are essentially *res nullius* from the value orientation of markets because they are not encased in property rights and traded in the market. They are therefore ministered to through ingenious extensions of market activity, the better to confer value, but they have relatively modest standing on their own as repositories of value. Enterprising social scientists, mindful of the esteemed categories of Market discourse, have tried to ameliorate this situation by recasting social communities as "social capital" and ecosystems as "natural capital." Current crusades for green technologies and a green economy, too, in effect subordinate Nature as a realm of intrinsic value so that it can be incorporated into the existing market economy and its growth imperatives.

This has been a recurrent problem of the environmental movement: how to foster and institutionalize the "land ethic" that Aldo Leopold famously wrote about in 1949.[21] As long as the intrinsic value of Nature is not recognized, ecological harm is likely to fester until the harms metastasize and become utterly undeniable, or until victims or environmentalists succeed in elevating them into political or legal controversies. Government has shown a limited capacity to anticipate and intervene to prevent future harms. In the United States, even in cases where federal regulators have statutory authority, they are unlikely to have the political clout to displease Congress and interfere with markets, whose decisions are seen presumptively as legitimate.[22] This helps explain why more than 70,000 chemicals are sold on the market without

over the long term, which is an investor priority. In practice, however, business interests tend to focus on short-term priorities over such long-term speculative risks whose potential costs they would not likely bear.

[21] Aldo Leopold, *A Sand County Almanac* 201–26 (1981). Leopold wrote: "[T]he 'key-log' which must be moved to release the evolutionary process [of cultivating a land ethic] is simply this: quit thinking about decent land-use as solely an economic problem. Examine each question in terms of what is ethically and esthetically right, as well as what is economically expedient. A thing is right when it tends to preserve the integrity, stability and beauty of the biotic community. It is wrong when it tends otherwise ... The fallacy the economic determinists have tied around our collective neck, and which we now need to cast off, is the belief that economics determines *all* land use. This is simply not true." *Id.* at 224–5.

[22] *See, e.g.,* Frank Ackerman & Lisa Heinzerling, *Priceless: On Knowing the Price of Everything and the Value of Nothing* 185–86 (2004); Douglas A. Kysar, *Regulating from Nowhere: Environmental Law and the Search for Objectivity* (2010); Thomas O. McGarity, Sidney Shapiro

independent pre-market testing for health effects,[23] why no regulatory scheme has been devised for nanotechnology despite warnings raised about it,[24] why the regulatory apparatus for deep-water oil drilling remains much the same as before the BP Gulf of Mexico oil spill,[25] and why little action has been taken to address global warming despite scientific warnings raised more than three decades ago.[26]

The point is that the market fundamentalism of our time is about enacting a distinct cultural episteme. It is an intellectual worldview that promises to generate wealth and progress by assigning private property rights to Nature, culture, and life itself. The problem with this default mode of governance is not just its selective priorities, but its totalizing tendencies. It is incapable of imposing limits on its own logic. The results can be seen in the patenting of genes, seeds, and other life forms; the trademarking of sounds, smells, and common words; and the selling of corporate naming rights to sports arenas, subway stations, and other civic facilities. Everything is for sale, little remains inalienable.

& David Bollier, *Sophisticated Sabotage: The Intellectual Games Used to Subvert Responsible Regulation* (2004).

[23] Mark Schaefer, *Children and Toxic Substances: Confronting a Major Public Health Challenge,* 102 Envtl. Health Persp. Supp. 155, 155 (1994): "Today, there are more than 70,000 chemicals in commerce in the United States, and little is known about their toxicological properties, despite the availability of high-quality, well-validated, toxicological testing methodologies." More than 1,000 new chemicals are introduced into the market each year, and information on the toxicological properties of all but a few of them is minimal or nonexistent. *Id.* at 156.

[24] *See* ETC Group & Nanogeopolitics, *The Big Downturn?* 16 (2011), available at http://www.etcgroup.org/upload/publication/pdf_file/nano_big4web.pdf (accessed May 23, 2011); Rick Weiss, *Nanotechnology Regulation Needed, Critics Say,* washingtonpost.com, Dec. 5, 2005, available at http://www.washingtonpost.com/wp-dyn/content/article/2005/12/04/AR2005120400729.html (accessed May 23, 2011).

[25] *See* Jason Leopold, *BP Still Being Awarded Lucrative Contracts,* truthout.org (Apr. 20, 2011), available at http://www.truthout.org/bp-still-being-awarded-lucrative-government-contracts (accessed Aug. 20, 2011). Writes Leopold: "BP continues to receive tens of millions of dollars in government contracts, despite the fact that the British oil company is under federal criminal investigation over the disaster in the Gulf of Mexico and twice violated its probation late last year." *Id.*

[26] *See* Bill McKibben, *The Race Against Warming,* washingtonpost.com (Sept. 29, 2007), available at http://www.washington post.com/wp-dyn/content/article/2007/09/28/AR2007092801400 .html?sub=AR) (accessed Aug. 20, 2011); Bill McKibben, *Climate of Denial,* Mother Jones, May/June 2005, available at http://motherjones.com/politics/2005/05/climate-denial ("The rest of the developed world took Kyoto seriously; in the eight years since then, the Europeans and the Japanese have begun to lay the foundation for rapid and genuine progress toward the initial treaty goal of cutting carbon emissions to a level 5 to 10 percent below what it was in 1990 . . . In Washington, however, the [industry] lobbyists did get things 'under control.' Eight years after Kyoto, Big Oil and Big Coal remain in complete and unchallenged power. Around the country, according to industry analysts, 68 new coal-fired power plants are in various stages of planning. Detroit makes cars that burn more fuel, on average, than at any time in the last two decades.") (accessed Aug. 20, 2011).

As such examples suggest, the market ethic of modern industrial societies rarely stays confined to the marketplace; it permeates other realms of life and institutions as a cultural force in its own right, crowding out other forms of value creation. A body of social psychology experiments has shown, for example, that people who are paid to perform certain tasks tend to do only minimally acceptable jobs, especially if they perceive the pay to be inadequate; by contrast, those who are offered no money often proceed to "do their best" and help each other.[27] Individuals cast in social isolation are likely to place a different value on goods than are individuals who see themselves as part of a larger group.[28]

This paradox has also been demonstrated by British sociologist Richard Titmuss, who documented that blood banks that buy blood (often from alcoholics and drug users) tend to acquire lower-quality supplies than blood banks that solicit from volunteers (who are more likely to have high-minded motives).[29] The introduction of money and market exchange can skew an individual's perceptions of the operative social order and how he or she chooses to relate to it. As we see in Chapters 7 and 8, this has significant implications for the governance frames that may best deal with managing Nature. Although there certainly may be a role for market-oriented solutions, governance institutions must somehow promote an ethic that honors nonmarket engagement and ideals as well (e.g., vernacular deliberation, voluntary social collaboration, long-term stewardship). In their current incarnation, however, our neoliberal Market regime and its partner, the State, are ill-equipped to foster these values.

That is why economists and others are questioning neoliberal capitalism anew, and why we argue for envisioning a system of governance that enshrines a more benign, richer, and constructive notion of value, especially as it pertains to the environment. The standard Market narrative for how value is generated and diffused (rational, self-interested individuals making free exchanges in free markets, ineluctably yielding the public good) fails to take account of other animating realities of life: the spectrum of human motivations and behaviors that lie beyond *homo economicus*; the influential role of cooperation in generating value; and the many moral, social, cultural, and environmental factors that are necessary to generate wealth. It is a narrative of value that is epistemologically and functionally deficient. It needs to be reimagined.[30]

---

[27] K. D. Vohs et al., *The Psychological Consequences of Money*, 314 Science 1154 (2006).

[28] *See* Mark Sagoff, *The Economy of the Earth: Philosophy, Law, and the Environment* (1988); *see also* M. A. Wilson & R. B. Howarth, *Discourse-Based Valuation of Ecosystem Services: Establishing Fair Outcomes Through Group Deliberation*, 41 Ecological Econ. 431 (2002).

[29] Richard M. Titmuss, *The Gift Relationship: From Human Blood to Social Policy* (1971).

[30] For an insightful overview of the impressive literature on cooperation and altruism – as studied by economists, social scientists, evolutionary scientists, and others – and the lessons being

A positive development since the financial crisis in 2008 has been the surge of innovative schools of economic thought seeking to expand basic notions of "the economy" and "value." These new approaches include complexity theory economics, especially as set forth by the Santa Fe Institute;[31] studies of empirical social and personal behaviors by behavioral economists;[32] neuroeconomics, which studies how evolution has shaped human propensities to cooperate and compete;[33] the Solidarity Economy movement, focused on building working projects and policies based on cooperation;[34] the "degrowth" movement, which seeks the means to arrest heedless economic growth;[35] and the efforts of a diverse array of ecological economists to force conventional economics to take account of ecological realities.[36]

Although their approaches vary a great deal, most of these schools of thought or political movements want to change the scope and character of property rights; rethink economic and social institutions and policies for managing resources; leverage local knowledge and participation in the stewardship of resources; and make more holistic, long-term cost accounting of our uses of Nature. In their different ways, these venturesome thinkers and activists are struggling to escape the gravitational pull of an economic paradigm based on the social norms, political frameworks, and scientific metaphysics of the eighteenth century.

taught by Internet-based commons, *see* Yochai Benkler, *The Penguin and the Leviathan: How Cooperation Triumphs over Self-Interest* (2011). Another important recent account of cooperation, by a leading expert on evolution and game theory, is Martin A. Nowak, *Super Cooperators: Altruism, Evolution and Why We Need Each Other To Succeed* (2011).

[31] *See* Santa Fe Institute, available at http://www.santafe.edu (accessed Aug. 2, 2011); *see also* Eric D. Beinhocker, *The Origin of Wealth: Evolution, Complexity and the Radical Remaking of Economics* (2006); John H. Miller, *Complex Adaptative Systems: An Introduction to Computational Models of Social Life* (2007).

[32] Behavioral economics examines the role of irrationality, cognitive biases, and other emotional filters that complicate or refute the classical paradigm of rational individuals seeking maximum economic utility through Market transactions. *See generally* Colin F. Camerer & George Loewenstein, *Behavioral Economics: Past, Present, and Future*, in *Advances in Behavioral Economics* 3 (Colin F. Camerer et al. eds., 2004).

[33] *See, e.g., Neuroecoomics*, Wikipedia, available at https://secure.wikimedia.org/wikipedia/en/wiki/Neuroeconomics (accessed July 22, 2011).

[34] *See* Jenna Allard, et al., *Solidarity Economy: Building Alternatives for People and Planet: Papers and Reports from the U.S. Social Forum 2007* (2007).

[35] *See* Conference Proceedings, Second Int'l Conf. on Econ. Degrowth for Ecological Sustainability and Soc. Equity in Barcelona, Spain (March 26–29, 2010), available at http://www.degrowth.org/Proceedings-new.122.0.html (accessed July 22, 2011); *see also* Richard Heinberg, *The End of Growth: Adapting to our New Economic Reality* (2011).

[36] *See, e.g.,* Michael Common & Sigrid Stagl, *Ecological Economics: An Introduction* (2005); Robert Costanza et al., *An Introduction to Ecological Economics* (1997); *Nature's Services: Societal Dependence on Natural Ecosystems* (Gretchen C. Daly ed., 1997).

Without probing more deeply into these insurgent, still-emerging approaches to economics and governance,[37] it is worth noting that many seek to understand the premises and logic of human social structures and economic behaviors at a basic level. They question, for example, the validity of certain binary oppositions such as "self-interest" versus "altruism," and "private interests" versus "public interest." They point out that such dualisms tend to lock us into prescriptive frameworks for understanding how institutions and policies can address problems. If we can escape these rigid axes of thought and consider frameworks that sanction new ways of seeing, being, and knowing, we might begin to get beyond the dominant knowledge system and its taxonomy of order. We just might be able to imagine a fresh synthesis for ecological governance.[38]

B. NEW GOVERNANCE MODELS ON THE INTERNET

New types of self-organized, distributed intelligence on the Internet – developed of necessity to meet the needs of a new, unconventional, and rapidly expanding creative and technological community – offer some highly suggestive governance models to guide our explorations. Open digital platforms are providing new ways of seeing, being, and producing. They are leveraging people's natural social inclinations to create, share, and collaborate, resulting in new sorts of collective, nonmonetized cultural, intangible wealth. Many of these models are based on the Commons Sector paradigm, meaning that their members sustainably manage a shared resource for the equitable benefit of their collectivity. Commons models generally embody a different type of social order than do the impersonal, transactional, self-servingly rational,

---

[37] *See, e.g.*, Samuel Bowles & Herbert Gintis, *A Cooperative Species: Human Reciprocity and Its Evolution* (2011); Eric D. Beinhocker, *The Origin of Wealth: Evolution, Complexity and the Radical Remaking of Economics* (2006); Colin Crouch, *The Strange Non-Death of Neoliberalism* (2012); David Graeber, *Debt: The First 5,000 Years* (2011).

[38] *See* Marianne Maeckelbergh, *The Practice of Unknowing*, Stir (U.K.) (Mar. 27, 2011), available at https://stirtoaction.wordpress.com/2011/03/27/the-practice-of-unknowing (surveying "alternative approaches to 'knowing' that [Maeckelbergh has] encountered through activism and anthropological fieldwork within the alterglobalization movement") (accessed July 22, 2011). Maeckelbergh concludes that the movements challenging multilateral organizations such as the WTO, the WB/IMF, and the G8/G20, are essentially challenging a "monoculture of knowledge" that de-legitimizes other ways of knowing and being. *Id.* These alternative ways of knowing are based on the conviction that "knowledge is collectively constructed"; that "knowledge is context specific, partial and provisional"; and that "a distinction must be made between knowing something and knowing better ... At heart of the struggle for self-determination, then, 'is a micro-politics for the production of local knowledge ... This micro-politics consists of practices of mixing, re-using, and re-combining of knowledge and information.'" *Id.*

money-based models typically fostered by property rights and market exchange. Instead, commons models tend to foster modes of social interaction and production that are more personal, relational, group-oriented, value-based, and nonmonetary. The community itself negotiates (and sometimes fights over) both the "constitutional rules" of the community and the "operational rules" that govern access, use, and oversight of a resource. Notable examples in the digital realm include free and open-source software communities such as GNU/Linux, wikis such as Wikipedia and its scores of cousins (i.e., server software programs that allow users to create and edit shared web pages freely), thousands of open-access scholarly journals, and the many open educational resource peer-production communities.[39]

We explore a fuller range of commons in Chapters 5 and 6, but here we wish to call attention to the ways in which the Internet is incubating a different type of economics and governance, one that recognizes the human propensity to cooperate and the right of everyone to participate in managing shared resources.[40] The "social Web," often known as Web 2.0, is starting to surmount the deficiencies of the price system by lowering the coordination and transaction costs among people, such that social communities can interact in ways that markets would not find profitable. "Precisely because a commons is open and not organized to maximize profit, its members are often

[39] There is a large literature on these different types of digital commons, but some landmark examples include Yochai Benkler, *The Wealth of Networks: How Social Production Transforms Markets and Freedom* (2006); Samir Chopra & Scott D. Dexter, *Decoding Liberation: The Promise of Free and Open Source Software* (2008); Christopher M. Kelty, *Two Bits: The Cultural Significance of Free Software* (2008); Mathieu O'Neil, *Cyber Chiefs: Autonomy and Authority in Online Tribes* (2009); John Willinsky, *The Access Principle: The Case for Open Access to Research and Scholarship* (2006); and Jonathan Zittrain, *The Future of the Internet and How to Stop It* (2008) (especially Ch. 6 – "The Lessons of Wikipedia," at 127).

[40] A skeptic might say that the new digital commons can flourish only because the resources they manage are nonrivalrous, infinite resources such as knowledge and culture. They therefore don't "run out" in the way that forests or fisheries do, and so the political conflicts over limited resources either do not exist or exist only in different ways. Digital commons are also easier to establish because they do not need to displace entrenched "legacy institutions" that already manage the resources – which is the norm in most instances of managing ecological resources. In short, the politics and management challenges of digital commons are arguably easier than those of natural resource commons. Yet, notwithstanding the tendency to segregate "commons of nature" from "digital commons," the story is, in truth, more complicated. The governance of code and information in "virtual spaces" is not disconnected from the "real world," as many people presume. Internet-based software platforms are increasingly being used by self-organized communities to influence or manage physical resources and social behavior in the "real world." Network-enabled governance models that honor participation, transparency, meritocratic leadership, and accountability are blending the digital and physical worlds. Online platforms are spurring major shifts in attitudes toward "group process," property rights, and resource management.

willing to experiment and innovate," writes David Bollier in his book *Viral Spiral*: "New ideas can emerge from the periphery. Value is created through a process that honors individual self-selection for tasks, passionate engagement, serendipitous discovery, experimental creativity and peer-based recognition of achievement.... A commons based on relationships of trust and reciprocity can undertake actions that a business organization requiring extreme control and predictable performance cannot."[41]

As a socially based, distributed network (rather than a centrally controlled, market-driven network), the Internet makes it relatively easy for self-organized peer production to occur. On open Web platforms, people can enter into transactions based on a much richer universe of relational information than price alone. Indeed, their transactions need not be based on eking the maximum economic value from the other party. Profit need not be the prerequisite for a relationship or transaction. Two parties – or thousands – can come together for casual and social reasons, and go on to self-organize enabling collaborative projects based on personal values and preferences, social reputation and affinities, geolocation, and other contextual factors. Seller-driven, centrally organized markets, by contrast, would find it prohibitively expensive and cumbersome to identify, organize, and exploit such myriad, on-the-ground attributes: evidence of the structural limitations of conventional (pre-Internet) markets.[42]

Self-selecting individuals who come together on open platforms equipped with specialized software tools (reputation systems, information meta-tagging tools, etc.) may find it fairly easy to establish a rudimentary commons or peer-production community. By aggregating and organizing personal and social data, sometimes in vast quantities, Internet users can collectively develop new types of social organization and governance from the bottom up. The protesters in Egypt, Libya, Syria, and other Middle Eastern countries, the flash mobs

---

[41] Bollier, *supra* note 17, at 142.

[42] There are many examples of markets that self-organize rapidly through online platforms. SourceForge is a website for programmers to affiliate with free software projects, some of which may involve payment; InnoCentive is an open "crowdsourcing" platform for soliciting and hiring experts for businesses that have specific research needs; Meetup.com is a platform for organizing in-person gatherings of people with shared interests. The point is that open network platforms can radically reduce the transaction costs of coordinating market activity, which means that people do not necessarily have to work through organizational hierarchies in order to achieve important goals. Indeed, self-organized commons with lower coordination and transaction costs (and greater social appeal) often out-perform conventional markets. For more, *see* Don Tapscott & Anthony D. Williams, *Wikinomics: How Mass Collaboration Changes Everything* (2008); David Bollier, *Aspen Inst., The Future of Work: What It Means for Individuals, Businesses and Governments* (2011), available at http://www.aspeninstitute.org/sites/default/files/content/docs/pubs/The_Future_of_Work.pdf (accessed Aug. 2, 2011).

in South Korea who used mobile phones to organize demonstrations and the Twitter users in Iran who did the same, the thousands of volunteers who have created Wikipedia – these are but a few examples of how vernacular participation and culture are giving rise to new types of social institutions that are more transparent and responsive than traditional institutions. Conventional markets often find themselves unable to compete with self-organized online social networks: They must somehow build business models "on top of" them.[43]

This is a very different "social physics" (as tech analyst John Clippinger calls it[44]) than that of twentieth-century institutional governance as embodied in centralized corporate and governmental bureaucracies. It is a type of bottom-up, participatory governance that devises its own institutional structures, as needed, compatible with both the resources to be shared and the social norms of the collectivity.

The transformational potential of the Web 2.0 paradigm for distributed governance may be seen in the emerging field of digital currencies. Although we generally regard existing monetary systems administered by national governments and banks ("fiat currencies") as natural facts of life, in fact they are political creations that determine how value is recognized and developed. Monopoly fiat currencies naturally flow among favored circuits of what constitutes value (e.g., activities that generate market profits) at the expense of communities of interest that have less access to the fiat currency. "The fundamental problem with our current monetary system," writes currency expert Bernard Litaer, "is that it is not sufficiently diverse, and as a result it dams and bottlenecks our creative energies, and keeps us trapped in a world of scarcity and suffering when we actually have the capacity to create a different reality

---

[43] Indeed, the rise of network-based social organization – "netarchic," in Michel Bauwens' term, *Netarchical Capitalism*, P2P Found., http://p2pfoundation.net/Netarchical_Capitalism (last modified Apr. 19, 2011) – poses a serious challenge for the "capitalist monetary economy," writes sociologist Adam Arvidsson, because the latter cannot develop reliable ways of measuring and thereby controlling the value generated by the "ethical economy" – the social realm "coordinated by respect, peer-status, networks, friends and other forms of inter-personal recognition." Adam Arvidsson, *Crisis of Value and the Ethical Economy*, P2P Found. (June 26, 2007), available at http://p2pfoundation.net/Crisis_of_Value_and_the_Ethical_Economy (accessed Mar. 19, 2011). There is a growing literature on "open business models." Prominent examples include Henry Chesborough, *Open Business Models: How to Thrive in the New Innovation Landscape* (2006); John Hagel III et al., *The Power of Pull: How Small Moves, Smartly Made, Can Set Big Things in Motion* (2010); Eric von Hippel, *Democratizing Innovation* (2005), available at http://web.mit.edu/evhippel/www/democ1.htm; Eric von Hippel, *The Collected Papers of Eric von Hippel*, available at http://web.mit.edu/evhippel/www/papers.htm (last modified Mar. 19, 2011).

[44] *See* John Henry Clippinger, *Social Physics*, http://www.jclippinger.com/social-physics (accessed Aug. 28, 2011).

by enabling our energies to move freely where they are most needed."[45] The Internet is helping to address this problem by becoming a rich hosting environment for hundreds of global complementary currencies, business-to-business currencies, and community currencies. These alternative currencies are diversifying and decentralizing the medium of money, and, in so doing, making it easier for communities to carry out economic exchanges that are important to them and form new sorts of social enterprises based on the currencies.[46] Alternative monetary systems, writes Adam Arviddson, a sociologist of networked culture, "can accomplish the coordination of scarce resources by means of media that are both disconnected from the global capitalist economy and thus oriented to alternative value flows, and that provide different protocols for action."[47]

Our chief point here is to emphasize that new ways of naming and managing value are enabling functional new forms of social organization and governance. This trend will intensify as more varieties of economic and social activity migrate online. One can easily imagine a new breed of institutional forms that blend digital and ecological concerns (i.e., the social and the biophysical) in more constructive ways. One can imagine collective decision-making that is more open, participatory, and transparent. One can imagine also management that is more efficient and responsive because knowledge is more easily aggregated and made public, and therefore is subject to criticism and improvement (a less politically corruptible feedback loop than the back corridors of legislatures). Governance that is more transparent and results-driven is also more likely to challenge the ideological posturing and "kabuki democracy" that now prevails in Washington, for example, further calling into question the latter's moral and political legitimacy.

---

[45] Bernard Lietaer, *Bird's Eye View: Currency Solutions for a Wiser World*, available at http://www.lietaer.com/birdseyeview (accessed Aug. 30, 2011). Lietaer is a leading expert on alternative currencies, and is most noted for his book *The Future of Money: Creating New Wealth, Work and a Wiser World* (2001).

[46] Some of the more prominent alternative currencies include Bitcoin, Flattr, Ithaca Hours, Local Exchange Trading Systems, Metacurrency, Open Bank Project, and Time Banking. *Alternative Currencies, Monetary Systems*, SocialCompare, available at http://socialcompare.com/en/comparison/alternative-currencies-monetary-systems (last modified Apr. 15, 2012, 11:16 pm) (containing a chart comparing these and other alternative currencies). For more on Bitcoin, arguably the most widely circulated digital currency today, *see Bitcoin – P2P Digital Currency*, Bitcoin Project, available at http://www.bitcoin.org (accessed May 26, 2012); *Babbage Blog – Virtual Currency: Bits and Bob*, The Economist (June 13, 2011), available at http://www.economist.com/blogs/babbage/2011/06/virtual-currency (accessed Aug. 30, 2011); Joshua Davis, *The Crypto-Currency*, New Yorker (Oct. 10, 2011), available at http://www.newyorker.com/reporting/2011/10/10/111010fa_fact_davis (accessed Oct. 30, 2011).

[47] Arvidsson, *supra* note 43.

To be sure, human conflict and ideology are not going to disappear. We are not suggesting that complex choices will be resolvable through plebiscites or that institutional leadership and resources are no longer needed. Many online commons have their own vexing constitutional problems and conflicts.[48] The governance models of digital spaces are still a work in progress. Our knowledge about human beings and social structures, our economic institutions and technologies, and our sense of identity and worldview have changed profoundly over time. The new digital commons point to a new episteme of value and the prospect of building institutional structures that can identify with, and protect, a wide spectrum of nonmarket values.[49]

C. IMAGINING NEW TYPES OF GOVERNANCE THAT GO BEYOND MARKET AND STATE

The State will not of its own provide the necessary leadership to save the planet. Nationally, where most environmental problems first arise, regulatory systems are captive to powerful special interests much if not most of the time. Internationally, where authority and control rests heavily on the will of coequal sovereign states, governments jealously guard their claimed territorial prerogatives. Forward-looking segments of the environmental movement and their allies are coming to this stark realization. It has become abundantly clear that the State is too indentured to Market interests and too institutionally incompetent to deal with the magnitude of so many distributed ecological problems. Evidence of this governance failure can be seen in the rapid decline of so many different ecosystem elements: atmosphere, biodiversity, desertification, glaciers, inland waterways and wetlands, oceans, coral reefs, and more.

But, then, what next? The regulatory State will continue to be, in at least the short run, the dominant governance system, and it will continue to share its authority with the "private governance" that large corporations and global investors visit upon countless communities and millions of people. Yet, the once-impregnable edifice of the State/Market is now seen, correctly, as vulnerable. Catastrophic events and popular protests in recent years have

---

[48] The governance difficulties of Wikipedia have been much-studied. *See, e.g.*, Andrew Lih, *The Wikipedia Revolution* (2009); Zittrain, *supra* note 39; Mayo Fuster Morrel, *Governance of Online Creation Communities: Provision of Platforms of Participation for the Building of Digital Commons, Self-Provision Model: Social Forums Case Study* (Sept. 2009), available at http://internet-politics.cies.iscte.pt/IMG/pdf/ECPRPotsdamFuster.pdf (paper presented at the European Consortium for Political Research General Conference in Potsdam on Oct. 21, 2009) (Aug. 26, 2012). An overview of different governance regimes for digital communities can be seen in Mathieu O'Neil, *Cyber Chiefs: Autonomy and Authority in Online Tribes* (2009).

[49] *See* Zittrain, *supra* note 39, which extensively discusses the "generativity" of online communities.

called into question the authority, credibility, and simple, functional competence of the State/Market, so much so that faith in the system has been profoundly shaken. Popular interest in reforming or transforming governance has soared.

The most salient recent catalyst, of course, is the 2008 financial crisis and its ongoing aftermath. The crisis exposed the self-serving policy delusions of the governing and financial elite and revealed the raw power they can mobilize to seize public resources to serve their private needs. The fallacy of the self-regulating, self-correcting "free market" – and the hidden costs it imposes on the majority of the population – became evident, yet made precious little difference in how the world is run. In the United States, Congress and the President continued to make massive, no-strings-attached bailouts of banks and other industries while slashing budgets for public services and infrastructure and ignoring bank illegalities in home foreclosures. The sense of taxpayer grievance was aggravated in 2010 when the US Supreme Court explicitly recognized corporations as "persons" for the purpose of allowing them to give unlimited sums to political campaigns. The Court in effect ratified the open secret that much of American policy-making and many candidates are now "bought" by corporations and wealthy individuals.

These realities were the tinder that ignited an improbable citizen protest called Occupy Wall Street in September 2011, unleashing frustrations and resentments against a system rigged to reward "the 1%" and override the interests of "the 99%." Unlike protests that seek specific policy change, the Occupy movement has declined to focus on particular policy demands lest it imply that the existing political system could indeed be responsive. What united the wildly diverse protesters is precisely the conviction that *the system itself is the problem*. New forms of governance are needed.

The protesters' willingness to enact creative, nonviolent resistance and to endure arrest, police brutality, and jail clearly struck a deep cultural chord. Within weeks, self-organized encampments spontaneously sprang up in scores of other American cities, and then around the world. In this, the Occupy movement was something of a "call and response" act echoing the earlier protests in the Middle East, Spain, and Greece, and taking the first Internet-driven mass mobilization, the Seattle World Trade Organisation protests of 1999, to sophisticated new levels. Each was a wildly popular uprising against a government that egregiously failed to respect the basic needs and dignity of its citizens.

These uprisings were notable also in their use of the Internet and digital technologies to enable self-organization and self-governance. Not only did digital networking help to coordinate the activities of thousands of strangers, but the technology helped protesters to outmaneuver the police and politicians by rapidly changing tactics and crowd activities. Even more impressive was the protesters' ability to use mobile phones, digital video cameras, and the like to present their case to a concerned world, outflanking government and corporate news media with a more credible message and on-the-ground reportage. Direct citizen communications capitalized on the public's long-simmering distrust of government and corporate media, and demonstrated the remarkable social power of blogging, texting, social networking, videocasting, and other forms of digital communication. The WikiLeaks release of US diplomatic cables gave a spanking confirmation of what many Americans already suspected – that the US government manages international policy-making and war-making in highly deceptive, mendacious ways, and with an overweening attentiveness to corporate interests. Why would its handling of Occupy protests be any different?

To traditionalists, all these developments are just another tedious chapter in the long and familiar struggle of citizens against governments. We demur. We believe the alter-globalization movement instigated by the Seattle protests, the Occupy movement, the Arab Spring, the Spanish Indignados, and the many other popular protests[50] represents something more profound and potentially transformative. It constitutes the early stages of a human rights struggle for a different, better model of governance, nationally and internationally, one empowered by powerful digital technologies and networks and suffused with a distinctive worldview and social ethic, what Richard Falk would call "a Grotian Moment," harking back to Hugo Grotius's seventeenth-century reformation of "the law of nations" – "a time in which a fundamental change in circumstances [signals] the need for a different world structure and a different international law."[51] Despite manifest differences among the many protest movements worldwide, each seeks to reclaim and revitalize democratic principles and human rights that have been suppressed by States intent on catering to commercial interests.

---

[50] For example, the Swedish Pirate Party now holds two seats in the European Parliament and is the most popular political party in that nation among voters younger than 30. The Party has spawned affiliates or is starting one in more than sixty nations and has won elections in a number of German regions. The Founder of the Pirate Party, Rick Falkvinge, explains the appeal of the party: "What it boils down to is a privileged elite who've had a monopoly on dictating the narrative. And suddenly they're losing it. We're at a point where this old corporate industry thinks that, in order to survive, it has to dismantle freedom of speech." Carole Cadwalladr, *Rick Falkvinge: The Swedish Radical Leading the Fight over Web Freedoms*, Guardian (U.K.) (Jan. 21, 2012), available at http://www.guardian.co.uk/technology/2012/jan/22/rick-falkvinge-swedish-radical-web-freedoms?INTCMP=SRCH (accessed Jan. 21, 2012).

[51] Richard Falk, *On the Recent Further Decline of International Law*, in *Legal Change: Essays in Honour of Julius Stone* 272 (A. R. Blackshield ed., 1983).

The struggles of the alter-globalization and Occupy movements, the Arab Spring, and others are attempts to get beyond the State/Market duopoly or, more accurately, to realign the relationship between the Commons Sector and the State/Market. The point is to win structural, systemic shifts in power and policy so that governance can be made more participatory, transparent, and accountable. The implications of these movements and their vision of governance have special promise for rights-based environmental protection.

Already, on the edges of mainstream environmental advocacy, seeds of a different style of governance and politics are starting to sprout. An emerging universe of eclectic, innovative players are pioneering new sorts of direct-action, postneoliberal environmental approaches. They have not yet reached a critical mass, nor even coalesced into new united fronts. They have many different attitudes toward politics and policy, and many are culturally marginalized or ridiculed (as was Rachel Carson initially, in 1962; it took another six or seven years for the environmental movement to go mainstream). Yet, the sheer size and diversity of new types of environmental advocacy, ranging well beyond traditional institutional advocacy and green technology, are impressive.

This much is certain: The current governance system for environmental issues is profoundly broken. There is today an entire genre of books that can be characterized as "collapse" books,[52] and insider critiques of the US environmental movement now find receptive audiences.[53] When environmental catastrophes such as the BP oil spill and the Fukishima nuclear disaster result in a great deal of public relations spin and few significant changes in public policy, the public can be excused for regarding the State with cynicism. Substantive solutions seem more remote than ever.

It is significant that the European Commission, the Organization for Economic Cooperation and Development (OECD), and several national governments have implicitly admitted that the prevailing paradigm of economics and public policy is limited, if not flawed.[54] Following the pioneering leadership

---

[52] *See, e.g.*, Lester R. Brown, *World on the Edge: How To Prevent Environmental and Economic Collapse* (2011); Diamond, *supra* Prologue note 20; Hansen, *supra* Prologue note 5; Lovelock, *supra* Prologue note 4; Robert L. Nadeau, *The Environmental Endgame: Mainstream Economics, Ecological Disaster, and Human Survival* (2006); McKibben, *supra* Prologue note 5; Orr, *supra* Prologue note 19; Speth, *supra* Prologue note 18.

[53] Michael Shellenberger & Ted Nordhaus, *The Death of Environmentalism: Global Warming Politics in a Post-Environmental World* (2004), available at http://thebreakthrough.org/PDF/Death_of_Environmentalism.pdf (accessed August 24, 2012).

[54] *See Beyond GDP*, Eur. Comm'n, available at http://www.beyond-gdp.eu/FAQ.html (accessed Aug. 24, 2012). The project, an initiative of the European Commission and several partners,

of the Bhutan government from of the 1990s, Europeans have launched new projects to develop new measures of wealth and progress that go beyond Gross Domestic Product.[55] "Beyond GDP" is clearly a rear-guard action at this moment in history, however, as a number of cultural and environmental visionaries try to get beyond consumerism itself. Critics such as Diane Coyle, John de Graff, Stephanie Kaza, Thomas Princen, and Juliet Schor are staking out ground for a new economics that does not rely on goods and services as a proxy for happiness and that entails different relationships with nature and social identities.[56] The Eurozone crisis of 2011–2012 has largely eclipsed these deeper inquiries into the structural, long-term problems of the dominant economic paradigm; avoiding default and bolstering short-term financial confidence became far more urgent. If anything, this "near-death experience" has only confirmed the widespread belief that certain fundamental premises of the global economic system need to be rethought.

Moving beyond mainstream environmentalism, one can quickly find a wide range of thoughtful initiatives and experiments dedicated to rethinking economics, revitalizing local economies, rebuilding foods systems, building alternative businesses and cooperatives, and reimagining environmental advocacy. What most of these projects share is a conviction that any serious solutions must address the pathologies of the growth economy.

In Chapter 3, we note efforts to secure legal standing for the ecological rights of future generations and to win recognition for "Nature's rights," even to the point of winning United Nations sympathy and potential endorsement. These initiatives, whatever their flaws, call attention to the struggle for a new international consensus that will recognize substantive, ecologically sound principles of law and commercial practices. Such frame-shattering approaches are shared by the burgeoning alter-globalization movement, which has flourished following the Seattle protests of 1999. It has become a large transnational movement that challenges the basic logic of global capitalism and its inevitable market enclosures.[57] The movement gained new adherents during the debt crises in

---

acknowledges the need for nonmarket metrics of value because "investments only to a limited extent account for the gains and losses in natural, economic and social assets – which are important aspects from a *long-term* sustainable development perspective." *Id.; see also* authorities cited in *supra* note 42.

55 Beyond GDP, *supra* note 54.

56 *See* Diane Coyle, *The Economics of Enough: How To Run the Economy as if the Future Matters* (2011); John de Graff, *Affluenza: The All-Consuming Epidemic* (2005); Stephanie Kaza, *Buddhist Writings on Greed, Desire and the Urge to Consume* (2005); Thomas Princen, *The Logic of Sufficiency* (2005); Juliet B. Schor, *Plenitude: The New Economics of True Wealth* (2010).

57 *See* Marianne Maeckelbergh, *The Will of the Many: How the Alterglobalisation Movement Is Changing the Face of Democracy* (2009).

Greece, Ireland, and Spain in 2011 when it became increasingly clear that the State/Market system was committed to salvaging and enriching itself at the expense of commoners.

Meanwhile, convinced that governments will fail to deal with the consequences of climate change and the coming historical moment known as Peak Oil,[58] scores of community groups in Canada, Ireland, the United Kingdom, and the United States, among other countries, have independently joined the "transition towns" movement. Their goal is to make their localities more economically self-sufficient and ecologically benign as inevitable economic and environmental calamities arrive.[59] Taking action and responsibility also animates the international Slow Food movement, which is trying to relocalize agriculture and food distribution.[60] The international Solidarity Economy movement, too, which is especially active in Europe and Brazil, is developing practical alternatives to global commerce that seek to empower local communities.[61] The World Social Forum is a prominent venue for discussions about getting "beyond growth," reflected most recently in its 2009 manifesto to "reclaim the commons."[62] This list could be supplemented by the many eco-digital commons movements, such as Open Source Ecology and Open Source Hardware, described in Chapter 6.[63]

Much more could be said about attempts by homegrown movements to get beyond regulatory politics and the corrupted State/Market. What is significant for our purposes is the desire of so many independent movements to reinvent democratic practice and develop new ways to integrate economic self-provisioning with environmental sensitivity and social justice. Although protean and evolving, these movements suggest receptivity to a new paradigm that can get beyond our "stuckness" in frameworks that can neither reform themselves nor usher in a new universe of possibilities.

---

[58] "Peak Oil" is a term used to describe the historical point when global oil production reaches its zenith, based on documented rates of extraction and knowledge of untapped reserves, after which oil production descends into a terminal decline. After this point in history is reached – perhaps as early as 2020 – the conjecture is that all sorts of economic and political disruption will ensue as nations clash to secure oil and scramble to make a transition to alternative fuel supplies. *See Peak Oil*, Wikipedia, available at https://en.wikipedia.org/wiki/Peak_oil (accessed Jan. 24, 2012).

[59] *See* Rob Hopkins, *The Transition Handbook: From Oil Dependency to Local Resilience* (2008).

[60] *See Slow Food International – Good, Clean, and Fair Food*, Slow Food, available at http://www.slowfood.com (accessed July 28, 2011).

[61] *See* Solidarity Econ., available at http://www.solidarityeconomy.net (accessed July 28, 2011).

[62] *See* Biens Communs, available at http://bienscommuns.org/signature/appel/?lang=en (accessed July 28, 2011).

[63] *See infra* Ch. 6, § A(3), at 158.

Establishing durable new systems of governance, however, will require the clarity and stability of law. The social and political expressions of the street need to find expression in a framework of law and policy that takes environmental and human well-being seriously. What might such a framework look like and how might it be actualized?

2

The Human Right to a Clean and Healthy Environment

There is little question that existing regulatory systems, national and international, have failed to assure a clean and healthy environment overall. Typically, they treat environmental damage in idiosyncratic and doctrinally restricted ways, after the fact, and with few requirements to restore natural systems or to compensate those who rely on them. Private property regimes focus largely on nuisance law (or the equivalent) to stop ongoing activity bothersome to individual rights, with little concern for collective harms. Public trust doctrines apply mainly to shorelines and waterfront properties, not to Nature more generally, and governmental regulatory schemes rely essentially on monetary sanctions to keep environmental misbehavior in check, demonstrating little if any interest in sanctions designed to encourage restorative and rehabilitative attitudes and practices.

In short, there are few legal principles and procedures designed to prevent environmental harm before the fact, to deal with nature in holistic ways, or to affirm and encourage creative environmental stewardship. An increasing number of national and subnational constitutional provisions have emerged in this regard in recent years, as have also a few doctrinal innovations (e.g., the precautionary principle, requirements of prior information disclosure and consultation with affected parties, mandatory impact assessments). Commonly, however, the application of these principles and procedures is hampered by multiple, often insuperable legal hurdles of justiciability (legal standing, ripeness, etc.) before crucial issues can even be heard in court. When this is not the case, legal decisions reflect a balancing of short-term economic benefits with often vaguely understood or scientifically uncertain long-term consequences. In such cases, economic and/or market considerations usually triumph over the environment, with ecosystemic, aesthetic, and other noncommercial considerations given the hindmost or neglected altogether.

Our challenge is to imagine a credible new architecture of law and policy that will enable varied societies to alter their governance of human activities, especially economic ones, in ways that assure a clean and healthy natural environment. At the same time, though accepting that creative alternative visions are not going to prevail without serious grounding in law, we recognize that it is not easy to see how existing systems of law and policy might evolve to enable more constructive results or, indeed, to effect a paradigm shift in thought, action, and governance. That is the primary focus of this book.

The explosion of dystopian narratives in western culture today suggests a widespread expectation that new forms of social order, law, and governance will arise only from the ashes of societal collapse or revolution. We believe there is a more benign, responsible way to make this necessary transition insofar as the environment is concerned: via *a reconceptualization of the human right to a clean and healthy environment achieved through new modes of commons-based governance.* Existing structures of law and policy must evolve to recognize and support commons- and rights-based ecological governance. "Green governance," as we call it, offers the possibility of surmounting the structural and procedural limitations of the State/Market and of enabling constructive new forms of direct, self-organized engagement and operational feedback that commands greater moral and social legitimacy. We outline this vision in Chapters 5 through 8.

We clarify at the outset that our notion of human rights is not one of formal law or legal process alone, but also one of active social practice. That is, we see human rights as *embodied* – as having corporeal and tangible substance in human activity, even if that substance is not always readily visible. Human rights are not to be seen as mere abstractions that may or may not be honored by administrative agencies, legislatures, and courts. As we explain in greater detail later in this chapter, the project to advance environmental human rights has foundered precisely because it depends on the State/Market and its legal underpinnings to vindicate its principles. Any great leap forward in human rights must necessarily imagine new types of sociopolitical governance and economic arrangements. At the outset the rights may be aspirational alone or merely symbolic, but if they are to be taken seriously they must be grounded in a functional system of governance that is truly capable of honoring a richer understanding of them.

We start this journey with a review of the current international legal status of human right to a clean, healthy, biodiverse, and sustainable environment. We focus on this right to environment for three primary reasons: first, because it is at present the only means internationally by which individuals and civil society can gain legal standing to effect definitive international environmental law-making and law-enforcing outcomes directly and peacefully; second, because nationally, especially in countries that have provisioned this right in their constitutions, codes, or statutes, it serves to mobilize political action in support of its recognition or in defense of ecosystems and victims of environmental degradation; and third, because in all venues, officially recognized or not, it carries with it a number of persuasive moral and strategic virtues that it shares with all other human rights. Human rights signal a public order of human dignity (of which environmental well-being is an essential component) and consequently challenge and make demands on State sovereignty and the parochial agendas of private elites. Also, because they embrace a sense of moral entitlement for the rights-holder, they are deemed juridically more elevated than commonplace standards, laws, or other policy choices, and in this way they facilitate the legal and political empowerment of ordinary citizens.

We review these virtues and more at greater length in Chapter 3, next. The need now is simply to emphasize that, for all the foregoing and other reasons, the human right to a clean and healthy environment provides a powerful narrative and means for envisioning and bringing about an effective, socially rooted system of ecological governance.[1]

There are skeptics, however, who say that the right does not exist except in moral terms; that it lacks the elements of authority and/or control requisite to making it count as law. Are they right? The answer is both "yes" and "no" – as Luis Rodriguez-Rivera signaled in the title (and text) of his helpful 2001 essay: *Is the Human Right to Environment Recognized under International Law? It Depends on the Source.*[2] Our own judgment, following a careful review of the relevant literature and practice, is that there does exist today a human right to a clean and healthy environment as part of our legal as well as moral inheritance, but that, however robust in particular applications, it is limited in its juridical recognition and jurisdictional reach.

It also is our judgment, as should by now be apparent, that the right to environment needs to be taken with an extra measure of seriousness, and that, for Earth itself to survive as an environment hospitable to life, the right must

---

[1] We use the phrase "clean and healthy environment" to encapsulate the numerous adjectives that, alone or in combination, are used to identify or define this right, e.g., "adequate," "decent," "balanced," "biodiverse," "resilient," "safe," "sustainable," and "viable," in addition to "clean" and "healthy." In no way, however, should our abbreviated usage be interpreted to diminish the right to an environment that is adequate, decent, balanced, biodiverse, resilient, safe, sustainable, and viable as well as clean and healthy. Nor should our use of the yet more abbreviated phrases "human right to environment" and "right to environment" be so construed.

[2] Luis E. Rodriguez-Rivera, *Is the Human Right to Environment Recognized Under International Law? It Depends on the Source*, 12 Colo. J. Int'l Envtl L. & Pol'y 1, 17 (2001).

be reimagined and reinvigorated, and as soon as possible. Many times since its inception, but particularly since the globalization of the Industrial Revolution over the past thirty years, powerful economic and political interests have suppressed and compromised this right. Its appropriation by large corporations and governments amounts to a theft of our ecological citizenship. This has occurred, if not by the barrel of the gun, then by the rule of law.[3] The private plunder of our common wealth[4] and the privileging of special interests over the common interest used to occur in gradual, almost invisible ways; increasingly, it occurs with cataclysmic instantaneity. Think, for example, of BP's 2010 Deepwater Horizon oil hemorrhage in the Gulf of Mexico.[5] Recovering the right to a clean and healthy environment – and finding effective instruments to give meaning to it – is a critical pathway to a planetary future fit for all living things.

In the last several decades, most recently due to heightened awareness of climate change and its consequences, environmental and human rights scholars (Rodriguez-Rivera included) have explored this question with acuity and at length.[6] So as not to interrupt unduly the principal focus of our project, however, we limit our discussion to a summary of their findings, together with some of our own. The details we leave to an addendum (see pp.

---

[3] *See, e.g.,* Laura Nader & Ugo Mattei, *Plunder: When the Rule of Law Is Illegal* (2008).

[4] Bollier, Silent Theft, *supra* Prologue note 3.

[5] The Deepwater Horizon oil "spill," as it is usually – and revealingly – characterized, is, of course, but one of a long list of ecological delinquencies. Appropriately, it was widely publicized and condemned, though not enough to prevent planning of further Gulf of Mexico drilling less than one year after the disaster. Many similar disasters escape widespread public notice and avoid responsible scrutiny entirely, as they commonly take place at the hands of artful corporate giants in developing countries, their victims either ignored or treated cavalierly, even with contempt. For a noteworthy exception, *see* Bob Herbert, Op–Ed., *Disaster in the Amazon*, N.Y. Times, June 5, 2010, at A21 (recounting "what has been described as the largest oil-related environmental catastrophe ever" – Texaco's operation from the early 1960s to 1992 of some 300 oil wells in Ecuador's Amazonian rainforest, fouling rivers and streams with polluting byproduct, contaminating the soils and ground water with toxic waste, poisoning the air and creating "black rain" via the burning of gas and waste oil into the atmosphere, and in the process destroying the lives and culture of the indigenous inhabitants, "upended in ways that have led to widespread misery"); *see also infra* Ch. 3 note 42 (describing the adjudicated response to this "catastrophe" by the Inter-American Commission on Human Rights [IACHR]).

[6] *See, e.g.,* Donald K. Anton & Dinah L. Shelton, *Environmental Protection and Human Rights* (2011); David R. Boyd, *The Environmental Rights Revolution: A Global Study of Constitutions, Human Rights, and the Environment* (2012); Alan E. Boyle & Michael R. Anderson, *Human Rights Approaches to Environmental Protection* (1996); Edith Brown Weiss, *In Fairness to Future Generations: International Law, Common Patrimony, and Intergenerational Equity* (1989); Cullinan, *supra* Prologue note 20; Earthjustice Legal Defense Fund, *Human Rights and the Environment* (2001); W. Paul Gormley, *Human Rights and the Environment: The Need for International Cooperation* (1976); Richard P. Hiskes, *The Human Right to a Green Future: Environmental Rights and Intergenerational Justice* (2009); *Human Rights and Climate Change*(Stephen Humphreys ed., 2010); *Human Rights and the Environment* (Maguelonne

Dejeant-Pons & Marc Pallemaerts eds., 2002); *Human Rights and the Environment: Cases, Law, and Policy*, at Chs. 2, 3, 5–8 (Svitlana Kravchenko & John E. Bonine eds. & contribs., 2008); Linda Hajjar Leib. *Human Rights and the Environment: Philosophical, Theoretical and Legal Perspectives* (2011); *Linking Human Rights and the Environment* (Romina Picolotti & Jorge Daniel Taillant eds., 2003); Edward A. Page, *Climate Change, Justice and Future Generations* (2006); *People's Rights* (Philip Alston ed., 2001); Philippe Sands, *Principles of International Environmental Law* 291–307 (2d ed. 2003); Sierra Club Legal Defense Fund, *Human Rights and the Environment: The Legal Basis for a Human Right to the Environment* (1992), Westra, *supra* Prologue note 20; Mariana T. Acevedo, *The Intersection of Human Rights and Environmental Protection in the European Court of Human Rights*, 8 N.Y.U. Envtl. L.J. 437 (2000); Sam Adelman, *Rethinking Human Rights: The Impact of Climate Change on the Dominant Discourse*, in *Human Rights and Climate Change*, *supra*, at 159; Gudmundur Alfredson & Alexander Ovsiouk, *Human Rights and the Environment*, 60 Nord. J. Int'l L. 19 (1991); Sumudu Atapattu, *The Right to Life or the Right to Die Polluted: The Emergence of a Human Right to a Healthy Environment Under International Law*, 16 Tul. Envtl. L.J. 65 (2002); Daniel Bodansky, Introduction, *Climate Change and Human Rights: Unpacking the Issues*, 38 Ga. J. Int'l & Comp. L. 511 (2010); Alan E. Boyle, *Human Rights or Environmental Rights? A Reassessment*, 18 Fordham Envtl. L. Rev. 471 (2008); Lynda M. Collins, *Are We There Yet? The Right to Environment in International and European Law*, 2007 McGill Int'l J. Sustainable Dev. L. & Pol'y 119; Caroline Dommen, *Claiming Environmental Rights: Some Possibilities Offered by the Human Rights Mechanism*, 11 Geo. Int'l. L. Rev. 1 (1998); Melissa Fung, *The Right to a Healthy Environment: Core Obligations Under the International Covenant on Economic, Social and Cultural Rights*, 14 Willamette J. Int'l L. & Disp. Resol. 97 (2006); Noralee Gibson, *The Right to a Clean Environment*, 54 Sask. L. Rev. 5 (1990); W. Paul Gormley, *The Legal Obligation of the International Community To Guarantee a Pure and Decent Environment: The Expansion of Human Rights Norms*, 3 Geo. Int'l Envtl. L. Rev. 85 (1990); W. Paul Gormley, *The Right to a Safe and Decent Environment*, 28 Indian J. Int'l L. 1 (1988); W. Paul Gormley, *The Right of Individuals to be Guaranteed a Pure, Clean and Decent Environment: Future Programs of the Council of Europe*, 1 Legal Issues Eur Integration 23 (1975); Gunther Handl, *Human Rights and Protection of the Environment: A Mildly 'Revisionist' View*, in *Human Rights, Sustainable Development and the Environment* 117 (A. Cançado Trindade ed., 1992); Gunther Handl, *Human Rights and the Protection of the Environment*, in *Economic, Social and Cultural Rights: A Textbook* (Asbjorn Eide et al. eds., 2d ed. 2001); Amy Hardberger, *Life, Liberty, and the Pursuit of Water: Evaluating Water as a Human Right and the Duties and Obligations It Creates*, 4 Nw. U. J. Int'l Hum. Rts 331 (2005); Iveta Hodkova, *Is There a Right to a Healthy Environment in the International Legal Order?*, 7 Conn. J. Int'l L. 65 (1991); John H. Knox, *Linking Human Rights and Climate Change at the United Nations*, 33 Harv. Envtl. L. Rev. 477 (2009); John H. Knox, *Climate Change and Human Rights Law*, 50 Va. J. Int'l L. 163 (2009); Svitlana Kravchenko, *Procedural Rights as a Crucial Tool to Combat Climate Change*, 38 Ga. J. Int'l & Comp. L. 613 (2010); Svitlana Kravchenko, *Right to Carbon or Right to Life: Human Rights Approaches to Climate Change*, 9 Vt. J. Envtl. L. 513, 514 (2008); John Lee, *The Underlying Legal Theory to Support a Well-Defined Human Right to a Healthy Environment as a Principle of Customary International Law*, 25 Colum. J. Envtl. L. 283 (2000); Marc Limon, *Human Rights Obligations and Accountability in the Face of Climate Change*, 50 Va. J. Int'l L. 5433 (2009); Andrzej Makarewicz, *La Protection Internationale du Droit y L'Environnement*, in *Environement et Droits de L'Homme* 77 (Pascale Kromarek ed., 1987); Linda A. Malone & Scott Pasternack, *Exercising Environmental Rights and Remedies in the United Nations System*, 27 Wm. & Mary Envtl L. & Pol'y Rev. 365 (2002); John G. Merrills, *Environmental Rights*, in *The Oxford Handbook of International Environmental Law* 666 (Daniel Bodansky et al. eds., 2007); R. S. Pathak, *The Human Rights System as a Conceptual Framework for Environmental Law*, in *Environmental Change and International Law: New Challenges and Dimensions* 205 (Edith B. Weiss ed., 1992); Neil

285–336) that we hope provides adequate supportive authority for the summary that follows.[7]

We hasten to stress, however, that our focus here is on the accepted formal or official law of the State system (nationally and internationally) – "State Law" we call it – which does not necessarily reflect the informal or unofficial law that emanates from most people's everyday perspectives and interactions. In general, these informal, socially based modes of law – the "pushing and pulling through reciprocal claim and mutual tolerance in [people's] daily competition for power, wealth, respect, and other cherished values"[8] – are ignored or seen as inconsequential by formal, State Law. Yet, they are an important type of law and potentially a vital wellspring for making State Law more responsive. We

Popovic, *In Pursuit of Environmental Human Rights: Commentary on the Draft Declaration of Principles on Human Rights and the Environment*, 27 Colum. Hum. Rts. L. Rev. 487 (1996); Lavanya Rajamani, *The Increasing Currency and Relevance of Rights-Based Perspectives in International Negotiations on Climate Change*, 22 J. Envtl. L. 391 (2010); Rodriguez-Rivera, *supra* note 2; Naomi Roht-Arriaza, *"First Do No Harm": Human Rights and Efforts to Combat Climate Change*, 38 Ga. J. Int'l & Comp. L. 593 (2010); Dinah Shelton, *Human Rights, Environmental Rights, and the Right to Environment*, 28 Stan. J. Int'l L. 103 (1991); Dinah Shelton, *The Right to Environment*, in *The Future of Human Rights Protection in a Changing World: Fifty Years Since the Four Freedoms Address, Essays in Honor of Torkel Opsahl* 197 (Asbjorn Eide & Jan Helgesen eds., 1991); Amy Sinden, *Climate Change and Human Rights*, 27 J. Land Res. & Envtl. L. 255 (2007); Heinhard Steiger et al., *The Fundamental Right to a Decent Environment*, in *Trends in Envtl. Pol'y & L.* 1 (Michael Bothe ed., 1980); Prudence E. Taylor, *From Environmental to Ecological Human Rights: A New Dynamic in International Law*, 10 Geo. Int'l Envtl. L. Rev. 309 (2010); Melissa Thorme, *Establishing Environment as a Human Right*, 19 Den. J. Int'l L. & Pol'y 301 (1991); Antonio Augusto A. Cançado Trindade, *The Contribution of International Human Rights Law to Environmental Protection, with Special Reference to Global Environmental Change*, in *Environmental Change and International Law: New Challenges and Dimensions* 244 (Edith Brown Weiss ed., 1992); Henn-Juri Uibopuu, *The Internationally Guaranteed Right of an Individual to a Clean Environment*, 1 Comp. L. Y.B. 101 (1977); Alan E. Boyle, *Human Rights and the Environment: A Reassessment?* (2009) (Draft Paper, UNEP/OHCHR High Level Expert Meeting on the New Future of Human Rights and the Environment: Moving the Global Agenda Forward, Nov. 30–Dec. 1, 2009) (on file with the authors); Jonas Ebbesson, *Participatory and Procedural Rights in Environmental Matters: State of Play* (2009) (Draft Paper, UNEP/OHCHR High Level Expert Meeting on the New Future of Human Rights and the Environment: Moving the Global Agenda Forward, Nov. 30–Dec. 1, 2009) (on file with the authors); Dinah Shelton, *Human Rights and the Environment: Past, Present and Future Linkages and the Value of a Declaration* (2009) (Draft Paper, UNEP/OHCHR High Level Expert Meeting on the New Future of Human Rights and the Environment: Moving the Global Agenda Forward, Nov. 30–Dec. 1, 2009) (on file with the authors).

7 See Addendum (titled *"The International Legal Status of the Human Right to a Clean and Healthy Environment"*), *infra* at 285.

8 Burns H. Weston, *The Role of Law in Promoting Peace and Violence: A Matter of Definition, Social Values, and Individual Responsibility*, in *Toward World Order and Human Dignity* 114, 117 (W. Michael Reisman & Burns H. Weston, eds., 1976).

must remember that "[l]aw does not live by executives, legislators, and judges alone"[9] and that it can and does exist beyond the formal corridors of power. It assuredly exists in our essentially "horizontal" and voluntarist international legal order, which by definition lacks a formal center; but it exists also in "vertical" and compulsory national legal orders, where behavioral codes of all sorts regulate diverse sectors of life (church canons, sports rules, norms of social etiquette) without formal State approval.

We call this important dimension of governance "Vernacular Law," and we deal with it at greater length in Chapters 4, 5, and 6.[10] For now, let us simply note that distinctions between formal/official and informal/unofficial present false dichotomies if invoked and applied too rigidly. Different orders of legal process are far more fluid and complementary – and therefore far more interpenetrating and interdependent – than is commonly acknowledged or recognized.

We turn now to our summary conclusions regarding the right to environment as formally or officially understood within the statist legal order. Five are particularly noteworthy.

1. *The human right to environment is today officially recognized juridically in three ways:*

- *as an entitlement derived from other recognized rights*, centering primarily on the substantive rights to life, to health, and to respect for private and family life, but embracing occasionally other perceived surrogate rights as well – e.g., habitat, property, livelihood, culture, dignity, equality or nondiscrimination, and sleep;[11]
- *as an entitlement autonomous unto itself*, dependent on no more than its own recognition and increasingly favored over the derivative approach insofar as national constitutional and regional treaty prescriptions proclaiming such a right are evidence;[12] and
- *as a cluster of procedural entitlements* generated from a "reformulation and expansion of existing human rights and duties"[13] (akin to the derivative substantive rights noted first) and commonly referred to as "procedural environmental rights" (i.e., the right to environmental information,

---

[9] *Id.*
[10] The term "Vernacular Law" originates and functions in the informal, unofficial zones of society, as we detail in Ch. 4, § B, *infra* at 104. In particular, *see infra* text accompanying notes at 99–107.
[11] For details, *see infra* Addendum § A, at 285–307 (especially note 83).
[12] For details, *see infra* Addendum § B, at 308–28.
[13] Shelton, *Right to Environment*, *supra* note 6, at 117.

to decisional participation, and to administrative and judicial recourse).[14]

2. All three of these official juridical manifestations of the human right to environment, however robust their particularized applications, are essentially limited in their legal recognition and jurisdictional reach.[15]

On the global plane, no treaty provides for a human right to environment explicitly in either its autonomous or derivative form; two, recognize its autonomous existence during peacetime and three, during wartime, but only implicitly and largely in passing;[16] and to date solely one global-level court decision affirms the right explicitly, though in its derivative form (via the rights to life and to health as surrogates for it),[17] as do also a few treaty-body rulings, but only implicitly.[18] Otherwise, the recognition and reach of the human right to environment is left largely to a series of progressive resolutions, declarations, charters, and other assorted instruments affirming the right in its autonomous form; all or most are technically nonbinding or at best disputed in their juridical quality or significance. Included among them is the historically prominent and influential 1972 Stockholm Declaration on the Human Environment, which, in the first instance in modern times, though tempered by the 1992 Rio Declaration on Environment and Development, affirmed the right to environment not only in the autonomous sense but, as well, in the

---

[14] For details, *see infra* Addendum § C, at 328–36; *see also* Malone & Pasternack, *supra* note 6 (reviewing environmental rights and remedies generally).

[15] For details, *see infra* Addendum §§ A–C, at 285–336.

[16] For peacetime expression, *see* Convention on the Elimination of All Forms of Discrimination against Women (CEDAW), art. 14(2)(h), Dec. 18, 1979, 1249 U.N.T.S. 13, *reprinted in* 19 I.L.M. 33 (1980) and III Basic Documents, *supra* Prologue note 13, at III.C.13; Convention on the Rights of the Child, art. 1, Nov. 20, 1989, 1577 U.N.T.S. 44, *reprinted in* 28 I.L.M. 1448 (1989) and III Basic Documents, *supra* Prologue note 13, at III.D.5. For wartime expression, *see* Geneva Convention (No. III) Relative to the Treatment of Prisoners of War, arts. 26 & 46, Aug. 12, 1949, 75 U.N.T.S. 135, *reprinted in* II Basic Documents, *supra* Prologue note 13, at II.B.4c; Geneva Convention (No. IV) Relative to the Protection of Civilian Persons in Time of War, arts. 89 & 127, Aug. 12, 1949, 75 U.N.T.S. 287, *reprinted in* II Basic Documents, *supra* Prologue note 13, at II.B.4d; and Protocol Additional (No. I) to the Geneva Conventions of Aug. 12, 1949, and Relating to the Protection of Victims of International Armed Conflicts. Art. 55, June 8, 1977, 1125 U.N.T.S. 3, *reprinted in* II Basic Documents, *supra* Prologue note 13, at II.B.4e.

[17] *See* Gabčíkovo-Nagymaros Project (Hung. v. Slovk.), 1997 I.C.J. 7 (Feb. 5).

[18] *See, e.g.,* Communication No. 67/1980, U.N. Doc. CCPR/C/OP/1, para. 8 (1984), 2 Selected Decisions of the Human Rights Committee 20 (1990) (dismissed on technical procedural grounds); Mrs. Vaihere Bordes and Mr. John Temeharo v. France, Communication No. 645/1995, U.N. Doc. CCPR/C/57/D/645/1995 (1996), 6 Selected Decisions of the Human Rights Committee 15 (1996) (same). For details of these cases, *see infra* Addendzim § A(1), at 286–94.

derivative sense via the rights to life and health.[19] Contemporary legal scholarship, however, influenced by frightening environmental trends, actual and
anticipated, evinces an increased willingness to reassess the juridical vitality
of this "soft law" (as it is often inadequately called).[20]

On the regional plane, the right to environment is recognized and supported
by several treaties: one each in Africa, Latin America, and the Middle East that
affirm it explicitly in its autonomous form;[21] two others in Europe that, with
the help of regionally authoritative regulatory and judicial decisions, embrace
it implicitly in its derivative guise;[22] and still another, the widely adopted
European Aarhus Convention, acclaimed by the United Nations and others
beyond Europe's frontiers, that honors the human right to environment in
terms of quite detailed procedural rights.[23]

[19] Stockholm Declaration of the United Nations Conference on the Human Environment [here-inafter "Stockholm Declaration"], para. 1, (June 16, 1972), U.N. Doc. A/CONF.48/14/Rev.1 at 3, U.N. Doc. A/CONF.48/14, at 2–65; Corr 1, 1972 U.N. Jurid. Y.B. 319, *reprinted in* V Basic Documents, *supra* Prologue note 13, at V.B.3. For the Rio Declaration, see U.N. Doc. A/CONF.151/26 (1992), *reprinted in* 31 I.L.M. 874 (1992) *and* V Basic Documents, *supra* Prologue note 13, at V.B.18.

[20] For further clarification of this scholarly trend, *see infra* Conclusion 4, at 21. *See also* Addendum at 285.

[21] *See* African Charter on Human and People's Rights ("Banjul Charter"), art. 24, June 27, 1981, OAU Doc. CAB/LEG/67/3/Rev. 5, *reprinted in* 21 I.L.M. 58 (1982) *and* III Basic Documents, *supra* Prologue note 13, at III.B.1; Additional Protocol to the American Convention on Human Rights in the Area of Economic, Social and Cultural Rights, art. 11, Nov. 17, 1988, O.A.S.T.S. *reprinted in* 28 I.L.M. 156 (1989) *and* III Basic Documents, *supra* Prologue note 13, at III.B.32a; Arab Arab Charter on Human Rights, Council of the League of Arab States, art. 38, May 22, 2004, 102d Sess, Rec 5437, *reprinted in* 12 Int'l Hum. Rts. Rep. 893 (2005) *and* III Basic Documents, *supra* Prologue note 13, at III.B.27.

[22] *See* European Convention for the Protection of Human Rights and Fundamental Freedoms (ECHR), arts. 2 (right to life) & 8 (right to private and family life), Nov. 4, 1950, 213 U.N.T.S. 221, C.E.T.S. 5, *reprinted in* III Basic Documents, *supra* Prologue note 13, at III.B.8; Charter of Fundamental Rights of the European Union, arts. 2 & 27, Dec. 7, 2000, C364 OJEC. 8, 2007 OJ (C303)1, *reprinted in* 40 I. L.M. 266 (2001) *and* III Basic Documents, *supra* Prologue note 13, at III.B.19 (now incorporated into the Consolidated Version of the Treaty on European Union the Treaty on the Functioning of the European Union, Dec. 30, 2010, 2010 OJ (C 83) 1, *reprinted in* I Basic Documents, *supra* Prologue note 13, at I.B.21). For leading judicial decisions interpreting one or more of these treaties, *see* Öneryildiz v. Turkey, No. 48939/99, Eur. Ct. H.R. 2004-XII (2005), 41 Eur. H.R. Rep. 20 (Nov. 30, 2004) (right to life); Lopez Ostra v. Spain, No.16798/90, 20 Eur. Ct. H.R. (ser. A), No. 303-C (1995), 20 Eur. H.R. Rep. 277 (Dec. 9, 1994) (right to private and family life); Taskin and Others v. Turkey, No. 46117/99, 2004-X, 42 Eur. H. R. Rep. 50 (Nov. 10, 2004) (right to private and family life, but dismissed on procedural grounds).

[23] UNECE Convention on Access to Information, Public Participation in Decision-Making and Access to Justice in Environmental Matters, June 25, 1998, 2161 U.N.T.S 447, U.N.Doc. ECE/CEP/43, *reprinted in* 38 I.L.M. 517 (1999) *and* V Basic Documents, *supra* Prologue note 13, at V.B.20 (also known and hereinafter cited as the "Aarhus Convention") (focusing

Individually and together, these diplomatic initiatives make for a distinctly
more receptive milieu for the human right to environment than prevails on
the global plane. However, excepting perhaps the procedural environmental
rights codified in the Aarhus Convention, the fact of their regionalism and
thus their inherent jurisdictional limits prevents finding in these eco-friendly
juridical practices the making of a global customary international law right to
environment.[24] This is all the more true in light of two additional facts: First,
the bulk of these practices are found in the developing world, still seeking full
effectual citizenship in the international legal order; and second, the right to
environment has been upheld in the African and Latin American regional systems principally with reference to the rights of native indigenous peoples and
according to national constitutional and treaty safeguards unique to them, at
least in part.[25] Even the popularity of the deservedly lauded procedural rights
detailed in the Aarhus Convention may be negatively interpreted partially as
vestiges of the ideological Cold War divide, which made room for certain procedural rights but thwarted the joinder of civil/political and economic/social
substantive rights.

principally on procedural environmental rights but not without first confirming in its preamble "that every person has the right to live in an environment adequate to his or her health
and well-being. . . ." At this writing, 45 European states plus the European Community are
party to the Aarhus Convention: Albania, Armenia, Austria, Azerbaijan, Belarus, Belgium,
Bosnia/ Herzegovina, Bulgaria, Croatia, Cyprus, Czech Republic, Denmark, Estonia, European Union, Finland, France, Georgia, Germany, Greece, Hungary, Iceland, Ireland, Italy,
Kazakhstan, Kyrgyzstan, Latvia, Lithuania, Luxembourg, Macedonia, Malta, Moldova, Montenegro, Netherlands, Norway, Poland, Portugal, Romania, Serbia, Slovakia, Slovenia, Spain,
Sweden, Tajikistan, Turkmenistan, Ukraine, United Kingdom.

[24] We note the possible exception of the Aarhus Convention, *supra* note 23, because it applies
not only to most of Europe (including Russia and the former Soviet bloc countries of Eastern
Europe) but also to eight of the nine former Soviet republics in Central Asia. While the
United States, a member of the U.N. Economic Commission for Europe (the Convention's
sponsor), is not a party to the agreement and withdrew from negotiations on it, it justified its
stance in part on the grounds that the Convention would not require the reporting of specific
pollutants, only waste as a whole. It is also to be noted that, at the time, the United States
was "one of the few nations that already has a well established system of pollution reporting"
and that much of the Aarhus Convention was already reflected in US domestic law. *U.S.
Backs Out of Register Treaty Group*, Environmental News Service, Nov. 25, 2002, available at
http://www.ens-newswire.com/ens/nov 2002/2002–11-25–10.html (accessed Nov. 25, 2002). All
of which points to a convention that resonates and possibly even persuades beyond its expressly
authorized jurisdiction. As stated by former U.N. Secretary-General Kofi Annan shortly before
the Convention's entry into force: "Although regional in scope, the significance of the Aarhus
Convention is global." Kofi Annan, *Forward to Economic Commission for Europe, The Aarhus
Convention: An Implementation Guide*, at v (2000).

[25] For more details, *see infra* Addendum §§ A–C, at 285–336.

On the national/local plane, as on the regional plane, legal support for the right to environment exists in both its derivative and autonomous forms, although in this setting more in constitutional and statutory mandates backed by judicial decisions from the lowest to highest of national tribunals than pursuant to international law.[26] Especially noteworthy are the growing numbers of new or amended national and subnational (provincial, state) constitutions that, explicitly and implicitly, provide for a right to environment in the autonomous sense.[27] Where these provisions appear to be taken as presumably intended (i.e., without judicially fabricated constraints upon subject-matter jurisdiction or proof of personal economic loss, as in the United States, for example[28]), they contribute to the building of a general principle of law recognized under international law as an authoritative "source" of law for the rendering of international legal judgments, judicial and otherwise.

The majority of these law-making and law-enforcing exercises, however, are restricted largely to the world's developing countries in Latin America, sub-Saharan Africa, and South Asia (especially India) and to the Eastern European countries formerly of the Soviet Union and Soviet bloc. In each case, however, it seems that they have been pursued largely for idiosyncratic reasons: in the first instance, to erect a protect ive shield against ecologically derelict business enterprise as experienced in the past, not least at the hands of foreign corporations (e.g., in Ecuador's Oriente, India's Bhopal, Nigeria's Ogoniland);

---

[26] *See infra* Addendum § C, at 328–36. For examples of, and commentary on, pertinent constitutional provisions, *see* Boyd, *supra* note 6; *Constitutional Rights to an Ecologically Balanced Environment* (Isabelle M. Larmuseau ed., 2007) [hereinafter *Constitutional Rights*].

[27] The United States is not among them at the federal level, though in 1968 Senator Gaylord Nelson of Wisconsin urged unsuccessfully for a constitutional amendment that would have recognized within the US Bill of Rights that "[e]very person has the inalienable right to a decent environment." H.R.J. Res. 1321, 90th Cong., 2d Sess. (1968). Similarly, in 2003, Representative Jesse Jackson, Jr. tendered without success a US constitutional amendment "respecting the right to a clean, safe, and sustainable environment." H.R.J. Res. 33, 108th Cong., 1st Sess. (2003).

[28] Eighteen US states have adopted constitutional provisions expressly affirming a state's duty to protect the environment or recognizing an autonomous right to a clean and healthy environment (or a component thereof, such as a right to clean water): Ala. Const. art. VIII; Cal. Const. art. X, § 2; Fla. Const. art. II, § 7; Haw. Const. art. XI; Ill. Const. art. XI; La. Const. art. IX; Mass. Const. art. XCVII, § 179; Mich. Const. art. IV, § 52; Mont. Const. art. IX, § 1; N.M. Const. art. XX; N.Y. Const. art. XIV; N.C. Const. art. XIV, § 5; Ohio Const. art. II, § 36; Pa. Const. art. I, § 27; R.I. Const. art. I, § 17; Tex. Const. art. XVI, § 59; Utah Const. art. XVIII; Va. Const. art. XI, § 1. Few of these provisions have major effect, however, owing to a largely judicial but widespread judgment that they are "non-self-executing" or "non-justiciable" or, in any event, subject to a strict "standing" requirement of personal economic injury. For details, *see* Matthew Thor Kirsch et al., *Upholding the Public Trust Doctrine in State Constitutions*, 46 Duke L. J. 1169 (1997); Dinah Shelton, *Environmental Rights in the State Constitutions of the United States*, in *Constitutional Rights*, *supra* note 26, at 111–24 (citing Kirsch et al.).

and in the second instance, as a demonstrative embrace of "environmental democracy" meant to enhance a nation's prospective membership in the European Union.[29] In other words, the generality of the incipient general principle appears to be limited.

In sum, a juridically recognized right to environment may be said to exist officially in Africa, Asia, Europe, and Latin America based on regional treaty, national constitutional authority, or both, but even then on a limited basis as follows:

- *in Africa* (i.e., sub-Saharan Africa), in its autonomous form courtesy of a regional treaty[30] backed by a treaty commission decision (invoking also, *sua sponte*, the derivative rights to life and health),[31] and in its derivative form (mainly the right to life) as pronounced in a few national judicial decisions interpreting constitutional mandates;[32]
- *in Asia* (i.e., South Asia, mainly India), in both its autonomous and derivative forms, via the enforcement by national courts largely of express constitutional authority – though to a degree of growing extraterritorial influence sufficient to suggest the emergence of at least a regional "general principle" voicing the right to environment;[33]
- *in Europe*, in three ways: (1) in its derivative form, mainly via the interpretative application by the European Court of Human Rights of the 1950 European Convention on Human Rights and Fundamental Freedoms;[34] (2) in its autonomous form, principally in Eastern Europe according to national constitutional mandates; and (3) in procedural terms throughout Europe and extending into Central Asia by virtue of the Aarhus Convention and national constitutional and statutory law;[35] and

---

[29] For more details, *see infra* Addendum §§ A–C, at 285–336.

[30] The 1981 Banjul Charter, *supra* note 21.

[31] The Social and Economic Rights Action Center and the Center for Economic and Social Rights v. Nigeria, African Commission on Human and Peoples' Rights, Comm. No. 155/96, Case No. ACHPR/COMM/A044/1, Oct. 27, 2001, available at http://www.umn.edu/humanrts/Africa/comcases/allcases.html (accessed Nov. 25, 2012).

[32] For details, *see infra* Addendum § B(3), at 316–24.

[33] Interestingly, legal scholars and activists appear yet to rely on this law-making authority to defend the standing of the right to environment.

[34] *See supra* note 22.

[35] *See* Bende Toth, *Public Participation and Democracy in Practice: Aarhus Convention Principles as Democratic Institution Building in the Developing World*, 30 J. Land Resources & Envtl. L. 295, 298–320 (2010) (describing how the three pillars of the Aarhus Convention are mirrored in United States federal law, and how they have been implemented domestically in Europe); *see also supra* note 17 (listing the European and Central Asian parties to the Aarhus Convention). Given the acclaim accorded the Aarhus Convention, *supra* note 23, by the United Nations and others outside Europe, and the preexisting pollution-reporting systems codified in the

- *in Latin America*, as in Africa, in its autonomous form courtesy of a regional treaty[36] backed by treaty commission decisions so far limited to the rights of indigenous peoples save one recent decision that implicitly recognizes an autonomous right to environment for all.[37]

3. *The same relatively favorable assessment cannot be made of the human right to environment on the global plane – or, for that matter, in all or most regions and nations of the world at this time – from the standpoint of statist legal process.*

The sum total of the legal and quasi-legal instruments affirming the human right to environment on the global plane, although possibly predictive of future decisional trends, cannot be said to reflect general customary international law at present or at least not in the eyes of the majority of the current world's formal/official governing elites. Neither the quantum nor strength of these communications supports such a conclusion.

On the regional and national planes, except for the possible but as yet uncertain extraregional impact of the Aarhus Convention relative to procedural environmental rights[38] and the occasional national court case invoking international legal authority to define or support a derivative or autonomous right to environment, few law-making and law-enforcing processes sympathetic to the right to environment have demonstrated juridical resilience beyond their regional or national frontiers, and few even within these frontiers. This makes it impossible or at best difficult to deduce from the sum of them a customary practice or general principle that might credibly validate a global right to environment. The full geographic compass of these procedural environmental rights is unclear as are the number of jurisdictions and different kinds of legal systems in which they are recognized and other such conditioning factors.

4. *A number of highly respected international human rights and environmental law scholars and practitioners demur from the foregoing assessment on the grounds that the right to environment – derivative, autonomous, or procedural – may be said to exist universally when pertinent "soft law" instruments and "the intrinsic value of the environment" are taken into account.*

---

domestic law of the United States, *see supra* note 28, it is credible to suggest that the right to procedural environmental rights as articulated in the Convention may be evolving into customary international law status.

[36] The 1988 Additional Protocol to the American Convention on Human Rights in the Area of Economic, Social and Cultural Rights (also known as the Protocol of San Salvador), *supra* note 21.

[37] *See* Case of the Saramaka People v. Suriname, Inter-Am. Ct. Hum. Rts., Ser. C, No. 172 (Nov. 28, 2007).

[38] *Supra* note 23.

Increasingly, international human rights and environmental law scholars and practitioners are calling for, or seriously entertaining, an expansive right to environment as a means to enhance environmental protection. Some of them argue that "soft law" expressions of environmental protection are not, as a practical matter, all that different from their "hard law" counterparts.[39] They do so, understandably, out of concern over current scientific forecasts, but also out of dissatisfaction with traditional international legal process which, they persuasively argue, is not up to the ecological challenges now facing the planet.[40] Among their grievances is "a traditionalist approach to the sources of international law" that "rejects as unpersuasive" the existence of an "expansive right to environment."[41] Rodriguez-Rivera states the case perhaps most succinctly:

> There are many instruments that serve as unmitigated sources for the recognition of the human right to environment in the international legal order, including: the thousands of international environmental soft law instruments; the many national constitutions and legislative acts; the dozens of international, regional, and national court decisions; the hundreds of non-governmental international organizations; the thousands of local or "grassroots level" community organizations, and, more importantly, the overwhelming and sweeping transformation in the valoration of environmental concerns in all levels of society. To ignore this voluminous evidence of the will of the people would be to ignore the evolution of international law during the last half-century.[42]

To this may be added former Indian Chief Justice R. S. Pathak's observation, echoed in Judge Weermantry's separate opinion in the World Court's

---

[39] Notable among them is Rodriguez-Rivera, _supra_ note 2; _see also_ Adelman, _supra_ note 6; Alan E. Boyle, _Soft Law in International Law-making_, in International Law 141 (M.D. Evans ed., 2006); _and_ Leib, _supra_ note 6. For further example, _see_ Patricia W. Birnie & Alan E. Boyle, _International Law and the Environment_ 254–59 (2d ed. 2002); Gormley, _supra_ note 6, at 233; Alexander Kiss & Dinah Shelton, _International Environmental Law_ 173–78 (1992); Alexander Kiss & Dinah Shelton, _International Environmental Law 1994_, Supplement 5–6 (1994); Sands, _supra_ note 6, at 294–307; Geoffrey Palmer, _New Ways to Make International Environmental Law_, 86 Am. J. Int'l L. 259 (1992); John H. Knox, _Climate Change and Human Rights Law_, 50 Va. J. Int'l Law 163 (2009), Rajamani, _supra_ note 6.

[40] Thus did New Zealand's former Prime Minister, Attorney-General, and Minister for the Environment Sir Geoffrey Palmer warn as long ago as 1991: "There is no effective legal framework to help halt the degradation.... There is no institutional machinery to evaluate gaps that may be found in the international framework of agreements or to develop means of assigning priorities among competing claims for attention." Palmer, _supra_ note 39, at 263.

[41] Rodriguez-Rivera, _supra_ note 2, at 44.

[42] _Id._ at 45.

Gabcikovo-Nagymaros Project case,[43] that a clean and healthy environment being indispensable to life itself, let alone to a life of dignity and the fulfillment of other rights and needs, is warrant enough to establish an autonomous right to environment on a universal basis.[44]

The fact remains, however, that all law, its existence and its reach, irrespective of its official or unofficial stature, is not about authority alone, but about authority *and* control jointly (not necessarily in equal measure, but jointly nonetheless). It also is fact that the statist legal world has yet to perform the control or applicative function to fulfill the right to environment (however defined) except in demonstrably limited, often idiosyncratic ways. It is not that the espoused right to environment does not have the content or justiciable standards necessary for statist endorsement and enforcement, as Gunther Handl has argued.[45] Nor is it that the will of the people should be ignored – indeed, the environment would likely be in better shape today had ordinary people been regularly consulted and given real voice yesterday. It is that, though State sovereignty is unquestionably in historic decline, it continues to define the substance and procedure of human rights; and the world's policy- and decision-making elites (with the notable exclusion of much of the developing world) simply have not yet accepted or recognized the right, or the combined soft and hard law authority on which it is said to stand, sufficiently to count as law universally or, indeed, as law at all.[46] The same control or applicative threshold we apply to customary international law in theory, but to all law in practice – the "bite" or "compliance pull" of sanction – has yet to be formally or officially crossed in a substantial or convincing way. It is the accepted authentication and application of durably enforceable norms over time that makes them socially as well as jurisprudentially significant.

---

[43] *Supra* note 17.

[44] *See* Pathak, *supra* note 6, at 211–14

[45] *See* Handl, *supra* note 6. Among developing countries at least, it may just come down to a lack of sufficient economic and technological capacity, not a lack of juridical intent, or so one might infer from Mark Drumbl, *Does Sharing Know Its Limits? Thoughts on Implementing International Environmental Agreements: A Review of National Environmental Policies, A Comparative Study of Capacity-Building*, 18 Va. Envtl. L.J. 281 (1999).

[46] For more details, *see infra* Addendum § A, at 285–307. While some may not currently recognize environmental rights as law, the myriad of "soft law" instruments endorsing such rights exemplify what Nobel Prize winner Amartya Sen calls the "proto-legal" connection between human rights and law – that is, the fact that human rights often form the grounds for adopting legislation, and in some cases might be called "law in waiting." Amartya Sen, *The Global Status of Human Rights*, Grotius Lecture to the International Legal Studies Program, American University, Washington D.C. (March 23, 2011).

5. *The human right to environment, in at least its derivative and autonomous modes if not also its procedural one, is unlikely to grow in normative recognition and jurisdictional reach as long as the state of international law and ecological governance within the current formal/official national and international legal orders remains unchanged.*

A fundamental problem with current national and international environmental law decision-making is a substantial tendency to rely on outmoded jurisprudence developed in a preindustrial era when environmental harm did not for the most part cross national boundaries. A consequential assumption (and legacy) of this jurisprudence is that both the economic benefits and the environmental costs of a State's policies remain within that State's territory. Jurists thus refrain from adjudicating the substantive issues of environmental law and policy that typically inform right-to-environment claims notwithstanding the implications of such deference for the environmental rights of humans and other species living outside the State's territory. Instead, deferring to likewise outmoded juridical–political notions of State sovereignty, jurists tend to limit themselves to procedural rights issues that, as demonstrated by the popularity of the Aarhus Convention,[47] appear less likely to offend national jurisdictional sensibilities. They therefore will focus on access to information, public participation in environmental decision-making, and recourse to just remedies.

This judicial resistance to substantive environmental decision-making is found similarly at the national level. US courts applying the political question doctrine, for example, will make the deferential calculus, often politically inspired, that substantive environmental issues are the province of the legislative and regulatory branches of government, not the judiciary.[48] The substantive issues raised by climate change, rapidly dwindling biodiversity, and other such major environmental problems, many of them transboundary in character, thus face significant theoretical and practical obstacles.

Commonly overlooked, however, is yet another and very serious obstacle to the future of the right to environment as presently conceived (derivative and autonomous especially). At all levels of State governance, most of the world's major industrial powers simply do not support the legal (as opposed to moral) recognition of the right to environment. Not surprisingly, China and the United States, the world's two largest emitters of greenhouse gases, are among

---

[47] *Supra* note 23.
[48] *See* Baker v. Carr, 369 U.S. 186 (1962) (outlining the political question doctrine in its formal posture).

them. Yet, nonsupport is far more widespread than this, at least to the extent that it may be measured by a nation's failure or refusal to constitutionalize the right to environment; as of this writing, fifty-six countries (most of them developing countries and former members of the Soviet Union or Soviet bloc) have no such constitutional provision. In addition, a majority of the G-20 countries and approximately half the world's top thirty-three economies (as determined by the International Monetary Fund) fail to meet this standard of support.[49] This roster of nations includes Australia, Canada, the European Union, Germany, India, Indonesia, Italy, Japan, Mexico, Saudi Arabia, and the United Kingdom, as well as China and the United States. Nonsupport correlates closely with countries that have advanced economies and that are operationally if not also ideologically committed to neoliberal economic dealing, domestically and internationally.

In contrast, a failure or refusal to embrace a treaty or constitutional endorsement of the right to environment (derivative, autonomous, or procedural) does not necessarily indicate a State's lack of attention to, or respect for, environmental well-being any more than does a treaty or constitution that solemnly proclaims the right to ensure its implementation. Numerous treaties and constitutions advocate the protection of environment and natural resources, and often assert a State's obligation to prevent harm to them. Such claims are also made by States with advanced economies otherwise unrestrained by treaty or constitution.

So it may just be that the environment is perceived by jurists in advanced economies to involve too many imponderables and indeterminacies to fashion and implement a workable right in relation to it.[50] But, then, how does one explain the numerous treaty- and constitution-based decisions where – as in South Asia, for example – judges and other decision-makers, of common law training, have somehow managed to overcome these uncertainties? No doubt these complexities are acute in the climate change and biodiversity contexts; but what explains the resistance outside these contexts? Since when are judges and other decision-makers unable to learn from environmental experts and specialists, even to enlist them as special masters of the court?

Perhaps then the fundamental problem is an instinctive conservatism among jurists about developing new or expanded norms and procedures to protect the environment. This is especially evident in settings where free

---

[49] *See* Int'l Monetary Fund, *World Economic Outlook Database*, April 2010, available at http://www.imf.org/external/pubs/ft/weo/2010/01/weodata/index.aspx (accessed Nov. 24, 2012).

[50] *See* in this connection Rajamani, *supra* note 6, at 409–10.

market sensibilities are strong or where emphatic assertions of extraterritorial jurisdictional reach are treated as suspect. Jurists can and often do make narrow interpretations of critical legal authority – in the United States, for example – minimizing or disregarding the broader community interests and policies at stake.

A case in point in the United States is *Flores v. Southern Peru Copper Corporation*, decided by the US Court of Appeals for the Second Circuit in 2003.[51] Peruvian residents and representatives of deceased residents brought personal injury claims against an American copper mining company under the US Alien Tort Claims Act (ATCA),[52] alleging that pollution from the mining company's Peruvian operations had caused them severe, even fatal lung disease. They asserted, too, that their fundamental human rights to life, health, and sustainable development (i.e., their derivative right to a clean and healthy environment) had been violated by this environmental degradation. But they did not succeed. The court held, among other findings, that (a) the rights to health and life were "insufficiently definite" to be binding norms of customary international law that could underwrite subject-matter jurisdiction under ATCA; and (b) the existence of a customary international law rule against intranational pollution was "not established" so as to provide a basis for jurisdiction under ATCA.

In reaching this decision, the court found each type of supporting authority provided by the plaintiffs – applicable treaties, General Assembly resolutions, decisions by international tribunals, and affidavits of international law experts – to be inadequate to validate their claims even though the authority provided appears to have exceeded the requirements relied on in the leading precedent, the court's own *Filártiga v. Peña-Irala*.[53] Moreover, it did so by using narrow grounds to distinguish the *Flores* decision from that of *Filártiga*, and without providing clear standards for future litigants as to what constitutes a violation of customary international law actionable under ATCA. One is led to wonder why it was so difficult for the court to do what its common law counterparts in Bangladesh, India, Nepal, and Pakistan have done when faced with similar issues.[54] One is led to wonder also whether *Flores* is not

---

[51] 406 F.3d 65 (2d Cir. 2003).

[52] 28 U.S.C. § 1350.

[53] 630 F.2d 876 (2d Cir. 1980).

[54] *See, e.g.*, Farooque vs. Government of Bangladesh (Bangladesh 1996) (upholding the plaintiffs' standing based on environmental harm that violated domestic and international legal provisions and made the plaintiffs "persons aggrieved" for purposes of establishing standing); K.M. Chinnappa v. Union of India, 2003 S.C.R. 742 (India 2002) (holding that mining on forest land violated the plaintiff's right to environment under the Stockholm Declaration and

in the tradition of the mid- to late-nineteenth-century US railroad cases, in which continental economic expansion and development in the name of Manifest Destiny led courts to rule against farmers, workers, and unions and "twist[ed] the law unduly in favor of the railroads and of other closely connected corporations."[55]

US resistance to the human right to a clean and healthy environment as expressed in *Flores* is evident on the international plane as well. In *Mossville Environmental Action Now v. United States*, a 2010 admissibility hearing before the Inter-American Commission on Human Rights (IACHR), hundreds of Mossville, Louisiana, residents (mostly African Americans) suffering from, or put at risk of, "various health problems caused by toxic pollution released from fourteen chemical-producing industrial facilities"[56] sought relief by claiming violations of their rights to life, health, privacy, and equal protection, as proclaimed in the 1948 American Declaration of the Rights and Duties of Man.[57] Although the IACHR held that the petitioners had alleged sufficient evidence to establish a *prima facie* case that environmental harm had violated their claimed rights, it did not reach this conclusion without vigorous opposition from the United States.[58] "[There is] no such right as the right to a healthy environment either directly, or as a component of the rights to life, health, privacy and inviolability of the home, or equal protection and freedom of

---

domestic constitutional provisions); Prakash Mani Sharma v. His Majesty's Government Cabinet Secretariat (Nepal 2003) (holding that the government must enforce essential measure to reduce pollution in the Katmandu Valley in order to comply with several constitutional provisions as well as international law); Anjun Irfan v Lahore Development Authority (2002) PLD 555 (Pak.) (holding that the constitutional right to life includes, *inter alia*, the right to an unpolluted environment); *see also infra* Addendum, § B, at 308–28.

[55] Fred Rodell, Nine Men: A Political History of the Supreme Court from 1790 to 1955, 146 (1955).

[56] Org. of Am. Sts., Report No. 43/10, Petition No. 232–05, OEA/Ser LV/II 138 (Mar. 17, 2010), at 1.

[57] American Declaration of the Rights and Duties of Man, adopted at Bogota by the Ninth International Conference of American States, 30 March-2 May 1948. OAS Res OAS Off Rec OEA/Ser L/V/I.4 Rev (1965), arts. I, II, V, IX, XI, & XXIII; *reprinted in* III Basic Documents, *supra* Prologue note 13, at III.B.27.

[58] Nor did the IACHR reach a decision entirely favorable to the petitioners. Finding that the petitioners had exhausted their available US remedies in respect of their claimed violations of their rights to equal treatment before the law and to privacy (involving the inviolability of the home), it declared these claims admissible. However, as it found petitioners not to have exhausted their available domestic remedies relative to their claimed violations of their rights to life and health, the IACHR denied their admissibility. It also should be noted that the petitioners did not claim explicitly that their right to a healthy environment had been violated, doubtless because the American Declaration does not expressly recognize such a right. But one may reasonably infer from the US defense that both the petitioners and the IACHR were assuming the existence of at least a derivative right to environment.

discrimination," the United States argued, and, furthermore, the United States should be considered a "persistent objector" whenever the claimed right is espoused against it.

Of course, the two cases cited are but two cases, and involve the United States only. No doubt others from within the United States and beyond can be cited in contradistinction to them. They are, however, symptomatic of a larger pattern of environmental disregard when free market values are at stake. In the United States, the courts have long resisted constitutionally recognized environmental rights and duties[59] and downgraded citizen suits authorized by key environmental protection statutes[60] while going out of their way to recognize corporations and unions as "persons" with a constitutional free-speech right to advocate independently for the election or defeat of candidates for federal office.[61] Similarly, the US Congress has balked at enacting effective climate change legislation[62] while rushing to encourage more offshore drilling even after the Deepwater Horizon oil disaster;[63] the Department of Interior has held competitive lease-sales of 758 million tons of coal in Wyoming's Powder River Basin;[64] and President Obama at this writing continues to be pressured by Congress and Big Oil to authorize a huge pipeline company with a history

---

[59] *See supra* notes 27–28 and accompanying text.

[60] *See, e.g.,* Lujan v. Defenders of Wildlife, 504 U.S. 555 (1992) (requiring that all plaintiffs, including civil society defenders of the environment, must suffer a concrete, discernible injury – not a "conjectural or hypothetical one" – to have standing to sue in federal court). "In these circumstances," observes Professor Sunstein, "the citizen suit is probably best understood as a band-aid superimposed on a system that can meet with only mixed-success. Instead of band-aids, modern regulation requires fundamental reform." Cass R. Sunstein, *What's Standing After Lujan? Of Citizen Suits, 'Injuries,' and Article III,* 91 Mich. L. Rev. 163, 222 (1992). For another leading U.S. Supreme Court decision limiting on procedural grounds ("ripeness") the capacity of environmentally concerned or damaged plaintiffs to secure hearing of their substantive claims, *see, e.g.,* Ohio Forestry Ass'n v. Sierra Club, 497 U.S. 726 1998, following Abbott Labs. v. Gardner, 387 U.S. 136 (1967) and *Lujan, supra.*

[61] Citizens United v. Federal Election Commission, 130 S.Ct. 876 (2010), holding unconstitutional a 62-year-old federal statute that prohibited corporations from making direct expenditures to support or oppose candidates in federal elections.

[62] *See* Carl Hulse & David M. Herszenhorn, *Democrats Call Off Climate Bill Effort,* N.Y. Times, July 23, 2010, at A15, available at http://www.nytimes.com/2010/07/23/us/politics/23cong.html (accessed Nov. 24, 2012).

[63] *See* Daniel Foster, Comment to the Corner, *Support for Offshore, ANWR Drilling Reaches New Heights,* National Review Online (Mar. 14, 2011, 2:19 pm), available at http://www.nationalreview.com/corner/262094/support-offshore-anwr-drilling-reaches-new-heights-daniel-foster (accessed Nov. 24, 2012).

[64] Press Release, US Dep't of the Interior, Salazar Announces Coal Lease Sales in Wyoming (Mar. 22, 2011), available at http://www.doi.gov/news/pressreleases/Salazar-Announces-Coal-Lease-Sales-in-Wyoming.cfm (accessed Nov. 27, 2012). These sales have prompted three environmental groups to sue the Bureau of Land Management, charging the Bureau with irresponsible stewardship of public land. M. J. Clark, *Coal Lease Sales Lead to Lawsuits,*

of major spills to carry oil to the American heartland from the tar sands of Alberta.[65]

The United States is not alone in these respects. Developmental policies in other countries – such as the European Union's Common Fisheries Policy (CFP) of continuous allocation of fishing quotas greater than the fish stocks can bear[66] – routinely fail to take account of the carrying capacity of natural systems and the secondary effects of extractive industries. Despite prominent scientific warnings, the two premier threats to Earth's ecosystems, climate change and biodiversity, have gone largely unaddressed except by the essentially dysfunctional Kyoto Protocol to the United Nations Framework Convention on Climate Change[67] and the 1972 Convention on Biological Diversity.[68] The ill-fated Copenhagen summit in December 2009 – the Fifteenth Conference of the Parties to the United Nations Framework Convention on Climate Change (COP 15) – never had a real chance of success.[69] Participating States would not even adopt the nonbinding Copenhagen Accord drafted by Brazil, China, India, South Africa, and the United States, though touted as a "meaningful agreement" by the United States.[70] Developed countries refused to commit to legally binding emission reductions and to providing financing and technology for developing country climate mitigation and adaptation needs, and the so-called Basic Countries (the rising developing nations bloc of Brazil, China, India, and South Africa) were prepared to block any imposition of binding emissions reductions on them lest this curb their economic growth.[71] Also,

Wyoming Business Report, Aug. 23, 2011, available at http://www.wyomingbusinessreport.com/article.asp?id=59357 (accessed Nov. 24, 2012).

[65] Lee-Anne Goodman, *State Department's Environmental Analysis Gives Pipeline an Initial Green Light* (Winnipeg Free Press, Canadian Press Online Edition, Aug. 26, 2011, 10:32 am), available at http://www.winnipegfreepress.com/arts-and-life/life/greenpage/state-dept-says-us-canada-oil-pipeline-wont-cause-big-environmental-problems-128464813.html (accessed Nov. 25, 2012).

[66] *See Eur. Comm'n, The Common Fisheries Policy: A User's Guide* (2008), available at http://ec.europa.eu/fisheries documentation/publications/pcp2008_en.pdf html (accessed Nov. 25, 2012).

[67] Dec. 10, 1997, FCCC/CP/1997/7/Add.1; *reprinted in* 37 I.L.M. 32 (1998) *and* V Basic Documents, *supra* Prologue note 13, at V.H.8a.

[68] June 5, 1992, 1760 U.N.T.S. 79; *reprinted in* 31 I.L.M. 818 (1992) *and* V Basic Documents, *supra* Prologue note 13, at V.N.14.

[69] Tom Zeller Jr., *Fault Lines Remain After Climate Talks*, N.Y. Times (Jan. 4, 2010), available at http://www.nytimes.com/2010/01/04/business/energy-environment/04green.html?ref=unitednationsframeworkconventiononclimatechange (accessed June 25, 2011).

[70] For the text of the Copenhagen Accord (Dec. 18, 2009), *see* U.N. Doc. FCCC/CP/2009/11/Add.1 at 5, available at http://unfccc.int/resource/docs/2009/cop15/eng/11a01.pdf (accessed June 25, 2011).

[71] In fairness, it should be noted that, although this agreement was initially opposed by many countries and NGOs because it contained no legally binding commitments for reducing

behind all this dubious maneuvering hover, it would seem, the ancient legal doctrines of *res or terra nullius* and *res communis* (singular) or *res communes* (plural) both of which, over time, have been artfully used by States to warrant their misbegotten, self-interested behavior.[72]

On final analysis, then, it may be that, in a highly decentralized and essentially voluntarist international legal order, the bottom-line commercial imperatives of the contemporary global political economy invariably trump human rights and environmental values. Clearly, it is not a system that invites widespread, much less universal, legal recognition and enforcement of a human right to a clean and healthy environment. Incredible though it may seem, many smart and sophisticated people appear to be incapable of understanding that our formal/official national and international legal orders are structurally organized to contribute to – and not prevent – the deterioration of the natural world. Elizabeth Kolbert of *The New Yorker* puts it crisply: "It may seem impossible to imagine that a technologically advanced society could choose, in essence, to destroy itself, but that is what we are now in the process of doing."[73]

What, then, do we conclude from these findings from the formal/official legal world? That the human right to a clean and healthy environment exists in legal as well as moral terms? Yes. That it is juridically most strongly recognized in its derivative versus autonomous form? Yes. That this acceptance is found principally in the developing worlds of Africa, Asia, and Latin America? Yes. That it is recognized also in expanded procedural terms principally in industrialized Europe? Yes. That there exists a growing but relatively small sentiment, and more regional and national than global, favoring an autonomous right to environment? Yes.

At bottom, it seems, it comes down mostly to a simple but profound truth: that as long as ecological governance remains in the grip of essentially unregulated (liberal or neoliberal) capitalism – a regime responsible for much if not most of the plunder and theft of our ecological wealth over the last

---

CO_2 emissions, as many as 141 countries, including the 27-member European Union, have "engaged" or are likely to have "engaged" with the Accord as of June 7, 2011, representing 87.24% of global emissions. *Who's on Board with the Copenhagen Accord?*, U.S. Climate Action Network (USCAN), available at http://www.usclimate network.org/policy/copenhagen-accord-commitments (accessed June 25, 2011). The central issue is, of course, the meaning or terms of "engagement."

[72] For explanatory discussion, *see infra* text accompanying Ch. 5 notes 5–11 and immediately following Ch. 7 note 44.

[73] Elizabeth Kolbert, *Field Notes from A Catastrophe: Man, Nature and Climate Change* 189 (2006).

century and a half – there never will be a human right to environment widely recognized and honored across the globe in any formal/official sense, least of all an autonomous one. Even the innovative use of the right in its disaggregated, derivative form (e.g., right to life, right to health, etc.) will face an uphill struggle. This is, truly, another inconvenient truth.

The roots of this failure to come to terms with humankind's systemic destruction of the environment run deep. They are reinforced, legitimized, and perhaps even sanctified by the Scientific Revolution of the sixteenth and seventeenth centuries as embodied in the philosophical views of Copernicus, Bacon, Galileo, Descartes, and Newton. We also are heirs to a religious anthropocentrism born of the Reformation, which encouraged so-called civilized humans to see themselves as separate from nature and, indeed, as its masters/beneficiaries rather than its servants/stewards. It has become normal to treat nonhuman species as things or objects to be exploited, not as fellow beings or subjects to be respected. As long as this worldview prevails – as long as we continue to insist that humans are outside Nature and that Nature has no limits – the mainstream economic and political paradigm will not take the right to environment seriously, and it will remain an idiosyncratic influence at best.[74] (It should be added that neither Soviet-based communism nor Chinese-style State capitalism has shown an ability to transcend this way of thinking and governing any more than the capitalist West.)

We recognize that worldviews cannot be summarily swept aside. We therefore take heart from a number of bold, creative attempts to stretch the boundaries of existing legal thought and action to arrest our planet's environmental decline and transform the law itself. Increasing numbers are arguing for establishing rights for people of the future – unborn generations – so that they might enjoy approximately the same earthly bounties we enjoy today. Indeed, two Latin American nations, Ecuador and Bolivia, are currently trying to win legal recognition for the rights of Nature itself. Other encouraging efforts are underway, as well. We now turn to these approaches to gauge their potential for fulfilling human rights principles that could secure and underwrite a clean and healthy environment.

---

[74] *Accord* Alberto Acosta, *Toward a Universal Declaration of Rights of Nature* (Aug. 24, 2010) (article for the AFESE Journal), available in unpaginated manuscript form at http://www. e-joussour.net/files/DDNN_ingl.pdf (accessed June 30, 2011); Cullinan, *supra* Prologue note 20, at Ch. 2 ("The Illusion of Independence").

3

The Quest for a New Rights-Based Pathway

Many environmentalists, frustrated by the failure of conventional policy advo-cacy to make significant headway, see the formal legal order of the State/Market as so deeply committed to narrow conceptions of economic progress and human well-being that it is simply incapable of entertaining more bracing, innovative approaches. Serious reductions in carbon emissions, for example, are typically dismissed as economically irrational or politically impractical. Environmental issues are cast as difficult tradeoffs (e.g., between economic growth and the environment, between human development and biodiversity), a view that conveniently allows the structural limits of the State/Market order to go unaddressed while marginalizing serious policy alternatives.

How, then, can effective new solutions be advanced within the existing legal system? In recent years, two alternative rights-based approaches to a clean and healthy environment have emerged. Each in its own way seeks to surmount the wall of resistance that has kept the right to environment largely in check. The first approach, *intergenerational environmental rights*, though well grounded in legal theory,[1] relies heavily on its ability to appeal to the moral conscience. The second, *Nature's rights*, chooses to alter the procedural playing field altogether by asserting that Nature has legal rights of its own.

Despite significant differences, the two approaches share several features between them. Each is autonomous or holistic rather than derivative or dis-aggregated in legal character. Each relies on both substantive and procedural environmental rights, in the sense that they reformulate and reconceptual-ize environmental rights and look to claimant surrogates to enforce them. In addition, each has been asserted officially, to date, at the national and subna-tional levels primarily. Politically, both approaches reflect a deep frustration

---

[1] *See, e.g.*, Burns H. Weston, *The Theoretical Foundations of Intergenerational Ecological Justice: An Overview*, 34 Hum. Rts, Q. 251 (2012).

with the environmental community's conventional terms of advocacy and the formal legal order's deep commitments to a neoliberal political and economic system.

A. INTERGENERATIONAL ENVIRONMENTAL RIGHTS

The assertion of intergenerational environmental rights focuses on the ecological rights of future generations. Born in modern times of the pioneering scholarship of Edith Brown Weiss[2] and continued by others[3] (including one of us[4]), it is premised on the twin understanding, first, that "the future" is a temporal space without outer limits (because such matters as the storage of radioactive waste make it unwise, except for cognitive convenience, to define the future narrowly[5]), and, second, that "future generations" includes all persons younger than 18 years[6] (i.e., children, as defined by Article 1 of

---

[2] *See* Brown Weiss's germinal book, *In Fairness to Future Generations, supra* Ch. 2 note 6, at 26. But *see also* the earlier essay collection *Responsibilities to Future Generations: Environmental Ethics* (Ernest Partridge ed., 1980).

[3] *See, e.g.*, Tracy Bach, *The Recognition of Intergenerational Rights and Duties in U.S. Law*, in Weston & Bach, *supra* Prologue note 12, at app. A (CLI Background Paper No. 6); Tracy Bach, *The Recognition of Intergenerational Rights and Duties in Foreign Law*, in Weston & Bach, *supra* Prologue note 12, at app. A (CLI Background Paper No. 7); Wilfred Beckerman & Joanna Pasek, *Justice, Posterity, and the Environment* (2001); *Fairness and Futurity* (Andrew Dobson ed., 1999); *Handbook of Intergenerational Justice* 53 (Jörg Chet Tremmel ed., 2006); Hiskes, *supra* Ch. 2 note 6; *Intergenerational Justice* (Axel Gosseries & Lukas H. Meyer eds., 2009); Page, *supra* Ch. 2 note 6; Jörg Chet Tremmel, *A Theory of Intergenerational Justice* (2009); Laura Westra, *Environmental Justice and the Rights of Unborn and Future Generations: Law, Environmental Harm, and the Right to Health* (2006); *see also Beyond Environmental Law: Policy Proposals for a Better Environmental Future* (Alyson C. Flournoy & David M. Driesen eds., 2010), especially *Part I: National Environmental Legacy Act*, at 1–169 [hereinafter Flournoy & Driesen]; Bradford C. Mank, *Standing and Future Generations: Does Massachusetts v. EPA Open Standing for Generations to Come?*, 34 Colum. J. Envtl. L. 1 (2009).

[4] *See* Weston, *supra* note 1; *see also* Burns H. Weston, *Climate Change and Intergenerational Justice: Foundational Reflections*, 9 Vt. J. Envtl. L. 375 (2008); Weston & Bach, *supra* Prologue note 12, at 17–27.

[5] Energy Inst., Inc. v. EPA, 373 F.3d 1251, (D.C. Cir. 2004), a case that concerned, *inter alia*, the temporal standard to be applied to activate safely a federal repository for spent nuclear fuel and high-level radioactive waste at Yucca Mountain, Nevada. The time frame contested ranged from between 10,000 to "hundreds of thousands of years after disposal, 'or even farther into the future." However, because it helps bring potentially vague future persons into meaningful focus, and thereby helps to mobilize much needed political energies, we recommend, for convenience only, a notion of future generations defined by three and a half generations of persons that exist from this day forward, a notion that is derived from the "one hundred year present" of the late sociologist Elise Boulding. *See* Elise Boulding, *The Dynamics of Imaging Futures*, 12 World Future Soc'y Bull. No. 5, at 7 (Sept.–Oct. 1978).

[6] I.e., children, as defined by Article 1 of the Convention on the Rights of the Child, *supra* Ch. 2 note 16.

the Convention on the Rights of the Child[7]). Pursuant to these rights, each generation receives a "natural and cultural legacy" in legal trust from previous generations; and each generation, in turn, holds this legacy in legal trust for generations in the future. This trust relationship grants to future generations a legal right to at least three conditions of ecological and cultural well-being that each living generation is legally obligated to fulfill:

- *conservation of ecological options* – each living generation shall "conserve the [planet's] natural and cultural resource base" and thus "not unduly restrict the options available to future generations in solving their problems and satisfying their own values";[8]
- *conservation of the quality of the planet* – each living generation shall "maintain the . . . planet so that it is passed on in no worse condition than the present generation received it," recognizing that future generations are "entitled to a quality of the planet comparable to the one enjoyed by previous generations";[9] and
- *conservation of equitable resource access* – each living generation shall "provide its members with equitable rights of access to the legacy [of resources and benefits received] from past generations . . . and conserve this access for future generations."[10]

As conditions or obligations of intergenerational ecological justice,[11] these three principles facilitate both the right to and reality of a clean and healthy environment for future generations (living and yet to be born) – assuming, of course, that the present generation has received a clean and healthy ecological legacy in the first place. These principles are also widely endorsed in the documentary literature (some of it predating Brown Weiss) and appear now to be increasingly accepted juridically.[12] One may assume this is so if for no other

---

7 *See supra* note 6.

8 Brown Weiss, *supra* Ch. 2 note 95, at 38, elaborated at 40–42.

9 *Id.* at 42–3.

10 *Id.* at 43–5.

11 In the literature, the terms "intergenerational justice" and "intergenerational equity" may be understood interchangeably. We prefer "intergenerational justice," however, because "equity" has lost some of its resonance since equity was combined with law into one cause of action; also, more importantly, because it evokes the sensibility of "social justice."

12 *See, e.g.,* Stockholm Declaration, *supra* Ch. 2 note 19; Convention for the Protection of the World Cultural and Natural Heritage, Nov. 16, 1972, 1037 U.N.T.S. 151, *reprinted in* 11 I.L.M. 1358 (1972) *and* V Basic Documents, *supra* Prologue note 13, at V.B.4; Convention on the Prevention of Marine Pollution by Dumping of Wastes and Other Matter, Dec. 29, 1972, 1046 U.N.T.S. 120, *reprinted in* 11 I.L.M. 1294 (1972) *and* V Basic Documents, *supra* Prologue note 13, at V.I.15; Convention on International Trade in Endangered Species of Wild Fauna and Flora (CITES), Mar. 3, 1973, 993 U.N.T.S. 243, *reprinted in* 12 I.L.M. 1085

reason than that they comport with both the ethical and pragmatic rationales that give intergenerational justice moral purpose and with the jurisprudential theories of social justice that give them legal standing[13] (i.e., distributive, reciprocity-based, and respect-based theories of social justice[14]).

(1973) *and* V Basic Documents, *supra* Prologue note 13, at V.N.7; Charter of Economic Rights and Duties of States, G.A. Res. 3281, U.N. GAOR, 29th Sess., Supp. No. 31, U.N. Doc A/9631, at 50 (Dec. 12, 1974); *reprinted in* 14 I.L.M. 251 (1975) *and* IV Basic Documents, *supra* Prologue note 13, at IV.H.5; Historical Responsibility of States or the Preservation of Nature for Present and Future Generations, G.A. Res. 35/8, U.N. GAOR, 35th Sess., Supp. No. 48, U.N. Doc A/35/48, at 15 (Oct. 30, 1980), *reprinted in* V Basic Documents, *supra* Prologue note 13, at V.B.10; U.N. World Charter for Nature, G.A. Res. 37/7, Annex, U.N. GAOR, 37th Sess., Supp. No. 51, U.N. Doc A/37/51, at 17 (Oct. 28, 1982), *reprinted in* 22 I.L.M. 455 (1983) *and* V Basic Documents, *supra* Prologue note 13, at V.B.12; The Rio Declaration on Environment and Development, June 13, 1992, U.N. Doc. A/CONF.151/26, *reprinted in* 31 I.L.M. 874 (1992) *and* V Basic Documents, *supra* Prologue note 13, at V.B.18 (hereinafter "Rio Declaration"); Declaration of The Hague, Mar. 11, 1989, U.N. Doc. A/44/340, *reprinted in* 28 I.L.M. 1308 (1989) *and* V Basic Documents, *supra* Prologue note 13, at V.H.5; U.N. Framework Convention on Climate Change, May 9, 1992, 1771 U.N.T.S. 107, *reprinted in* 31 I.L.M. 849 (1992) *and* V Basic Documents, *supra* Prologue note 13, at V.H.8; Convention on Biological Diversity, *supra* note 89. Also, see several regional seas conventions, such as the Revised Barcelona Mediterranean Sea Convention, June 10, 1995, U.N. Doc. UNEP (OCA)/MED IG.6, Annex, *reprinted in* V Basic Documents, *supra* Prologue note 13, at V.I.34; UNESCO Declaration on Responsibilities Towards Future Generations, Nov. 12, 1997, available at http://unesdoc.unesco.org/images/0011/001102/ 10220e.pdf#page=75 (accessed June 25, 2011); Aarhus Convention, *supra* Ch. 2 note 23; Declaration of Bizkaia on the Right to Environment, United Nations Educational, Scientific and Cultural Organization, 30th Sess., Doc. 30C/INF.11 (Feb. 12, 1999), *reprinted in* III BASIC DOCUMENTS, *supra* Prologue note 13, at III.S.5; Resolution on International Mother Earth Day, G.A. Res. 63/278, U.N. GAOR, 63d Sess., Supp. No. 49, U.N. Doc. A/RES/63/49, at 4 (Apr. 22, 2009), *reprinted in* V Basic Documents, *supra* Prologue note 13, at V.B.26. Especially noteworthy is the 1998 Aarhus Convention, *supra*, which builds on the "conservation of access" principle in considerable detail. For helpful insight, see Jeremy Wates, *The Aarhus Convention: Promoting Environmental Democracy*, in *Sustainable Justice: Reconciling Economic, Social and Environmental Law* 393 (Marie-Claire Cordonier Segger & C.G. Weeramantry eds., 2005).

[13] For extensive treatment of the ethical rationales, *see Moral Ground: Ethical Action for a Planet in Peril* (Kathleen Dean Moore & Michael P. Nelson eds., 2010); *see also* Weston (2008), *supra* note 4, at 397–405 (including pragmatic rationales); Weston (2012), *supra* note 1. Additionally, *see* Dinah Shelton, *Nature in the Bible*, in Man and the Environment: Essays in Honor of Alexandre Kiss 63 (1998). Also noteworthy, although addressing *intra*generational concerns more implicitly than explicitly, is *White Paper on the Ethical Dimensions of Climate Change* (Donald Brown et al., eds., undated), available at http//rockethics.psu.edu/climate (accessed Apr. 28, 2012).

[14] The respect-based theory of social justice that we favor builds on two distinct but conceptually related intellectual traditions: the relational metaphysics and "process philosophy" of Alfred North Whitehead, on the one hand, and the values that underlie human rights law and policy, on the other, the core value of which – respect – honors difference, freedom, of choice, equality of opportunity, and aggregate well-being in value processes. For further elaboration and justification, see references cited in note 4, *supra*.

These theories of intergenerational justice have been affirmed in some quarters of everyday law and policy. In the *Bamaca Vélasquez* case decided by the Inter-American Court of Human Rights in November 2000, for example, World Court[15] Judge Cançado Trindade of Brazil, in his separate opinion when he was President of the regional court, observed:

> Human solidarity manifests not only in a spatial dimension – that is, in the space shared by all peoples of the world – but also in a temporal dimension – that is, among the generations who succeed each other in the time, taking the past, present and future altogether.... It is the notion of human solidarity, understood in this wide dimension, and never that of State sovereignty, which lies on [sic] the basis of the whole contemporary thinking on the rights inherent to the human being.[16]

This kind of thinking has scant following in statist circles internationally, however. The far-sighted, eloquent argument famously put forward by the United States in the 1893 *Bering Sea Fur Seals Arbitration*[17] (United States v. Great Britain) in defense of intergenerational environmental rights has not been resurrected in most contemporary international jurisprudence; and though an impressive array of international instruments express concern for the ecological legacy we leave to future generations,[18] either they do not have the force of law or, if considered binding, they lack enforcement procedures adequate to moving from the aspirational to the justiciable.[19]

There are notable exceptions that both explicitly and implicitly strive to conserve ecological options, maintain ecological quality, and/or provide ecological

---

[15] Officially known as the International Court of Justice.

[16] Judgment of Nov. 25, 2000, Inter-Am. Ct. H.R. (Ser. C) No. 70, ¶ 23 (July 25, 2000).

[17] *See* IX Fur Seal Arbitration 2–8 (Washington: Government Printing Office 1895). In a passage that could have been written with present-day greenhouse gases and climate change in mind, the US expressed the ideal of intergenerational justice as a Whitehead-informed, respect-based theory would have it:

> The earth was designed as the permanent abode of man through ceaseless generations. Each generation, as it appears upon the scene, is entitled only to use the fair inheritance. It is against the law of nature that any waste should be committed to the disadvantage of the succeeding tenants. The title of each generation may be described in a term familiar to English lawyers as limited to an estate for life; or it may with equal propriety be said to be coupled with a trust to transmit the inheritance to those who succeed in at least as good a condition as it was found, reasonable use only excepted. That one generation may not only consume or destroy the annual increase of the products of the earth, but the stock also, thus leaving an inadequate provision for the multitude of successors which it brings into life, is a notion so repugnant to reason as scarcely to need formal refutation. *Id.* at 65–66 (footnotes omitted).

[18] *See, e.g.*, all the instruments cited in note 12, *supra*.

[19] For confirmation, see Weston & Bach, *supra* Prologue note 12, at 35–36, 44–45, and 52–53.

access to benefit future generations. Good examples are the 1992 conventions on climate change and biological diversity[20] and the 1998 Aarhus Convention on Access to Information, Public Participation in Decision-Making and Justice in Environmental Matters.[21] But the principal legal recognition of an inter-generational right to the core elements of a clean and healthy environment is found mainly at the national and subnational levels – in constitutions, statutes, regulations, and judicial and other third-party decisions, both explicitly and implicitly.[22]

For example, an amendment to the Constitution of France provides that "[e]ach person has the right to live in a balanced environment which shows due respect for health";[23] and in the French Civil Code the amendment is made subject to the principle of sustainable development which, the Code states, makes it necessary "[to] protect the health of current generations without compromising the ability of future generations to meet their own needs."[24] The Basic Law of Germany, in contrast, recognizes the ecological rights of future generations implicitly (dwelling on duty in lieu of right): "Mindful . . . of its responsibility toward future generations, the state shall protect the natural foundations of life and animals."[25] Similarly implicit is the Constitution of the Commonwealth of Pennsylvania as amended in 1971 to mark the first Earth Day, proclaiming that "[t]he people have a right to clean air, pure water, and to the preservation of the natural, scenic, historic and aesthetic values of the environment" and that these resources "are the common property of all the people, including generations yet to come," held in trust by the Commonwealth for all their benefit.[26] Likewise, the Constitution of the State of Montana as amended in 1972 mandates that "the state and each person shall maintain and improve a clean and healthful environment in Montana for present and future generations."[27]

Also illustrative are such legislative initiatives as Japan's Basic Environmental Law of 1993, which provides, among other things, that "environmental

---

[20] *Supra* note 12.

[21] *Supra* Ch. 2 note 23.

[22] *See* Weston & Bach, *supra* Prologue note 12.

[23] 19 Const. 1958, Charte de l'Environnement de 2004, available at http://www.assemblee-nationale.fr/english/8ab.asp (English transl., accessed June 25, 2011).

[24] Code Civil [C. Civ.] art. L110–2, available at http://195.83.177.9/code/liste.phtml?lang=uk&c=40 (accessed June 25, 2011).

[25] Grundgesetz für die Bundesrepublik Deutschland [Grundgesetz] [GG] [Basic Law], May 23, 1949, BGBl. 1, art. 20(a), available at https://www.btg-bestellservice.de/pdf/80201000.pdf (English transl., accessed June 25, 2011).

[26] Pa. Const. art. I, § 27.

[27] Mont. Const. art. IX, §1.

conservation shall be conducted appropriately to ensure that the present and future generations of human beings can enjoy the blessings of a healthy and productive environment."[28] New Zealand's 1996 Resource Management Amendment Act was designed in part to "[s]ustain the potential of natural and physical resources . . . to meet the reasonably foreseeable needs of future generations."[29] In addition, the US Congress, in enacting the 1994 National Environmental Policy Act (NEPA), declared its intention "[to] create and maintain conditions under which man and nature can exist in productive harmony, and fulfill the social, economic and other requirements of present and future generations of Americans," facilitated in part by mandated environmental impact assessments.[30]

Similar intentions lie behind the establishment in the United States of state public trusts and parks such as the Alaska Permanent Fund (created "to benefit all generations of Alaskans"[31]) and New York State's Adirondack Park (the largest protected area in the contiguous United States, within which state-owned land is mandated to remain "forever wild"[32]). Not to be overlooked are tribal codes such as those giving voice to the "seventh generation principle,"[33] extending responsibility for the environment far into the future.[34] Worldwide, various as one should expect, one finds favorably disposed administrative directives and regulations, both national and subnational, developed to interpret and oversee environmental actions and laws with an eye to the ecological

---

[28] Kankyō kihonhō [Basic Environmental Act], Law No. 91 of 1993, art. 3, available at http://www.env.go.jp/en/laws/policy/basic/ch1.html (accessed June 25, 2011).

[29] Resource Management Act 1991 § 5, available at http://www.legislation.govt.nz/act/public/1991/0069/latest/DLM230265.html (accessed June 25, 2011); *see also* Weston & Bach, *supra* note Prologue 12, at 97 n.115 (listing New Zealand as a country whose laws expressly reference the environmental rights of future generations).

[30] 42 U.S.C. § 4331(A) (1970).

[31] Alaska Stat. § 37.13.020 (2004).

[32] N.Y. Const. art. XIV; *see also* Nicholas Robinson, *"Forever Wild": New York's Constitutional Mandates to Enhance the Forest Preserve* (Feb. 15, 2007), available at http://digitalcommons.pace.edu/cgi/viewcontent.cgi?article=283&context=lawfaculty (accessed June 25, 2011).

[33] E.g., the Dine Natural Resources Protection Act of 2005, available at http://www.sric.org/uranium/DNRPA.pdf (accessed June 25, 2011).

[34] *See* Weston & Bach, *supra* Prologue note 12, at 31 (discussing the mission statement of the Great Lakes Indian Fish and Wildlife Commission invoking the "Anishinaabe Way" that embraces the "Seventh Generation" principle in ecosystem management); N. Bruce Duthu, *The Recognition of Intergenerational Ecological Rights and Duties in Native American Law*, in Weston & Bach, *supra* Prologue note 12, at app. A. *See generally* Brian Edward Brown, *Religion, Law, and the Land: Native Americans and the Judicial Interpretation of Sacred Land* (1999).

rights of future generations. It appears, however, that there are exceedingly few judicial decisions.[35]

In sum, the intergenerational right to a clean and healthy environment is backed by powerfully persuasive ethical and moral arguments,[36] and also is established in law as a matter of principle. Overall, however, legal recognition of intergenerational environmental rights has been hemmed in by doctrines of nonjusticiability – the idea that courts lack the authority to adjudicate these rights for one technical reason or another (e.g., "ripeness," "standing") – so that legal recognition is limited in scope and practice. On the one hand, then, the right must be understood as still emerging; on the other hand, the rights of future generations could plausibly be applied to climate change and other such large-scale hazards.[37]

B. NATURE'S RIGHTS

On September 28, 2008, the people of Ecuador approved, by a 2-to-1 margin, a new constitution that for the first time in modern history recognizes

---

[35] For six known cases granting intergenerational relief, *see* Nat'l Wildlife Fed'n v. Burford, 835 F.2d 305, 326 (D.C. Cir. 1987) (stating that "denying the motion could ruin some of the country's great environmental resources – and not just for now but for generations to come"); Weyerhaeuser Co. v. Costle, 590 F.2d 1011 (D.C. Cir. 1978) (reasoning that "the health and safety gains that achievement of the [Clean Water] Act's aspirations would bring to future generations will in some cases outweigh the economic dislocation it causes in the present generation"); Concerned About Trident v. Rumsfeld, 555 F.2d 817 (D.C. Cir. 1976) (holding that the Navy's environmental impact statement [EIS] was insufficient because it limited the EIS analysis to environmental harms up to a time only seven years away and thus held that the EIS "fail[ed] to ensure that the environment will be preserved and enhanced for the present generation, much less for our descendants"); Cape May Cnty. Chapter, Inc., Izaak Walton League of Am. v. Macchia, 329 F. Supp. 504 (D.N.J. 1971) (holding that an environmental group had standing to sue in a representative status in a class action suit on behalf of future generations to prevent the dredging and development of an island off the coast of New Jersey); Oposa v. Factorian, G.R. No. 101083 (S.C., July 30, 1993) (Phil.) (noting in dicta that minors, their parents, and the Philippine Environmental Network had standing to sue for their own generation and for successive generations based on the concept of intergenerational responsibility and the right to a balanced and healthful ecology), available at http://www.lawphil.net/judjuris/juri1993/jul1993/gr_101083_1993.html; Gray v Minister for Planning [2006] NSWLEC 720, ¶ 116 (Austl.) (reasoning that environmental impact assessments are key considerations because they include the public interest and enable the "present generation to meet its obligation of intergenerational equity by ensuring the health, diversity and productivity of the environment is maintained and enhanced for the benefit of future generations").

[36] For such arguments, *see* references in note 4, *supra*.

[37] *See generally* Tremmel, *supra* note 3.

legally enforceable ecosystem rights. Chapter 7 ("Rights of Nature") of Title II ("Fundamental Rights") of the new constitution[38] grants Nature "the right to integral respect for its existence and for the maintenance and regeneration of its life cycles, structure, functions and evolutionary processes."[39]

In short, the new constitution of Ecuador puts Nature on the same legal footing as individuals and governments, corporations, and other legal persons. Title II treats the natural world – or "Pacha Mama [Goddess Earth], where life is reproduced and occurs" – as having protective rights of its own; when threatened, they can be adjudicated via human surrogates, thus granting Nature legal standing – potentially even beyond Ecuador, depending on the construct of the dispute. The constitution stipulates that "all persons, communities, peoples and nations can call on public authorities to enforce the rights of Nature."[40] It adds that "Nature has the right to be restored" and that "[t]his restoration shall be apart from the obligation of the State and natural persons or legal entities to compensate individuals and communities that depend on affected natural systems."[41]

This constitutional innovation was inspired by indigenous communities in Ecuador demanding environmental protection of their traditional habitats from exploitation and abuse by large, predominantly corporate interests (as in Texaco's defilement of Ecuador's Oriente rainforest[42]). It must be understood

---

[38] To our best knowledge, no official translation of the 2008 Ecuador Constitution has yet been released. For Title II, Chapter Seven, we therefore rely on an English language rendition provided by the Edmund A. Walsh School of Foreign Service at Georgetown University, offering also the original Spanish version of the Constitution. *See Ecuador: Constitutions*, Georgetown Univ., available at http://pdba.georgetown.edu/constitutions/ecuador/ ecuador.html (accessed Jan. 31, 2011). A somewhat different English translation is provided also by the Community Environmental Legal Defense Fund (CELDF), a Pennsylvania-based NGO dedicated to providing legal assistance to governments and community groups working to reconcile human affairs with the natural environment. *See Articles of the Constitution Adopted September 28, 2008*, Community Envtl. Legal Def. Fund, available at http://celdf.org/rights-of-nature-ecuador-articles-of-the-constitution (accessed June 25, 2011). CELDF having assisted Ecuador's Constitutional Assembly in the drafting of Title II, Ch. 7, we believe it to be a worthy translation also.

[39] Ecuador Constitution of 2008, *supra* note 38, at tit. II, ch. 7, art. 1.

[40] *Id.*

[41] *Id.* art. 2.

[42] *See* Inter-Am. Comm'n H.R., Report on the Situation of Human Rights in Ecuador, OEA/Ser.L/V/II.96, doc. 10 rev. 1 (1997), at Ch. VIII. Reporting on the human rights situation of some 500,000 indigenous peoples in Ecuador's interior (known as the Oriente), the IACHR observed that "severe environmental pollution" resulting from decades of developmental activities, mostly of oil drilling concessionaires (Texaco and Ecuador's state-run Petroecuador primarily) that dumped close to 16 million gallons of oil and 20 billion gallons of petroleum waste into roughly 17,000 acres of pristine rainforest, had so despoiled the Oriente environment as to threaten the physical and cultural lives of the indigenous inhabitants of the

as an historic, audacious lifting of the right to a clean and healthy environment to a new, higher level of legal recognition and activism. Not only are plaintiffs stripped of the need to prove self-injury to have legal standing – a hallmark of most judicial systems today – the autonomous right *to* a clean and healthy environment is converted into an autonomous right *of* the environment itself to be clean and healthy. "The essence of Nature's Rights," affirms former President of Ecuador's Constituent Assembly Alberto Acosta in a vigorous and eloquent defense of Ecuador's constitutional daring, "is rescuing the '*right to existence*' of human beings *themselves* . . . . [H]uman beings cannot live apart from Nature."[43]

This "Rights of Nature" idea is certainly not without its critics and detractors.[44] Indeed, it faces an uncertain future in Ecuador itself at this writing. Although lawsuits for the constitutional protection of Nature's Rights in particular circumstances have been filed (and at least one of them successfully litigated[45]), Ecuador has yet to appoint an environmental ombudsperson as called for by the new constitution. Nor has it adopted legislation establishing

---

area, in violation of their internationally as well as constitutionally guaranteed rights to life and health. Stated the Commission in its ruling:

> The Commission recognizes that the right to development implies that each state has the freedom to exploit its natural resources, including through the granting of concessions and acceptance of international investment. However, the Commission considers that the absence of regulation, inappropriate regulation, or a lack of supervision in the application of extant norms may create serious problems with respect to the environment which translate into violations of human rights protected by the . . . American Convention on Human Rights [which] is premised on the principle that rights inhere in the individual simply by virtue of being human. Respect for the inherent dignity of the person is the principle which underlies the fundamental protections of the right to life and to preservation of physical well-being. Conditions of severe environmental pollution which may cause serious physical illness, impairment and suffering on the part of the local populace are inconsistent with the right to be respected as a human being.

Id. at 89; *see also supra* Prologue note 3; Lucy Mayhew, *Rights of Nature*, 253 Resurgence Mag. 8 (2009).

[43] Acosta, *supra* Ch. 2 note 74 (citing Swiss jurist Jörg Leimbacher, Die Rechte der Natur 27 (1988)).

[44] *See, e.g.*, Wesley J. Smith, *Beware "The Rights of Nature*," DAILY CALLER (Dec. 30, 2011), available at http://dailycaller.com/author/wsmith (accessed Jan. 21, 2012).

[45] The case, brought by the Global Alliance for the Rights of Nature, the Ecuadorian Coordinator of Organizations for the Defense of Nature and the Environment (CEDENMA) and Fundación Pachamama under Article 71 (Nature's Rights) of the Ecuadorian Constitution, concerned a three-years old road-widening project of the Government of the Province of Loja which was depositing large quantities of rock and excavation debris in the Vilcabamba River adjacent to the roadway. The project had been undertaken without investigation of its environmental impact. The Provincial Court of Loja ruled in favor of nature

institutional support for effective environmental management from a Nature's
Rights perspective. This may be due, at least in part, to a tactical political
shift by Ecuador's socialist President Rafael Correa, who prompted Ecuador's
new constitution and presided over its signing. Recently, Correa introduced a
new mining law allowing for large-scale, open-pit metal mining in the pristine
Andean highlands and Amazon rainforest, a move that has been criticized as a
capitulation to mining interests at the expense of indigenous peoples as well as
Nature.[46] He also is alleged to have used the protection of Nature as an excuse
for expanding his governmental powers and possibly his personal fortune.[47]
Carlos Zorilla, Executive Director of the Ecuadorian Defensa y Conservación
Ecológica de Intag (Organization for the Defense and Conservation of the
Intag; a grassroots group comprising farmers, peasants, and priests), has put it
this way: "As exciting as these [Nature's Rights] developments are, it was also
inevitable that the people in power would, and will, find ways to circumvent,
undermine, and ignore those rights."[48]

Still, Ecuador's "Rights of Nature" provisions have helped set in motion
what has come to be called the "Pachamama" or "Earth Jurisprudence" movement, now spreading in sub-Saharan Africa, Australia, Canada, India, Nepal,

(principally the Vilcabamba River), issuing a "constitutional injunction" (Granted Constitutional Injunction 11121–2011-0010) to put an end to the environmental damage and ordering comprehensive redress of the harm caused to the river. *See* Gonzalo Ortiz, *Nature's
Rights Still Being Wronged*, INT'L Press Service News Agency (June 3, 2011), available at
http://ipsnews.net/news.asp?idnews=55922 (accessed Jan. 21, 2012). For details, including the
specifics of the injunction, *see* Natalia Greene, *The First Successful Case of the Rights of Nature
Implementation in Ecuador*, Siber Ink, available at http://www.siberink.co.za/siber-ink-blog/
vilcabamba-ecuador-ron-case-complete.pdf (accessed Jan. 21, 2012).

[46] *See, e.g., El Presidente de Ecuador, Rafael Correa, Irrita a EEUU y la Comunidad Indígena
[The President of Ecuador, Rafael Correa, Irritates the United States and the Indigenous Com-
munity]*, America Economica (Jan. 30, 2012), available at http://www. americaeconomica.com/
smartphone/noticia.php?noticia=12151&name=POL%C3%8DTICA (accessed Jan. 30, 2012);
see also Indigenous Ecuadorian Group Sues for "Genocide," Herald Sun (Austl.) (Mar. 30, 2011,
4:39 pm), available at http://www.heraldsun.com.au/news/breaking-news/indigenous-group-
sues-for-genocide/story-e6frf7k6–12260308632 31 (accessed Mar. 30, 2011); *Ecuador's Constitutional Rights of Nature*, Project Censored Media Democracy in Action (May 8, 2010), available at http://www.projectcensored.org/top-stories/articles/18-ecuadors-constitutional-rights-
of-nature (accessed Mar. 30, 2011).

[47] *See Indígenas, Dispuestos a Dialogar con Gobierno de Rafael Correa [Indigenous Peoples
Willing to Engage in Dialogue with Government of Rafael Correa]*, El Universo (Guayaquil,
Ecuador) (Feb. 8, 2012), available at http://www.eluniverso.com/2011/05/12/1/1355/indigenas-
dispuestos-dialogargobierno-rafael-correa.htm (accessed Feb. 8, 2012); *Rafael Correa se Alinea
a las Mineras Transnacionales [Rafael Correa Aligns Himself with Transnational Mining Companies]*, Conflictos Mineros (Ecuador) (Jan. 30, 2012), available at http://www.
conflictosmineros.net/contenidos/12-ecuador/9077-rafael-correa-se-alinea-a-las-mineras trans
nacionales (accessed Feb. 8, 2012).

[48] As quoted in Ecuador Constitution of 2008, *supra* note 38.

New Zealand, the United Kingdom, and even the United States.[49] The movement has been most conspicuous, however, in the Plurinational State of Bolivia, under the leadership of Aymara Indian President Evo Morales.

In 2008, President Morales convened and hosted the World People's Conference on Climate Change and the Rights of Mother Earth,[50] an achievement that prompted the United Nations (UN) General Assembly in 2009 to declare Morales the World Hero of Mother Earth.[51] The conference, held in the small town of Cochabamba, where an historic "water war" helped sweep Morales into power, resulted in a proposed Universal Declaration of the Rights of Mother Earth[52] and a People's Agreement.[53] Doubtless energized by the conference, President Morales and his supporters succeeded in winning UN General Assembly approval of a resolution declaring April 22 International Mother Earth Day.[54] Introduced several weeks after its adoption to the G-77

[49] For some of the details, *see* Cullinan, *supra* Prologue note 20, at 178–91. Regarding the United States, *see* Lili DeBarbieri, *In Bolivia, Ecuador and Pittsburgh, Nature Has Rights*, Ethical Traveler (June 2, 2011), available at http://www.ethicaltraveler.org/2011/06/in-bolivia-ecuador-and-pittsburgh-nature-has-rights; *see also* Community Envtl. Legal Def. Fund, *supra* note 38 ("Nature's Rights"). The most recent country to join the Nature's Rights movement officially is New Zealand when, on August 30, 2012, after prolonged litigation, the Crown government agreed to give legal personhood to the Whanganui River under the name Te Awa Tupua – said to be "the first time a river has been given legal identity." Kate Shuttleworth, *Agreement Entitles Whanganui River to Legal Identity*, The New Zealand Herald, Aug. 30, 2012, available at http://www.nzherald.co.nz/nz/news/article.cfm?c_id=1 & objectid=10830586 (accessed Sept. 8, 2012). Under the agreement, the river, New Zealand's third largest, will be protected by two guardians, one appointed by the Crown and the other by the Whanganui River iwi (the local Māori people). *See* Sandra Postel, *A River in New Zealand Gets A Legal Voice*, National Geographic News Watch, Sept. 4, 2012, available at http://newswatch.national geographic.com/2012/09/04/a-river-in-new-zealand-gets-a-legal-voice (accessed Sept. 8, 2012).

[50] World People's Conference on Climate Change and the Rights of Mother Earth, available at http://pwccc.wordpress.com (accessed Dec. 19, 2011) [hereinafter "PWCCC"].

[51] *See* H.E. Miguel D'Escoto Brockmann, President of the United Nations Gen. Assembly, Remarks at the Mother Earth Special Event (Apr. 22, 2009), available at www.un.org/esa/socdev/unpfii/documents/MEDSE_PGA_ en.doc.

[52] PWCCC, available at http://pwccc.wordpress.com/2010/02/07/draft-universal-declaration-of-the-rights-of-mother-earth-2 (accessed June 25, 2011). For an updated version, *see* *Universal Declaration of the Rights of Mother Earth*, Climate & Capitalism, available at http://climateandcapitalism.com/?p=2268 (accessed June 25, 2011); *see also* Cormac Cullinan, *The Universal Declaration of the Rights of Mother Earth: An Overview*, in Does Nature Have Rights? Transforming Grassroots Organizing To Protect People and the Planet (2011), available at http://canadians.org/rightsofnature (accessed June 25, 2011) (draft form, published by the Council of Canadians, Fundacion Pachamama, and Global Exchange).

[53] PWCCC, available at http://pwccc.wordpress.com/support (accessed June 25, 2011).

[54] International Mother Earth Day, GA Res. 63/278, U.N. GAOR, 63d Sess., Supp. No. 49 (vol. III), U.N. Doc. A/RES/63/49, at 4 (May 1, 2009), *reprinted in* V Basic Documents, *supra* Prologue note 13, at V.B.26.

countries and UN Secretary-General Ban Ki-moon, the resolution expressed the General Assembly's conviction that, to achieve a just balance among the socioeconomic and environmental needs of present and future generations, "it is necessary to promote harmony with Nature and the Earth."[55]

Significantly, these achievements – and implicitly the Pachamama Movement itself – won further General Assembly support in its February 2010 Resolution 64/196 (Harmony with Nature), requesting a report from the Secretary-General on the same theme,[56] which he submitted in August 2010.[57] It also is noteworthy that Secretary-General Ban Ki-moon issued a Mother Earth Day 2010 statement declaring that "protecting the Earth must be an integral component of the strategy to achieve the MDGs [Millennium Development Goals[58]] . . . that world leaders have pledged to try to achieve by 2015, along with other ambitious targets to halve poverty, hunger and disease."[59] Although not legally enforceable officially, actions such as these can help garner support for Nature's Rights that eventually could lead to widespread legal recognition.

Especially instructive in this regard is the proposed Universal Declaration of the Rights of Mother Earth that emanated from the World People's Conference in Bolivia in 2008, which has since been submitted to the UN General Assembly for consideration[60] and which served as a prelude to Bolivia's new Ley de Derechos de La Madre Tierra (Law of Mother Earth), adopted as Law Number 71 by Bolivia's Plurinational Legislative Assembly in December 2010.[61] Clearly drawing inspiration from the 1948 Universal Declaration of

---

[55] *Id.*, at pmbl.

[56] Resolution on Harmony with Nature, GA Res. 64/196, U.N. GAOR, 64th Sess., Supp. No. 49 (vol. I), U.N. Doc. A/RES/64/49, at 267 (Feb. 12, 2010), *reprinted in* V Basic Documents, *supra* Prologue note 13, at V.B.27.

[57] U.N. Secretary-General, *Harmony and Nature*, U.N. Doc. A/65/314 (Aug. 19, 2010).

[58] *See* United Nations Millennium Declaration, GA Res. 55/2, U.N. GAOR, 55th Sess., Supp. No. 49, U.N. Doc A/55/49, at 4 (Sept. 8, 2000), *reprinted in* III Basic Documents, *supra* Prologue note 13, at III.V.5.

[59] *See* U.N. News Centre, Safeguarding Earth Crucial to Development, Human Well-being, Ban Stresses (Apr. 22, 2010), available at http://www.un.org/apps/news/story.asp?NewsID=34445&Cr=&Cr1= (accessed Jan. 22, 2012).

[60] Submission by the Plurinational State of Bolivia to the AWG-LCA, *Additional Views on Which the Chair May Draw in Preparing Text to Facilitate Negotiations Among Parties*, FCCC/AWGLCA/2010/MIS (Apr. 30, 2010).

[61] *See Law of the Rights of Mother Earth*, Wikipedia, available at http://en.wikipedia.org/wiki/Law_of_the_Rights_of_ Mother_Earth (accessed Jan. 22, 2012); *see also Bolivia's Law of Mother Earth Would Give Nature and Humans Equal Protection*, Huffpost Green, available at http://www.huffingtonpost.com/2011/04/13/bolivias-law-of-mother-earth_n_848966.html (accessed June 25, 2011); John Vidal, *Bolivia Enshrines Natural World's Rights with Equal Status for Mother Earth*, guardian.co.uk (Apr. 10, 2011), available at http://www.guardian.co.uk/environment/2011/apr/10/bolivia-enshrines-natural-worlds-rights (accessed June 25, 2011).

Human Rights[62] and the 2000 Earth Charter,[63] it begins with an acknowledgment that "[w]e, the peoples and nations of Earth . . . are all part of Mother Earth, an indivisible, living community of interrelated and interdependent beings with a common destiny."[64] Thereafter, in Article 1(1), it asserts that "Mother Earth is a living being," and in Article 2 specifies the "Inherent Rights of Mother Earth":

> (1) Mother Earth and all beings of which she is composed have the following inherent rights:
>   (a) the right to life and to exist;
>   (b) the right to be respected;
>   (c) the right to regenerate its bio-capacity and to continue its vital cycles and processes free from human disruptions;
>   (d) the right to maintain its identity and integrity as a distinct, self-regulating, and interrelated being;
>   (e) the right to water as a source of life;
>   (f) the right to clean air;
>   (g) the right to integral health;
>   (h) the right to be free from contamination, pollution, and toxic or radioactive waste;
>   (i) the right to not have its genetic structure modified or disrupted in a manner that threatens it integrity or vital and healthy functioning;
>   (j) the right to full and prompt restoration of the violation of the rights recognized in this Declaration caused by human activities;
> (2) Each being has the right to a place and to play its role in Mother Earth for her harmonious functioning.
> (3) Every being has the right to well-being and to live free from torture or cruel treatment by human beings.

Thus, Bolivia and the Pachamama Movement seek generally to shift away from the anthropocentric rights paradigm of environmental protection; and,

---

[62] Universal Declaration of Human Rights (UDHR), G.A. Res. 217A, U.N. GAOR, 3d Sess., 1st plen. mtg., U.N. Doc. A/810, at 71 (Dec. 10, 1948), *reprinted in* III BASIC DOCUMENTS, *supra* Prologue note 13, at III.A.1.

[63] The Earth Charter, adopted at The Hague by the Earth Charter Commission, 29 June 2000. *See Earth Charter in Action*, Earth Charter Commission, available at http://www.earthcharterinaction.org/content/pages/Read-the-Charter.html (accessed June 25, 2011).

[64] Universal Declaration of the Rights of Mother Earth, *supra* note 224, pmbl. For an anthology of commentary on the Declaration, *see The Rights of Nature: The Case for a Universal Declaration of the Rights of Mother Earth* (2011), available at http://canadians.org/rightsofnature (accessed Jan. 22, 2012), published jointly by the Council of Canadians, Fundación Pachamama, and Global Exchange.

as with Ecuador's constitutional evolution, they have won growing numbers of adherents and supporters.[65]

Although the Mother Earth declaration details "[o]bligations of human beings to Mother Earth,"[66] it does not identify the mechanisms and procedures through which those obligations might be enforced – an omission that appears to have given President Morales room to maneuver in ways that have caused some to question the depth of his commitment to Nature's Rights and the rule of law. Recently, for example, after Morales announced plans to build a highway through the Amazon Basin that would encroach on the ancestral lands of indigenous communities, protestors who reacted indignantly were subjected to a violent government crackdown that led to four deaths. The conflict fueled a growing concern that, as in the case of Ecuador's President Correa and despite pleas for forgiveness, President Morales was seizing extraconstitutional power and sanctioning land grabs at the expense of indigenous peoples and peasant communities.[67] If the UN General Assembly does in fact endorse Bolivia's revolutionary initiative, its action will be valuable if it helps point the way to practicable and effective legal and social governance mechanisms and to operational arrangements that obtain at different levels of social governance in Bolivia and worldwide.

These paradigm-shifting developments in Ecuador and Bolivia, it should be noted, have received scant attention in the United States media (and seemingly other non-Latino media) except as passing objects of bemused curiosity, even derision.[68] Perhaps this is to be expected. Such shifts are rarely if ever popular

[65] *See* text accompanying note 50, *supra*. *See also* The Rights of Nature, *supra* Ch. 2 note 38.

[66] Universal Declaration of the Rights of Mother Earth, *supra* note 60, art. 3.

[67] *See, e.g., 2011 Bolivian Protests*, Wikipedia, available at http://en.wikipedia.org/wiki/2011_Bolivian_protests#cite_note-FT 2010–269-0 (accessed Feb. 12, 2012); Carlos A. Quiroga L., *Indígenas Reviven Conflicto por Carretera en Bolivia* [*Indigenous Peoples Revive Conflict over the Highway*], Reuters América Latina (Jan. 30, 2012), available at http://lta.reuters.com/article/domesticNews/idLTASIE80ToFD 20120131 (accessed Feb. 12, 2012) *Defensor del Pueblo Pide a Evo No Promulgar Ley de Consulta por ser Inconstitucional* [*Public Defender Asks Evo to Not Enact the Consultation Act Because It Is Unconstitutional*], Los Tiempos (Feb. 10, 2012), available at http://www.lostiempos.com/diario/actualidad/politica/20120210/defensor-del-pueblopide-a-evo-no-promulgar-ley-de-consulta-porser_159947_334202.html (accessed Feb. 12, 2012); *El Gobierno Evadió la Consulta y Hoy la Defiende como "Derecho"* [Government Evaded Query, Now Defends It as "Right"], Los Tiempos (Feb. 10 2012), available at http://www.lostiempos.com/diario/actualidad/economia/20120209/el-gobierno-evadio-la-consulta-y-hoy-ladefiende-como_159751_333762.html (accessed Feb. 12, 2012); ¿*Más Leyes Inconsultas?* [*Need More Unwise Laws?*], Los Tiempos (Feb. 10, 2012), available at http://www.lostiempos.com/diario/opiniones/columnistas/20120208/mas-leyes-inconsultas_159593_333413.html (accessed Feb. 12, 2012).

[68] *See, e.g.,* Nita Still, *Lies and Deceptions*, siskiyoudaily.com (July 19, 2011, 9:01 am), available at http://www.siskiyoudaily.com/opinions/letters_to_the_editor/x121482358/-Lies-and-deceptions

at their outset. Moreover, the Pachamama Movement seeks to catalyze a great socioeconomic shift away from the anthropocentric conceits dominant in free-market countries such as the United States.

It is arguably remarkable, therefore, that it was a law professor from North America, not Latin America, who first provided the intellectual foundations for Nature's Rights: Christopher Stone of the University of Southern California in a now canonical essay *Should Trees Have Standing? – Toward Legal Rights for Natural Objects.*[69] Stone's plea for the "rights of Nature," published in 1972, gave legal voice to Aldo Leopold's "land ethic."[70] Stone pointed out that the law routinely transmutes the fictional into justiciable reality: "We have been making persons out of children although they were not, in law, always so. And we have done the same, albeit imperfectly some would say, with prisoners, aliens, women (especially of the married variety), the insane, Blacks, and Indians."[71] The US judiciary has even vested corporations with First Amendment rights.[72] Joint ventures, trusts, municipalities, ships, and other inanimate right-holders, too, have been endowed with legal personhood. Until now, however, legal innovation to recognize the interests of Nature has never taken root. As Stone conceded, "[t]hroughout legal history, each successive extension of rights to some new entity has been . . . a bit unthinkable,"[73] adding that "[w]e are inclined to suppose the rightlessness of rightless 'things' to be a decree of Nature, not a legal convention acting in support of some status quo."[74]

(accessed Feb. 12, 2012); Jonathan Wachtel, *U.N. Prepares To Debate Whether 'Mother Earth' Deserves Human Rights Status*, foxnews.com (Apr. 18, 2011), available at http://www.foxnews.com/world/2011/04/18/prepares-debate-rights-mother-earth (accessed Feb. 12, 2012).

[69] 45 S. Cal. L. Rev. 450 (1972); *see also Christopher D. Stone, Should Trees Have Standing: And Other Essays on Law, Morals, and the Environment* (2010); Susan Emmenegger & Axel Tschentscher, *Taking Nature's Rights Seriously: The Long Way to Biocentrism in Environmental Law*, 6 Geo. Int'l Envtl. L. Rev. 545 (1994) (revisiting the subject twenty-two years after the publication of Stone's essay). *See* yet more recently The Rights of Nature, *supra* Ch. 2, note 38; *Should Trees Have Standing? 40 Years on* (Anna Grear ed., 2012).

[70] Aldo Leopold, *A Sand County Almanac* 201–26 (1981). Leopold wrote: "[T]he 'key-log' which must be moved to release the evolutionary process [of cultivating a land ethic] is simply this: quit thinking about decent land-use as solely an economic problem. Examine each question in terms of what is ethically and esthetically right, as well as what is economically expedient. A thing is right when it tends to preserve the integrity, stability and beauty of the biotic community. It is wrong when it tends otherwise. . . . The fallacy the economic determinists have tied around our collective neck, and which we now need to cast off, is the belief that economics determines *all* land use. This is simply not true." *Id.* at 224–25.

[71] Stone, *supra* note 69, at 2.

[72] Citizens United v. Federal Election Commission, 130 S.Ct. 876 (2010).

[73] Stone, *supra* note 69, at 2.

[74] *Id.*

Stone's idea that natural objects should have rights gave rise to US Justice William O. Douglas's spirited dissent in *Sierra Club v. Morton*[75] in which he wrote approvingly of it. Yet, Douglas's endorsement provoked skepticism, even disdain at the time,[76] and as late as 2009, Stone's idea roused antipathy.[77]

Today, however, Ecuador's and Bolivia's assertions are causing some lawyers and policy-makers to revisit Stone's argument and see merit in it. President Obama's top science advisor, John Holdren, for example, has described Stone's arguments as "tightly reasoned."[78] Presumably this is due in part to the gravity and urgency of climate change and other large-scale environmental threats; but one can sense also not a little professional frustration with a system of environmental laws and regulations that "don't actually protect the environment" but, "at best . . . , merely slow the rate of its destruction."[79] So

---

[75] 405 U.S. 727, 741 (1972).

[76] *See*, for example, the derisive verse penned by attorney John M. Naff, Jr., under the title *Reflections on the Dissent of Douglas, J.* in Sierra Club v. Morton, 58 A.B.A. J. 820 (1972):

> If Justice Douglas has his way –
> O Come not that dreadful day –
> We'll be sued by lakes and hills
> Seeking a redress of ills.
> Great Mountain peaks of name prestigious
> Will suddenly become litigious.
> Our brooks will babble in the courts,
> Seeking damages for torts.
> How can I rest beneath a tree
> If it may soon be suing me?
> Or enjoy the playful porpoise
> While it's seeking habeas Corpus?
> Every beast within his paws
> Will clutch an order to show cause.
> The Courts besieged on every hand,
> Will crowd with suits by chunks of land.
> Ah! But vengeance will be sweet
> Since this must be a two-way street.
> I'll promptly sue my neighbour's tree
> For shedding all its leaves on me.

[77] Persons sympathetic to Stone's thesis, for example, are reported to have been identified as "radical," a McCarthy-style ploy well known to marginalize people and ideas. *See*, e.g., Christopher Neefus, *In the 70s, Obama's Science Adviser Endorsed Giving Trees Legal Standing to Sue in Court* (July 29, 2009), available at http://www.cnsnews.com/node/51756 (accessed June 25, 2011).

[78] As quoted in Neefus, *supra* note 77. According to this source, Holdren supports Stone's thesis and thus also the idea of Rights of Nature.

[79] Mari Margil, *Stories from the Environmental Frontier*, in *Exploring Wild Law: The Philosophy of Earth Jurisprudence* (Peter Burdon, ed., 2011), as quoted in Peter Burdon, *The Rights of Nature: Reconsidered*, 49 Austl. Human. Rev. 69, 70 (2010).

says, at any rate, the Associate Director of the Community Environmental Legal Defense Fund (CELDF), a nongovernmental not-for-profit environmental law firm based in south-central Pennsylvania.[80] CELDF is helping communities across the United States develop and adopt Rights of Nature ordinances that put the power of legal protest into the hands of local citizens without their having to prove personal environmental harm to achieve standing. It also assisted delegates to Ecuador's Constitutional Assembly in rewriting that country's constitution, specifically in the drafting of the Rights of Nature language, drawing on the Rights of Nature ordinances that CELDF has promoted at home.[81] "[E]nvironmental protection cannot be attained," CELDF asserts on its website, "under a structure of law that treats natural communities and ecosystems as property."[82] This is a crude but essentially accurate judgment. Adds Peter Burdon, paraphrasing the CELDF website: "[B]y every measurable statistic, the environment is in worse condition today than thirty years ago when the first environmental protection law was passed."[83]

Of course, this sort of initiative (national or international) does not in itself change the economic practices and cultural norms that are primarily to blame for our environmental predicament. Local environmental ordinances are subservient to the higher laws of State and constitution, and national and even international environmental priorities are subservient to the higher interests of the Market and national security – as we have seen, for example, in the politics of the Kyoto Protocol, the UNFCC's COP 15 in Copenhagen, and COP 16 in Cancun, and the UN Conference on Sustainable Development in Rio de Janeiro.[84] As Stone correctly foresaw, the supposed theoretical barriers to change have deeper origins in powerful "psychic and socio-cultural aspects" that are not easily overcome.[85] At the same time, the growing appeal

---

[80] *See Community Envtl. Legal Def. Fund,* available at http://www.celdf.org. In particular, *see* the CELDF's *April 2010 Draft Rights of Nature Ordinance,* available at http://www.celdf.org/-1–6 (each accessed June 25, 2011).

[81] *See Rights of Nature,* CELDF, available at http://www.celdf.org/rights-of-Nature (accessed June 25, 2011).

[82] *Rights of Nature, supra* note 80, says CELDF's Co-founder and Executive Director Thomas Linzey, quoting an unidentified source, "the only thing that environmental regulations regulate are environmentalists." *Of Corporations Law, and Democracy: Claiming the Rights of Communities and Nature,* 25th Annual E. F. Schumacher Lecture (Oct. 2005), available at http://neweconomicsinstitute.org/publications/lectures/of-corporations-law-and-democracy (accessed June 25, 2011).

[83] Burdon, *supra* note 79, at 72.

[84] "UNFCC" is the acronym for "United Nations Framework Convention on Climate Change." The acronym "COP" is shorthand for "Conference of the Parties" to the 1992 Climate Change Convention.

[85] Stone, *supra* note 69, at 7.

of CELDF's work, nationally and transnationally, suggests a promising new vanguard for environmental advocacy that could ultimately transform environmental law.

C. FOUR SYSTEMIC COMPLICATIONS

Both the intergenerational and Nature's Rights approaches to environmental protection and sustainability have their own complexities, well beyond the psychic and socio-cultural ones. They necessarily raise fundamental questions of economic and political governance and moral philosophy. They also challenge the worldwide corporate-led, bigger-better/-more value system within which most of us live (or, in the name of development, seek to live). Finally, society and lawyers have a quite natural tendency to treat the unfamiliar cautiously if not apprehensively.

At the same time, new approaches require that we contend with significant issues that arise from the official legal systems within which they exist. Three procedural issues – legal surrogacy, legal standing, and uncertainty in determining future damage – stand out; so also does a fourth – anthropocentrism – although arguably it is more substantive than procedural.

1. *Legal Surrogacy*

The intergenerational rights and Nature's Rights approaches equally share unresolved questions concerning the threshold issue of qualified representation. To function, each approach requires surrogates to represent their beneficiaries – future generations in the first instance, Mother Nature in the second. Each therefore raises a host of representational issues that appear not to have been thoroughly or widely vetted: Should the surrogate be a "guardian" (as recommended vis-à-vis future generations in preparation for the 1992 UN Conference on Environment and Development [UNCED] conference in Rio[86]),

---

[86] In anticipation of the 1992 U.N. Conference on Environment and Development (UNCED) Earth Summit in Rio and in furtherance of Principle 1 of the 1972 Stockholm Declaration (*supra* Ch. 2, note 19) declaiming that "Man . . . has the solemn responsibility to protect and improve the environment for present and future generations," the Maltese delegation submitted to the Preparatory Committee a proposal to institute a guardian officially to represent the interests of future generations. Except for the earnest musings of scholars, however, little if anything has been done in this regard in the statist arena vis-à-vis future generations; nor in relation to Nature's Rights, it seems, except, so far, in Ecuador and Bolivia. But for scholarly work, *see*, for example, Stone, *supra* note 69, at ch. 5; *see also* Cullinan, *supra* Prologue, note 20; Weston & Bach, *supra* Prologue, note 12; and the scholars cited in notes 3–4, *supra*.

or would an "ombudsperson" or even an "everyman" model be more appropriate (each of them options under Article 3 of the Universal Declaration of the Rights of Mother Earth[87])? Who, in short, should serve in surrogate capacity? What kind of individual, institution, or agency, and with what geopolitical reach? How should the surrogate be selected? What background, training, and experience should the surrogate have? What obligations should the surrogate be required to fulfill, and what functions should he, she, or it be expected to perform? For whom or what, exactly, should the surrogate be authorized to speak? What guidelines or standards of judgment should the surrogate be expected to follow, and who should author them in the first place? To whom should the surrogate account? And so forth.[88]

None of these operational questions is easily answered, but neither are they insurmountable. Every legal system, certainly the most advanced, has had to wrangle with these and related issues every time it has had to deal with the rights and interests of women, children, and unborn, mentally retarded, and/or elderly infirm persons, for example. The current statist legal framework notwithstanding, it seems reasonable to believe that the world can handle these issues when its own sustainability is at stake.

2. *Legal Standing*

Even if surrogates for future generations and Mother Nature succeed at establishing their credentials, they run up against other, potentially insurmountable threshold criteria of justiciability. Prominent in this regard is the much-litigated doctrine of legal standing or *locus standi*, requiring a personal stake in the outcome of a case to bring suit. This principle is common within many legal systems in one form or another inasmuch as it helps to keep the legal process "tied to its ultimate sources of legitimacy."[89] In *Lujan v. Defenders*

---

[87] *Supra* note 60. Article 3(2)(h) of the Mother Earth Declaration provides as follows: "Human beings, all States, and all public and private institutions to defend the rights of Mother Earth and of all beings...."

[88] For some conscientious answers to these kinds of representational questions, see WESTON & BACH, *supra* Prologue note 12, at 81 (Recommendation 10: Adopt a Model Executive Order Establishing an Office of Legal Guardian for Future Generations and Provide for the Training and Certification of Legal Guardians, authored mostly by Carolyn Raffensperger).

[89] David Johnson, *The Life of the Law Online*, First Monday (Feb. 6, 2006), available at http://www.ucmp.berkeley.edu/cambrian/cambrian.php (accessed June 30, 2011). For helpful exploration of legal standing and related doctrines without as well as within the United States, *see*, for example, Constitutional Rights, *supra* Ch. 2, note 26.

of Wildlife (1992),[90] the US Supreme Court articulated a highly restrictive three-part test to determine whether the "standing" requirement is met: Plaintiffs must prove (a) actual personal injury, (b) which can be fairly traced to defendants' alleged harmful acts, and (c) is likely capable of favorable redress – or face dismissal of their claims without consideration of their merit.[91] The Nature's Rights approach exempts surrogates from such traditional standing requirements because it measures claimed environmental damage not by human loss of use of an ecosystem but by harm done to the ecosystem itself, and thus presupposes or explicitly grants legal standing to those who would defend the environment (e.g., everyman under Ecuador's constitution[92]), generally residents of US municipalities.[93]

The intergenerational rights approach, however, does not have the same warrant, especially in free-market economies such as that in the United States. Legal standing in the United States has much to do with the Article III "cases and controversies" clause of the US Constitution which, over the years, the Supreme Court has interpreted to sharpen the adversarial nature of cases and to define the US judiciary's boundaries within the separation of powers mandated by the Constitution.[94] For example, as the post-*Lujan* case of *Friends*

---

[90] 504 U.S. 555 (1992). For helpful elaboration and analysis, *see* Robin Kundis Craig, *Standing and Environmental Law: An Overview*, (FSU Coll. of Law, Pub. Law Research Paper No. 425), available at http://papers.ssrn.com/sol3/papers.cfm?abstract_id=1536583 (accessed June 30, 2011).

[91] Among many critiques of this and like US decisions for being too restrictive, especially in environmental cases, *see*, for example, Robin Kundis Craig, *Removing the "Cloak of a Standing Inquiry": Pollution Regulation, Public Health, and Private Risk in the Injury-in-Fact Analysis*, 29 Cardozo L. Rev. 149, 176–83 (2007); Neil Gormley, *Standing in the Way of Cooperation: Citizen Standing and Compliance with Environmental Agreements*, 16 Hastings W.-N W. J. Envtl. L. & Pol'y 397, 398 (2010); Sunstein, *supra* Ch. 2, note 20.

[92] *See supra* note 40 and accompanying text.

[93] *See, e.g.*, Section 7 of the April 2010 Draft Rights of Nature Ordinance of the Community Environmental Law Defense Fund (CELDF), *supra* note 38.

[94] U.S. Const. art. III, § 2 provides: "The judicial power shall extend to all cases, in law and equity, arising under this Constitution, the laws of the United States, and treaties made, or which shall be made, under their authority – to all cases affecting ambassadors, other public ministers and consuls; – to all cases of admiralty and maritime jurisdiction; – to controversies to which the United States shall be a party; – to controversies between two or more states; – between a state and citizens of another state; – between citizens of different states; – between citizens of the same state claiming lands under grants of different states, and between a state, or the citizens thereof, and foreign states, citizens or subjects." Addressing the meaning of "cases" and "controversies," Chief Justice Earl Warren explained on behalf of the 8–1 majority in Flast v. Cohen, 392 U.S. 83, 95 (1968):

In part, those words limit the business of federal courts to questions presented in an adversary context and in a form historically viewed as capable of resolution through the judicial process. And in part those words define the role assigned to the judiciary in a tripartite allocation of power to assure that the federal courts will not intrude into areas committed to the other

of the Earth, Inc. v. Laidlaw Environmental Services (TOC), Inc.[95] and the writings of qualified scholars[96] make clear, the doctrine of legal standing in environmental cases, like all legal norms, is subject to interpretation, and thus open to possible other influencing factors, whether or not stated. In the intergenerational rights context, legal standing decisions may be the consequence, at least in part, of an understandable bias favoring the property rights of presently living generations or, alternatively, of ignorance or misunderstanding of theories of intergenerational ecological justice,[97] perhaps the result of bias but in any case inviting extra caution. When plaintiffs are members of future generations, the assumed complexities in dealing with an abstract group of individuals (if they be not persons younger than 18 years) make this "standing" hurdle particularly challenging, as the few known cases granting relief for intergenerational ecological harms would seem to affirm.[98]

In contrast, an alternative, favorable scenario within the formal or official legal framework is possible, even within market economies. "Australia, New Zealand, Germany, Japan, France, Israel, The Philippines, the U.K., and Sweden," reports Tracy Bach, "all provide examples of how different countries, with different legal systems, have inserted the rights of future generations into their governing law."[99] Not to be overlooked, although yet to gain real traction, is a posterity proposal within the US constitutional system for a new and independent doctrine of equitable standing for future generations based on the US Constitution's Preamble: "We the People of the United States, in Order to form a more perfect Union, ... to ourselves and our Posterity, do ordain ... "[100]

On final analysis, however, given the worldwide paucity of cases on the ecological rights of future generations, it is not likely that the courts will take the lead in recognizing such rights. More likely they will invoke another

---

branches of government. Justiciability is the term of art employed to give expression to this dual limitation placed upon federal courts by the "case and controversy" doctrine.

[95] 528 U.S. 167 (2000).

[96] *See, e.g.*, the scholars cited in Ch. 3, note 91, *supra*; *see also* Joseph M. Stancati, *Victims of Climate Change and Their Standing to Sue: Why the Northern District of California Got It Right*, 38 Case W. Res. J. Int'l L. 687, 704–06 (2007); Justin R. Pidot, *Global Warming in the Courts: An Overview of Current Litigation and Common Legal Issues* 3–4 (Georgetown Envtl. Law & Policy Inst. 2006), available at http://www.law.georgetown.edu/gelpi/current_research/documents/GlobalWarmingLit_CourtsReport.pdf (accessed June 30, 2011).

[97] For an attempt at enlightenment, *see* Weston (2012), *supra* note 1.

[98] *See* cases cited in note 35, *supra*.

[99] Bach (No. 7), *supra* note 3, at 17. For further evidence, *see* Constitutional Rights, *supra* Ch. 2, note 26.

[100] *See* John Edward Davidson, *Tomorrow's Standing Today: How the Equitable Jurisdiction Clause of Article III, Section 2 Confers Standing upon Future Generations*, 28 Colum. J. Envtl. L. 185 (2003).

nonjusticiability doctrine known in the United States as the "political question doctrine," leaving it to the administrative and legislative branches to untangle the legal – and political – complexities involved.[101] They probably will apply it to Nature's Rights as well, which, under this doctrine, will most likely not be exempted if and when challenged.[102] Still, future generations and Mother Nature stand at Law's gate, hoping that the gatekeepers are listening. At bottom it is a matter of moral/political values and choice.

3. Uncertainty of Future Damage

Assuming they have avoided or overcome the difficulties of surrogacy and legal standing, claimants espousing the ecological rights of future generations and Nature's Rights must, like all who seek redress for alleged environmental damage, demonstrate environmental loss in fact and extent. Often – in the case of intergenerational rights claims especially – this requires having to estimate and prove the likelihood that future damage will occur, at once or cumulatively over time. In this setting, decision-makers in the present must account for the probabilistic nature of consequences in the future, which can be especially difficult to establish for events that occur gradually over the long term. The likelihood that a given cost or benefit will materialize in the future is affected both by scientific uncertainty in projecting outcomes and by the possibility of unforeseen external influence. This difficulty is reflected in the aphorism "a bird in the hand is worth two in the bush," which economists have taken to heart with the mathematical tool of discounting, the practice of reducing future costs and benefits by a set percentage so they can be compared with the immediate consequences of a decision.[103]

---

[101] *See* Baker v. Carr, 369 U.S. 186 (1962) (outlining the political question doctrine). *But see* James R. May, *Climate Change, Constitutional Consignment, and the Political Question Doctrine*, 85 Denv. U. L. Rev. 919 (2008) (arguing that courts often misapply the political question doctrine in the context of environmental litigation).

[102] While legal standing poses an obstacle for the Nature's Rights approach in the judiciary, it does not create the same difficulty for local legislative initiatives, which are gaining traction in municipalities like Pittsburgh, Pennsylvania, and over two dozen others. *Rights of Nature FAQs*, Community Envtl. Legal Def. Fund, available at http://celdf.org/-1-27 (accessed Aug. 24, 2011).

[103] The issue is complicated, as briefly explained in Weston & Bach, *supra* Prologue note 12, at 54:

> Economists believe that benefits received in the future generally have less value than those received in the present, because people have a "positive pure time preference," meaning that they prefer to receive benefits now rather than in the future. Economists also believe that because society will continue to become richer and consume more, benefits consumed now have greater marginal utility than those in the future, when

A form of cost–benefit analysis, discounting has the effect of favoring short-term benefits at the expense of long-term costs. Such a trade-off is not only problematic for the future damaged claimant, it often involves continued and widespread environmental degradation in exchange for temporary economic benefit. Not surprisingly, it works well for those who would champion corporate and state economic interests over individual and community environmental interests.

Discounting future environmental consequences has its own practical and moral difficulties.[104] Economists often cannot agree on an accurate discount rate for a given problem, and "the precise discount value chosen can result in very different regulatory choices."[105] In addition, some question how a discount rate could be set to account for projected costs that are "catastrophic" and "irreversible,"[106] as in the case of climate change, for example. Arguably more important, discounting provokes an ethical question of fairness because its cost–benefit trade-offs privilege present market interests over future nonmarket interests.

Both the intergenerational rights claimant and the Nature's Rights claimant are disadvantaged by this supposedly neutral tool. As Cass Sunstein and Arden Rowell note with respect to the intergenerational rights claimant (but applicable to the Nature's Rights claimant as well), "the moral obligations of current generations should be uncoupled from the question of discounting, because neither discounting nor refusing to discount is an effective way of ensuring that those obligations are fulfilled. The moral issues should be investigated directly, and they should be disentangled from the practice of discounting."[107] Accordingly, it may be argued, discounting is an inherently unsatisfactory tool for addressing the crucial and controversial issue of future damage uncertainty in environmental decision-making.[108]

---

any particular cost or benefit will constitute a smaller portion of society's total wealth. In addition, economists highlight the "opportunity cost" of spending resources now rather than later. The cost of regulatory action now theoretically means forgoing the opportunity to invest the money instead, let it grow in value, and then have greater wealth with which to purchase benefits in the future.

[104] *See* Joseph H. Guth, *Resolving the Paradoxes of Discounting, in* Weston & Bach, *supra* Prologue note 12, at app. A (CLI Background Paper No. 12).

[105] Weston & Bach, *supra* Prologue note 12, at 55.

[106] *See* Ackerman & Heinzerling, *supra* Ch. 1 note 48, at 185–86; Kysar, *supra* Ch. 1 note 48, at 71–98; McGarity, Shapiro, & Bollier, *supra* Ch. 1 note 48.

[107] Cass R. Sunstein & Arden Rowell, *On Discounting Regulatory Benefits: Risk, Money, and Intergenerational Equity*, 74 U. Chi. L. Rev. 171, 199 (2007).

[108] For detailed overviews of the deficiencies of discounting, *see* Weston & Bach, *supra* Prologue note 12, at 55–59, and Guth, *supra* note 104; *see also* Ackerman & Heinzerling and Kysar, *supra* note 106.

There are, thus, no easy formulae or techniques that will reduce the problem of uncertainty to an unambiguous mathematical calculation. The uncertainty-of-future-damage argument in the cloak of discounting is in reality a methodological subterfuge, a diversionary straw man.[109] Decision-makers should rely, rather, on meticulous investigation and analysis of future costs and benefits on a case-by-case basis, using qualitative criteria, and strive to "relate environmental science with social values in the search for rational policies."[110]

4. *Anthropocentrism*

Critics have taken issue both with the anthropocentrism that inheres in intergenerational rights and with its absence in the case of Nature's Rights. Even so, this is not, as one might therefore think, a lose–lose situation.

In the case of the intergenerational rights approach, the fundamental underlying concern is whether *any* human rights approach (intergenerational ecological rights included) can honor sufficiently the interdependence of human and nonhuman life, as well as the importance of natural processes and ecosystems, given that all human rights are by definition anthropocentric. This complaint is most commonly made by those who profess "deep ecology," a philosophical outlook that has greatly influenced many green movements and activist organizations. But the concern is exaggerated in our view. The anthropocentrism of intergenerational rights is scarcely egoistic at all, and it is in any event far less human-centered than the traditional human rights–based approach, which focuses largely on persons unknown in potentially distant futures.[111] Intergenerational rights reflect, at bottom, another way of thinking, talking, and acting on behalf of Mother Nature. Because of its strong moral pull, it should be understood as one of the most conceptually cogent human rights approaches to environmental well-being currently available to us. It takes the long planetary view, not the all-too-familiar myopia of the present that has brought us such major environmental calamities as climate change and drastic species depletions.

In the case of Nature's Rights, the fundamental and obvious fact is that it is a *non*-anthropocentric ecological right, not a *human* right. This, of course, provokes the question: Does the Nature's Rights approach essentially mean the

---

[109] For more on these issues, *see* McGarity et al., *supra* note 106, especially at 67–102.

[110] Bryan G. Norton, *Sustainability: A Philosophy of Adaptive Ecosystem Management*, at xii (2005).

[111] Furthermore, observes Linda Hajjar Leib, intergenerational rights should not be tagged as anthropocentric for being conceived, like human rights generally, "beyond the mere immediate materialistic interests of human beings to the preservation of the integrity and dignity of humanity in its spiritual and ecological dimensions." Leib, *supra* Ch. 2 note 95, at 66–7.

abandonment of human rights approaches to environmental protection and sustainability altogether? The answer, for the reasons just mentioned, certainly must be "no" when it comes to the intergenerational rights approach. The same must be said of the more widely practiced derivative, autonomous, and procedural approaches to environmental human rights insofar as they prove ecologically wise and legally feasible. Now is not the time to abandon any human rights strategy that, even if only periodically, can break through the walls of resistance and benefit the environment.

The answer to the question can be in the negative also when it comes to the Nature's Rights approach, provided that the right to environment is conceived in procedural terms. That is, the right to environment must be conceived as a human right to *represent* Mother Nature (not oneself or other members of the human species alone) in the quest for a clean and healthy environment. Such a right is comparable to the procedural environmental rights – access to information, public participation in environmental decision-making, and recourse to just remedies – that in recent years have been much lauded as part of an "expansive right to environment."[112]

To invoke a procedural human right to represent Mother Nature is not mere word play; it gives to the Nature's Rights approach a power that currently is not guaranteed by any legislative, administrative, or judicial modality anywhere – except, as previously noted, in Ecuador, where it is enshrined in the country's new constitution (though not yet in applicative legislation),[113] and in Bolivia's recently adopted "Law of the Rights of Mother Earth."[114] It is thus much needed. In theory and often in practice, contesting on human rights grounds unleashes the power to assert maximum claims on society (an attribute to which we alluded earlier in and which we explore in Chapter 4), among other advantages.[115]

This truth applies to the intergenerational rights approach as well. Indeed, it applies to all approaches to the right to a clean and healthy environment. For all the hurdles that a rights-based approach to a clean and healthy environment must surmount to succeed, it remains a powerful way – arguably *the* most powerful way – to achieve environmental (and social) well-being via legal (and political) means. No other approach challenges the official status quo as rights-based advocacy does, both in the public sector and increasingly in the private sector as well. When properly aligned with such environmental values as cleanliness, wellness, biodiversity, and sustainability, a right-based

---

[112] For details, *see infra* Addendum § C, at 328–36.
[113] *See supra* text accompanying notes 38–48.
[114] *See supra* note 61.
[115] See, respectively, *supra* Ch. 2, at 29–30, and *infra* ch. 4, §A, at 87.

approach provides the most comprehensive available gateway to a socially constructed paradigm of ecological governance based on principles of respect and collective responsibility.[116]

There is little question that the push for intergenerational human rights and Nature's Rights are positive developments that could yield important gains if allowed to expand conceptually beyond the essentially normative shift they currently represent. To the extent that they must advance through a legal system that has trouble accepting their basic premises without being conceived in postneoliberal institutional and procedural terms as well, these legal gambits are not likely to produce the kinds of dramatic environmental improvements we need. The truth is that we need to enlarge our sense of law and the social structures that enable it to work. The neoliberal political and economic superstructure is so alienated from Mother Earth that its legal system is not likely to sanction an autopoietic transformation, which is why we must look beyond the conventional structures of law and adjudication and enlarge our fundamental understanding of law and how it is formulated and enforced.

The Commons, we believe, can serve as an holistic, integrated platform for a new paradigm of law and policy that could help secure a clean, healthy, biodiverse, and sustainable environment – the central focus of Part II. We also believe that a human right to commons- and rights-based ecological governance, alone or in concert with other rights-based strategies, can greatly facilitate the conceptual transition to a genuinely eco-friendly governance framework. Its great promise lies in its ability to help reshape social practice, material provisioning, and environmental stewardship in ways that advance human rights while bringing the law of humans into greater alignment with the laws of nature.

---

[116] For elaboration on these themes, see *infra* Ch. 4, § A, *infra*, at 87.

4

Making the Conceptual Transition to the New Paradigm

Barring some game-changing ecological disaster, huge economic and political forces will continue to resist the rights-based legal initiatives described in the preceding two chapters. This is not surprising, considering the hostility with which earlier challenges to the State/Market paradigm have been met. In 1988, Chico Mendes was murdered for organizing indigenous people in Brazil to protect the Amazon's rain forests from ranchers and corrupt government officials.[1] In 1995, Ken Saro-Wiwa of Ogoniland was hanged for protesting the disastrous oil drilling operations of the Nigerian government junta and its corporate cronies.[2] Such brutal reactions echo the terror inflicted by King John's sheriff on thirteenth-century commoners for using forests to meet their basic subsistence needs, as sanctioned by centuries of custom.

The opposition to change is not just economic and political; it is also historical and philosophical. It has deep roots.

Renowned biologist E. O. Wilson takes a long view:[3] "According to the archeological evidence," he writes, "we strayed from Nature with the beginning of civilization roughly ten thousand years ago. That quantum leap beguiled us with an illusion of freedom from the world that had given us birth. . . ." He adds: "A wiser intelligence might now truthfully say of us at this point: here is a chimera, a new and very odd species come shambling into our universe, a mix of Stone Age emotion, medieval self-image, and godlike

---

[1] *See, e.g.,* Alex Shoumatoff, *The World Is Burning: Murder in the Rain Forest* (1990); Andrew Revkin, *The Burning Season: The Murder of Chico Mendes and the Fight for the Amazon Rain Forest* (2004).

[2] *See, e.g.,* Craig W. McLuckie & Aubrey McPhail, *Ken Saro Wiwa: Writer and Political Activist* (2000). *See also* Addendum, *infra* at 285, in text accompanying notes 49–56.

[3] E.O. Wilson, *The Fate of Creation Is the Fate of Humanity,* in *Moral Ground, supra* Ch. 3 note 13, at 21.

technology. . . . The combination makes the species unresponsive to the forces that count most for its own long-term survival."

The Scientific Revolution and Reformation of the sixteenth and seventeenth centuries aggravated the problem by elevating reductionist, quantitative, and individualistic modes of thought. This worldview gives more credence and prestige to that which can be seen and measured, while relegating intangible moral and social concerns to the contingent worlds of philosophy, politics, and other "values discourses." Not surprisingly, economics became, in the eighteenth century, an autonomous "scientific" discipline, while humanistic, moral, and ethical issues became subordinate, secondary matters.[4] Modern Western jurisprudence continues to perceive issues of distributive justice – for example, socioeconomic and environmental rights – as matters to be dealt with, *if at all*, less by courts or law, strictly speaking, than by the administrative and legislative institutions of government and by politics. This tendency is abundantly evident in the conservatively leaning rulings of the US judiciary in recent years. As international and comparative law scholar Ugo Mattei has observed:

> The birth of the Welfare State in the early twentieth century was... considered as an *exceptional intervention* by regulation (by means of fiscal policy) into the market order, with the specific aim to guarantee some social justice to the weaker members of society. In the West, since then, social justice was never able to capture again the core of rights discourse, and consequently has remained constantly at the mercy of fiscal crisis: no money, no social rights![5]

Ecological rights as social rights have befallen the same fate.

Indeed, as we note in Chapter 1, the most serious and urgent problem of our time may well be the myriad enclosures of nature, from waterways and land, to genes and the atmosphere. By the light of contemporary economic thought and culture, however, this is not seen as alarming because humankind stands apart from Nature, and so may treat it as an object; the Market and State are simply carrying out their "natural" functions. In this framework of thought, it is no wonder that it is difficult to secure a meaningful right to the environment and ecologically responsible forms of governance: Such initiatives violate our

---

[4] *See, e.g.,* Cullinan, *supra* Prologue note 20, at pt. 2; Ugo Mattei, *The State, the Market, and Some Preliminary Questions about the Commons* (DG III Social Cohesion of the Council of Europe project: Human Rights of People Experiencing Poverty, Mar. 28, 2011), available at http://works.bepress.com/ugo_mattei/40 (accessed June 25, 2011).

[5] Mattei, *supra* note 4, at 1 (English version) (emphasis added).

prior epistemological and cultural commitments. They defy entrenched ways of perceiving, thinking, and acting.

The formidable task ahead is somehow to develop ways of seeing, thinking, and acting that enable us to recalibrate humankind's relationship to Nature. We must devise new cultural mores, social practices, and policy tools to nourish this new relationship and cultivate ways to see, think, and act anew. Needed, in a sense, is "a Copernican revolution in ethics"[6] that can be secured only by imagining the general outlines of a different economic, political, legal, and cultural order, however provisionally. We agree with E. O. Wilson that "[w]e took a wrong turn when we launched the Neolithic revolution" and that "[w]e have been trying ever since to ascend *from Nature* instead of *to Nature*."[7] The result is that humankind has created unprecedented environmental threats that within the next five to ten years could cause truly catastrophic harms within the lifetimes of the majority of the world's current population. T. S. Eliot put it this way in 1939: "We are being made aware that the organization of society on the principle of private profit, as well as public destruction, is leading to both the deformation of humanity by unregulated industrialism, and to the exhaustion of natural resources, and that a good deal of our material progress is a progress for which succeeding generations may have to pay dearly."[8] It is already seventy-four years later.

As Wilson reassuringly adds, however, "[i]t is not too late for us to come around, without losing the quality of life already gained, in order to receive the deeply fulfilling beneficence of humanity's natural heritage." We cautiously agree with this assessment, and do not regard it as wishful thinking. As we note in Chapter 1, we are at a historically propitious moment for reimagining our economic order and its relationship to Nature. The standard economic narrative is crumbling in the face of its own limitations, giving way to new frameworks for understanding value. New types of self-organization and collaboration on the Internet are pointing toward new forms of governance, resource management, and culture. In addition, new opportunities to change and broaden human rights advocacy on behalf of a clean and healthy environment, beyond the possibilities sanctioned by the neoliberal policy framework, are now emerging like green sprouts through the concrete.

How, then, do we make the transition to the green governance paradigm we propose? How do we proceed? Before we explain our full vision in Part II, it is helpful, we believe, to outline how we might make the *conceptual* transition

---

[6] Kate Rawles, *A Copernican Revolution in Ethics*, in *Moral Ground, supra* Ch. 3 note 13, at 88.
[7] E. O. Wilson, *supra* note 3, at 23–4.
[8] T.S. Eliot, *The Idea of a Christian Society* 62 (1940).

to the new paradigm – one that, with a healthy mixture of ecological realism and creative imagination, can be recognized by State Law, both nationally and internationally, yet also be grounded in everyday practices and culture.

From today's vantage point, the transition to commons- and rights-based ecological governance may seem improbable, if not impossible. It helps to remember, however, that a certain naïve optimism and creativity have animated all great social movements. The suffragette movement, the civil rights and antiapartheid movements, the antiwar movement – all found ways to make the impossible possible.

In this case, we see green governance as a vision of "on the ground" practice that can reorient our imagination and thinking, and in turn inform the political struggles and social transformations that must inevitably occur to achieve that vision. To that end, the transition to green governance must start by asserting a foundation of values and principles profoundly different from that which defines and maintains the State/Market today.

As we state in the Prologue, a new regime must find ways to cultivate and uphold, first, a logic of respect for nature, sufficiency of provisioning, interdependence, shared responsibility, and fairness among all human beings and, second, an ethic of integrated global and local citizenship that insists on transparency and accountability in all activities affecting the integrity of the environment. Without such core commitments, the current deficiencies of the State/Market political and legal regime will remain intact.

On final analysis, however, the real challenge is to make these core commitments operational as a matter of law and social practice. Somehow the existing economic and political priorities of the State/Market – as well as our own cultural habits and consciousness – must be transformed.

We do not presume to have all the answers to this formidable challenge. But we do believe that there exist at least three foundational and interconnected precepts – understood also as tasks – that are critical to the evolutionary challenge of redesigning our mental operating systems and moving forward:

1. Embrace anew the power of human rights to effect progressive change, especially when reenvisioned as a more theoretically inclusive, operationally grounded force;
2. Persuade State Law to honor the environmentally germane moral convictions and social practices that emanate from the everyday life of ecological commons, what we call the "Vernacular Law" of the commons;[9] and

---

[9] For an elaborated definition and elucidation of "Vernacular Law," *see* § B, *infra* at 104–12.

3. Promote new policy structures and procedures that encourage and reward distributed, self-organized governance and bottom-up innovation as elements of complex systems (in contrast to bureaucratically driven, top-down forms of "command-and-control" regulation). We call this precept "Self-Organized Governance and Collaboration in Complex Adaptive Systems."

These three foundational and interconnected precepts are vital for at least three reasons

First, a properly recognized approach to human rights has access to great moral and legal authority and legitimacy. Also, when human rights are reenvisioned to embrace new "sources of law" (i.e., new law-making processes such as Vernacular Law) and new applications of human rights principles to the corporate as well as the public sector, their moral and legal authority and legitimacy are further amplified.

Second, Vernacular Law exercised through commons has a legitimacy, efficacy, and creative flexibility that the centralized bureaucratic State and concentrated Market do not. If commons-based Vernacular Law is given the space to work in tandem with State Law so as to serve as an authoritative basis for "official" normative change, it could generate substantive improvements in ecological governance and thereby operationalize the right to the environment.

Third, Self-Organized Governance can mobilize bottom-up energies and local knowledge that will be needed to develop ecologically appropriate policies and practices. Working in synergy with Vernacular Law, it could enact a new vision of human rights through ecological commons.

We believe that, in combination, these key precepts for transitioning to green governance – Human Rights, Vernacular Law, and Self-Organized Governance – can promote socioecological practices that will improve the biodiversity and sustainability of the planet and enhance the well-being of all life on it, present and future.

We also believe that it is important to take seriously the lessons of Chapter 2 and reimagine and establish the human right to environment in form and substance different from previous incarnations. It needs to be made more inclusive in its application (to embrace structural and procedural issues equally with normative ones) and more integrated with people's everyday social and production practices. We have specifically in mind *a new procedural human right to commons- and rights-based ecological governance*. This right would not in principle privilege any right or cluster of rights (liberty, equality, or solidarity rights) over another except as a particular fact or context warrants. It would affirm, however, what Sam Adelman might call a "meta right" – "a foundational right that would, where necessary, take precedence over other rights" notwithstanding the problematic of "a hierarchy at odds with the assertion that all rights are equal and indivisible."[10] Alternatively, it would affirm a "species right" ("a new category of... right which transcends traditional categorizations, highlights the truly universal nature of the threat, and which we hold not simply as individual human beings but rather by virtue of our membership [in] the species *homo sapiens*.... "[11]). This meta-right should be treated with the sanction of State Law, both national and international.

It is credible as well as necessary to do this. The human right would embody the spirit of Article 28 of the Universal Declaration of Human Rights,[12] namely: "Everyone is entitled to a social and international order in which the rights and freedoms set forth in this Declaration can be fully realized." It would resonate with the United Nations (UN) Declaration on the Right and Responsibility of Individuals, Groups and Organs of Society to Promote and Protect Universally Recognized Human Rights and Fundamental Freedoms.[13] Additionally, it would complement – indeed, reinforce and extend – in the same procedural universe, the values and policies embedded in the understandably popular Aarhus Convention on Access to Information, Public Participation in Decision-Making and Access to Justice in Environmental Matters.[14] Most important, this new meta- or species right would make way for a sensibly collaborative and nonproprietary alternative to the ecologically dysfunctional State/Market regulatory system at the heart of our worldwide environmental crisis: It would lend support to commons-based governance practices that invite stakeholder engagement and innovation, and therefore be politically attractive.

Given the substantial constraints and limited success the right to environment has had to date, how might a human rights framing of commons- and rights-based ecological governance have a chance of succeeding? How can it succeed when, in particular, it aims at nothing less than remaking the ecological governance paradigm itself? The answer lies in the fact that, in addition to addressing the jurisprudential issues posed by the human right to environment,

---

[10] Adelman, *supra* Ch. 2 note 6, at 172.
[11] *Id.* at 173. Out of respect for all life on Earth, however, it would be helpful to view the species *homo sapiens* living among all other species.
[12] *Supra* Ch. 3 note 62.
[13] G.A. Res. 53/144, Annex, U.N. GAOR, 53d Sess, Supp. No. 49, (Vol. 1), UN Doc A/RES/53/144, at 261 (Mar. 8, 1999) (adopted without recorded vote). Article 7 provides that "[e]veryone has the right, individually and in association with others, to develop and discuss new human rights ideas and principles and to advocate their acceptance."
[14] *Supra* Ch. 2 note 21.

environmental and human rights specialists are now beginning to confront the systemic barriers. These developments, together with sympathetic and synergetic energies that grassroots activists are already mobilizing, give reason for genuine optimism.

Historically, few environmental and human rights specialists have considered seriously how to liberate environmental rights from the systemic paradigm within which it has been imprisoned; the citadels of State sovereignty and market economics have been entirely too entrenched and imposing to allow venturesome alternative visions. Another impediment has been the intellectual self-isolation of disciplines and their propensity to focus on narrow topics rather than to "think big" in collaborative and holistic ways. Stephen Humphreys has noted the fundamental dissimilarities between the legal worlds of climate change and international human rights: "One is a regime of flexibility, compromise, soft principles and differential treatment; the other of judiciaries, policing, formal equality and universal truths. Faced with injustice, one regime tends to negotiation, the other to prosecution."[15] But as Humphreys hastens to emphasize "Neither *on its own* seems quite up to the challenge presented by climate change."[16]

Fortunately, this discerning viewpoint has begun to take hold, albeit primarily in relation to climate change. Three distinctive though not incompatible system-oriented approaches to ecological governance are noteworthy.

The first and most comprehensive approach, albeit focused essentially on the United States, may be found in the work of the Center for Progressive Reform (CPR), a US-based network of university-affiliated legal, economic, and scientific scholars founded "to restore and preserve existing regulatory and common law methods of [environmental] protection . . . under attack by regulated industries and the think tanks and lobbying organizations they support."[17] The CPR works to develop "new or revised ways to protect people and the environment" and, to this end, endeavors to provide "more and better information about health, safety, financial and environmental risks," to hold environmentally irresponsible business enterprises accountable for "their risk-producing actions through new forms of corporate governance," and to open regulatory processes to "greater public scrutiny, particularly by facilitating the participation of groups representing the public interest."[18]

[15] Stephen Humphreys, *Conceiving Justice: Articulating Common Causes in Distinct Regimes*, in Human Rights (Humphreys ed.), *supra* Ch. 2 note 6, at 316–17.
[16] *Id.* at 317 (emphasis added).
[17] *About the Center for Progressive Reform*, Center for Progressive Reform, available at http://www.progressivereform.org (accessed May 4, 2012).
[18] *Id.*

Especially noteworthy for present purposes are the two core complementary "policy proposals for a better environmental future" of CPR scholars Alyson C. Flournoy and David M. Driesen and their associates: a proposed National Environmental Legacy Act (NELA) and a proposed Environmental Competition Statute (ECS).[19] The NELA proposal, drawing on lessons learned from the US National Environmental Policy Act (NEPA),[20] aims to ensure in concrete terms a public natural resource legacy for future generations. The ECS proposal is offered to stimulate movement toward new clean technologies. Designed to help establish "a new generation of environmental law," each seeks to break from the complex system of regulatory statutes and standards of "the first generation . . . that proved more difficult to implement than its creators anticipated" and from the "second generation [that] carried out regulatory reforms *ostensibly* guided by a desire for economic efficiency."[21]

The second, more modest system-oriented approach is grounded in the idea, proffered with transboundary eco-damage in mind, that the burden of vindicating claims for environmental loss must shift from the individual victim to the State (particularly, one may assume, where the loss is large). As Dinah Shelton points out, the current system requires that, in most instances, victims of transboundary environmental degradation must themselves endure the frustration of vindicating their claims through individual or group human rights litigation while their governments look passively on.[22] Instead, she argues, States should be seen as legally obligated to protect the environmental rights of their inhabitants. This principle is based on each State's sovereignty over its natural resources (a fundamental principle of the international legal order), the international law of State responsibility for transboundary environmental harm, and principles of equity as well as international human rights law.

Shelton does not invoke the Responsibility to Protect (R2P) doctrine launched by the UN in 2005 to require States to safeguard their populations against genocide, war crimes, crimes against humanity, and ethnic cleansing.[23]

---

[19] *See* Flournoy & Driesen, *supra* Ch. 3 note 3, at 1–169 (NELA), 171–267. For an earlier summary of the NELA proposal, *see* Flournoy's Recommendation 5 in Weston & Bach, *supra* Prologue note 12, at 72.

[20] 42 U.S.C. §§ 4321–4347.

[21] Flournoy & Driesen, *supra* Ch. 3 note 3, at xix (emphasis added).

[22] Dinah Shelton, *Equitable Utilization of the Atmosphere: A Rights-Based Approach to Climate Change*, in *Human Rights and Climate Change*, *supra* Ch. 2 note 6, at 91.

[23] For convenient summary, *see* *Responsibility to Protect*, Wikipedia, available at http://en .wikipedia.org/wiki/Responsibility_to_protect (accessed May 15, 2012).

Nor from a legal standpoint need she have done so given that the doctrine originated out of concern for internally displaced persons and that UN officials, the Secretary-General included, have denied that R2P applies to environmental calamities. It is not unreasonable to imagine, however, that an R2P claim alleging a crime against humanity could apply when, in cases of extreme transboundary harm (e.g., loss of habitat due to global warming, floods, nuclear accidents, or major toxic leaks or spills), governments have failed or refused to take at least obvious precautions against such harms or those who perpetrate them.[24] Nor is it unreasonable to think that, in cases of extreme *intra*territorial harm (e.g., Katrina, Fukushima), governments unresponsive to victims within their jurisdiction could be held similarly accountable or that legislation to this effect could be enacted where necessary. The implications of recognizing such a principle are profound.[25]

The third and here final approach – a recommendation of Linda Hajjar Leib – advocates the "reconfiguration of the human rights system" so as to "provide a broad legal and policy framework necessary to take on the complexities of environmental issues and the multiplicity of duty-bearers involved."[26] The plan is inspired by the concept of sustainable development and its "three pillars" – economic development, social equity, and environmental protection – which have been the "dominant global discourse relating to environment and development"[27] since Principle I of the Rio Declaration on Environment

---

[24] Support for this idea is implicit in remarks made at U.N. headquarters in New York by Jean Ziegler, Special Rapporteur on the Right to Food, who condemned the growing use of crops to produce biofuels as a replacement for petrol as a crime against humanity "because it has created food shortages and sent food prices soaring, leaving millions of poor people hungry." *See* Edith M. Lederer, *Production of Biofuels "Is A Crime,"* The Independent (Oct. 27, 2007), available at http://www.independent.co.uk/environment/green-living/production-of-biofuels-is-a-crime-398066.html (accessed May 15, 2012). To similar but more profound effect, *see infra* note 21.

[25] Consider, for example, the implications, both normative and systemic, of philosopher Thomas Pogge's contention that the occurrence and persistence of extreme global poverty, which causes one-third of all human deaths annually (including 18 million who die from preventable diseases), is attributable not to random misfortune but to a global State/Market order that systematically seconds developing countries often by deliberate and predictably negligent policy choices (e.g., installing oppressive rulers, bribing them with weapons, waging unnecessary wars). Such malfeasance, Pogge argues, constitutes a crime against humanity. *See* Thomas Pogge, *World Poverty and Human Rights: Cosmopolitan Responsibilities and Reforms* (2d ed. 2008). Imagine how Pogge's argument would fare relative to the deliberate failure of governments to cut their carbon emissions and "severe climate change harm" were substituted for "persistent extreme poverty."

[26] Leib, *supra* Ch. 2 note 6, at 109.

[27] *Id.* at 123. The "three pillars" of sustainable development are economic development, social equity, and environmental protection.

and Development in 1992.[28] Leib proposes a two-level conceptualization of rights. The first level, a trio of "generalist" or "umbrella" rights, consists of the Right to Democracy (extracted from the International Covenant on Civil and Political Rights[29]), the Right to Development (extracted from the International Covenant on Economic, Social and Cultural Rights[30]), and the Right to Environment, a newly conceived bundle of justiciable (to some extent aspirational) "environmental human rights" designated "sub-rights" incorporated into a new "Covenant on Environmental Rights." This Covenant would be akin to the 1966 covenants that make up the International Bill of Human Rights[31] and is composed of such entitlements as the rights of nature, the right to a clean environment, the right to natural resources, the right to water, the right to food, and indigenous land rights.[32]

Taken altogether, Leib contends, these umbrella rights and their subrights could serve "to enhance cooperation among states in addressing the human rights implications of ecological problems and the development of distinct environmental human rights in both the international and the domestic spheres."[33]

Skeptics might dismiss Leib's proposal as so much wordplay or label shuffling. But it is not. Rather, it forges a discursive/linguistic shift that consolidates the fragmentation of current environmental and human rights themes and trends which, in theory and if taken seriously, hold out the prospect of a more coherent institutional or operational architecture than currently exists. As has often been said, there is nothing more practical than a good theory, especially at a time when States need desperately to find common meanings to manage common problems.

There is much good to be said about each of these proposals, modest though they be. The first proposal, bearing in mind the widespread imitation of NEPA around the world, holds out the prospect of nationally based progressive

---

[28] *Supra* Ch. 2 note 19. Article I provides: "Human beings are at the centre of concerns for sustainable development. They are entitled to a healthy and productive life in harmony with nature."

[29] Dec. 16, 1966, 993 U.N.T.S. 171, *reprinted* in III Basic Documents, *supra* Prologue note 13, at III.A.3 [hereinafter ICCPR].

[30] Dec. 16, 1966, 993 U.N.T.S. 3, art. 12(1), *reprinted in* III Basic Documents, *supra* Prologue note 13, at III.A.2 [hereinafter ICESCR].

[31] I.e., the ICCPR, *supra* note 29, and the ICESCR, *supra* note 30, together with the UDHR, *supra* Ch. 3 note 62; *see also* note 90, *infra*.

[32] Leib, *supra* Ch. 2 note 6, at 136–55. The author emphasizes that the list "is by no means exhaustive or unique." *Id.* at 136.

[33] *Id.* at 125.

initiatives to serve as an engine for equivalent reforms elsewhere. The second proposal puts the finger directly on the State, a key player in the ecological governance process that has tended more to exacerbate than to confront and remedy ecological crises. The third proposal opens the door to imagining how, at least conceptually, we might reorganize our understanding of environmental rights so as to be more effective in dealing with crisis.

Due partly to their deliberate modesty, however, the three proposals share a common problem: each accepts the existing global State/Market system as a given and thus, logically, does not confront it or seek to transition away from it (except marginally). Perhaps these proposals will do some good in the short term, and because social change – especially legal change – rarely happens swiftly or predictably, they may have a welcome impact in the years ahead. Yet, absent an overhaul of the current regulatory framework or a radical shift from it, none is likely to prove sufficient over the long term. As Adelman convincingly argues when contemplating a rights-based approach to climate change (but applicable to other environmental threats as well), there is no getting around the need to confront "the enduring pre-eminence of the principle of [territorial] sovereignty in the international system"[34] and "the notion that the market is a private sphere subject to different rules from the public domain of politics."[35]

Let us be blunt: history has shown that neither the State nor the Market has been very successful at setting limits on Market activity. The simple truth is that neither wants to. Setting limits on State/Market exploitation of nature slows economic growth, diminishes profits, and potentially reduces tax revenues. We believe, however, that a commons- and rights-based approach to ecological governance that emerges from an energetic dedication to the three foundational and interconnected precepts of Human Rights, Vernacular Law, and Self-Organized Governance, is potentially a powerful means for challenging the State/Market's primary commitments and values.

A. THE POWER OF HUMAN RIGHTS

In Chapters 2 and 3, we mention in passing some reasons why a human rights approach to commons- and rights-based ecological governance is potentially a powerful means for both achieving green governance and administering it. Here, in some detail, we explain why.

---

[34] Adelman, *supra* Ch. 2 note 6, at 167.
[35] *Id.* at 162.

1. *Human Rights as "Trumps"*

In his germinal book *Taking Rights Seriously*, legal philosopher Ronald Dworkin asserts unequivocally – and correctly – that when a claimed value or good is categorized as a right it "trumps" most if not all other claimed values or goods.[36] By framing perceived environmental entitlements as human rights, rights-holders (e.g., commoners) can assert maximum claims on society, juridically more elevated than commonplace standards, laws, or other policy choices which, in contrast to human rights, are subject to everyday revision and rescission for lack of such ordination. A proximate analogy is the distinction between a contractual or statutory claim and a constitutional one. As Alexander Kiss and Dinah Shelton have written, "[r]ights are inherent attributes of human beings that must be respected in any well-ordered society. The moral weight this concept affords exercises an important compliance pull."[37] One, of course, can dispute whether human rights are inherent attributes of human beings. The concept and its moral weight derive in major part from the world's many religions, and the association is particularly apparent when it comes to the natural environment and environmental rights.[38] Human rights steeped in religious tradition exercise, for obvious reasons, an especially strong compliance pull. Importantly for present purposes, they also provide powerful motivation for fervent discourse and ardent political engagement.

Thus, when human abuse of a natural resource or ecosystem is designated the wronging of a right, or when a proposed new right – to commons- and rights-based ecological governance, for example – is authoritatively recognized as such, there results an opportunity for empowerment and mobilization that otherwise is lacking. A human right is not merely a regulatory prohibition that can be changed or discarded at will. A rights-based approach to ecological governance can enhance the status of the environmental interests of human

---

[36] Ronald Dworkin, *Taking Rights Seriously* 91–3, 189–91, 269 (1977).

[37] Alexander Kiss & Dinah Shelton, *Guide to International Environmental Law* 238 (2007).

[38] For a comprehensive overview, *see*, e.g., *Faiths & Ecology*, ARC-Alliance of Religions and Conservation, available at http://www.arcworld.org/faiths.htm (accessed Apr. 9, 2012), documenting the ecological views of Bahá'í, Buddhism, Christianity, Daoism, Hinduism, Islam, Jainism, Judaism, Shintaoism, Sikhism, and Zoroastrianism. *See also* Dinah Shelton, *Nature in the Bible*, in *Man and the Environment: Essays in Honor of Alexander Kiss* 63 (1998), identifying where, throughout the Christian Bible, "we are reminded that humans do not own the earth and its resources." To similar effect, *see Climate Inst. (Austl.), Common Belief: Australia's Faith Communities on Climate Change* 8–39 (2006), reporting "a dialogue on the morality of climate change" among Anglicans, Bahá'ís, Baptists, Buddhists, Catholics, Evangelical Christians, Greek Orthodox, Hindus, Jews, Lutherans, Muslims, and Sikhs, among others (including The Salvation Army).

beings and other living things when balanced against competing objectives, granting such interests formal legal and political legitimacy.[39]

In sum, rights are not matters of charity, a question of favor or kindness to be bestowed or taken away at pleasure. They are high-level public order values or goods at the apex of public policy. They carry with them a sense of entitlement on the part of the rights-holder and obligatory implementation on the part of the rights-protector – intergovernmental institutions, the State, society, the family. They are values or goods deemed fundamental and universal; and while not absolute, they nonetheless are judged superior to other claimed values or goods. To assert a right to freedom from degrading and otherwise abusive environmental behavior is, thus, to strengthen the possibility of life informed by dignity and well-being. It bespeaks duty, not optional benevolence, and for this reason bespeaks political empowerment as well.

2. *Human Rights as Interdependent Agents of Human Dignity*

Central to the concept of human rights, as just intimated, is the notion of a "public order of human dignity," an *ordre publique* "in which values are shaped and shared more by persuasion than by coercion, and which seeks to promote the greatest production and widest possible sharing, without discriminations irrelevant of merit, of all values among all human beings."[40] This notion of public order, encapsulating "the basic policies of an international law of human dignity,"[41] is embedded in the International Bill of Human Rights.[42]

In the struggle for a clean and healthy environment, a rights-based approach to ecological governance thus signals more than environmental protection per se. It signals also that norms of nondiscrimination, justice, and dignity must be central in all aspects of ecological governance, the way in which it is achieved as well as the way in which it functions thereafter, including the manner in which it processes and resolves environmental grievances within its jurisdiction. The human right to a clean and healthy environment is part of a complex web of interdependent rights that extends protection beyond one

---

[39] *See* Patricia W. Birnie, Alan E. Boyle, & Catherine Redgwell, *International Law and the Environment* 255 (3d ed. 2009) (citing the arguments advanced by the U.N. Sub-Commission on the Prevention of Discrimination and Protection of Minorities for adopting its proposed Declaration of Principles on Human Rights and the Environment in 1994).

[40] Myres S. McDougal, *Perspectives for an International Law of Human Dignity*, in Myres S. McDougal et al., *Studies in World Public Order* 987 (1987).

[41] Myres S. McDougal, Harold D. Lasswell & Lung-chu Chen, *Human Rights and World Public Order: The Basic Policies of an International Law of Human Dignity*, at iv (1980).

[42] *See supra* note 31 and accompanying text.

domain to many others. Most if not all human rights depend on the satisfaction of other human rights for their fulfillment.

Treating freedom from abusive environmental practices as a human right thus raises the stakes against those who would damage our natural world. It recognizes, write international environmental law scholars Patricia Birnie, Alan Boyle, and Catherine Redgwell, the "vital character of the environment as a basic condition of life, indispensable to the promotion of human dignity and welfare, and to the fulfillment of other human rights."[43] It thus transforms the struggle for ecological governance in the common interest into a struggle for human dignity and ecological well-being, thereby adding to the moral gravitas that makes such governance and its achievement compelling, thereby better capturing responsible attention and heightened pressure in the search for enduring solutions.

3. *Human Rights as a Crucible for Human Security and Democracy*

"Is not peace, in the last analysis, basically a matter of human rights," President John F. Kennedy once famously asked, "the right to live out our lives without fear of devastation – the right to breathe air as nature provided it – the right of future generations to a healthy existence?"[44] Herein lies another, commonly overlooked virtue of human rights activism and governance. When peace is broadly conceived to include more than the absence of war, such as "security in position, expectation, and potential with regard to all basic community values,"[45] then, quite obviously, "the interrelationship of peace and human rights . . . passes beyond that of interdependence and approaches that of identity."[46] Peace in this sense – what today scholars like Mary Kaldor call "human security" (emphasizing the security of the individual in contrast to that of the State, i.e., "freedom from fear" and "freedom from want"[47]) – becomes

---

[43] Birnie et al., *supra* note 39, at 278–79; *see also* Boyle (2008), *supra* Ch. 2 note 6, at 483; Boyle (2009), *supra* Ch. 2 note 6, at 1–13.

[44] John F. Kennedy, A Strategy of Peace, Commencement Address at American University (June 10, 1963), available at http://www.jfklibrary.org/Research/Ready-Reference/JFK-Speeches/Commencement-Address-at-American-University-June-10-1963.aspx (accessed Apr. 9, 2012).

[45] Myres S. McDougal & Florentino P. Feliciano, *The International Law of War*, at xviii (1994).

[46] *Id.*

[47] *See* Mary Kaldor, *Human Security* (2007). *See also* United Nations Development Programme (UNDP), *Human Development Report: New Dimensions of Human Security*, at Ch. 1 (1994), available at http://hdr.undp.org/en/reports/global/hdr1994 (accessed May 15, 2012) (endorsing "universalism of life claims" to validate "sustainable human development," as follows: "Universalism of life claims is the common thread that binds the demands of human development today with the exigencies of development tomorrow, especially with the need for environmental preservation and regeneration for the future.").

more or less synonymous with the fulfillment of human rights, as Kennedy suggested.

Reversing the logic, to fulfill human rights is to promote peace. Mutual respect is the foundation of peace and human security; it is also at the innermost core of all human rights. In virtually any societal context, taking human rights seriously, committing to mutual tolerance and reciprocal forbearance, even making only a good faith effort to do this, is more likely than most other stratagems to bring peace and tranquility to social order, to secure and sustain human security.

This is particularly true when contemplating the life-enhancing and life-sustaining qualities of Nature, when human rights are understood to embrace the right to a clean and healthy environment. As James Quilligan observes (pinpointing basic needs dependent on environmental well-being and recognized as human rights almost everywhere outside the United States), "The basic reason for alleviating material insecurity – through food, clean water, housing, health care, education, jobs and self-sustaining livelihoods – is to ensure people's personal safety and survival in conditions of peace and dignity."[48] As a crucible for peace or human security, in other words, human rights inspire and energize society's most respectful and cooperative instincts. At a time when even conventional representative democracy, not just autocracy, is showing itself to be appallingly dysfunctional, human rights offer a way to regenerate and reignite the democratic process. This convenient truth applies as much to the struggle for green governance as it does to its ongoing expression within green governance once achieved. This truth alone should persuade the most doubting of Thomases to join in the great transition.

4. *Human Rights as a Mobilizing Challenge to Statist and Elitist Agendas*

As markers of preeminent societal values and agents of human dignity, human rights challenge and make demands on State sovereignty and power, a point that bears special notice when it comes to imagining a new human right to commons- and rights-based ecological governance. Scores of human rights conventions entered into force since World War II require States to cede bits of sovereign power in the name of human dignity. Legal obligations of great solemnity, many environmental treaties and declarations, may be counted among them. They include the 1972 Stockholm Declaration on the Human Environment, the 1982 World Charter for Nature, the 1986 Legal Principles

---

[48] James B. Quilligan, *Commons for Peace*, Kosmos, Fall/Winter 2011, at 15 (an issue devoted to "the changing nature of human security").

for Environmental Protection and Sustainable Development adopted by the Experts Group on Environmental Law of the World Commission on Environment and Development (WCED), the 1992 Rio Declaration on Environment and Development, and the 2002 Johannesburg Declaration on Sustainable Development.[49]

Proof that human rights challenge and make demands on State sovereignty and power is found, too, in the many occasions in which States, intergovernmental institutions, nongovernmental organizations (NGOs), professional associations, corporations, trade unions, faith-based groups, and others have relied successfully on this "corpus juris of social justice"[50] to measure and curb State behavior. Invoking criteria informed and refined by human rights, including environmental rights, critics question the legitimacy of political regimes, and hence their capacity to govern noncoercively or at all. In short, the worldwide recognition of human rights as both a moral and legal beacon for assessing the actual behaviors of governments can be powerfully influential – a dynamic now seen in political and market players vying to claim a "green" public image and reputation.

All of this is well known. To be sure, there is considerable posturing and gaming of perceptions in efforts to claim unwarranted moral standing. Yet most States are keenly aware of their interdependencies. They know that, however much they may resist human rights pressures from within and without, their national interest and desired self-image depend on their willingness to play by the rules or to be perceived as doing so, especially when those rules weigh heavily on the scales of social and political morality. Even the most powerful States are vulnerable to what has come to be called "the mobilization of shame" in defense of human rights.[51] There is no principled reason why States that encourage or tolerate release of greenhouse gases into the atmosphere –

---

[49] Stockholm Declaration, *supra* Ch. 2 note 19; World Charter for Nature, G.A. Res 37/7, Annex, U.N. GAOR, 37th Sess., Supp. No. 51, UN Doc A/37/51, at 17 (1983), *reprinted in* 22 I.L.M. 455 (1983) *and* V Basic Documents, *supra* Prologue note 13, at V.B.12; WCED Expert Grp. on Envtl. Law, *Environmental Protection and Sustainable Development: Legal Principles and Recommendations*, U.N. Doc. WCED/86/23/Add.1 (1986), *reprinted in* V Basic Documents, *supra* Prologue note 13, at V.B.13; the Rio Declaration, *supra* Ch. 2 note 19; Johannesburg Declaration on Sustainable Development (Sept. 4, 2002), available at http://www.un.org/esa/sustdev/documents/WSSD_POI_PD/English/POI_ PD.htm (accessed July 23, 2011).

[50] C. Van Boven, *Survey of the Positive Law of Human Rights*, in 1 *The International Dimensions of Human Rights*, at 87, 88 (Karl Vasak ed., revised and edited for the English transl. by Philip Alston, 1982).

[51] *See, e.g., Robert F. Drinan, The Mobilization of Shame: A World View of Human Rights* (2001).

or other abusive, degrading, or hazardous environmental practices – cannot or should not be targeted and shamed.

But not only States. Today, human rights claims are used increasingly to challenge and make demands on the particularist agendas of private elites. Writes Adelman: "[n]on-state actors, especially transnational corporations, "must be brought fully within the ambit of human rights as duty bearers."[52] Why? Most obviously because the cross-sectoral nature and cause of much environmental degradation – the anthropogenic pollution of the atmosphere via greenhouse gases, for example – demands that industrial enterprises be held accountable. This is especially compelling, one may argue, when it comes to economic interests that often are more powerful than the countries within which they operate. Arguably even more important, human rights enshrine respect as their core value, an entitlement to equality and nondiscriminatory treatment that belongs to all human beings everywhere. "Equality or non-discrimination," writes Virginia Leary once wrote, "is a leitmotif running through all of international human rights law."[53]

There is no question that these principles are often disregarded, much as law itself is often violated. Still, the widespread recognition of human rights across space and time places a significant moral burden, and often a political and legal one as well, on those who treat other human beings in disrespectful, discriminatory ways; increasingly, similar burdens are being placed on those who mistreat the natural environment. The potential of human rights norms to dislodge or seriously burden private exclusive interests that commit and perpetuate environmental abuse is thus likewise manifest – yet another persuasive reason to join the great transition.

5. *Human Rights as Legal and Political Empowerments*

As noted, human rights carry with them a sense of entitlement on the part of the rights-holder. They embrace also a corollary of a "right of the individual to know and act upon his [sic] rights"[54] – which implies, of course, a duty of satisfaction or redress on the part of the State and other actors to respond

---

[52] Adelman, *supra* Ch. 2 note 6, at 173.
[53] Virginia A. Leary, *The Right to Health in International Human Rights Law*, 1 Health & Hum. Rts. 26, 37 (1994).
[54] This quotation is from Paragraph 7 of the 1975 Helsinki Accords, officially known as the *Final Act of the Conference on Security and Co-operation in Europe: Declaration on Principles Guiding Relations Between Participating States, Respect for Human Rights and Fundamental Freedoms, Including the Freedom of Thought, Conscience, and Religion or Belief* (Aug. 1, 1975), *reprinted in* 14 I.L.M. 1292 (1975) *and* I Basic Documents, *supra* Prologue note 13, at

to right-to-know requests. The essence of rights discourse (or human rights law) is that, in Michael Freeman's pointed alert, "if you have a right to x, and you do not get x, this is not only a wrong, but it is a wrong against *you*."[55] This extends inexorably to environmental rights-holders, both living and unborn, principal or surrogate. The 1998 Aarhus Convention on Access to Information, Public Participation in Decision-Making and Access to Justice in Environmental Matters,[56] for example, states clearly its objective that "to contribute to the protection of the right of every person of present and future generations to live in an environment adequate to his or her health and well-being, each [State] Party shall guarantee the rights of access to information, public participation in decision-making, and access to justice in environmental matters in accordance with the provisions of this Convention."[57] Although regional in intent, the Convention's impact has been to serve as a model for environmental procedure everywhere.

At least five specific ways may be identified by which human rights accomplish this empowerment.[58] Each validates Cicero's great insight that "freedom is participation in power";[59] and each bears obvious relevance to environmental protection, both the pursuit and practice of it.

1. Because human rights entail fundamental values of superior legal and moral order, their violation correspondingly entails greater moral condemnation than do other wrongs. As a consequence, they provide a level of accountability that transcends that of other legal obligations, thus giving victims of rights violations the authority to hold violators accountable, even to the point of criminal liability. This is what distinguishes rights from benefits or from being the beneficiary of another's obligation.[60] It is what makes possible, for example, "the mobilization of shame" and the condemnation of the international community, commonly without even having to go to formal court. The "truth and

---

I.D.10. Although we wish to distance ourselves from the gendered language often found in international law discourse, we will leave further quotations unamended without comment.

[55] Michael D.A. Freeman, *Human Rights: An Interdisciplinary Approach* 61 (2002).

[56] *Supra* Ch. 2 note 23.

[57] *Id.* art. 1.

[58] For much of what follows in this subsection, we are indebted to Ronald C. Slye, *International Human Rights Law in Practice: International Law, Human Rights Beneficiaries, and South Africa: Some Thoughts on the Utility of International Human Rights Law*, 2 Chi. J. Int'l L. 59, 73–6 (2001).

[59] E.g., *Marcus Tullius Cicero Quotes*, Goodreads, available at http://www.goodreads.com/quotes/show/106593 (accessed Feb. 10, 2012).

[60] Jack Donnelly, *The Concept of Human Rights* 1–3 (1985); Jack Donnelly, *Universal Human Rights in Theory and Practice* 9–12 (1989).

reconciliation" processes of Argentina, Chile, El Salvador, Ghana, Guatemala, Haiti, Malawi, Nepal, Nigeria, the Philippines, Serbia and Montenegro, South Africa, South Korea, and elsewhere are proof enough.[61] On occasion, they can be more effective than their more formal legal counterparts in overcoming impunity.[62]

2. Although closely related by virtue of their superior legal and moral standing, human rights help shift legal and moral burdens to redistribute power. This attribute is particularly helpful when victims of harm seek to hold powerful economic and political forces accountable, typically the case in large-scale environmental crises. Climate change in particular requires that we address the problem of power imbalance "between the interests that stand to gain from climate change regulation and those that stand – in the short run at least – to lose."[63] Framing climate change as a human rights problem helps to empower politically weaker interests with serious substantive and/or procedural claims in their struggles against the powerful – as could be the case, for example, in seeking recognition of a right to green governance. "By acting as 'trumps,'" Amy Sinden writes, "human rights effectively put a thumb on the scale in favor of the weaker party in order to correct for the distorting effects of power."[64] Imagine British Petroleum's Deepwater Horizon disaster approached in this light.

3. Human rights generate legal grounds for political expression and action, again (as we note in Chapter 2) because they entail greater moral force than do ordinary legal obligations. This is abundantly seen in the many global and regional conferences and other gatherings commonly called under the auspices of the UN and such regional organizations as the Council of Europe, the Organization of American States, and the African Union. Each provides a forum in which the voices of human rights victims and advocates can be heard. The history of the anti-apartheid movement is replete with examples.[65] The

---

[61] *See, e.g., International Conflict Management Collection,* U.S. Inst. of Peace, available at http://www.usip.org/library/truth.html (accessed July 1, 2011).

[62] *See Truth and Justice: The Morality of Truth Commissions* (Robert I. Rotberg & Dennis Thompson eds., 2000); *see also* Martha Minow, *Between Vengeance and Forgiveness: Facing History After Genocide and Mass Violence* (1998); John Dugard, *Reconciliation and Justice: The South African Experience, in The Future of International Human Rights* 399 (Burns H. Weston & Stephen P. Marks eds., 1999) [hereinafter Weston & Marks].

[63] Sinden, *supra* Ch. 2 note 6, at 264.

[64] *Id.* at 270.

[65] Also illustrative, particularly when they find the strength to function independently of their state clients, are the conferences and high-level meetings of the U.N.'s specialized agencies and programs that commonly deal with environmental or environmentally-related issues, often

Occupy movement has provided another. The adoption of new resolutions and treaties, the recommendation of new norms and mechanisms, the reinterpretation of existing international and domestic norms and procedures – these and other such activities contribute to legal and political empowerment because "[t]he more fortunate are called upon to assist the less fortunate as an internationally recognized responsibility."[66] The authority of the sponsoring organizations and participants, and the resulting rights vocabulary and action plans, help to fortify all varieties of human rights projects.

4. Human rights provide access to international institutions dedicated specifically to their promotion and vindication. This includes the widely accepted "thematic mechanisms" of the UN; the ad hoc tribunals relative to heinous human rights disasters in the former Yugoslavia, Rwanda, Sierra Leone, and Cambodia, and specialized treaty bodies at the global level; and the regional human rights regimes of Europe, the Americas, and Africa. The effectiveness of these institutions as enforcement mechanisms is not consistent and often cumbersome and time-consuming, particularly at the global level. Nevertheless, they confirm that, given sufficient political will, perpetrators of human suffering can be prosecuted on the international plane using formal legal tools to remedy or otherwise mitigate abuses and thereby help prevent future abuse.[67] As Kiss and Shelton note, there is now an "extensive jurisprudence in which the specific obligations of states to protect and preserve the environment are detailed."[68] Both these formal legal tools and less formal techniques, such as civil society mobilization of shame, can deter violations of individual and group environmental rights.

5. Human rights discourse and strategy encourage the creation of initiatives both within and beyond civil society that are designed to facilitate the meeting of basic needs. For many years, Cold War rivalries stifled any such efforts (except for the 1975 Helsinki Accords[69]) until the fall of the Berlin

---

of large scale – e.g., the Food and Agriculture Organization (FAO), the International Maritime Organization (IMO), the World Health organization (WHO), the U.N. Development Programme (UNDP), the U.N. Environmental Programme (UNEP), the U.N. Human Settlements Programme (UN-HABITAT), the Office of the U.N. High Commissioner for Human Rights (OHCHR), and the U.N. High Commissioner for Refugees (UNHCR) as well as other intergovernmental organizations.

[66] Mary Robinson, *Foreword* to Marta Santos Pais, A Human Rights Conceptual Framework for UNICEF (1999) (Innocenti Essay No. 9, Florence: UNICEF International Child Development Centre), available at http://www.unicef.org/cfc/essay-o.pdf (accessed July 1, 2011).

[67] *See*, generally, *Guide to International Human Rights Practice* (Hurst Hannum ed., 4th ed. 2004).

[68] Kiss & Shelton, *supra* note 37, at 238.

[69] *Supra* note 54.

Wall in 1989. Since 1989, however, they have proliferated, especially in the human rights NGO advocacy and scholarly communities. This is of profound importance because such initiatives foster the provision of basic needs, including, obviously, a clean and healthy environment. Assuring people that they have the material basis to act on their rights is the very definition of empowerment.[70]

There are, to be sure, some predictable objections to a rights-based strategy that would fundamentally shift the ways we currently go about governing the natural environment. Five arguments resistant to human rights are especially conspicuous: the claimed immutability of State sovereignty, the claimed irrelevance of public international law to private actors, the claimed sanctity of corporate sovereignty, the claimed indeterminacy of human rights, and the claimed absence of human rights theory. In our highly interdependent and interpenetrating world, it is hard to take the first three of these claims seriously, especially when applied to the global environment: the first holds little favor beyond China and Russia; the second collapsed with the "war on terrorism"; and the third has been called repeatedly into question since the end of the Cold War and the widespread globalization of capital that followed.[71] It is therefore unnecessary to contest these arguments here.[72] The last two, however, are less obviously vulnerable and thus merit at least brief rebuttal.

Rebutting the Claimed Indeterminacy of Human Rights

Some scholars criticize the language of human rights as lacking conceptual clarity, noting that there are conflicting schools of thought as to what constitutes a right and how to define human rights.[73] For this reason, they claim the concept to be indeterminate and therefore distrust its capacity to address

---

[70] *See, e.g.*, Richard Pierre Claude, *What Do Human Rights NGOs Do?*, in *Human Rights in the World Community: Issues and Action* 424 (Richard Pierre Claude & Burns H. Weston eds. & contribs., 3d ed. 2006).

[71] *See, e.g.*, the landmark essay by Steven R. Ratner, *Corporations and Human Rights: A Theory of Legal Responsibility*, 111 Yale L. J. 443 (2001), *also* available at http://yalelawjournal.org/the-yale-law-journal/article/corporations-and-human-rights:-a-theory-of-legal-responsibility (accessed Feb. 15, 2012).

[72] *But see* Burns H Weston & Mark B. Teerink, *Rethinking Child Labor: A Multifaceted Human Rights Problem*, in *Child Labor and Human Rights: Making Children Matter* 3, 12–15 (Burns H. Weston ed., 2005) (contesting these claims at some length albeit, obviously, in the context of combating child labor).

[73] For an insightful account, with discussion of other views, *see* Alan Gewirth, *The Community of Rights* (1996).

real world social ills effectively or at all.[74] They observe that there are many unresolved theoretical questions about rights: whether the individual is the only bearer of rights (in contradistinction to such entities as families; groups of common ethnicity, religion, or language; communities; and nations); "whether rights are to be regarded as...constraints on goal-seeking action or as parts of a goal that is to be promoted"; "whether rights – thought of as justified entitlements – are correlated with duties"; and, not least, "what rights are understood to be rights to."[75] A certain level of well-being? A certain access to certain resources in one's life pursuit? A certain quality of opportunity in that pursuit? The relatively recent debate over "Asian values" and its underlying tension between cultural relativist and universalist approaches to human rights make clear that all this questioning is no idle intellectual chatter.[76] It is present in political discourse as well and thus serves as a possible explanation for resistance to a rights-based approach to ecological governance.

The claimed indeterminacy of human rights, however, is less problematic than sometimes perceived. The core of the human rights concept is as well-defined and clearly articulated as any social or legal norm, a fact proven by the numerous widely accepted human rights norms increasingly enforced.[77] Moreover, even conceding that unresolved theoretical issues relating to human rights remain, this fact does not of itself detract from the broadest and most effective actualization of the fundamental principles and values on which

---

[74] The concept of indeterminacy has been much discussed in several modern approaches to language and literature, contending that the meaning of a text never can be fully determined because its author's original intention is subject to the unfixed nature of the author's makeup and experience, because it is the consequence of the particular cultural and social background of the reader, and because language itself generates its own meaning over time. This contention, Michael Freeman points out, is prominent particularly when it comes to concepts such as "human rights": abstract, oftentimes ambiguous, and therefore a challenge to the philosophical discipline of conceptual analysis, which can seem remote from the experiences of human beings. Freeman, *supra* note 55, at 2.

[75] Martha C. Nussbaum, *Capabilities, Human Rights, and the Universal Declaration*, in Weston & Marks, *supra* note 62, at 25, 26–7.

[76] On cultural relativism versus universalism in human rights law and policy, *see* Burns H. Weston, *The Universality of Human Rights in a Multicultured World: Toward Respectful Decision-Making*, in Weston & Marks, *supra* note 56, at 65; Burns H. Weston, *Human Rights and Nation-Building in Cross-Cultural Settings*, 60 Me. L. Rev. 1 (2008).

[77] *See* Samuel Moyn, *The Last Utopia: Human Rights in History*, at Ch. 5 (2010). "Today, it seems, self-evident that among the major purposes – and perhaps the essential point – of international law is to protect individual human rights." *Id.* at 176; *see also* Kenneth Cmiel, *The Recent History of Human Rights*, 1 Am. Hist. Rev. 117 (2004); Burns H. Weston, *Human Rights*, in *Encyclopædia Britannica* (15th ed., 2005 printing), available at http://www.britannica.com/EBchecked/topic/275840/human-rights (accessed June 1, 2011).

there is virtually universal agreement – for example, the human right to a clean and healthy environment.

Thus, while the concept or language of rights, like most legal language, sometimes suffers ambiguity, it is not to be discarded in the struggle for a clean and healthy environment simply for this reason. Rather, as with any human system, incomplete and imperfect, one must make use of those elements that are established and effective while working to improve and clarify those that remain vague or incomplete, just as we do all other legal norms as a matter of course all the time.

Rebutting the Claimed Absence of Human Rights Theory

Perhaps the most confounding of the alleged unresolved theoretical issues about human rights is the claimed absence of a theory to justify human rights in the first place.[78] In the presence of ongoing philosophical and political controversy about the existence, nature, and application of human rights in a multicultural world, a world in which Christian natural law justifications for human rights are now widely deemed suspect or obsolete, one must exercise caution when adopting a human rights approach to social policy lest one be accused of cultural imperialism. It is not enough to say, as Michael Freeman argues, that human beings possess human rights simply for being human, as does, for example, the 1993 Vienna Declaration and Programme of Action, which proclaims that "[h]uman rights and fundamental freedoms are the birthright of all human beings."[79] Writes Freeman: "It is not clear why one has *any* rights simply because one is a human being."[80]

We do not disagree. But neither do we accept that there exists no theory to justify human rights in our secular times, and therefore no theory exists to justify a human rights approach to the environment and its governance. The concept of human rights is or can be firmly established on sound theoretical grounds.

First, there is the proposition, formally proclaimed in both the 1948 Universal Declaration of Human Rights and the yet more widely adopted – and revalidating – 1993 Vienna Declaration, that human rights derive from "the

---

[78] The late philosopher Richard Rorty, for one, contended that there is no theoretical basis for human rights on the grounds that there is no theoretical basis for any belief. *See* Richard Rorty, *Human Rights, Rationality, and Sentimentality*, in *On Human Rights* 116, 126 (Stephen Shute & Susan Hurley eds., 1993).

[79] Vienna Declaration and Programme of Action of the World Conference on Human Rights, U.N. Doc. A/Conf.157/24, at 20–46 (June 5, 1993), *reprinted in* 32 I.L.M. 1661 (1993) *and* III Basic Documents, *supra* Prologue note 13, at III.V.2 [hereinafter "Vienna Declaration"].

[80] Freeman, *supra* note 55, at 60–1 (emphasis in original).

inherent dignity... of all members of the human family"[81] or, alternatively, from "the dignity and worth inherent in the human person."[82] Although this proposition informs us little more than the assertion that human rights extend to human beings simply for being human, it does point the way. Unless one subscribes to nihilism, it is the human being's inherent dignity and worth that justify human rights. Of course, the obvious question remains: how does one determine the human being's inherent dignity and worth?

Noteworthy in this regard is the work of Martha Nussbaum and Amartya Sen on "capabilities and human functioning." In their search for a theory that answers at least some of the questions raised by rights talk, they have pioneered the language of "human capabilities" as a way to speak about, and act on, what fundamentally is required to be human – "life," "bodily health," "bodily integrity," "senses, imagination, and thought," "emotions," "affiliation" ("friendship" and "respect"), "other species," "play," and, not least, "control over one's environment" ("political" and "material").[83] Although Nussbaum and Sen do not reject the concept of human rights as such[84] – indeed, they see it working hand in hand with their concept of capabilities, jointly signaling the central goals of public policy – they propose an emphasis on human capabilities as the theoretical means by which to restore "the obligation of result." This would thereby move the discussion from the abstract to the concrete without having to rely on controversial transempirical metaphysics to cut across human differences.[85]

---

[81] UDHR, *supra* Ch. 3 note 62, at pmbl., para. 1.

[82] Vienna Declaration, *supra* note 79, at pmbl., para. 2.

[83] *See* Nussbaum, *supra* note 75; *see also* Amartya K. Sen, *Equality of What?*, Tanner Lecture on Human Values at Stanford University, Tanner Lectures on Human Values (1979). For another early advocacy of a capabilities approach to human rights, *see* Bernard Williams, *The Standard of Living: Interests and Capabilities*, in Amartya K. Sen, *The Standard of Living* 94 (1987); *see also The Quality of Life* (Martha Nussbaum & Amartya K. Sen eds., 1993).

[84] In her essay linking the capabilities approach with the 1948 UDHR, Nussbaum acknowledges that the language of rights retains an important place in public discourse, providing a normative basis for discussion, emphasizing the importance and basic role of the entitlements in question and peoples choice and autonomy, and establishing the parameters of basic agreement. *See* Nussbaum, *supra* note 75, at 59.

[85] This line of theoretical argument, interestingly, parallels the reason why the Commons is empowering in contemporary times: it enables individuals, as members of communities, to participate in the fulfillment of their own, most fundamental human needs and capabilities, at a time in history when a Leviathan State/Market has arrogated such functions to itself, often to the detriment of commoners. This is not to say that the modern Market and State do not need to play important (but different) roles; it is to say that human existence and the Commons are more intimately bound up with each other as a matter of historical experience, and that re-validating the Commons is more likely to empower basic human capabilities and human functioning, if not grander, more elevated human aspirations as well.

A theory of human rights can be found, we believe, in the idea of necessity driven by enlightened self-interest – no need to consult some transempirical source. "A just society," Burns Weston writes,[86]

> whether operating across space or time or both, requires rights as a matter of necessity to guarantee its possibility. And to ensure its probability (or "compliance pull"[87]), it must be defined by values freely and equally chosen by its members in rational contemplation of the self-interest – *their* self-interest – that inheres in mutually tolerant and reciprocally forbearing attitudes and behaviors. Of course, enlightened altruism can, does, and should contribute to the building of just societies as well, and therefore should be encouraged always. But in the "nasty, brutish, and short" Hobbesian world in which many if not most humans live, enlightened self-interest can greatly motivate respect for others. This is, indeed, the lesson that many evolutionary scientists are coming to embrace. As Martin Nowak puts it, "our ability to cooperate goes hand in hand with succeeding in the struggle to survive."[88] Darwinian competition notwithstanding, individually and as a species we are more likely to survive and thrive if we honor the values that underwrite human rights law and policy in its most inclusive aspect. What goes around comes around, as they say, with the prospect of a society in waiting – local, global, present, future – that honors a public order of human dignity – the essence of human rights – marked by the widest possible shaping and sharing of all basic values among all human beings.

Such a society, we recognize, can be validated by intellectual constructs in an imagined Lockean "initial position" – as in the Rawlsian "veil of ignorance" construct, for example, akin to Immanuel Kant's "categorical imperative."[89] We believe, however, that a preferable, more straightforward approach would be simply to postulate a just society as an empirically measurable, verifiable preference in the here and now (i.e., *sans* intellectual contrivance) when it is inclusively determined in the inclusive interest.

In any event, however enunciated or substantiated, the necessity idea comes down to a kind of share-and-share-alike Golden Rule, as intimated earlier, anchored in respect and driven by self-interest as well as empathetic altruism by all humans, present and future, to satisfy the fundamental requirements of socioeconomic and political justice – the minimum conditions of what it means to be human, the minimum conditions for a life of human dignity in

---

[86] Weston, *supra* Ch. 3 note 1, at 263–4.
[87] *See* Thomas M. Franck, *The Power of Legitimacy Among Nations* 26 (1990).
[88] Martin A. Nowak with Roger Highfield, *Super Cooperators: Altruism, Evolution, and Why We Need Each Other To Succeed*, at xvi (2011).
[89] *See* John Rawls, *A Theory of Justice* §§ 1–4, 9, 11–17, 20–30, 33–5, 39–40 (1971).

a clean, healthy, ecologically balanced, and sustainable environment. In the words of former UN High Commissioner for Human Rights Louise Arbour, "[h]uman rights are not a utopian ideal. They embody an international consensus on the minimum conditions for a life of dignity."[90]

IN SUM, making the transition to green governance using a human rights approach – and making human rights a lodestar for such governance – is conceptually not difficult to comprehend or endorse. Especially when understood holistically, it can both enable and operationalize the new paradigm.

What appears problematic, however, is the public's insufficient understanding of the power and potential of human rights beyond what is known by scholars, jurists, and activists who make it their specialty; the truly full human rights message has not yet reached the vast majority of the lay public worldwide. Doubtless, there are many reasons for this condition. Too slavish an adherence to outmoded conceptions of human rights is certainly one of them. As historian Samuel Moyn observes, "human rights are not so much an inheritance to preserve as an invention to remake – or even leave behind – if their program is to be vital and relevant in what is already a very different world than the one in which it came so recently."[91] There are other reasons: too much resistance from the State/Market system, too little financial support, too little human rights education, too little imagination, and so forth.

If the environmental science is to be believed, however, and if commons- and rights-based ecological governance is to be realistically wished for on a widespread basis, then this state of affairs cannot be allowed to endure. To make the shift, a "bottom-up" engagement of assorted commoners and sympathetic others everywhere – concentrated in focus and strong in conviction – is required. Necessarily this would include a large-scale and sustained commitment to human rights education,[92] akin to the work of the UN Decade for Human Rights Education (1995–2004)[93] and its follow-up World Programme

---

[90] Statement by Ms. Louise Arbour, High Comm'r for Human Rights, to the Open-Ended Working Group Established by the Commission on Human Rights to Consider Options Regarding the Elaboration of an Optional Protocol to the International Covenant on Economic, Social, and Cultural Rights (Jan. 14, 2005), available at http://www.unhchr.ch/huricane/huricane.nsf/newsroom (accessed Feb. 16, 2012).

[91] Moyn, *supra* note 77, at 9.

[92] *See, e.g.,* Richard Pierre Claude, *The Right to Education and Human Rights Education,* in Human Rights in the World Community, *supra* Ch. 4, note 70, at 211.

[93] *See, e.g., United Nations Decade for Human Rights Education,* Office of the U.N. High Comm'r for Human Rights, available at http://www2.ohchr.org/english/issues/education/training/decade.htm (accessed Feb. 16, 2012).

for Human Rights Education (2005-ongoing).[94] A prime example is the work of the People's Movement for Human Rights Education (PDHRE), a New York–based NGO "dedicated to human rights learning for social and economic transformation."[95] Particularly pertinent is its Human Rights Cities program, the purpose of which is "to develop and advance learning about human rights *as a way of life*,"[96] to enable all members of a community – from ordinary citizens and community activists to policy-makers and local officials – "to pursue . . . community-wide dialogue[s] and launch actions to improve the life and security of women, men and children based on human rights norms and standards."[97] The inescapable point is that to move from what is said and written (lexis) to on-the-ground tactics (praxis) that can give tangible meaning to what it means to take a human rights approach to commons- and rights-based ecological governance requires an informed citizenry.

On final analysis, then, there is no good theoretical reason why a human rights strategy should not be pursued – and as we have seen, many good theoretical reasons why it should. There remains, to be sure, the haunting question of whether humanity has the political will to attend to the important work of enacting and enforcing laws and policies that can help save Planet Earth. But that key issue is one of moral and political choice, and that choice is, to us, obvious. When joined to the struggle against contaminating, degrading, and otherwise abusive treatment of the natural environment, human rights can be a uniquely powerful tool for achieving as well as informing ecological governance in the common interest. Richard Hiskes puts it well. The emergence of environmental human rights, he avers, "ushers in a new chapter in the development of human rights as a central focus of human political endeavor."[98]

---

[94] *World Programme for Human Rights Education*, Office of the U.N. High Comm'r for Human Rights, available at http://www2.ohchr.org/english/issues/education/training/programme.htm (accessed Feb. 16, 2012).

[95] *See* People's Movement for Human Rights Learning, available at http://www.pdhre.org (accessed Feb. 16, 2012). *See also* the work of Human Rights Education Associates (HREA), available at http://www.hrea.org/decade (accessed Feb. 16, 2012), in particular its follow-up to the U.N. Decade for Human Rights Education in the form of HREA's Global Consultation on the (U.N.) World Programme for Human Rights Education.

[96] *See Human Rights Cities* in People's Movement for Human Rights Learning, *supra* note 95, at http://www.pdhre.org/projects/ hrcommun.html (accessed Nov. 30, 2012) (emphasis added).

[97] *See* Stephen P. Marks & Kathleen A. Modrowski with *Walther Lichem, Human Rights Cities: Civic Engagement for Societal Development* 45 (2008), available at http://www.pdhre.org/ Human_Rights _Cities_Book.pdf (accessed May 15, 2012).

[98] Hiskes, *supra* Ch. 2 note 6, at 151.

B. THE POTENTIAL OF VERNACULAR LAW

"Vernacular Law," it will be recalled, is the term we use to distinguish informal or unofficial law from what we call "State Law." Vernacular Law originates in the informal, unofficial zones of society and is a source of moral legitimacy and power in its own right. This helps explain why colonial powers often used law to repress local languages in favor of their controlling mother tongues, and why postcolonial governments have also used law to consolidate the rule of their linguistic culture in multilingual settings.[99] Such political uses of law and language point to the real power of Vernacular Law.

The terms used to describe this realm of unofficial law vary. Legal scholars have used the words "informal," "customary," "grass-roots," "indigenous," "common," and "local" law. Perhaps the most extensive treatment of the subject is an anthology of dozens of essays titled *Folk Law: Essays in the Theory and Practice of Lex Non Scripta*,[100] which surveys the history of unwritten, customary law in a variety of cultural contexts. Although cultural anthropologists might call it "subaltern jurisprudence," the colonial and postcolonial origins of the term "subaltern" render it insufficient even if illuminating.

We are concerned to emphasize the "living law" nature of this form or level of legal process – its character as an evolving, communicative life pulse. We therefore elected the term "Vernacular Law," inspired by the late Ivan Illich's essays on "Vernacular Values," first published in *CoEvolution Quarterly*, and the basis of his book *Shadow Work* (1981). As a later commentator on Illich's essays describes it, the "vernacular domain" evokes a "sensibility and rootedness...in which local life has been conducted throughout most of history and even today in a significant proportion of subsistence- and communitarian-oriented communities," that is, "places and spaces where people are struggling to achieve regeneration and social restoration against the forces of economic globalization."[101]

Legal scholar Michael Reisman elucidates this theme in his germinal study *Law in Brief Encounters*, calling this neglected legal process "microlaw."[102]

---

[99] *See, e.g.*, Robert J. Gordon, *Vernacular Law and the Future of Human Rights in Namibia* (NISER Discussion Paper No. 11, The Namibian Inst. of Soc. and Econ. Research, Univ. of Namib., Nov. 1991).

[100] 1 & 2 Folk Law: Essays in the Theory and Practice of Lex Non Scripta (Alison Dundes Renteln & Alan Dundes eds., 1994).

[101] Trent Schroyer, *Beyond Western Economics: Remembering Other Economic Cultures* 69 (2009).

[102] W. Michael Reisman, *Law in Brief Encounters* 3 (1999). Reisman writes: "Mainstream contemporary legal theory – with its emphasis on the state as the centerpiece of any legal system and, for many theorists, its primary, if not exclusive, source of law – misdirects our attention

Especially significant for present purposes is his observation that "[w]hen assessments [of formally organized legal systems] yield discrepancies between what people want and what they can expect to achieve, macrolegal changes may not be effective. Microlegal adjustments may be the necessary instrument of change."[103] Reisman continues: "In everyone's life, microlaw has not only *not* been superseded by state law but remains . . . the most important and continuous normative experience."[104] Reisman is addressing Vernacular Law, or the sensibilities or expectations of "right" and "wrong," of "practical" and "ineffective," that emerge from the everyday lives of "ordinary" people. They may be self-conscious or unself-conscious, but the social protocols that people develop over time in a given societal setting constitute an undeniable form of law.

There are, as one might expect, many variants.[105] In Chapter 2 we identify three relatively conspicuous examples: the canons of the church, the rules of the sporting field, the codes of social etiquette.[106] At the other extreme, Reisman includes "looking, staring, and glaring," "standing in line and cutting in," and "rapping and talking to the boss."[107] In addition, somewhere in between there exists a seemingly inexhaustible number and variety of Vernacular Law systems, each with its own protocols for what is acceptable and unacceptable, what constitutes a sanction, and other rules for negotiating relationships. These systems can be seen in the management of indigenous communities, peasant collectives, farmers' markets, businesses and factories, interbusiness dealings (e.g., "gentlemen's agreements"), specialized trades (e.g., magicians' secrets, bakers' recipes), labor unions, academic institutions and classrooms, hospitals and wards, civil society organizations (NGOs), neighborhood associations, fraternal and sororal orders, social clubs, the family, and, obviously not to be overlooked, the commercial market – and at all levels. Such State Law as may govern any of these domains has an informal complement and antecedent – socially negotiated, based on practical experience, and sometimes tacit – that acts in concert with State Law's more formal components.

---

from the full realm of law. The law of the state may be important, but law, *real* law, is found in all human relations, from the simplest, briefest encounter between two people to the most inclusive and permanent type of interaction. Real law is generated, reinforced, changed, and terminated continually in the course of almost all human activity." *Id.*

[103] *Id.* at 4.

[104] *Id.* (author's emphasis).

[105] As Reisman puts it: "That legal systems, like Mariushka dolls, occur within legal systems within legal systems is hardly rare. Legal anthropologists have demonstrated the prevalence, within the apparently unitary nation-state, of groups with effective political and legal organizations that are independent of and substantively different from those of the state." *Id.*, at 149.

[106] *See supra* text accompanying Ch. 2 notes 8–9.

[107] Reisman, *supra* note 102, at Chs. 1–3.

The fugue of State and Vernacular Law may be subtle, but Vernacular Law – "the most important and continuous normative experience," says Reisman of his functionally equivalent "microlaw" – is a cardinal process for establishing the legitimacy of State Law and adapting it to new human and ecological (or other) circumstances as necessary.

Vernacular Law is of great interest to us because commons governance depends critically on the informal, socially negotiated values, principles, and rules that a given community develops. It constitutes a form of cultural ballast that gives a commons stability and self-confidence, even in the absence of formal law.

Perhaps the most salient arena for Vernacular Law today is the Internet – where, cyberlaw practitioner and professor David R. Johnson informed us in 2006, "[w]e are on the brink of a Cambrian explosion of differentiation of legal organisms."[108] The Internet acts as a great hosting infrastructure for countless digital commons. As it has exploded in scope and become a pervasive cultural force around the world, so Vernacular Law – self-organized, self-policing community governance – has become a default system of law in many virtual spaces (notwithstanding the lurking presence of State Law or corporate-crafted law that may enframe these commons). For millions of "digital natives" born into a highly networked cultural environment, Vernacular Law is such a familiar, natural mode of governance that the legacy institutions of the real world such as the US Congress, courts, and large corporations are seen as unduly complicated, unresponsive, archaic, and/or corrupt. "It is commonplace," Johnson writes, "that the law has grown too complex for anyone to deal with ... Expenditure of energy (money) to drive a case down to any given scale in the legal fractal can produce just about any tangent, any result. In consequence, law has become a form of force – its invocation is often a use of power rather than an appeal to justice."[109]

As one might expect, it cannot be said that digital or other examples of Vernacular Law systems are pure in the sense that they are completely unrelated to State Law. The very idea of the uninvolved, noninterfering State in itself communicates an implicit if not explicit policy of official deference and tolerance – a stance that is desirable if not indispensable for the effective governance of modern heterogeneous societies. Clearly, there are times when even the tolerant State will intervene if events within these systems are perceived

---

[108] David Johnson, "The Life of the Law Online," *First Monday* Feb. 6, 2006, at 8, available at http://firstmonday.org/htbin/cgiwrap/bin/ojs/index.php/fm/article/view/1314/1234 (accessed Feb. 20, 2012).

[109] *Id.* at 5.

to compromise the policies or existence of the dominant order. But a due regard for the opinions of "the street," as worked out through Vernacular Law, is essential to any system of formal law.

It must be said that not all Vernacular Law systems are virtuous in the sense of working for the well-being of their constituents and possibly even the broader society beyond. In point: black markets, inner-city gang operations, Internet pirates, and other criminal arrangements (from the vantage point of State Law at least). Yet, these more problematic forms of Vernacular Law cannot be summarily dismissed as criminal; quite possibly their existence points to the failures of State Law to meet needs that may be entirely legitimate.

What is key for present purposes is not the number or varieties of Vernacular Law systems that can be identified. Rather, it is that, from time to time, when the State and/or its State Law fails to meet the needs, wants, and expectations of the peoples whom they are supposed to serve, then – in Reisman's words – "microlegal adjustments [e.g., assertions of Vernacular Law] may be the necessary instrument of change."

No more appropriate demonstration of this truth is to be found than at Runnymede in 1215 when King John of England[110] was forced to make concessions to his feudal baron subjects in armed rebellion against his ruinous foreign policy and arbitrary rule. The resulting "peace treaty," the Great Charter or Magna Carta, restricted the King's absolute power and settled a number of long-standing disputes in early thirteenth-century English society. The document established new terms of agreement to resolve seven basic conflicts, writes historian Peter Linebaugh, "between church and monarchy, between individual and the state, between husband and wife, between Jew and Christian, between king and baron, between merchant and consumer, between commoner and privatizer."[111]

The conflict that most concerns us is this last conflict, the terms of peace of which were spelled out in a companion document, the Charter of the Forest, adopted by King Henry III, son and successor of King John (1166–1216), in 1217. The Charter of the Forest formally recognized the Vernacular Law of the English commoners, that is, their traditional rights of access to, and use of, royal lands and forests. The rights were essentially rights of subsistence, because the commoners depended on the forests for food, fuel, and economic security through their traditional rights of pannage (pasture for their pigs), estover (collecting firewood), agistment (grazing), and turbary (cutting of turf

---

[110] Son of Richard the Lionhearted, but not his equal.
[111] Peter Linebaugh, *The Magna Carta Manifesto: Liberties and Commons for All* 45 (2008).

for fuel), among other practices.[112] Recognition of these rights also amounted to a form of protection against State terror, which the sheriff had inflicted on commoners for using the King's forests. The Charter of the Forest was later incorporated into the Magna Carta and considered an integral part of it.[113]

As is well known, the Magna Carta underlies many constitutions and statutes in the English-speaking world, including in the U.S. Constitution, the International Bill of Human Rights,[114] and the three leading regional human rights conventions of Europe, the Americas, and Africa.[115] Subject to minor adjustments, the Charter of the Forests remained in force from 1215 to 1971, when it was superseded by the U.K.'s Wild Creatures and Forest Laws Act of 1971.[116]

What is most notable about this early history of Anglo-American law is its frank recognition of Vernacular Law as an instrument to help State Law make restorative "macrolegal" adjustments to honor environmental needs and demands. In modern parlance, we might say that Vernacular Law provided the building blocks and feedback loops to inform the State Law enforced by the State. The social practices and traditions of commoners shape normative expectations that, if generally complied with, constitute law. As Linebaugh puts it, "[c]ommoners think first not of title deeds, but of human deeds: How will this land be tilled? Does it require manuring? What grows there? They begin to explore. You might call it a natural attitude."[117]

At the same time, if anarchy or war or other violent confrontation is to be avoided, it cannot be assumed that restorative State Law adjustments will

---

[112] For brilliant insight into these historic events and their influence upon contemporary thought and practice, see *id.*

[113] Linebaugh writes: "The two charters were reissued together in 1225. McKechnie states, 'it marked the final form assumed by Magna Carta.' Subsequently, the two were confirmed together. By 1297 Edward I directed that the two charters become the common law of the land. After a law of Edward III in 1369, the two were treated as a single statute. Both charters were printed together at the commencement of the English *Statutes-at-Large*." *Id.* at 39.

[114] I.e., the UDHR, *supra* Ch. 3 note 62; the ICESCR, *supra* Ch. 4 note 30, art. 12(1); and the ICCPR, *supra* Ch. 4 note 29. Each of these core human rights instruments is reprinted in Title III of Basic Documents, *supra* Prologue note 13, at III.A.1, III.A.2, and III.A.3, respectively.

[115] *See* ECHR *supra* Ch. 2 note 22; American Convention on Human Rights, Nov. 21, 1969, 1144 U.N.T.S. 123, O.A.S.T.S. 36, OEA/Ser.L/V/II.23, Doc. 21, Rev. 6, *reprinted in* 9 I.L.M. 99 (1970) *and* III Basic Documents, *supra* Prologue note 13, at III.B.32; Banjul Charter, *supra* Ch. 2 note 21. Each of these fundamental human rights instruments is reprinted in Title III of Basic Documents, *supra* Prologue note 13, at III.B.8, III.B.32, and III.B.1, respectively.

[116] Wild Creatures and Forest Laws Act, 1971, c. 47 (Eng.).

[117] Linebaugh, *supra* note 111, at 45. Linebaugh continues: "Second, commoning is embedded in a labor process; it inheres in a particular praxis of field, upland, forest, marsh, coast. Common rights are entered into by labor. Third, commoning is collective. Fourth, being independent of the state, commoning is independent also of the temporality of the law and state. Magna Carta does not list rights; it grants perpetuities. It goes deep into human history." *Id.*

be made without some self-conscious intervention. Revolutions often occur precisely because State Law refuses to make necessary accommodations with Vernacular Law. As Johnson notes, law must be viewed as a living social organism, one that "causes its own form of order and persistence" that is capable of rejecting dysfunctional components from time to time. As a living social system, Vernacular Law does this. State Law, however, is more likely to be beholden to abstract logic and syllogisms that, over time, fail to account for shifting economic, technological, and other realities, not to mention social mores and practices. State Law, then, can too easily become ossified and unresponsive, a captive of special interests that is made to serve narrow, private, and short-term goals.

"The problem is," writes Johnson, "that our current legal system lacks the most fundamental mechanism, used by more rapidly replicating and adapting biological organisms, to keep undesirable levels of complication under control. We haven't had competition for survival."[118] Johnson continues:

> In biology, if an organism becomes too complicated [or outmoded or corrupted] for its own good, it fails to mate and its line dies out – replaced by other systems, with other kinds of order. Because of the particular nature of law's meta –meta-story [of, by, and for the people], its historical rooting of legitimacy in a particular geographic area, we've developed only one legal organism per country. We haven't had a real competition for survival among rule sets. The competition is only between the rule of (our one) law and, presumably, anarchy. So the tendency of all rule sets to become more complicated [or outmoded or corrupted] over time, especially when written by people considering only parts of the system in analytical isolation, has not been checked by evolutionary forces. We replicate the law by telling (slightly different versions of) its story every day.[119]

"But," Johnson rues, "we tell only one story and we don't shorten the story very often because we don't have to compete very hard for our own attention."[120]

In her study of the history of property law, Yale law professor Carol Rose notes that custom is "a medium through which a seemingly 'unorganized' public may organize itself and act, and in a sense even 'speak' with the force of law . . . Over time, communities may develop strong emotional attachments to particular places and staging particular events in those places . . . "[121] Medieval

---

[118] Johnson, *supra* note 108, at 6.
[119] *Id.*
[120] *Id.*
[121] Carol M. Rose, "Comedy of the Commons: Custom, Commerce, and Inherently Public Property," in *Property and Persuasion: Essays on the History, Theory, and Rhetoric of Ownership* 134 (1994).

courts were known to elevate custom over other claims, as when they upheld the right of commoners to stage maypole dance celebrations on the medieval manor grounds even after they had been expelled from tenancy.

Courts were and are generally hostile toward claims of traditional rights (or in our terms, rights based on Vernacular Law) because, as one court put it, they are "forms of community unknown in this state."[122] As Rose writes, citing *Delaplace v. Crenshaw & Fisher* (1860),[123] "a claim based on custom would permit a 'comparatively... few individuals' to make a law binding on the public at large, contrary to the rights of the people to be bound only by laws passed by their own 'proper representatives.' Indeed, if the customary acts of an unorganized community could vest some form of property rights in that community, then custom could displace orderly government."[124]

Courts have been uneasy with the idea of informal communities as a source of law because they are not formally organized or sanctioned by the State, and courts themselves are generally creatures of the State. But as Rose notes, this is precisely why such law is so compelling and authoritative a substitute for government-made law; it reflects the people's will in direct, unmediated ways:

> It was a commonplace among British jurisprudes that a general custom, the "custom of the country," is none other than the common law itself. Looked at from this perspective, custom is the means by which an otherwise unorganized public can order its affairs, and even do so authoritatively.

Custom thus suggests a route by which a commons may be managed – a means different from ownership either by individuals or the rule of organized governments. The intriguing aspect of customary rights is that they vest property rights in groups that are indefinite and informal yet nevertheless capable of self-management. Custom can be the medium through which such an informal group acts; indeed, the community claiming customary rights was in some senses not an "unorganized'" public at all, even if it was not a formal government either.[125]

---

[122] As quoted in Rose, *supra* note 121, at 157. Rose comments: "Certainly this remark reflected the general American hostility to the feudal and manorial basis of customary claims. But it also focused precisely on the informal character of the 'community' claiming the right; the remark suggested that if a community were going to make claims in a corporate capacity, then the residents would have to organize themselves in a way legally authorized by the state." *Id.* at 123–24.

[123] 56 Va. (15 Gratt.) 457 (1860).

[124] *Id.* at 124.

[125] *Id.*

In Chapters 5 and 6, where we discuss some of the virtues of commons as a governance solution, we return to Rose's idea that the Commons can result in a *comedy* (i.e., greater value creation through participation), not a *tragedy*.

For now, the point we wish to emphasize is that the Vernacular Law praxis called the Commons, particularly that of the ecological Commons, is a necessary instrument of change for a State/Market world order that is failing to act as a responsible steward of our planet. Through ecological and other commons, Vernacular Law (what some approximate with the term "wild law"[126]) is simultaneously an institution and process that safeguards common-pool resources or ecosystems while providing for an equitable distribution of the fruits borne of them. In its broad architecture, the Commons is a paradigm of beneficent ecological governance because it can help address, among other issues, the State/Market's compulsive externalizing of costs; the ethics of monetizing all value; the growth imperatives of neoliberal economics; the legal prejudices against collective stewardship and long-term commitments; and our cultural alienation from nature.

Unlike the dominant State Law system, the Vernacular Law of the ecological commons is, if properly conceived and structured, inherently predisposed to welcome and support a human right to a clean and healthy environment. It is well suited as a source of law on which State Law can rely for enlightened interpretation and application. As Ugo Mattei observes, "commons are an ecological-qualitative category based on inclusion and access" and thus create "an institutional setting reflecting long term sustainability and full inclusion of all the global commoners, including the poorest and most vulnerable (human and non-human)."[127] By contrast, the dominant State/Market order is an economic-quantitative paradigm of unrelenting territorial sovereignty and competitive privatism in property ownership; it produces scarcity by fostering exclusion and concentration of power in a few hands. Embracing the Vernacular Law of the ecological commons as an authoritative source of law, we submit, would prod the dominant State Law system to provide greater substantive support to the human right to a clean and healthy environment.

---

[126] *See, e.g.,* Cullinan, *supra* Prologue note 20, at 30 ("[T]he term 'wild law' cannot easily be snared within the strictures of a conventional legal definition. It is perhaps better understood as an approach to human governance, rather than a branch of law or a collection of laws. It is more about ways of being and doing than the right thing to do."). We hasten to add, however, that, while we agree with Cullinan's existential sentiments, we do not agree with his jurisprudential outlook, too tied as it is, we believe, to a kind of Austinian positivism that insists that law, to be law, requires the apparatus of the state, everything else being "positive morality."

[127] Mattei, *supra* note 4, at 5 (English version).

We clarify and expand on these and other virtues of commons governance in Chapters 5–8. Suffice it to say here that the primary task of the ecological commons is not to do battle with the State or Market. It is, rather, to establish or restore effective authority and control over ecological resources at the appropriate scale, through delegations of management authority as necessary, and with distributed initiative and innovation.

It also is necessary for ecological commons to be assertive agents of normative, institutional, and procedural change, alone and in cooperation with the State and Market. The goal always should be to advance the logic of respect for nature, sufficiency, interdependence, shared responsibility, and fairness, to the maximum extent possible. The ethic should foster an integrated global and local citizenship that insists on transparency and accountability in all environmental dealings. Additionally, commons governance should strive to ensure internally that the substance and practice of human rights values and principles are honored, based on the understanding that human rights and effective ecological governance go hand in hand.

C. THE NECESSITY OF SELF-ORGANIZED GOVERNANCE AND COLLABORATION IN COMPLEX ADAPTIVE SYSTEMS

Arguably the greatest challenge of all is imagining how to induce the dominant State/Market order, nationally and internationally, to recognize the need to embrace commons- and rights-based ecological governance and to cooperate in making it happen. To this end must be brought to bear, of course, all the skills and tools known to effective persuasion, and at all levels of social organization – while also maintaining a healthy realism about entrenched political systems. No amount of persuasion is likely to yield progress if it is focused exclusively or even primarily on the formal legal order and its array of sanctioned political action. The "top down" strategies favored by guardians of the current order will tend to reflect the interests of the "haves" over the "have nots" and a fierce commitment to preserving the existing order. Or, it will seek to co-opt the quest for fundamental change.

Without dismissing appropriate "top-down" initiatives altogether, we believe the greatest promise lies in "bottom-up" or grassroots-driven approaches, especially those that are inclusive and cross-sectoral. This is not just a political opinion: profound discoveries in the evolutionary sciences and the rise of complexity science over the past generation validate the power of bottom-up forms of social organization and governance. Extensive empirical research shows that some of the most robust, stable forms of governance are distributed, self-organized, and collaborative. It is thus important to survey this field, even if briefly, because these scientific fields point to a different framework for under-standing human agency, the evolution of cooperation, and the dynamics of governance in a networked environment.

The worldview that has prevailed for the past several centuries is familiar but archaic. As we have previously noted, it sees humanity as separate from Nature, and posits a fairly static, mechanical worldview in which knowable causes produce measurable effects in linear patterns. In this mindset, the point is to improve the rigor of our instruments and empirical analysis so that we might identify cause and effort more clearly, and then regulate and control isolated elements of nature or human society. To do this, we strive to refine our scientific knowledge to come up with better designs and implementations. Governance is focused on amassing the most extensive fact base and objective expert knowledge so that we can devise more reliable (usually, bureaucratic) systems for achieving desired results.

Complexity science has opened the door to some quite different frame-works for understanding human and ecological phenomena. The field draws on the lessons of evolution, chemistry, and biology to identify fundamental principles governing what it calls "complex adaptive systems." Frequently cited complex adaptive systems include the self-organizing dynamics and behavior of the brain, cells, ant colonies, the biosphere, the stock mar-ket, and Internet communities. Remarkable parallels can be traced between the behaviors of natural, physical systems and social and economic sys-tems. Much of the pioneering work in complexity sciences has emerged from the Santa Fe Institute, a theoretical research institute that blends elements of physics, biology, chemistry, economics, mathematics, and the social sciences.[128] Among the leading thinkers in this field are the Nobel Laureate physicist Murray Gell-Mann, psychologist and electrical engineer John Holland, economist Brian Arthur, and theoretical biologist Stuart Kauffman.[129]

---

[128] As the Wikipedia entry for the Santa Fe Institute notes: "Recent research has included studies of the processes leading to the emergence of early life, evolutionary computation, metabolic and ecological scaling laws, the fundamental properties of cities, the evolutionary diversification of viral strains, the interactions and conflicts of primate social groups, the history of languages, the structure and dynamics of species interactions including food webs, the dynamics of financial markets, and the emergence of hierarchy and cooperation in the human species, and biological and technological innovation." *Santa Fe Institute*, Wikipedia, available at https://en.wikipedia.org/wiki/Santa_Fe_Institute (accessed Feb. 20, 2012).

[129] Important books explaining complexity science include *The Economy as an Evolving Complex System II* (Brian Arthur, Steven Durlauf & David Lane eds., 1997); Stuart Kauffman, *Origins of Order: Self-Organization and Selection in Evolution* (1993); John H. Holland, *Hidden Order: How Adaptation Builds Complexity* (1995) and *Emergence: From Chaos to Order* (1998).

Complexity science proposes a conceptual framing of the world based on the observable behavior of complex natural systems. Stable, successful systems are not constructed from advance blueprints devised by brilliant minds (e.g., God as the absent watchmaker); they can be shown to have self-organized from the free interplay of adaptive agents following simple principles operating at the local level, with no big-picture knowledge or teleological goals at the outset. Instead of presuming that an *a priori*, comprehensive design system is possible and can yield the best outcomes, complexity theory takes its cues from bio-physical evolution. It asserts that the best results will arise if intelligent, living agents are allowed to evolve over time toward optimum outcomes in suitable environments. The schemas or agents that survive and thrive will be the ones capable of prevailing against competitors and reproducing; less capable agents will be shunted to niches or die, according to principles of natural selection.

Microbes, ants, humans, and diverse other organisms exhibit characteristics of complex adaptive systems. Each is nested within larger complex systems that are dynamic and constantly shifting; and yet each flourishes by embody-ing some highly predictive theories, as distilled in schema that are useful in exploring resources and regularities in a particular environment (the "fitness landscape"). The species with the most adaptive schema (e.g., DNA, organism functions, culture) and the most refined feedback loops will be better equipped to learn from its environment and thus adapt, evolve, and grow. Evolutionary scientists increasingly believe that natural selection manifests itself more at the group level than through individual organisms.

What do these bodies of thought have to do with our search for green governance? They suggest that human communities can evolve into higher, more complex forms of organization without the directive control of a central sovereign or bureaucracy. Given a sufficiently defined and hospitable fitness landscape, self-organization based on local circumstances can occur. Just as biological and chemical systems exhibit autocatalytic features that generate "order for free," so human communities have inborn capacities to create sta-ble order. Indeed, this is one of the key insights of the late Nobel laureate Elinor Ostrom's empirical research of natural resource commons, and the countless self-organized communities on the Internet constitute a kind of exis-tence proof. The capacity for self-organization is often overlooked, especially by mainstream economics and its model of *homo economicus*. Yet, commons

An excellent overview of economics as a complex adaptive system can be found in Eric D. Beinhocker, *The Origin of Wealth: Evolution, Complexity and the Radical Remaking of Eco-nomics* (2006). Two useful popular accounts include Murray Gell-Mann, *The Quark and the Jaguar* (1994) and M.Mitchell Waldrop, *Complexity: The Emerging Science at the Edge of Order and Chaos* (1992).

are fully capable of yielding robust, flexible, and durable forms of managing ecological resources. These advantages stem in part from the fact that commons governance systems arise organically from the governed themselves in ways that are mindful of the resource, local conditions, and cultural norms; externally imposed or arbitrary systems may or may not be as adaptive.

The point is that effective governance need not be imposed through a comprehensive grid of uniform general rules embodied in formal State Law and administered by centralized legislatures, regulators, and courts. Complexity science demonstrates that governance can be a highly distributed, evolving form of social practice and tradition; and it can arise from Vernacular Law that is rooted in communities of decentralized agents responding to particular local circumstances. The twentieth-century mind may be convinced that governance and organization must be based on uniform, top-down expertise and command, but the lessons of evolutionary sciences and complexity science suggest that new modes of diversified, locally appropriate governance are entirely feasible, based on what we know about bio-physical and social systems.

We have several reasons for focusing on governance through the lens of the evolutionary sciences and complexity science. Like our arguments for looking to human rights theory and practice and the Vernacular Law of commons, these sciences suggest how we might make the conceptual transition to a green governance paradigm.

First, this perspective helps us reassert the fundamental truth that human beings are part of Nature, and not ahistorical supercreatures that stand apart from it and control it with a dispassionate Cartesian objectivity. Acknowledging human immersion in nature and its processes is essential if our governance institutions are to be capable of working respectfully and dynamically *with* Nature, rather than merely exploiting it as an Other.

Second, complexity and evolutionary sciences confirm that the most efficient and flexible systems of governance will respect the natural proclivities of lower-order governance units in a large, complex system. The quest to impose coercive control from a centralized governance body, without the active participation and consent of the governed at the relevant scale, is ultimately futile. Subsidiarity matters. Complex, higher levels of organization are sustainable only if they take account of the inherent needs and dynamics of their constituent subsystems and members at all scales. Governance involves an organic, integrated whole that has its own history and peculiarities; that systemic whole is not a clockwork machine of modular, interchangeable parts, as legislation and regulation often seem to assume.

Seen from this perspective, planetary governance to address climate change is not likely to succeed unless it can honor the elemental needs and energies of the lower-order governance units; the centralized mandates of an international body will simply be flouted and thereby fail to achieve the cooperation and compliance needed. Coercive centralized systems, moreover, tend to ignore the affirmative benefits of an open, integrated governance system. Vital collaboration and innovation can emerge only if the governed at the most distributed scales are accorded basic rights of autonomy, human dignity, and intelligent agency. Commoners have something vital to contribute and function as a kind of stabilizing flywheel in governance and participatory innovators. Governance is not simply a matter of political leaders, lawyers, and experts imposing their supposedly superior knowledge and will.

Finally, complexity theory offers another critical concept that can help us understand governance in complex adaptive systems: the idea of *emergence*. The agents within any complex adaptive system are motivated by local circumstances and knowledge; they do not deliberately plan or create a higher, more sophisticated level of social organization. Yet, when the micro-behaviors of agents reach a critical stage of interconnection and intensity, and tap into some new flow of energy or resource, an emergent new system arises in an almost mysterious fashion.

"Living systems always seem to emerge from the bottom up, from a population of much simpler systems," writes science journalist M. Mitchell Waldrop.[130] A mix of proteins, DNA, and other biomolecules coevolved to produce a cell. Neurons in the brain come together to produce cognition, emotions, and consciousness. A collection of ants self-organize into a complex ant colony. "In the simplest terms," complexity author Steven Johnson writes when identifying what all these systems share in common, complex systems "solve problems by drawing on masses of relatively stupid elements, rather than a single, intelligent 'executive branch.' They are bottom-up systems, not top-down. They get their smarts from below."[131] Johnson continues: "In a more technical language, they are complex adaptive systems that display emergent behavior. In these systems, agents residing on one scale start producing behavior that lies one scale above them: ants create colonies, urbanites create neighborhoods; simple pattern-recognition software learns how to recommend new books. The movement from low-level rules to higher-level sophistication is what we call emergence."[132]

The point is that there is abundant evidence of emergence in the world, and it has important lessons for human organization, particularly since the

---

[130] Waldrop, *supra* note 129, at 278.
[131] Steven Johnson, *Emergence: The Connected lives of Ants, Brains, Cities and Software* 18 (2001).
[132] Id.

Internet has arisen as an infrastructure for individuals to coordinate their social interactions on a global scale. The paradigmatic example may be free and open-source software. The story is often told of Linus Torvalds, a twenty-one-year-old computer science student in Helsinki, Finland, who in 1991 released the kernel of a computer operating system to his online newsgroup. Within a few months, he had received hundreds of suggestions and additions to it. This collaboratively created software code soon merged with another set of programs built by free-software hackers. Soon, a fully functional operating system had arisen out of the collaborations of tens of thousands of programmers. The self-organization of individual programmers, each with his or her own local motivations, propelled the emergence of a higher level of organizational complexity now known as Linux. The code, managed as a commons that is international in scale, rivals the operating systems produced by many corporate software makers.

A similar dynamic of emergence can be seen in the rise of Wikipedia, the Web encyclopedia now published in more than two hundred different languages. The Internet enabled people to coordinate their expertise and public-spirited concern into a massive information resource that draws on the talents and expertise of tens of thousands of volunteers. Creative Commons, the nonprofit that developed a suite of copyright-based licenses to promote the sharing of creative works online, is another transnational phenomenon borne aloft by the initiatives of millions of individuals who both devised the legal licenses and then used them on their music, videos, books, and online writings. One can point also to the open-access publishing movement, a sector of academic publishing that now produces more than 8,000 free, openly available journals, and the Open Educational Resources (OER) movement, which produces freely available course curricula and textbooks.

Social activism exhibits the attributes of emergence, too, as can be seen in the remarkable rise of the Occupy movement, which began with a small corps of campers in a Wall Street park. As *New York Times* columnist Nicholas D. Kristof reported: "The square is divided into a reception area, a media zone, a medical clinic, a library and a cafeteria. The protesters' Web site includes links allowing supporters anywhere in the world to go online and order pizzas (vegan preferred) from a local pizzeria that delivers them to the square."[133] The protest was a stellar model of civic virtue and self-governance, proving once again the instinctive nature of commoning. This local protest

---

[133] Nicholas D. Kristof, *The Bankers and the Revolutionaries*, N.Y. Times (Oct. 1, 2011), available at https://www.nytimes.com/2011/10/02/opinion/sunday/kristof-the-bankers-and-the-evolutionaries.html?r=2&partner=rssnyt&emc=rss (accessed Nov. 8, 2011).

quickly evolved into a national and international movement as the Internet enabled the sharing of news about the "occupation" through blog posts, Twitter "tweets," text messaging, and homemade videos of police brutality posted to YouTube. The transformation of a series of small protests into a massive cultural phenomenon, albeit with a future yet undetermined, is an example of how emergence works in the networked communications environment.

In the Internet era, indeed, emergence is arguably the default form of organization in forming new political movements. Bottom-up activism at the local level is capable of joining up with kindred actions in other locations, converging into something larger and more organized, with only the most minimal forms of top-down leadership and coordination. Thus the past decade has seen "flash mob" protests in South Korea organized by cell phones; the Tahrir Square protests in Cairo along with the similar protests of the Arab Spring in 2011; and the M15 demonstrations in Spain protesting the illegitimacy of the corporation-dominated government policy.

The coalescence of local activity into more intensive, coordinated forms of advocacy at national and international levels can also be seen in activism challenging the privatization of water; the Landless Workers movement that has organized peasant farmers internationally; the Transition Town movement that seeks to relocalize economic activities in anticipation of Peak Oil and climate change; and the Pirate Party, an actual political party that arose in Sweden to fight draconian copyright laws and Internet restrictions. The party now holds two seats on the European Parliament, numerous regional and local elected positions, and has spawned Pirate Parties in more than fifty nations.

Emergence thus constitutes what we may call a "bottom-up" theory of governance. If agents capable of learning are allowed to co-evolve in a sufficiently hospitable fitness landscape, they can self-organize higher levels of governance and organization. This does not mean that top-down structures no longer matter, but it does mean that those structures must be capable of promoting the bottom-up capacities of lower-level agents. Honoring basic rights, freedoms, and the self-directed intelligence of individual agents in an open, flexible system (with certain necessary structures and supports) helps produce a stable, resilient system.

As should now appear obvious, the science of complex adaptive systems bears certain resemblances to theories of democratic governance, but especially to the idea of the Commons as a system of ecological governance. As we observe in Chapter 5, the Commons can be seen as a class of complex adaptive systems that blend ecological forces with sociopolitical governance. Situating the Commons into the framework of complexity science helps us identify some useful principles in crafting governance systems. For example, history matters and can greatly affect present behavior and future options. Small changes in one corner of a commons can have dramatic, nonlinear effects on the entire Commons over time. Additionally, the Commons as a complex adaptive system depends on constant, co-evolving flows of participation. As commons historian Peter Linebaugh would put it, "There is no commons without commoning."[134]

A complexity science approach to governance helps us understand why conventional forms of top-down governance are less capable than complex adaptive systems. Conventional forms of governance presume that they can reliably identify and control relevant boundaries, such as national borders, but a terrestrially based system of governance, for example, fails to take account of the transnational and mobile character of, say, the atmosphere, oceans, fish, wildlife, and so forth. Nature does not respect political boundaries. International treaty organizations and UN bodies may attempt to compensate for this failure, but, rooted in the political priorities of State/Market, this alternative tends to be ineffectual. Conventional top-down governance structures are more brittle and inflexible because they generally choose *not* to adapt and co-evolve. Indeed, for political reasons, they often shut down or punish vital feedback loops that could provide valuable information about the actual state of their environment and the efficacy of governance.

The science of complex adaptive systems, by contrast, presumes that any given living system is open and nested within larger complex systems. Strict, controllable boundaries are not assumed. This puts aside the dream of acquiring perfect information and absolute control that the Newtonian worldview encourages and that the bureaucratic mind seeks to apply. What matters instead are the co-evolving capacities of complex adaptive agents. If they can develop the inner skills and feedback loops to respond rapidly and flexibly to the fitness landscape, without producing negative externalities, they are more likely to thrive. As we see in Chapter 5, this is an apt description of a commons.

When seen through the lens of complexity science, it is easier to understand not only how small-scale ecological commons can self-organize and function, but also how we might organize governance systems for large-scale ecological commons. The constituent parts of a complex adaptive system need only respond to local circumstances; none is required to have a comprehensive or sophisticated grasp of the larger whole to play a meaningful, essential role. The system's interconnections help solve problems that would otherwise defy

---

[134] *See* Linebaugh, supra note 117 *passim; see also, e.g.,* Peter Linebaugh, "Some Principles of the Commons, Counterpunch (Jan. 8–10, 2010), available at http://www.counterpunch.org/2010/01/08/some-principles-of-the-commons (accessed Feb. 20, 2012).

the bounds of human rationality. Think of the various systems of the human organism: none (including the brain) knows and controls everything. The human body is a networked allocation of talents and responsibilities, with each performing vital – but partial, local – functions. The same can be said for artificial intelligence in computing systems. Researchers in the natural and behavioral sciences commonly use "agent-based models" in networked computer systems to simulate complex situations and gain knowledge that goes beyond standard modes of deduction and induction.

This metaphor is helpful for understanding new forms of commons- and rights-based ecological governance; although complex, it is a more dynamic and robust way of coordinating people and managing resources. Conventional top-down regimes tend to be static, oriented toward command-and-control, and centrally administered. They are less capable of learning and adapting. In a commons regime, by contrast, it is the internal relationships across different scales and systems that matter most. Open flows of information, the development of trust, and collaborative learning help the complex adaptive system/commons flourish.

What matters, then, is not structures of control based on arrogant dreams of perfect knowledge, but structures that enable these relationships and flows of information to flourish, so that bottom-up energies, innovation, and consent may manifest and generate emergent forms of new organization. We explore the implications of complex adaptive systems for commons- and rights-based governance at greater length in Part II, next.

PART II

5

The Commons as a Model for Ecological Governance

In this chapter, we outline the potential of the Commons as a model or template for ecological governance favorable to the rights of both Nature and human beings.[1] We do so, first, by describing the near-forgotten history of commons, its rediscovery by social scientists over the past thirty years, and the burgeoning global commons movement that is now emerging. We do so also by clarifying how the worldwide commons movement is demonstrating a range of innovative, effective models for assuring diverse expressions of the right to a clean and healthy environment

Both the past and contemporary history of commons are important because they show the feasibility of commons governance in a wide variety of circumstances over centuries. In the past thirty years, contemporary scholarship has rediscovered commons, illuminating their cooperative management principles as a counterpoint to conventional economics and particularly its growth imperatives, artificially created scarcities, and fealty to consumption as a preeminent goal. A key lesson we shall learn is that commons have a natural vitality conducive to environmental (and social) well-being.

The overriding challenge for our time, as several times emphasized, is to devise an architecture of law and public policy that can legally recognize and support this vitality. Commoners (sometimes the general public, other times

---

[1] Hereinafter, as here, we use the phrase "the Commons" or more precisely "the ecological Commons" (capitalizing "Commons") as convenient shorthand for a distinct paradigm of ecological resource governance and management (as when commoners manage one or more ecosystems or natural resources directly themselves) or governance according to commons principles (as when commoners delegate their managerial authority conditionally). We refer to "commons" (lowercase) in all other, more generic instances. For more on our use of the term "commons" generally, *see supra* Prologue note 21; *see also supra* Ch. 4 note 117 and accompanying text on the definition of "commoning" by historian Peter Linebaugh.

a distinct community) must be empowered to prevent market enclosure of their shared natural resources and directly advance and defend their human and ecological rights – and the State must at least sanction, if not affirmatively support, such activity. Either way, it is clear that the State cannot play this role without first understanding the value proposition of commons and then adopting suitable legal principles and policies to support them.

Let us be clear. The challenge is not to establish a separate and "pure" ecological Commons governance system, untouched by either the State or the Market. This is arguably impossible in any case. Commons tend to be inscribed within larger systems of power, and are intertwined with the State and Market in complicated ways. It is important, however, that State Law and public policy empower the ecological Commons and broader Commons Sector on their own terms so that they can preserve their essential integrity and value proposition. This chapter seeks to advance this perspective by examining the history, scholarship, and contemporary emergence of the Commons paradigm.

A. THE CHARACTERISTICS OF COMMONS

We have argued so far that the Commons as an ecological governance paradigm may be understood less as an ideology than as an intellectual scaffolding that can be used to develop innovative legal and policy norms, institutions, and procedures relative to a given resource or set of resources. These new structures, however, do not evolve of themselves, nor are they State-directed. Instead, they are animated by commoners who have the authority to act as stewards in the management of the given resource. A commons constitutes a kind of social and moral economy. It is also a matrix of perception and discourse – a worldview – that can loosely unify diverse fields of action now seen as largely isolated from one another.

But what is a commons *exactly*?

In its broadest sense, a commons is a governance system for using and protecting "all the creations of nature and society that we inherit jointly and freely, and hold in trust for future generations."[2] Typically, a commons consists of non-State resources controlled and managed by a defined community of commoners, directly or by delegation of authority. Where appropriate or needed, the State may act as a trustee for a commons or formally facilitate specific commons, much as the State chartering of corporations facilitates Market activity. A commons, however, generally operates independent of State control and need not be State sanctioned to be effective or functional.

---

[2] *The State of the Commons: A Report to Owners from Tomales Bay Institute* 3 (2003).

Although commons and particularly ecological commons often are associ-ated with physical resources (land, air, water) or, more precisely, pools of shared physical resources, they are equally – indeed, most importantly – sociocultural phenomena. A commons is primarily about the self-determined norms, prac-tices, and traditions that commoners themselves devise for nurturing and pro-tecting their shared resources. In this acute sense, it is to be distinguished from a *common-pool resource* (CPR), a term often used to describe a good (often depletable) that is usually expensive to prevent others from using, though not impossible. Economists would say that a CPR is "subtractible" – it can be used up or become congested so that one person's use may limit another's use.

To distinguish a CPR from a commons is important because there are many possible economic, political, and social arrangements for protecting and maintaining a CPR. One can imagine *a private owner* managing a forest CPR, for example, exercising exclusive control of the right to sell access and use rights. Or one can imagine *government* taking charge of a river irrigation system and deciding who may have what quantities of water, and under what terms. Or, as so often happens, a CPR could be treated as an *open-access regime* in which there are no preexisting property rights or rules for managing the resource; everyone would treat the water, fish, or timber as free for the taking.

A commons, however, is a quite a different thing. It is a regime for managing a CPR that eschews individual property rights and State control. It relies instead on common property arrangements that tend to be self-organized and enforced in complicated, idiosyncratic social ways, and it generally is governed by what we call *Vernacular Law*, the unofficial norms, institutions, and procedures that a peer community devises to manage community resources on its own. State Law and action may set the parameters within which Vernacular Law operates, but it does not directly control how a given commons is organized and managed.[3]

In this way, commons operate in a quasi-sovereign manner, largely escaping the centralized mandates of the State and the structures of Market exchange while mobilizing decentralized participation on the ground. A commons enacts new forms of governance without becoming government. In a sense, it mediates the tensions that normally exist between conventional politics and society, and between Nature and community. Drawing on its self-created Ver-nacular Law, a commons asserts its own form of moral and social sovereignty,

---

[3] An analogy might be State chartering and oversight of corporations: general policy principles and accountability are required, but much leeway is granted to how basic responsibilities are implemented.

developing new norms for defining legitimate social action and new rule sets for community governance.

As we shall see later in this chapter, commons governance and resource management can take many forms. Among the more salient are *subsistence commons* such as forests, fisheries, wild game, arable land, pastures, and irrigation and drinking water; *social and civic commons* such as public schools and libraries, parks, community festivals, civic associations, and affinity groups; and *global commons* such as the planetary atmosphere, oceans, the polar regions, biodiversity, and the human genome. This last class of commons tends to be more aspirational than juridical at this point in history, and thus might best be thought of as CPRs in need of governance structure, preferably commons and rights based. In addition, there are *digital commons* on the Internet, such as free and open-source software, wikis like Wikipedia,[4] open-access publishing, collaborative Web archives, and content pools tagged with Creative Commons licenses.

Studying commons requires that we transcend the limitations of conventional economics by taking into account the larger individual, social and ecological context of economic activity – and, indeed, the *particularity* of a given resource and governance system. We must scrutinize the actual costs and benefits of economic activity in their entirety and see them holistically, in context, and not just as they affect individuals. We must evaluate a community's values, norms, and social practices. The theater of relevant inquiry extends well beyond the financial and quantitative factors that a for-profit business enterprise regards as germane. To study commons is to venture into anthropology, environmental science, political science, and social psychology, as well as culture, the empirical study of specific stewardship practices, and the law. There is no universal template of a commons for the simple reason that each is grounded in particular, historically rooted, local circumstances.

The study of economics remains essential, however, if only because commons are chronically vulnerable to "Market enclosures," which occur when private business enterprises, often with the overt or tacit support of government and State Law, privatize and commodify ecological resources in ways that may destroy a commons and damage its CPR. Enclosure is about dispossession. It privatizes and commodifies resources that may be legally owned or used by a distinct community (a rainforest, a lake, an aquifer) or that morally belongs to everyone (the human genome, the atmosphere, wilderness).

---

4 Wikis are simple web pages that many different people can edit sequentially, enabling the knowledge and perspectives of groups to be synthesized.

Enclosure typically aims to reap private market gains from a common asset without taking account of its full, long-term market and nonmarket value. It also seeks to dismantle the commons-based culture (egalitarian co-production and co-governance) and supplant it with a market order (money-based producer/consumer relationships and hierarchies). Markets tend to have thin commitments to localities, cultures, and ways of life because such commitments may "interfere" with market exchange and thereby diminish (monetary) wealth creation. For most commons, however, socially rooted commitments to a particular place, resource, and community are essential.

This power to enclose a commons stems in large part from the metaphors and rhetorical terms that valorize private property rights. In this regard, John Locke's writings continue to provide the prevailing moral logic and legal justifications for private property rights – and, not incidentally, for the dispossession and slaughter of indigenous peoples and other victims of colonial economic and political expansion. Locke starts by asserting that lands lying outside the legal jurisdiction of the State and international agreements amount to *terra nullius*, or empty land (sometimes referred to as *res nullius*, or a nullity).[5] He declares that such resources belong to no one and are therefore free for the taking.

By this reckoning, a resource considered *res nullius* becomes valuable only as individuals apply their labor and ingenuity (by extracting it from the land, improving it, making it marketable, etc.), which is said to confer a moral justification for private ownership. To victimized commoners who may have used a resource in a collective fashion for nonmarket, subsistence purposes, however, such acts of appropriation, or enclosures, are experienced as profound violations. For them, naming a commons as a commons is the first step toward protecting and reclaiming collective resources. It is a way of reclaiming what they once enjoyed as a matter of right; in a larger sense, it is about reclaiming their identities, traditions, and culture. The commons is seen as a way of asserting a different set of cultural and productive relationships with natural resources.

In a sense, enclosure is invisible to mainstream political culture because the law chooses to enshrine a different "epistemic imaginary," as Kathryn Milun

---

[5] Kathryn Milun notes that Locke's *Two Treatises of Government* (1690) "is the preamble for the justification of the European natural rights theory of property which dispossessed Native Americans of the land." She adds, "Historical references to both *terra nullius* and *res nullius* domains show that global commons and Indigenous peoples are caught in an epistemic imaginary where metaphors of vacant, empty space support a legal rhetoric that legitimates dispossession." Kathryn Milun, *The Political Uncommons: The Cross-Cultural Logic of the Global Commons* 8, 11 (2010).

puts it.[6] The law sees only the virtues that flow from private property rights and market activity, as well as from the associated cultural ramifications: the less attractive aspects of colonial conquest amount to offstage phenomena. Issues of coercion, disenfranchisement, underpayment, or simple trespass do not exist as a matter of law or cultural perception because the law's field of vision has already declared this theater of action *terra nullius*. Quite literally, the law has no way of representing the commons or enclosure within its epistemological framework. As Kathryn Milun notes in her book, *The Political Uncommons*, "International law is like a radar system. It creates a gridded screen where certain peoples and cultures appear and others disappear. They disappear because they fall under the radar: they have no standing in the jurisdictional radar system and therefore cannot be seen on the grid."[7]

The logical failing of Locke's epistemic imaginary is its conceit that any element of Nature can truly exist as *res nullius* – an inert object that can be privately owned without regard for its connections to a given community, humanity as a whole, or larger natural ecosystems. From time immemorial, indigenous peoples and peasants have relied on open-access CPRs for subsistence and cultural survival, without the legal formality of a title or contract as required in western State Law. Surely their customary subsistence use constitutes some form of moral and historical entitlement that should not be regarded as a nullity simply because a commercial enterprise or State took pains to appropriate something that did not belong to it in the first place. Similarly, as inhabitants of the planet, every human being may not have formal legal ownership of the atmosphere or oceans, yet we do have at least a collective ethical entitlement to their preservation as healthy planetary ecosystems – some say even a *legal* entitlement, in fairness to future generations at least.[8]

Usually omitted from Locke's theory of private property rights is his significant added qualification: that any private appropriations are limited to "at least where there is *enough, and as good, left in common for others.*"[9] Locke does not develop this idea; he is, after all, intent on establishing the moral and legal justifications for private property. Still, he did raise the issue, doubtless because it simply could not be ignored: the exercise of private property rights can encroach on and even destroy resources that belong to everyone.

Nonetheless, the State/Market even today tries hard to disguise this hidden tripwire in the Lockean theory of private property rights. It has become

---

[6] *Id.* at 2.

[7] *Id.* at 49.

[8] *See, e.g.,* Brown Weiss, *supra* Ch. 2 note 6; *see also* Weston (2012), *supra* Ch. 3 note 1; and Weston (2008), *supra* Ch. 3 note 4.

[9] John Locke, *Two Treatises of Government* 329 (1965) (emphasis added).

accustomed to talking about oceans, outer space, biodiversity, and the Internet as resources that belong to no one, or as *res nullius*, therefore justifying unchecked private exploitation in the Lockean tradition, while simultaneously calling such resources "global commons" that belong to everyone, or are *res communes*.[10] This rhetorical feint allows the State/Market to have it both ways: it can plunder planetary CPRs in an imperialistic, free-market tradition (ignoring the sovereign needs of Nature and extraterritorial human beings) and yet imply that these planetary resources are being managed as a commons for the benefit of everyone and nonmarket purposes when, in fact, they are not.[11] This rhetorical strategy continues to this day – an issue that we revisit in Chapter 7, Section C.

Beyond such excursions into legal philosophy, contemporary enclosures are typically justified in fairly mundane terms – that they are a necessary means to increase production of material wealth. This rationale has made enclosure a pervasive dynamic. Multinational bottling companies are laying claim to groundwater supplies and freshwater basins that once sustained local ecosystems and communities.[12] Agriculture-biotech companies are actively

[10] *See, e.g.* David Bollier, "Global Enclosures in the Service of Empire," in *The Wealth of the Commons: A World Beyond Market and State* 213 (David Bollier & Silke Helfrich eds., 2012), which describes how NATO is actively setting policies for the "global commons" of oceans, outer space, and the Internet. It essentially regards these resources as *res nullius* whose governance can be unilaterally imposed on them (by NATO countries) without regard to other considerations.

[11] Kathryn Milun summarizes helpfully: "*Res nullius* . . . is the doctrine through when the cultural logic of empty space works in international law. Once a space is declared legally 'empty' of the social relations of belonging, [it] can achieve the status of *res communis* (things [sic] which belong to everyone) if states can agree on the proper conventions. Without such conventions, these commons remain *res nullius* and legally open access to a seemingly limitless exploitation, privatization and a variety of unrelated practices. Much of the global commons today endures in this latter state. Here, it tends to be framed in a rhetoric of *res communis*, space that belongs to everybody, even as in practice it is treated as *res nullius*, space that belongs to nobody. Understanding the paradoxical and dynamic relation between *res nullius* and *res communis*, I argue, allows us to better understand the rhetorical strategies that keep the global commons malingering in its present dispossessive state." MILUN, *supra* note 5, at 6. Some of the confusion between *res communis* and *res nullius* must be traced to the academic custom of talking about the atmosphere, biodiversity, and telecommunications as "global commons" even though none has been legally recognized or actually managed as commons. In a technical sense, as we observe in our text immediately preceding note 4, *supra*, such planetary resources remain common-pool resources, not commons, until they are subject to a viable governance regime that benefits all relevant commoners and draws upon their participatory "commoning" practices.

[12] *See, e.g.*, Maude Barlow, *Blue Covenant: The Global Water Crisis and the Coming Battle for the Right to Water* (2007); Elizabeth Royte, *Bottlemania: Big Business, Local Springs and the Battle over America's Drinking Water* (2008); Alan Snitow & Deborah Kaufman with Michael Fox, *Thirst: Fighting the Corporate Theft of Our Water* (2007).

supplanting conventional crops with proprietary, genetically modified crops whose seeds are sterile or may not be shared.[13] High-tech industrial trawlers are eclipsing coastal fishing fleets and overexploiting ocean fisheries to the point of exhaustion.[14] Biotech companies and universities have now patented approximately one-fifth of the human genome.[15] Many companies enjoy free or cut-rate access to minerals, grazing areas, and timber on public lands.[16]

Enclosures are often tolerated and even welcomed by some because one person's enclosure is another person's idea of freedom, progress and prosperity. The private economic gains generated by converting natural resources into marketable products are enormous. Enclosures also tend to produce secondary, spillover benefits for society, such as jobs, products, and economic growth. Yet these gains can be illusory or unsustainable. When the scope of property rights and Market activity compromises the integrity of ecosystems, "economic development" is but another name for cannibalizing Nature's capital. In such circumstances, Market activity becomes ecologically destructive and antisocial, and does not provide a net gain for society. As economist Herman Daly pointed out in his 1996 book, *Beyond Growth*,[17] the core problem with modern-day economic theory is that it fails to differentiate between mere growth in the volume of Market activity (e.g., Gross Domestic Product) and healthy, socially beneficial development that can be ecologically sustained over time.

Commons offer a vocabulary for talking about the proper limits of Market activity – and enforcing those limits. Commons discourse helps force a conversation about the Market externalities that often are shunted to the periphery of economic theory, politics, and policy-making (as discussed in Chapter 1). It asks questions such as the following: How can appropriate limits be set on the Market exploitation of Nature? What legal principles, institutions, and procedures can help manage a shared resource fairly and sustainably over time, sensitive to the ecological rights of future as well as present generations?

There is a rich body of academic literature that explores many of these questions, and much of it is focused on the use of natural resources in the

---

[13] *See, e.g.*, Keith Aoki, *Seed Wars: Controversies and Cases on Plant Genetic Resources and Intellectual Property* (2008).

[14] *See, e.g.*, Charles Clover, *The End of the Line: How Overfishing Is Changing the World and What We Eat* (2008); Daniel Pauly & Jay Maclean, *In a Perfect Ocean: The State of Fisheries and Ecosystems in the North Atlantic Ocean* (2003).

[15] Kyle Jensen & Fiona Murray, "Intellectual Property Landscape of the Human Genome," 310 Science 239, 239 (2005).

[16] *See, e.g.*, David Bollier, "The Abuse of the Public's Natural Resources," in Bollier, *supra* Prologue note 2, at 85–97.

[17] Herman E. Daly, *Beyond Growth: The Economics of Sustainable Development* (1996).

so-called developing world. There has been far less examination of how modern, industrialized countries might balance Market activity and the environment more prudently. This is due in part to the intellectual premises and worldview of neoliberal economics, which, since the collapse of the Soviet Union in 1991 especially, has become the dominant framework for political culture and public policy in industrialized societies worldwide.

In this political and cultural context, the idea and practice of commons as a system of management and culture has been largely marginalized and ignored over the past generation – doubtless a reason why the right to environment has surfaced in recent years as a serious if struggling claim against the dominant order. Mainstream economists presume that individual property rights and Market exchange are the most efficient, responsible means for allocating access to, and use of, natural resources and for generating material wealth and progress. Political scientist and political economist Francis Fukayama famously proclaimed "the end of history" in 1991 to celebrate the triumph of neoliberal markets and liberal democracy.[18] It is no surprise that in respectable circles commons are generally seen as failed management systems, inefficient, quaint vestiges of premodern life, or all three. Yet, the history of the Commons tells a different story.

B. A BRIEF HISTORY OF COMMONS LAW AND THE RIGHT TO THE ENVIRONMENT

Commons history extends into the deep mists of prehistory as a set of social practices and, as societies became more organized, into formal law as well. It has flourished as if by spontaneous self-organization in human societies with and without the support of larger systems of power. Formal law is by no means essential to the functioning of a commons, though it can certainly help many types of commons function more effectively, if only by reducing the threat of enclosure. In any case, "commoning" – the social practices by which commoners manage their shared resources – has been a pervasive and durable governance system for assuring judicious and equitable access to and use of Nature.[19]

The instinct to establish commons may be a deeply rooted aspect of humanity. A growing body of scientific evidence suggests that social trust and cooperation may be an evolutionary force hard-wired into the human species.[20]

---

[18] Francis Fukayama, *The End of History and the Last Man* (1992).
[19] For a definition of "commoning" steeped in history, *see supra* Ch. 4 note 117.
[20] Samuel Bowles & Herbert Gintis, *A Cooperative Species: Human Reciprocity and Its Evolution* (2011).

If true, many eighteenth- and nineteenth-century notions of human beings as autonomous, selfish, rational individuals, on which entire political and economic philosophies and institutional structures are built, deserve to be revisited and rethought. The idea of *homo economicus*, which modern-day economists and political theorists presume to be a universal norm, may in fact have little basis in fact or history.

The more relevant matrix of human behavior, according to many evolutionary scientists, may be social exchange. When geneticists, evolutionary biologists, and mathematical game theorists evaluate the "fitness" of an evolutionary adaptation or mutation, they often look for traits that cannot be displaced by other mutations or phenotypes. These traits are called "evolutionary stable strategies" (ESS) and, as such, are regarded as deep and enduring aspects of human nature. In summarizing some of this literature, Clippinger and Bollier write:

> Recent studies have argued that the notion of "reciprocal altruism" is an ESS. So are many innate "social contracting algorithms" of the human brain. What makes this evidence especially compelling is that the ESS approach can successfully predict what kinds of "strategies" and even special competences will emerge in different social exchange networks. For example, many different species – vampire bats, wolves, ravens, baboons, and chimpanzees – exhibit similar social behaviors and emotions such as sympathy, attachment, embarrassment, dominant pride, and humble submission. Both ravens and vampire bats can detect cheaters and punish them accordingly – a skill needed to thwart free-riders and maintain the integrity of the group.

> This indicates that "cooperative strategies" have evolved in different species and, because of the evolutionary advantages that they offer, become encoded in their genome. While much more needs to be learned in this area, evolutionary sciences appear to be identifying some of the basic principles animating the "social physics" of human behavior.[21]

If human beings are neurologically hard-wired to be empathetic and cooperative, as many studies suggest, and if this occurs at the species level and not just at an individual level, then rational-actor models of human behavior – which

---

[21] John Clippinger & David Bollier, "A Renaissance of the Commons: How the New Sciences and Internet Are Framing a New Global Identity and Order," in Rishab Aiyer Ghosh, *CODE: Collaborative Ownership and the Digital Economy* 266–7 (2005). A fuller treatment of these themes can be found in John Clippinger, *A Crowd of One: The Future of Individual Identity* (2007).

are the basis for so many game theory and "prisoner's dilemma" scenarios – may misrepresent how human beings actually behave "in the field."

In many respects, it makes sense to see social exchange as the framework in which humans and societies develop. Personal identity cannot really exist, after all, without history and culture; people are not really decontextualized, atomistic units. Language is thought to have arisen as a way to serve important social bonding purposes, and evolutionary anthropologists and geneticists have documented the presence of reciprocal altruism in various species.[22] This suggests that principles of natural selection may be manifested in the genes and physiology of *homo sapiens*, and that by the light of twenty-first-century science, cooperative behaviors may constitute a contemporary form of natural law.[23]

Social Darwinism is a cautionary history about presuming more about human nature than scientific evidence can support. Still, it is encouraging that many scientists believe that cooperation is an inborn human capacity that enhances our long-term struggle to survive. This is a more hopeful, socially constructive storyline for political theory and economics than that of the Hobbsean savage that has prevailed for centuries.

Abundant evidence of commoning can be found throughout human history. Hunter–gatherer and foraging societies were often nomadic, following seasonal and migratory changes for subsistence, which makes it unlikely that they allowed private-property rights in land.[24] Cooperation and collective action were certainly factors in the development of prehistoric agriculture. As one scholar argues, territoriality and storage were necessary for agricultural experimentation: neither could have evolved among individuals acting in purely selfish ways. "No family is strong enough to defend its fields or stores of food in

---

[22] See, e.g., Leda Cosmides & John Tooby, *Evolutionary Psychology: A Primer* (2002); Elliot Sober & David Sloan Wilson, *Unto Others: The Evolution and Psychology of Unselfish Behavior* (1998).

[23] See, e.g., Robert Axelrod, *The Evolution of Cooperation*, Revised Edition (2006); Axelrod, *The Complexity of Cooperation: Agent-Based Models of Competition and Collaboration* (1997); Peter Kollock, "Social Dilemmas: The Anatomy of Cooperation," 24 *Ann. Rev. Soc.* 183–214 (1998).

[24] In instances where hunter–gatherers did attach themselves to a fixed piece of land (becoming so-called "central-place foragers"), they developed communal plots of land for shared use. In the Rio Asana valley of the Andean Highlands, for example, residential structures were grouped around a single public structure that was "used as a dance floor, public space or . . . as a probable focus of intensive, restricted worship." Mark Aldenderfer, "Costly Signaling, the Sexual Division of Labor, and Animal Domestication in the Andean Highlands," in *Behavioral Ecology and the Transition to Agriculture* 167, 180 (Douglas J. Kennet & Bruce Winterhalder eds., 2006) [hereinafter "Behavioral Ecology"].

settings where everyone is motivated wholly by self-interest," writes Robert L. Bettinger.[25] Religion also played some role in prehistoric conceptions of land ownership.

Water provides the earliest clear examples of communal resource use and management, perhaps because water is indispensable to life. Most societies have developed systems for sharing water used for navigation, fishing, irrigation, and drinking. Collective management was made easier by the constant flow of water through the hydrological cycle, which made the private capture and enclosure of water difficult (a barrier that modern-day appropriators have overcome through innovative technologies and antisocial laws).

In eastern Africa, early nomadic Somalians who traveled great distances across deserts dug wells by hand at regularly spaced intervals to provide drinking groundwater for their caravans of people and cattle. These wells later served as the foundation for small desert communities and larger cities.[26] Since around 1000 B.C.E.,[27] civilizations in southwest Asia, North Africa, and the Middle East arose as people built *qanats* – water delivery systems consisting of a mother well and long, gently sloping underwater delivery tunnels – to secure reliable water supplies.[28]

In Mesopotamia, where the Euphrates was prone to flood and uncontrolled irrigation led to pollution of the soil, State ownership of riparian lands and irrigation works helped spread risks and prevent the degradation of common goods.[29] The Code of Hammurabi (circa 1750 B.C.E.) provided that "[i]f a man has opened up his channel for irrigation, and has been negligent and allowed the water to wash away a neighbors field, he shall pay grain equivalent to

---

[25] Robert L. Bettinger, "Agriculture, Archaeology, and Human Behavioral Ecology," in *Behavioral Ecology, supra* note 24, at 310–11. Yet, alongside cooperation in agriculture, the idea of exclusive private property also took root. As some scholars have argued, "It is inconceivable that, from the very beginning, the first farmers did not exclude outsiders from sharing the fruits of their labour." D.C. North & R.P. Thomas, "The First Economic Revolution," 30 *Econ. Hist. Rev.* 229, 235 (1977). This does not imply a sense of individual ownership of the land, however. While some enclosure would have been necessary as a practical measure to demarcate fields and contain herds of livestock, "[e]arly societies probably did not conceive of land as an asset, and investment, or a factor of production," according to John P. Powelson, *The Story of Land: A World History of Land Tenure and Agrarian Reform* (1988). Particular tracts of land were often associated with people, such as clans or tribes, who lived upon it and could defend it: "Much land was group-owned if it was owned at all," writes Powelson. *Id.* at 3. In early Mesopotamia, collectively owned land belonged to a god or goddess, not individuals.

[26] Thomas V. Cech, *Principles of Water Resources: History, Development, Management, and Policy* 2 (2d ed., 2005).

[27] "Before the Common Era," a secular alternative to B.C., "Before Christ."

[28] CECH, *supra* note 26, at 2.

[29] Joshua Getzler, *A History of Water Rights at Common Law* 10 (2004).

[the crops of] his neighbors," demonstrating strict social justice regulation of the common irrigation works.[30]

The elaborate aqueducts and civil hydraulic systems of the Roman Empire were indispensable to the development of that civilization. Public rights of access to the water works were protected by the *Lex Quinctia* of 9 B.C.E., which declared: "It is not the intent of this law to revoke the right of persons to take or draw water from these springs, mains, conduits, or arches to whom the curators of the water supply have given or shall give such right, except that it is permitted with wheel, water regulator, or other mechanical contrivance, and provided that they dig no well and bore no aperture into it."[31]

The Ancient Romans were the first society in recorded history to have made explicit laws regarding distinct categories of property, including common property. According to Gaius, writing in approximately 161 C.E., things (*res*) were classified according to whether they should or should not be privately owned. There were several categories of property that could *not* be privately owned.[32] The first of these were *res communes*, or things owned in common to all: "Public things are regarded as no one's property; for they are thought of as belonging to the whole body of the people."[33] Although such things could not be owned, the law recognized a right to enjoy them: "deliberate interference with enjoyment could result in a delictual remedy [a civil wrong allowing compensation or punitive damages] for insulting behavior."[34]

Res communes – a category of law enshrined by Emperor Justinian in 535 C.E. – is of particular importance to us as the first legal recognition of the Commons:

> By the law of nature these things are common to mankind – the air, running water, the sea and consequently the shores of the sea.... Also all rivers and ports are public, so that the right of fishing in a port and in rivers is common to all. And by *the law of nations* the use of the shore is also public, and in the same manner, the sea itself. The right of fishing in the sea from the shore *belongs to all men....*[35]

---

[30] Code of Hammurabi §§ 55–6, *as rendered in* J.N. Postgate, *Early Mesopotamia: Society and Economy at the Dawn of History* (1992).

[31] Lex Quinctia de Aquaeductibus, art. 9 (P. Birks trans.), *cited in* Getzler, *supra* note 29, at 11.

[32] Gaius, Institutes of Gaius 2.1, *cited in* Andrew Borkowski & Paul du Plessis, *Textbook on Roman Law* 154 (2005).

[33] *Id.*

[34] Borkowski & du Plessis, *supra* note 32, at 154.

[35] J. Inst. 2.1 (Thomas C. Sandars trans., 1876), available at http://www.fordham.edu/halsall/basis/535 institutes.html#I.%20Divisions%20of%20things (accessed Aug. 7, 2001) (follow link for Book Two, Title 1) [hereinafter Institutes].

Through this codification, neither the State nor ordinary citizens could make proprietary claims on resources that belong to everyone. This concept is arguably the earliest manifestation of what in American law is known as the "public trust doctrine," a concept that has analogues in most legal systems of the world and indeed in many of the world's major religions.[36] We return to the public trust doctrine in Chapter 8.

Another category of property that private individuals could not own was *res publicae*, or public things, which belong to the State.[37] This category included public roads, harbors, ports, certain rivers, bridges, and conquered enemy territory.[38] Provincial land was further subdivided into senatorial and imperial provinces – the former belonged to the Roman people, but the latter belonged to the Emperor.[39] There were other categories of property enumerated as well.[40]

It is worth pausing to note an early instance of a political tension that recurs throughout history: the State's assertion of power to act as a trustee for the public interest versus the inherent rights of the people to manage *res communes* as self-organized commons. The State and commoners often have different ideas about how best to manage *res communes* for the common good.

For example, when the Roman Empire claimed rights to manage water through a centralized, formal body-of-water law, a unitary legal regime displaced the plural systems of customary water rights that had prevailed in conquered territories. Although the centralization of Roman law in theory made water management more rational, uniform, and fair, it also gave political elites special opportunities to assert their own privileged access to water and

---

[36] As noted by Mary Christina Wood, "[l]eaders of the world's major religions have declared a spiritual duty to protect Nature." *See* Carrie McGourty, *Prayer To End Climate Change,* ABC World News (Sept. 7, 2007), available at http://abcnews.go.com/WN/GlobalWarming/Story?id=3572327&page=1 (accessed Aug. 7, 2001), *in Advancing the Sovereign Trust of Government To Safeguard the Environment for Present and Future Generations (Part I): Ecological Realism and the Need for a Paradigm Shift,* 39 Envtl. L. 65 n.112 (2009); *see also* Weston (2008), *supra* Ch. 3 note 4, at notes 154–7 and accompanying text.

[37] Borkowski & du Plessis, *supra* note 32, at 154.

[38] *Id.*

[39] *Id.*

[40] Things that were intended for the use of a public corporate body – such as a municipality or colony – were termed *res universitatis*: public streets and buildings, theaters, parks, racecourses, and stadia. Finally, *res nullius* described things belonging to no one, including wild animals, abandoned property, and "divine" things; the last of which were further divided into *res sanctae*, or things considered to be protected by the gods such as city walls and gates; *res religiosae*, or tombs, sepulchers, mausoleums, cenotaphs, and some land used for burial; and *res sacrae*, or things formally consecrated and dedicated to the gods like temples or shrines. *Id.* at 154–55.

to dispossess less favored parties in the provinces.[41] Petty and grand corruption of the formal legal system also opened the door for the legal privatization and overexploitation of scarce water supplies – in other words, State-sanctioned enclosures.

This pattern was replicated in the sixteenth to nineteenth centuries when the European colonial powers imposed Roman water law on their new colonies.[42] The State effectively dispossessed small-scale, traditional, local users of water – a process that returned in the late twentieth century, when states instituted compulsory permit systems for water usage, and in our times, as international investors buy rights to land and water traditionally used by commoners. In each case, national governments claimed to act as public trustees, but their permit systems and investment policies served to displace and delegitimize local, traditional commons management, which was likely more ecologically benign. State-based permitting of water use appears to be "finishing the unfinished business of colonial dispossession."[43]

This tension between dominant systems of power and commons continued after the fall of the Roman Empire and the beginning of the Dark Ages. Kings and feudal lords throughout Europe started claiming the right of access to "public resources" previously protected as *res communes* under Roman law.[44] In thirteenth-century England, following the Norman Conquest, a series of monarchs claimed increasingly large swaths of forest for their own recreation and profit at the expense of barons and commoners. Rather than viewing the forests as a commonly owned asset of the people, the Normans proclaimed all such land to be the exclusive property of the king: "It was the supreme status symbol of the king, a place of sport."[45] Kings "bypassed the customs of the forests that had prevailed since Anglo-Saxon times."[46]

These royal encroachments on commons had a devastating impact on medieval English life, which was highly dependent on forests to meet basic needs. As historian Peter Linebaugh notes, whole towns were timber-framed, the tools and implements of the commoner were all wood-wrought, and wood was the primary source of light and heat.[47] Noted the English naturalists

[41] As skillfully documented and described in B. van Koppen et al., Roman Water Law in Rural Africa: Dispossession, Discrimination and Weakening State Regulation? (paper presented at the International Association for the Study of the Commons conference, Hyderabad, India, January 2011) (on file with authors).

[42] *Id.*

[43] *Id.*

[44] *See* Geoffrey Hindley, *A Brief History of the Magna Carta* (2008).

[45] *Id.*

[46] Linebaugh, *supra* Ch. 4 note 111, at 34.

[47] *Id.* at 33–4.

Garrett Jones and Richard Mabey: "More than any other kind of landscape they [forests] are communal places, with generations of shared natural and human history inscribed in their structures."[48] Thus, when the king expanded his claims over the forest, he drastically reduced commoners' access to food, firewood, and building materials, while his sheriffs meted out brutal punishments to anyone trying to reclaim commons resources.[49] In everyday terms, this meant that commoners were denied access to common pastures for their cattle. Livestock were not allowed to roam the forests. Pigs, a major source of food, could not eat acorns from the forest. Commoners could not take wood, timber, bark, or charcoal from the forest to fix their homes and build fires for meals. Private causeways and dams often made it impossible to navigate rivers. Women, especially widows, depended on commons to gather food and fuel, and disproportionately suffered, particularly as targets of witch hunts, as commons were enclosed.[50]

As described in Chapter 4, a long series of armed conflicts culminated in the signing of the Magna Carta in 1215 and the Charter of the Forest in 1217.[51] The latter formally recognized and protected certain rights of commoners, such as stipulated rights of pasturage (grazing for their cattle), piscary (fishing in streams), turbary (cutting of turf to burn for heat), estovers (forest wood for one's house), and gleaning (scavenging for what's left in the fields after harvest).[52] The Charter remained the law governing the English commons for almost 800 years, making it one of the longest-standing laws of England until it was superseded, as previously noted, by the Wild Creatures and Forest Laws Act in 1971.[53] As such, the Charter continues to have a special influence as the legal basis for managing commons in England.[54] In the years after its

---

[48] Gareth Lovett Jones & Richard Mabey, *The Wildwood: In Search of Britain's Ancient Forests* (1993).

[49] *Id.* (quoting J.R. Maddicott, *Magna Carta and the Local Community*, 102 Past & Present 37, 72 (1984)).

[50] *See*, especially, Silvia Federici, *Caliban and the Witch: Women, the Body and Primitive Accumulation* (2004). Peter Linebaugh writes: "Wherever the subject is studied, a direct relationship is found between women and the commons. The feminization of poverty in our own day has become widespread precisely as the world's commons have been enclosed." LINEBAUGH, *supra* Ch. 4 note 111, at 40.

[51] *See supra* text accompanying Ch. 4 notes 113–16.

[52] A compelling account of this history may be found in William F. Swindler, *Magna Carta: Legend and Legacy* 44–103 (1966); *see also* Linebaugh, *supra* Ch. 4 note 111, at 102, 223.

[53] *Supra* note 116.

[54] George Shaw-Lefevre Eversley, *Commons, Forests and Footpaths* (1910), available at http://books.google.com/books/about/Commons_forests_and_footpaths.html?id=dORCAAAAIAAJ, remains a standard, influential text on the law governing the 1.3 million acres of common land in England and Wales. The Open Spaces Society (U.K.), is the nation's leading citizens' advocate and defender of such commons. Open Spaces Soc'y, available at http://www.oss.org.uk (accessed Aug. 7, 2011).

ratification, the Magna Carta was regularly invoked by commoners, barons, and kings alike to affirm their mutual commitment to its principles.

What formal State Law officially guarantees, however, often requires enforcement by a commons itself, through complicated forms of community self-policing, as we find today, for example, in certain Amish communities in the United States. In eighteenth-century England, a community often staged an annual "beating of the bounds" perambulation around the perimeter of a commons to identify – and knock down – any enclosures of it, such as a fence or hedge.[55] This was a community's way of monitoring its shared resources and assuring collective access to them. Beating the bounds assured the long-term integrity of a commons. Similarly, to ensure that the CPR would not be overused and ruined, commoners insisted on certain "stints," both simple and elaborate, that set strict limits on commoners' use rights. As Lewis Hyde writes, "The commons were not open; they were stinted. If, for example, you were a seventeenth-century English common farmer, you might have the right to cut rushes on the common, but only between Christmas and Candlemas (February 2). Or you might have the right to cut branches of trees, but only up to a certain height and only after the tenth of November."[56]

Here, then, is a general lesson to be drawn from the history of English commons: although State Law is vital, so is the vernacular practice of commoners. The two must be aligned and supportive of each other. That, arguably, is why the Magna Carta was necessary in the first place, to affirm in writing that traditional values and practice would be honored. Commons have been and remain a critical governance system for assuring that "ordinary" people will have clear rights to access and use natural resources for their household and subsistence needs (as distinguished from commercial purposes).

The English battles to reclaim and preserve commons of the thirteenth century have cast a long shadow. Their influence on American jurisprudence can be seen in the US Declaration of Independence's bold proclamation, "We the People," which once again cast the interests of commoners against those of the monarch and State. The English Commons as a source of inalienable rights also influenced various constitutional provisions, especially those of the Bill of Rights. When Congress debated the Thirteenth, Fourteenth, and Fifteenth Amendments to the US Constitution, it often invoked the Magna Carta as shorthand for "common rights" that are sufficiently fundamental to warrant constitutional protection.[57]

---

[55] Lewis Hyde, *Common as Air: Revolution, Art, and Ownership* 32–8 (2010).
[56] *Id.* at 34.
[57] *See* Linebaugh, *supra* Ch. 4 note 111, at 251.

Legal recognition of the ecological Commons, and thus the commoners' right to environment, has come in many other guises over the centuries as well. Following are several of the more significant commons-based legal regimes:

Common Land. Commoners around the world have relied on shared lands for subsistence throughout history and today.[58] There has been a long history of prehistoric agriculture, as noted earlier and today more than 1.6 billion people actively use the world's forests (which comprise approximately 30 percent of the global land mass), often as commons. Another one billion people rely on drylands (which constitute some 40 percent of the global land mass) for their subsistence.[59] In the contemporary world, other commons-based subsistence uses of fisheries, irrigation systems, oceans and lakes, and other natural resources are widespread. But because so many commons are based on traditional usage, and are unrecognized by formal property rights, these lands tend to be highly vulnerable to corporate and State enclosure.[60] At the same time, formal recognition of the Commons is growing, as suggested by a landmark ruling of the Supreme Court of India in 2011 (requiring a real estate developer to vacate a village pond he had unlawfully enclosed)[61] and by growing advocacy on behalf of the Commons.[62] It is precisely the lack of clear legal protection for commons that makes them attractive targets for investor "land grabs," often in collusion with governments.[63]

---

[58] An important repository of literature of this history can be found at the Digital Library of the Commons. *Digital Library of the Commons*, Ind. U., available at http://dlc.dlib.indiana.edu (accessed July 26, 2011). Another is the Netherlands-based Institutions for Collective Action, a website with considerable literature about European commons prior to 1900. Institutions for Collective Action, available at http://www.collective-action.info (accessed July 26, 2011).

[59] *See* Ruth Meinzen-Dick et al., *Securing the Commons* 1 (CAPRi Policy Brief No. 4, May 2006), available at http://www.capri.cgiar.org/pdf/polbrief_04.pdf (accessed July 26, 2011).

[60] *See, e.g.,* Liz Alden Wily, Int'l Land Coal., *The Tragedy of Public Lands: The Fate of the Commons Under Global Commercial Pressure* (2011), available at http://www.landcoalition .org/es/publications/tragedy-public-ands-fate-commons-under-global-commercial-pressure (accessed July 26, 2011).

[61] Singh v. Punjab, [2001] 2 S.C.R. 250, available at http://www.elaw.org/system/files/Jagpat+ Singh+judgment_details.doc (accessed July 26, 2011).

[62] The Foundation for Ecological Security, a nonprofit organization in India, is a leading example. *See, e.g.,* its book, *Vocabulary of the Commons* (2011) and report on its advocacy in Rajasthan, *Spaces for the Poor: Working with Communities and Commonlands in Central Aravalis, Rajasthan,* available at http://www.boell.de /downloads/20101029_ Spaces_for_the_poor.pdf (accessed July 26, 2011).

[63] Hernando de Soto has famously cited this problem in *The Mystery of Capital: Why Capitalism Triumphs in the West and Fails Elsewhere* (2002), but his prescription is exclusively for more secure private property rights, not for more secure commons property rights. As a result, even if private property rights to land are established among poor, rural populations, powerful economic and political actors can still in effect enclose commonly held lands by buying up and consolidating smaller units of disaggregated property rights.

Wildlife. Like the oceans and atmosphere, wildlife has enjoyed a unique status outside of private property at least since the Roman Empire.[64] Under Roman law, wild animals could become the property of anyone who captured or killed them (subject to the restriction that private landowners enjoyed the exclusive right to possess wildlife on their land).[65] This restriction, however, was more "a recognition of the right of ownership in land than an exercise by the State of its undoubted authority to control the taking and use of that which belonged to no one in particular, but was common to all."[66] This classification of wildlife as a commons carried into medieval Europe; to maintain a common supply of fish, the Veronese code in the eleventh and twelfth centuries provided that fishnets were to have meshes two fingers wide, multihooked lines were prohibited, and no one was permitted to fish during the month of February.[67]

Endangered Species. In enacting the Endangered Species Act of 1973, the US Congress recognized that "various species of fish, wildlife, and plants in the United States have been rendered extinct as a consequence of economic growth and development untempered by adequate concern and conservation."[68] The law formally recognized the "esthetic, ecological, educational, historical, recreational, and scientific value [of fish, wildlife, and plant species] to the Nation and its people."[69] The U.S. government has also pledged, through various international agreements, to conserve endangered species.[70]

Wilderness Conservation. Even in ancient Persia (now Iran), there were forestry conservation laws in effect as early as 1700 B.C.[71] Pharoah Akhenaten established Nature reserves in Egypt in 1370 B.C. George Perkins Marsh, a diplomat from Vermont, saw barren tracts of Nature in the Mediterranean, and

---

[64] *See, e.g.,* Convention on the Conservation of Migratory Species of Wild Animals (Bonn Convention), June 23, 1979, 1651 U.N.T.S. 333 *reprinted in* 19 I.L.M. 15 (1980) *and* V Basic Documents, *supra* Prologue note 13, at V.N.8; *see also* Michael J. Bean & Melanie J. Rowland, *The Evolution of National Wildlife Law* 8 (3d ed. 1997).

[65] Bean & Rowland, *supra* note 64.

[66] Geer v. Connecticut, 161 U.S. 519, 523 (1896).

[67] Ronald E. Zupko & Robert A. Laures, *Straws in the Wind: Medieval Urban Environmental Law – The Case of Northern Italy* 85 (1996).

[68] 16 U.S.C. § 1531(a)(1).

[69] *Id.* § 1531(a)(3).

[70] *Id.* § 1531(a)(4): "[T]he United States has pledged itself as a sovereign state in the international community to conserve to the extent practicable the various species of fish or wildlife and plants facing extinction. . . . " *E.g.,* Convention on International Trade in Endangered Species of Fauna and Flora (CITES), Mar. 3, 1973, 993 U.N.T.S. 243, *reprinted in* 12 I.L.M. 1085 (1973) *and* V Basic Documents, *supra* Prologue note 13, at V.N.7.

[71] *See, e.g.,* J. Louise Mastrantonio & John K. Francis, *A Student Guide to Tropical Forest Conservation* (1997), available at http://www.fs.fed.us/global/lzone/student/tropical.htm (accessed July 26, 2011).

theorized that the environmental collapse was caused by reckless deforestation. In his 1864 book, *Man and Nature*, Marsh predicted a similar future for the United States if forests were not protected. The book became a best-seller and the "fountainhead of the conservation movement," in the words of one historian.[72] Partly a result: the State of New York began to regulate the private use of the forests in the Adirondack Mountains, and in 1885 reorganized its holdings in the Adirondacks as a forest preserve under a forest commission.[73] Although New York State protection of the Adirondacks was not without faults,[74] it was the first of many steps toward the robust national and state park programs (including the present Adirondack Park) that the United States enjoys today.

Oceans and Seas. Hugo Grotius, often called the "father of international law," argued in his famous treatise *Mare Liberum* (1609) that the seas must be free for navigation and fishing because the law of Nature prohibits ownership of things that appear "to have been created by nature for commons things."[75] Powerfully motivating Grotius, who at the time was legal counsel to the Dutch East India Company, was the concern of that company to break the hegemony of Portugal and Spain, which were bent on establishing dominion over the seas and lands divided between them along a line close to that assigned by Pope Pius VI. A formidable reply to Grotius's theory of freedom of the seas came in John Seldon's 1635 treatise, *The Closed Sea or Two Books Concerning the Rule Over the Sea*, which relied on historical data and State practice to argue that the seas were not common everywhere and had in fact been appropriated in many cases, especially in waters immediately surrounding nations.[76] Even so, in the age of European colonialism marked by conquest and enclosure, common access to the high seas was protected by international law, and remains so in the modern United Nations Convention on the Law of the Sea,[77] which

---

[72] Karl Jacoby, *Crimes Against Nature: Squatters, Poachers, Thieves and the Hidden History of American Conservation* 15 (2001).

[73] *Id.* at 16. *See also* text immediately following *infra* Ch. 7 note 64.

[74] *Id.* at 17 (noting that state protection of the Adirondacks had dire consequences for the approximately 16,000 people already living there). Mark Dowie chronicles this recurring dynamic – the displacement of indigenous commoners to establish modern-day commons – in his book *Conservation Refugees: The Hundred-Year Conflict Between Global Conservation and Native Peoples* (2009).

[75] Kemal Baslar, *The Concept of the Common Heritage of Mankind in International Law* 30 (1998); *see also* Arthur Nussbaum, *A Concise History of the Law of Nations* 103 (1954 rev. ed.).

[76] Nussbaum, *supra* note 75, at 111; Ram Prakash Anand, *Origin and Development of the Law of the Sea* 105 (1982).

[77] Dec. 1, 1982, 1833 U.N.T.S. 3, *reprinted in* 21 I.L.M. 1261 (1982) *and* V Basic Documents, *supra* Prologue note 13, at V.I.22.

recognizes freedom on the high seas as well as the exclusive rights enjoyed by coastal States in waters immediately offshore.

Antarctica. One of the most unusual and durable global commons involves Antarctica, managed as a cooperative regime of research scientists since the entry into force of the 1959 Antarctic Treaty in 1961.[78] As many as seven countries had asserted plausible territorial claims to the Antarctic land mass, but two major research projects – International Polar Years and International Geophysical Years – had demonstrated the feasibility of scientific cooperation. The advantages of continuing this cooperation were seen as a highly attractive alternative to potential political or military strife. Too, the potential economic gains to be had from making territorial claims on Antarctica were minimal, which made it easier to forge acceptable treaties. Antarctica is one of the rare global commons that has been highly stable because it met many important principles of a successful commons: a well-defined user community, clearly delineated and well-recognized boundaries, and moral and political legitimacy for decisions that have constituted the Antarctica commons regime.[79]

Space. Although the iconic photograph of Neil Armstrong and Buzz Aldrin planting an American flag in the lunar Sea of Tranquility in 1969 evokes an image of conquest, colonization, and manifest destiny, the United States never did stake a claim to lunar territory.[80] Indeed, such a claim would have violated the 1967 Outer Space Treaty,[81] which declares outer space, the moon, and other celestial bodies to be the "province of all mankind,"[82] and "not subject to national appropriation by claim of sovereignty, by means of use or occupation, or by any other means."[83] However, both States and private actors are vested with the enjoyment and freedom to share the use of, and exploit, the

---

[78] Dec. 1, 1959, 402 U.N.T.S. 71, 12 U.S.T. 794, *reprinted in* 19 I.L.M. 860 (1980) *and* V Basic Documents, *supra* Prologue note 13, at V.D.1.

[79] *See, e.g.,* Christopher C. Joyner, *Governing the Frozen Commons: The Effectiveness and Legitimacy of the Antarctic Treaty System* (1998); *see also* Susan J. Buck, *The Global Commons: An Introduction* 45–74 (1998); Juan Barcelo, *The International Legal Regime for Antarctica*, 19 Cornell Int'l L. J. (1986); Martin Holdgate, *Regulated Development and Conservation of Antarctic Resources, in* The Antarctic Treaty Regime 128 (Gillian Triggs ed., 1987); Donald R. Rothwell, *The Antarctic Treaty: 1961–1991 and Beyond*, 14 Sydney L. Rev. 62 (1992) Karen N. Scott, *Institutional Developments Within the Antarctic Treaty System*, 52 Int'l & Comp. L. Q. 473 (2003).

[80] Harlan Cleveland, *The Global Commons: Policy for the Planet* 5 (1990).

[81] Treaty on Principles Governing the Activities of States in the Exploration and Use of Outer Space, including the Moon and Other Celestial Bodies, Jan. 27, 1967, 610 U.N.T.S. 205, 18 U.S.T. 2410, *reprinted in* 6 I.L.M. 386 (1967) *and* V Basic Documents, *supra* Prologue note 13, at V.P.21.

[82] *Id.* art. I.

[83] *Id.* art. II.

Green Governance

available resources of space and celestial bodies without discrimination.[84] As a result, the commons of space is largely uncontrolled and unregulated, and runs the risk of inviting self-interested actors to irresponsibly degrade, exploit, and overuse the resources of the space environs – a "tragedy of the unmanaged commons."[85] The accumulation of debris in heavily used orbital regions such as Low Earth Orbit and Geostationary Earth Orbit could cause these regions to become overcrowded. As astronaut Ed Mitchell once noted, "[i]f there were only one gram of debris per cubic kilometer, out to a thousand kilometers from Earth, the average useful life of a satellite orbiting in that space would be no more than seven hours."[86] The answer, as space law scholar Professor Shane Chaddha argues, is to impose and enforce "appropriate mechanisms and disincentives controlling entry to, and the exploitation of, the resource."[87] Such governance is currently lacking.

This brief overview of commons-based legal regimes shows that, despite the inevitable struggles to achieve commons management for large-scale CPRs, commons have been a durable cross-cultural institution for assuring that people can have direct access to, and use of, natural resources, or that government can act as a formal trustee on behalf of the public interest. The regimes have acted as a kind of counterpoint to the dominant systems of power over the centuries (tribes, monarchs, feudalism, republics) because legally recognized commons for a coastal region, forest, or marshland address certain ontological human wants and needs that endure: the need to meet one's subsistence needs through cooperative uses of shared resources; the expectation of basic fairness and respectful treatment; and the right to a clean, healthy

---

[84] Shane Chaddha, *Hardin Goes to Outer Space – "Space Enclosure"* 2 (Feb. 8, 2011), available at http://ssrn.com/abstract=1757903 (accessed July 26, 2011); *see also* Gyula Gál, Space Law 200 (trans. I. Móra, 1969) ("It results from the *res omnium communis* character that such stuffs of cosmic origin can be appropriated by the exploiting state without acquiring sovereignty over the given celestial body. Exploitation of the fish of the high seas and the minerals of the sea-bottom rests on the same legal ground."); Glenn H. Reynolds & Robert P. Merges, Outer Space: Problems of Law and Policy 80 (2d ed., 1997) ("[T]he conclusion may be drawn that States and other natural and juridical persons have the right of free and equal access to space environment.... Moreover, their rights are also extended to exploration, exploitation, and use.").

[85] Shane Chaddha, *A Tragedy of the Space Commons?* (Apr. 8, 2010), available at http://ssrn.com/abstract=1586643 (accessed July 26, 2011).

[86] Cleveland, *supra* note 80, at 3; *see also* H. A. Baker, *Space Debris: Legal and Policy Implications* 10 (1988).

[87] Chaddha (2010), *supra* note 85, at 3; *see also* Mancur Olson, *The Logic of Collective Action* 2 (1971) (asserting that if members of a large community rationally seek to maximize their personal welfare, they will not act to achieve their common or group objectives unless there is either coercion to force them to do so, or some separate incentive distinct from the benefits of the group objective).

environment. In this sense, the various historical fragments of what may be called "commons law" constitute a legal tradition on which we can draw to advance human environmental rights.

The history of commons also reveals a constellation of tensions between power and commons. For example, in modern times, the State/Market duopoly is threatened by the rise of new commons because the latter are capable of exposing the limited competencies of the State and Market and may out-compete one or both of them in meeting people's needs. A commons may siphon consumer demand and moral allegiances away from the State/Market system by enabling new types of political self-determination and non-Market self-provisioning. People may be attracted to participate in commons because they may provide greater everyday flexibility, social satisfactions, and local responsiveness than do existing, concentrated State or Market bureaucracies. The leaders of State and Market are likely to be displeased by citizens and consumers who redirect their energies and allegiances to the Commons or general Commons Sector lest they diminish industry revenues, economic growth, and tax revenues – or more generally call into question the cultural hegemony of the State/Market system.

In a deeper sense, the rise of the Commons Sector may aggravate tensions between two visions of law: (1) the State and its commitment to formally administered law; and (2) the commoners and their reliance on vernacular practices that are informal, situational, and custom-based. As formal law becomes subject to elaborate gaming by giant corporate players (who routinely use lawyers and lobbyists to shape law and its enforcement to serve their purposes), individual citizens are increasingly alienated or excluded from the legal system, making a mockery of the State's nominal commitment to equality, due process, and the common good. The Commons Sector, by contrast, including the Commons proper, may deliver greater actual benefits to citizens in ways that are more accessible, participatory, transparent, and accountable than is State-based governance. Thus, commons governance may serve to expose the collusion and corruption of State/Market management of collective resources and its negative consequences for the citizenry.

This may help explain why, despite its rich history over millennia, the Commons has tended to be subordinate to the prevailing system of political power in any given society. One might venture to say that the Commons resembles a yin to the yang of power, as embodied in a given political system. And yet the Commons often serves such elemental human needs and ecological purposes that even political power must on occasion recognize and concede its existence and value, much as King John did in signing the Magna Carta. Or, sometimes political power affirmatively recognizes the value of *not* allowing

State or Market to enjoy absolute dominion over a natural resource, as in land conservation preserves or Antarctic scientific commons. The perennial question is how far can commoners advance the value-proposition of commons governance within a given system of power? What sorts of structural protections can be secured for commons governance through law, social practice, and technology?

Ultimately, the Commons and the modern State/Market system may clash because each embodies a different set of ontological and epistemological premises.[88] The State/Market alliance has its own implicit vision of people as rational, utility-maximizing citizen-consumers who believe in the benefits of technological progress and ever-rising Gross Domestic Product. Its system of formal law rests on a foundation of positivism, behavioralism, and administrative regularity, and therefore tends to be perplexed by the idea of the Commons as a self-governing, generative, evolving system of management. On the other hand, the State/Market has important roles to play in serving as public trustee of many common assets, in stopping enclosures of commons, and in setting general protocols, boundary conditions, and legal rules that can help new commons arise. We elaborate on this vision and its complications in Chapter 8.

C. SOCIAL SCIENTISTS REDISCOVER THE COMMONS

Despite the long history of the ecological Commons and its manifest significance, modern economics has largely dismissed it as an historical curiosity. Perhaps it was inevitable that as post-World War II Market culture soared to new heights, the Commons would be seen as having little relevance – or, as one scholar put it, as "no more than the institutional debris of societal arrangements that somehow fall outside modernity."[89] Two leading introductory economics textbooks – Samuelson & Nordhaus[90] and Stiglitz & Walsh[91] – ignore the Commons entirely.

Much of the dismissive neglect of the Commons can be traced to an influential essay, "The Tragedy of the Commons," a parable about the inevitable collapse of any shared resource that biologist Garrett Hardin published in the

---

[88] *See, e.g.*, Uskali Mäki, *The Economic World View: Studies in the Ontology of Economics* (2001); *see also* James Quilligan, *The Failed Metaphysics Behind Private Property: Sharing Our Commonhood*, Kosmos (May 4, 2011), available at http://www.kosmosjournal.org/kj02/library/kosmos-articles/failed-metaphysics.shtml (accessed July 26, 2011); Maeckelbergh, *supra* Ch. 1 note 38.

[89] Arun Agarwal, *Common Resources and Institutional Sustainability*, in Nat'l Research Council, Comm. on the Human Dimensions of Global Change, *The Drama of the Commons* 42 (2002).

[90] Paul A. Samuelson & William D. Nordhaus, *Economics* (17th ed. 2001).

[91] Joseph E. Stiglitz & Carl E. Walsh, *Economics* (3d ed. 2002).

journal *Science* in 1968.[92] If you have a shared pasture on which many herders can graze their cattle, Hardin wrote, no single herder will have a rational incentive to hold back. And so he will put as many cattle on the physical commons as possible, take as much as he can for himself. The pasture will inevitably be over-exploited and ruined: A "tragedy." The tragedy narrative implied that only a regime of private property rights and markets could solve the tragedy of the Commons. If people had private ownership rights, they would be motivated to protect their grazing lands.

But Hardin was not describing a commons. He described a scenario in which there were no boundaries to the grazing land, no rules for managing it, and no community of users. That is not a commons; it is an open-access regime or free-for-all. A commons has boundaries, rules, social norms, and sanctions against free-riders. A commons requires that there be a community willing to act as a steward of a resource. Yet Hardin's misrepresentation of actual commons stuck in the public mind and became an article of faith thanks to economists and conservative pundits who saw the story as a useful way to affirm their anthropocentric ethics and economic beliefs. So, for the past two generations the Commons has been widely regarded as a failed paradigm.

Happily, contemporary social science scholarship has done much to rescue the Commons from the memory hole to which it was consigned by mainstream economics. The late Nobel laureate Elinor Ostrom of Indiana University was the most prominent academic to rebut Hardin and, over time, rescue the Commons as a governance paradigm of considerable merit. Sometimes working with political scientist Vincent Ostrom, her husband, Elinor Ostrom's work concentrated on the institutional systems for governing CPRs – collective resources over which no one has private property rights or exclusive control, such as fisheries, grazing lands, and groundwater, all of which are certainly vulnerable to a "tragedy of a commons" outcome.

Writing in her path-breaking book, *Governing the Commons*, published in 1990, Ostrom stated the challenge she was addressing:

> The central question in this study is how a group of principals who are in an interdependent situation can organize and govern themselves to obtain continuing joint benefits when all face temptations to free-ride, shirk, or otherwise act opportunistically. Parallel questions have to do with the combinations of variables that will (1) increase the initial likelihood of self-organization, (2) enhance the capabilities of individuals to continue self-organized efforts over time, or (3) exceed the capacity of self-organization to solve CPR problems without eternal assistance of some form.[93]

---

[92] Garrett Hardin, *The Tragedy of the Commons*, 162 Science 1243 (1968).
[93] Ostrom, *supra* Prologue note 20, at 42.

Ostrom's achievement has been to describe how many communities of resource-users can and do develop shared understandings and social norms – and even formal legal rules – that enable them to use CPRs sustainably over the long term. Some commons, for example – such as the communities of Swiss villagers who manage high mountain meadows in the Alps, and the Spaniards who developed *huerta* irrigation institutions – have flourished for hundreds of years, even in periods of drought or crisis. The success of such commons can be traced to their social authority and administrative capacities to allocate access and use rights to finite resources, among other factors such as responsible rules for stewardship and effective punishments for rule-breakers. *Governing the Commons* has had a far-reaching impact on the American legal academy, particularly in general property theory, environmental and natural resource law, and, since the mid-1990s, intellectual property.[94]

Scholars of CPRs and common property (who now associate their work under the more general term "commons"[95]) have developed a formidable literature exploring how CPRs can be managed as commons: What property rights in land or water or forests work well in a particular circumstance? What participatory systems and sanctions are needed? What interactions with statutory law and with markets affect the performance of commons? Analyses of these questions have shown how pastoralists in semi-arid regions of Africa, lobstermen in the coastal coves of Maine, communal landholders in Ethiopia, rubber tappers in the Amazon, and fishers in the Philippines, have negotiated cooperative schemes to manage their shared resources in sustainable ways.

In *Governing the Commons*, Ostrom identified seven basic design principles of successful commons that are now regarded as a default framework for discussion, plus an eighth principle applicable to larger, complex commons:

1. *Clearly defined boundaries.*
   Individuals or households who have rights to withdraw resource units from the CPR must be clearly defined, as must the boundaries of the CPR itself.

---

94 Carol M. Rose, "Ostrom and the Lawyers: The Impact of Governing the Commons on the American Legal Academy" (Ariz. Legal Studies Discussion Paper No. 10–37, Oct. 31, 2010), available at http://papers.ssrn.com/sol3/papers.cfm? abstract_id=1701358 (accessed July 27, 2011).

95 The study of commons was initially characterized as a study of *common-pool resources*; but in 2003, the International Association for the Study of Common Property changed its name to the International Association for the Study of the Commons. "See Time To Change the IASCP Mission Statement?," *CPR Digest* (Dec. 2003), available at http://www.iasc-commons.org/sites/all/Digest/cpr67.pdf (accessed July 27, 2011).

2. *Congruence between appropriation and provision rules and local conditions.*

   Appropriation rules restricting time, place, technology, and/or quantity of resource units are related to local conditions and to provision rules requiring labor, material, and/or money.

3. *Collective-choice arrangements.*

   Most individuals affected by the operational rules can participate in modifying the operational rules.

4. *Monitoring.*

   Monitors, who actively audit CPR conditions and appropriator behavior, are accountable to the appropriators or are the appropriators.

5. *Graduated sanctions.*

   Appropriators who violate operational rules are likely to be assessed graduated sanctions (depending on the seriousness and context of the offense) by other appropriators, by officials accountable to these appropriators, or both.

6. *Conflict-resolution mechanisms.*

   Appropriators and their officials have rapid access to low-cost local arenas to resolve conflicts among appropriators or between appropriators and officials.

7. *Minimal recognition of rights to organize.*

   The rights of appropriators to devise their own institutions are not challenged by external governmental authorities. **For CRPs *that are parts of larger systems:***

8. *Nested enterprises.*

   Appropriation, provision, monitoring, enforcement, conflict resolution, and governance activities are organized in multiple layers of nested enterprises.

Each commons has evolved its own particular rules tailored to the specific "physical systems, cultural views of the world, and economic and political relationships that exist in the setting," Ostrom has noted.[96] Yet, despite profound differences among commons, she concludes, they tend to exhibit many similarities:

> Extensive norms have evolved in all of these settings that narrowly define "proper" behavior. Many of these norms make it feasible for individuals to live in close interdependence on many fronts without excessive conflict. Further, a reputation for keeping promises, honest dealings, and reliability in

---

[96] Ostrom, *supra* Prologue note 20, at 89.

one arena is a valuable asset. Prudent, long-term self-interest reinforces the acceptance of the norms of proper behavior. None of these situations [small-scale commons studied in *Governing the Commons*] involves participants who vary greatly in regard to ownership of assets, skills, knowledge, ethnicity, race or other variables that could strongly divide a group of individuals.[97]

"The most notable similarity of all, Ostrom adds, "is the sheer perseverance manifested in these resources systems and institutions."[98] She writes: "The resource systems clearly meet the criterion of sustainability [and] of institutional robustness. . . . They have endured while others have failed."[99]

Ostrom has studied some CPRs in modern, industrialized settings, such as institutional collaboration in providing police and other municipal services in major American cities;[100] an inter-governmental collaboration to protect Los Angeles groundwater basins from overuse and ruin;[101] and "new commons" on the Internet.[102] Two critical fora for much of this work have been the Ostrom-founded Workshop on Political Theory and Policy Analysis at Indiana University and the International Association for the Study of the Commons (IASC). A large body of transdisciplinary fieldwork and theoretical studies of international scope are now housed at the Workshop-associated Digital Library on the Commons at Indiana University.[103] However, while a handful of commons scholars have addressed the challenges posed by global CPRs such as the atmosphere, most of the "Bloomington school" scholarship has focused on small, subsistence-based commons in rural areas.

Ostrom, it must be emphasized, does not regard her eight design principles as a strict blueprint for successful commons because many contingent,

[97] *Id.* at 88–89.
[98] *Id.* at 89.
[99] *Id.*
[100] Elinor Ostrom & G.P. Whitaker, "Does Local Community Control of Police Make a Difference? Some Preliminary Findings," 17 *Am. J. Pol. Sci.* 48 (1973).
[101] Instead of allowing a race to over-pump scarce water supplies, government at multiple levels collaborated to establish a governance system that remained, in Ostrom's words, "largely *in* the public sector without [government] being a central regulator. . . . No one 'owns' the basins themselves. The basins are managed by a *polycentric set* of limited-purpose governmental enterprises whose governance includes active participation by private water companies and voluntary producer associations. This system is neither centrally owned nor centrally regulated." Elinor Ostrom, "Public Entrepreneurship: A Case Study in Ground Water Basin Management" 315–16 (1965) (unpublished dissertation), available at http://dlc.dlib.indiana.edu/dlc/bitstream/handle/10535/3581/eostr001.pdf?sequence=1 (accessed July 27, 2011).
[102] Charlotte Hess & Elinor Ostrom, "Ideas, Artifacts and Facilities: Information as a Common-Pool Resource," 66 *Law & Contemp. Probs.* 111 (2003).
[103] *See Digital Library, supra* note 58.

situational factors affect the performance of commons. Rather, she sees the principles as general guidelines. Other scholars have formulated their own lists for sustainable commons, whose enumerated factors tend to overlap with Ostrom's design principles (implicitly affirming them) while organizing them in different ways. Arun Agarwal writes, "[I]t is reasonable to suppose that the total number of factors that affect successful management of commons is greater than 30, and may be closer to 40."[104] With this caveat, we note the following list of significant factors that condition the management of successful commons:[105]

The character of the resource determines whether it is finite and depletable, such as a forest or the atmosphere, for example; or whether it is self-replenishing to some degree, such as a fishery; or "limitless" in scale, such as language, knowledge traditions, and Internet resources.

The geographic location and scale of a resource will dictate a particular type of management. A village well requires different management rules than a regional river or global resource like the oceans.

The experience and participation of commoners matters. Indigenous communities that have centuries-old cultural traditions and practices will know far more about their resource than outsiders. Long-time members of free software networks will be more expert at designing programs and fixing bugs than newcomers.

Historical, cultural, and natural conditions can affect the workings of a commons. A nation that has a robust civic culture is more likely to have healthy commons institutions than a nation where civil society is barely functional.

Reliable institutions that are transparent and accessible to the commoners matter. Some may be State-sanctioned commons institutions that rely upon official law, such as trusts, while others may be informal, self-organized commons (such as subsistence forests or fisheries) that function below the threshold of conventional law.

The state of technology affects the state of a commons. New technology such as the Internet can facilitate the formation of new commons. But technology can also be a force for artificially restricting access to a shared resource, as it

---

[104] Agarwal, *supra* note 89, at 65. Agarwal was comparing Ostrom's studies of the Commons with those by Robert Wade, *Village Republics: Economic Conditions for Collective Action in South India* (1988) and Jean-Marie Baland & Jean-Philippe Platteau, *Halting Degradation of Natural Resources: Is There a Role for Rural Communities?* (1996).

[105] This list is derived from Silke Helfrich et al., *The Commons: Prosperity by Sharing* (2011), available at http://www.boell.de/economysocial/economy/economy-commons-report-10489.html (accessed July 27, 2012).

has done with software encryption and content-controls. Much depends upon whether a technology is accessible to commoners and under what terms.

Despite a profusion of important analyses of commons, we hasten to add, a great deal remains unknown or under-developed, both theoretically and empirically, and thus these factors cannot be considered authoritative and complete. As Agarwal explained when assessing the state of commons scholarship in 2003: "One significant reason for divergent conclusions of empirical studies of commons is that most of them are based on the case study method [which itself exhibits a] multiplicity of research designs, sampling techniques and data collection methods. . . . It is fair to suggest that existing work has not yet fully developed a theory of what makes for sustainable common-pool resource management."[106] Not surprisingly, there are few generalized conclusions about how to foster what we call the "Commons Sector." Public policy, for its part, barely recognizes the Commons as a governance alternative.

The dream of a unifying theory may indeed be a chimera, precisely because the success of commons seems to reside in their highly particularistic governance rules and circumstances. "The differences in the particular rules take into account specific attributes of the related physical systems, cultural views of the world, and economic and political relationships that exist in the setting," Ostrom writes. "Without different rules, appropriators could not take advantage of the positive features of a local CPR or avoid potential pitfalls that might be encountered in one setting but not others."[107] For mountain commons, the uncertainty may be the timing or location of rainfall. For forest commons, it may be the peculiar habits of wild pigs or the growth cycle of trees. Local commoners are more likely to know such things, and have a greater personal motivation in dealing with them, than remote politicians and bureaucrats.

Even apart from the particularity of commons or the case study method, commons scholarship faces some vexing methodological quandaries. For example, in studying the success of a given commons, it is not necessarily self-evident which factors (such as cultural values, geography, and social practices) are "contextual" and which are primary. Researchers may disagree about which methodologies are most appropriate for gathering and assessing data from the field, and therefore whether comparisons between commons are valid. These sorts of issues make it difficult to formulate broad generalities about commons as they now exist.

Even so, the empirical academic descriptions of commons as they now exist suggest an array of normative attributes that we believe can and should be incorporated into the governance of ecological commons, from local to global.

---

[106] Agarwal, *supra* note 89, at 45.
[107] Ostrom, *supra* Prologue note 20, at 89.

Implicit in the academic literature on commons is a set of normative values such as inclusive participation, basic fairness, transparent decision-making, and respect for all members of a community. While social scientists may be understandably chary of advocating such principles as a normative template for commons, given the variations in the political economy that enframe most commons, we have no such inhibitions. If the Commons is to serve as a vehicle for improved ecological governance, we must balance the particularities and context of each commons with general principles of ecological sustainability and human rights. In Chapters 7 and 8, we elaborate on those principles.

Ostrom, for her part, recognized that studying commons can be difficult because they tend to be nested within larger systems of economic and political governance, and thus can be affected by many exogenous variables. Her theoretical solution to this problem is *polycentrism*, the idea that nested tiers of governance provide the best way to manage resources. "Each unit [of governance] may exercise considerable independence to make and enforce rules within a circumscribed scope of authority for a specified geographical area," Ostrom notes[108] "In a polycentric system, some units are general-purpose governments, whereas others may be highly specialized. Self-organized resource governance systems, in such a system, may be special districts, private associations, or parts of a local government."[109]

Polycentric governance helps assure that decision-making can occur at the location closest to the resource and commoners themselves, which tends to enhance the quality of decision-making and its legitimacy. This principle is known as *subsidiarity*, which holds that governance should occur at the lowest, most decentralized level possible in order to be locally adaptive; one-size-fits-all governance structures tend to be less effective, less flexible, and more coercive.

While there are inefficiencies and redundancies in polycentric governance systems – chiefly through overlapping authority, resources, and information – there also is a greater robustness because sub-optimal performance at one level of governance can be compensated for by other tiers of governance. Also, polycentric systems tend to share information more easily and therefore have greater access to local knowledge and better feedback loops. This enhances the quality of decision-making, institutional learning, and system resilience.[110]

---

[108] Interview by Paul Dragos Agilicia with Elinor Ostrom, Rethinking Governance Systems and Challenging Disciplinary Boundaries, at 12 (Nov. 7, 2003) (transcript available at http://mercatus.org/sites/default/files/publication/Rethinking_Institutional_Analysis_Interviews_with_Vincent_and_ Elinor_Ostrom.pdf (accessed July 27, 2011).

[109] *Id.* at 12–13.

[110] Elinor Ostrom, *Understanding Institutional Diversity* 281–86 (2005). For more on resilience, *see* Brian Walker & David Salt, *Resilience Thinking: Sustaining Ecosystems and People in a Changing World* (2006).

As a system that has evolved in response to resource-users themselves, a polycentric system is open to diverse sources of information and innovation, and thus is less dependent on any single, rigid policy approach or ideology. Polycentrism avoids the dysfunctionality of centralized, top-down administration by "rational experts" who impose overly broad solutions on everyone. Rather, trial-and-error experimentation from the "bottom up" allows the development of rule-sets that are tailored to the particular resource, community, and local circumstances, and that can evolve in the future. This is particularly important in devising large-scale commons, as we discuss in Chapter 7.

Commons scholarship pioneered by Ostrom and hundreds of academics has rescued the Commons from the misleading "tragedy" myths while building invaluable analytic models for understanding how commons function. In so doing, scholars have helped validate the Commons as a viable, practical way to manage ecological resources sustainably. Needless to say, the complexity embodied by polycentrism makes it extremely difficult to tease out general principles. In any case, polcycentrism and the academic commons literature have remained largely confined to the academy and a handful of policy professionals; they have not aspired to speak to the lay public or the press, let alone political activists.[111]

But as we will see in Chapter 6, the Commons has become in recent years an organizing template for an eclectic, loosely coordinated new international movement that rejects the prevailing neoliberal premises of State/Market politics and policy. Moving beyond the abstract models of social scientists, the Commons has become a living political vision and set of cultural practices associated with new forms of ecological stewardship, participatory politics, and policy alternatives, often empowered by the Internet. We turn now to this noteworthy phenomenon, which in turn will help us understand, in Chapter 7, the contours of a new architecture of law and policy that could support the ecological Commons.

---

[111] As an institutional matter, this disinclination to "get political" or to affiliate with the political struggles of commoners may be changing. The 2011 conference of the International Association for the Study of the Commons was co-hosted by an activist-minded group in India, the Foundation for Ecological Security; and Professor Ostrom, since winning her Nobel Prize until her death in 2012, supported a number of efforts seeking political or policy change. Notwithstanding these sympathies, the academic orientation and methodologies of most social scientists remains resolutely apolitical.

6

The Rise of the Commons Movement Globally

Traditional commons scholarship has historically shown little interest in political or economic ideology, or in instigating political change through activist campaigns. It therefore comes as something of a surprise that, in a separate universe beyond the perimeter of scholarship, a diverse global movement of commoners began to emerge in the late 1990s and early 2000s.[1] This commons-based advocacy – for indigenous culture, subsistence commoning, urban spaces, free software, open-access scholarly publishing, shareable videos and music, and much else – has been less interested in academic theories about commons, however potentially apt, than in improvisational innovation in the *building* of practical new models of commoning outside the control of the State/Market.

Some commoners are interested in cheap, nonmarket self-provisioning, period, whereas others see themselves participating in a larger political and cultural struggle to upend market capitalism, or save it from itself. In any case, the scope, energy, and creativity of the global commons movement suggest the appearance of something quite new and likely to be a powerful force in the future, especially now that the commons-friendly Internet is globally pervasive. The power of the movement stems from the fact that its motivations are political, cultural, and economic all at the same time. In addition, it got a fortuitous boost when Elinor Ostrom won the Nobel Prize in 2009 for her analysis of economic governance, especially the commons.

The global commons movement, composed of direct practitioners engaged in political struggle, has developed some ways of understanding commons that are different from those of academics. In a sense, the commons projects of

---

[1] David Bollier, A *New Politics of the Commons*, 15 Renewal (U.K.), no. 4, 2007, at 10–16, available at http://www.renewal.org.uk/articles/a-new-politics-of-the-commons (accessed July 28, 2011).

these practitioners speak more eloquently than any of the (infrequent) books and treatises that they may write. Despite manifest differences among various commoners in their commons structures and practices, however, they tend to share a general set of fundamental commitments – to participation, openness, inclusiveness, social equity, ecological respect, and human rights.

Though not without political implications, commons projects tend to escape ideological capture perhaps because they have a kind of prepolitical character. As German commons advocate Silke Helfrich notes, one of the great virtues of commons is that it "draws from the best of all political ideologies." *Conservatives* like the tendency of commons to promote responsibility; *liberals* are pleased with the focus on equality and basic social entitlement; *libertarians* like the emphasis on individual initiative; and *leftists* like the idea of limiting the scope of the Market. As Helfrich points out, it is important to realize that "commons is not a discussion about objects, but a discussion about *who we are and how we act*. What decisions are being made about *our* resources?"[2] This kind of discussion may not conform easily to established political categories, especially at the local level, but this perspective points to the most significant fulcrums of change: identity, social relationships, and social practice.

Notwithstanding the transideological appeal of commons, commoners tend to be skeptical of the State and the Market if only because commoning itself tends to run athwart the laws enacted by the State/Market regime – for example: copyright law, which makes many types of online sharing problematic; and property and trade law, which makes collective management of land and other natural resources difficult. Thus, it is not unusual for some commoners to become politicized as they seek to defend their traditional community practices (even if other commoners, such as free software programmers and other tech commoners, may feel quite "in sync" with Market culture and its values.) Most share a skepticism of Market fantasies of unlimited growth, perfect control through technology, and faith in "bigger, better, faster" as a mode of transcendence. They generally reject claims that absolute private property rights should prevail and that commercial market outcomes should trump sustainability, equality, fairness, and other humane values.

As a strange admixture of centrists, conservatives, hobbyists, libertarians, social democrats, socialists, subsistence peasants, and the apolitical, most commoners eschew the search for a "unified-field theory" of political philosophy. Commoners tend to be focused on what works in their unique circumstances

---

[2] *Quoted in* David Bollier, *The International Commons Conference: An Interpretive Summary* (2010), available at http://www.boell.de/downloads/economysocial/ICC_report-Bollier.pdf (accessed July 28, 2011).

and are wary of overemphasizing ideology and abstractions. Some commoners function exclusively in local contexts; others are locally oriented but connected to transnational networks; and still others traverse a mix of local, national, regional, and global networks and have a well-developed commitment to the Commons *qua* commons. Theory is seen as seriously lagging behind social practice, goes the thinking, so useful knowledge is better gleaned from vernacular practice than from academics or other experts. Although there are perhaps a handful of commons "stars" with developed critiques and philosophies – free software advocate Richard Stallman, copyright scholar-activist Lawrence Lessig, Indian activist Vandana Shiva, and author Raj Patel come to mind – the movement's leadership tends to be decentralized and diversified, not charismatic and coordinated.

To understand why the Commons is a compelling ecological governance solution, therefore, one must first become familiar with some of the leading types of commons and noteworthy projects that currently exist. There is no canonical or comprehensive taxonomy of commons, in part because commons can be approached from so many perspectives (e.g., the specific resource being managed, their scale and geographic location, their law and policy governance structures, types of community norms).[3] As an extremely heterogeneous phenomenon, the international commons movement is not a unified, monolithic entity; it is, rather, a diverse, loosely coordinated network of projects and players. Its participants generally do not see themselves through the lens of traditional commons scholarship;[4] they focus instead on their situational challenges or their broader class of commons compatriots.

This emerging Commons Sector is notable as a means of production that integrates cultural with natural realms. It meets people's needs in ways that do not necessarily involve either the State or the Market (at least directly), by opening a conversation between economic and social practices relative to the use of nature and the inherent dynamics of nature itself. Commons are not about technocratic, top-down management of a static common-pool resource (CPR); they are, rather, an always-evolving interaction between the vernacular

---

[3] One of the earliest and most comprehensive attempts to make systematic sense of the proliferation of "new commons" is the work of commons scholar Charlotte Hess, *Mapping the New Commons* (July 2008), available at http://papers.ssrn.com/sol3/papers.cfm?Abstract_id=1356835 (accessed July 28, 2011).

[4] As Charlotte Hess has noted: "Much of the impetus of new commons today is considerably beyond the academic application of traditional commons analysis to new types of shared resources. The upsurge of new commons literature documents a new way of looking at what is shared or what *should be* shared in the world around us. It focuses on who shares them, how we share them, and how we sustain them for future generations." *Id.* at 1.

needs, practices, values, and norms of a community and a given natural source. If market economics posits an imaginary theater of action, the marketplace, animated by the rational *homo economicus* trucking and bartering to maximize her or his self-interest and utility, a commons envisions a theater of human cooperation in managing a shared resource, a social-economic-ecological paradigm known as "commoning." It presumes a more integrated, complicated, and subtle field of human activity than does rational actor theory, and does not presume that individual organisms or resources can be abstracted from their surroundings and propounded as universal, interchangeable schema.

It helps, nonetheless, to have a rough mental map of this world. In this spirit, we offer the following suggestive (i.e., noncomprehensive) overview of commons that are managing collective resources today.[5]

A. SALIENT CONTEMPORARY COMMONS

Six broad classes of contemporary commons are noteworthy: subsistence commons, indigenous peoples' commons, Internet commons, social/civic commons, businesses embedded in commons, and State-based commons.

1. *Subsistence Commons*

These commons, sometimes known as "traditional commons," are typically associated with forests, fisheries, water, arable land, wild game, or other natural resources. In many cases, these commons have long histories rooted in specific communities and bioregions. Rights of access and other rules tend to be based on informal social customs rather than on formal law or regulatory supervision. For example, in the *Zanjera* irrigation communities in the Philippines, landowning farmers and tenant farmers (whose participation enables them to

---

[5] A single taxonomy of commons is unlikely given that a commons may arise whenever a self-styled community decides that it wishes to manage a resource in a collective manner, with a special regard for equitable access, use, and sustainability. The idiosyncratic nature of a commons is well-illustrated by a motley clan of surfers at the Banzai Pipeline beach on the North Shore of Oahu, Hawaii, called "The Wolfpak," the subject of a documentary film, *Bustin' Down the Door*. The Wolfpak constitutes a commons because it is a social collective that manages usage of a scarce local resource – great surfing waves – that its members cherish and use themselves. Wolfpak members are protective of the waves and each other, and have evolved their own rules for the orderly, fair use of the resource and community stability. According to Matt Higgins, members of the Wolfpak "determine which waves go to whom, and punish those who breach their code of respect for local residents and the waves." *On North Shore of Oahu, Enforcing Respect for Locals and the Waves*, N.Y. Times (Jan. 23, 2009), available at http://www.nytimes.com/2009/01/23/sports/othersports/23surfing.html?scp=1&sq=wolfpack&st=cse (accessed July 28, 2011).

acquire land and irrigation water, if they are without money) join together to build common irrigation works for land that was previously dry.[6] In Mexico, a communal land system known as *ejidos* was the foundation for decentralized, locally controlled peasant and indigenous farming, forestry, and other land use – until the North American Free Trade Agreement (NAFTA) forced its elimination.[7]

In New Mexico, native Hispanic-Americans continue to manage *acequias* (a community-operated waterway system) as a "bio-cultural" institution for irrigation under a governance system begun by their forebears in the early 1600s under Spanish colonization.[8] Under the sanction of state law, *acequias* in New Mexico blend community life, culture, and local politics with stewardship of the scarce waters of the arid region. Community members are expected to participate in the annual cleaning of the water ditches and other shared responsibilities, and allocations of the limited water are made without overexploiting it, even in times of drought. The *acequias* have been vital to soil and water conservation, aquifer recharge, wildlife and plant habitat preservation, and energy conservation – and stand in stark counterpoint to the insatiable water demands of nearby towns and real estate developers.

In dozens of small villages in India's Andhra Pradesh region, *dalit* women have emancipated themselves from their jobs as bonded farm laborers by establishing their own seed-sharing commons, rejuvenating poor farmlands near their villages.[9] Their march to food sovereignty began with the village *sanghams*, self-organized voluntary associations, through which women found and then replicated many lost millet-based grain seeds that generations of villagers had grown before the Green Revolution displaced the seeds. The traditional millet crops are far more ecologically suited to the semiarid landscape of the region; the biodiverse farming methods that the women have resurrected rely on dozens of nearly forgotten seeds that yield more reliable harvests and more nutritious food supplies than do commercial seeds, which often are genetically modified and require expensive synthetic pesticides and fertilizers. The shift

[6] *See* OSTROM, *supra* Prologue note 20, at 82–8.

[7] *See* María Teresa Vásquez Castillo, *Land Privatizaion in Mexico: Urbanization, Formation of Region and Globalization in Ejidos* (2004); *The Transformation of Rural Mexico: Reforming the Ejido Sector* (Wayne A. Cornelius & David Myhre eds., 1998).

[8] *See, e.g.,* Stanley G. Crawford, *Mayordomo: Chronicle of an Acequia in Northern New Mexico* (1988); Sylvia Rodriguez, *Acequia: Water Sharing, Sanctity and Place* (2006).

[9] *See* Jaideep Hardikar, *Crops of Truth*, New Internationalist (Sept. 24, 2010), available at http://www.newint.org/features/2010/09/01/seeds-rural-south-india (accessed July 28, 2011); David Bollier, *The Seed-Sharing Solution*, bollier.org (Jan. 19, 2011), available at http://bollier.org/seed-sharing-solution; DECCAN DEVELOPMENT SOCIETY, available at http://ddsindia.com/www/ default.asp (accessed May 17, 2012).

from market-based monoculture crops to seed-sharing cooperatives and tradi-tional farming has enabled families to become virtually self-sufficient in food.

Subsistence commons may appear small and inconsequential in the bigger scheme of things, but it is important to realize that an estimated two billion people in poor, rural parts of the world depend on commons of forests, fisheries, and other natural resources for their daily food.[10] Conventional economists are prone to overlook the importance of subsistence commons because they lie outside the Market and often do not entail formal property rights or Market exchange. Yet, subsistence commons play a vital role in meeting people's basic human needs, and generally do so with a greater attentiveness to long-term ecological sustainability and social equity than conventional markets.[11]

2. *Indigenous Peoples' Commons*

These commons, based on traditional ecological knowledge, vary immensely and cannot be easily categorized because of the enormous variations in land-scapes, tribal cosmologies, cultural practices, and so forth. That said, ecolo-gist Fikret Berkes has called traditional ecological knowledge "a cumulative body of knowledge, practice and belief, evolving by adaptive processes and handed down through generations by cultural transmission, about the rela-tionship of living beings (including humans) with one another and with their environments."[12] Indigenous commons are arguably some of the purest com-mons because many have evolved in isolation from dominant, external systems of power over the course of centuries or longer. Thus, indigenous peoples gen-erally regard the earth as an animate being to which duties are owed – "Mother Earth" or "Pachamama" in Latin America – and not as an inert object to be exploited as any individual or group may see fit. Indigenous peoples generally see themselves as having enduring relationships of reciprocity with their local ecosystems that they express and reinforce through rituals that affirm continu-ity among one's ancestors, the present generation, and future generations.

[10] Press Release, Int'l Assoc. for the Study of Commons, Pol'y Forum, 12th Biennial Conference, Gloucestershire, Cheltenham, Eng. (July 14–18, 2008), available at http://resources.glos.ac.uk/ news/politicalvoice.cfm (accessed July 28, 2011); *see also* Ruth Meinzen-Dick et al., *supra* Ch. 5 note 59, at 1 ("Over 1.6 billion people live in and actively use the 30% of the global land mass that is forest and close to 1 billion people use the 40% of the land mass that is drylands. These areas, although often classified by national law as public lands, are in many places actively managed by their inhabitants, very often through common property arrangements.").

[11] *See, e.g.,* Maria Mies & Veronika Bennholdt-Thomsen, *The Subsistence Perspective: Beyond the Globalised Economy* (1999); Veronika Bennholdt-Thomsen, *Subsistence: Perspectives for a Society Based on Commons,* in *Wealth of the Commons, supra* Ch. 5 note 10, at 82.

[12] Fikret Berkes, *Sacred Ecology: Traditional Ecological Knowledge and Resource Management* 8 (1999).

"Tribal regulation and stewardship of resources are interwoven with religious teachings, interfamilial covenants, and family place within society," write Mary Christina Wood and Zachary Welcker.[13] "Tribal leaders also speak of natural law, which designates them as stewards of plants, animals, water and air. Natural law is premised on the attainment of balance in nature, as practiced through ancient stewardship covenants with Mother Earth. This legal structure has maintained a remarkable rhythm of life for generations."[14] Among indigenous cultures, ecological management is regarded as a trust that confers affirmative duties on the community to protect resources for future generations, as a matter of both religious conviction and tribal law.

As suggested by Bolivia's embrace of Nature's rights, discussed in Chapter 3, indigenous commons implicitly challenge some of the philosophical premises of modernity itself and therefore posit a quite different set of human relationships with nature. As Dartmouth College professor N. Bruce Duthu writes:

> The idea of "property" in the Western tradition . . . implies an orientation toward the Market use of resources without special regard for the long-term ecological consequences or the social meanings of nature to people; the price system presumes a basic equivalence among like-priced elements of nature. Societies that have a more direct, subsistence relationship to nature may therefore find property- and Market-based sensibilities alien and even offensive.[15]

This background helps explain why the modern, industrialized nations of the world dismiss out of hand Bolivia's proposed United Nations declaration to recognize Nature's rights; it presumes a set of relationships to Earth that secular, industrialized market societies cannot fathom.[16]

Multinational corporations often aspire to own property rights in the agroecological or ethnobotanical knowledge developed by indigenous peoples over centuries. This tendency, which has provoked charges of biopiracy,[17] has prompted many indigenous peoples to take affirmative steps to develop legally

---

[13] Mary Christina Wood & Zachary Welcker, *Tribes as Trustees Again (Part I): The Emerging Tribal Role in the Conservation Trust Movement*, 32 Harv. Envtl. L. Rev. 373, 385 (2008).

[14] *Id.*

[15] N. Bruce Duthu, *The Recognition of Intergenerational Ecological Rights and Duties in Native American Law*, in Weston & Bach, *supra* Prologue note 12, at app. A (Background Paper No. 3), *also* available at http://www.vermontlaw.edu/Documents/CLI%20Policy%20Paper/BP_03%20-%20(Duthu).pdf (accessed July 28, 2011).

[16] On Nature's rights, *see supra* Ch. 3, § B, at 55–66.

[17] *See, e.g.*, Vandana Shiva, Protect or Plunder? Understanding Intellectual Property Rights (2001).

defensible traditional knowledge (TK) commons to prevent outsider con-
fiscation of an indigenous community's TK and attendant environmental
rights.[18] Another commons-based strategy to prevent biopiracy and inappropriate patents is the Traditional Knowledge Digital Library, an Indian database
of public-domain medical knowledge of remedies and treatments that can be
used to challenge patent applications that seek to privatize TK.[19]

3. Internet Commons

As we explore briefly in Chapter 1, the rise of the Internet over the past
twenty years has propelled the Commons paradigm forward as a functional
alternative to market-based forms of property and resource management in
online spaces. In digital commons, enormous value is being created by large
numbers of people freely interacting with each other without the hope or
expectation of financial rewards. Money and markets do not necessarily drive
creative activity and wealth creation in online contexts. Life on the Internet
is demonstrating, in the words of Harvard law professor Yochai Benkler, that
"behaviors that were once on the periphery – social motivations, cooperation,
friendship, decency – move to the very core of economic life."[20] "What we are
seeing now is the emergence of more effective collective action practices that
are decentralized but do not rely on either the price system or a managerial
structure for coordination."[21]

Benkler's term for this phenomenon is "commons-based peer production."
By that, he means systems that are collaborative and nonproprietary, and based
on "sharing resources and outputs among widely distributed, loosely connected
individuals who cooperate with each other."[22] There are countless examples
of these phenomena,[23] from the millions of socially minded travelers who use

---

[18] Elan Abrell et al., *Natural Justice, Implementing a Traditional Knowledge Commons: Opportunities and Challenges* (2009), available at http://www.naturaljustice.org/images/naturaljustice/
implementing%20tkc.pdf (accessed July 28, 2011).

[19] Traditional Knowledge Digital Library, available at http://www.tkdl.res.in/tkdl/langdefault/
common/Home.asp?GL=Eng (accessed July 28, 2011).

[20] Yochai Benkler, Remarks at the International Commons Summit in Dubrovnik, Croat. (June
15, 2007).

[21] Yochai Benkler, *The Wealth of Networks: How Social Production Transforms Markets and
Freeedom* 63 (2006).

[22] *Id.* at 60.

[23] A dizzying array of such projects are described in Benkler, *supra* note 21; Lawrence Lessig,
Remix: Making Art and Commerce Thrive in the Hybrid Economy (2008); Clay Shirky, *Here
Comes Everybody: The Power of Organizing Without Organizations* (2008); Jonathan Zittrain,
The Future of the Internet – And How to Stop It (2008). More details on CouchSurfing can
be found at CouchSurfing, available at http://www.couchsurfing.org (accessed June 10, 2012);

the Couchsurfing website to arrange free lodging and hospitality across the world to the amateur-volunteers who help NASA classify the craters of Mars through online collaboration. The Commons paradigm is being enacted by the tens of thousands of people who have contributed more than 22 million entries to Wikipedia in 285 languages by 2012 and by the hundreds of thousands of programmers who produce free software and open-source software such as GNU Linux, the highly respected computer operating system. It is part of the daily lives of the millions of Internet users, including scholars and governments, who use Creative Commons licenses to authorize the legal copying, sharing, and/or modification of their copyrighted works. By mid-2012, scientists and other scholars had created more than 8,300 open-access journals whose contents are freely available in perpetuity, bypassing commercial publishers that charge exorbitant subscription fees and assert strict copyright controls.

The full implications of commons-based peer production for the economy and society are too complicated to explore here. We do wish to note their importance for ecological governance, however.

We wish as well to clear away the misconception that "natural resource commons" and "digital commons" are utterly separate and distinct. This confusion is understandable because natural resources tend to be depletable and rivalrous whereas the content of digital commons can readily expand because the incremental cost of reproduction of digital files is virtually nil. Notwithstanding this important difference, digital and ecological commons are starting to bleed into each other as Internet platforms become a pervasive reality of modern life for managing all sorts of resources and social communities. It is now routine for people to use the Internet to organize themselves into commons to generate new types of shared ecological knowledge and manage natural resources in more open, participatory, and nonbureaucratic ways.

We call these new regimes *eco-digital commons*. They are exemplified by smart phones, cameras on mobile devices, motion sensors, and global positioning systems (GPS) that, when networked through telephone and Internet systems, enable new forms of participatory information aggregation that take wiki-style mass-participation to new levels. As described in a 2009 report by the Woodrow Wilson International Center for Scholars on participatory sensing,

on NASA Clickworkers, in Benkler, *supra* note 21, at 69–70; on Wikipedia, in Zittrain, *supra*, at 127–48; on Creative Commons licenses, at Creative Commons, available at http://www.creativecommons.org (accessed June 10, 2012); on GNU Linux at *GNU Operating System*, Free Software Found, available at http://www.gnu.org/licenses/gpl.html (accessed June 10, 2012); and on open access journals, at Directory of Open Access Journals, available at http://www.doaj.org (accessed September 6, 2012), and *OA Tracking Project*, Open Access Directory, available at http://oad.simmons.edu/oadwiki/OA_tracking_project (accessed June 10, 2012).

citizen-scientists using electronic devices have helped collect environmental data during events such as the Audubon Society's Christmas Bird Count, World Water Monitoring Day, and the University Corporation for Atmospheric Research's Project BudBurst.[24] In one study, participants took cellphone photos of plants at the fruiting stage of their life cycle and then uploaded them to a central website. Large-scale bodies of such citizen-generated data can reveal important information about the state of climate change and other ecological trends.

"Using people's everyday mobile phones to collect data in a coordinated manner could be applied to scientific studies of various sorts, such as accessing fishermen's extensive knowledge to identify and locate fish pathologies in the field or documenting the spread of an invasive species."[25] The report notes that GPS-equipped mobile phones might also be used to photograph diesel trucks as part of a campaign to understand community exposure to air pollution. The North American Butterfly Association invites people to submit counts of butterflies in their localities.[26] Rarebirds.com is a location-based database of bird sightings that draws upon volunteer submissions.[27] Using data from the National Oceanic and Atmospheric Administration, a software app for iPads and iPhones provides near-real-time warnings of the presence of North Atlantic right whales in Massachusetts Bay shipping lanes, helping vessels to steer clear of them.[28] New types of self-organized digital commons make it possible to create new bodies of community knowledge (such as the traditional knowledge database mentioned earlier in this chapter), raise alerts about polluters,[29] and advance the standards of ecological stewardship. Types of data that were once too expensive or unreliable to

---

[24] See Jeffrey Goldman et al., *Woodrow Wilson Int'l Ctr. for Scholars, Participatory Sensing: A Citizen-Powered Approach to Illuminating the Patterns That Share Our World* 10 (2009), available at http://www.wilsoncenter.org/sites/default/files/participatory_sensing.pdf (accessed Feb. 25, 2011).

[25] *Id.* at 11.

[26] See *Butterfly Counts*, N. Am. Butterfly Assoc., available at http://naba.org/butter_counts.html (accessed Feb. 25, 2011).

[27] See *Rare Bird Reporting System*, rarebirds.com, available at http://www.rarebirds.com (accessed Feb. 25, 2011).

[28] More information about EarthNC's app, "Whale Alert – Ship Strike Reduction for Right Whales," is available at *Whale Alert*, Apple iTunes, available at http://itunes.apple.com/us/app/whale-alert-ship-strike-reduction/id511707112?mt=8 (accessed Feb. 25, 2011).

[29] Citizen-compiled bodies of pollution data have been made by The Right-to-Know Network, Right-to-Know Network, available at http://www.rtknet.org (accessed July 28, 2011); the Sunlight Foundation, Sunlight Found, available at http://www.sunlightfoundation.com (accessed July 28, 2011); and the UMass Political Economic Research Institute's report, *Toxic 100: Top Corporate Polluters in the United States*, Political Econ. Research Inst., http://www.peri.umass.edu/Toxic-100-Table.265.0.html (accessed July 28, 2011).

collect may be gathered and applied in conventional policy-making and standards enforcement.

The open-source ethos recently inspired the System of Rice Intensification (SRI), which is a new form of agroecological innovation.[30] Farmers in some forty countries, from Sri Lanka to Cuba to India, are using the Internet to develop higher-yielding, ecologically benign rice-farming methods. SRI emerged outside the scientific establishment as a kind of open-source collaboration to escape the dependency on proprietary seeds and pesticides. A key goal is to achieve "knowledge *swaraj*" ("self-rule" in Hindi).[31] Over the past twenty years, some 250,000 Indian farmers have committed suicide as a result of intense market pressures and the loss of their traditional farming practices and identities.[32] In this context, SRI has been a powerful commons-based platform that bypasses ecologically regressive Market-based agricultural practices (genetically modified seeds, chemical fertilizers, and pesticides). It has bridged the local and the global, enabling bottom-up, transnational collaboration to improve rice yields on marginal plots of land around the world.

The power of the eco-digital commons can also be seen in the fledgling open-source hardware movement, a diversified set of engineering projects that is applying open-source principles to the development of eco-friendly farming machines and tools. One leading advocate for this idea is the Open Source Hardware and Design Alliance, a federation that promotes the user freedom to copy, share, and redistribute innovative ideas.[33] Another leading project, Open Source Ecology, explains the movement's thinking: "By using permaculture and digital fabrication together to provide for basic needs and open source methodology to allow low cost replication of the entire operation, we hope to empower anyone who desires to move beyond the struggle for survival and 'evolve to freedom'."[34]

---

[30] *See, e.g., System Rice Intensification,* Wikipedia, available at http://en.wikipedia.org/wiki/System_of_Rice_Intensification (accessed Aug. 29, 2011).

[31] C. Shambu Prasad, *Knowledge Swaraj, Agriculture and the New Commons: Insights from SRI in India* (paper for panel on "Knowledge Swaraj and Knowledge Commons," 13th Biennial Conference, Int'l Assoc. for the Study of the Commons in Hyderabad, India, Jan. 11, 2010).

[32] The Center for Human Rights and Global Justice, NYU Law School estimated in a 2011 report that more than 250,000 Indian farmers had committed suicide over the past 16 years. In 2009, official figures counted 17,368 farmer suicides. Ctr. for Human Rights and Global Justice, Every Thirty Minutes: Farmer Suicides, Human Rights, and the Agrarian Crisis in India 1 (2011), available at www.chrgj.org/publications/docs/every30min.pdf (accessed July 28, 2011).

[33] *See* Open Source Hardware and Design Alliance, available at http://www.ohanda.org (accessed Feb. 25, 2011).

[34] *See* Open Source Ecology, available at http://openfarmtech.org/wiki (accessed Feb. 25, 2011).

By helping people inexpensively copy and manufacture useful equipment, Open Source Ecology aims "to define a new form of social organization where it is possible to create advanced culture, thriving in abundance and largely autonomous, on the scale of a village, not nation or state."[35] A signature project is the Global Village Construction Set – a set of machines that includes a sawmill, pyrolysis oil, solar heating units, an agricultural microcombine, a manual well-drilling rig, and many other machines – all of which would be open source, inexpensive, and locally replicable by design.[36] One project, the LifeTrac, is a low cost, multipurpose, open-source tractor that has modular components, hydraulic quick couplers, lifetime design, and a design for disassembly.[37]

Yet another example of digital technologies improving ecological management is the Global Innovation Commons, a massive database of energy-saving technologies whose patents have expired, been abandoned, or simply have no protection.[38] The idea behind the project is to let entrepreneurs and national

---

[35] As Open Source Ecology explains: "Economy creates culture and culture creates politics. Politics sought are ones of freedom, voluntary contract, and human evolution in harmony with life support systems. Note that resource conflicts and overpopulation are eliminated by design. We are after the creation of new society, one which has learned from the past and moves forward with ancient wisdom and modern technology." *Global Village Construction Set*, Open Source Ecology, available at http://opensourceecology.org/wiki/Global_Village_Construction_Set (accessed Aug. 3, 2011).

[36] *See Global Village Construction Set, supra* note 35.

[37] *See LifeTrac*, Open Source Ecology, available at http://opensourceecology.org/wiki/LifeTrac (accessed Aug. 29, 2011).

[38] David C. Martin, founder of the Global Innovation Commons, points out that a great many patents are simply duplicates of innovations made decades ago. *See Global Innovation Commons*, available at http://www.globalinnovationcommons.org/content/about (accessed Feb. 28, 2011). Patent applications often disguise this fact by using colorful and complicated language, however, and overworked government patent examiners, struggling with limited resources and seeking to avoid legal hassles, often grant new patents that are not truly warranted. The Global Innovation Commons challenges a key rationale for patents – that they are essential in promoting innovation. Patents in fact often serve to *impede* innovative technologies and make them unaffordable – at precisely the time when all countries of the world, rich and poor, need to adopt cutting-edge energy technologies to cut carbon emissions. The World Bank, a partner on this project, has estimated that the technologies in the GIC database could save more than $2 trillion in potential license fees by enabling countries to choose open, shareable technologies and eschew more expensive proprietary systems. The Global Innovation Commons states: "In the Global Innovation Commons, we have assembled hundreds of thousands of innovations – most in the form of patents – which are either expired, no-longer maintained (meaning that the fees to keep the patents in force have lapsed), disallowed, or unprotected in most, if not all, relevant markets. This means that, as of right now, you can take a step into a world full of possibilities, not roadblocks. You want clean water for China or Sudan – it's in here. You want carbon-free energy – it's in here. You want food production for Asia or South America – it's in here." *Id.*

governments query the database on a country-by-country basis to identify useful technologies that are in the public domain. When identified, these technologies for energy, water, and agriculture are prime candidates for being developed at lower costs than patented technologies.

Some may dismiss these eco-digital commons as fringe novelties of marginal significance. We see them as beacons of governance innovation that will increasingly challenge conventional State and Market mechanisms. Despite inevitable resistance, eco-digital commons will surge ahead because, consistent with human rights values, they empower people to take responsibility to achieve better, more responsive, and more flexible solutions in the face of costly and deteriorating performance by large-scale State and Market institutions.

4. *Social and Civic Commons*

There is a wide variety of commons that are ingeniously leveraging our social inclinations to cooperate to develop new types of self-provisioning. To the extent that conventional markets are less mindful of their ecological impact and more intent on maximizing consumption, social and civic commons provide new means of humane ecological governance. Some are utterly familiar, such as public libraries, parks, and land trusts. But there is a wave of innovation going on right now, seen in such as examples as community tool sheds, which let participants share garden tools, and websites that enable the sharing of books (BookMooch) and household items (Freecycle.org).[39]

The international Time Banking movement lets volunteers earn time credits for providing services to people, such as lawn mowing or legal advice, which they can then spend for other services.[40] Time Banking has been highly successful in helping elderly and poor people with little money but lots of time to meet basic needs. The systems help people escape from their dependency on markets while building social relationships in a community.

---

[39] Other examples include collective bicycle programs in such cities as Montreal and London, *Bicycle Sharing System*, Wikipedia, available at http://en.wikipedia.org/wiki/Bicycle_sharing_system (accessed Aug. 7, 2011); car-sharing businesses such as Zipcar, Zipcar, available at http://www.zipcar.com (accessed Aug. 7, 2011); the ShareStuff website, iShareStuff, available at http://www.isharestuff.com (accessed Aug. 7, 2011); and the chronicler of the sharing social ethic, Shareable, Shareable, available at http://www.shareable.net (accessed Aug. 7, 2011). For more examples of community-based sharing, *see* Rachel Botsman & Roo Rogers, *What's Mine Is Yours: The Rise of Collaborative Consumption* (2010).

[40] *See* TimeBanks, available at http://www.timebanks.org (accessed July 28, 2011); *see also* Edgar Cahn & Jonathan Rowe, *Time Dollars: The New Currency That Enables Americans To Turn Their Hidden Resource – Time – into Personal Security and Community Renewal* (1992) available at http://www.timebanks.org (accessed July 28, 2011).

The same applies to blood and organ donation systems, which help people obtain needed blood and organs without the inequities, expense, and indignities of treating body parts and plasma as market commodities. A similar ethic animates the Slow Food and Slow Money movements, which are attempting to reimagine the food supply system and financial markets so that they might become more respectful of personal and community needs, above and beyond the Market. Another growing field of experimentation is trying to establish alternative currencies that can substitute for or complement the "fiat" national or multinational currencies.[41]

Social and civic commons do not necessarily have direct ecological implications. They do foster, however, an ethic of community engagement as well as relationships and styles of practice, which help incubate new models of commons- and rights-based ecological governance. A good example is the Solar Commons, a Phoenix-based project that will use municipal rights-of-way for solar panels to generate and sell electricity. The revenues will be collected by the Solar Commons, a nonprofit trust, and used to support affordable housing.[42]

5. Businesses Embedded in Commons

It is tempting to try to segregate commons and markets into two entirely different realms. In reality, they often interpenetrate and have mutual dependencies. No market can function without some measure of community stability, culture, and trust; and most commons operate within a larger market and private property context. In his book, *The Great Transformation*, economist Karl Polanyi showed that, historically, markets were embedded in communities and therefore were subservient to social norms, religious beliefs, and cultural values.[43] It was only in the "Great Transformation" of the nineteenth century that markets began to disembed themselves from social control and assert their autonomy as the default ordering principle for nature, labor, communities, and culture.

---

[41] Leading examples include Bitcoin, available at http://www.bitcoin.org (accessed July 28, 2011); Flattr, available at http://www.flattr.org (accessed July 28, 2011); Ithaca Hours, available at http://www.ithacahours.info (accessed July 28, 2011); Metacurrency, available at http://www.metacurrency.org (accessed July 28, 2011); Open Bank Project, available at http://www.openbankproject.com (accessed July 28, 2011); and WIR Bank, available at http://www.wir.ch (accessed July 28, 2011).

[42] *See* Solar Commons, available at http://solarcommons.org (accessed July 28, 2011).

[43] Karl Polanyi, *The Great Transformation: The Political and Economic Origins of Our Time* (1944).

What is happening today (in part because of the Internet) is that communities are reasserting greater sovereignty over the structure and behaviors of conventional markets. They are also creating entirely new types of market structures that are embedded in communities.[44] Commons of shared values and practices are becoming hosting environments for socially embedded businesses. This trend is perhaps best exemplified by local agricultural systems (farmers, distributors, retailers, safety compliance co-ops) that are bypassing national and global vendors.[45] Farmers' markets, community-supported agriculture (CSA), the Slow Food movement, and local cooperatives are examples of businesses embedded in commons (as distinct from national and global businesses whose first loyalties are to capital markets and public investors). Another class of examples is open-source software companies, which depend on communities of volunteer programmers to produce their software and pioneer new ideas. Hundreds of software vendors such as IBM, Oracle, and Red Hat are keenly aware that their business success depends on respectfully interacting with open-source programming communities (most notably, by respecting the community ethic that code must be legally shareable and modifiable without permission or payment).[46]

The growing power of commoners as drivers of market activity can be seen in the new websites that enable ordinary people to band together to finance new products. The popular Kickstarter website lets people invest funds in proposed artistic projects, and has collected and distributed more than $150 million to date. Spot.us is a vehicle for user-commissioned journalism. Sellaband hosts fan-financed music. "Crowdsourcing" has become a major way for serious research intermediaries like InnoCentive to service corporate research needs, especially in pharmaceuticals, through decentralized, self-selected participation.[47] The Web and digital technologies are enabling new, socially driven forms of "collaborative consumption" in which people can share, barter, lend, trade, or rent their cars, apartments, tools, and other possessions.[48]

M.I.T. professor Eric von Hippel has written extensively about how communities of users – for example, cyclists, windsurfers, amateurs of all sorts – are

[44] Bollier, *supra* Ch. 1 note 17, at 229–52 (Chapter 10: "The New Open Business Models").
[45] *See generally* Steve Martinez et al., *Local Food Systems: Concepts, Impacts, and Issues* (2010) (USDA Economic Research Report No. 97), available at http://books.google.com/books?id=wVTjlY75WW8C&lpg=PP1&dq=local%20food&pg=PP1#v=onepage&q&f=true (accessed Aug. 9, 2011).
[46] *See* Christopher M. Kelty, *Two Bits: The Cultural Significance of Free Software* (2008); Steven Weber, *The Success of Open Source* (2004).
[47] *See* InnoCentive, available at http://www.innocentive.com (accessed July 28, 2011).
[48] Botsman & Rogers, *supra* note 39.

neglected but powerful sources of research and development (R&D) innovation for businesses.[49] The idea of center-pivot irrigation sprinklers, Gatorade, the mountain bike, desktop publishing, email, and the sports bra were all dreamed up by ordinary people immersed in affinity groups, not by corporate R&D departments. The counterintuitive point is that the Commons is a serious engine of innovation in its own right, often with important Market impact.[50]

With the right enabling structures, commons and markets can be constructively synergistic rather than adversarial. Commoners can readily become co-producers and co-innovators with the Market. First, however, markets must be prevented from enclosing commons, and commoners must devise the legal frameworks and other systems that give them a shared, protected space for collaboration and generativity.

6. State Trustee Commons

Even though commons are generally seen as a self-organized governance regimes that are separate from both the State and Market, it makes sense to recognize State trustee commons as a hybrid category of commons. Pursuant to its many constitutional, statutory, and common law commitments, the State often acts as a formal trustee or steward of CPRs, from the airwaves and public lands to federally funded research and national parks. Purists may demur, but we prefer to recognize these trustee or steward initiatives as a distinct class of commons while acknowledging their mixed status – part State, part commons. Where the CPR is of large scale or spans major political boundaries – the atmosphere or the oceans, for example – they would seem especially necessary.

It is important to make this distinction to underscore the political stake of commoners in resources under government control. The State has its own

---

[49] *See* Eric von Hippel, *Democratizing Innovation* (2005), available at http://web.mit.edu/evhippel/www/democ1.htm (accessed July 28, 2011); *see also* C.Y. Baldwin & E.A. von Hippel, *Modeling a Paradigm Shift: From Producer Innovation to User and Collaborative Innovation* (Working Paper, MIT Sloan Sch. of Mgmt. 2009) ("We conclude that innovation by individual users and also open collaborative innovation increasingly compete with – and may displace – producer innovation in many parts of the economy. We argue that a transition from producer innovation to open single user and open collaborative innovation is desirable in terms of social welfare, and so worthy of support by policymakers."), available at http://papers.ssrn.com/sol3/papers.cfm?abstract_id=1502864 (accessed July 28, 2011).

[50] David Bollier, The Commons as a Different Engine of Innovation, The Illahee Lecture in Portland, Or. (May 11, 2011), available at http://www.bollier.org/commons-different-engine-innovation (accessed July 28, 2011).

sovereign powers, to be sure, but its many alliances with Market-based con-
stituencies have made it an unreliable steward of ecological and cultural commons alike, as borne out by the historical record. In Chapter 8, we explore
how the State might serve as a more responsible trustee for certain collective
resources and how it can use its powers to sanction new types of commons-
based governance approaches. Prominent, for example, could be the *State-
sanctioned common assets trust*, a delegation of stewardship authority to better
manage water, oil revenues, public lands, and Social Security funds for the
public benefit. Another could be *State-supervised rentals* in which government
agencies oversee auctions or rentals of common assets, such as the right to harvest fish from fisheries; use the airwaves for broadcasting and telephony; use
public lands for mining, grazing, and timber; and pollute the atmosphere in
specified amounts.

Calling these types of governance regimes "state trustee commons" articu-
lates a fact that is too easily forgotten when assessing State management and
regulation of the airwaves, public lands, taxpayer-funded research, and the like:
*These resources belong to the people, not to the State. The State is acting merely
as an administrative and fiduciary agent of the people; it is not the "owner."*
Emphasizing this fact helps clarify that the State has stewardship obligations
that go beyond providing subsidized infrastructure, resource giveaways, and
legal privileges to politically powerful industries.

Irrespective of category, the strength of the Commons as an ecological governance paradigm receptive to human rights values stems from its commitments
to a broader array of operative variables – social, economic, ecological – and to
its more complex sense of human capacities. Unlike the neoclassical, liberal
economic worldview that sees a universe of individuals pursuing rational self-
interest for material gain as an engine of inexorable progress,[51] the Commons
worldview puts forward a much broader, richer ontology of social existence
and value. Instead of insisting on narrowly contrived, instrumental metrics of
value (namely, price), the Commons matrix enables us to see more subtle
and diverse forms of value – value that is ecologically complex; that cannot
necessarily be monetized; that is embedded in human relationships and community; and that embraces collective and long-term needs. The ontological
frame of the Commons is not an arid theoretical issue, but its primary, practical
virtue.

---

[51] Jonathan Rowe, *The Tragedy of Economics: Market Theory vs. Human Nature*, On
the Commons (Feb. 8, 2009), available at http://onthecommons.org/tragedy-economics-
market-theory-vs-human-nature (accessed July 29, 2011); Mäki, *supra* Ch. 5 note 88.

We do not wish to leave the impression, however, that commons are self-actualizing or free from the usual problems of administration, politics, technical challenges, and so forth. Our point is that, as a general paradigm for ecological governance, the Commons offers several critical capacities that are sorely missing from the neoliberal State/Market system:

- *the ability to set and enforce sustainable limits* to resource consumption;
- *the capacity to uphold the inalienability of certain resources and values*, so that markets will not over-exploit or abuse them;
- *the ability to use resources to meet everyone's basic needs in an equitable way*, thereby helping to reduce inequality and insecurity and thus pressures for greater exploitation of nature;
- *a framework for redefining "development"* in ways that re-integrate production and governance, enterprise and accountability, and economic provisioning with ecological values; and
- *a process that highlights people's interdependencies on nature and each other*, which in turns helps heal the alienation from nature and others that market individualism encourages.

Together these special capacities suggest a practical way to escape the growth imperative of the contemporary economy, an imperative that lies at the core of so many ecological crises. The Commons can help us escape the growth compulsion, writes commons advocate Silke Helfrich, "because all those things that are produced in commons do not have to be made artificially scarce [as the private property system and markets require]. There is no incentive to create artificial scarcity because commons do not produce goods to be exchanged, but rather to foster and maintain social relationships, satisfy needs, and solve problems. Directly."[52]

In sum, when commons-based alternatives are available, it is easier for individuals to insulate themselves from unregulated markets and their logic of maximal production, consumption, debt, and capital accumulation. They can bypass the Market or establish a more orderly, co-equal transactional relationship with it. They can more readily meet their needs directly while maintaining control over their cultural norms. Access to commons in general and the Commons in particular reduces the social exclusion and material deprivation that characterizes most Market societies. It enhances participation

---

[52] Silke Helfrich, *Commons Jenseits des Wachstums* [*The Commons Beyond Growth*], CommonsBlog (May 23, 2011), available at http://commonsblog.wordpress.com/2011/05/23/commons-jenseits-des-wachstums (Ger.), translated at http://www. bollier.org/commons-antidote-relentless-growth (each accessed July 29, 2011). For more on this theme, *see* Wolfgang Hoeschele, *The Economics of Abundance: A Political Economy of Freedom, Equity, and Sustainability* (2010).

in more open, deliberative settings. It fosters self-determination in meeting one's needs. All of these are fundamental to the effectuation of human rights.

B. TENSIONS BETWEEN MODERN STATE LAW AND THE COMMONS

Whereas the particular logic of the Commons gives it many inherent advantages over existing modes of governance, it also brings with it some deep philosophical tensions with the liberal polity. Many commons embody notions of human existence and relationships (ontology), systems of knowledge (epistemology), and cultural assumptions (worldview) that are quite different from those assumed by modern liberal society.

For example, Western legal systems tend to give juridical recognition to individuals only (juridical persons as well as natural persons), and chiefly to vouchsafe their private property rights, personal liberties, and commercial interests. The idea of recognizing collective rights for nonmarket interests is alien to the very premises of Western liberal polity and law, which, for the most part, favors the worldview and interests of unregulated markets. One could say, truly, that this is one of the purposes of Western law – the consequence of which, as in any legal system, is to constitute the categories of legitimate thought and adjudication. Not surprisingly, the idea of the Commons is invisible and virtually unthinkable in Western law in the modern era.

An emblematic example in the United States is the Dawes Act of 1887, which made it illegal – or extralegal – for Native Americans to presume to be commoners.[53] The Act's prime sponsor, Republican Senator Henry L. Dawes of Massachusetts, believed that life on the reservations made "Indians" indolent, uninterested in their own advancement, and unfit for citizenship. "To solve the 'Indian problem'," writes Lewis Hyde, a commons scholar, "the Dawes Act began the process of breaking up tribal holdings and giving individual Indians deeds to private plots of land. Land would no longer be owned 'in the entirety' by a tribe but 'in severalty' by individuals. Thus [were tribal lands made alienable and converted into salable commodities, and thus also] did Jefferson's vision of a nation of small farms and yeomen farmers settle, a century later, over the Indian lands, a civilizing enclosure for a once native commons."[54]

---

[53] General Allotment Act of 1887, 25 U.S.C. §§ 331–4, 339, 341–2, 348–9, 354, 381 (2009). The General Allotment Act is commonly referred to as the Dawes Act.

[54] Lewis Hyde, *Invisible Commoners: Native Americans' Communal Approach to Land Was Consciously Dismantled by 19th Century U.S. Leaders*, On the Commons (July 5, 2005), available at http://www.onthecommons.org/invisible-commoners (accessed July 29, 2012).

As a condition of becoming American citizens, the Dawes Act required that Native Americans give up their commons-based way of life and become property-owning individuals. Hyde writes:

> A few years before the act was passed, the Supreme Court had ruled that Native Americans could be denied the right to vote because they were not U.S. citizens, a decision which those in favor of assimilation sought to remedy by adding a citizenship provision to the [Dawes] bill. After the process of [land] allotment had been completed, the Act said, "every Indian . . . who has voluntarily taken up . . . his residence separate and apart from any tribe . . . and has adopted the habits of civilized life, is hereby declared to be a citizen of the United States. . . . "

> The law would seem to have embodied a hidden syllogism: all U.S. citizens have private, alienable holdings; Indians accepting allotment will have such holdings; therefore such Indians, living "separate and apart," will be citizens. In this way does one kind of self become a citizen, enfranchised and visible to the law, while others drop out of sight. As if to underscore that point the Dawes Act actually says that when it comes to hiring "Indian police," those who have accepted allotment "shall be preferred." Those who accept allotment are not just recognized by the law, they embody the law.[55]

As this history shows, modern law itself can be a formidable barrier to those who wish to maintain their commons or establish new ones. Behaving as a commoner is in many respects an affront to citizenship – if that citizenship is essentially synonymous with individualism, private ownership, and a commitment to the Market alienability of everything. It is why the State/Market resists demands for indigenous people's rights and recognition of the rights of nature; they run counter to the deep logic of liberal political theory and thereby challenge existing configurations of political power and culture.

As a practical matter, the lexical prejudices of modern law can be skirted through practical expedients, and often are. We might add that such evasions are not entirely to be scorned. They are responsible for important forms of collective governance such as public libraries, national parks, and land trusts, all of which exist within a legal system with different constitutive priorities. Indigenous peoples have often won *sui generis* legal regimes for themselves; Native Americans have a qualified sovereignty over tribal territories. Yet attempts to win legal recognition for commoning within the Western legal tradition are irregular and difficult.[56] They tend to require ingenious "legal hacks" or anomalous innovations to transcend the epistemological

[55] *Id.*
[56] *See* Mattei, *supra* Ch. 4 note 4.

premises of the law. The challenge frequently comes down to devising service-able "work-arounds" or exceptions that can protect collective, non-State and non-Market interests without structurally altering the core premises of liberal legal discourse.[57]

In this sense, notwithstanding the venerable historical precedents of com-mons law detailed earlier in this section, the movement to devise legal protec-tions for the commons can border on being an extralegal enterprise. The histor-ical legal doctrines recognizing the commons may exist, but they have largely been forgotten (Charter of the Forest),[58] reinterpreted or ignored (Magna Carta),[59] deliberately flouted, limited, or overturned (habeas corpus, torture prohibitions;[60] Native American land commons[61]), or kept in check to suit the economic and cultural priorities of modern, liberal societies (public trust doctrine).[62]

Western legal categories are tenaciously resistant to the idea of commons, in part because they are embedded in centuries-old ontological premises that we rarely think about. Descartes, as previously noted, famously separated body

---

[57] Exemplary legal work-arounds include the General Public License for software, based on copyright ownership; the Creative Commons licenses for creative works, also based on copy-right ownership; and land trusts that create "property on the outside, commons on the inside," in Professor Carol Rose's phrase. *See* Carol M. Rose, *The Several Futures of Property: Of Cyberspace and Folk Tales, Emission Trades and Ecosystems*, 83 Minn. L. Rev. 129, 144 (1998).

[58] Historian Peter Linebaugh writes: "Over the great arch of English history some parts of Magna Carta, namely, Chapter 39, evolved in creative response to events while other parts, such as chapter 7 providing the widow with her reasonable estovers of common, and the entire Charter of the Forest, collected dust among the muniments." Linebaugh, *supra* Ch. 4 note 111, at 72.

[59] "Contemplating the history of Magna Carta seemed to give the [U.S. Supreme] Court courage to make changes of its own: 'the words of Magana Carta stood for very different things at the time of the separation of the American colonies from what they represented originally . . . What Magna Carta has become is very different indeed from the immediate objects of the barons of Runnymede.'" Linebaugh, *supra* Ch. 4 note 390, at 191 (quoting Green v. U.S., 356 U.S. 165, 189 (1958) (Frankfurter, J., concurring)). Linebaugh also writes: "Following the Palmer raids in 1919 . . . the liberties of Magna Carta – no torture, habeas corpus, due process of law, trial by jury – and the principles of the Forest Charter – subsistence, no enclosure, neighborhood, travel and reparations – began to disappear." *Id.* at 230.

[60] *See, e.g.*, David Cole, *The Torture Memos: Rationalizing the Unthinkable* (2009).

[61] *See, e.g.*, Wood & Welcker, *supra* note 13; *see also* S. James Anaya, *Brief of Lone Wolf, Principal Chief of the Kiowas, to the Supreme Court of American Indian Nations*, 7 Kan. J.L. & Pub. Pol'y 117, 142 (1997); N. Bruce Duthu, *Incorporating Discourse in Federal Indian Law: Negotiating Tribal Sovereignty Through the Lens of Native American Literature*, 13 Harv. Hum. Rts. J. 141, 171 (2000).

[62] *See, e.g.*, Mary Christina Wood, *Advancing the Sovereign Trust of Government To Safeguard the Environment for Present and Future Generations* (pts. 1 & 2), 39 Envtl. L. 43, 91 (2009) (the article's two parts are subtitled *Ecological Realism and the Need for a Paradigm Shift* and *Instill-ing a Fiduciary Obligation in Governance*); *see also* Mary Christina Wood, *Nature's Trust: En-vironmental Law for a New Ecological Age* (forthcoming from Cambridge University Press).

from mind and subject from object, formalizing the individual's separation from nature and community.[63] In Western law, a person's desires and motivations – and therefore rights and liberties – are formally assigned to the individual, whose rationality and self-interest are seen as the animating forces of economic and social order.[64] It should come as no surprise that Garrett Hardin's tragedy parable sees individual selfishness as limitless and cooperation as illogical and unsustainable. In the episteme of modern law, the idea that there might be an integrated, organic community that preexists the individual and might actually influence individual predilections and desires makes little sense.[65] It lies outside the logic of the legal system and the culture, both of which are framed around the sovereign individual. Identity is seen as self-made, not relational and community-based. Context and culture are seen as incidental, not controlling. No wonder modern legal systems have trouble comprehending commons! No wonder it is difficult to inscribe the enabling

[63] *See supra* text accompanying Ch. 2 note 74.

[64] Philosopher Richard Tarnas writes:

> It has been said that Descartes and Kant were both inevitable in the development of the modern mind, and I believe this is correct. For it was Descartes who first fully grasped and articulated the experience of the emerging autonomous modern self as being fundamentally distinct and separate from an objective external world that it seeks to understand and master. Descartes 'woke up in a Copernican universe'; after Copernicus, humankind was on its own in the universe, its cosmic place irrevocably relativized. Descartes then drew out and expressed in philosophical terms the experiential consequence of that new cosmological context... For if the human mind was in some sense fundamentally distinct and different from the external world, and if the only reality that the human mind had direct access to was its own experience, then the world apprehended by the mind was ultimately only the mind's interpretation of the world. . . . Everything that this mind could perceive and judge would be to some undefined extent determined by its own character, its own subjective structures. The mind could experience only phenomena, not things-in-themselves; appearances, not an independent reality. In the modern universe, the human mind was on its own.

Richard Tarnas, *The Passion of the Western Mind: Understanding the Ideas That Have Shaped Our World View* 416 (1993).

[65] This point is well made by Ugo Mattei:

> The commons can be described only from a phenomenological and holistic perspective and their understanding is therefore incompatible with the above mentioned reductionism [of the Anglo-American empiricist tradition in economics, political science, sociology, analytical philosophy and the law]. . . . In this respect, commons are an ecological-qualitative category based on inclusion and access, whereas property and State sovereignty are rather economical-qualitative categories based on exclusion (produced scarcity) and violent concentration of power into a few hands.

Mattei, *supra* Ch. 4 note 4.

legal principles for cooperation within an individualist legal framework. As Ugo Mattei explicates:

> Commons, unlike private goods and public goods, are not commodities and cannot be reduced to the language of ownership. They express a qualitative relation. It would be reductive to say that we have a common good: we should rather see to what extent we are the commons, in as much as we are part of an environment, an urban or rural ecosystem. Here, the subject is part of the object. For this reason commons are inseparably related and link individuals, communities and the ecosystem itself.[66]

Commons also poses a challenge to Western law because, as described in Chapter 3, they are not creatures of State law (except by way of benign tolerance). The inner gyroscope of commons has traditionally been its self-generated community values and procedures (which may sometimes be supported by exogenous structures of authority and power). For the most part, commons tends to govern itself through what we have called "Vernacular Law" or, in Michael Reisman's term, "microlaw."

These meta-issues complicate the regeneration of commons law that can manage ecological resources in the twenty-first century. Yet, though these issues counsel for humility in moving forward and wariness of theoretical purity or political correctness, they do not prevent commons renewal. When it comes to commons, *praxis* trumps State law theory, and human agency and presence must be given their due in the formation of commons-based institutions. Vernacular experimentation yields all sorts of knowledge about commons and commoning that may forever be inscrutable to official or formal law.[67]

Our point with this excursus into the tensions between modern State Law and the Vernacular Law of commons is to make the reader self-conscious of the State/Market's principled aversion to the Commons. As we suggest in our brief account of John Locke in Chapter 5, this aversion cuts deeply, implicating ontology, epistemology, and worldview. Anyone who seeks to forge a new, regenerated body of Commons Law must grapple with the limitations of contemporary language in expressing the dynamics and logic of the Commons and with the power of Market-oriented State Law to render the Commons

---

[66] *Id.*

[67] A good example is the General Public License for software, which made possible the flowering of free software and open source software. The GPL was the product of vernacular experimentation. So, too, with countless small-scale resource commons whose governance systems have evolved through *in situ* innovation over time, not through scholarly theory.

invisible and less able to constitute themselves as recognized legal institutions. The deeply engrained habits of language, perception, culture, and worldview are not easily overcome, but if our natural environment – from local to global – is ever to be fundamentally and enduringly clean, healthy, balanced, and sustainable, it is essential that we confront the general inability of the State/Market to see the Commons and Commons Sector and therefore to protect them.

Given this daunting array of challenges, the befuddled skeptic may wonder how we might realistically go about the task of regenerating a commons- and rights-based ecological law system within the framework of modern, liberal society. The short answer is this: the Commons always plays the hand that it is dealt. It must find ways of working within legacy systems of law designed for different purposes while simultaneously advancing paradigm-shifting social practices that may gestate into a different sort of legal process. Theoretical purity and abstract ideals are ultimately less important than creating practical and protectable platforms on which commoners can be commoners.[68]

---

[68] A good example is the free culture movement's acceptance of copyright law as the philosophical basis for building its Creative Commons licenses that enable sharing in myriad content commons. Some left-wing critics have denounced the acceptance of copyright law, but this alleged sell-out has achieved something that a frontal attack on copyright law never would have achieved – the amassing of a diversified constituency whose everyday practices are grounded in working commons, which represents a significant political/cultural base.

7

Imagining a New Architecture of Law and Policy to Support the Ecological Commons

Having introduced the Commons and explained its promise as a governance template favorable to the rights of human beings and nature, we turn now to the challenge of building an architecture of law and policy that can support it. How might law and policy recognize and support the Commons as a salutary paradigm of ecological governance?

Achieving this goal will require remodeled legal processes for both State and Vernacular Law and practice. Indeed the two must mutually constitute each other in an iterative upward spiral: State Law and Policy will give recognition and visibility to diverse "tribes" of commoners, and their active commoning will help regenerate the authority and reach of Commons Law and policy. This conjoining of State and Vernacular Law and practice is essential if we are to rehabilitate the State as a trustee of common assets at all levels – local, national, regional, and global – and the permutations among them.

We believe the basic architecture of law and policy to support commons- and rights-based ecological governance (green governance) must be developed in three distinct yet interrelated fields:

1. *General internal governance principles and policies* that can guide the development and management of commons;
2. *Macro-principles and policies* that the State/Market can embrace to develop laws, institutions, and procedures friendly to the Commons and "peer governance"; and
3. *Legal institutional structures and policies* that can operationalize the principles of small-scale commons and human rights in large-scale and planetary commons.

Imagining a legal and policy architecture that can support rights-based ecological commons in their many varieties, secure them against enclosure, assure their responsible operation, and unleash their generative stewardship is a universal responsibility of the highest order. However it is structured, an ambitious project that addresses these key issues is imperative if we are to establish green governance that can preserve Earth's natural (and social) environment free of irretrievable harm.

We do not presume to set forth, however, a fully developed theory or comprehensive plan for a new multilateral system of governance. If history is any guide, such grand ambitions must be discussed and negotiated inclusively and over time if they are to change minds, institutional commitments, and the course of history. This challenge is all the more pronounced because the current liberal polity is structurally biased against (or simply confounded by) proposed laws, policies, and strategies that support ecological commons. Invariably, many proposals will provoke philosophical opposition and thus require makeshift legal approaches. But as suggested in Chapters 5 and 6, theory must follow practice, and practice must be guided by situational opportunities.

We therefore take for granted that Commons Law and policy structures are likely to emerge in irregular, unpredictable ways over time, and for this reason our orientation is more practical and improvisational than theoretical and directive. The best results are likely to emerge from on-the-ground experimentation and political struggles that can "road test" any proposed legal and policy architecture and then expand its scope and complexity incrementally over time. An empty legal and policy formalism that nominally supports the Commons and the right to environment but fails to engage commoners in these tasks or deliver practical results is of little use to anyone.

To be transformative, a new body of Commons Law and policy must be richly braided with Vernacular Law principles rooted in evolving social and administrative practice. This is important not just for the efficacy of internal governance of commons, but also as a way to discover stable principles and policies that can guide State and Market support of the Commons. Most ecological commons, for example, can yield important localized knowledge rooted in the customary practices of people who love and depend on the natural resource and intimately understand its ecological cycles and peculiarities. It should be obvious that long-standing policies of the State/Market will thus need to be changed to recognize and advance commoning. Astute strategies that can successfully validate, protect, and support clean and healthy ecological commons for all must be devised. This will take time, imagination, and political struggle.

At the same time, though it is premature to declare that our ecological governance proposal will lead to a paradigm shift, we believe it has the philosophical coherence and functional promise to stimulate the dialogue that is needed for a fruitful journey forward. A paradigm of commons- and rights-based ecological governance is compelling because it comprises at once a rich legal tradition that extends back centuries, an attractive cultural discourse that can organize and energize people in personal ways, and a widespread participatory social practice that, at this moment, is producing practical results in projects big and small, local and transnational.

For a shift of this paradigm to take place, however, the countless commons that now exist must be seen as organically connected to a much larger worldview that deserves formal recognition and support by State Law and public policy. Needed is a coherent vision of State Law that can enable diverse commons-based endeavors to be seen as part of a larger whole and a collaboration to make that shared vision a political and cultural reality. For generations, State Law has given legal recognition and generous backing to the "free market," extending similar support to the Commons could unleash tremendous energy and creativity in safeguarding and improving planetary ecosystems. It also could help to transform the State and Market in many positive ways, reducing the cronyism, corruption, and secrecy that presently mark each and forcing corporations to internalize the many costs and risks they now displace onto common-pool resources (CPRs) and communities.

A. INTERNAL GOVERNANCE PRINCIPLES OF COMMONS

The great achievement of the late Elinor Ostrom and her colleagues has been to take wildly heterogeneous commons – generally small-scale ones – and develop structured, intelligent ways to assess how and why they do or do not function well. Ostrom's eight general design principles, which tend to be present to some significant degree in most successful commons, provide a valuable "beachhead" for understanding commons governance.[1] Yet another key lesson from the academic literature is that much of the success of a commons depends on contextual factors that are peculiar to a given resource, culture, political rule, legal polity, geography, or history. Universal principles therefore have limited applicability in designing commons.

In an attempt to deal with such variability among commons, Ostrom developed what is known as the Institutional Analysis and Development (IAD) framework, a standard research methodology for investigating commons regimes as they exist in diverse contexts and in nested, multitiered

---

[1] *See supra* text accompanying Ch. 5 notes 93–111.

environments.[2] The IAD is a meta-theoretical research framework for assessing variables in commons across disciplinary boundaries.[3] It consists of using case studies to develop practice-based taxonomies of management approaches; identifying the most significant variables at play; and ensuring adaptations of the overall framework as new information is learned. Special attention is given to the interplay of biophysical resources, community attributes and the rules-in-use, or governance mechanisms, as they play out in action situations, or deliberative social spaces. Much of commons literature uses the IAD framework as a methodology to draw larger conclusions about discrete resource commons.

Among the most useful analytic concepts of the IAD framework is its differentiation of commons rule making in three overlapping stages: (1) operational rules which deal with transient, everyday situations within a commons; (2) collective-choice rules which involve decisions about how the operational rules may be changed; and (3) constitutional rules which address decisions about how the collective-choice rules may be changed. These differentiations help us understand some of the structural dynamics within which trust, cooperation, and reciprocity are negotiated, and therefore to have a more refined understanding of how to build and grow a commons.

In the ensuing pages, we focus mostly on the collective-choice and constitutional rules because, in contrast to the operational rules, they have the more enduring impact on the stability and success of commons governance over time. Our purpose is not to survey the large commons literature or propose definitive rules for each and every type of commons.[4] It is, rather, to build on, and extrapolate from, the analytic insights of Ostrom and her collaborators to imagine policies and legal principles that could extend existing commons, which typically are geophysically small, to commons that might or should be created to cope with more complicated national and transnational ecological issues, and even global ones such as the atmosphere or the oceans. These large-scale CPRs entail many more complexities than do small-scale

[2] *See* Elinor Ostrom, *A Diagnostic Approach for Going Beyond Panaceas*, 104 Proc. Nat'l Acad. Sci. 15181 (2007).

[3] Elinor Ostrom, *The Institutional Analysis and Development Approach*, in *Designing Institutions for Environmental and Research Management* 68–90 (E.T. Loehman & D.M. Kilgour eds., 1998). For an overview of how the IAD framework has been used, *see* Graham R. Marshall, *Economics for Collaborative Environmental Management: Renegotiating the Commons* (2005).

[4] However, a useful compendium of research of diverse ecological commons can be found in CAPRI (CGIAR Systemwide Program on Collective Action and Prop. Rights), *Resources, Rights and, Cooperation: A Sourcebook on Property Rights and Collective Action for Sustainable Development* (2010) (International Food Policy Research Institute, Washington, D.C.), available at http://www.capri.cgiar.org/sourcebook.asg (accessed June 11, 2012).

ones and, furthermore, require grappling more intensively with the neoliberal global economy and political struggles to create alternatives to it. State trustee commons, for example, are nominally subject to law but are inherently creatures of politics and therefore must be approached from a broader perspective than, say, the IAD framework or small-scale commons.

In our analysis of the internal governance of commons, then, we shift from small-scale commons (a realm studied in the literature with dispassionate scientific observation) to large-scale commons (a realm in which creative political struggle and moral commitment also play important roles). In sharp contrast to small-scale commons which have a great number of bounded variables, large-scale commons are driven by a messy, wide-open set of nonrational, situational, historically specific, nonreplicable variables – for example, culture, history, ideology – that are far less amenable to scientific methodologies.

With this proviso in mind, we tender seven core principles in areas that we believe do, or feasibly can, influence the internal governance of commons, large and small. These principles are grounded in the belief that the natural environment is the common heritage of all humankind, present and future, and that it should therefore be accorded maximum protection.

1. *Principles of Social Cooperation, Trust, and Problem Solving*

Ostrom's eight core design principles, published in 1990, remain the most solid foundation for understanding the internal governance of commons as a general paradigm.[5] In a book-length study published in 2010 examining the ability of self-organized groups to develop collective solutions to CPR problems at small- to medium-scales based on evidence derived from multiple methodologies, Poteete, Janssen, and Ostrom offer a more recent summary of the key factors in cooperation.[6] Ostrom summarizes the research as follows:

A large number of variables increase the likelihood that self-organization could be effective in solving collective action problems. Among the most

---

[5] *See supra* text between Ch. 5 notes 95 and 96. However, there have been a number of valuable adaptations of Ostrom's eight principles by various commoners seeking to make them reflect the experiential, subjective experience of commoning. One such adaptation is "Nine Core Principles," set forth by the American commons advocacy group, On the Commons, http://onthecommons.org/work/nine-core-commons-principles (accessed Sept. 13, 2012). Another adaptation is "Eight Points of Reference for Commoning," developed by the first German Sommerschool on the Commons held in Bechstedt, Thuringia, in June 2012, http://www.bollier.org/blog/eight-points-reference-commoning (accessed Sept. 13, 2012).

[6] Amy R. Poteete et al., *Working Together: Collective Action, the Commons, and Multiple Methods in Practice* (2010).

important are the following: (1) reliable information is available about the immediate and long-term costs and benefits of actions; (2) the individuals involved see the resources as important for their own achievements and have a long-term time horizon; (3) gaining a reputation for being a trustworthy reciprocator is important to those involved; (4) individuals can communicate with at least some of the others involved; (5) informal monitoring and sanctioning is feasible and considered appropriate; and (6) social capital and leadership exist, related to previous successes in solving joint problems.

The exact structure that will enhance cooperation cannot be specified at a general level, as many specific features of a particular dilemma affect what has a chance of working. The crucial factor is that a combination of structural features leads many of those affected to trust one another and to be willing to do an agreed-upon action that adds to their own short-term costs because they do see a long-term benefit for themselves and others and they believe that most others are complying.[7]

Ostrom notes that "extensive empirical research on collective action . . . has repeatedly identified a necessary central core of trust and reciprocity among those involved that is associated with successful levels of collective action."[8] In addition, "when participants fear they are being 'suckers' for taking costly actions while others enjoy a free ride,"[9] it enhances the need for monitoring to root out deception and fraud.

In sum, effective commons manifest a Vernacular Law of social cooperation, trust, and reciprocity without which they simply cannot succeed. The distinctive rules of this Vernacular Law, implicit in Ostrom's observational summary, must therefore be made an integral part of commons- and rights-based ecological governance. To ensure their legitimacy, however, they in turn must be served by self-determined laws and policies that guarantee to commoners the right to be clearly informed, to participate in decisions that affect their interests, and to redress by competent internal mechanisms and processes for violations of these procedural human rights. Also, to further underwrite their authoritativeness – indeed, to reinforce the integrity of the entire self-governing process – green governance must account as well (and transparently, as typically is its wont) for the fragile and complex interdependence of living ecosystems, the aesthetic value of the environment, and the interests of future generations.

---

7   Elinor Ostrom, *A Multi-Scale Approach to Coping with Climate Change and Other Collective Action Problems*, Solutions (Feb. 24, 2010), available at http://www.thesolutionsjournal.com/node/565 (accessed Aug. 2, 2011).
8   Id.
9   Id.

2. *Human Rights and Nature's Rights Principles*

Both human rights and nature's rights are implicit in ecological commons governance. If any commons is to cultivate trust and reciprocity and therefore enhance its chances of stable management, its operational, collective, and constitutional rules must be seen as fair and respectful. To this end, ecological commons must embody the values of human dignity as expressed in, for example, the Universal Declaration of Human Rights[10] and nine core international human rights conventions that have evolved from it or from such of them as may be applicable.[11] In addition, they must affirm the values expressed in the Universal Declaration of the Rights of Mother Earth which was adopted by the World's People's Conference on Climate Change in Cochabamba, Bolivia, in 2008 and received for official consideration by the United Nations (UN) General Assembly in 2010.[12] The very point of well-managed ecological commons is to ensure that the CPR – be it local (e.g., a prairie or lake), global (e.g., the atmosphere or an ocean), or somewhere in between (e.g., a forest or river) – is kept clean, healthy, biodiverse, and sustainable. To the maximum extent possible, each ecological commons should make human rights and nature's

---

[10] *Supra* Ch. 3 note 62.

[11] The Office of the U.N. High Commissioner for Human Rights (OHCHR) identifies the following instruments as the "nine core international human rights instruments" (the second and third of which, together with the 1948 Universal Declaration of Human Rights, *supra* Ch. 3, note 62, comprise the "International Bill of Human Rights"): the International Convention on the Elimination of All Forms of Racial Discrimination (ICERD), Dec. 21, 1965, 660 U.N.T.S. 195, S. Exec. Doc. C/95-2, *reprinted in* III Basic Documents, *supra* Prologue note 13, at III.I.1; the 1966 International Covenant on Economic, Social and Cultural Rights (ICESCR), *supra* Ch. 4, note 30; the 1966 International Covenant on Civil and Political Rights (ICCPR), *supra* note Ch. 4, note 29; the Convention on the Elimination of All Forms of Discrimination against Women (CEDAW), Dec. 18, 1979, 1249 U.N.T.S. 13, *reprinted in* 19 I.L.M. 33 (1980) *and* III Basic Documents, *supra* Prologue note 13, at III.C.12; the Convention against Torture and Other Cruel, Inhuman or Degrading Treatment or Punishment (CAT), Dec. 10, 1984, 1465 U.N.T.S. 85, U.S.T. 100–20, *reprinted in* 24 I.L.M. 535 (1984) *and* III Basic Documents, *supra* Prologue note 13, at III.K.2; Convention on the Rights of the Child (CRC), Nov. 20, 1989, 1577 U.N.T.S. 3, *reprinted in* 28 I.L.M. 1448 (1989) *and* III Basic Documents, *supra* Prologue note 13, at III.D.5; International Convention on the Protection of the Rights of All Migrant Workers and Members of Their Families (ICRMW), Dec. 18, 1990, G.A. Res. 45/158, Annex, U.N. GAOR, 45th Sess., Supp. No. 49, U.N. Doc. A/45/49 (1991), at 262, *reprinted in* 30 I.L.M. 1517 (1991) *and* III Basic Documents, *supra* Prologue note 13, at III.O.9; Convention on the Rights of Persons with Disabilities (CRPD), Dec. 13, 2006, U.N. Doc. A/61/611, *reprinted in* 46 I.L.M. 443 (2007) *and* III Basic Documents, *supra* Prologue note 13, at III.E.4; International Convention for the Protection of All Persons from Enforced Disappearance (CPED), Dec. 20, 2006, G.A. Res. 61/177, Annex, U.N. GAOR, 61st Sess., Supp. No. 49, (vol. I), U.N. Doc A/61/49, at 408, *reprinted in* 2007 Int'l. Hum. Rts. Rep. 582 *and* III Basic Documents, *supra* Prologue note 13, at III.K.5.

[12] *See supra* Ch. 3 notes 50–65 and accompanying text.

rights an explicit, integral part of its Vernacular Law system, with differences
or conflicts between them in their interpretation and application resolved in
ways that best promote the integrity, biodiversity, and overall health of Earth.
In addition, State Law and policy should encourage if not formally promote
such rights to the maximum extent possible, including the facilitative procedural right of everyone to participate in commons- and rights-based ecological
governance to the extent feasible. Put another way, people should have a right
of commoning – a human right to participate in the governance of resources
that are important to their basic needs and culture.

3. Control and Subsidiarity Principles

The scale of a commons matters, particularly when its (physical) resources
are rooted in a local geography. Unlike markets, in which corporate growth
and consolidation are seen as natural behaviors, commons have a tendency
to remain discrete and closely tethered to local and regional resources, land-
scapes, and cultural practices. One's identity and aspirations tend to be bound
up with one's proximity to and control of the shared resource (e.g., food,
water, or landmarks). Consolidating the governance of shared resources into
a single, centralized institutional entity can erode people's sense of personal
affiliation and commitment – the "social capital"[13] – that make for responsible
and discerning stewardship.

   Thus, commons governance by default should aspire to devolve to the lowest
possible level and adhere to the principle known as subsidiarity, as explained
in Chapters 5 and 6.[14] For many reasons, this has been true in customary commons practice, so much so that one may view the principle as another expression, here constitutive in character, of commons Vernacular Law. Besides
bolstering the internal robustness of a commons, local control and subsidiarity
have many economic benefits. They can lower the transport costs of trade
external to the region (and thus the ecological footprint), insulate localities
from the predations and volatility of global markets, and capture the positive
externalities of locally cooperating and trading enterprises, thereby enhancing regional resilience. The principle of "comparative advantage" proclaimed

---

[13] Although the term "social capital" is widely used by social scientists, it is profoundly misleading
about the inner logic and dynamics of social community. Intensive use of "social capital" does
not deplete it (as the term "capital" implies). Rather, it enlarges it. In social relationships, the
principle of "the more, the merrier" applies, as Professor Carol Rose puts it in her essay on "the
comedy of the commons." *See supra* Ch. 4 note 121, at 141. When we escape the economistic
lens, it is easier to see these self-reinforcing social dynamics of commons.

[14] *See* in particular text accompanying and following Ch. 5 note 108, *supra*.

by economist David Ricardo is logical only if one ignores the ecological and social externalities that are routinely generated by large-scale and global market transactions. When actual nonmarket costs are re-integrated into the analysis, and the nonmarket human satisfactions of localism are counted as benefits, the "commons advantage" becomes more evident, if not compelling.

4. *Money and Principles of Shared Assets*

A factor that often is crucial in the success of a commons is the ability of commoners to limit or ban the monetization of shared assets. Are the fish, timber, or crops produced by a commons alienable for sale in the Market and, if so, on what terms? If people can opt out of their commons obligations by buying their way out, or by selling community assets at the expense of the community, it begins to erode the community by casting others as "suckers." Relationships of trust and reciprocity will flourish best – and make a commons more likely to succeed – when money does not compromise the integrity of relationships and community.

This is not to say that the resources of commons can never be monetized, just that any engagements with markets must be strictly controlled to preserve the sense of fairness that is critical to a commons's social and political cohesion.[15] In traditional commons, commoners have the right to use a shared resource for subsistence or household purposes, but not for commercial, profit-making purposes. Where commercial gain is permitted, it is generally in ways that are carefully stipulated and for renewable units of a resource, not for exploitation of the capital asset itself. Furthermore, the ethic of commons generally seeks to prevent whatever money making that does occur from poisoning community relationships.

The basic point is that commoners should have collective control over the surplus value that they create collectively. This is yet another principle learned from commons Vernacular Law and therefore to be incorporated into commons- and rights-based ecological governance. Internal relations should

---

[15] For example, free software communities allow programs developed through software commons – and any ancillary services such as consulting – to be sold in the Market, but since the program code is still available at no cost and with no restrictions, community relationships remain more or less intact. For more on the problems and benefits of paying developers in volunteer free and open-source projects, *see* Benjamin Mako Hill, *Financing Volunteer Free Software Projects*, Advogato (June 10, 2005), available at http://www.advogato.org/article/844.html (accessed Apr. 3, 2012). Similarly, in ecological commons, care must be taken to regulate how the fruits of the commons may be sold in the market lest some participants in the commons over-exploit the resource for personal gain, a form of free-riding that lessens the shared commitment to commoning.

not be cash-driven or market-mediated (except with explicit consent of commoners and clear rules for personal use and alienability). Such oversight of the marketization of common resources helps assure that a richer palette of human motivation and community commitment can flourish and that beggar-thy-neighbor individualism and profit seeking do not drive out cooperative impulses. No one wants to be a sucker.

5. Principles Concerning the Just Allocation of Property Rights

Related to the operational rules for handling money in a commons is the proper, just allocation of property rights. Although we are accustomed to thinking of property rights as unitary bundles of rights that authorize absolute individual dominion over a given resource, property rights have always been subject to conditions mandated by the State and communities. Nonetheless, tenacious Western mythologies about private property rights tend to blind us to the reality that property can be collectively owned and apply to indivisible collective resources, too. Indeed, collective property regimes are well known and evident in most if not all legal systems worldwide. They also can be divided into highly specific parcels of access and use rights, also widely sanctioned in law. An obvious but often-overlooked point, however, is this: property rights are not self-evident and do not inhere in the resource itself. They reflect social and political priorities that may or may not be fair, functional, or ecologically appropriate.[16] Natural resources have a life of their own apart from the property regimes that may be superimposed on them; their natural dynamics are independent and severable from the legal regimes that may be used to manage them.

In other words, the structure of collective property rights is important not only in assuring internal fairness within a commons, but also in structuring, morally and legally, the ways in which people use – and therefore protect – a natural resource. Choosing the most appropriate configuration of property rights for a given ecological resource helps assure its sustainability.

How, then should property rights be structured for shared resources? In the following figure, geographer Wolfgang Hoeschele offers a decision-tree chart for choosing property rights regimes that will maximize fairness and minimize the scarcity of a natural resource.[17] The chart reflects certain

---

[16] *See* Silke Helfrich, *Commons Don't Simply Exist – They Are Created*, in *The Wealth of the Commons, supra* Ch. 5 note 10, at 61.

[17] HOESCHELE, *supra* Ch. 6 note 52. A discussion of the chart is found at pages 150–65 of Hoeschele's book. The chart is available also at http://p2pfoundation.net/Choosing_the_Right_Form_of_Common_Property (accessed Aug. 4, 2011). Hoeschele also offers an excellent account of how markets artificially create scarcity in their business models as a necessary step in commoditizing resources.

commons-friendly criteria in determining what particular property rights regimes and institutional structures should govern different classes of ecological resources. Nonrenewable, rivalrous resources such as oil and minerals, for example, are best managed through "Common or state property with equitable revenue sharing," Hoeschele argues, because such resources produce large rents and have regional economic impact.

A commons approach to property rights and institutional control is a structural commitment to managing resources in ways that minimize social inequities and ecological harm. A corporation or industry has every incentive to monopolize ownership and control to the detriment of everyone else; they are in the business of creating choke points (proprietary products, copyright and patent restrictions, anticompetitive advantages, branding dominance, etc.) to create artificial scarcity and discourage competition. Why, then, should business enterprises, which do not create the minerals and other resources of nature, enjoy privileged, free, or tax-subsidized access to the gifts of nature and private equity stakes in them? If all human beings have a moral entitlement to Earth's natural wealth, as even political philosopher John Locke acknowledged, private exploiters of common wealth should pay a fair rent to use it.

Unfortunately, the State has a long history of giving politically connected industries privileged access to our common assets, without fair payment of rents. An important legal strategy for regenerating commons generally – and green governance in particular – is to establish new institutional regimes that charge fair market rates for the use of Earth's natural wealth and resources, where appropriate and ecologically sustainable. It is a principled cousin of the legal "polluter pays" principle; rents should be charged for everything from depletable minerals, the catch from renewable fisheries and forests, and the dumping of pollution into unowned spaces such as the oceans and atmosphere. Commons activist Peter Barnes has argued, for example, that polluters should have to pay rent for the right to emit pollutants into the atmosphere. The waste-absorption capacities are finite; and, in any case, who owns the sky? We all do.[18]

6. *Property Rights Use Principles*

Closely related to principles concerning the just allocation of property rights are principles concerning the proper use of property rights. One such principle, present in commons Vernacular Law but well known in State Law systems as well, is the precautionary principle mentioned earlier in this chapter. Another principle accepted by both systems is the polluter-pays principle.

---

[18] *See* BARNES, *supra* Ch. 1 note 6.

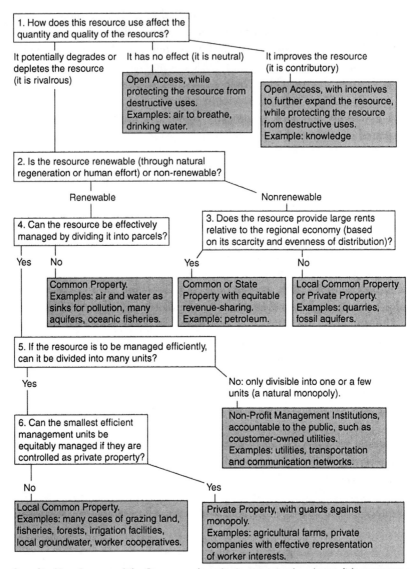

1. How does this resource use affect the quantity and quality of the resourcs?

It potentially degrades or depletes the resource (it is rivalrous)

It has no effect (it is neutral)

Open Access, while protecting the resource from destructive uses. Examples: air to breathe, drinking water.

It improves the resource (it is contributory)

Open Access, with incentives to further expand the resource, while protecting the resource from destructive uses. Example: knowledge

2. Is the resource renewable (through natural regeneration or human effort) or non-renewable?

Renewable

Nonrenewable

4. Can the resource be effectively managed by dividing it into parcels?

Yes   No

Common Property. Examples: air and water as sinks for pollution, many aquifers, oceanic fisheries.

3. Does the resource provide large rents relative to the regional economy (based on its scarcity and evenness of distribution)?

Yes

No

Common or State Property with equitable revenue-sharing. Example: petroleum.

Local Common Property or Private Property. Examples: quarries, fossil aquifers.

5. If the resource is to be managed efficiently, can it be divided into many units?

Yes

No: only divisible into one or a few units (a natural monopoly).

Non-Profit Management Institutions, accountable to the public, such as coustomer-owned utilities. Examples: utilities, transportation and communication networks.

6. Can the smallest efficient management units be equitably managed if they are controlled as private property?

No

Yes

Local Common Property. Examples: many cases of grazing land, fisheries, forests, irrigation facilities, local groundwater, worker cooperatives.

Private Property, with guards against monopoly. Examples: agricultural farms, private companies with effective representation of worker interests.

Scarcity, Abundance, and the Commons: In order to promote abundance, it is necessary to adapt property rights to each type of resource use. In most cases, this involves some kind of common property.
For more details, see Wolfgang Hoeschele, 2010, *The Economics of Abundance,* **Gower Publ.**

The first of these principles pays heed to the legal (and moral) proposition that if a proposed action risks harm to the public or the environment, the burden of proof, absent a scientific consensus that it is harmful, falls on those who pursue the action. The polluter-pays principle requires as a matter of law (and morality) that the costs of pollution or other environmental degradation must be borne by the risk taker or others who cause it. Each principle is premised on the notion that property rights, like most rights, are not absolute and that their exercise must conform to the wider social-order standards of environmental well-being. Each in its own way seeks to internalize the environmental externalities of economic activity, so that the price of goods and services reflects the true cost of production and that, in each case, financial compensation alone is increasingly understood not to be the full extent of liability for the harm caused.

Applying these principles in commons ecological practice tends to be less complicated because that is a key goal of commons-based ecological stewardship in the first place: to internalize externalities and anticipate long-term problems. Still, these issues can and do arise even in commons settings. For example, a fishery commons may grant the right to individual commoners to reap private commercial gains from their catch. When there are large-scale CPRs, State and Market actors (individuals and groups) may be involved, which further complicates the ability of a commons to apply the polluter-payers principle. This is one area in which the authority and interests of the State, Market, and Commons sectors must be renegotiated so that the general proclivities of commons can be used to better align property rights with ecological protection.

7. *Conflict Resolution Principles*

Given the cooperative nature of commons, conflicts and disputes within commons- and rights-based ecological governance systems are not best settled by adversarial litigation or other such decision-making processes. They should be settled, instead, to the maximum extent feasible, through self-organized dispute resolution systems, using techniques and procedures that favor dialogue, mutual respect, and restorative outcomes among the disagreeing parties.

B. MACRO-PRINCIPLES AND POLICIES TO GUIDE THE STATE/MARKET IN SUPPORTING THE COMMONS SECTOR

Historically, the governance of a traditional commons has had little to do with the State/Market except for the latter conceding its existence. But often even that is not forthcoming because the State/Market is predisposed to enclose commons to monetize its resources and consolidate State/Market power.[19] Traditional commons therefore remain vulnerable and in need of affirmative protection by State Law and public policy.

For larger-scale CPRs – national, regional, and global – the State must play a more active role in establishing and overseeing commons. The State may have an indispensable role to play in instances where a resource cannot be easily divided into parcels (the atmosphere as a waste sink, oceanic fisheries) or where the resource generates large rents relative to the regional economy (e.g., petroleum), as Hoeschele noted. In such cases, it makes sense for the State to intervene and devise appropriate management systems. *State trustee commons*, as we call them, typically manage, among other things, hard and soft minerals, timber, and other natural resources on public lands and in national parks, wilderness areas, rivers, lakes, and other bodies of water; State-sponsored research; and civil infrastructure. In such instances, the State claims to act as a trustee on behalf of commoners.

When a commons is administered by the State as trustee for the citizenry, a quite different matrix of power, politics, and management arises than is present in traditional commons. There is a fundamental structural tension between commoners and the State/Market in the administration of collective assets because the State has strong economic incentives to forge deep political alliances with the Market. As a result, the State/Market often chooses to advance its matrix of interests (privatization, commoditization, globalization) despite the adverse consequences for commoners. Any successful regime of Commons Law must therefore recognize this reality and take aggressive action to ensure that the State/Market does not betray its trust obligations, particularly by colluding with market players in acts of enclosure.

The legal details for assuring the integrity of State trustee commons will naturally vary from one resource domain to another. By way of general orientation, however, we offer the following eight macro-principles and policies – or tenets – to guide State policy relative to the commons- and rights-based ecological governance. These principles reflect fragments of Vernacular and State Law policy and practice that come down to us from many sources. They constitute, like Ostrom's findings, important guideposts for defining and developing

---

[19] The international "land grab" of arable lands in Africa, Asia, and Latin America are a prime example of this phenomenon. *See, e.g.*, Liz Alden Wiley & Jeffrey Hatcher, *Rights to Resources in Crisis: Reviewing the Fate of Customary Tenure in Africa* (2012), available at http://www.rightsandresources.org/publication_ details.php?publicationID=4699 (accessed Apr. 3, 2012).

a law of the ecological commons.[20] Although we do not presume them to be exhaustive, these macro-principles and policies do suggest a normative framework that can inform appropriate State policies to support all ecological commons and, indeed, the entire Commons Sector.

1. *Commons- and Rights-based Ecological Governance as a Practical Alternative*

   Commons- and rights-based ecological governance, or green governance, is a system for using and protecting all the creations of nature and related societal institutions that we inherit jointly and freely and hold in trust for future generations. These creations must be managed democratically, by the consent of the governed, in keeping with human rights principles grounded in respect for nature as well as for human beings. One such right is the right to participate in the governance of wealth and resources important to people's basic needs and culture. It is a system of governance by which communities of varying sizes and kind assert their commitments to manage shared resources, allocate them fairly, and preserve them unimpaired for present and future generations. Where appropriate or needed, as determined by the commoners, the State may act as a trustee for them to protect and maintain their shared resources.

2. *The Earth Belongs to All*

   The services and infrastructure of Earth are necessary for present and future humans and other beings to be fully biological and social creatures, and thus must be understood as the common heritage of all humankind, belonging to all natural beings present and future. They are to be respected as such and therefore desirably governed as an ecological commons through State trustees, traditional commons, or acceptable hybrids. Optimally, to protect, conserve, and restore (where necessary) the integrity, health, and sustainability of Earth and its vital ecological balances, cycles, and processes, the State should facilitate and safeguard commons- and rights-based governance of Earth's ecological resources. In these critical respects, the State should strive to work as a generous partner, not a stern overlord, of the Commons.

3. *State Duty to Prevent Enclosures of Commons Resources*

   The State has an affirmative duty to prevent enclosures of commons

---

[20] Many of these principles and policies were derived from a set of recommended "tenets" authored by Carolyn Raffensperger, Burns H. Weston & David Bollier in *Climate Legacy Initiative, Recommendation No. 1 ("Define and Develop a Law of the Commons for Present and Future Generations")*, in Weston & Bach, *supra* Prologue note 12, at 63–4.

and commons resources because commons serve the needs of basic provisioning, social equity, and ecological protection in ways the State and Market do not or cannot. To this end, it should formally recognize commons and commons resources and, through its State Law, public policy, and resources (budget, expertise, convening powers), enable and facilitate responsible commons management. These duties apply especially to subsistence and indigenous commons that have long preceded States and are vital to people's cultural identities.

4. *State Trustee Commons*
   Due to the size, geographic scope, or market value of CPRs, the State is sometimes needed to serve as a trustee of certain resources belonging to commoners (the public or a defined community) and to future generations (including children alive today). To this end, the State, under State Law, must create transparent, accountable management systems to ensure that commons and/or commons resources entrusted to it are adequately protected and that beneficial interests are well served. Commoners' rights should not be alienated or diminished except for the purpose of protecting the commons for future generations.

5. *State Chartering of Commons*
   As warranted, governments may charter parties to manage a commons as deputized guardians or fiduciaries obligated to uphold the fundamental governing principles of the Commons. This tenet is especially compelling when stewardship by identifiable commoners can be shown to serve the general public.

6. *Precautionary and Polluter-Pays Principles*
   These two widely recognized environmental law principles (explicated in Section A (6)) must apply with special emphasis to the State and Market because both have a structural aversion to internalizing the ecological costs of their activities. The State must strive to prevent private property owners and commercial activity from externalizing risk, damage, and costs onto the natural environment (in general) and the Commons (in particular). This obligation stems from the State's general duty to protect, conserve, and restore (where necessary) the integrity, health, and sustainability of our Earth and its duty, in particular, to facilitate and safeguard green governance of Earth's ecological resources.

7. *Private Property and Commons*
   All systems of private property must affirmatively serve the common good, particularly ecological and human well-being. As warranted by circumstances, therefore, legal limitations on private property may be

asserted to ensure the long-term viability of ecological systems. These shifts of private privilege versus collective and ecological need may come through changes in property law, tort law, diverse environmental laws, and/or the power of eminent domain (the "taking" of private property for public use and subject to payment of just compensation). Ultimately, even private property and markets are subject to the exigencies of the common good.

8. ***The Human Right to Establish and Maintain Ecological Commons Designed for Environmental and Social Well-Being***
   Given the recurrent, demonstrated failures of the State and Market to protect the Commons, commoners have the fundamental human right, sanctioned by national and international law, to establish and maintain commons to protect their vital ecosystem resources. The State must facilitate and safeguard this right as part of its larger mission to assure ecological sustainability, nourish communities, and enhance human life and dignity.

––––––––

The seven core legal (and moral) principles of internal commons governance described in Section A of this chapter, and the immediately foregoing eight legal (and moral) macro-principles and policies conditioning State practice relative to the Commons, together represent a synthesis of key legal and normative principles for commons- and rights-based ecological governance. (For an indication of how this synthesis could serve to generate political and legal mobilization in support of such green governance worldwide, see *A Universal Covenant Affirming the Human Right to Commons- and Rights-based Governance of Earth's Natural Wealth and Resources* in the Appendix to this volume).

To be sure, this proposed law of the ecological commons is likely to be operationalized in different ways in different societies. Even so, this law nonetheless insists on the prioritization in all ecological commons of environmental sustainability, human rights, personal participation and responsibility, transparency and accountability, social equity, and intergenerational benefit.

Fortunately, the liberal State offers a serviceable (if limited) framework for pursuing many types of commons-based solutions. But building within this framework requires that we reconceptualize the neoliberal State/Market as a "triarchy" – the *State/Market/Commons* – that realigns authority and provisioning in new ways.[21] The State maintains its commitments to representative

––––––––

[21] The term "triarchy" is Michel Bauwens', who expounds on the topic at the P2P Foundation blog, P2P Found., available at http://blog.p2pfoundation.net/the-new-triarchy-the-

governance and management of public property just as private enterprises in the Market sector continue to own capital to produce saleable goods and services. The State, however, must shift its focus to become a "Partner State,"[22] assisting not just the Market sector but also the Commons Sector, and working to ensure its health and continuing well-being and thereby the health and well-being of nature and society.

A Partner State would assume, among other things, an active obligation to promote peer governance in multiple societal contexts (e.g., in ecosystems, cyberspace, education, local communities). As Michel Bauwens, founder of the Foundation for Peer to Peer Alternatives, explains:

> Rather than seeing itself as sovereign master, the State must be seen as embedded in relationships, and as in need of respecting these multiple relationships. This is probably best translated by the concept of multistakeholdership. We can probably expect that the nation-state, along with the newly emerging sub- and supraregional structures,[sic] will continue to exist, but that their policies will be set through a dialogue with stakeholders. The key will be to disembed the state from its primary reliance on the private sector, and to make it beholden to civil society, i.e. the Commons, so that it can act as a center of arbitrage. Despite the recent greater subsumption of the state to private interests (in the neoliberal era) – which of course has never been total since the balance of forces is not based on a complete defeat of the citizenship – many supraregional institutes, and in particular non-state governance institutions such as the standards bodies, but also policy-making at the U.N., already exhibit many features of multistakeholdership.[23]

Of course, this vision will require us to revise some deeply held prejudices about the proper role of the State relative to the economy and the environment.

Free-market doctrine holds that the State should generally refrain from intervening in markets. But in actual practice, as we know well, the State is extensively involved in shaping and subsidizing markets, and especially in helping or acquiescing in companies' enclosures of commons.[24] The State provides politically important industries with free and discounted access to public resources, regulatory privileges, research subsidies, tax breaks, special legal immunities and protections, and much more, based on the assumption

---

commons-enterprise-the-State/2010/08/25 (accessed Aug. 4, 2011). Peter Barnes has also been an early expositor of the Commons Sector, especially in his *Capitalism 3.0: A Guide to Reclaiming the Commons* (2006).

[22] The term "Partner State" is the creation of Michel Bauwens, *supra* note 21 and *infra* note 23.

[23] Michel Bauwens, *Peer Governance as a Third Mode of Governance*, P2P Found. (June 9, 2010), available at http://blog.p2pfoundation.net/peer-governance-as-a-third-mode-of-governance/2010/06/09 (accessed Aug. 5, 2011).

[24] *See, e.g.*, Neil Fligstein, *The Architecture of Markets: An Economic Sociology of Twenty-First Century Capitalist Societies* (2001).

that greater market activity will enhance the common good. This is a dubious proposition, of course, when so much of market growth is systemically diminishing the value of nonmonetized common wealth such as oceans, the atmosphere, biodiversity, and other ecosystem services, not to mention levels of health, education, employment, and other indicia of human welfare. Indeed, as we document in Chapters 2 and 3, the State allied with the Market is actually in the business of abridging or shrinking the right to a clean and healthy environment.

The first imperative for the State must be, therefore, to stop colluding with industry in giving away the public's common wealth in its many forms[25] and enter into a new Partner State social contract with civil society, reconstituted as commoners. The first principle for the Partner State must be to stop enclosures of commons, and its second principle must be to serve as a conscientious trustee of collective wealth.

Beyond these basic injunctions, the Partner State has many constructive roles to play in the development of a robust Commons Sector.[26] It can and must adopt legal principles that explicitly protect common assets and commoning,[27] and it can and must provide legal authorization for establishing new types of commons institutions (without directly managing them, to the extent possible). Centuries ago, the State came up with the innovative idea of chartering corporations as collective enterprises to serve public purposes. Today, using the same rationale of advancing the public good, the State can and should empower the establishment of commons-based institutions: a different sort of institutional vehicle for advancing the public good, environmentally and otherwise.

Of course, supporting the Commons Sector would represent a significant shift in focus and process for the bureaucratic State, which is accustomed to issuing regulations and delivering program-based services to passive citizen-consumers (especially in the case of market failures). Despite its manifest problems and attempts to eradicate it or significantly improve its performance, the bureaucratic State remains entrenched the world over.

It may be countered that bureaucracy, despite its limited competence, is simply an inexorable reality of a large, complex, technological Market society. Yet in a sense that is precisely the point: the planetary ecosystem and human

---

[25] *See, e.g.,* Bollier, *supra* Prologue note 3; Raj Patel, *The Value of Nothing: How to Reshape Market Society and Redefine Democracy* (2010); James Ridgeway, *It's All for Sale: The Control of Global Resources* (2004); Jennifer Washburn, *University Inc.: The Corporate Corruption of Higher Education* (2005).

[26] Bauwens, *supra* note 21.

[27] To some commoners, "common assets" is an oxymoron because it implies a propertization of resources that is alien to the commons. To the extent that one accepts the idea of "state-based commons," however, or commons that have regulated intercourse with markets, "common assets" is a useful term.

rights can no longer survive government bureaucracy and conventional politics as the means to control Market excesses. The State/Market's propensity to overexploit resources and commoditize everything can no longer be sustained. It is destroying the Earth's natural systems and shattering human communities.

Is there a serious alternative? We believe there is, and that the Commons is part of it. A hint of a possible direction can be seen in the so-called Blue Labour movement in the United Kingdom, which, dissenting from its liberal allies, wants changes in how government attempts to help people meet their needs.[28] Blue Labour calls for "a new politics of reciprocity, mutuality and solidarity" inspired by economist Karl Polanyi and opposition to neoliberalism and globalization. It actually makes an ontological critique of the State/Market that the Commons is well equipped to address. Writes Labour Party activist Jon Wilson:

> The free market and the centralized, statistically obsessed State try to subordinate the local peculiarities of life to universal values, whether those values are established by the price mechanism or [even] a language of universal rights. In reality our lives only make sense within concrete contexts and relationships. If the market or centralized State annihilate those local contexts, life literally loses its meaning... The problem with the liberal idea of the identical, relation-less self-determining individual is not that it is bad (although it is that) but that it is a false description of the way human beings act.[29]

Many liberal internationalists scoff at the aspirations of those who seek stronger autonomy, tradition, and meaning through localism; to them, it smacks of conservative parochialism and a regression to tribalism over universal rights. But it is precisely the failure of the liberal State and international bodies to fulfill their stated commitments to universal human (and ecological) rights that has engendered cynicism about State governance, as Wilson's analysis implies. What confidence can be put in a high-minded commitment to principles that in reality are only selectively and irregularly applied – empty commitments that are embraced or disregarded as it suits the passing political convenience and budgetary priorities?

The deeper skepticism, in any case, is whether a governance system espousing universal rights is capable of making good on those rights in people's particular local contexts. Does the governance system inspire deep allegiance and meaning? Does it meet people's everyday needs? "Ideologies, however appealing, cannot shape the whole structure of perceptions and conduct unless

---

[28]   *See Blue Labour*, Wikipedia, available at https://secure.wikimedia.org/wikipedia/en/wiki/Blue_ Labour (accessed Aug. 5, 2011).

[29]   Jon Wilson, *Blue Labour Realism*, opendemocracy.net (June 14, 2011), available at http://www. opendemocracy.net/our kingdom/jon-wilson/blue-labour-realism (accessed Aug. 5, 2011).

they are embedded in daily experiences that confirm them," the late historian Christopher Lasch once wrote. The core problem may be that liberal universalism – yoked as it has been to the State/Market and abstractly expressed – is not generally perceived as a personal or local phenomenon. This may help explain why it often has trouble securing the allegiance of "the street," or at least of religious fundamentalists and racial and ethnic bigots who see political opportunity in pitting "the local" against larger principles of law and justice.

One of the most important challenges facing global governance in the future, we believe, is to devise better ways to integrate the language of universal rights with local, lived experience so that the former is more than an abstraction mouthed by remote politicians, judges, and lawyers. State support for the Commons is an attractive solution because it provides a realistic way to link universal legal principles with localized, lived experience. Indeed, a Commons Sector could be the basis for a political culture dedicated to a new understanding of universal human and ecological rights.

From this perspective, we also believe the Partner State could work with a fledgling Commons Sector to develop a new constellation of self-organized, bottom-up governance systems that can evolve their own locally appropriate expertise, rules, and relationship-driven solutions. The particulars would, of course, vary from one resource domain to another, from one locality or region to another, and from one State system to another. At bottom, however, the State would assume a different role, guided by the principles enumerated earlier in this chapter. Instead of administering universal programs with little regard for local context or the personal participation of citizens (the liberal approach), or abandoning a government role altogether because it amounts to "paternalism" and the "nanny-state" (the conservative approach), the State would adopt policy structures that invite and support commons-based approaches that enable new forms of participation, responsibility, and self-organized governance. The State would establish, for example, basic governance protocols – legal and technical – that authorize and assist commoners in coming up with management solutions that work best for them and a given resource. The principles of polycentrism and subsidiarity would help assure that the most appropriate tiers of government would take on differential roles but would have the end result that commoners proximate to the resource or problem would have the greatest discretion in fashioning management schemes.[30]

---

[30] A likely problem, at least initially, would be the inclination of national governments to displace their obligations onto lower levels of government without providing adequate legal authority or support, all the while cloaking such action in high-minded reformist rhetoric. Such subterfuges would have to be challenged.

Some commons can and will thrive if there is minimal State oversight and they are left essentially alone to do what they do best (though with clear legal authorization from the State and basic performance parameters). No experts or politicians were necessary to instruct indigenous peoples how to devise traditional commons in rural Asia, for example, or farmers to launch Community-Supported Agriculture projects, or programmers to design GNU Linux and other breakthrough free/open-source software programs. Many commons self-organize without much or any government supervision. Such commons niches could become much more expansive and robust, however, if they enjoyed a more formal rapprochement or *modus vivendi* with the State. It is important that the State recognize the value proposition of the Commons as a governance paradigm and be willing to provide adequate legal recognition and resource support, without overbearing supervision.

A vivid historical model for Partner State support of the Commons can be seen in the role played by the Pentagon's DARPA (Defense Advanced Research Projects Agency) in creating the Internet – for example, developing a set of minimalist technical protocols known as TCP/IP[31] which, along with supportive regulation, enabled extremely diverse computer networks to connect with each other on one single system, the Internet. The TCP/IP protocols amount to a governance architecture, a set of shared rules that enable collective action. The beauty of the architecture is that each node of the network is free to self-implement and innovate within the overarching framework of minimalist, collective standards.

This might be restated as follows: the distributed creativity of commoners is empowered through minimalist design principles at the center;[32] and the model might be called "State governance in the service of commons formation and stewardship." This model contrasts sharply with conventional public

---

[31] TCP/IP stands for "Transmission Control Protocol/Internet Protocol." *See Internet Protocol Suite*, Wikipedia, available at https://secure.wikimedia.org/wikipedia/en/wiki/Internet_Protocol_Suite (accessed Aug. 5, 2011). Besides TCP/IP, there were important regulatory protocols that facilitated the Internet's growth, such as telecommunications regulations. *See Janet Abbate, Inventing the Internet* (2000).

[32] This same design concept was also responsible for the World Wide Web. The hypertext transfer protocol (HTTP) invented by Tim Berners-Lee established a shared governance protocol for Web communication. This in turn unleashed an explosion of self-organized digital commons (as well as business models "built atop" this commons-based technical and social infrastructure). Critically, the "policy protocols" were as simple and limited as possible. To be sure, supplementary laws have been needed for privacy, security, and so forth, but the basic design rules have enabled countless self-regulating commons to arise on a new platform, the Web.

administration, which tends to centralize authority, expertise, and decision-making at the expense of local control and capacity.

Commons scholar James B. Quilligan notes that public administration generally seeks "the greatest good for the most people" – a worthy ambition, to be sure. Too often, however, it has resulted in lowest-common-denominator, one-size-fits-all systems that may not serve anyone well. It focuses on abstract, universal clients who embody the statistical mean and has few ways to host participatory co-production and co-management to serve needs defined by the clients themselves. Predictably, conventional top-down administration is usually more mindful of its own institutional self-interests (reputation, political support, revenues, etc.) than the on-the-ground needs of the people or ecosystems being served. Ivan Illich spent much of his life documenting dehumanizing and ineffective results when societal problems are defined by institutional experts as "needs" that require professional interventions.[33] People are objectified and dispossessed, and their human dignity and agency diminished.

The Partner State would strive to advance a different approach. It would seek to enable people to have real – not just nominal – opportunities for participation, interaction, and responsibility to craft solutions appropriate to their self-defined needs. In supporting commons, the Partner State would likely enable decision-making that takes account of people's actual needs and their neighborhoods, local economies, historical traditions, and natural landscape and climate.[34] Writes Quilligan: "[W]hen consumers are co-producers of the goods and services they receive and organize, their practical and applied knowledge are embodied directly in their commoning. As co-producers, the motivations, knowledge, and skills of resource users become part of the production praxis, leading to new ways of interacting and coordinating social and economic life."[35]

---

[33] *See* Ivan Illich, *Deschooling Society* (1971); Ivan Illich, *Tools for Conviviality* (1973); Ivan Illich, *Medical Nemesis* (1982).

[34] Trent Schroyer puts it well: "In so far as the actual forms of material provisioning vary, so the substantive rationality of specific orders of life differ. The ideal and material are always unified in so far as people meet their needs within a specific environmental context and to which they are oriented by their culturally acquired competences and stocks of knowledge, and are part of a human group that has a shared concept of the good life. Meeting their substantively defined 'needs' requires solutions of specific technical problems of means, not problems defined exclusively in terms of price or the maximizing of economic goals. . . . Application of formal economizing principles to non-market oriented life orders is economistic in that it produces knowledge that is coercive to indigenous practices in so far as it disvalues and displaces social solidarities and embedded knowledge." Trent Schroyer, *supra* Ch. 4 note 101, at 33–4.

[35] James B. Quilligan, Social Charters: Praxis of the Commons (unpublished essay) (on file with authors).

Additionally, the Partner State could feasibly advance "biophilic design" or "ecological design," a holistic, place-based approach in technology, production, and usage that emulates natural processes.[36] Such approaches are not incompatible with market activity, but they do imply a rejection of centralized provisioning of technology and infrastructure, which tend to be relatively more brittle, costly, and unreliable. Industrialized models of provisioning seek to consolidate and streamline production and distribution, all in the name of efficiency, whereas ecological commons with biophilic design seek to fortify natural diversity and local stability. What neoliberal economics regards as inefficient and redundant in ecological commons, commoners regard as essential to resilience, robustness, and durability.

To the outdated twentieth-century mind schooled in traditional, top-down bureaucratic control, decentralized commons are counterintuitive at best and incomprehensible at worst. Commons do not conform to principles of mechanistic, "rational" order and do not exhibit linear causality. They are subject to too many incalculable and qualitative variables in ways that blithely transgress established political boundaries (local, national, regional, global). Yet, successful commons are actually more stable, resilient, and self-healing than are command-and-control systems precisely because they are nested within a dynamic, living ecosystem of players. They enjoy an invisible means of support whose subtleties and time horizons are not evident to the positivist, instrumentalist mind. Ecological commons are also more stable because they are rooted in familiar local circumstances, and therefore are more insulated from the vagaries and manipulations of global markets, whose chief motive is not long-term stewardship, but monetization of the local resource. The local embeddedness of commoners gives them a sophisticated knowledge of native resources and context that often is invisible to scientists, companies, and public agencies accustomed to thinking in abstract, universal terms.

The Partner State has a keen incentive to support Commons governance. With many more richly nuanced, self-correcting feedback loops than markets, commons are more capable of rapid, self-healing action. As we note in Chapter 1, markets overrely on price as an indicator of value and ignore externalities as much as possible (lest the very articulation of the externality is used to force internalization of costs to the detriment of a firm's bottom line).

---

[36] *See, e.g.,* Janine M. Benyus, *Biomimicry: Innovation Inspired by Nature* (2002); John H. Clippinger, *The Biology of Business: Decoding the Natural Laws of Enterprise* (1999); Ian McHarg, *Design with Nature* (1969); Donella H. Meadows, *Thinking in Systems: A Primer* (2008); David Orr, *The Nature of Design: Ecology, Culture, and Human Intention* (2004); Nikos A. Salingaros, *Twelve Lectures on Architecture: Algorithmic Sustainable Design* (2010); Sim van der Ryn & Stuart Cowan, *Ecological Design* (2007).

Because they tend to be committed to a fuller spectrum of (nonmonetized) value and because many are local, commons are more willing and able, by contrast, to internalize costs that markets typically try to displace onto nature and future generations. Their cultural commitments are able to guide and stabilize resource management; and their rich histories, traditions, and ethical norms are valuable sources of moral guidance, wisdom, and flexibility, all on a decentralized scale. They also tend to perform invaluable social functions such as subsistence support, reductions in inequality, and greater social cohesion.

The social/moral gyroscope of traditional commons is most evident among indigenous peoples, who tightly integrate governance, culture, and ecosystem needs. Such governance is able to express and enforce an ethic of "enough," unlike the market ethic which presumes (and celebrates) limitless appetites that are never satiated – the "hungry ghost" phenomenon.[37] The Partner State may see the technocratic virtues of relying on commons, but it may not appreciate that its support of commons could also help address, in piece-meal, project-driven ways, some of the deeper pathologies of market culture and modernity. Unlike legislatures and bureaucracies, for example, properly constituted commons are more capable of declaring certain resources to be off-limits to the market or usable only under controlled, stipulated terms. Instead of making social reconstruction and local self-determination dependent on market growth (no growth, no social well-being), the Commons integrates these social goals into the very process of commoning. Examples include community forests, regional water supplies, local food systems, and coastal fisheries. The establishment of commons does not eliminate political maneuvering, competition, and antisocial behaviors, but it does create institutional and social frameworks that can contain such energies and channel them in more constructive ways than, say, laissez-faire markets or State/Market alliances.

In a world with a flourishing Commons Sector, the State's role changes. As Michel Bauwens puts it:

> On the one hand, market competition will be balanced by co-operation, the invisible hand will be combined with a visible handshake. On the other hand, the state is no longer the sovereign authority. It becomes just one participant among others in the pluralistic guidance system and contributes

---

[37] Christopher Alexander's classic work on "pattern languages" in architecture is a contemporary example of how profound forms of order – aesthetic, spiritual, cultural, functional – have manifested themselves over time through cooperative experimentation and reflection. *See* Christopher Alexander, Sara Ishikawa & Murray Silverstein, *A Pattern Language: Towns, Buildings, Construction* (1997). The essential point is that these other values must be integrated into the governance and design of a system as a way to surmount the commodity fetishism and market values that otherwise prevail.

its own distinctive resources to the negotiation process. As the range of networks, partnerships, and other models of economic and political governance expands, official apparatuses remain at best first among equals. The state's involvement would become less hierarchical, less centralized, and less directive in character. The exchange of information and moral suasion become key sources of legitimation and the state's influence depends as much on its role as a prime source and mediator of collective intelligence as on its command over economic resources or legitimate coercion.[38]

Moving from a world dominated by the State/Market to one of the Partner State and peer governance entails considerable transformation, of course – and not just in legal systems. Given the immense breadth and depth of today's environmental crisis, the Partner State would have to share elements of its traditional sovereignty with both established and new commons-based institutions; and, for the same reason, it would have to collaborate in the invention of new policy structures (normative, institutional, and procedural) that could work effectively with commons of large scale – national, regional, and global – as well as those of relatively small scale. We turn now to this challenge: imagining appropriate policy structures to support the workings of large-scale commons.

C. THE SPECIAL CHALLENGE OF LARGE-SCALE ECOLOGICAL COMMONS

In the traditional commons studied by scholars, the smaller the community and its base of resources, the more tractable the challenges of governance. This appears to be an anthropological reality. Evolutionary scientists invoke "Dunbar's number" (named after British anthropologist Robin Dunbar) as a crude measure of the maximum size of functional social groupings. Based on the processing capacity of the brain's neocortex, anthropologists consider 150 persons (or between 100 and 230 persons, depending on how one defines a community) to be the "theoretical cognitive limit to the number of people with whom one can maintain stable social relationships."[39] As Wikipedia summarizes the idea, "[t]hese are relationships in which an individual knows who each person is, and how each person relates to every other person. Proponents

---

[38] Michel Bauwens, *Peer Governance as a Third Mode of Governance*, P2P Found. (June 9, 2010), available at http://blog.p2pfoundation.net/peer-governance-as-a-third-mode-of-governance/2010/06/09 (accessed Aug. 5, 2011) (drawing upon peer governance scholar Bob Jessop).

[39] *See Dunbar's Number*, Wikipedia, available at https://en.wikipedia.org/wiki/Dunbar%27s_number (accessed Mar. 3, 2012).

assert that numbers larger than this generally require more restrictive rules and enforced norms to maintain a stable, cohesive group."[40]

If we accept the rough validity of Dunbar's number, a major challenge for commons-based management is how to devise structures that can enable governance systems for groups larger than 150 people while maintaining some measure of social commitment, participation, stability, and accountability. Specifically, we must imagine new ways to enable group cohesion, shared identity and purpose, the legitimacy of governance, participation, rule making, monitoring, enforcement, and other modes of group governance to function in larger contexts with more people. This must be done not only with respect to large-scale CPRs that are devoid of effective governance mechanisms and procedures altogether, but for existing commons whose governance is deficient. We must imagine new institutions of law, policy, and social practice (including software) that can help us replicate the principles of smaller commons in larger ecological settings. The Internet and its ability to do precisely this is perhaps the most significant fact of our time in this regard; it serves as a remarkable hosting infrastructure for scaling the size of social governance and the management of online resources.[41]

Unlike the Internet, however, the structures of national and international institutions and procedures do not readily lend themselves to conscientious hands-on management of large-scale CPRs, particularly when they traverse international political boundaries. Besides the familiar problems of bureaucracy in managing interstate CPRs, there are complicated jurisdictional and coordination problems for transboundary resources. Fisheries, forests, oceans, fresh water systems, genetic life forms and species, seeds, climate and atmosphere, not to mention the airwaves, Internet, and ethnobotanical knowledge, should arguably be treated as common goods; they are gifts of nature, the creations of social communities, or legacies from earlier generations. Yet, the State and Market generally are not prepared to recognize these resources as common goods. Not surprisingly, neither the private sector of property and commerce nor the public sector of government provisioning and regulation are capable of imagining and implementing suitable governance regimes.

The root problem is precisely the artificial, misleading dichotomies of public and private, government and market – dichotomies that have defined twentieth-century models of centralized scientific and bureaucratic governance. Such dualities shut down the conceptual space for commons-based

---

[40] *Id.*
[41] *See* Bollier, *supra* Ch. 1 note 17.

resource management that draws on people's shared commitments, collective practices, and social identities. It is now possible to see that these default paradigms have not succeeded in protecting against major environmental devastation and degradation since the first Earth Day some forty years ago. Besides being too rigid and remote from on-the-ground problems, these management systems are dangerously amenable to capture and corruption by the corporate sector and compliant politicians. Although governmental structures certainly have important environmental roles to play, we nonetheless must be wary of letting them set the agenda for achieving the types of change that are needed; we cannot afford to invest our hopes in more of the same.

This is particularly true for large-scale common goods, which governments have trouble recognizing because of their "pervasive commitment to free markets in driving global economic integration and sovereign reciprocity in making global decisions," as James Quilligan notes.[42] As a result, all sorts of large-scale and global CPRs are classified as either private or public goods. This classification dictates that they be treated either as raw inputs for market exploitation or as public resources to be managed by fiscally beleaguered and bureaucratic governments. In either case, the standard public/private categorization precludes serious consideration of managing the CPR as a commons, which could in fact provide responsible, equitable, and sustainable stewardship.

Governments and multilateral intergovernmental bodies such as the UN and the World Bank frequently talk about "global public goods," but the concept is really a deception, Quilligan notes, because it implies the existence of a global framework or process by which to provide public goods to the citizens of the world. The term "public goods" makes sense when used at the national level, where sovereign governments are nominally able to provide public goods to the citizens within their borders. At the international level, however, the logical extension of the notion of global public goods is essentially meaningless because there is no sovereign order with authority over global resources and no recognized world citizenry in the technical sense to whom such authority would minister. As Quilligan writes, "[n]ational governments simply do not have the interdependent power or legitimacy, nor are they designed, to protect, manage and distribute resources for the world's people as a whole."[43]

---

[42] James Quilligan, *Why Distinguish Common Goods from Public Goods?*, in *The Wealth of the Commons, supra* Ch. 5 note 10, at 73.

[43] *Id.* at 80.

The challenge, therefore, is to develop and facilitate the formation and governance of new sorts of international institutions and procedures (bilateral and multilateral) capable of managing large-scale CPRs and, likewise, to facilitate the formation and governance of large-scale CPRs at national and local levels. These institutions and procedures must be focused not on maximizing output from ecosystems, as currently they do, but, rather, on managing sustainable capacity. To this end, as suggested by our previous discussions about the Internet and complexity science, we must look to minimalist, flexible policy structures that can provide an overarching framework for (and focus on) governance while simultaneously enabling distributed, locally tailored solutions to arise from the bottom up to the maximum extent possible. Ideally, a superstructure of shared protocols should authorize and support a multitude of self-organized, diversified solutions originating from commoners themselves, or at least be directly answerable to them. The design challenge will be to enable the governance of CPRs at the lowest levels feasible (subsidiarity) without micromanaging them through excessive top-down control that commonly spells centralized bureaucracy and political interference. Such a balance would then allow Vernacular Law to express itself and unanticipated forms of locally responsive self-organization to arise, leading over time to the evolution of higher, emergent properties of organization and governing processes.

Given the State's tight partnership with the Market in pursuing neoliberal priorities, governance structures that empower commoners are not likely to be enthusiastically embraced. As we have several times observed, such changes would require a shift in cultural attitudes and political struggle. As environmental crises and social unrest intensify, the State/Market may come to see the wisdom of acknowledging its limitations in addressing ecological problems through conventional means. Faced with its own ineffectual governance, worsening ecological problems, and consequent dwindling legitimacy, the State/Market may see genuine advantage in authorizing the emergence of a new Commons Sector that honors the rich knowledge, passion, ingenuity, and commitment that commoners can bring to the management of their resources if given the chance.[44]

---

[44] The City of San Francisco, for example, established in 2012 a "Sharing Economy Working Group" that has convened numerous city departments, neighborhood and community stakeholders, and "sharing economy companies" to assess how municipal policies and resources can support socially based business models and development, as exemplified by car-sharing, open workspaces, tool sharing, and other collective practices of the "sharing economy." *See* Sharable, available at http://www.shareable.net/channel/cities; *see also infra* notes 67–68 (accessed Mar. 3, 2012).

Such a shift in the governance paradigm surely qualifies as a "Grotian Moment," an epochal shift in the configuration of the powers exercised by the nation-state,[45] but we should not shrink from this prospect. Rather, we should embrace it, because little progress will be made against the planet's myriad ecological crises unless the State and international order can jettison John Locke's notions of *res and terra nullius* – the so-called empty slate of nature – as deadly fictions. As we note in Chapter 5, these doctrines have been used to justify ecological plunder and the slaughter and marginalization of indigenous peoples, all in the interest of colonial economic and political expansion, which continues to this day.[46] This doctrine presumes that there is an untouched realm of nature that is separate and apart from humankind and market activity. It is time to liberate modern-day environmental law from this cultural mythology that impedes ecological progress and social justice, both nationally and internationally, and move, instead, toward a more equitable, just, and environmentally sane system based on a doctrine of *res communes* that treats humankind's environmental rights as if they really mattered.

Part of the problem in making this leap is our inability to imagine larger commons-based governance structures. Our tacit assumption is that the only realistic governance options available to us are those that form existing frameworks of institutional governance – for example, representative legislatures, regulatory bureaucracies, and Western-style litigation and jurisprudence. The fact is that some attractive systems of open, participatory, and effective governance are now being developed on the Internet (for activities in the real world, not just cyberspace) that may well have future applications for large-scale, common-pool governance systems. One such innovation, LiquidFeedback, has been developed by the German Pirate Party to enable active membership participation in initiating and debating policy proposals, independent of party leadership. The platform enables members to retain their relative sovereignty (vis-à-vis their leaders, board, and executive staff) by letting members participate in all processes and by assigning their votes to trusted individuals of their choice as proxies, who can then aggregate fluid voting blocs of power. The system, characterized as a "bridge between direct and representative democracy," has helped the Party develop and maintain strong internal coordination, aggressive policy positions, and mass mobilizations, leading to surprising electoral victories.[47] The future will likely produce other software-enabled innovations

---

[45] As noted earlier, the term "Grotian Moment" originated with international law scholar Richard Falk. For explication, *see supra* Ch. 1 note 51 and accompanying text.

[46] *See* text accompanying *supra* Ch. 5 notes 418–21.

[47] As Andreas Nitsche of the German Pirate Party explains: "LiquidFeedback is an online system for discussing and voting on proposals in an inner party (or inner organizational) context and

in large-scale, participatory governance, some of which may be adaptable, at least within liberal democracies, to commons and conventional government processes.

Still, difficult theoretical and practical questions remain. One such question is how to cede, in whole or in part, State control of large-scale ecological resources to commons governance. This can be a problem when large-scale CPRs are located within the geographic boundaries of the State, including within and across intra-State boundaries at the provincial or lesser subnational level. Another, even more difficult question is how to delegate authority over large-scale CPRs that are transnational or even global in expanse.

Neither of these challenges is insurmountable if one considers that the State has on many occasions affirmatively authorized (and thereby created) new vectors of institutional governance with wide-ranging jurisdictions and impact. State chartering of corporations and labor unions are two notable examples. The licensing of public utilities is another. The State has even consented to the establishment of new multinational governance structures (as well as bilateral ones) that cede certain sovereign authority to multilateral treaty bodies, as in the case of the Antarctic Treaty System (operational since 1959),[48]

---

covers the process from the introduction of the first draft of a proposal to the final decision. Although we want everybody to be able to participate in the development of ideas, we believe at the first instance many drafts will be created by small groups or even individuals. This is no problem providing that everybody can find out about the initiative; everybody can contribute by making suggestions; everybody can create an alternative initiative; and everybody can vote in the end. . . . The basic idea: a voter can delegate his vote to a trustee (technically a transitive proxy). The vote can be further delegated to the proxy's proxy, thus building a network of trust. All delegations can be done, altered, and revoked by topic. I myself vote in environmental questions, Anne represents me in foreign affairs, Mike represents me in all other areas but I can change my mind at any time." LIQUIDFEEDBACK, available at http://liquidfeedback.org/mission (accessed May 6, 2012). Within the German Pirate Party, thus, LiquidFeedback has helped to minimize the unilateral power of elected leaders and boards of directors and made them more directly accountable to its large membership. This, in turn, has helped to ensure a more open, substantive dialogue about what members want irrespective of tactical political considerations. The system thereby avoids the familiar pattern of leaders trying to temper members' demands for change and pleas to be "politically realistic." Instead of elected leaders and boards neutralizing dissent and co-opting power threats, members can collectively determine how they really feel about issue x or y, and demand that the organization publicly advocate those positions. For further details in LiquidFeedback, *see* David Bollier, *LiquidFeedback – What a Genuine Democratic Process Looks Like*, bollier.org (May 7, 2012), available at http://www.bollier.org/blog/liquidfeedback-what-genuine-democratic-process-looks (accessed May 14, 2012). *See also* Simone Kaiser & Gunther Latsch, *Pirate Party Woos Voters with Transparency*, Der Spiegel (Ger.) (Mar. 15, 2012), available at http://www.spiegel.de/international/germany/0,1518,818683,00.html%20 (accessed May 15, 2012).

[48] *See The Atlantic Treaty*, Antarctic Treaty Sys., available at http://www.ats.aq/e/ats.htm (accessed Mar. 8. 2012).

for example, or the International Monetary Fund (since 1945, the European Union (since 1993), and the World Trade Organization (since 1995).[49] Although as a practical matter, legally and otherwise, initiatives such as these have not always been easy to effect (e.g., the establishment of the International Seabed Authority in 1994[50]), it is entirely plausible for the State system to authorize similar types of international governance of large-scale ecological resources and processes that can leverage the considerable advantages of the Commons.

There is, moreover, a small but growing literature on the challenges of multilevel governance that deals with the interplay of commons institutions at different levels.[51] This literature seeks to assess how decision-making authority should be allocated among players at different levels and how governance might be structured to produce the most effective, equitable, and sustainable outcomes. Elinor Ostrom, one of the first scholars to point to the challenges of multilevel governance in her 1990 book *Governing the Commons*, posits a final, eighth design principle for CPRs that are part of larger systems. Design Principle 8 states that, in successful large-scale commons, "appropriation, provision, monitoring, enforcement, conflict resolution and governance activities are organized in multiple layers of nested enterprises."[52] Returning to this topic in 2005, Ostrom elaborated on the special governance problems posed by large-scale CPRs, stressing the need for "polycentric" systems of governance

[49] *See Universal Postal Union*, Wikipedia, available at http://en.wikipedia.org/wiki/Universal_Postal_Union; Int'l Monetary Fund, http:// www. imf.org/external/index.htm; European Union, http://europa.eu/index_en.htm; *World Trade Organization*, Wikipedia, http://en .wikipedia.org/wiki/World_Trade_Organization (each accessed Mar. 4, 2012); *see also* Universal Postal Union, http://www.upu.int; Int'l Monetary Fund, http://www.imf.org/external/ index.htm; world trade org., http://www.wto.org (each accessed Mar. 4, 2012).

[50] *See* Int'l Seabed Auth., http://www.isa.org.jm/en/home (accessed Mar. 4, 2012); *see also International Seabed Authority*, Wikipedia, http://en.wikipedia.org/wiki/International_Seabed_Authority (accessed Mar. 4, 2012). Additionally, *see* the brief discussion at and following note 70, *infra*.

[51] Three panels at the Biennial Conference of the International Association for the Study of Commons (IASC) held in Bali, Indonesia, in June 2006, dealt with "community-based conservation in a multi-level world," which in turn gave rise to a special issue of the *International Journal of the Commons* on this topic (vol. 2, no. 1), edited by Fikret Berkes. Other notable essays include Douglas A. Kysar, *Global Environmental Constitutionalism: Getting There from Here* (Yale Law Sch. Pub. Law Working Paper No. 244), available at http://papers.ssrn.com/sol3/papers.cfm?abstract_id=2001958#%23 (accessed Apr. 2, 2012); Yishai Blank, *Federalism, Subsidiarity, and the Role of Local Governments in an Age of Global Multilevel Governance*, 37 Fordham Urb. L.J. 509 (2010); and Liesbet Hooghe & Gary Marks, "*Unraveling the Central State, But How? Types of Multi-Level Governance*," 97 Am. Pol. Sci. Rev. 233 (2003).

[52] Ostrom, *supra* Prologue note 20, at 101.

in nested configurations and the importance of "subsidiarity" – the pushing of decision-making down to the lowest feasible levels.[53]

The central point of this more distributed, flexible system of governance is that it can more closely track the dynamic, complex realities of natural ecosystems than top-down bureaucratic systems typically do. As noted earlier, top-down systems tend to be more rigid and unable to adapt to the evolving circumstances of a forest, fishery, farmland, or waterway. They tend also to marginalize or override local knowledge and participation and thus to bolster the interests of political elites who dominate the governance process. Multi-level commons governance, in contrast, aspires to overcome these problems by building higher-order systems of governance on top of smaller-scale, simpler units of commons governance. Such governance recognizes that socioecological governance (i.e., the blending of social norms and practices with ecological realities, as in a commons) is not static and fixed; it is, rather, constantly changing and in dynamic, nonlinear ways. Accordingly, small-scale commons must develop their own stable social relationships, practices, and adaptive learning to give rise to and support large-scale commons. Graham R. Marshall, an Australian commons scholar, sees multilevel governance resulting from "larger, more inclusive organizational units emerging from and then 'nesting' . . . smaller, more exclusive units that manage to self-organize sooner."[54]

It is not difficult to imagine the top-down creation of institutional structures for managing large-scale commons, but the danger is that government and corporate interests could capture such governance systems, replicating the problems that afflict existing regulatory systems. Therefore, however large-scale governance systems are instituted, it is important that they be firmly rooted in a broader network of commoners who have a real stake in related, smaller-scale resource systems. National and subnational parks, multijurisdictional aquifers, even the atmosphere could benefit from such an approach that honors subsidiarity and stakeholder engagement.

The literature on multilevel commons governance explores the logic of nested systems, especially in contrast to conventional top-down hierarchies, and it notes how nested systems tend to be more robust and resilient (i.e., capable of enduring disruptions and adapting to new circumstances). These capacities are enhanced also by the principles of subsidiarity and polycentrism (Ostrom's term) that seek to nest authority at the right level of governance.

[53] Elinor Ostrom, *Understanding Institutional Diversity*, at ch. 9 (2005). *See* especially *id.* at 255–88.
[54] G. R. Marshall, *Economics for Collaborative Environmental Management: Renegotiating the Commons* 47 (2005).

As a theoretical matter – and in selected circumstances – this principle helps explain what multilevel commons governance might look like.

Yet, theoretical principles can go only so far in helping to design effective governance of large-scale CPRs. As Mary Robinson (1997–2002 UN High Commissioner for Human Rights) has complained, within the context of European Union integration, "the chief advantage of subsidiarity seems to be its capacity to mean all things to all interested parties – simultaneously."[55] Broad theoretical principles may provide some useful guidance, but they also are subject to highly variable interpretations, not to mention irregular adoption by different political processes.

Paola Carozza has observed, however, that criticisms of the subsidiarity principle typically derive from a failure to understand that it is "a general principle, not a clear rule,"[56] and that the detailed criteria by which it operates "are not suited to abstract reasoning *ex ante,* but instead need to be worked out over time, and the conclusions . . . will always be contextual and dynamic, containing the fluidity and flexibility of phronesis (practical judgment)."[57] In other words, the most decisive arena may be that of practical experimentation and the politics that inevitably comes with it. As commons scholars Lars Carlsson and Annica Sandström concede, "institutional variety is immense, not only in terms of property rights and mixtures thereof, but also in the ways different societies have chosen to organize human affairs. Building institutions is a matter of trial and error, as no blueprint exists for the endeavor."[58] Similarly, Graham R. Marshall notes that "policy makers are beginning to take seriously the challenge of decentralizing environmental governance in ways that actually deliver the community ownership and voluntary cooperation that they previously assumed would arise automatically. But knowledge to face this challenge remains limited."[59]

These cautionary notes are particularly apt when it comes to creating commons for large-scale CPRs. Existing scholarship and institutional precedents can be immensely useful, but they do not necessarily provide guidance on what is possible or needed at this moment in history. Nor does existing

---

[55] Mary Robinson, *Constitutional Shifts in Europe and the US: Learning from Each Other,* 32 Stan. J. Int'l L. 1, 10 (1996).
[56] Paola G. Carozza, *Subsidiarity as a Structural Principle of International Human Rights Law,* 97 Am. J. Int'l L. 38, 79 (2003).
[57] *Id.*
[58] Lars Carlsson & Anica Sandström, *Network Governance of the Commons,* 2 Int'l J. Commons 33, 34 (2008).
[59] Graham R. Marshall, *Nesting Subsidiarity and Community-Based Environmental Governance Beyond the Local Scale,* 2 Int'l J. Commons 92 (2008), available at http://www.thecommonsjournal.org/index.php/ijc/article/view/50/19 (accessed Mar. 27, 2012).

scholarship venture into this trickier, more problematic terrain. Who shall be the agent of change, and how shall new sorts of large-scale commons be politically achieved? Even a supposedly ideal large-scale commons design cannot be summarily imposed by a cadre of policy experts and politicians; there must be active participation and consent by commoners themselves, and, inescapably, political struggle with the State and Market interests. The path toward instituting any large-scale commons regime is therefore likely to be historically and politically idiosyncratic, and propelled at least as much by social movements as by policy experts.

It also is likely that the fruits of practical experimentation and its attendant politics will precede our theoretical understanding of multiscale commons governance – if only because the relative handful of existing models was created several generations ago, often under quite different political and economic circumstances. In that spirit, we heed the hard-won insights of commons scholarship that draws on hundreds of case studies while recognizing the necessity of the arcane arts of activism, politics, and law. There simply are too many variables to design and build a multilevel commons regime as if it were a machine; it must grow organically and fitfully over time as part of the politics and culture of its host society, which is itself a complex adaptive system.

These dynamics aside, it is nonetheless fair to ask how the internal governance principles and policies that operate within smaller-scale commons might be adapted and applied to work at larger scales. How can the normative framework for ecological commons that we outline in preceding Sections A and B be made functional in larger systems that rely on the State, multiple jurisdictions, or international (usually intergovernmental) institutions?

This challenge must be divided into two fields of inquiry and innovation: (1) the challenge of devising governance regimes for large-scale CPRs that are *intrastate* or *transboundary* in character; and (2) the challenge of devising governance regimes for large-scale CPRs that are *planetary* in character, such as the atmosphere, space, the oceans, and biodiversity.[60] Scale matters, as does the legacy system of governance that already exists. If a system of commons-based governance is to be established for large-scale CPRs, it will require different institutional and procedural designs than those needed for planetary CPRs, and probably even some normative variances.

Large-scale CPRs can be *intrastate* in character, both nationally and subnationally – for example, the Black Forest in Germany and Alaska's Denali

---

[60] We, of course, concede that large-scale ecological CPRs are nested within planetary CPRs; so, from a policy standpoint, the division between the two should not be considered sharp or absolute.

National Park and Preserve. Also, they can be *transboundary* in character, both nationally and internationally – for example, the Mississippi River, the Ogallala Aquifer, and Lake Champlain in the United States, in the first instance; and, in the second instance, the Amazon rain forest, the North American Great Lakes, the Mekong and Nile rivers, and the Aral Sea between Kazakhstan and Uzbekistan. Arguably, intrastate CPRs are more amenable to new sorts of commons-based governance than are transboundary CPRs, which immediately implicate two or more political jurisdictions, bodies of law, cultural traditions, and so forth. The complexities may therefore be said to be more significant in transboundary commons regimes than in intrastate ones.

For certain large-scale CPRs, there exist already some interesting governmental bodies that have commons or commons-like attributes or that might be modified to incorporate the commons principles enumerated in Sections A and B earlier in this chapter. Prominent examples involving the United States – local, provincial, and transnational – include the following:

- *The Water Replenishment District (WRD) of Southern Los Angeles County*, managing groundwater for approximately 4 million residents in 43 cities across a 420-acre service area.[61] Authorized by the California State Legislature in 1955 and established in 1959 by a 4-to-1 vote of the people, the WRD was formed to protect the groundwater resources of the Central and West Coast groundwater basins underlying the area. Prior to 1959, decades of overpumping caused coastal groundwater levels to drop below sea level and allowed salty sea water intrusion to contaminate coastal groundwater. Today, the WRD "protects the basins through groundwater replenishment, deterrence of sea water intrusion, and groundwater quality monitoring of contamination through assessments on water pumped from the WRD service area."[62] As Ostrom observes in a detailed study, however, the WRD "is only one public enterprise among a half dozen agencies that are actively involved in the management program . . . [I]nstead of one central governmental authority, a polycentric public-enterprise system has emerged to achieve a very sophisticated management system."[63] She further observes: "The overall costs of this system are quite low."[64]

---

[61] *See* WRD: Water Replenishment Dist. of S. Cal., available at http://www.wrd.org/index.php (accessed Mar. 11, 2012).

[62] *Our History*, WRD: Water Replenishment Dist. of S. Cal, available at http://www.wrd.org/about/water-district-history.php (accessed Mar. 11, 2012).

[63] Ostrom, *supra* note 20, at 133.

[64] *Id.*

- *The Adirondack Park*, the largest publicly created park in the contiguous United States, comparable in size to the State of Vermont, and forming the southernmost part of the Eastern forest-boreal transition eco-region (the largest boreal forest in the world). Created by New York State in 1892 amid concerns about clear-cutting deforestation and the pollution of water resources, the Park has been constitutionally protected since 1894 to remain "forever wild." It is administered exclusively by the New York State Adirondack Park Agency (responsible for developing and maintaining a master plan for the use of all state lands in the Park) in cooperation with the New York State Department of Environmental Conservation (responsible for the care, custody, and control the state lands) – each pursuant to New York State environmental laws as determined by the New York State legislature.[65]
- *The Waterton-Glacier International Peace Park*, combining Waterton Lakes National Park in Canada and Glacier National Park in the United States, established by separate national legislation and operational since 1932. Designated a UN Educational, Scientific and Cultural Organization (UNESCO) International Biosphere Reserve and inscribed on UNESCO's World Heritage List,[66] the Park is thus subject to some, albeit minimal, international environmental accountability.[67]

Likewise, notable are the multiple river commissions that manage the hydrology and navigation of the Danube, Rhine, Mosel, and Sava rivers and river

---

[65] *See About the New York State Adirondack Park Agency*, N.Y. State Adirondack Park Agency, available at http://apa.ny.gov/About_Agency/index.html; *Citizen's Guide to Adirondack Park Agency Land Use Regulations*, N.Y. State Adirondack Park Agency, available at http://apa.ny. gov/Documents/Guidelines/CitizensGuide.pdf (each accessed Mar. 9, 2012).

[66] For a list of the International Biosphere Reserves recognized as such to date, *see List of Biosphere Reserves*, UNESCO, available at http://www.unesco.org/mab/doc/brs/brs_whc.pdf (accessed Mar. 8, 2012). To view UNESCO's World Heritage List, *see World Heritage List*, UNESCO, available at http://whc.unesco.org/en/list (accessed Mar. 8, 2012).

[67] The Park is joined by ten other transnational ecological sites similarly managed and similarly designated and/or recognized: in chronological order of designation/recognition: the Fertö/Neusiedlersee Cultural Landscape between Austrian and Hungary; the Belovezhskaya Pushcha/Białowieża Forest between Belarus and Poland; the W National Park of Niger extending into Benin/Burkina Faso; the Talamanca Range-La Amistad Reserves/La Amistad National Park between Costa Rica and Panama; the Mount Nimba Strict Nature Reserve between Côte d'Ivoire and Guinea; the Caves of Aggtelek Karst and Slovak Kars between Hungary and Solvakia; the Danube Delta between between Romania and Ukraine; the Pyrénées – Mont Perdue between France and Spain; the Uvs Nuur Basin between Mongolia and Russia; and the Kluane/Wrangell-St Elias/Glacier Bay/Tatshenshini-Alsek between Canada and the United States. For details, *see List of Biosphere Reserves, supra* note 66.

basins of Europe[68] and the world's largest consolidated nature reserve (and new "peace park") in southern Africa – the Kavango Zambezi Transfrontier Conservation Area (Kaza TFCA), established by treaty among Angola, Botswana, Namibia, Zambia, and Zimbabwe. The Kaza TFCA was founded in 2011 to manage more than 444,000 square kilometers (similar in size to Sweden) comprising multiple resource use areas including national parks, game reserves, forest reserves, conservancies, game/wildlife management areas, and communal lands.[69]

Imagining commons-based governance structures for open-access planetary resources such as the atmosphere, space, oceans, and biodiversity is a more daunting challenge. Here, the task is less about adapting existing institutions or inventing new types or models (however complicated) than about inventing essentially novel, unprecedented systems of governance. The sheer scale of planetary CPRs and their complexities – when set against the arbitrary jurisdictions and vagaries of political governance – create staggering challenges in devising effective commons governance. Yet, given the manifest failure of the nation-state and existing multilateral bodies to address scientifically documented environmental problems (e.g., desertification, loss of fresh water, species extinction, ocean pollution, climate change), we cannot shrink from imagining bold new ways of applying commons principles to the management of planetary CPRs.

At present, there are only a few planetary CPRs that are managed in some limited way as commons. The most notable are Antarctica, the deep seabed, and the Moon (as well as other celestial bodies), as we describe in Chapter 5. Each of these governance regimes has significant deficiencies and reflects the political culture of its founding moment, yet they also provide crude templates for imagining future commons-based systems.

- *The Antarctic Treaty System*, operational since 1961,[70] has proven to work reasonably well among its twelve States Parties[71] as a vehicle for multilateral cooperation on scientific research, even if it has been less effective in matters of resource extraction and military uses where relations between the members have become strained since recent discoveries of oil, gas,

---

[68] *See, e.g.*, RIS (EU River Services), available at http://www.ris.eu/background/parties_involved/ european_river_commissions (accessed Mar. 28, 2012). *See generally* Hilal Elver, *Peaceful Uses of International Rivers – The Euphrates and Tigris Rivers Dispute* (2002).

[69] *See Peace Parks Foundation – The Global Solution*, Peace Parks Found., available at http://www.peaceparks.org/index.php?pid =100&mid=1 (accessed Mar. 28, 2012).

[70] *See* Antarctic Treaty Sys., *supra* note 48.

[71] Argentina, Australia, Belgium, Chile, France, Japan, New Zealand, Norway, Russia, South Africa, the United Kingdom, and the United States.

and other minerals on Antarctica's continental shelf. But its standstill on
territorial claims and, since 1991, its Madrid Protocol 50-year moratorium
on mineral activity,[72] have so far prevented the States Parties from taking
actions aimed at preserving their continental shelf claims under the 1982
UN Convention on the Law of the Sea (UNCLOS), actions that could
prove environmentally threatening or damaging.[73]

- *The 1994 International Seabed Authority,* an independent treaty organization established under a 1994 agreement on the implementation of Part
XI of the 1982 UNCLOS to regulate, especially in relation to polymetallic nodules, all mineral-related activities in the international seabed area
beyond the limits of national jurisdiction.[74] Originally, at the behest of
the Group of 77 countries of the global South in the 1970s, Part XI provided for a UN entity called The Enterprise, which would perform these
functions under the principle of "the common heritage of mankind."[75]
It was to be funded by half the proceeds of all private or state seabed
mining projects to assure the developing world a share of the common
seabed resource heritage that otherwise their economies and technologies could not afford. Numerous Western countries, however, led by
Germany, the United Kingdom, and the United States, objected to Part
XI, principally on the grounds that its implementation terms were unfa-
vorable to their economic and security interests, and for this reason they
refused to ratify the 1982 UNCLOS even while expressing agreement
with the remainder of it. Not until 1994, following many preparatory
negotiations, were differences about the seabed provisions resolved and
The Authority officially established. Not until 2001, when The Authority

---

[72] *See* Protocol on Environmental Protection to the Antarctic Treaty, Oct. 4, 1991, XI Special
Consultative Meeting of Antarctic Treaty Parties (ATSCM)/2, *reprinted in* 30 I.L.M. 1461 (1991)
and V Basic Documents, *supra* Prologue note 13, at V.D.1b.

[73] UNCLOS, art. 76, Dec. 10, 1982, 1833 U.N.T.S. 3, *reprinted in* 21 I.L.M. 1261 (1982) *and* V
Basic Documents, *supra* Prologue note 13, at V.I.22.

[74] *See* Agreement Relating to the Implementation of Part XI of the United Nations Convention
on the Law of the Sea of 10 December 1982, July 28, 1994, 1836 U.N.T.S. 3, *reprinted in* 33
I.L.M. 1309 (1994) *and* V Basic Documents, *supra* Prologue note 13, at V.I.22b; *see also* Int'l
Seabed Auth., *supra* note 50.

[75] UNCLOS, *supra* note 73, art. 136; *see also* U.N. General Assembly Declaration of Principles
Governing the Sea-Bed and the Ocean Floor, and the Subsoil Thereof, Beyond the Limits of
National Jurisdiction, Dec. 17, 1970, G.A. Res. 2749, U.N. GAOR, 25th Sess., Supp. No. 28,
U.N. Doc. A/RES/2749 (XXV), at 24, *reprinted in* 10 I.L.M. 220 (1971) *and* V Basic Documents,
supra Prologue note 13, at V.I.11. For an insightful review of the common heritage principle
and its distinction from *res nullius* and *res communis* principles, *see* Christopher C. Joyner,
Legal Implications of the Concept of the Common Heritage of Mankind, 35 Int'l & Comp. L.Q.
190 (1986).

first signed seabed exploration contracts with a mix of governments and organizations,[76] did the seabed regime become operational – but only as a faint shadow of The Enterprise originally intended, "in effect preserving the 'open access' policy of *res nullius*."[77] Since then, The Authority – headquartered in Kingston, Jamaica, and governed by an Assembly (composed of 161 member States plus the European Union as of May 15, 2011), a Council (The Authority's executive body), and a Secretariat (numbering approximately 40 staff persons) – has added one new seabed contractor to its authorized list;[78] legislated technical regulations The Authority and all contractors must follow when locating and evaluating polymetallic nodules (including the submission of annual activity reports); and issued guidelines to safeguard the seabed environment.[79] To date, however, for lack of technology capable of retrieving deep seabed minerals at costs competitive with land-based mines, no polymetallic nodules have been extracted from the seabed area. Also, the United States, with one of the most advanced technology capabilities in the world, is the only major maritime power that has not ratified the 1982 UNCLOS – nor, indeed, the 1994 implementation agreement.

- *The 1967 Outer Space Treaty*[80] and its satellite *1979 Moon Treaty*[81] turn over jurisdiction of all celestial bodies to the world community, including the orbits around such bodies, and declares them, as in the case of the deep seabed, to constitute part of "the common heritage of mankind." Although the Outer Space Treaty, representing the basic legal framework of international space law, outlaws the placement of nuclear and

[76] The seven contractors were and include still: Yuzhmorgeologya (Russian Federation); Interoceanmetal Joint Organization (IOM) (Bulgaria, Cuba, Slovakia, Czech Republic, Poland and Russian Federation); the Government of the Republic of Korea; China Ocean Minerals Research and Development Association (COMRA) (China); Deep Ocean Resources Development Company (DORD) (Japan); Institut français de recherche pour l'exploitation de la mer (IFREMER) (France); and the Government of India.

[77] Milun, *supra* Ch. 5 note 5, at 120.

[78] I.e., the Federal Institute for Geosciences and Natural Resources of Germany.

[79] The Authority has also sponsored conferences and workshops on various aspects of seabed exploration with emphasis on measures to protect the marine environment, and established an endowment to aid experienced scientists and technicians from developing countries to participate in deep-sea research.

[80] Treaty on Principles Governing the Activities of States in the Exploration and Use of Outer Space, Including the Moon and Other Celestial Bodies, Jan. 27, 1967, 18 U.S.T. 2410, 610 U.N.T.S. 205, *reprinted in* 6 I.L.M. 386 (1967) *and* V Basic Documents, *supra* Prologue note 13, at V.P.1.

[81] Agreement Governing the Activities of States on the Moon and Other Celestial Bodies, Dec. 5, 1979, 1363 U.N.T.S. 3, *reprinted in* 18 I.L.M. 1434 (1979) *and* V Basic Documents, *supra* Prologue note 13, at V.P.3.

other weapons of mass destruction in orbit of Earth or otherwise station-
ing them in outer space, it does not prohibit the placement of conventional weapons in orbit or elsewhere in outer space. In addition, though
the Moon Treaty was intended to establish a regime for the use of the
Moon and other celestial bodies similar to that of the deep seabed under
UNCLOS, it *has not* been ratified by any nation capable of engaging
in self-launched manned space exploration or with plans to do so (e.g.,
China, the European Union, India, Japan, Russia, the United Kingdom,
and the United States) – and, indeed, *has* been ratified by only 15 States
as of October 2012. Nonetheless, both treaties establish the precedent of
recognized outer space commons, and thus have potential value relative
to future governance in the earth–space environment.

At bottom, however, these few existing commons or commons-like regimes
that we have for governing planetary CPRs are not as functional, full-bodied, or
all-embracing as they need to be. The Antarctic Treaty System has never been
treated as part of "the common heritage of mankind" and thus is restricted
in its State Party participation. The UN Convention on the Law of the Sea
was a major diplomatic achievement that validated the principle of "the common heritage of mankind," but the principle has been undermined by the
United States and other industrial powers by their refusal to participate in
the treaty's seabed terms. In addition, the Outer Space and Moon treaties,
although declaring the moon and other celestial bodies to be part of the "common heritage of mankind," do not prevent the indiscriminate use of space as
a junkyard for dead satellites and other orbital debris.

It would be natural for some to consider these large-scale and planetary
precedents as the final word on what can be achieved, especially when
estimable scholars and policy experts look to the usual bodies – national
governments and international agencies – to address ecological crises. Given
the disappointing history of such governance institutions, however, especially
in relation to planetary-scale CPRs, we believe it is imperative to imagine
structurally different, multilevel approaches. We must find ways to develop
innovative stewardship regimes with multilateral participation and accountability to commons- and rights-based principles.

The major goal should be to facilitate a new, alternative political dynamic
to governance dominated by the State/Market and its ecologically ineffectual
programs. As a practical matter, decentralized experimentation and bottom-
up energies must play a more significant role in addressing global problems.
As both a moral and political matter, commons- and rights-based principles
must play a more significant role in governance. The rise of a Commons

Sector, or federation of commons acting as stewards for CPRs of various sizes and types, could bring different perspectives and greater political influence than now prevails. A Commons Sector, after all, would be asserting its direct stewardship interests in a resource. In part because commoners would be assuming an affirmative responsibility for managing a given resource, however partially, they would have greater political standing and moral legitimacy than would "interested citizens" petitioning governments whose prior allegiances to corporate players tend to preempt civil society.

We concede that the challenge of devising new commons- and rights-based governance systems is a bold departure with many speculative uncertainties. Yet, when balanced against the known, gross failures of the status quo, such uncertainties do not appear especially intimidating. What matters is that new frameworks for managing large-scale or planetary CPRs embody certain commons- and rights-friendly norms in their constitutional design and everyday operations. They must act as hosting infrastructures for the effective management of ecological commons at different scales, and yet be coordinated and interconnected; and they must do the same with respect to human rights doctrines, principles, and rules, especially the environmental and environment-related ones. These large-scale and planetary commons must apply the principle of subsidiarity so that authority is not needlessly centralized, but distributed as widely as possible, so that responsibility and innovation can flourish at levels closest to the resource usage and the human beings most affected by them.

"Governance" in traditional discourse suggests a force of control and management external to the average person, a separation. That is not the case with the Commons, where law derives from the community itself (Vernacular Law) and which may or may not then be codified. Governance should not be seen simply as a more ingenious external form of control, but, rather, as a system that honors self-maintaining "generative rules" that internalize governance devised by citizen commoners themselves. External policies by a large-scale commons framework can stipulate the outer boundaries of legitimate social action (e.g., the harvesting of timber, fish, or irrigation water shall not exceed *x* amount), and must respect certain human rights norms and meet certain performance standards; commoners themselves, however, must have the authority and budgets to develop their own rule sets within those parameters. Such an allocation of decision-making authority in the context of stewardship procedures and institutions would lend greater legitimacy to the final rules. It would enable commoners to draw on local knowledge and priorities, and provide space for diversity of implementation and innovation. Recognizing the internal governance of a commons also reduces the need for external State intervention and control, which may otherwise be perceived as arbitrary or politically motivated and therefore resisted. A key point of subsidiarity in commons-based governance is to unleash latent cooperative energies by assuring that the resulting benefits are internally shared in equitable ways – not simply captured by privileged outsiders or moneyed interests.

Government bureaucracies whose mission is maximum control, uniform rules, and formal accountability are not likely to understand the sensibility embodied in commons-based ecological governance structures. The idea that commons can coevolve over time as complex adaptive systems and give rise to new properties of organization and administration is alien to conventional control systems. Yet, one can imagine stewardship arrangements that provide a general framework for performance within general parameters and then guide and leverage the intelligence of independent players in the complex adaptive system. Indeed, this is much the role played by independent judiciaries in democratic societies, and its efficacy as a governance paradigm is quite evident in Internet contexts. If nations could be persuaded to delegate policy- and decision-making authority for one or more ecological systems to a multilateral trustee with proper authority, policy perspective, and accountability, there could begin a process of realigning the conversation away from the brokering of international economic interests (i.e., minimally credible actions and the most effective evasions) and toward a serious grappling with serious problems.

We have in mind, for example, such innovations as a reconstituted UN Trusteeship Council or new Environmental Security Council (as once proposed, respectively, by Kofi Annan and Mikhail Gorbachev); an independent global environmental body (such as the Global Environment Facility); the creation of a World Environment Organization equal to the World Health Organization, International Labor Organization, and World Trade Organization; an upgrading of the UN Environment Programme into a UN Environment Organization; or the clustering of multilateral environmental agreements, a reformation of the World Trade Organization, and the establishment of public policy networks.[82] These are reform options that, as Maria

---

[82] For helpful discussion of these and other proposals, *see* Maria Ivanova, *International Environmental Governance Reform: Options and Implications* (Draft Report: International Environmental Governance, Chatham House Workshop, July 26–27, 2007), available at http://www.chathamhouse.org/sites/default/files/public/Research/Energy,%20Environment%20and%20Development/260707ieg2.pdf (accessed Mar. 29, 2012). *See also* Reforming International Environmental Governance: From Institutional Limits to Innovative Reforms (W. Bradnee Chambers & Jessica F. Green eds., 2005), available at http://i.unu.edu/media/publication/000/002/344/reforming-iegov.pdf (accessed Mar. 29, 2012); Peter H. Sand, *Sovereignty Bounded: Public Trusteeship for Common Pool Resources?*, 4 Global Envtl. Pol. 47 (2004).

Ivanova points out, "fall into two categories: those that advocate the establishment of a more authoritative and better endowed international environmental organization and those that argue against such a strategy contending that a focus on improving other elements of the global governance system would be more effective."[83] For reasons that are by now obvious, we strongly favor the first option. Of course, to function well, any such stewardship arrangement would have to have real enforcement authority and a coherent network of political support.

A key objective is to break the hammerlock of the State/Market on large-scale ecological policies or at least open some space for innovative alternatives to grow so that a different order of governance might begin to take hold. Also, governance structures must affirmatively draw on Vernacular Law and human rights law and find new ways to integrate each into existing policies and decision-making.

An apt metaphor is gardening. The gardener attempts to provide a hospitable environment and modest interventions (pruning, watering, fertilizing) to enhance the natural proclivities of the various plants. But the gardener does not "make" the plants grow; he or she can only create only a favorable environment for growth. The plants will invariably enact their own developmental responses. Governments already take such an attitude toward business development and market growth by trying to provide a business-friendly environment, and this is something of the point for commons-based governance as well: to nourish the agency and innovation of the participants-members, not to stifle or prescribe those capacities. Commons principles must be enacted over time, not simply declared. They must grow over time, much as large life forms (such as mammals) have come to integrate myriad heterogeneous subsystems that interconnect and function as a coherent, organic whole. In large living systems, the control system is not just the brain. It consists of many quasi-autonomous subsystems connected in vital interdependencies across different scales by way of various signaling protocols. Although this is an abstract metaphor, it characterizes the evolutionary development of the European Union, whose increasingly successful governance of diverse State interests suggests some convincing, general design principles for planetary commons.

The intrastate and transboundary governmental bodies mentioned in this chapter are precedents on which new commons-based solutions could be built. In some instances, innovative governments are already taking steps in this direction. The State of Rajasthan in India, for example, has formally

---

[83] Ivanova, *supra* Ch. 1 note 36, at 6.

recognized the value of natural resource commons within its borders,[84] and the mayor of Naples, Italy, has been a prominent backer of new sorts of commons governance at the local level.[85] A key point of these initiatives is to create a policy structure that understands the commons as a living system and that expressly looks to co-production and co-management among its many constituent players.

Commons- and rights-based governance – green governance – acknowledges that no single solution will work in ecological systems that are geographically diverse and complex. It recognizes the active, contributing roles that a diverse base of local and regional commons must play in addressing large-scale ecological problems. It also asserts that the internal governance of even large or planetary commons can be knit together through the principles of subsidiarity and "scale-linking structures."

This vision of commons-based governance echoes the political theory known as "cosmopolitan democracy," advanced principally by David Held and Daniele Archibugi, Richard Falk, and Mary Kaldor.[86] The concept holds that global governance should be decentralized, with decisions made as much as possible by the people affected by them. The idea is to promote global governance without world government and the centralized hierarchies of control that characterized – and, in too many instances, ravished – much of the twentieth century.

Chapter 8, next, suggests a number of practical, catalytic legal strategies for making large-scale commons work more effectively. Municipal law, for example, can be adapted to facilitate commons governance, and federal and

---

[84] *Rajasthan Takes Lead in Policy for Common Land*, Times of India (Sept. 30, 2011), available at http://articles.timesofindia times.com/2011–09-30/jaipur/30229410_1_water-policy-encroachment-facilitator (accessed Apr. 2, 2012); *see also* Draft Rajasthan Common Land Policy 2010, available at http://www.rajpanchayat.gov.in/common/RCLP_2010.pdf (accessed Apr. 2, 2012).

[85] *See, e.g.*, Anthony Quattrone, *Naples Is Becoming a Laboratory for Social Innovation*, Naples Pols. (Aug. 1, 2011), available at http://naplespolitics.com/2011/08/01/naples-is-becoming-a-laboratory-for-social-innovation (accessed Apr. 2, 2012); *see also* David Bollier, *The Mayor of Naples Champions the Commons*, bollier.org (Jan. 30, 2012), available at http://www.bollier.org/mayor-naples-champions-commons (accessed Apr. 2, 2012).

[86] *See* Daniele Archibugi, *The Global Commonwealth of Citizens: Toward Cosmopolitan Democracy* (2008); *Cosmopolitan Democracy: An Agenda for a New World Order* (Daniele Archibugi & David Held, eds., 1995); Richard Falk, On Humane Governance: Toward a New Global Politics (1995); David Held, *Democracy and the Global Order* (1995); David Held, *Cosmopolitanism: Ideals and Realities* (2010); Mary Kaldor, *New and Old Wars* (1999); Mary Kaldor, *Global Civil Society: An Answer to War* (2003); Kaldor, *supra* Ch. 4 note 47. *See also* Daniele Archibugi, *Cosmopolitan Democracy and Its Critics: A Review*, 10 Eur. J. Int'l Rel. 437 (2004), especially at 438 where the author identifies "an increasingly vast literature."

provincial governments can support the formation and expansion of commons via constitutive enactments and economic incentives and rewards. The blending of online platforms and natural resource management can help create more transparent, accountable commons-based governance. New sorts of commons trusts can both protect a natural resource and act as a trustee for revenues generated by it.

The challenges of establishing planetary commons are obviously more complex and vexing; indeed, they are essentially unprecedented. For now, therefore, it is difficult to suggest specific structures that can both transcend the pathologies of the State/Market and enact new commons- and rights-based principles from the bottom up. The global base of commoners will likely have to grow and mature before such ideas will be seen as compelling. This said, there have been serious attempts to rethink how planetary governance of major global interests might be achieved. In the early 1970s, Richard Falk and Saul Mendlovitz led the World Order Models Project (WOMP), which acknowledged that, "to interpret and come to grips with the crises plaguing the contemporary global political and social system," scholars and intellectuals have "a special and important [obligation] to discern trends, detect signals warning us of emerging... problems, to think seriously and critically about alternative solutions and possible future worlds, as well as recommend strategies for achieving those solutions and worlds."[87] Regrettably, no doubt because it emerged before the environmental movement became a political force, WOMP did not address specifically the global environmental *problématique*.[88] It did demonstrate, however, the importance of imagining the grand contours and specifics of preferred world futures as a way to think creatively about the globe, its crises, and their potential solutions.

---

[87] Saul H. Mendlovitz, *Introduction to On the Creation of a Just World Order: Preferred Worlds for the 1990s*, at vii (Saul H. Mendlovitz ed., 1975). For the other WOMP studies, *see* Richard A. Falk, *A Study of Future Worlds* (1975); Johan Galtung, *The True Worlds: A Transnational Perspective* (1980); Horacio H. Godoy & Gustavo Matus Lagos, *Revolution of Being: A Latin American View of the Future* (1977); Rajni Kothari, *Footsteps Into the Future: Diagnosis of the Present and a Design for an Alternative* (1974); Ali A. Mazrui, *A World Federation of Cultures: An African Perspective* (1976). Other books inspired by WOMP include Falk (1995), *supra* note 86; Samuel S. Kim, *China In and Out of the Changing World Order* (1991); *Preferred Futures for the United Nations* (Saul H. Mendlovitz & Burns H. Weston eds., 1995); *The Quest for a Just World Order* (Richard A. Falk, Samuel S. Kim & Saul H. Mendlovitz eds., 1984); *The United Nations and a Just World Order* (Richard A. Falk, Samuel S. Kim & Saul H. Mendlovitz eds., 1991). WOMP was responsible also for the launching and publication in 1975 of the theoretical journal *Alternatives: A Journal for World Policy*.

[88] *But see* Richard A. Falk, *This Endangered Planet: Prospects and Proposals for Human Survival* (1971). *See also generally* Falk (1995), *supra* note 86.

A particularly thoughtful, recent essay in this regard is one by Arnaud Blin and Gustavo Marín, especially pertinent because it explores how the Commons, as part of a "global social contract," could serve as the philosophical and practical foundation for world governance generally.[89] The authors write: "The sudden powerlessness of the most powerful actor of the global stage [the nation-state] has been caused by the onrush of globalization, which with breathtaking speed has overtaken the traditional actors of international politics and rewritten the rules of the game of economics. By doing so, it has also fostered the need to devise and uphold what can be described as the global interest, one that should inevitably take precedence over the outdated and ineffectual individual 'national interests' that have for centuries determined the direction of international affairs."[90]

Proper governance of large-scale and planetary CPRs is, thus, a subject worthy of another WOMP-style book. It is obviously important – indeed, essential – and it requires more research, dialogue, and creative experimentation. However, for both large-scale and planetary commons, it is vital that human rights and Nature's rights principles be deeply embedded in the constitutional structure and operational norms; that subsidiarity of control and decision-making be honored; and that the internal and macro-principles enumerated in Sections A and B of this chapter be respected even while recognizing a diversity of forms. The goal should be to replicate on a larger scale as much as possible the principles and norms of smaller-scale commons.

In time, new forms of commons governance and a Commons Sector can begin to assert a set of interests that are today grievously ignored or marginalized by the State/Market system. This is likely to be an evolutionary process. If successful commons can be established at local and regional levels, one can imagine their operations giving rise to demands for larger governance structures, much as geographically based markets have given rise to larger structures to facilitate their operation on national and global scales. A base of commoners who step up to their responsibilities and succeed in acting as stewards of their resources will be able to push for large-scale and planetary commons. Finding the ways to advance those interests – politically, economically, culturally, and last but not least juridically – remains an unmet but heroic challenge.

---

[89] Arnaud Blin & Gustavo Marín, *The Commons and World Governance: Toward a Global Social Contract* (April 2012), available at http://rio20.net/en/propuestas/the-commons-and-world-governance-towards-a-global-social-contract (accessed June 14, 2012).

[90] *Id.*, at 1.

8

Catalytic Strategies for Achieving Green Governance

The cold reality is that new forms of commons- and rights-based governance, however compelling or meritorious, will not materialize on their own. They must be propelled by real people who see them as holding genuine answers to their needs and aspirations. In addition, they must somehow secure the sanction of law. Yet, this ambitious and necessary project immediately encounters a significant challenge: an "institutional void" of policy-making. As Dutch political scientist Maarten Hajer explains:

> As established institutional arrangements often lack the powers to deliver the required or requested policy results on their own, they take part in transnational, polycentric networks of governance in which power is dispersed. The weakening of the state here goes hand in hand with the international growth of civil society, the emergence of new citizen-actors and new forms of mobilization. In such cases action takes place in an "institutional void": *there are no clear rules and norms according to which politics is to be conducted and policy measures are to be agreed upon.* To be more precise, there are *no generally accepted* rules and norms according to which policy making and politics are to be conducted. (emphasis in original)[1]

Hajen makes a persuasive case that "classical-modernist political institutions" are no longer trusted or seen as legitimate and, accordingly, many citizen-actors have pioneered their own "new political spaces" to advance policies and practices that they regard as more efficacious, trusted, and legitimate. Classical-modernist political institutions are those based on "a differentiation between politics and bureaucracy, the commitment to ministerial responsibility and the idea that policy making should be based on expert knowledge." The operation

[1] Maarten Hajer, *Policy without Polity? Policy Analysis and the Institutional Void*, 36 Pol'y Sci. 175 (2003).

of these institutions has critically depended on "societal processes and cultural adherences" that, in today's twenty-first-century Internet culture, simply do not exist any longer. Political and cultural authority has splintered into countless fragments.

By Hajen's reckoning, the Commons Sector can be seen as one of those political and cultural forces now developing new political spaces. It seeks to accomplish things that "established institutions are – for a variety of reasons – unable to resolve in a manner that is perceived to be both legitimate and effective."[2] Because confidence in government institutions, both political and bureaucratic, is fairly low, successful policy-making today means that "trust and cultural adherence have to be actively organized," writes Hajen, " . . . [and] political conflicts often cannot be solved simply by producing more knowledge. Interventions to resolve key problems, finally, often cannot be based on the territorial sovereignty of a particular government."[3]

These trends suggest that, although the State as a system of power will continue, the nature of its sovereignty may well change in the years ahead. Pressures from new citizen-actors will push for a devolution of sovereignty down to local and regional levels in various novel forms, and up to the global level to manage global common-pool resources more effectively.

Our final challenge, then – how, in the predominantly statist ordering of our planet, does one construct new legal frameworks for protecting CPRs as commons? – is a perplexing puzzle and mostly uncharted territory. Although there are any number of State-administered programs that serve "the public interest" (a term that is itself an artifact of the classical-modernist paradigm), few if any of these programs recognize the Commons as a distinct governance paradigm and value proposition. Any rights that may exist are attached generally to citizens as individuals (who, in a well-functioning democracy, have the primary right to petition their government); they are not rights guaranteed to commoners to exercise some meaningful measure of direct responsibility and control over shared, defined resources. In any case, although the State may be the only source of "official" power and law, it cannot necessarily command the full energy and commitment of commoners.

There is thus a paradox facing anyone attempting to institute catalytic strategies of law and policy that could advance commons projects as a matter of enforceable State Law. State Law alone cannot provide the legitimacy or effective interventions to make a commons successful and foster its beneficial activities. Yet, in our largely State-centric world order, its authorization is

---

[2] *Id.* at 176.
[3] *Id.* at 188.

usually necessary for any projects that have national or transnational impact or that impinge on local or subnational State authority. Thus, in the new political spaces that commoners and others are developing in the face of the "institutional void," attention must continue to be paid to the State.

Given this reality, if there is to be a viable Commons Sector that can challenge the excesses of the State/Market and press for sane ecological practices, State Law must somehow find a *modus vivendi* with commoners (currently known as "civil society") and their Vernacular Law systems. A working rapprochement must be found to mediate the interests of an aging classical-modernist institutional order and the emergent governance institutions of the Commons and global networks.

Our purpose in urging greater delegation and devolution of State governance to commons – illustrative of the Partner State relationship – is to empower cooperating individuals to participate in the governance of shared ecological resources as a matter of established State Law. By authorizing diverse forms of distributed (i.e., decentralized and quasi-autonomous) commons working at numerous levels and sometimes working in collaboration with the State, the State can "provide for the common welfare" in ways that neither the State nor the Market can do alone. By carving out legal frameworks that provide recognized "open spaces" for commons governance, the State can leverage the energies and innovation of commoners to address ecological needs. A flourishing Commons Sector can also temper the State's distressingly broad delegations of authority via corporate chartering that have resulted in so much environmental abuse (among other antisocial behaviors).[4]

Of course, a significant challenge – perhaps *the* most significant challenge – is the liberal polity's indifference or hostility to most collectives (corporations excepted). This means that commoners must perforce use ingenious innovations to make their commons legally cognizable and protected. For this reason, our methodology in proposing policy structures that can affirmatively support the formation and maintenance of commons sensitive to ecological and human rights is to build on concrete projects and precedents based on real world experience.

The legal strategies described later in this chapter are drawn from a number of exemplary commons models and supportive bodies of existing law. Because legal regimes vary immensely around the world, our proposals should be understood as general approaches that will require modification and refinement

---

4 *See* Program on Corps., Law & Democracy (POCLAD), available at http://www.poclad.org (accessed Aug. 6, 2011). On the history of corporate chartering, *see* Ralph Nader et al., *Taming the Giant Corporation: How the Largest Corporations Control Our Lives* (1976).

for any given jurisdiction. We start first with commons that entail minimal entanglement with the State and move on to ones that have greater state involvement, concluding with State trustee commons, State leasing of commons, and the daunting challenges of establishing new sorts of multilateral commons institutions for the atmosphere, oceans, and other global commons.

A. VERNACULAR LAW COMMONS

This is the classic, default way for a commons to operate: a collective asserts its community rules and norms in its management of resources, and sanctions those who may violate them. This is a traditional and often effective form of Vernacular Law, as our notice of "micro-law" and other variants has shown.[5] Peer sentiment, pressure, and sanctions can define and stabilize a community and unite its members in working together to protect the resources of a commons. This is how, indeed, most subsistence commons have functioned over time, without exogenous institutional backup by the State or civil-society institutions. Such commons can be self-policing and stable without the kind of external authority that Hobbes erroneously theorized was essential to restrain barbarism in a "state of nature."[6]

Contemporary examples of using peer sentiment to encourage cooperation abound, even in modern industrial contexts. A good example is the use of peer norms by electric utilities to incentivize and shame rate-payers into reducing their usage of electricity and gas. A 2008 study showed that utility customers are more likely to reduce their consumption when they are informed about the actual conservation habits of the majority of their neighbors than when they are being exhorted to conserve.[7] In a completely different arena, the Open Knowledge Foundation in the United Kingdom has developed the Panton Principles, a series of public criteria for assessing whether scientific data are legally open and shareable. Institutions that meet the designated criteria

---

[5] *See supra* Ch. 4.

[6] An external civil authority may be necessary to help *scale* the size of social cooperation in a commons but not necessarily, as peer-based cooperation on the Internet demonstrates. In any case, as archeologists and neuro-scientists have shown, the cooperative impulse appears to precede the rise of civil institutions and law.

[7] Jessica M. Nolan *et al., Normative Social Influence Is Underdetected,* 34 Personality & Soc. Psychol. Bull. 913 (2008). Using such finding, an electricity and gas provider in the Northeast United States National Grid has expanded its program to inform homeowners on their monthly statements how their energy usage compares to their neighbors. *See* Jim Witkin, *Utilities Finding Peer Pressure a Powerful Motivator,* N.Y. Times (Feb. 22, 2010), available at http://green.blogs.nytimes.com/2010/02/22/utilities-finding-peer-pressure-a-powerful-motivator/ (accessed Aug. 2, 2011).

can legally claim adherence to the Panton Principles and its halo of social esteem.[8]

The point is that social norms can be an effective and efficient way of encouraging positive behavior and cooperation in ways that precede or complement formal legal requirements. Indeed, the rules of social etiquette and State Law itself would not work at all if they did not comport with the basic sentiments of Vernacular Law. But as a voluntary enterprise constrained only by social approval or opprobrium, community norms are also limited instruments of enforcement. They may or may not be adequate to protect an ecological commons.

B. "PRIVATE LAW WORK-AROUNDS"

Devising ingenious adaptations of private contract and property law is a potentially fruitful way to protect commons. The basic idea is to use conventional bodies of law serving private property interests, but to invert their purposes to serve collective rather than individual interests. The most notable example may be the General Public License, or GPL, which is a software license devised by Richard Stallman and the Free Software Foundation in 1986 to ensure that any code contributed to a software commons cannot be legally privatized and must remain always legally free to modify, copy, and share.[9] Copyright owners can choose to attach the GPL to their software to guarantee that the code and any subsequent modifications of it will be forever free for anyone to use. The GPL was a seminal legal innovation in helping to establish commons for software code.

Drawing inspiration from the GPL is Creative Commons (CC), a nonprofit organization that devised a series of free, standardized public licenses that enable copyright holders to ensure that their works may be copied, modified, and shared, as stipulated by six basic licenses.[10] Users affix the licenses to their copyrighted works, whether text, music, video, or any other content, and in so doing make their work legally free to be shared and reused in online digital commons.

---

[8] *See* Panton Principles, available at http://pantonprinciples.org (accessed Aug. 6, 2011); *see also* Open Data Commons, available at http://www.opendatacommons.org/guide (accessed Aug. 6, 2011).

[9] *See GNU General Public License*, Free Software Found., available at http://www.gnu.org/licenses/gpl.html (accessed Aug. 6, 2011); *see also* Chopra & Dexter, *supra* Ch. 1 note 39; Andrew M. St. Laurent, *Understanding Open Source & Free Software Licensing* (2004).

[10] For more on the licenses, see *About the Licenses*, Creative Commons, available at http://creativecommons.org/licenses (accessed Aug. 6, 2011).

Essentially, both the GPL and CC licenses turn copyright law on its head. The GPL has enabled the rise of GNU Linux, the popular computer operating system, and thousands of free and open-source software programs, because the GPL assures volunteer programmers that their work will not be privately appropriated but will remain in the Commons instead. Similarly, the CC licenses enable creative works to escape automatic and strict copyright protection (which, for works created today, would be locked up until approximately the year 2153) and instead make the works shareable on stipulated terms. These copyright-based licenses have been critical to the formation of commons of digital content, which are now a significant productive and cultural force on the Internet. To date, more than seventy nations have adapted the CC licenses to their legal jurisdictions, and an estimated 400 million online artifacts are now shareable under CC licenses.[11]

The GPL and CC licenses are not special cases. Both have been emulated by other creative sectors. Richard Jefferson of CAMBIA, a nonprofit research institute in Australia dedicated to open-source biology, has created an open platform for the sharing of biological research by creating shareable research tools (patented and then given open licenses) to assure that any research produced by using the tools will be available to all.[12] Science Commons, a project started by Creative Commons, has created a private-law innovation, CC0 (CC Zero), which creates legal and technical protocols for the scientific community to develop its own reputation-based system for sharing data.[13] Databases that meet stipulated standards are authorized to use an Open Access Data mark.

These digital tools for sharing are significant for ecological commons for two reasons. First, digital networking infrastructures are increasingly becoming the platforms on which political and social governance occur. The configuration of these platforms, especially via software design, therefore has political and social implications for how people may manage resources and interrelate to each other. "Code is law," as Professor Lawrence Lessig famously declared[14] – and

[11] *See* Creative Commons, The Power of Open (2011), available at http://thepowerofopen.org (accessed Aug. 6, 2011).

[12] *See* Cambia, available at http://www.cambia.org/daisy/cambia/home.html (accessed Aug. 6, 2011).

[13] The peculiar nature of data makes them very complex and legally inappropriate to attempt to make them proprietary via copyright law (and thus, by transference, shareable via Creative Commons licenses). *See* CC0 FAQ, Creative Commons, available at http://wiki.creativecommons.org/CC0_FAQ (accessed Aug. 6, 2011).

[14] Lawrence Lessig, *Code and Other Laws of Cyberspace* 20 (1999). Lessig writes: "There is regulation of behavior in cyberspace, but that regulation is imposed primarily through code. What distinguish different parts of cyberspace are the differences in regulations effected through

the structural design of software on open networks is fostering greater participation, transparency, and collaborative innovation as a matter of Vernacular Law. Second, as we explain in Chapter 6, relative to eco-digital commons, digital systems are increasingly being integrated into ecological monitoring, management, and rules enforcement, so the structure of the systems (open/closed, commons/proprietary) can have far-reaching "constitutional" implications.

Beyond these "side door" uses of private-law work-arounds to help ecological commons, such work-arounds also can directly establish ecological commons. Perhaps the most pervasive is the community land trust. Like the GPL and CC licenses, conservation trusts do not provoke hostility from private property devotees because the trusts are the voluntary and consensual choice of property owners. No one is coerced by the State to dedicate her/his private property to collective or intergenerational interests.[15]

A number of examples of eco-minded trusts serving the interests of indigenous peoples and poorer countries rely on private-law work-arounds to property and contract law. The Global Innovation Commons developed by entrepreneur/activist David C. Martin (see Chapter 6) is a massive international database of lapsed patents that enables anyone to manufacture, modify, and share ecologically significant technologies.[16] The Heritable Innovation Trust, also developed by Martin, uses contract law to help indigenous cultures protect their traditional knowledge commons in the face of trade conventions that subvert their control.[17] The Traditional Knowledge Digital Library works within the framework of patent law to assure that formally registered traditional knowledge will be treated as a protected commons. It is a database of public-domain medical knowledge that can be used to document a specific body of traditional knowledge as "prior art" and therefore render it ineligible for patents and available to commoners. The Library seeks to thwart a practice often known as "biopiracy" in which multinational corporations assert patent ownership over ethnobotanical or agrobiological knowledge that has customarily been freely shared.

---

code. In some places life is fairly free, in other places controlled, and the difference between them is simply a difference in the architectures of control – that is, a difference in code." *Id.* at 20. Lessig does not mean to imply that code alone is law, of course, but that code in the digital age is a powerful new modality of law – one that obviously intersects with other modalities of law, most notably State Law, Market governance and social norms.

[15] There is an ironic edge to this claim, however, because much of the growth of conservation trusts has been fueled by sizeable tax incentives that taxpayers underwrite.

[16] *See supra* Ch. 6 note 38 and accompanying text.

[17] *See* Heritable Innovation Trust, available at http://www.heritableinnovationtrust.org (accessed Aug. 6, 2011).

Property law professor Carol Rose has called commons that leverage property and contract law to serve collective interests "property on the outside, commons on the inside."[18] It is an apt description of the general category of private-law work-arounds.

C. LOCALISM AND MUNICIPAL LAW AS A VEHICLE
FOR PROTECTING COMMONS

Some of the most innovative work in developing ecological commons (and knowledge commons that work in synergy with them) is emerging from local and regional circumstances, particularly municipal governments and activists. The reason is simple: the scale of such commons makes participation more feasible and the rewards more evident. Local commons are also attractive because they provide practical opportunities to reduce consumption and thus the demands on natural systems.[19] Here, we reference some of the more imaginative movements and projects now under way.

Perhaps the most salient projects are part of a burgeoning relocalization movement in the United States and UK that are attempting to bolster local self-sufficiency. As one Bay Area group describes it, re-localization is "the process by which a region, county, city or even neighborhood frees itself from an overdependence on the global economy and invests its own resources to

---

[18] Rose, *supra* Ch. 6 note 57.

[19] Jeffrey Sterling proposes new sorts of "demand-side reduction cooperatives" in local communities as practical ways to reduce consumption:

> The basic idea is that siloed supply side companies are not in the business of reducing demand; they are in the business of increasing supply which damages the environment and is not sustainable. Creating community-run demand side reduction coops (that are voluntary) will make a community resilient, sustainable and will create work for community members. Having a community-owned [Internet] cloud will make the integration of demand side reduction services into the life of a community possible. Also establishing performance based contracts where demand reductions are measured will make it possible for demand side reduction services to be cash flow positive because demand reduction decreases the need for supply which keep the money in the community. Among Sterling's examples: Catching rainwater in cisterns for graywater and freshwater supply that eliminated the need for the next groundwater well or dam. Superinsulating all homes in a community to reduce the number of new power plants or a new gas pipeline. Creating a smart microgrid that will provide peaking power megawatts as an independent power producer and provide solar collectors for peak cooling as well as battery backup storage and essential power to computers in the home.

> *Quoted in* Michael Bauwens, *A Sustainability Proposal: Demand-Side Reduction Cooperatives*, P2P Found., available at http://blog.p2pfoundation.net/a-sustainability-proposal-demand-side-reduction-cooperatives/2011/07/26 (accessed Aug. 6, 2011).

produce a significant portion of the goods, services, food, and energy it consumes from its local endowment of financial, natural, and human capital."[20]

The Transition Town movement is the most visible and organized relocalization effort, with self-organized groups in more than 300 towns, mostly in the UK, Ireland, Canada, and the United States. These groups are actively taking steps to mitigate the anticipated disruptions of Peak Oil and climate change.[21] They are attempting to promote permaculture, rebuild local infrastructures with ecological design principles, cultivate local provisioning of food, build renewable fuel sources, and insulate their communities from the vagaries of the global economy and technologies. The movement frankly admits: "We truly don't know if this will work. Transition is a social experiment on a massive scale. What we are convinced of is this: If we wait for governments, it will be too little, too late. If we act as individuals, it'll be too little. But if we act as communities, it might just be enough, just in time."[22]

Local commons are playing significant roles in re-imagining the food production and distribution systems. Community-Supported Agriculture (CSA) farms have grown tremendously over the past twenty years in the United States as a way for consumers and farmers to interact directly and share the economic risks and the social pleasures that come from a commons-based market. Part of a larger movement to revamp local food systems and culture, CSAs and their members share a commitment to wholesome, pesticide-free food and the local landscape, economy, and community.[23] The Slow Food movement is an international movement that "unites the pleasure of food with responsibility, sustainability and harmony with nature," according to Italian Carlo Petrini, the founder and president of Slow Food International (SFI). This global, grassroots movement has more than 100,000 members organized in 1,300 *convivia*, or local chapters, which are committed to "practice small-scale and sustainable production of quality foods."[24]

Another type of local commons that is surging in visibility is the community forest in which self-organized local groups, sometimes with the participation of local governments, buy and manage large tracts of forest land for the benefit

---

[20] John Talberth et al., *Building a Resilient and Equitable Bay Area: Towards a Coordinated Strategy for Economic Localization* (2006), *also available at* http://www.sustainable-economy. org/art?cid=5 (accessed Aug. 6, 2011); *see also* Rob Hopkins, *The Transition Handbook: From Oil Dependency to Local Resilience* (2008).

[21] *See Transition Towns*, Wikipedia, available at http://en.wikipedia.org/wiki/Transition_Towns (accessed Aug. 6, 2011).

[22] *See What Is a Transition Initiative*, Transition Network, available at http://www. transitionnetwork.org/support/what-transition-initiative (accessed Aug. 7, 2011).

[23] *See* Local Harvest, available at http://www.localharvest.org/csa (accessed Aug. 7, 2011).

[24] *See* Slow Food Int'l, available at http://www.slowfood.com (accessed Aug. 7, 2011).

of the community. Commoners share in the management, decision-making, and benefits of the forest, such as recreation, ecosystem protection, nature education, community building, and selective timber harvests. Forest commons are pervasive in poorer, rural countries. "[I]n the developing world, nearly 145 million hectares are communally administered and an additional 180 million hectares are owned by communities and indigenous groups," according the India-based publication *Common Voices*.[25] Community forests are growing in popularity in developed countries as well,[26] in part because they engage people in everyday stewardship of their local resource and offer an attractive way to reimagine ecological governance beyond the options available via the State or Market.[27]

The Community Environmental Legal Defense Fund (CELDF), previously noted in our discussion of Nature's rights,[28] is a project that helps local communities assert local, democratic self-control over community resources threatened by large corporations such as big-box retailers and natural gas drillers.[29] Special attention is paid to how to use municipal ordinances, home rule charters, and other legal strategies to preserve local governance over things that matter to the community. The Institute for Local Self-Reliance provides a range of innovative strategies and working models for local self-sufficiency.[30] The Foundation for the Economics of Sustainability is a major resource on locally based ecological economics.[31] The City of Linz, Austria, is notable for announcing its intention of becoming the first "regional information commons" by using the Internet to make local information and creative works as open, accessible, and shareable as possible. The city government aims to transform city politics, governance, and culture by building a vast ecosystem of

---

[25] Found. for Ecological Sec., *An Introduction to Forest Commons*, Common Voices, no. 3, 2011, at 5, *also* available at http://iasc2011.fes.org.in/common-voices-3.pdf (accessed Aug. 12, 2011).

[26] For example, the town of Gorham, New Hampshire, manages a community forest of 4,900 acres; Grand Lake Stream, Maine, has a 340,000-acre forest; both towns have year-round populations of about 150 people. *See* Trust for Public Land, Community Forest Collaborative, *Community Forests: A Community Investment Strategy* (2007), available at http://www.northernforest.org/data/uploads/docs/Community_ForestsA_Community_Investment_Strategy.pdf (accessed Aug. 7, 2011).

[27] *Id.*

[28] *See supra* Ch. 3 notes 79–83 and accompanying text.

[29] *See* Community Envtl. Legal Def. Fund, available at http://www.celdf.org/index.php (accessed Aug. 7, 2011).

[30] *See* Inst. for Local Self-Reliance, available at http://www.ilsr.org (accessed Aug. 7, 2011).

[31] *See* Found. for the Econ. of Sustainability, available at http://www.feasta.org (accessed Aug. 7, 2011).

open-information commons that would enable new types of commons-based ecological practices.[32]

A number of other cities are taking steps to fortify local commons in their midst. Mayor Ed Lee of San Francisco has appointed a Sharing Economy Working Group to promote new sorts of collective projects (car sharing, open workspaces, tool sharing, etc.) and socially based business models and development policies.[33] Mayor Luigi de Magistris of Naples, Italy, has appointed an Assessor of the Commons to take account of local commons systems and has convened municipal officials throughout Italy to help improve city government's support for local commons.[34]

It is tempting to regard local commons as ultimately less important than the policies made by more concentrated centers of power at regional, national, or international levels. Quite the contrary. Just as any complex ecosystem depends on the most ordinary organisms – plankton in the oceans, microscopic bacteria within animals, as well as the intermediate, organically connected systems – so any efforts to secure large-scale or planetary commons will depend on the creation of effective "scale-linking" systems, as we describe in Chapter 7, Section C. Large-scale commons governance will depend on the engagement, stability, and resilience that must exist among "subordinate" commons at local and regional levels. Indeed, large-scale and planetary commons are not likely to flourish if created by fiat by the nation-state or international treaties; new types of interlinked, commons-based governance are needed at many different levels.[35] This challenge is discussed in greater depth in Section J of this chapter.

D. FEDERAL AND PROVINCIAL GOVERNMENTS AS SUPPORTERS OF COMMONS FORMATION AND EXPANSION

The next higher stages of government can and should play supportive roles in developing the Commons Sector, much as they reflexively attempt to

---

[32] *Linz Open Commons*, Open Commons, available at http://opencommons.public1.linz.at (accessed Aug. 7, 2011); David Bollier, *The City of Linz Pioneers a Regional Information Commons*, bollier.org (May 4, 2011), available at http://bollier.org/city-linz-pioneers-regional-information-commons (accessed Aug. 7, 2011).

[33] See a twenty-part series of policy papers called "Policies for a Shareable City," written by lawyers at The Sustainable Economies Law Center in cooperation with Shareable, a Bay Area nonprofit. *See* Sustainable Economies Law Center, available at http://www.theselc.org (accessed Apr. 10, 2012).

[34] *See* David Bollier, *The Mayor of Naples Champions the Commons*, bollier.org (Jan. 30, 2012), available at http://www.bollier.org/mayor-naples-champions-commons (accessed Apr. 10, 2012).

[35] Some of the strategies for fostering commons at different scales in the context of climate change are examined in a collection of essays edited by Brian Davey. *Sharing for Survival: Restoring the Climate, the Commons and Society* (Brian Davey ed., 2012).

support market activity. State and national governments usually have commerce departments that host conferences, assist small businesses, promote exports, and so on. Other government programs may provide generous research and development support for market activity.

We already have noted Yale law professor Carol Rose's analysis of how the managed commons can produce a "comedy of the commons"[36] – not a tragedy – because the principle of "the more, the merrier" in a commons generates greater collective value than private ownership or markets might produce. This analysis is confirmed as well in a masterful analysis by Brett M. Frischmann of the economic and social rationale for treating infrastructure as commons.[37] Although the institutional schemes for treating "environmental infrastructure" as "regulated semicommons" can be quite complicated and hybrid, as Frischmann explains,[38] the essential point deserves emphasizing: given the value proposition of the Commons, it often makes much more economic and ecological sense for government to support commons development so that the benefits can be shared by all rather than privatized by a few.

One likely objection is that the benefits of commons cannot be easily measured and plugged into the kind of cost–benefit analyses that economists regard as "hard proof" of benefit. Studies of the quantitative and monetary benefits of "Nature's services" may quell some objections, but ultimately an observer must come to accept the *qualitative* benefits of commons as an epistemological reality. Commons routinely have publicly beneficial spillover effects that are subtle and diffuse in impact, subject to long time frames, and difficult to track in cause-and-effect ways.

National and subnational governments could help amplify these benefits by establishing or facilitating "translocal structures" that can federate local and other subnational state-based commons. Locally oriented commons such

---

[36] Rose, *supra* Ch. 6 note 57. *See also supra* Ch. 5 note 94.

[37] Brett M. Frischmann, *Infrastructure: The Social Value of Shared Resources* (2012); *see also* Brett M. Frischmann, *An Economic Theory of Infrastructure and Commons Management*, 89 Minn. L. Rev. 917 (2005), available at http://papers.ssrn.com/sol3/papers.cfm?abstract_id= 588424 (accessed Aug. 7, 2011).

[38] In practice, the dominant approach in the environmental area is a mixed strategy that regulates some uses and sustains a commons for others. In essence, environmental infrastructure resources often are sustained through complex institutional arrangements that form something akin to semicommons property regimes, although often through regulatory regimes rather than pure property regimes. This approach to constructing semicommons (1) assigns and regulates private rights (access, use, exclusion and/or exchange) for certain fields of use, such as diversion for industrial purposes; (2) defines commons in terms of community rights (access and use) for certain fields of use, such as recreational use; and (3) sustains the integrity of the resource for nonhuman users and future generations. Brett M. Frischman, *Environmental Infrastructure*, 35 Ecology L.Q. 102 (2008), available at http://papers.ssrn.com/sol3/papers.cfm? abstract_id=1123732 (accessed Aug. 7, 2011).

as CSAs and the Slow Food movement could have greater impact if government were to help them reach out to companion commons in other localities, enabling them to reap the positive externalities of mutual association. The power of such mutual support can be seen in the development of the System of Rice Intensification commons (see Chapter 6), a self-organized international network of rice farmers whose collaboration has spawned innovative, ecologically responsible ways of improving crop yields.

Translocal collaboration of commons has a particularly promising future now that the Internet is becoming ubiquitous even in rural areas of poor countries. When local commoners involved in agriculture, sustainable forestry, and seed sharing can link up with international commoners in the same field, all sorts of innovative ecological practices can emerge and be improved on and propagated rapidly. Some excellent examples of this can be seen in work done by groups such as Appropedia, a website/wiki in which local actors collaborate in developing solutions for sustainability, poverty reduction, and international development using appropriate technology;[39] the Global Villages Network, which uses networking technologies to help local communities address local development and improve their lives;[40] and Akvo.org, which works transnationally to promote new water and sanitation projects at the local level.[41]

E. EXPANDING AND STRENGTHENING THE PUBLIC TRUST DOCTRINE

The State often functions as a public trustee for present and future generations or for some designated subsets of them. We call this a stewardship *public trustee commons* as a way to emphasize that the resources belong to the people, not the government. A State trustee commons is a hybrid commons, as we note in Chapter 6. It does not exemplify the classic structures and relationships of a traditional commons described by Ostrom and colleagues, particularly in its scale and bottom-up management. Yet, it is legally intended to serve many of the same functions, to wit, stable stewardship of the resource, equitable access and benefits to commoners, transparency and accountability, and the sanctioning of transgressors against the commons.

The State's role as a trustee of the Commons is often mandated by the *public trust doctrine*, a legal principle that can reliably be traced back at least

---

[39] *See* Appropedia, available at http://www.appropedia.org/Welcome_to_Appropedia (accessed Aug. 7, 2011).
[40] *See* Global Villages Network, available at http://www.globalvillages.org (accessed Aug. 7, 2011).
[41] *See* akvo.org, http://www.akvo.org (accessed Aug. 7, 2011).

as far as the Roman Empire.[42] The public trust doctrine formalizes the idea that a society's governing bodies have an affirmative duty to protect natural resources for the health and well-being of present and future generations. The doctrine has traditionally applied to rivers, the sea, and the coastal shoreline, protecting such activities as navigation, fishing, and recreation. The idea is that the unorganized public has sovereign ownership interests, over and above those of the State itself. The State may hold the legal title to the land or water, but the public is the beneficial owner. As a trustee, the State must exercise the highest duty of care in managing property that is necessarily held in common by all. This means, among other things, that the State may not sell or transfer common property to other parties.

In the United States, the courts have long recognized the public trust doctrine as a means of ensuring that the government protect public assets for present and future generations. When the Illinois legislature tried to transfer ownership of shoreline property along Lake Michigan held in public trust by the State of Illinois, the US Supreme Court issued a landmark ruling in 1892 – *Illinois Central Railroad Co. v. Illinois*[43] – prohibiting such a transfer as unconstitutional. The salience of the public trust doctrine grew in the 1970s in response to an influential law review article on the public trust doctrine by Joseph Sax.[44] Paradoxically, judicial interest in the public trust doctrine waned in the heyday of the environmental movement, in the 1970s, largely because the enactment of numerous environmental statutes of sweeping scope eclipsed interest in a common-law doctrine. The courts have not significantly developed the public trust doctrine over the past four decades.[45]

This does not mean that the scope of the public trust doctrine could not be significantly expanded. Mary Christina Wood, a leading scholar of the doctrine, argues persuasively in her 2012 book *Nature's Trust* that the courts

---

[42] Charles F. Wilkinson, *The Headwaters of the Public Trust: Some Thoughts on the Source and Scope of the Traditional Doctrine*, 19 Envtl. L. 425, 429 (1989).

[43] 146 U.S. 387 (1892).

[44] Joseph L. Sax, *The Public Trust Doctrine in Natural Resource Law: Effective Judicial Intervention*, 68 Mich. L. Rev. 471 (1970).

[45] "The trust concept has remained underdeveloped in at least six respects. First, it has primarily evolved within the courts, having less of a presence in the other two branches of government. Second, it has been applied primarily to state government. Third, it has been interpreted as applicable to primarily water and wildlife resources rather than the full span of natural resources. Fourth, it has never been infused into the statutory and regulatory structure that now dominates the field of natural resources law. Fifth, it has not been invoked to define transboundary responsibilities for common resources (like the oceans and atmosphere) in which many states or nations have interests. And sixth, it has not been linked to other important societal realms, such as the economic and moral realms." Mary Christina Wood, *supra* Ch. 1 note 10, at 66.

can and should apply the public trust doctrine to a far broader array of natural resources, including protection of the Earth's atmosphere.[46] She believes the courts could justifiably apply the public trust doctrine to

> ... the full "ecological res," including the atmosphere, air, soils and forests – all of which carry as much importance as water resources to human survival and civilization. Failure to recognize these natural resources as assets in the trust simply perpetuates a misguided assumption underlying much of environmental law today – that natural assets are capable of severance and partition. In arguing for a holistic approach to the scope of protected assets, the discussion aims to align environmental legal doctrine with the ecological realities of Nature.[47]

The enactment of numerous environmental statutes, Wood points out, does not mean that the public trust doctrine is inoperative, but it does require that courts step up and recognize the ancient provenance and purpose of the doctrine, construe it as having the stature of a constitutional principle, and apply its principles to contemporary public needs, namely, planetary survival. Wood writes that the doctrine "is most appropriately viewed as a fundamental, organic attribute of sovereignty itself" and that the "beneficiary class" that is covered by the doctrine includes not just the present generation but future generations.[48] It expresses the idea that the State has intergenerational responsibilities, something that native nations for millennia have practiced and many religious traditions honor by calling on humans to act as stewards of Creation's doing.

To be clear, the public trust doctrine is not the same as the commons paradigm. It is a venerable principle of State Law that can reinforce the Commons by recognizing the importance of commonly held use rights. Public trust doctrine can be invoked as an antidote to the "tragedy of the commons"

---

[46] Mary Christina Wood, *Nature's Trust, supra* Ch. 6 note 62. *See also* Mary Christina Wood, *Atmospheric Trust Litigation Around the World, in Fiduciary Duty and the Atmospheric Trust* (Ken Coghill, Charles Sampford & Tim Smith eds., 2012); Mary Christina Wood, *Atmospheric Trust Litigation, in Climate Change Reader* 1018 (W.H. Rodgers, Jr. & M. Robinson-Dorn eds., 2011).

[47] Wood, *supra* Ch. 1 note 10, at 89.

[48] *Id.* at 69, 71 ("The role of natural resources in realizing the perpetual human self-interest does not diminish over time, because the fabric of ecology is as vital to each future generation as it was to each past generation, though the modes of resource utilization may change over time. From this it can be surmised that any government deriving its authority from the people never gains delegated authority to manage resources in a way that jeopardizes present or future generations or diminishes the people's use of resources that have public benefit. The trust's attribute of sovereignty, then, is fundamentally one of limitation, not power, organically comprised as a central principle of governance itself.")

by requiring the State to uphold its responsibilities to protect resources that belong to the citizenry at large – or, in the case of transboundary resources such as oceans or mountain ranges, to act as a "tenant in common" (with other jurisdictions) to protect those resources. As an attribute of State sovereignty, the public trust doctrine provides a legal framework for the State to define common ownership of natural resources and authorizes State action to protect them. That State sovereignty, however, is based on people's original grant of authority to the State to protect earthly resources that are essential to their survival; the State can, if it chooses, lay the legal groundwork for the establishment of commons governance over CPRs that are part of the State's public trust.

In this sense, the public trust doctrine may be seen as having shared origins with the Vernacular Law of the Commons, which is philosophically linked also to natural law and human rights. The public trust doctrine is a legal instrument of State power; the Commons asserts its own moral and political authority as Vernacular Law, independent of the State. But both the public trust doctrine and the Vernacular Law of the Commons have solid grounding in natural law, which today expresses itself, relative to the natural environment especially, in terms of what today we call human rights law.

By seeing the State as a trustee of the Commons, we can entertain a more constructive array of State management options, such as the innovative commons trusts mentioned later in Sections G, H, and I of this chapter. However, a prior political hurdle is the capture of State administrative and legislative bodies by special interests, which forces us to ask the following question: How can the State be made to uphold its public trust responsibilities?

The first, most obvious approach is through judicial enforcement of the public trust doctrine and, we urge, a more muscular interpretation of the doctrine to address contemporary environmental realities, such as the deterioration of the atmosphere. This requires more concerted test cases and "judicial education" to bring the public trust doctrine to the fore.[49] One such attempt, the US-based Atmospheric Trust Litigation project, has organized a series of fifty federal and state lawsuits that seek a declarative judgment affirming the applicability of the public trust doctrine to Earth's atmosphere.[50] The lawsuits also seek injunctive relief that forces US federal and state governments to reduce carbon emissions in fulfillment of their duty to protect the Earth's atmosphere. Atmospheric protection may be the most urgent potential application of the

---

[49] Regarding *necessary* judicial education, *see* Joseph H. Guth, *Law for the Ecological Age*, in Weston & Bach, *supra Prologue* note 22, app. I (Background Paper 11).

[50] The Atmospheric Trust Litigation, the brainchild of University of Oregon law professor Mary Christina Wood, is being coordinated by Our Children's Trust, a nonprofit organization. Our Children's Trust, http://www.ourchildrenstrust.org (accessed Aug. 7, 2011).

public trust doctrine, but, consistent with the analysis set forth by Wood and others, the doctrine could and should be applied to other ecological systems – the oceans, wetlands, forests, species habitat, and more.

There may be new openings to expand the public trust doctrine as a result of the US Supreme Court's ruling in *PPL Montana, LLC v. Montana*, on Feb. 22, 2012.[51] The decision, the first US Supreme Court reference to the public trust doctrine in many years, reaffirmed that states have *carte blanche* authority to determine the scope of the doctrine within their borders. It also favorably cited the landmark *Mono Lake* ruling, which upheld the paramount authority of the public trust doctrine even in the face of the federal "equal footing doctrine," the constitutional basis for state authority over riverbeds, for example.[52]

Despite its relative underuse in recent decades, the public trust doctrine offers a powerful, venerable legal tool to uphold the principle that the State must act as a conscientious trustee of ecological commons.

F. STATE TRUSTEE COMMONS

State trustee commons – some established pursuant to the public trust doctrine, others established by statute – are generally administered by government agencies, as overseen by the legislature. They attempt to protect a specified realm of common assets through regulatory programs and enforcement. Prominent examples include national parks, forestry, fisheries and wildlife management, wilderness protection, and wetlands management. Some state trustee commons oversee the leasing of public assets such as land containing oil, groundwater supplies, minerals, timber, and grasslands for cattle grazing. There are many other State trustee commons that do not involve natural resources (such as federally financed research, databases and information, the Internet, federal highways, museums), but we will focus here on those involving ecosystem resources.

The recurrent problem with State trustee commons is the "fox in the chicken coop" scenario: regulated industries have captured the leadership and policy-making of agencies, effectively neutering or countermanding their statutory

---

[51] 132 S.Ct. 1215 (2012), available at http://www.supremecourt.gov/opinions/11pdf/10-218.pdf (accessed May 15, 2012).

[52] The Court wrote: "While equal footing cases have noted that the State takes title to the navigable waters and their beds in trust for the public, the contours of that public trust do not depend upon the Constitution. Under accepted principles of federalism, the States retain residual power to determine the scope of the public trustover waters within their borders, while federal law determines riverbed title under the equal-footing doctrine." *Id.* at 1235 (citing Shively v. Bowlby, 152 U.S. 1, 49, 15–17, 24, 26 (1894)).

missions to protect the common wealth. In the United States at least, the very centralization of authority in federal agencies that is intended to make decision-making more expert and consistent has instead provided rich opportunities for political cronyism, corruption, and "split the difference" stewardship of common assets. Even sincere, well-intentioned, politically committed agency leaders find it difficult to overcome the innumerable impediments to good regulation contrived by recalcitrant legislators and regulated industries.[53]

Reforming the administrative State is well-nigh impossible given the larger political priorities of the State/Market. There are two possible responses: (1) intensify citizen pressures on regulatory agencies to carry out their statutory obligations (which may be deficient in the first place) through research, standard setting, and enforcement; and (2) devise new structural roles for administrative agencies that leverage commons-based solutions. The first option has been the centerpiece of the environmental movement for the past generation, and it has yielded, as noted earlier, irregular and dwindling results, if not outright failure. Regulatory watchdogs clearly need to continue their Sisyphean work, but if we are ever going to get ahead of the curve of relentless environmental decline, structural changes will be essential. We therefore propose, in Sections G, H, and I that follow, several structural changes that would make administrative agencies more effective, reliable trustees of the Commons.

G. ECO-DIGITAL INNOVATIONS: CROWDSOURCING, PARTICIPATORY SENSING, WIKIS, AND MORE

In the twentieth century, the administrative State "hollowed out" democratic participation by centralizing authority and implementation and relying on bureaucratic systems, political appointees, and scientific experts. Such decision-making has actually served to exclude citizens from participating in the creation and enforcement of government regulations and has ensured that regulated industries have privileged access and influence over policy and enforcement. Fortunately, various digital networking technologies now make it possible to reinvent the administrative process so it can be more transparent, participatory, and accountable.

In Chapter 6, we note a number of important crowdsourcing and participatory sensing innovations.[54] Government-hosted wikis are other vehicles for

---

[53] McGarity et al., *supra* Ch. 1 note 22; *see also* Ch 1 notes 23 and 24 for further references on the failures of the regulatory state.

[54] On the meaning of "crowdsourcing," see *Crowdsourcing*, Wikipedia, available at http://en .wikipedia.org/wiki/Crowdsourcing (accessed Aug. 30, 2011). For more on crowdsourcing, *see supra* Ch. 1 note 42 and *infra* note 58.

eliciting public sentiment and suggestions in ways that can materially affect policy outcomes.[55] The State of Florida recently posted special software on its website and invited the public to suggest how the state's electoral districts should be redrawn.[56] This public participation is coming *before* the maps have been drawn, so citizens are not simply commenting after the fact on proposed maps. This kind of "distributed participation" through Internet technologies enables citizens to inform and pressure the State, and force it to respond to public opinion.

In 2009, the US Patent and Trademark Office established an expert network called Peer To Patent that "harnesses citizen-experts to improve patent quality by helping identify prior art relevant to pending patent applications."[57] The effort is part of a much larger dynamic of using open platforms to capture the "wisdom of the crowd" to serve larger societal purposes. The Smithsonian Institution is now using social media, such as its Smithsonian Commons project, to encourage free and unrestricted online sharing of Smithsonian resources and social networking as a way to enhance the museum's mission.[58] This resembles the pioneering "Clickworkers" initiative launched by NASA in 2000 to recruit volunteers to classify the craters of Mars, now carried on by its "Be a Martian!" website.[59] In Colorado, "collaborative conservation" has enabled farmers, industries, and households to save water and help protect endangered fish in the Upper Colorado Basin, using a broader range of recovery

55 On the meaning of "wikis," *see Wiki*, Wikipedia, available at http://en.wikipedia.org/wiki/Wiki (accessed Aug, 30, 2011).
56 *See* Greg Allen, *Florida Begins Redistricting Hearings* (National Public Radio broadcast June 23, 2011), transcript available at http://www.npr.org/2011/06/23/137376145/politics-embroil-floridas-redistricting-hearings (accessed Aug. 8, 2011); Amateur software applications such as "Dave's Redistricting," Dave Bradlee, *Do Your Own Redistricting*, Dave's Redistricting, available at http://gardow.com/davebradlee/redistricting/launchapp.html (accessed Aug. 8, 2011), are democratizing the ability to map legislative districts, which in turn is providing heightened public visibility and accountability for that highly politicized process.
57 *See* Peer To Patent, available at http://www.peertopatent.org (accessed Aug. 8, 2011).
58 For example, the museum is using crowdsourcing to help identify unknown people in archival photos and to solve curatorial mysteries. Elizabeth Olson, *Smithsonian Uses Social Media to Expand Its Mission*, N.Y. Times (Mar. 10, 2011), available at https://www.nytimes.com/2011/03/17/arts/design/smithsonian-expands-its-reach-through-social-media-and-the-public.html?_r=1 (accessed Aug. 8, 2011); *see also Smithsonian Commons*, Wikipedia, available at http://smithsonian-webstrategy. wikispaces.com (accessed Aug. 8, 2011).
59 "Virtual Volunteering" is a growing phenomenon. *See Virtual Volunteering*, Wikipedia, available at https://secure.wikimedia. org/wikipedia/en/wiki /Virtual_volunteering (accessed Aug. 8, 2011). NASA's current website for "clickworking" is its "Be a Martian" website, at *Be a Martian*, NASA, http://beamartian.jpl.nasa.gov/welcome (accessed Aug. 8, 2011).

tools that would otherwise have been available under traditional regulation and the Endangered Species Act.[60]

At the moment, "virtual commoning" innovations are highly eclectic and irregular, but they point to some compelling new ways of rehabilitating administrative regulation and engaging citizens to play direct, collaborative roles in monitoring and managing ecological resources. Crowdsourcing and "virtual participation" platforms quicken people's sense of affiliation, responsibility, and stewardship and produce more informed, democratically responsive policy.[61] By leveraging such participation, the State could do a better job of carrying out its public trust and statutory responsibilities.

H. ESTABLISHING COMMONS TRUSTS TO MANAGE COMMON ASSETS AND DISTRIBUTE REVENUES

Commons scholar Peter Barnes has pointed out that the trust is a familiar legal form that can serve as a template for designing new sorts of commons institutions.[62] In Barnes's formulation, the trust is to the Commons as the corporation is to the marketplace: "The essence of a trust is a fiduciary relationship. Neither trusts nor their trustees may ever act in their own self-interest; they're legally obligated to act solely on behalf of beneficiaries."[63] He continues: "Trusts are bound by numerous rules, including the following: Managers must act with undivided loyalty to beneficiaries. Unless authorized to act otherwise, managers must preserve the corpus of the trust. It's okay to spend income, but not to diminish the principal. Managers must ensure transparency by making timely financial information available to beneficiaries."[64]

One of the great virtues of the stakeholder trust as an institutional form is its ability to safeguard long-term interests structurally, especially those of

---

[60] John Loomis, Portland State Univ., *Collaborative Conservation: Endangered Fish Recovery in the Upper Colorado Basin*, YouTube (May 26, 2011), available at http://www.youtube.com/watch?v=zJsdZ4ukMJs (accessed Aug. 8, 2011).

[61] Tim Kassar, a professor of psychology at Knox College, has studied extensively the need for personal and social changes to meet ecological challenges. He writes: "A growing body of psychological research suggests that if these efforts incorporated more knowledge about human identity (including our values, our sense of social identity, and the ways we cope when threatened), greater progress towards a more sustainable (and socially just) world might be forthcoming." Lecture by Tim Kassar, *Human Identity and Environmental Challenges*, available at http://www.pdx.edu/sustainability/events/tim-kasser-lecture-human-identity-and-environmental-challenges (accessed Aug. 8, 2011).

[62] Barnes, *supra* Ch. 7 note 21, at Ch. 6 ("Trusteeship of Creation").

[63] *Id.* at 83.

[64] *Id.*

future generations. The legal principles for managing trusts are familiar and well-established, and can be adapted to serve the interests of protecting natural resources, as land trusts already do. One abiding limitation with trusts, as with other centralized institutions, is assuring the faithful execution of the trust's mission – or the "agency" problem, as it is known in contract law. How does the trust prevent conflicts of interest or corruption of its executives? Besides the standard audit and accountability measures, one could imagine leveraging the oversight of commoners themselves. Ingenious combinations of stakeholder trusts, with broad participation and transparency among beneficiary-members and open-source style, could minimize this problem.

A number of state-sanctioned common assets trusts manage revenues on behalf of commoners, and a number of new ones have been proposed in recent years. The Alaska Permanent Fund, created by the Alaska state legislature in 1980, diverts a royalty on all oil drilled on state lands to the Fund, which then distributes dividends to all Alaskan households each year – usually on the order of $1,500 per household – from its $32 billion endowment.[65] The US Social Security system is an intergenerational risk-insurance commons that serves commoners as a quasi-independent trust. The Land and Water Conservation Fund is a state-sanctioned trust that channels offshore oil and gas drilling revenues to acquire land for parks, forests, and open spaces and to develop recreational projects.[66]

The "stakeholder trust" is a legal regime that could be adapted to ensure that the public receives its due entitlements from the Market exploitation of natural resources (in cases where Market use of the resource is appropriate and sustainable). Currently, the US government leases access to public lands (for mineral extraction, oil, timber, and cattle grazing) and ocean fisheries, but the revenues collected are grossly lower than open markets would pay for similar resources, and the revenues do not begin to compensate for the ecological harm and overuse that occurs.[67] In a few cases, the government holds auctions for the use of common assets, such as telecommunications companies' use of the electromagnetic spectrum for wireless services and polluters' use of the sky to get rid of sulfur dioxide and nitrogen oxide. Other common assets, such as the broadcast airwaves and the atmosphere (as a repository for pollution), are treated as free resources that industry may use without payment.

---

[65] For quick insight, see *Alaska Permanent Fund*, Wikipedia, available at http://en.wikipedia.org/wiki/Alaska_Permanent_Fund (accessed Feb. 28, 2011).

[66] See *Land and Water Conservation Fund*, U.S. Forest Service, Land and Realty Mgmt., available at http://www.fs.fed.us/land/staff/LWCF/index.shtml (accessed July 29, 2011).

[67] Bollier, *supra* Prologue note 3, at Ch. 6 ("The Abuse of the Public's Natural Resources").

In all of these cases, and others, commons trusts may be suitable vehicles for capturing revenues generated from common assets and channeling some portion of them to the public directly. For example, to help control carbon emissions and prevent global warming, Peter Barnes has proposed a US-based Sky Trust – also known as "cap-and-dividend."[68] This scheme auctions pollution rights to industry and places the revenues in a trust fund owned by all citizens. Over time, the Sky Trust would distribute dividends to everyone, much as the Alaska Permanent Fund does. The beauty of the system is that it would use market incentives to discourage pollution, reward those who reduce their carbon use, and help consumers offset higher prices.

There are other trust-based proposals. A number of environmental economists have proposed the establishment of a global Earth Atmospheric Trust based on the Sky Trust idea.[69] An Ocean Trust has also been proposed that would rely on the public trust doctrine.[70] A charitable trust model has been proposed for genomic biobanks, which are large-scale databanks of biologic specimens and medical information used in pharmacogenomic research.[71]

One of the most ambitious new proposals to apply trust principles to manage commons is legislation calling for the creation of a Vermont Common Assets Trust. The law seeks to declare that certain natural resources within the state's borders are common assets that belong to all citizens of the state.[72] The trust's foremost duty would be to protect designated common assets for present and future generations. Where appropriate, the trust would generate revenues from leasing those assets (such as selling water extraction rights to bottlers or timber-harvesting rights to logging companies). The money would not flow through the legislature, but would be managed directly by the trust. The legislation would also expand the scope of the public trust doctrine. Instead of covering just navigable waters and shorelines, the public trust doctrine would explicitly apply to "undisturbed habitats, entire ecosystems, biological diversity, waste absorption capacity, nutrient cycling, flood control, pollination, raw materials,

---

[68] *See* Cap and Dividend, available at http://capanddividend.org (accessed Aug. 8, 2011).

[69] Peter Barnes et al., *Creating an Earth Atmospheric Trust: A System to Control Climate Change and Reduce Poverty*, 319 Science 724 (2008).

[70] Peter H. Sand, *Public Trusteeship for the Oceans*, in *Law of the Sea, Environmental Law and Settlement of Disputes* 521 (Tafsir Malick Ndiaye & Rüdiger Wolfrum eds, 2007).

[71] David E. Winickoff & Richard N. Winickoff, *The Charitable Trust as a Model for Genomic Biobanks*, 349 New Eng. J. Med. 1180 (2003).

[72] H. 385, Gen. Assemb., 2010–2011 Legis. Sess. (Vt. 2011), available at http://www.leg.state.vt.us/docs/2012/bills/Intro/H-385.pdf (accessed Aug. 8, 2011); *see also* David Bollier, *The Vermont Common Assets Trust*, bollier.org (Mar. 10, 2011), available at http://bollier.org/vermont-common-assets-trust (accessed Aug. 8, 2011).

fresh water replenishment systems, soil formation systems, and the global atmosphere." It would also apply to "social assets such as the Internet, our legal and political systems, universities, libraries, accounting procedures, science and technology, transportation infrastructure, the radio spectrum and city parks."

Finally, it is useful to entertain the model of State trusts that provide direct services and financial benefits. A great example is the North Dakota State Bank, which takes an equity stake in loan packages that are offered to businesses and consumers, and so reduces the levels of risk that private, commercial banks must assume.[73] It also makes direct loans to South Dakota farmers, students, and businesses at reasonable rates, and it acts as the repository for the funds administered by all North Dakota state agencies. The bank got its start in 1919 when out-of-state bankers and grain dealers were manipulating markets and credit to farmers in the state, hurting the ability of farmers to buy and sell crops and finance farm operations.

I. STATE CHARTERING OF NEW TYPES OF COMMONS TRUSTS

Rather than rely exclusively on centralized bureaucracies to monitor environmental quality and enforce laws – an approach that has yielded disappointing results – an attractive alternative would be for the State to charter new types of commons trusts. It would therefore be useful to develop a model statute for state chartering of ecosystem trusts that are accountable to future generations and have some property rights over ecosystems resources. This is an area that merits further research and statutory creativity: it is one thing to argue that

---

[73] *See* Bank of N.D., available at http://www.banknd.nd.gov (accessed Aug. 8, 2011). Although the State earns about 0.25 percent less interest on funds deposited in the Bank of North Dakota than in commercial banks, it does not pay state or federal taxes. Nor does it pay deposit insurance; essentially the State of North Dakota is the guarantor of funds: a great way for taxpayers to leverage their collective equity for collective benefit. (If government is going to act as a guarantor for banks, why not reap some margin from doing so to benefit the general public?) Because the Bank of North Dakota is not obliged to maximize returns for private investors, but to serve the common good – within the bounds of responsible banking practices – it can spend time and energy trying to make deals work rather than summarily rejecting them as too risky or not lucrative enough. After all, the bank realizes that putting together a successful loan package could have enormous effects on community development – something that is lesser priority for commercial banks. As a result, the Bank of North Dakota is often willing to take extra steps to try to make local development projects work. In 2009, the Bank of North Dakota had profits of $58.1 million (on a loan portfolio of $2.67 billion), which was the sixth consecutive year of record profits. Over the past decade, the bank has channeled about $300 million to the state treasury, where it supplements the budget of the state government. *See* David Bollier, *Why Not State Banks?*, bollier.org, (Feb. 26, 2010), available at http://bollier.org/why-not-state-banks (accessed Aug. 12, 2011); Barbara Dudley, *The State Bank Solution*, The Nation, June 27, 2011, at 19.

commoners ought to have a right to such trusts to protect their interests; it is another to make it a practical step for commoners to create and manage them on their own. The trusts might go by different names and have different delegations of authority, but the basic idea would be for commoners to act as stewards of designated resources, for both their own benefit and the wider public's, and to work as partners with the State in protecting CPRs.

A classic example is the *acequias* sanctioned by the State of New Mexico, as we describe in Chapter 5.[74] The New Mexico state government authorizes indigenous peoples to manage their own *acequias* with designated water allocation rights. This delegation of stewardship empowers distinct communities to manage their own water resources responsibly. Grounded by deeply rooted traditions and cultural practice, *acequias* have been able to prevent overexploitation of scarce water supplies and assure greater social equity in allocations.

Critics may argue that *acequias* and other indigenous commons are special cases, because they draw on centuries-old traditions and practices that are alien to modern-day citizens. In a way, however, that is precisely the point: to try to emulate and develop modern-day analogues of indigenous commons by working through formally sanctioned commons trusts. Mary Christina Wood notes that Native Americans have entered into a variety of fruitful partnerships with the conservation land trust movement, with benefits to both parties. Ordinary citizens and environmental groups are pleased to be protecting more land from development, and the Native organizations are happy to use conservation easements and other private-law tools as ways to "regain access to cultural resources and apply management expertise to land from which tribes have been excluded for generations," Wood explains.[75]

The partnerships can be seen as crucibles for forging a new land ethic based on active commoning. Wood writes:

> Land trusts often lack a cultural and historical relationship to the lands they conserve, and their management does not encompass any religious or spiritual approach to Nature. Moreover, their market approach to conservation, combined with their neutral demeanor toward the development industry, reinforces the social acceptability of viewing land as a market asset and exploiting it for profit.
>
> ... [By contrast, tribes] are positioned to spread their own land ethic when they return as trustees of aboriginal lands... The consistent expression of intergenerational responsibility and stewardship obligations towards Nature,

---

[74] *See supra* Ch. 6 note 8 and accompanying text.
[75] Wood & Welcker, *supra* Ch. 6 note 13, at 373, 398.

grounded in timeless cultural practices, has the potential to proliferate a type of respect that is still foreign to the majority society . . . [76]

Wood points out that the abiding challenge is to find ways to demonstrate how humans can live in a symbiotic relationship to the land, something that Native Americans, through their spiritual relationships to aboriginal land, have been able to achieve. "A generalized land ethic of the kind Aldo Leopold espoused," Wood writes, "is often not enough to overcome a community's entrenched outlook on private property rights. By bringing spiritual, cultural and historical context to threatened resources through a uniquely Native worldview, tribal trustees may be able to spread a reverence for Nature, a will for conservation and a penchant for natural abundance that the mainstream environmental movement has not yet been able to achieve."[77]

The point of commons trusts is to grow a participatory culture of stewardship that can persist and cherish the resources that need to be protected. State Law must find ways to support vernacular community practice. What's happening on the ground, in everyday life, in a specific location, among people who love that place, is a strong base from which to grow a sustainable land ethic. In the case of Native Americans, the idea of the land trust works well – despite its grounding in the liberal polity of individualism and private property rights – because the trust is based on the kind of stewardship principles that lie at the heart of tribal aboriginal management.

Although *acequias* and land trusts are notable forms of commons trusts, others deserve to be studied further and emulated. There are a number of Commons/State partnerships that combine the best of State authority with commons-based participation. The Adirondack Mountain Club, for example, has close working relationships with the US Forest Service in the management of its land and hiking trails. The Alpine Stewardship Volunteer Program works to protect alpine vegetation, and the Trail Stewardship program maintains more than 3,500 miles of the Appalachian Trail.[78] In New York City, a group of citizens entered into a partnership with the city government to preserve and maintain an elevated trestle structure that had once carried freight trains; they turned it into a lovely elevated park, High Line Park; formed a commons-like nonprofit (Friends of the High Line, responsible for 70 percent of the park's budget); and actively maintain it.[79] Of course, partnerships such as these not

---

[76] *Id.* at 428.

[77] *Id.*

[78] *See Become a Volunteer Alpine Steward*, Appalachian Mountain Club, available at http://www.outdoors.org/volunteers/information/information-alpine.cfm (accessed Aug. 8, 2011).

[79] *See* High Line, available at http://www.thehighline.org (accessed Aug. 8, 2011).

only have great potential for empowering citizens, they can also make it easy for the State to shirk its budgetary responsibilities. Voluntarism and philanthropy can easily become a subterfuge that allows the cutting of social services budgets to be disguised as a high-minded way of helping people (as exemplified in the United States, for example, by President George H.W. Bush's "Thousand Points of Light" campaign, and in the U.K. by Prime Minister Cameron's "Big Society" policy agenda).

Beyond voluntarism, commons trusts can be imagined as significant forms of commons governance. James B. Quilligan has proposed the idea of a "social charter" as a means by which producer/consumers can enter into cogovernance of a resource with or without the formal authority of the State. Quilligan writes:

> A social charter is a formal declaration which outlines the rights and incentives of a community – involving both local jurisdictions and the multijurisdictional environment – in the supervision and protection of a common resource. The charter describes patterns of relationships between the resources and its users, managers and producers, allowing them all an opportunity to voice the mutual interests and responsibilities emerging from their rights to these common goods. The social charter empowers a geographical group and a broader association of stakeholders to hold a commons in trust for its beneficiaries, thereby safeguarding these vulnerable resources from the growing pressure to exploit them.[80]

As a practical matter, the State may well object to social charters that flout its established authority, a problem for which commoners have little redress. Or, the State could try to co-opt social charters, using them to mask State control. As Quilligan notes, "Social charters generated by states often disempower those who use and manage a local commons. They put the locus of power in government and function more as a complaint mechanism or quality control procedure than as a means of honoring the rights of people to their commons."[81] But such co-optation of State chartering need not be inevitable particularly if there is a well-organized group of commoners eager to assume certain responsibilities.

A number of American states have been introducing new forms for *corporate charters* for socially beneficial purposes.[82] Surely, innovative charters for

[80] Quilligan, *supra* Ch. 5 note 88.
[81] *Id.; see also Social Charters FAQ*, P2P Found., available at http://p2pfoundation.net/Social_Charters_FAQ (accessed Aug. 8, 2011).
[82] Maryland, New Jersey, Virginia, and Vermont have authorized people to create a "Benefit Corporation," which does not require the corporation to make profitability its fiduciary priority;

commons-based initiatives deserve serious exploration as well. The point is to legitimize the idea that commoners can and should come together to create their own governance mechanisms.

J. NEW TYPES OF MULTILATERAL FRAMEWORKS THAT CAN MANAGE LARGE-SCALE COMMON-POOL RESOURCES

In Chapter 7 we considered the special challenge of large-scale ecological commons – specifically, how to devise structures that might enable commons- and rights-based governance of large-scale CPRs while maintaining some measure of social commitment and participation among commoners in relation to them.[83] An inescapable conclusion was that large-scale commons will require the delegation of authority to governmental and intergovernmental institutions and processes working cooperatively. Here, we emphasize the need for new multilateral policies, institutions, and practices that foster interdependency in environmental stewardship among States, much as global trade policies, institutions, and practices are structured to facilitate commercial interdependencies among States.

Such ideas, we recognize, run against the grain of the neoliberal polity. Proof positive are such failures as the Kyoto Protocol and the Copenhagen climate change summit. Aggressive environmental cooperation threatens the core priorities of the State/Market agenda.

However, attempts to nurture a new transnational ethic of environmental stewardship must start somewhere. One of the most prominent starting points is the Earth Charter[84] – a "people's charter" that sets forth "fundamental ethical principles for building a just, sustainable, and peaceful global society in the 21st century."[85] The charter was finalized in 2000 after ten years of worldwide discussion and adopted by 4,500 organizations, including many governments. Its preamble provides:

companies are authorized to combine the profit motive with the goal of making "a positive impact on society and the environment." Jamie Raskin, *Plan B for Corporations*, The Nation, June 27, 2011, at 14. In 2008, the Vermont legislature formally conferred "legal personhood" on online communities that wish to form limited-liability partnerships. The law enables people to come together as virtual businesses, with dispersed partners who may live anywhere, and avoid the usual requirements that the company host in-person board meetings, maintain a physical office, and file paper documents with the state.

[83] See *supra* Ch. 7, § C.

[84] Adopted at The Hague by the Earth Charter Commission, June, 29, 2000, available from the Earth Charter Initiative, available at http://www.earthcharter.org (accessed Aug. 8, 2011), *reprinted in* V Basic Documents, *supra* Prologue note 13, at V.V.3.

[85] See Earth Charter Initiative, *supra* note 84.

We stand at a critical moment in Earth's history, a time when humanity must choose its future. As the world becomes increasingly interdependent and fragile, the future at once holds great peril and great promise. To move forward we must recognize that in the midst of a magnificent diversity of cultures and life forms we are one human family and one Earth community with a common destiny. We must join together to bring forth a sustainable global society founded on respect for nature, universal human rights, economic justice, and a culture of peace. Towards this end, it is imperative that we, the peoples of Earth, declare our responsibility to one another, to the greater community of life, and to future generations.[86]

More recent is the proposed Universal Declaration of the Rights of Mother Earth, which emerged from the People's Conference on Climate Change and the Rights of Mother Earth in Bolivia in 2008[87] as an attempt to extend the ethic of interdependency to Mother Earth itself.[88] The Declaration notes that "[w]e, the peoples and nations of Earth . . . are all part of Mother Earth, an indivisible, living community of interrelated and interdependent beings with a common destiny."[89]

Beyond the symbolic and norm-changing value of these and like declarations, it is important to develop actual governance systems, in whatever limited forms, that can demonstrate the functional value of new collaborative governance. One way to do this is to empower commoners to act as trustees of a given natural resource for their own benefit as well as for stipulated larger interests of humanity and Mother Earth – and then develop administrative and legal linkages between these commons and larger international legal institutions. A good example is the Potato Park in Peru, a *sui generis* legal regime that gives indigenous tribes explicit stewardship rights over a wide variety of rare potatoes considered to be part of the agroecological landscape and tribal culture.[90] A specified region has been designated an Indigenous Biocultural Heritage Area, which enshrines an holistic, community-led, and rights-based approach

---

[86] *Read the Charter*, Earth Charter Initiative, available at http://www.earthcharterinaction.org/content/pages/Read-the-Charter.html (accessed Aug. 12, 2011), *reprinted in* V Basic Documents, *supra* Prologue note 13, at V.V.3.

[87] *See supra* text accompanying Ch. 3 notes 52–53.

[88] For the text of the Declaration, see *supra* Ch. 3 note 60 and accompanying text.

[89] *Id.*

[90] *See* Alejandro Argumedo, *The Potato Park, Peru: Conserving Agrobiodiveristy in an Andean Indigenous Biocultural Heritage Area*, in Protected Landscapes and Agrobiodiversity Values (Thora Amend et al. eds., 2008); *see also The Ayllu System of the Potanto Park, Cusco, Peru*, Satoyama Initiative to United Nations U. Inst. of Advanced Stud. (May 3, 2010), available at http://satoyama-initiative.org/en/case_studies-2/area_americas-2/the-ayllu-system-of-the-potato-park-cusco-peru (accessed June 12, 2012).

to conservation while protecting and enhancing local livelihoods and biocultural diversity. Management practices in the Potato Park are based on the traditional knowledge and cultural practices of indigenous Peruvians. Such a scheme empowers local and regional commoners with direct responsibilities and entitlements, and preserves their cultural traditions and livelihoods as well. But the regime serves also the larger interests of the world in preserving the ecological biodiversity of the region (especially of the potatoes), preventing biopiracy, and enabling managed scientific access to noteworthy plants.[91]

Another innovative governance idea, proposed by the government of Ecuador, aims to create a United Nations (UN)-administered trust to protect a region renowned for its biodiversity and containing huge supplies of untapped oil. The region is also home to a number of indigenous peoples living in voluntary isolation. Under the Yasuní Ishpingo Tambococha Tiputini (ITT) Trust Fund initiative, the government of Ecuador plans to renounce the exploitation of the oil and preserve the lands of the Yasuní National Park intact, if industrialized countries contribute at least half the market value of the oil into a special trust fund to be administered by the United Nations Development Programme (UNDP).[92] Revenues from the trust fund would be used to support renewable energy sources, reforestation, and social development within Ecuador. The plan represents a huge financial sacrifice for the Ecuadorian government, which depends on oil for half its tax revenues and 20 percent of its gross domestic product (GDP), yet the Ecuadorian government recognizes the long-term importance of protecting the remarkable natural biodiversity within its border. It also believes that the world should share the burden in helping to reduce the release of additional carbon into the atmosphere.

Within the dominant economic framework, Ecuador's aversion to drilling the oil is compared to a "beggar sitting on a gold sack."[93] The Yasuní-ITT initiative is an attempt to reconceptualize the idea of "wealth" by developing a new ethic and relationships with nature. The basic idea is to treat nature as a subject in relationship to humankind, and not merely as an insensate object

---

[91] A related example is the collaboration between Native Americans and land trusts, often with the help of state governments, in re-introducing sustainable management of land, wildlife, and bodies of water, as described in text accompanying notes 54–6, *supra*.

[92] Ecuador Yasuní ITT Trust Fund: Terms of Reference (2010), available at http://yasuni-itt.gob.ec/wp-content/uploads/tr_english.pdf (accessed Feb. 25, 2011).

[93] An anthropocentric observation first made by Alexander von Humboldt, a German naturalist and geographer (1769–1859), but echoed by many political and corporate leaders in the centuries since. *Cited by* Acosta, *supra* Ch. 2 note 74.

to be exploited. "This is the core of Nature's Rights," explains Alberto Acosta, economist at Facultad Latinoamericana de Ciencias Sociales (FLACSO) and the former president of the Constituent Assembly of Ecuador; "[w]e have to stress over and over again that human beings cannot live apart from Nature."[94] The Yasuní ITT trust is an attempt to go beyond the rhetoric of such claims by advancing a specific administrative and legal system that embodies a different notion of prosperity and progress. "Wealth and well-being cannot be defined any longer as the accumulation of material goods," as Acosta puts it.[95]

Acosta has called the Yasuní-ITT Initiative a new way to imagine a global commons of interdependent participants and a new way to realign relationships among the industrialized nations and poorer nations. The richer countries of the global North "have a huge ecological debt to the world's poorest countries," he said, citing the history of colonialism and imperialism, and the $90 billion in environmental damage that British Petroleum, Chevron, and Texaco have inflicted on Peruvian lands.[96] The Yasuní-ITT Initiative offered a practical scheme for exercising "co-responsibility in protecting the Amazon," he said, which is why the tagline for the proposal (which still is seeking full funding) is "An opportunity to rethink the world."[97]

The Yasuní-ITT Initiative gives us a glimpse into how we might construct a multilateral system of interconnected "nested commons" at different scales (local, provincial, national, regional, global). But there are others such as the Global Innovation Commons of patent-free technologies having ecological value, the Earth Atmospheric Trust, and the Ocean Trust – all mentioned earlier in this chapter.[98] The limited histories of commons-based legal systems for Antarctica, the oceans, and space also provide some templates for future innovation.

One familiar legal principle that could be pressed into service to promote joint stewardship of global ecosystems is the public trust doctrine. In a series of lawsuits known as Atmospheric Trust Litigation, plaintiffs are seeking to force the US government to reduce carbon emissions into the atmosphere.[99] Under the public trust doctrine, the lawsuits argue, the State is "a sovereign

---

[94] *Id.*

[95] *Id.*

[96] Alberto Acosta, Remarks at the International Commons Conference in Berlin, Ger. (Nov. 2, 2011), *as reported in* David Bollier, *The International Commons Conference: An Interpretive Summary* 8–9, available at http://www.boell.de/downloads/economysocial/ICC_report–Bollier.pdf (accessed Aug. 8, 2011); *see also* Alberto Acosta, *The Yasuní-ITT Initiative, or the Complex Construction of Utopia*, in Wealth of the Commons, *supra* Ch. 5 note 10, at 418–23.

[97] Acosta, *Yasuní-ITT Initiative*, *supra* note 96.

[98] *See supra* notes 16, 69, and 70 and the respective accompanying texts.

[99] *See supra* note 31 and accompanying text.

trustee of natural resources with an organic fiduciary obligation to protect the atmosphere in order to ensure the survival and prosperity of present and future generations of citizen beneficiaries. Positioned along with other sovereigns, government is co-tenant of the atmosphere and therefore holds a correlative duty to prevent waste to the asset."[100] This is a significant legal claim because co-tenancy makes all nations, as sovereigns, jointly responsible for protecting a common asset, the atmosphere. As the lawsuit states, "[C]o-tenants have a right against other co-tenants for waste and for failure to pay necessary expenses [in protecting an asset]." Thus, one nation could sue another for a breach of its fiduciary obligations under the public trust doctrine.

These are the types of legal innovations, by no means exhaustive, that must be pursued to establish interdependent governance. The first hurdle to overcome is the idea that we can avoid such governance.

▶ *Developing a Scheme of Nested and/or Networked Commons That Can Work Dynamically Together*

A central problem with existing international environmental and human rights law – the right to environment included – is its dependence on a territorially based, consensual system of global governance in which rigid State sovereignties are empowered, essentially alone, to make the legal and political decisions about problems that international environmental and human rights law are supposed to solve. Another is that, however high-minded their rhetoric, sovereign States typically act tenaciously in their own self-interest, generally perceived in neoliberal economic terms, with little to no regard for the ecological and social needs of the wider community of which they are a part. If, however, our planet is to survive in a manner truly hospitable to life on it, international environmental and human rights law – indeed, national and international law in general – must change. Law as a creature of sovereign hierarchies must adapt to a world of interdependent, interpenetrating networks, both ecological and social.

Over the past twenty years, the Internet has significantly dissolved institutional and geographic boundaries, making them far more porous, if not indefensible. This poses serious challenges to conventional forms of law, not just in terms of geographic control, but equally in terms of maintaining legitimacy and efficacy. It also opens up new opportunities to reimagine standard forms of law, which are often too remote and detached from on-the-ground moral, socioeconomic, political, and cultural realities, especially when seen

[100] Wood, *Atmospheric Trust Litigation* (2011), *supra* note 46; *see also supra* note 50.

against the many nimble Internet communities that have outflanked stodgy government bureaucracies and politicians (e.g., the Arab Spring, the Wiki-Leaks disclosures of US government cables).

When law is controlled mostly by elite policy-makers and administered through arcane and often corrupt legal systems, even as open networks enable a divergent public narrative to emerge, citizens understandably become cynical about formal law. They are not truly agents of its creation and interpretation, even in nominal democracies. And when they do become engaged, perhaps as a result of crisis or demagoguery, there may not be vehicles for implementing governmental laws and policies. Elinor Ostrom put it this way on winning the Nobel Prize: "I'm not denigrating that officials can do something very positive, but what we have ignored is what citizens can do, and the importance of real involvement by the people involved, as opposed to just having somebody in Washington or at a far, far distance, make a rule. How does that get all the way down to management of forests, fisheries, irrigation systems, etc.? So we have to look from the ground up."[101]

A new system of multilateral ecological governance, therefore, must reimagine the role of the State and multilateral institutions and their policy priorities. This requires the development of a new vision of societal development beyond maximum capital accumulation and economic growth. A vision of the "good life" beyond material acquisition and an economics of sufficiency must be developed. This will, of course, entail both profound shifts in all aspects of life over many years and realignments of international political relationships. As Ecuador's Alberto Acosta has put it: "The impoverished and structurally excluded countries must, on one hand, try to find options for a decent and sustainable lifestyle, which do not represent a caricatured re-issue of the western way of life."[102] Acosta continued: "While, on the other hand, the 'developed' countries will have to solve the growing problems of international unfairness that they have caused and, particularly, incorporate criteria of sufficiency into their societies before attempting to support, at the expense of the rest of mankind, the logic of efficiency understood as permanent accumulate of material possessions."[103]

The State must move from serving as the sovereign master of a closed, hierarchical system to the light-touch host of an open, diverse network.

---

[101] Professor Elinor Ostrom, Press conference at Indiana University, following the announcement of her shared award of the 2009 Nobel Prize in Economic Sciences (carried live via satellite and streamed live on the Internet at http://broadcast.iu.edu/ceremon/Nobel, Oct. 12, 2009) (accessed Aug. 21, 2011).

[102] Acosta, *Yasuní-ITT Initiative*, *supra* note 96.

[103] *Id.*

In other words, *there must be means for the agency of commoners at lower levels of governance to be expressed rapidly, dynamically, and interactively at the higher macro-levels levels of law.* This capacity is important for the quality of information, the flexibility and speed of response, and the overall legitimacy of international governance, ecological and otherwise. A crude model for such transnational, networked collaboration is the rapid response of health researchers and public health agencies to the outbreak of the severe acute respiratory system (SARS) virus in 2002.[104] Networked collaboration was widely seen as essential to the quick containment of an infectious disease that otherwise had catastrophic potential; one can only wish that such fierce cooperation could animate efforts to reduce carbon emissions into the atmosphere.

If online networks could knit together diverse commoners and make them a visible and coordinated political force in international legal fora, it would become possible to make law conform more closely to vernacular morality and practice and to change the political climate for new initiatives. In ecological design, there is a term to describe how natural phenomena at different spatial scales interconnect. "Nature's processes are inherently *scale linking,* for they intimately depend on the flow of energy and materials across scales," write Sim van der Ryn and Stuart Cowan.[105] "The waste oxygen from blue-green algae is absorbed by a blue whale, whose own waste carbon dioxide feeds an oak tree. Global cycles link organisms together in a highly effective recycling system crossing about seventeen tenfold jumps in scale, from a ten-billionth of a meter (the scale of photosynthesis) to ten thousand kilometers (the scale of the Earth itself)."[106]

Taken as a metaphor, if not a functional template, scale linking must find expression in national and international law to overcome the structural frictions and missing feedback loops that make existing institutions so ineffective. The Vernacular Law of commons at all levels needs to be integrated

---

[104] During the SARS outbreak, the World Health Organization convened regular teleconference meetings that allowed more than a dozen national public health agencies and leading medical laboratories to share information with each other rapidly. This collaborative approach enabled medical authorities to identify the virus and develop diagnostic tests and treatment regimes in a matter of weeks, not months, as would have been required had national health systems worked independently of each other. For a case-study of this success, *see* Stephen S. Morse, *Int'l Relations and Sec. Network, SARS and the Global Risk of Infectious Diseases* (2006), available at http://kms1.isn.ethz.ch/serviceengine/Files/ISN/18142/ipublicationdocument_singledocument/42a87936–86b3–4e4b-94e1-bdbbccceb27c/en/casestudy_emerging_disease.pdf (accessed Aug. 31, 2011); *see also* Peter J. van Baalen & Paul C. van Fenema, *Instantiating Global Crisis Networks: The Case of SARS,* 47 Decision Support Sys. 277 (2009).

[105] Ryn & Cowan, *supra* Ch. 7 note 36, at 33.

[106] *Id.*

into the actual formulations of national and international law. The obvious vehicle for reimagining new types of scale-linked multilateral institutions is the Internet. Software platforms are just one channel among many in political relationships, and they are constitutive in the ways in which they can structure relationships, communication, and implementation. Properly designed platforms could enable the emergence of new voices and venues for consensus building in multilateral governance. The LiquidFeedback software used by the German Pirate Party, mentioned in Chapter 7, is a rudimentary example of how an online platform could help reimagine more participatory, constructive modes of governance. By allowing information and participation to flow from the bottom up, from diverse levels and locations, the overall system of governance would be more capable of addressing the myriad, distributed complexities of ecosystem problems.[107] The principles of polycentrism and subsidiarity could be designed into such a system.

Admittedly, what we propose is a general concept, not an implementation. But the virtue of such a system of networked multilateral governance is that it could help us get beyond the dysfunctional premises of the current system, provide new platforms for commoners to represent their ecological and human rights interests, and thereby help make governance more aligned with ecological (and social) needs.

▶ Human Rights as an Integral Aspect of Multilateral Ecological Governance

We have argued previously that human rights, both substantive and procedural, are an indispensable element in the governance of any one commons. Likewise, they are necessary in the design and operation of multilateral ecological governance wherein the State, the Market, and the Commons safeguard and enhance the ecosystems on which all life depends. Indeed, international governance of the ecosystem complexities that now confront all of humankind cannot be solved without the flows of information and participation that human rights principles help ensure.

Central to such governance, therefore, just as in the design and governance of individual commons, must be a commitment to all the values of human dignity as expressed in the 1948 Universal Declaration of Human Rights and the nine core international human rights conventions that have evolved from it or

---

[107] One vision of governance has been put forward by Christian Arnsperger in an essay, *Fostering New Governance Through Participatory Coordination and Communalism*, P2P Found., available at http://p2pfoundation.net/Six_Framework_Conditions_for_Global_Systemic_Change (accessed Aug. 30, 2011)

such of them as may be applicable.[108] Also central must be recognition and validation of the right to environment as traditionally (derivatively, autonomously) and expansively (procedurally) espoused, as applied to unborn future generations, and as represented in the entitlement of all persons to serve as trustee surrogates on behalf of the rights of Nature. Likewise, the multilateral design must recognize and validate the proposed right of everyone to commons- and rights-based ecological governance at all levels of social organization.[109] This is not a matter merely of preference. It is a matter of necessity. Without rights, as previously observed, there is no guarantee of justice. Without *these* rights, there is no guarantee of environments that can sustain life on Earth.

The future of commons- and rights-based governance, thus, must rest with our ability to adapt State Law to recognize the imperatives of Vernacular Law and, in so doing, sanction new sorts of institutional forms and political spaces for the Commons to thrive. Although the Commons can easily be seen as a threat to the State/Market, it also is quite credible to see it as a complementary, constructive force, one that provides forms of governance, social organization, and personal affiliation and affection that neither the State nor the Market can or will provide. Indeed, the Commons has flourished to date largely because traditional State and Market institutions have failed to protect basic ecological systems and satisfy elemental human needs. There is a serious institutional void, as Hajer astutely notes.

The path forward, then, requires us to show great ingenuity and courage in developing new institutions and modes of law to address the singular ecological and social challenges of our time. A blind reliance on existing precedents will not be enough to escape the old paradigms of law and policy that are, at root, a large part of the problem. Selective precedents of the past also embody important principles that we can build on and tailor to suit new needs and circumstances. The urgent, immediate need is to start a new conversation with the proper framing of questions, an openness to change, and a willingness to see the rich potential of green governance in helping us protect Mother Earth and at the same time advance human rights. We hope the preceding pages can help guide this conversation in the planet-saving journey ahead, a journey we must take or risk unprecedented collective peril.

---

[108] *See supra* Ch. 7 notes 10–11 and accompanying text.
[109] *See* Appendix for a draft covenant to this effect.

Epilogue

We have sketched, we hope, a persuasive vision for ecological governance in a worldwide context, one that can break the normative, institutional, and procedural impasse imposed by conventional economic, political, and legal thought. Our goal has been to outline a substantive framework and ethos for green governance and the human right to a clean, healthy, biodiverse, and sustainable environment that can help both to actualize such governance and to condition its operation.

Climate change, in both its geophysical and social dimensions, has been a driving force in this endeavor, but it has not been the sole catalyst. Our concern is with the global environmental *problématique* in all its sorrowful manifestations, and from this broader perspective we have outlined what we believe is a practical pathway for moving forward comprehensively while mindful of varied, discrete circumstances. We need solutions that address ecological and social problems together, in an integrated and effective way, thus providing holistic and realistic ways to achieve a paradigm shift that can help save our planet and its myriad forms of life. Like Rachel Carson and the many others who have followed in her footsteps, we are motivated by "a sense of wonder" at the miracle we call Earth and seek to protect it and all who inhabit it as inclusively as possible.

It may appear optimistic or naïve to expect that the State, already deeply indentured to the neoliberal Market order, would wish to help establish a commons- and rights-based approach to ecological governance, let alone a vibrant Commons Sector. Why would the guardians of the current State/Market wish to dismantle or modify that system?

The answer is: they don't. But as the folk wisdom says, "Nature always bats last." Systems of governance that can no longer deliver on their cherished mythologies and flout Nature's order have been known to disappear. At a certain point – sooner rather than later, we fervently hope – the merits of embracing the positive, constructive agenda of the Commons will be seen as more attractive than desperate attempts to salvage a profoundly flawed paradigm. The dysfunctionalities of existing systems of government and law cannot be denied, repressed, or finessed forever.

In the face of a global political economy that refuses to curb its material appetites and admit the reality of biophysical limits, it is no exaggeration to say that the fight for a new ecological governance system is tantamount to a fight for human survival. It comes as no surprise, therefore, that with ecosystems collapsing and economic woes deepening, public demands for systemic change will intensify. Even now, governments and international bodies realize that their future legitimacy will depend on effective governance, social fairness, and popular trust – all of which are currently in short supply.

It might be claimed that commons- and rights-based ecological governance is a utopian enterprise. The reality is, however, that it is the neoliberal project of ever-expanding consumption on a global scale that is the utopian, totalistic dream. The mythological vision of human progress through ubiquitous market activity simply cannot be fulfilled; it demands more than Nature can deliver and inflicts too much social inequity and disruption in the process. The first step toward ecological sanity requires that we recognize our myriad ecological crises as symptoms of an unsustainable cultural, socioeconomic, and political worldview.

Our first aspiration, then, is that this book provoke a focused dialogue on the merits of a commons- and rights-based framework of ecological governance and the virtues of reimagining the role of the State and Market as part of a new State/Market/Commons triarchy. We are especially interested in joining a dialogue with potential partners, whether they be individual commoners, nongovernmental organizations, governments, academies, faith-based institutions, or foundations. We have established the Commons Law Project for this very purpose: to help continue the needed conversation and deliberation, to marshal resources, and to advance creative policy thinking and activism about the Commons, ecological survival, and human rights.[1]

Shifting paradigms is never easy, especially when the process implicates the many everyday elements of people's lives. In the course of human history, it is unlikely that *any* society, let alone all of humanity, has faced as many complex, transformational challenges in such a foreshortened period of time,

---

[1] *See* Commons Law Project, available at http://www.commonslawproject.org (accessed May 15, 2012).

as we do today. The shift to ecological wellness will entail epochal shifts in law, business practices, personal lifestyles, cultural attitudes, and, of course, worldviews about nature, humanity, and governance institutions.

The way forward, therefore, must be "polychromatic," with multiple, eclectic nodes of transformational change. It will not – cannot – be a centrally coordinated and implemented process, but one that is driven by countless players around the world, in different resource domains, with different cultural perspectives. State Law must surely play a significant role in this transition, and at all levels from local to global. The social change needed will also require active forms of Vernacular Law, working in tandem with supportive State Law whenever possible.

Formal and informal legal arrangements created specifically to promote and protect the environment are indispensable components of a comprehensive strategy for the realization of commons- and rights-based ecological governance. In truth, however, they are by no means the only components – indeed, not assuredly the most effective or important in many instances. Effective and just ecological governance will require broad and deep social change across many disciplines and domains. The simple fact is that we humans are deeply imbued with the pernicious belief that Nature is, with modest exception, a commodity for ownership and maximum profit, much as, appallingly, we once bought and sold human beings at auction.

Indeed, the road ahead will be not unlike the nineteenth-century struggle to abolish slavery and render it illegal, against the full weight of deeply engrained, powerful, yet also powerfully contentious moral and economic worldviews. Abolitionist William Lloyd Garrison spoke of the necessity of dismantling the "higher than the Alps" ethical establishment of his day "brick by brick, and foot by foot, till it is reduced so low that it may be overturned without burying the nation in its ruins."[2] We must do the same with the present-day State/Market ideology that doggedly resists constraints on the unfettered use of private property and its heedless exploitation of Nature. For this we must invoke all manner of nonviolent strategy, extralegal and quasi-legal as well as legal, including the active engagement of all manner of civil society everywhere, and the State as well to the extent compatible and feasible.

Discounting revolutionary and other tumultuous times, history has shown that political cultures will absorb a new set of values and practices if they are allowed to engage in a cycle of peaceful activism structured to fulfill their high

---

[2] William Lloyd Garrison 54 (George M. Frederickson ed., 1968) *quoted in* Roderick Frazier Nash, The Rights of Nature: A History of Environmental Ethics 212 (1989).

aspirations. Enacting a few laws is not enough; the entire gamut of what legal and political science scholars call "policy- and decision-making functions" must be put into play if, over time, a society is to succeed at metabolizing the new worldview and ethos.

Here, based on previous transformations in societal values, we outline a multifaceted typology of seven of these functions that modern society must undergo if it is to realize new forms of commons- and rights-based ecological governance – and in so doing regenerate the human right to a clean and healthy environment. We do not presume that our catalogue reflects an always-precise, exclusive fit; it is intended, rather, to be heuristic, suggestive, *not* definitive – and a tool for charting a course forward.

First, there must be *the means for information-retrieval and dissemination*, so that research into Commons and State/Market ecological governance can be done. We must initiate and strengthen research methodologies (case studies, correlation studies, experimental studies, prototypes, etc.) and develop monitoring and surveillance systems that can assess the performance of different systems of ecological governance. This knowledge must be globally accessible, most logically through the Internet and specialized knowledge commons on it. Curricular initiatives (from K-12 to college-level course to adult education), mass-media programming, and new sources of scientific and technical information on ecological commons will also be needed.

Second, *resources and skills to promote and advocate commons- and rights-based ecological governance* at all levels must be developed. These capacities must be cultivated in the emerging Commons Sector and in human rights and environmental advocacy circles. They must also include new administrative, financial, and logistical support within such bodies as the United Nations (UN), the UN Environment Programme, the International Labor Organization, the International Monetary Fund, the World Bank, the Office for the High Commissioner for Human Rights (OHCHR), free trade agreements (FTAs), regional human rights systems, and other relevant intergovernmental organizations (IGOs). We will need new forms of collaboration among the State and commons, nongovernmental organizations, and civil society actors, including private-sector lobbies. In addition, the State itself must provide commoners with platforms and opportunities to learn from each other and to participate in State policy-making that affects their interests.

Third, *prescriptive initiatives* are needed to identify and mandate life-sustaining natural resources and ecosystems as commons. State institutions, both national and international, must assist in the effective and humane management of such commons through regulations, legislation, and agreements and through corporate and industry codes of cooperative conduct. In particular, State institutions must support initiatives to establish a recognized human right to commons- and rights-based ecological governance and help to define or determine the precise meaning and intent of this right. More broadly, they must recognize and develop human and environmental rights prescriptions that support commons.

The *ability to invoke the law* to protect ecological commons is a fourth vital need. This function entails the initiation, strengthening, and expansion of complaint procedures (including shareholder and tort actions) that can protect commons- and rights-based ecological governance. Nongovernmental organizations (NGOs) must develop the capacity to monitor the implementation of commons- and rights-based principles and to challenge perceived violations. Commons and commoners must be able to access justice institutions to redress perceived State or Market violations of their rights.

The *will to apply and enforce the law* is a fifth function that is critical to the new paradigm of ecological governance. The State must ratify and enforce national and international law-making instruments directed at establishing and protecting ecological commons and commons- and rights-based ecological governance projects and systems. This will require new, strengthened, and expanded law enforcement mechanisms and procedures. Economic strategies such as consumer boycotts, economic embargoes, and trade sanctions should be fostered in support of commons- and rights-based ecological governance projects and systems.

The *termination of regressive public policies and laws* is a sixth important function. Legal systems that impede the establishment or effective operation of commons- and rights-based ecological governance should be repealed. Private contractual and other arrangements that interfere with commons- and rights-based ecological governance should be intercepted and cancelled.

Finally, a seventh function must be developed, in the form of *systems for appraisal and recommendation of Commons policies*, capable of comparing the short- and long-term effectiveness of Commons versus State/Market governance in protecting natural resources and ecosystems. The means for reforming misguided or unsuccessful practices must be available, along with the ability to make concrete recommendations for enhanced performance via a new system of triarchical governance by State, Market, and Commons. To this end, people who need to understand the theory and practice of commons in general (ecological or otherwise) – families, teachers, legal and public health specialists, environmental and human rights experts, corporate and labor personnel, governmental and intergovernmental officials, and others – must have access to education and training about commons- and rights-based ecological governance. At the broadest transformational level, strategies must be developed – for households, workplaces, public media, and other venues – to transform the myths and values that shape how people think and act relative to the natural environment, and toward those who seek to protect and enhance it (e.g., ecological commoners). We need new types of broad and deep education to promote stewardship of Nature rather than simply economic and technological mastery of it.

In sum, a strategy worthy of commons- and rights-based ecological governance requires the instigation of a multitude of mechanisms and techniques – from systematic research and documentation, to education and schooling, to domestic legislative programs, to national and international enforcement measures, to long-term initiatives of social transformation – on all fronts at all levels, from the most local to the most global. Also needed will be strategies to engage all elements of society: individuals, families, communities, academic institutions, trade unions, business enterprises, faith-based groups, NGOs and nongovernmental associations, government agencies, IGOs, and others. Perhaps most important, strategies of engagement must proceed self-consciously, proactively, and with imagination and energy if the rights that attend ecological well-being are to be secured.

At a more specific level, several challenges have a special urgency in moving forward. As we noted in Chapter 7, a key priority is to design and establish commons governance regimes for large-scale and planetary resources. These structures cannot simply replicate the flaws of existing international bodies: they must be grounded, instead, in a different set of values and priorities and integrated with systems of smaller-scale commons governance. Another urgent challenge is to restore some measure of commons- and rights-based ecological governance in societies that have already privatized ownership of much of their land and natural resources. We need to develop practical legal strategies and theoretical frameworks to help us confront the environmental *problématique* holistically. Finally, among many additional problems that surely will arise, there are practical challenges in unleashing the imagination and commitment of commoners themselves. To this end, the State must explore legal innovations that can sanction social charters, ecological trusts, State/Commons partnerships, and other vehicles to formally recognize and, in keeping with fundamental human rights principles, empower self-organized commons.

Human rights have been a persistent theme throughout this book, and for good reason. They provide a strategic pathway to the regeneration of the right to environment in the commons renaissance and an indispensable element in the governance of any one commons. Also, human rights have a deep and powerful role to play in advancing a new, more integrated vision of ecological stewardship, sustainable economics, and commons-based governance. We make these critical points in Chapter 4, Section A of Chapter 4. Shifting the ecological governance paradigm via human rights, we argued, unleashes the power to assert maximum claims on society and valorizes environmental well-being as indispensable to human dignity. It challenges statist and elitist agendas, and carries with it a sense of legal and political entitlement on the part of the rights-holder and duties of implementation on the part of the rights-protector. The commons paradigm itself has deep roots in human rights as a body of legal and moral advocacy – while also bringing forward additional advantages: a venerable body of historical law, a distinct analytic and popular discourse, and a rich inventory of functional models. We believe this is an attractive framework for reimagining the world and thereby addressing myriad ecological challenges more effectively.

We come, then, to the end – and the beginning. We seek green governance and a human right to a clean, healthy, biodiverse, and sustainable environment that can be instrumental in both its achievement and its operation. If we are truly to achieve this vision, we must gird ourselves for the ambitious task of imagining alternative futures; mobilizing new energies and commitments; deconstructing archaic institutions while building new ones; devising new public policies and legal mechanisms; cultivating new understandings of human rights, economics, and commons; and, perhaps most daunting of all, reconsidering some deeply rooted prejudices about governance and human nature.

The good news is that some of this work to imagine and build an alternative future is already underway, fueled by a surging corps of activists, academics, and other project leaders around the world.[3] In Berlin, the newly established Mercator Research Institute on Global Commons and Climate Change is explicitly exploring how the Commons can guide future climate research and policy. Asian academics and activists convened a "Re-thinking Property" conference in Bangkok. Thousands of activists went to Rio de Janeiro to pressure the official Rio+20 environmental summit to formally embrace the Commons as a promising strategy. Members of Occupy Wall Street met in 2012 to explore the synergies between the Occupy and Commons movements. The mayor of Naples, Italy, has rallied Italian municipal officials to protect local commons, and has pushed an exploratory effort to win a Europe-wide vote on a European Directive on the Commons. A UN agency launched a

---

[3] This good news and the examples of it that follow are amply documented in *Epilogue* in The Wealth of the Commons, *supra* Ch. 5 note 10, at 434–37.

new online course on the commons just as a fledgling School of Commoning in London offered a twelve-part lecture series on the Commons.

Clearly, this kind of disparate, spontaneous interest in the Commons suggests the stirrings of a larger, more serious movement – one that is willing to dream big dreams, take risks, think creatively, and organize aggressively. But it will need to walk before it runs and to deal with existing national and international policy institutions while inventing new systems of commons governance and practices.

An appropriate beginning, we believe, is to (1) welcome Bolivia's Nature's Rights initiative at the UN and improve on it if we can; (2) advocate for an equivalent initiative recognizing the ecological rights of future generations; (3) press for UN Security Council and/or General Assembly resolutions declaring the atmosphere, the oceans, and other large-scale common-pool resources to be global commons; and (4) in keeping with the Universal Covenant we propose next in our Appendix, urge the importance all manner of constitutional, legislative, administrative, judicial, and private sector initiative – at the United Nations, in City Hall, and *all* points in between – that affirms the Universal Human Right to Commons- and Rights-based Ecological Governance – the human right to green governance – as a common standard of achievement for all humankind. But time is short. We cannot delay. Seamus Heaney says it just right:

> Two sides to every question, yes, yes, yes . . .
> But every now and then, just weighing in
> Is what it must come down to . . . [4]

---

[4] Seamus Heaney, *Weighing In, in* The Spirit Level 22–3 (1996).

Universal Covenant Affirming a Human Right to Commons- and Rights-Based Governance of Earth's Natural Wealth and Resources[*]

PREAMBLE

The 1948 Universal Declaration of Human Rights assertion that "Everyone is entitled to a social and international order in which the rights and freedoms set forth in this Declaration can be fully realized"[1] necessarily mandates a clean and healthy environment, without which human beings cannot fully enjoy their rights.

The principles set forth in the 1972 Stockholm Declaration of the United Nations Conference on the Human Environment[2] unequivocally stipulate that "Man has the fundamental right to freedom, equality and adequate conditions of life, in an environment of a quality that permits a life of dignity and well-being;"[3] and that "[the environment] must be safeguarded for the benefit

---

[*] Prepared for the Commons Law Project by Burns H. Weston and David Bollier with assistance from Samuel M. Degree, Matthew J. Hulstein, and Dinah L. Shelton in the early stages and Jonathan C. Carlson and Anne Mackinnon in the final stage. Copyright © 2012 by Burns H. Weston and David Bollier. This Covenant (or "Green Governance Covenant") may be copied and shared under a Creative Commons Attribution-NonCommercial-ShareAlike 3.0 license (https://creativecommons.org/licenses/by-sa/3.0/us). Indeed, it is encouraged that it be so shared and acted upon widely – adjusted to situational circumstance as needed, of course. To that end, the Covenant is available for downloading, printing, and dissemination on the Commons Law Project website (http://www.commonslawproject.org).

[1] Universal Declaration of Human Rights (UDHR), art. 28, G.A. Res. 217A, at 71, U.N. GAOR, 3d Sess., 1st plen. mtg., U.N. Doc. A/810 (10 Dec 1948), *reprinted in* III INTERNATIONAL LAW AND WORLD ORDER: BASIC DOCUMENTS, at III.A.1 (Burns H. Weston & Jonathan C. Carlson eds., 1994–) (hereinafter "BASIC DOCUMENTS" for all five titles), *available at* http://nijhoffonline.nl/subject?id=ILWO (accessed July 3, 2012).

[2] Stockholm Declaration of the United Nations Conference on the Human Environment (16 June 1972), U.N. Doc A/CONF.48/14/Rev.1 at 3, *available at* http://www.unep.org/Documents.Multilingual/Default.asp?documentid=97&articleid=1503; *reprinted in* V BASIC DOCUMENTS, *supra* note 1, at V.B.3.

[3] *Id.*, Principle 1.

of present and future generations through careful planning or management, as appropriate."[4]

The scientific validity of global climate change and its underlying human causes is authoritatively substantiated by the United Nations Intergovernmental Panel on Climate Change (IPCC) with ominous environmental predictions for the near- and long-term future (the loss of land, forests, freshwater systems, and biodiversity and the increasing frequency of severe weather patterns, including intensified storms, prolonged draught, hurricanes, monsoons, typhoons, and climate shifts) accompanied by hardships to humankind (famine, displacement, disease, and violence) and to other living beings.

Other worsening environmental crises with stressful and life-imperiling consequences for humans and other beings include the depletion of nonrenewable resources, the improper disposal of hazardous wastes, the defilement of precious food and water supplies, and the overall contamination and degradation of delicate ecosystems;

The long history of State and Market abuse and destruction of nature has accelerated since the advent of an essentially unregulated globalization of capital, with investor and corporate interests, often with the active partnership of governments, unrelentingly exploiting polluting energy resources and increasingly commercializing water and other natural wealth and resources once considered beyond the reach of technology and markets.

The lack of international consensus for the principles embodied in the 1997 Kyoto Protocol[5] to the 1992 United Nations Framework Convention on Climate Change[6] and the 1992 Convention on Biological Diversity,[7] as well as the failure of these and other environmental instruments to protect the natural environment sufficiently to safeguard life on Earth for present and future generations, is regrettably well known.

The continuing failure of the world's leaders to acknowledge or address the most fundamental causes of the accelerating ecological and social devastation of our planet, as manifested at the COP 15/MOP 5 2009 United Nations Climate Change Conference in Copenhagen and the 2012 Rio+20 United Nations Conference on Sustainable Development in Rio de Janeiro, is beyond dismaying.

---

4   *Id.*, Principle 2.
5   FCCC/CP/1997/7/Add.1, *reprinted in* 37 I.L.M. 32 (1998) *and* Basic Documents, *supra* note 1, at V.H.8a.
6   1771 U.N.T.S. 107, *reprinted in* 31 I.L.M. 849 (1992) *and* Basic Documents, *supra* note 1, at V.H.8.
7   1760 U.N.T.S. 79, *reprinted in* 31 I.L.M. 818 (1992) *and* Basic Documents, *supra* note 1, at V.N.14.

State and Market leadership has either forgotten or neglects the fact that the authority of the State and the power of private business enterprise stem from the people as sovereign, and from the institutions of civil society that they have created to serve collective human interests.

Also forgotten or neglected, often not even understood, is the reality that the interests of humanity are interdependent with the interests of other creatures that cohabit our planet, and that therefore humanity cannot be adequately protected and sustained without recognizing and defending the rights of Nature and of all beings within its surround.

It thus appears that a new system of ecological governance capable of recognizing Nature's worth and of embracing greater civil society participation must be developed if Nature is to be adequately protected and nourished.

The world community has recognized Antarctica, the deep seabed, and outer space as within "the interest of all mankind" or part of the "common heritage of mankind" in the 1959 Antarctic Treaty,[8] the 1982 United Nations Convention on the Law of the Sea,[9] and the 1967 Treaty on Principles Governing the Activities of States in the Exploration and Use of Outer Space, Including the Moon and Other Celestial Bodies.[10]

However, the deep seabed's "common heritage" status was subsequently denied by powerful State and Market forces whose self-interests were threatened by it; the Outer Space Treaty has yet to be put to the real test of competing economic, political, and strategic priorities; and the Antarctic regime, though so far unbeaten, is increasingly threatened to be compromised by the same kinds of forces and priorities.

The global proliferation of the Internet and new digital technologies, on the other hand, is today enabling imaginative new forms of informal, self-organized, collaborative governance on open platforms that provide powerful means for aggregating and distributing ecological information, coordinating collective responses, enlisting the knowledge and innovation of commoners, and improving management systems, all of which are enabling important "eco-digital" commons that can help preserve our planet and other vital ecological interests.

For millennia, human communities have successfully and sustainably managed the use of ecological resources through commons-based governance, and

---

[8] 402 U.N.T.S. 71, *reprinted in* 19 I.L.M. 860 (1980) *and* BASIC DOCUMENTS, *supra* note 1, at V.D.1.

[9] 1833 U.N.T.S. 3, *reprinted in* 21 I.L.M. 1261 (1982) *and* BASIC DOCUMENTS, *supra* note 1, at V.I.22.

[10] 610 U.N.T.S. 205, *reprinted in* 6 I.L.M. 386 (1967) *and* BASIC DOCUMENTS, *supra* note 1, at V.P.1.

these practices have long been sanctioned by national and international law, as has also the right of individuals and groups to establish and maintain commons to protect their vital ecosystems (the right of commoning).

The historical record and social science research demonstrate the ability of communities of varying sizes and kinds to manage natural wealth and resources equitably, allocate access and use rights fairly, and preserve resources essentially unimpaired for present and future generations, thus serving as responsible long-term stewards of ecological resources.

International law and policy increasingly validate these truths as, for example, in the 1992 People's Earth Declaration[11] – adopted by the International NGO forum of 170,000 civil society participants at the Global Forum that met parallel to the 1992 United Nations Conference on Environment and Development (UNCED) – which proclaims that "[o]rganizing economic life around decentralized relatively self-reliant local economies that control and manage their own productive resources and have the right to safeguard their own environmental and social standards is essential to sustainability."

Especially notable is the 1998 Convention on Access to Information, Public Participation in Decision-Making and Access to Justice in Environmental Matters,[12] which codifies the central importance of public participation in setting environmental policy and calls on its State Parties to take every reasonable step to foster such participation.

Also validating is the 2005 Paris Declaration on Biodiversity,[13] in which scientists participating in the International Conference on Biodiversity Science and Governance – organized by the French Government, sponsored by UNESCO, and attended by over 1,000 participants representing governments, inter-governmental organizations and non-governmental organizations, as well as academia and the private sector – urged governments, policy-makers, and citizens to take the actions necessary to ensure that "biodiversity [be] integrated without delay, based on existing knowledge, into the criteria considered in all economic and policy decisions as well as environmental management."

[11] Adopted June 12, 1992, *reprinted in* V BASIC DOCUMENTS, *supra* note 1, at V.K.2; *also available at* http://habitat.igc.org/treaties/at-01.htm (accessed July 3, 2012).

[12] UNECE Convention on Access to Information, Public Participation in Decision-Making and Access to Justice in Environmental Matters, 25 June, 1998, 2161 U.N.T.S 447, U.N.Doc. ECE/CEP/43, *reprinted in* 38 I.L.M. 517 (1999) and V BASIC DOCUMENTS, *supra* note 1, at V.B.20; *also available at* http://live.unece.org/fileadmin/DAM/env/pp/documents/cep43e.pdf (accessed July 3, 2012).

[13] Adopted Jan. 28, 2005. *reprinted in* 8 J. INT'L WILDLIFE LAW AND POLICY 263 (2005) *and* V BASIC DOCUMENTS, *supra* note 1, at V.K.4; *also available at* htttp://www.unesco.org/new/fileadmin/MULTIMEDIA/HQ/SC/pdf/Paris_declaration_biodiversity.pdf (accessed July 5, 2012).

Noteworthy, too, is a growing recognition of the severity of humankind's abuse of its planetary environment, the unprecedented threat it poses to future generations, and the disastrous harm it has begun already to unleash upon nature and society worldwide.

Hence the emergence of a proposed crime of "ecocide," first in a 1972 Proposed International Convention on the Crime of Ecocide born of the use of Agent Orange during the Vietnam war;[14] more recently urged as a fifth international crime of peace under the 1998 Rome Statute of the International Criminal Court;[15] and today, in the context of the evolving disasters resulting from the excessive emission of greenhouse gases into the atmosphere and the scant State or Market resolve to stop it, seriously contemplated as a crime against humanity.[16]

Hence also the 2000 Earth Charter[17] – created by a global consultation process and endorsed by organizations representing millions of people around the world – which calls for "a sustainable global society founded on respect for nature, universal human rights, economic justice, and a culture of peace" and to these ends affirms it to be "imperative that we, the peoples of Earth, declare our responsibility to one another, to the greater community of life, and to future generations."

And hence, too, the 1997 UNESCO Declaration on the Responsibilities of the Present Generation Towards Future Generations[18] and the 2010 Draft Universal Declaration of the Rights of Mother Earth,[19] the purposes of which are self-evident from their titles.

---

[14] Adopted by the Emergency Conference against Environmental Warfare in Indochina, at Stockholm, June 1972. *Available at* 4 Bull. Peace Proposals 93 (1973). *Reprinted in* V BASIC DOCUMENTS, *supra* note 1, at V.V.1 (accessed July 5, 2012).

[15] Adopted by the United Nations Diplomatic Conference of Plenipotentiaries on the Establishment of an International Criminal Court, July 17, 1998, UN Doc. A/CONF.183/9 (July 17, 1998); *reprinted in* 37 I.L.M. 999 (1998) *and* I BASIC DOCUMENTS I.H.18, *supra* note 1.

[16] *See, e.g.*, Polly Higgins, *Closing the Door to Dangerous Industrial Activity: A Concept Paper for Governments to Implement Emergency Measures* http://www.eradicatingecocide.com/wp-content/uploads/2012/02/Ecocide-Concept-Paper.pdf (accessed July 11, 2012).

[17] Adopted at The Hague by the Earth Charter Commission, June 29, 2000, *available from* the Earth Charter Commission at http://www.earthcharter.org, *reprinted in* V BASIC DOCUMENTS, *supra* note 1, at V.K.3.

[18] Adopted Nov. 12, 1997 on the report of UNESCO Commission V at the 27th plenary meeting of the UNESCO General Conference. *Available at* http://unesdoc.unesco.org/images/0011/001102/110220e.pdf#page=75 (accessed July 5, 2012).

[19] Adopted Apr. 22, 2010 by the World People's Conference on Climate Change and the Rights of Mother Earth at Cochabamba, Bolivia. *Available at* http://celdf.org/downloads/FINAL%20UNIVERSAL%20DECLARATION%20OF%20THE%20RIGHTS%20OF%20MOTHER%20EARTH%20APRIL%2022%202010.pdf (accessed July 5, 2012).

Energizing, then, is the World Social Forum's 2009 Reclaim the Commons Manifesto[20] calling upon "all citizens and organizations to commit themselves to recovering the Earth and humanity's shared inheritance and future creations" and in so doing "demonstrate how commons-based management – participatory, collaborative and transparent – offers the best hope for building a world that is sustainable, fair and life-giving."

THEREFORE, keenly aware of the urgency of taking decisive, collective action to transform existing systems and structures of ecological governance so as to reduce climate change, loss of biodiversity, and other severe threats to Earth's life-giving and life-sustaining capacity,

WE, _____,

CALL UPON all citizens, organizations, and governments of the world to commit themselves to recovering the Earth and humanity's shared inheritance and future creations, and in furtherance of this pledge

AFFIRM a Universal Human Right to Commons- and Rights-based Ecological Governance as a common standard of achievement for all humankind, and to this end

ADOPT, PROCLAIM, AND IMPLEMENT this Universal Covenant, *mutatis mutandi*, by all manner of constitutional, legislative, administrative, judicial, and private sector initiative to facilitate the prompt and sustained recognition and observance of its ascribed definitions, principles, rights, and duties at all levels of social organization at home and around the world.

ARTICLE I. COMMONS- AND RIGHTS-BASED ECOLOGICAL GOVERNANCE

All natural persons have a human right to commons- and rights-based ecological governance (green governance).

1. Commons- and rights-based ecological governance is a system for using and protecting all the creations of nature and related societal institutions that we inherit jointly and freely, hold in trust for future generations, and manage democratically in keeping with human rights principles grounded in respect for nature as well as human beings, including the right of all people to participate in the governance of wealth and resources important to their basic needs and culture.

---

[20] Opened for signature at the World Social Forum in Belém do Pará (Brazil), January 2009. *Available at* bienscommuns.org. *Reprinted in* V Basic Documents, *supra* note 1, at V.K.5 (accessed July 5, 2012).

2. Typically, commons- and rights-based ecological governance consists of non-State management and control of natural wealth and resources by a defined community of natural persons (commoners), directly or by delegation, as a means of inclusively and equitably meeting basic human needs. It generally operates independently of State control, and it need not be State-sanctioned to be effective or functional.

3. Where appropriate or needed, the State may act as a guardian or trustee for commons- and rights-based ecological governance or formally facilitate its principles and practices by establishing commons-like State institutions to manage publicly owned natural wealth and resources.

ARTICLE II. PRINCIPLES OF INTERNAL GOVERNANCE

1. The natural environment is the common heritage of all humankind, belonging to all natural persons present and future, and shall be respected as such by all commons- and rights-based governance systems.

2. Commons- and rights-based governance systems shall at all times responsibly account for the fragile and complex interdependence of living ecosystems, social and cultural norms, the aesthetic value of the environment, the interests of future generations, and the ultimate dependence of humankind on our Earth for health and survival.

3. Social cooperation, trust, and reciprocity are essential to the success of commons- and rights-based ecological governance.

   a. To these ends the self-determined constitutive and operational rules of green governance systems must be conducive to ensuring that

      1) reliable information is available about the immediate and long-term costs and benefits of actions as measured in both quantitative and qualitative terms;

      2) individual commoners understand that their shared resources are important for their own interests and long-term security, and therefore are motivated to act as trustworthy, reciprocal and openly communicative commoners in the shared management of ecological resources;

      3) informal as well as formal monitoring of resource use and sanctioning of rules-violators are feasible and considered appropriate; and

      4) the culture, leadership and historical continuity of a commons enable it to adapt and learn in addressing ecological management challenges over time.

b. To these ends also the self-determined constitutive and operational rules of green governance systems shall guarantee to all involved individuals and groups:

    1) the right to be informed, which includes

        a) the right to prior notice of proposed decisions and policies that may significantly affect their common assets, governance covenant, community ethos, and cultural identity;

        b) the right to clear and complete information on the ecological impact of activities that may significantly affect their common assets, governance covenant, community ethos, and cultural identity;

        c) the right to effective access to legislative, administrative, judicial, or other proceedings during which decisions that may have significant ecological impact upon the common assets are under discussion; and

    2) the right to participation, which includes

        a) when practical, the right to participate directly in decisions affecting their common assets, governance covenant, community ethos, and cultural identity;

        b) in the absence of a practical opportunity for direct participation, the right to adequate representation of their interests in the stewardship of common assets;

        c) the right to consistent and meaningful access to any representative ecological decision-makers as well as effective mechanisms of communication and accountability;

        d) the right to timely and accessible public hearings before decisions are made that may significantly affect their common assets, governance covenant, community ethos, and cultural identity; and

    3) the right to recourse, for themselves or as surrogates for future generations, from competent internal decision-making institutions or processes for redress of violations of their rights to ecological information and participation.

4. Human rights (applicable to both present and future generations) and nature's rights (applicable to all species present and future) are likewise essential to the success of commons- and rights-based ecological governance, including the human right to commons- and rights-based ecological governance recognized in this Universal Covenant.

    a. To this end, commons- and rights-based ecological governance shall embody the values of human dignity as expressed in the 1948

Universal Declaration of Human Rights[21] and such human rights treaties evolved from it that have been designated "core international human rights instruments" by the Office of the United Nations High Commissioner for Human Rights.[22]

b. To the same end, commons- and rights-based ecological governance shall embody the values expressed in the Universal Declaration of the Rights of Mother Earth adopted by the World People's Conference on Climate Change and the Rights of Mother Earth in 2008 and submitted by the Plurinational State of Bolivia to the United Nations for consideration in 2010.[23]

c. If and when the application of human rights and nature's rights differ or conflict, such disagreement shall be resolved in a way that best promotes the integrity, balance, and health of Earth for the benefit of present and future generations and other beings.

5. Commons- and rights-based ecological governance shall be based on the principle of local control and subsidiarity to the maximum extent feasible. Green governance by default should aspire to the lowest level of policy- and decision-making possible, with conscientious and generous support from institutions of greater scale and authority.

6. To protect common assets, commons- and rights-based ecological governance systems shall conscientiously adhere to a precautionary approach when threats of damage to ecological resources are serious or potentially irreversible. Lack of full scientific certainty shall not be used as justification for postponing cost-effective measures to prevent environmental degradation.

7. Commoners shall have collective control over the surplus value they create through the collective management of their shared wealth and resources. To this end, commons- and rights-based ecological governance shall not be cash-driven or market-mediated except with the explicit consent of commoners and clear rules for personal use and resource alienability. The freedom of commoners to limit or ban the monetization of their shared assets shall not be compromised.

8. Property rights granted by commons- and rights-based governance systems for use of natural wealth and resources to individuals or groups (public, private or commons-based) are not absolute; they must conform

---

[21] *Supra* note 1.
[22] *See* Office of the United Nations High Commissioner for Human Rights (OHCHR) at http://www2.ohchr.org/english/law/index.htm#core (accessed July 5, 2012).
[23] *Supra* note 17.

to the principles and practices of commons- and rights-based ecological governance as recognized and reaffirmed in this Universal Covenant.

9. Conflicts and disputes within commons- and rights-based ecological governance systems shall be settled through self-organized dispute resolution systems to the maximum extent feasible, using techniques and procedures that favor dialogue, mutual respect, and restorative outcomes among the disagreeing parties.

ARTICLE III. PRINCIPLES AND POLICIES TO GUIDE STATE SUPPORT OF COMMONS- AND RIGHTS-BASED ECOLOGICAL GOVERNANCE

1. Earth belongs to everyone, and its services and infrastructure are necessary for the well-being and survival of all humans and other species. The State shall therefore facilitate and safeguard commons- and rights-based governance of Earth's wealth and resources as part of its mission to protect, conserve, and restore (where necessary) the integrity, health, and sustainability of the vital ecological balances, cycles, and processes that nourish communities and enhance life on Earth. In these critical respects, the State shall strive to work as a generous partner, not a stern overlord, of green governance systems.

2. In furtherance of foregoing Article III (1), the State and its agents at all levels shall:

    a. recognize and promote the full implementation and enforcement of the principles, rights, and obligations proclaimed or reaffirmed in this Universal Covenant, including the human right to commons- and right-based ecological governance recognized herein;

    b. without financial burden, assist commoners in fulfilling their rights to current, timely, and clear ecological information, including but not limited to:

        1) the compilation, maintenance, and regular updating by all public authorities of environmental information relevant to their functions,

        2) the assessment of the ecological impact of any activity that may significantly impact the environment, especially large-scale common-pool resources and prompt publication thereof on the Internet, with opportunities for public dialogue, and

        3) the facilitation of crowdsourcing of knowledge, information, and new initiatives to assist State activities designed to support the Commons Sector.

c. further and similarly assist the public by guaranteeing its rights to participation in ecological decision- and policy-making and to justice in environmental matters, ensuring, *inter alia*, that individuals exercising their rights, including their rights to petition government, are not penalized, persecuted, or otherwise harassed or disadvantaged for raising and expressing their ecological concerns;

d. fully and actively support the right of all individuals and groups, sanctioned by national and international law and reaffirmed in this Universal Covenant, to protect, conserve, and restore (where necessary) their vital ecosystems via commons governance in national, subnational, and transnational settings;

e. in exercise of its partnership with commons- and rights-based ecological governance, collaborate with established and new green governance systems in the invention, recommendation, and initiation of new policy structures (normative, institutional, and procedural) that could work effectively to manage large-scale national, transboundary and global common-pool resources; and

f. cooperate fully with other States, appropriate intergovernmental organizations (including the United Nations and its system of organizations), and civil society in respect of vital ecological matters largely beyond the limits of the State's territorial jurisdiction, in particular in respect of large-scale transboundary and global common-pool resources, and the invention, recommendation, and initiation of effective new policy structures for the management of them.

3. In keeping with foregoing Articles I(4) and III(1), when ecological or economic conditions require, the State may:

a. serve as a trustee of common-pool resources belonging to commoners if the commoners so authorize or if protection of a given resource so requires it; and

b. charter or otherwise authorize responsible parties to manage common-pool resources as ecological commons when such stewardship can be shown to serve the public interest;

c. provided, however, that in each of the foregoing instances the State, its agents, and its surrogates shall create transparent and accountable ecological management systems under State law that are compatible with commons- and rights-based ecological governance principles, rights, and duties, and that beneficiary interests are well served with effective accountability systems. Commoners' rights shall not be alienated or diminished except for the purpose of protecting the commoners' shared resources for future generations.

4. The State has an affirmative duty to prevent enclosures of ecological commons and common-pool resources. To this end, it shall formally recognize such commons and resources by State law to the maximum possible.

5. The State has an affirmative duty also to ensure that private property owners – individuals and commercial interests alike – shall exercise maximum caution not to externalize environmental risks, damage, or costs onto the environment in general or ecological commons in particular, or otherwise act in ways that are incompatible with the principles, rights, and duties of commons- and rights-based ecological governance. To this end, the State shall, among other environmentally protective policies, conscientiously adhere to:

   a. a precautionary approach to prevent human activities from causing species extinction, the destruction of ecosystems, or the disruption of ecological cycles onto ecological commons in particular and the wider environment in general – the lack of full scientific certainty never to be used as justification for postponing cost-effective measures to prevent environmental degradation, especially when such degradation is serious or potentially irreversible; and

   b. the principle that the polluter, not the general public or the commoner, remedies any harm that may occur despite best efforts – the remedy, however, shall not to be considered the equivalent of the ecological loss if it be in the form of financial compensation exclusively and therefore shall not to be considered exhaustive of remedial responsibility, which shall include, but not be limited to, restoration of the integrity and health of the damaged resource to the maximum extent possible.

6. The State has an affirmative duty to eliminate nuclear, chemical, and biological weapons, all of which are antithetical to a clean and healthy environment, including common-pool ecological resources (managed or unmanaged).

ARTICLE IV. DUTIES OF MARKET ACTORS TOWARDS COMMONS-
AND RIGHTS-BASED ECOLOGICAL GOVERNANCE

1. Market actors, comprised of both natural and juridical persons, shall honor and respect the existence and expansion of commons- and rights-based ecological governance and, to the extent possible, support the human right to commons-and right-based ecological governance recognized in this Universal Covenant. To this end, they shall:

    a. act in accordance with the principles, rights, and duties recognized in this Universal Covenant, including the full realization of the human right to commons- and right-based ecological governance recognized in this Universal Covenant;

    b. recognize and promote their full implementation to the maximum of their capabilities;

    c. cooperate fully with State officials in their efforts to facilitate commons- and rights-based ecological governance systems, in particular by providing, when requested, clear, current, and timely environmental information to State and Commons officials alike; facilitating active commoner participation in ecological governance; and helping to ensure commoner access to justice in environmental matters, when needed.

2. Market actors shall conscientiously establish and apply effective norms to protect, conserve, and restore (where necessary) the natural resources with which they become involved, including the shared resources of ecological commons. In this regard, they shall assess fully and transparently any proposed activity of their own that might impact adversely the environment in general and common-pool ecological resources in particular. If ecological harm results nonetheless, the market actor, not the general public or commoners, shall remedy the harm. The remedy, however, shall not to be considered the equivalent of the ecological loss if it be in the form of financial compensation exclusively, and therefore shall not be considered exhaustive of the market actor's responsibility, which shall include, but not be limited to, restoration of the integrity and health of the damaged resource to the maximum extent possible.

3. Market actors shall cooperate fully with ecological commons systems, State officials, intergovernmental organizations, and civil society in the management of vital ecological resources, both within and beyond the limits of their domiciles (in the case of natural persons) or executive and operational headquarters (in the case of juridical persons), in particular in respect of large-scale transboundary and global common-pool resources. Market actors shall be invited to help invent, recommend, and initiate effective new policy structures for Market activity that are consistent with commons- and rights-based ecological management.

4. At no time shall private actors seek to undermine or otherwise compromise commons- and rights-based ecological governance systems. They shall undertake, instead, to partner with green governance systems, not to compete with them, in the preservation, conservation, and,

where necessary, restoration of vital ecological resources, including vital common-pool ecological resources.

5. Market actors shall at all times cooperate with the State in fulfillment of its affirmative duty to eliminate nuclear, chemical, and biological weapons, as well as other toxic substances antithetical to a clean and healthy environment, including common-pool resources whether managed or unmanaged.

ARTICLE V. (DUTIES OF UNITED NATIONS AND OTHER INTERGOVERNMENTAL ORGANIZATIONS)

1. The United Nations and its system of organizations shall contribute to the extent of their capacities to the creation, support, and proliferation of commons- and rights-based ecological governance through the mobilization of financial cooperation, technical assistance, and other methods and means of promoting such governance.

   a. To this end, the Member States of the United Nations and the intergovernmental organizations that have agreed to achieve eight Millennium Development Goals (MDGs)[24] by 2015, including "ensuring environmental sustainability," shall strive both before and, if possible, after 2015, to make the creation, support, and proliferation of commons-and rights-base ecological governance an integral part of the MDG policy frame.

   b. The United Nations and its system of organizations shall contribute also to the full realization of the human right to commons- and rights-based ecological governance recognized and defined in this Universal Covenant. In this regard,

      1) the General Assembly shall formally recognize this right to green governance, and, in accordance with Article 22 of the Charter of the United Nations, shall establish and actively support a subsidiary organ empowered to refer cases to the International Court of Justice for compulsory advisory opinions on all matters pertinent to said right; and

      2) the United Nations shall use its good offices to establish a permanent Ecological Governance Oversight Panel (or equivalent) charged with responsibility to help safeguard the human right to commons- and rights-based ecological governance for present and future generations. The Panel shall have legal standing before

---

[24] Millennium Development Goals, http://www.un.org/millenniumgoals (accessed July 8, 2012).

the Human Rights Council and all other relevant United Nations bodies, both treaty and non-treaty, on all matters pertinent to this right.

2. All other appropriate intergovernmental organizations – including but not limited to such global institutions as the International Monetary Fund (IMF), the World Bank, and the World Trade Organization (WTO); and such regional systems as the African Union (AU), the Association of Southeast Asian Nations (ASEAN), the European Union (EU), and the Organization of American States (OAS) – shall

   a. at all times cooperate with the United Nations and its system of organizations in their efforts to promote and protect both commons- and rights-based ecological governance and the full realization of the universal right of all natural persons to it as set forth in this Universal Covenant; and

   b. to the extent of their financial, technical, and other capacities take initiatives of their own to promote and protect both green governance and the full realization of the universal right of all natural persons to it as set forth in this Universal Covenant.

The International Legal Status of the Human Right to a Clean and Healthy Environment

The human right to environment is today officially recognized juridically in essentially three ways:

- as an entitlement derived from other recognized rights, centering primarily on the substantive rights to life, health, and respect for private and family life but occasionally embracing other perceived surrogate rights as well – for example: habitat, property, livelihood, culture, dignity, equality or nondiscrimination, and sleep;
- as an entitlement autonomous unto itself, dependent on no more than its own recognition and increasingly favored over the derivative approach insofar as national constitutional and regional treaty prescriptions proclaiming such a right are evidence; and
- as a cluster of procedural entitlements generated from a "reformulation and expansion of existing human rights and duties" (akin to the derivative substantive rights noted first above) and commonly referred to as "procedural environmental rights."

We assess each of these three approaches in the pages following.

A. AS DERIVED FROM OTHER RECOGNIZED RIGHTS

Most human rights treaties, declarations, and other international instruments do not reference the natural environment explicitly. This is so mainly because the majority of those instruments came into being before the environment – especially the global environment – became widely understood to require universally concerted attention and protection.[1] As a result, the human right

---

[1] For example, while the first Earth Day took place in the United States in 1970, the first *international* Earth Day did not come to pass until 1990, and then at the hands of an individual

to a clean and healthy environment has developed over time as an entitlement derived from other rights that had already been recognized before it became desirable and fashionable, nationally as well as internationally, to champion the right to a clean and healthy environment as an autonomous right, complete unto itself.[2]

Predominant are the internationally recognized human rights to life and to health, which are frequently conjoined in environmental discussions and contexts. As the United Nations (UN) General Assembly presciently "determined" more than three decades ago in a resolution titled "Historical responsibility of States for the preservation of nature for present and future generations," the preservation of nature is "a prerequisite for the normal life of man."[3] Similarly, but more recently, in the 1997 case of the *Gabcíkovo-Nagymaros Project* (Hung. v. Slovk.), the International Court of Justice observed that "[t]he protection of the environment is . . . a vital part of contemporary human rights doctrine, for it is a *sine qua non* for numerous human rights such as the right to health and the right to life itself."[4]

As implied, however, the right to a clean and healthy environment is not derived exclusively from the rights to life and health. Indeed, in many decisions – diplomatic, parliamentary, judicial, administrative – these substantive rights are themselves commonly cited in conjunction with the right to respect for private and family life.

1. *The Environment and the Substantive Rights to Life, Health, and Respect for Private and Family Life*

The right to life is arguably the most fundamental and uncontested of international human rights. As stated by the Human Rights Committee, commenting on Article 6 of the 1966 International Covenant on Civil and Political Rights (ICCPR),[5] the right to life is "the supreme right from which no derogation

---

citizen, not a government or intergovernmental organization. *See Earth Day*, Wikipedia, available at http://en.wikipedia.org/wiki/Earth_Day (accessed Nov. 28, 2010).

[2] For helpful, extended elucidation, *see* Dinah Shelton, *Human Rights and the Environment: What Specific Environmental Rights Have Been Recognized?*, 35 Denv. J. Int'l L. & Pol'y 129 (2006).

[3] G.A. Res. 35/8, U.N. GAOR, 35th Sess., Supp. No. 48, U.N. Doc. A/35/48, at 15 (Oct. 30, 1980).

[4] 1997 I.C.J. 7, 88 (Sept. 25) (separate opinion of Judge and Vice-President Weeramantry). Judge Weeramantry added: "It is scarcely necessary to elaborate on this, as damage to the environment can impair and undermine all the human rights spoken of in the Universal Declaration and other human rights instruments." *Id.* at 91–2.

[5] ICCPR, Dec. 16, 1966, 993 U.N.T.S. 171, *reprinted in* III International Law and World Order: Basic Documents at III.A.3 (Burns H. Weston & Jonathan C. Carlson eds., Titles I-V, 1994)

is permitted even in times of public emergency. . . . It is basic to all human rights."[6]

The right to life was first officially recognized in Article 3 of the 1948 Universal Declaration of Human Rights (UDHR),[7] which states that "everyone has the right to life, liberty, and security of person," a principle that continues across a wide spectrum of international human rights instruments – global and regional, binding and nonbinding. The right is now widely understood to protect not only against the arbitrary deprivation of life as provided in Article 6 of the ICCPR expressly,[8] but as well, explicitly and implicitly, against "other aspects" of the right[9] – for example, the death penalty; denial to children of water, food, and medicine; abuse of the disabled; the imperilment of refugees; genocide; and war crimes.[10]

[hereinafter Basic Documents for all five titles], available at http://nijhoffonline.nl/subject?id= ILWO (accessed May 1, 2012) (hosting many other multilateral treaties bearing upon the natural environment, globally, regionally, directly, and indirectly). Article 6(1) of the ICCPR provides: "Every human being has the inherent right to life. This right shall be protected by law. No one shall be arbitrarily deprived of his life." The Committee, established pursuant to ICCPR Articles 29–47, monitors the ICCPR's implementation.

[6] Human Rights Committee, *General Comment No. 14: Nuclear Weapons and the Right to Life*, at art. 6, available at http://www.unhchr.ch/tbs/doc.nsf/(Symbol)/ 9c882008fd898da7c12563ed004a3b08?Opendocument (accessed Nov. 28, 2010).

[7] UDHR, Dec. 10, 1948, G.A. Res. 217A, U.N. GAOR, 3d Sess., 1st plen. mtg., U.N. Doc. A/810, at 71 (1948), *reprinted in* I Basic Documents, *supra* note 5, at III.A.1.

[8] *Id.*

[9] Office of the U.N. High Commissioner for Human Rights (OHCHR), available at http://www.universalhuman-rightsindex.org/hrsearch/search.do?accessType=catgory&lang= en&categories=48&orderBy=country&clusterCategory=category&annoType=observations (accessed Nov. 28, 2010).

[10] In addition to UDHR art. 3 and ICCPR art 6, see, for example, Second Optional Protocol to the International Covenant on Civil and Political Rights, G.A. Res. 44/128, at 206, U.N. GAOR, 44th Sess., Supp. No. 49, U.N. Doc. A/44/49, at 206 (Dec. 15, 1989), *reprinted in* 29 Int'l Legal Materials 1464 (1990) [hereinafter "I.L.M."] *and* III Basic Documents, *supra* note 5, at III.A.5; Convention on the Rights of the Child [hereinafter "CRC"], arts. 23(1) & 37, Nov. 20, 1989, 1577 U.N.T.S. 3, *reprinted in* 28 I.L.M. 1448 (1989) *and* III Basic Documents, at III.D.5; International Convention on the Protection and Promotion of the Rights and Dignity of Persons with Disabilities, art. 10, G.A. Res. 61/106, U.N. GAOR, 61st Sess., Supp. No. 49, U.N. Doc. A/61/49, at 65 (Dec. 13, 2006), *reprinted in* 46 I.L.M. 443 (2007) *and* III Basic Documents, at III.E.4; Convention Relating to the Status of Refugees, art. 33, July 28, 1951, 189 U.N.T.S. 150, *reprinted in* III Basic Documents, at III.G.4; Convention on the Prevention and Punishment of the Crime of Genocide, Dec. 9, 1948, 78 U.N.T.S. 277, *reprinted in* III Basic Documents, at III.J.1; Rome Statute of the International Criminal Court, July 17, 1998, U.N. Doc. A/CONF.183/9, *reprinted in* 37 I.L.M. 999 (1998) and I Basic Documents, at I.H.13.

For comparable embrace of the right to life regionally, see, for example, European Convention for the Protection of Human Rights and Fundamental Freedoms (ECHR), art. 2, Nov. 4, 1950, 213 U.N.T.S. 221, C.E.T.S. No. 5, *reprinted in* III Basic Documents, *supra* note 5, at III.B.8; Protocol (No. 6) to the ECHR Concerning the Abolition of the Death Penalty,

Much the same can be said of the right to health, likewise high among international law's human rights priorities. Beginning with UDHR Article 25(1), which proclaims that "everyone has the right to a standard of living adequate for the health and well-being of himself and of his family, including food, clothing, housing and medical care and necessary social services," it, too, is reaffirmed among a broad array of instruments (again, global and regional, binding and nonbinding). The most prominent among them is, arguably, the 1966 International Covenant on Economic, Social and Cultural Rights (ICESCR). "The States Parties to the present Covenant," the ICESCR stipulates broadly, "recognize the right of everyone to the enjoyment of the highest attainable standard of physical and mental health."[11] In its General Comment 14 of August 11, 2000, the Committee on Economic, Social and Cultural Rights (CESR), charged to oversee the implementation of the ICESCR, identified this right to embrace "a wide range of socio-economic factors that promote conditions in which people can lead a healthy life,

---

Apr. 28, 1983, 1496 U.N.T.S. 281, C.E.T.S. No. 114, *reprinted in* 22 I.L.M. 538 (1983) *and* III Basic Documents, at III.B.8(f); Charter of Fundamental Rights of the European Union, art. 2, Dec. 7, 2000, C364 O.J.E.C. 8, 2007 O.J. (C303) 1, *reprinted in* 40 I.L.M. 266 (2001) *and* III Basic Documents, at III.B.19, now incorporated into the Consolidated Version of the Treaty on the Functioning of the European Union, Dec. 1, 2009, 2010 O.J. (C 83) 1, *reprinted in* I Basic Documents, at I.B.13(h); American Declaration of the Rights and Duties of Man (ADRDM), art. 1, Mar. 30-May 2, 1948, O.A.S. Res. XXX, O.A.S. Off. Rec. OEA/Ser.L/V/1.4(Rev.), *reprinted in* III Basic Documents, at III.B.27; American Convention on Human Rights, art. 1, Nov. 22, 1969, 1144 U.N.T.S. 123, O.A.S.T.S. 36, O.A.S. Off. Rec. OEA/Ser.L/V/II.23, Doc. 21, Rev. 6, *reprinted in* 9 I.L.M. 99 (1970) *and* III Basic Documents, at III.B.32; African Charter on Human and People's Rights ("Banjul Charter"), art. 4, June 27, 1981, O.A.U. Doc. CAB/LEG/67/3/Rev. 5, *reprinted in* 21 I.L.M. 58 (1982) *and* III Basic Documents, at III.B.1; African Charter on the Rights and Welfare of the Child, art. 5, July 11, 1990, O.A.U. Doc. CAB/LEG/24.9/49, *reprinted in* III Basic Documents, at III.B.3.

[11] ICESCR, Dec. 16, 1966, 993 U.N.T.S. 3, art. 12(1), *reprinted in* III Basic Documents, *supra* note 5, at III.A.2; *see also* the Universal Declaration on the Eradication of Hunger and Malnutrition, para. 1, Nov. 16, 1974, U.N. Doc. E/CONF.65/20 (1974), *reprinted in* III Basic Documents, at III.N.1; International Convention on the Elimination of All Forms of Racial Discrimination (ICERD), art. 5(3), Dec. 21, 1965, 660 U.N.T.S. 195, *reprinted in* III Basic Documents III.I.1; Convention on the Elimination of All Forms of Discrimination Against Women, arts. 11(1)(f) & 12(1), Dec. 18, 1979, 1249 U.N.T.S. 13, *reprinted in* 19 I.L.M. 33 (1980) *and* III Basic Documents, at III.C.12; CRC, *supra* note 10, art. 24; International Convention on the Protection and Promotion of the Rights and Dignity of Persons with Disabilities, *supra* note 10, art. 25.

For comparable embrace of the right to health regionally, see, for example, the 1981 Banjul Charter, *supra* note 10, art. 4; Additional Protocol to the American Convention on Human Rights in the Area of Economic, Social and Cultural Rights, art. 10, Nov. 17, 1988, O.A.S.T.S. No. 69 (1988) *reprinted in* 28 I.L.M. 156 (1989) *and* III Basic Documents, at III.B.32(a); African Charter on the Rights and Welfare of the Child, *supra* note 10, art. 14; July 11, 1990 European Social Charter (Revised), arts. 3, 7, 8, 11 & 23, May 3, 1996, C.E.T.S. No. 163, *reprinted in* III Basic Documents, at III.B.10.

and extends to the underlying determinates of health, such as . . . a healthy environment."[12]

These texts and others like them affirming the rights to life and/or health are rich with interpretative opportunity. As evidenced by UN General Assembly Resolution 35/8 and the *Gabčíkovo-Nagymaros Project* case quoted above,[13] they make possible, among other things, the now widespread legal judgment that environmental harms that threaten or negate basic human life and health should be and in fact are recognized to fall within the scope of these two rights. "It is scarcely necessary to elaborate on this," the World Court stated further in *Gabčíkovo-Nagymaros*, "as damage to the environment can impair and undermine all the human rights spoken of in the Universal Declaration and other human rights instruments."[14] These 1980 and 1997 pronouncements surely were influenced by the earlier 1972 Stockholm Declaration, which made the linkage between the rights to life and health and the environment explicit for the first time.[15] "Both aspects of man's environment, the natural and the man-made," it proclaims, "are essential to his well-being and to the enjoyment of basic human rights – even the right to life itself."[16] "Man," it continues, "has the fundamental right to freedom, equality, and adequate conditions of life, in an environment of a quality that permits a life of dignity and well-being, and he bears a solemn responsibility to protect and improve the environment for present and future generations."[17] Not surprisingly, then, although for the first time in a human rights treaty, the 1989 Convention on the Rights of the Child requires its States Parties to take into consideration "the dangers and risks of environmental pollution" when implementing a child's right to health through the application of technology and the provision of nutritious foods and drinking water.[18] Many of the international agreements directed at curbing the illicit movement and discharge of toxic substances also draw on the

---

[12] U.N. Econ. & Soc. Council (ECOSOC), *General Comment 14, Substantive Issues Arising in the Implementation of the International Covenant on Economic, Social and Cultural Rights*, para. 4, U.N. Doc. E/C.12/2000/4 (Aug. 11, 2000).

[13] *See supra* text accompanying notes 3–4.

[14] Gabčíkovo-Nagymaros Project, 1997 I.C.J. 7, 88–89 (Sept. 25).

[15] In the instance of the 1997 *Gabčíkovo-Nagymaros* case, possibly also by the World Charter for Nature adopted by the U.N. General Assembly Oct. 28, 1982. *See* G.A. Res. 37/7, Annex, U.N. GAOR, 37th Sess., Supp. No. 51, U.N. Doc. A/37/51, at 17 (Oct. 28, 1982), *reprinted in* 22 I.L.M. 455 (1983) *and* V Basic Documents, *supra* note 5, at V.B.12.

[16] Stockholm Declaration of the United Nations Conference on the Human Environment, para. 1, June 16, 1972, U.N. Doc. A/CONF.48/14/Rev.1 at 3, U.N. Doc. A/CONF.48/14 at 2–65 and Corr. 1, 1972 U.N. Jurid. Y.B. 319, *reprinted in* V Basic Documents, *supra* note 5, at V.B.3 [hereinafter "Stockholm Declaration"].

[17] *Id.*, princ. 1.

[18] CRC, *supra* note 10, art. 24(2)(c).

Stockholm Declaration and state explicitly their purpose: to protect human life and health.[19] This purpose is shared strongly by the former UN Commission on Human Rights, which, in addition to appointing, in 1995, a Special Rapporteur to assess the human rights impact of such environmental hazards,[20] unequivocally proclaimed in more than one resolution that these hazards "constitute a serious threat to the human rights to life, health and a sound environment for everyone."[21] More recently, the successor UN Human Rights Council has adopted resolutions expressing concern that climate change bears serious implications for the "full" or "effective enjoyment of human rights."[22]

It is against this jurisprudential backdrop that, in addition to the 1997 World Court decision in the *Gabcíkovo-Nagymaros Project* case cited and quoted above,[23] human rights treaty bodies, tribunals, and commissions, especially at the regional level, have confirmed with increasing resolve in recent years the link between human rights and the right to environment. Sometimes this linkage is made via the right to life exclusively, but more often it is with reference to the rights to life, health, and, in time, respect for private and family life in combination or coextensively.

On the global plane, two major treaty bodies have been active in this regard: the CESR, charged to oversee the implementation of the ICESCR,[24] principally by means of a periodic reporting system; and the Human Rights Committee, with equivalent responsibility for the ICCPR[25] but, unlike the

[19] *See, e.g.*, Basel Convention on the Control of Transboundary Movements of Hazardous Wastes and Their Disposal, Mar. 22, 1989, 1673 U.N.T.S. 57, *reprinted in* 26 I.L.M. 649 (1989) *and* V Basic Documents, *supra* note 5, at V.M.4; Convention on the Prevention of Marine Pollution by Dumping of Wastes and Other Matter, Dec. 29, 1972, 1046 U.N.T.S. 120, *reprinted in* V Basic Documents, at V.I.15; Convention on the Transboundary Effects of Industrial Accidents, Mar. 17, 1992, 2105 U.N.T.S. 457, *reprinted in* V Basic Documents, at V.R.2.

[20] *See* U.N. Commission on Human Rights, Resolution 1995/81 (Adverse Effects of the Illicit Movement and Dumping of Toxic and Dangerous Products and Wastes on the Enjoyment of Human Tights), para. 7, E/CN.4/RES/1995/81.

[21] *E.g.*, U.N. Commission on Human Rights Resolution 1999/23 (Adverse Effects of the Illicit Movement and Dumping of Toxic and Dangerous Products and Wastes on the Enjoyment of Human Rights), pmbl., E/CN.4/RES/1999/81; Commission on Human Rights Resolution 2000/72 (Adverse Effects of the Illicit Movement and Dumping of Toxic and Dangerous Products and Wastes on the Enjoyment of Human Rights), pmbl., E/CN.4/RES/2000/72.

[22] *See, e.g.*, U.N. Human Rights Council Resolution 7/23 (Human Rights and Climate Change) (Mar. 28, 2008), available at http://www2.ohchr.org/english/issues/climatechange/docs/Resolution_7_23.pdf (accessed Nov. 28, 2010); U.N. Human Rights Council Resolution 10/4 (Human Rights and Climate Change) (Mar. 25, 2009), available at http://www2.ohchr.org/english/issues/climatechange/docs/ Resolution 104.pdf (accessed Nov. 28, 2010).

[23] *See supra* text accompanying notes 3–4 and 13–14.

[24] The Committee was established pursuant to ECOSOC Resolution 1985/17 of May 28, 1985, to perform the monitoring functions assigned to the U.N. Economic and Social Council (ECOSOC) in Part IV of the ICESCR, *supra* note 11.

[25] *Supra* note 11, pt. IV.

ICESCR, operating like an adjudicative tribunal. In this setting, the CESR has on numerous occasions received reports from the ICESCR's States Parties relative to environmental issues perceived to implicate rights prescribed in the Covenant.[26] Yet, though the CESR sometimes proactively asks for specific environmental information where human rights harms may be involved (a stratagem that recently has been enhanced by follow-up procedures to facilitate compliance),[27] it is primarily the Human Rights Committee that has produced the most informative, albeit limited, jurisprudence. This can be seen, first, in the Committee's 1984 decision in *E.H.P. v. Canada*[28] (shortly after the ICCPR's entry into force); and second, in the Committee's 1996 case of *Bordes and Teneharo v. France*.[29] Accuracy compels acknowledging, however, that these two decisions did not confirm the right-to-life/environment

---

[26] Noteworthy are, for example, the "periodic reports" submitted to the CESR by Ukraine transmitting information on the environmental consequences of the 1986 Chernobyl disaster relative to ICESCR Article 12 (Right to Physical and Mental Health). *See, e.g.,* Economic and Social Council (ECOSOC), *Implementation of the International Covenant on Economic, Social and Cultural Rights: Fourth Periodic Reports Submitted by States Parties Under Articles 16 and 17 of the Covenant on the Basis of the Programmes Referred to in Economic and Social Council Resolution 1988/4*, add. (Ukraine), E/C.12/4/Add.2, § III (art. 12), at 50 (Mar. 21, 2000).

[27] *See* Committee on Economic, Social and Cultural Rights, *Working Methods: Overview of the Present Working Methods of the Committee*, pt. III, available at http://www2.ohchr.org/english/bodies/cescr/working methods.htm (accessed Nov. 28, 2010).

[28] Communication No. 67/1980, U.N. Doc. CCPR/C/OP/1, para. 8 (1984), 2 Selected Decisions of the Human Rights Committee 20 (1990). While declaring the communication (i.e., petition) inadmissable for failure to exhaust local remedies, the HRC found that the storage of radioactive waste in close proximity to the homes of a group of Canadian citizens "raises serious issues with regard to the obligation of States parties [to the 1966 ICCPR] to protect human life (article 6 (1))." *Id.* For the text of Article 6(1), see *supra* text accompanying note 6.

[29] Mrs. Vaihere Bordes and Mr. John Temeharo v. France, Communication No. 645/1995, U.N. Doc. CCPR/C/57/D/645/1995 (1996), available at http://www1.umn.edu/humanrts/undocs/html/DEC64557.htm (accessed Nov. 28, 2010). Bordes and Temeharo, Tahitian citizens, claimed that France's underground nuclear tests on the nearby South Pacific Mururoa and Fangataufa atolls had resulted in "a violation of their right to life and their right to their family life" under ICCPR Articles 6(1) and 17(1). *Id.* at para. 5.5. For the text of Article 6(1), *see supra* text accompanying note 6. ICCPR Article 17(1) provides in part that "[n]o one shall be subjected to arbitrary or unlawful interference with his privacy, family, home or correspondence. . . . " The HRC dismissed the case on the procedural grounds that the complainants did not substantiate that they were "victims" within the meaning of Article 1 of the Optional Protocol to the ICCPR, Dec. 16, 1966, 999 U.N.T.S. 171, 999 U.N.T.S. 302, *reprinted in* 6 I.L.M. 383 (1967) *and* III Basic Documents, *supra* note 5, at III.A.4 (providing in part that "[a] State Party to the Covenant that becomes a Party to the present Protocol recognizes the competence of the Committee to receive and consider communications from individuals subject to its jurisdiction who claim to be victims of a violation by that State Party of any of the rights set forth in the Covenant"). However, at para. 5.9 of its decision, the Committee nevertheless reiterated its observation in its General Comment 14 that "it is evident that the designing, *testing*, manufacture, possession and deployment of nuclear weapons are among the greatest threats to the right to life which confront mankind [sic] today" (emphasis added in the original).

linkage in so many words, but only implicitly. However, we see this bridge crossed unequivocally in the many cases decided in the European (Strasbourg), Inter-American, and African human rights systems, in addition to the World Court's *Gabcíkovo-Nagymaros Project* decision.

The European Human Rights System

Before the 1980s, when concern for the natural environment first began to take hold internationally, the former European Commission of Human Rights and the European Court of Human Rights were deterred from making the connection between right to life and right to environment by the historically understandable omission of any mention of the environment in the 1950 European Convention on Human Rights and Fundamental Freedoms (ECHR)[30] and its protocols.[31] Thereafter, however, not only the right to life, but also, even more so, the right to respect for private and family life became a part of the European Court's dominant repertoire when assessing claims seeking protection from environmental harms under the ECHR.

Numerous cases decided by the Court, variously responding to claims of violation of ECHR Articles 2 (right to life) and 8 (respect for private and family life), are illustrative – for example, the oft-cited cases of *Öneryildiz v. Turkey* (Article 2)[32]

---

[30] *Supra* note 10.

[31] According to Daniel I. García San José, *Environmental Protection and the European Convention on Human Rights* 7 (2005), two early applications seeking protection from environmental harms under the Convention were declared inadmissable by the former European Commission on Human Rights for being "incompatible *ratione materiae* with the Convention": Dr. S. v. F.R.G., App. No. 715/60 (unpublished, Aug. 5, 1969) and X & Y v. F.R.G., App. No. 7407/76, 5 Eur. Comm'n H.R. Dec. & Rep. 161 (May 13, 1976).

[32] 41 Eur. Ct. H.R. 20 (2004). The first right to life case brought to the European Court relative to an environmental harm, the Court held in *Öneryildiz* that the Turkish government was responsible for deaths caused by a methane explosion at a municipal rubbish disposal site, primarily on the grounds that there had been a violation of Article 2 of the European Convention, *supra* note 10, in both "its substantive aspect [unanimously agreed to], on account of the lack of appropriate steps to prevent the accidental death of nine of the applicant's close relatives"; and "its procedural aspect [by 16 to 1 vote], on account of the lack of adequate protection by law safeguarding the right to life," *id.*, para. 71. Article 2 "must be construed," the Court explained, "as applying in the context of any activity, whether public or not, in which the right to life may be at stake, and a fortiori in the case of industrial activities, which by their very nature are dangerous, such as the operation of waste-collection sites. . . ." *Id.* Interestingly, the Court referenced Article 56 of the 1982 Turkish Constitution (as amended), providing for the autonomous environmental entitlement that "[e]veryone has the right to live in a healthy, balanced environment" and that "[i]t is the duty of the state and citizens to improve the natural environment, and to prevent environmental pollution." *Id.* para. 52; *see also infra* note 174). Also interesting is that it referenced the 1993 European Convention on Civil Liability for Damage Resulting from Activities Dangerous to the Environment (C.E.T.S. No. 150) and the 1998 European Convention on the Protection of the Environment through Criminal Law (C.E.T.S. No. 172), neither of which, the Court acknowledged, had been signed or ratified by a majority of the member states of the Council of Europe, Turkey included, at the

and *López Ostra v. Spain* (Article 8).[33] So also are a growing number of
cases that have followed or been guided by these precedents.[34] A number
of cases note the connection between the rights to life and environment,

time – indeed, they have yet to enter into force even at this writing. One may conclude from
these invocations that the European Court's commitment to a clean and healthy environment
is strong, to protect and preserve the right to life at least.

[33] 20 Eur. Ct. H.R. 277 (1994). In *López Ostra*, the European Court's first major Article 8
decision and preceding *Öneryildiz* by ten years, the applicants, Spanish nationals and residents,
complained that the negligent operation of a tannery waste treatment facility a few meters from
their home violated their right to respect for their private and family life guaranteed by Article
8. The facility began operations in 1988 without a license from the municipality as required
by law. Subsequently, a malfunction at the facility caused a release of "gas fumes, pestilential
smells and contamination" that resulted in health problems and a nuisance to the applicants
such that they were forced to sell their house and move from the area. Important for present
purposes is that the Court ruled for the applicants and thereby validated their claim under
Article 8 because the Spanish authorities had failed to take steps to protect the applicant
and her family from the environmental problems caused by the facility and because "severe
environmental pollution [can] affect individuals' well-being and prevent them from enjoying
their homes in such a way as to affect their private and family life adversely, without, however,
seriously endangering their health." *Id.*, para. 51. Also important is that the Court found the
government to have exceeded its "margin of appreciation" in the delicate task of "striking a
fair balance between the interest of the town's economic well-being – that of having a waste-
treatment plant – and the applicant's effective enjoyment of her right to respect for her home
and her private and family life." *Id.*, para. 58.

[34] For a case following *Öneryildiz*, but arising from deaths caused by a natural disaster
(mudslide) rather than human activity, *see* Budayeva v. Russia, App. No. 15339/02,
available at http://cmiskp.echr.coe.int/tkp197/view.asp?Item=1&portal=hbkm&action=html&
highlight=Budayeva&sessionid=78977336&skin=hudoc-en (Mar. 20, 2008) (accessed Nov. 28,
2010); *see also* Öçkan v. Turkey, App. No. 46771/99, available at http://cmiskp.echr.coe.int/
tkp197/view.asp? item=1&portal=hbkm&action=html&highlight=%D6%E7kan%20%7C%
20Others%20%7C%2046771/99&sessionid= 78977447&skin=hudoc-en (Mar. 28, 2006) (available in French only) (accessed Nov. 28, 2010).

For a case similar to and following *López Ostra*, *see* Giacomelli v. Italy, 45 Eur. Ct. H.R.
38 (2006). For other cases following *López Ostra*, *see* Moreno Gómez v. Spain, [2004] Eur.
Ct. H.R. 633; Fadeyeva v. Russia, 45 Eur. Ct. H.R. 10 (2005); Ledyayeva v.
Russia, App. Nos. 53157/99, 53247/99, 53695/00 & 56850/00, available at http://cmiskp
.echr.coe.int/tkp197/view.asp?item=1&portal=hbkm&action=html&highlight=Ledyayeva&
sessionid=78977336&skin=hudoc-en (2005) (accessed Nov. 28, 2010), *reprinted in* 25
Hum. Rts. L.J. 108 (2004), available also in Russian at http://www.supcourt.ru/vs-court‗
detale.php?id=1961 (accessed Nov. 28, 2010); Öçkan (2006), *supra*; Tatar v. Romania,
App. No. 67021/01, available at http://cmiskp.echr.coe.int/tkp197/portal.asp?sessionSimil
(accessed Nov. 28, 2010), ar=78977336&skin=hudoc- en&action=similar&portal=hbkm&
Item=2&similar=frenchjudgement(2009) (French only); *see also* Guerra v. Italy, 26 Eur. Ct.
H.R. 357 (1998) (wherein the European Court ruled that because it found a violation under
Article 8, there was no need to consider an additional claim under Article 2 (right to life)).
To like effect, *see* Taskin v. Turkey, 42 Eur. Ct. H.R. 50 (2004), wherein the Court ruled that
because it found a violation under Article 8 and 6.1 (right to a fair hearing), there was no need
to consider an additional claim under Articles 2 and 13 (right to an effective remedy). For a
López Ostra precursor by 16 years, *see* Arrondelle v. United Kingdom, 19 Eur. Comm'n H.R.
Dec. & Rep. 186 (1980); *see also* cases cited in note 59, *infra*.

but the applicants have *not* been victorious. These include cases in which the Court has dismissed or rejected the claim for failure to exhaust local remedies, to substantiate victim standing, or to establish a firm causal link, disproportionate harm, impermissible risk, or an abuse of a state's discretionary authority ("margin of appreciation").[35] In none of these cases since the 1980s has the Court challenged the underlying causes of action based on the right to life or respect for private and family life. Indeed, they are implicit in the typically procedural grounds for dismissal or rejection. On the basis of these cases alone, the right to a clean and healthy environment may be understood to be accepted as law, however implicitly, in the European human rights system.

One case before the European Committee on Social Rights (established to monitor the European Social Charter (ESC)[36]) relative to the right to health (or, more precisely, "the right to protection of health") confirms this conclusion. In *Marangopoulos Foundation for Human Rights v. Greece*, responding to a 2005 complaint alleging violations of the ESC's right to health provisions (Article 11) stemming from environmentally hazardous lignite mining operations, the Committee, in 2006, held, by 9 votes to 1, "that Greece has not managed to strike a reasonable balance between the interests of persons living in the lignite mining areas and the general interest, and finds that there thus has been a violation of Article 11 §§1, 2 and 3 of the Charter [right to protection of health]."[37] A significant element of this ruling is that the Committee saw fit

---

[35] *See, e.g.*, Baggs v. United Kingdom, 44 Eur. Comm'n H.R. Dec. & Rep. 13 (1985); Powell & Raynor v. United Kingdom, 12 Eur. Ct. H.R. 355 (ser. A) (1990); Hatton v. United Kingdom, 34 Eur. Ct. H.R. 1 (2003); Kyrtatos v. Greece, 40 Eur. Ct. H.R. 16 (2003); Borysewicz v. Poland, App. No. 71146/01 (Jan. 10, 2008); Fägerskiöld v. Sweden, App. No. 37664/04 (Mar. 25, 2008); Kania v. Poland, App. No. 12605/03, (Jul. 21, 2009), available at http://cmiskp .echr.coe.int/tkp197/view.asp?item=1&portal=hbkm&action=html&highlight=Leon%20|% 20Agnieszka%20|%20Kania%20|%20v.%20|%20Poland&sessionid=78978536&skin=hudoc - en (accessed Nov. 28, 2010).

[36] *Supra* note 11.

[37] Emphasizing the link between the rights to health and environment in particular detail, the Committee found: (1) the Greek National Action Plan for greenhouse gas emissions in the framework of the Kyoto Protocol to be "limited and have little dissuasive effect" and (2) the initiatives of the public power corporation operating the Greek lignite mines to adapt plant and mining equipment to the "best available techniques" to have been "slow." It also found (3) that the Greek authorities "[did] not apply ... satisfactorily" domestic legislation concerning information about and public participation in the procedure for approving environmental criteria for projects and activities; (4) that the Greek government "[did] not provide sufficiently" precise information to amount to a valid education policy for persons living in lignite mining areas"; and (5) that "very little [was] done" to organize systematic epidemiological monitoring of those concerned and that "no morbidity studies [were] carried out." The Committee quoted Resolution CM/ResChS(2008)1 of the Committee of Ministers of the Council of Europe adopted Jan. 16, 2008 at the 1015th meeting of the Ministers' Deputies, Council of Europe, available at https://wcd.coe.int/ViewDoc.jsp?id=1235523&Site=CM&BackColor

to pass judgment on the Greek government's lackluster response to its Kyoto Protocol obligations, although this was not required to reach the judgment that it did. It thus sent a clear message that, in future cases, it is likely to take a quite liberal view of the environmentally based claims that may be brought to it, at least in relation to the right to protection of health.

The Inter-American Human Rights System

The bridge between environmental harm and the rights to life and health has been crossed in the inter-American human rights system so far successfully in four known cases. Each involved the lives and well-being of indigenous peoples: three before the Inter-American Commission on Human Rights (IACHR) – its 1985 case of *Yanomami v. Brazil*;[38] its 1997 Report on the Situation of Human Rights in Ecuador;[39] and its 2004 decision in *Maya*

Internet=9999CC&BackColor Intranet=FFBB55&BackColorLogged=FFAC75 (accessed Nov. 28, 2010). The resolution incorporates and endorses the CESR's decision on the merits of Dec. 6, 2006, available at Council of Europe, available at http://www.coe.int/t/dghl/monitoring/social charter/Complaints/CC30 Meritsen.pdf, transmitted by the CESR to the Committee of Ministers the same day.

[38] Case 7615, Inter-Am. C.H.R., Report No. 12/85, OEA/Ser.L/V/II.66, doc. 10, rev. 1 (1985). In this case, the IACHR found that, by reason of Brazil's "failure . . . to take timely and effective measures in behalf of the Yanomami Indians" in the construction of the Northern Circumferential Highway across territory "occupied for ages beyond memory by the Yanomami Indians," it brought about an invasion "by highway construction workers, geologists, mining prospectors, and farm workers desiring to settle in that territory" that resulted in loss of habitat, disease, even bloodshed. In so doing, said the Commission, approximately two decades *before* the European human rights system first admitted environmental injury into the protective custody of the right to life and the right to health, Brazil violated "the right to life, liberty, and personal security (Article I) . . . and the right to the preservation of health and to well-being (Article XI)" of the Yanomami people, referencing rights recognized in the American Declaration of the Rights and Duties of Man. In the same breath, it found a violation also of the right to residence and movement (Article VIII).

[39] Report on the Situation of Human Rights in Ecuador, Inter-Am. C.H.R., OEA/Ser.L/V/II.96, doc. 10, rev. 1, at ch. VIII (1997). Reporting on the human rights situation of some 500,000 indigenous peoples in Ecuador's interior (known as the Oriente), the IACHR observed that "severe environmental pollution" resulting from decades of developmental activities, mostly of oil drilling concessionaires (Texaco and Ecuador's state-run Petroecuador primarily) that dumped close to 16 million gallons of oil and 20 billion gallons of petroleum waste into roughly 17,000 acres of pristine rainforest, had so despoiled the Oriente environment as to threaten the physical and cultural lives of the indigenous inhabitants of the area, in violation of their internationally as well as constitutionally guaranteed rights to life and health:

> The Commission recognizes that the right to development implies that each state has the freedom to exploit its natural resources, including through the granting of concessions and acceptance of international investment. However, the Commission considers that the absence of regulation, inappropriate regulation, or a lack of supervision in the application of extant norms may create serious problems with respect to the environment

Indigenous Community of the Toledo District v. Belize[40] – and one before the Inter-American Court relative to multiple rights in addition to the rights to life and health, the 2001 case of *The Mayagna (Sumo) Awas Tingni Community v. Nicaragua.*[41] In one such case before the Commission and involving the human rights impact of climate change, the case of the *Inuit v. United States,* the bridge has yet to be successfully crossed.[42]

It is, of course, arguable that the four processed cases are of limited general utility because they involve indigenous peoples and their essentially unique identity with, and commitment to, the natural environment, and

> which translate into violations of human rights protected by the . . . American Convention on Human Rights [which] is premised on the principle that rights inhere in the individual simply by virtue of being human. Respect for the inherent dignity of the person is the principle which underlies the fundamental protections of the right to life and to preservation of physical well-being. Conditions of severe environmental pollution which may cause serious physical illness, impairment and suffering on the part of the local populace are inconsistent with the right to be respected as a human being. *Id.*

[40] Case 12.053, Inter-Am. C.H.R., Report No. 40/04, OEA/Ser.L/V/II.122, doc. 5, rev. 1, at 727 (2004). In this case, the IACHR found that, among other infractions, logging and oil concessions granted by the Government of Belize without "meaningful consultation" with the Maya people "violated the right to property enshrined in Article XXIII of the American Declaration to the detriment of the Maya people" and violations of the right to life under ADRDM Article I and the right to health and well-being under Article XI subsumed therein. *Id.* para. 156.

[41] Inter-Am. Ct. H.R. (ser. C) No. 79 (Aug. 31, 2001). In this case, the Inter-American Court held that the Government of Nicaragua, for having ignored and rejected the territorial claim of the indigenous community and granted a logging concession within its traditional land without consulting the Community (in a manner similar to what took place in the 2004 Maya Indigenous Community case described in note 40, *supra*), breached a combination of articles enshrined in the American Convention on Human Rights, *supra* note 11, including Articles 4 (Right to Life), 11 (Right to Privacy), and 17 (Rights of the Family).

[42] In December 2005, Sheila Watt-Cloutier (an Inuk woman and Chair of the Inuit Circumpolar Conference or ICC), on behalf of herself, sixty-two other named individuals, and all Inuit of the Arctic regions of the United States and Canada affected by the impacts of climate change filed with the IACHR a petition requesting the Commission's assistance in obtaining relief "from human rights violations resulting from the impacts of global warming and climate change caused by acts and omissions of the United States." In addition to other claimed violations of international law by the United States, the Petition alleged breaches of the rights to life, health, family life, and other rights proclaimed in the 1948 American Declaration, *supra* note 10, originally adopted as a legally non-binding instrument but today considered a source of legal obligation for member states of the Organization of American States, including the United States. The IACHR rejected the petition without prejudice in November 2006. In January 2007, the ICC requested a hearing with the IACHR to assist the Commission in exploring and better understanding the relationship between global warming and human rights. This hearing was granted, and took place in March 2007. The IACHR has not issued a report since that hearing. For a convenient summary of the details, *see* Kathryn Milun, *The Political Uncommons: The Cross-Cultural Logic of the Global Commons* 2–6 (2011). For the text of the petition, *see* CIEL, available at http://www.ciel.org/Publications/ICC_Petition_7Dec05.pdf (accessed Sept. 24, 2011); for transcripts of relevant testimony at the hearing, *see* CIEL, available at http://www.ciel.org/Climate/IACHR_Inuit_5Mar07.html (accessed Sept. 24, 2011).

the world community's growing deference to their special rights to cultural, socioeconomic, and political self-determination.[43] But to so argue would require rationalizing the 2007 Inter-American Court of Human Rights decision in *Case of the Saramaka People v. Suriname.*[44] Although the Court was not asked to rule on the rights to life and health, it nonetheless spelled out standards it considered mandatory to ensure economic development friendly to the human rights of the indigenous people involved. The Court did not cite the Bonn Guidelines on Access to Genetic Resources and Fair and Equitable Sharing of the Benefits Arising out of their Utilization, adopted pursuant to the Convention on Biological Diversity,[45] but the standards it issued paralleled them. The Bonn guidelines are applicable to indigenous and nonindigenous populations alike. In any event, as evidenced by the decisions rendered in the European human rights system, in cases having nothing to do with indigenous peoples, the legal judgment that the rights to life and/or health are fundamentally dependent on a clean and health environment is manifest.

The African Human Rights System

The African human rights system is unique among the regional human rights systems in that its governing instrument, the 1981 African (or Banjul) Charter on Human and Peoples' Rights,[46] was the first human rights treaty to embrace both first- and second-generation rights and to include, in Article 24, an autonomous right to a "general satisfactory environment."[47] When given the chance, therefore, the commission and a later court established to oversee the Charter's implementation are conceptually freer than their two regional counterparts to extend human rights protection to environmental claims.

---

[43] *See, e.g.,* ILO Convention (No. 169) Concerning Indigenous and Tribal Peoples in Independent Countries, June 27, 1989, 2 ILO Conventions & Recommendations 1436 (1989), ILO Off. Bull. 59 (1989), *reprinted in* 28 I.L.M. 1382 (1989) *and* III Basic Documents, *supra* note 5, at III.F.2; United Nations Declaration on the Rights of Indigenous Peoples, G.A. Res 61/295, U.N. GAOR 61st Sess., Supp. No. 49, vol. III, U.N. Doc. A/61/49, at 15 (Sept. 13, 2007), *reprinted in* 46 I.L.M. 1013 (2007) *and* III Basic Documents, *supra* note 5, at III.F.5.

[44] 2007 Inter-Am. Ct. H.R., Ser. C, No. 172 (Nov. 28, 2007).

[45] Convention on Biological Diversity, June 5, 1992, 1760 U.N.T.S. 79, *reprinted in* 31 I.L.M. 818 (1992) *and* V Basic Documents, *supra* note 5, at V.N.14, available at http://www. cbd.int/doc/publications/cbd-bonn-gdls-en.pdf (accessed Nov. 28, 2010). We are indebted to Professor Dinah Shelton for this insight in Human Rights and Environment: Past, Present, and Future Linkages and the Value of a Declaration 13–14 (unpublished draft paper to the UNEP-OHCHR High-Level Meeting on the New Future of Human Rights and Environment: Moving the Global Agenda Forward, Nov. 30–Dec. 1, 2009), available at http://www.unep.org/environmentalgovernance/LinkClick.aspx?fileticket=vmjUL305H0% 3d&tabid=2004&lang uage=en-US (accessed Nov. 28, 2010).

[46] *Supra* note 10.

[47] Article 24 provides in full as follows: "All peoples shall have the right to a general satisfactory environment favorable to their development."

Because the African system is the youngest of the three regional systems, its experience is necessarily more limited. Indeed, to our best knowledge, it has ventured into the environmental rights realm in only one instance at this writing. In a landmark case factually reminiscent of the environmentally devastating oil company operations in Ecuador's Oriente interior noted above,[48] the Banjul Charter was comprehensively applied.

The case, *The Social and Economic Rights Action Center and the Center for Economic and Social Rights v. Nigeria*, decided by the African Commission on Human and Peoples' Rights in 2001,[49] concerned the decades-long operations of the Shell Petroleum Development Corporation in consort with the Nigerian National Petroleum Development Company that resulted in the severe spoliation of the environment of Ogoniland in the Niger River Delta region of southeast Nigeria on the Gulf of Guinea. The Nigerian government, a military government at the time, had not enforced its environmental laws or otherwise curbed the consortium's destructive oil practices (oil spills, the dumping of industrial waste into the Niger River Delta, the flaring of natural gas into the atmosphere, all reminiscent of the environmentally devastating oil company operations in Ecuador's Oriente interior noted above[50]). For these acts, the government was found to have disregarded its duty "to respect, protect, promote, and fulfill"[51] the obligations it assumed when it became party to the Charter. It was therefore held to have violated a number of the human rights guaranteed to the native Ogoni people in the Banjul Charter, including the right to life (Article 4),[52] the right to health (Article 16), and the right to a "generally satisfactory environment" (Article 24).[53] "These rights,"

---

[48] *See supra* note 39.

[49] African Commission on Human and Peoples' Rights, Comm. No. 155/96, Case No. ACHPR/COMM/A044/1, Oct. 27, 2001, available at http://www.umn.edu/humanrts/africa/comcases/allcases.html (2001) (accessed Nov. 28, 2010) [hereinafter "SERAC & CESR v. Nigeria"]. For a helpful and favorable summary of this case, *see* Bernard H. Oxman & Dinah Shelton, *Decision Regarding Communication 155/96 (Social and Economic Rights Action Center/Center for Economic and Social Rights v. Nigeria), Case No. ACHPR/COMM/AO44/1*, 96 Am. J. Int'l L. 937 (2002).

[50] *See supra* note 39.

[51] SERAC & CESR v. Nigeria, *supra* note 49, at para. 44.

[52] Involving killings that included the Nigerian junta hanging in 1995 of writer and political activist Ken Saro-Wiwa. Craig W. McLuckie & Aubrey McPhail, *Ken Saro Wiwa: Writer and Political Activist* (2000).

[53] Specifically, the Commission held that the military government violated the right to life (art. 4) by facilitating and engaging in widespread "terrorisations and killings," and by "the pollution and environmental degradation to a level humanly unacceptable [that] has made living in [Ogoniland] a nightmare" for individuals and the entire Ogoni community alike. *Supra* note 49, at para. 67; *see also supra* note 52. Violations of the right to health it coupled with violations of the right of peoples to a "general satisfactory environment favorable to their development,"

the Commission continued, "recognise the importance of a clean and safe environment that is closely linked to economic and social rights in so far as the environment affects the quality of life and safety of the individual."[54] That the Banjul Charter itself took this broad view played an important, perhaps even definitive, role.[55] Nevertheless, as Oxman and Shelton correctly observe, "the [Commission's] decision that all rights in the African Charter are enforceable and may be subject to the system's communication procedure advances the African system well ahead of other regional systems. Those systems have moved tentatively toward allowing petitions for economic, social, and cultural rights, and which only partially recognize a right to environment."[56]

National Decision Making

National legal processes that honor the human rights–environment linkage can be important to confirming the human right to a clean and healthy environment for two principal reasons: first, because they can jointly create, if sufficiently similar and numerous, general principles of law recognized as law-making or law-enforcing "sources of law" for pertinent national and international decisions; second, because they can and frequently do shape both

---

and, in so doing, affirmed a broad conception of the right to health that in fact tied it, in the Commission's collective mind, to most if not all the other rights it adjudged the Nigerian government to have violated: non-discrimination (art. 2); the right to property (art. 14); the right to housing, as implied in the duty to protect the family (art. 18[1]); the right to food (as implied in arts. 4, 16, and 22); and the right of peoples to freely dispose of their wealth and natural resources (art. 21). State obligations to safeguard each of the rights cited by it, the Commission ruled, "universally apply to all rights and entail a combination of negative and positive duties," *id.* at para. 44, thus suggesting a broadly conceived justiciable right to a clean and healthy environment.

[54] *Id.*, para. 51. Interestingly, the Commission supported this interpretative proposition by quoting with approval the late French law professor Alexandre Kiss, an environmental and human rights law scholar well known for his holistic view of the right to a clean and healthy environment: "an environment degraded by pollution and defaced by the destruction of all beauty and variety is as contrary to satisfactory living conditions and the development as the breakdown of the fundamental ecologic equilibria is harmful to physical and moral health." Alexandre Kiss, *Concept and Possible Implications of the Right to Environment, in Human Rights in the Twenty-First Century: A Global Challenge* 551, 553 (Kathleen Mahoney & Paul Mahoney eds., 1993).

[55] As pointed out by Oxman & Shelton: "The Commission gives the right to environment meaningful content by requiring the state to adopt various techniques of environmental protection, such as environmental impact assessment, public information and participation, access to justice for environmental harm, and monitoring of potentially harmful activities. The result offers a blueprint for merging environmental protection, economic development, and guarantees of human rights." *Supra* note 49, at 942 (footnote omitted). For further discussion of an autonomous human right to a clean and healthy environment, *see* § B, *infra* at 308.

[56] *Id.*

national and international legal and policy decisions. These decisions are typically part of a reciprocal process of give and take, in ways binding or conclusive as well as influential in the more limited sense of providing guidance, especially where the respective legal systems are similar or compatible.

In recent years, however, national decisions that focus exclusively on the rights to life, health, and/or respect for private and family life as safeguards against environmental injury are less readily found or widespread. The same may be said, indeed, of any specific cluster of such substantive rights. This is so, it appears, because of the "greening" influence of the 1972 Stockholm Declaration and its successors;[57] the trend has been to encourage more an autonomous than a derivative right to a clean and healthy environment (a theme to which we turn in Subsection B, later in this text). Still, nationally based decisions in the derivative tradition do continue, and while documentary inaccessibility and language barriers preclude comprehensiveness at this time, those we have come upon are worthy of attention if only because they tend to mirror their international counterparts. Some we have found in Latin America and sub-Saharan Africa reveal symmetry between the civil and common law systems. The majority, however, appear to emanate from South Asia.

Latin America

A "Background Paper" for a 2002 Joint UN Environment Programme-Office of the High Commissioner for Human Rights (UNEP-OHCHR) Expert Seminar on Human Rights and the Environment conveniently reports six cases that focus on the rights to life and health in Argentina, Chile, Colombia, and Costa Rica.[58] Interestingly, these cases closely track the international legal and policy decisions surveyed above, involving actionable deprivations of the right to life and health – although apparently not of the right to respect for private and family life – resulting from environmental harm, with conspicuous attention given to the rights of indigenous peoples and distinct indications of a trend toward an autonomous right to a clean and healthy environment.[59]

---

[57] *See supra* note 16.

[58] *See* Adriana Fabra & Eva Arnal, *Review of Jurisprudence on Human Rights and the Environment in Latin America* (Background Paper No. 6, Joint UNEP-OHCHR Expert Seminar on Human Rights and the Environment, Jan. 14–16, 2002), available at http://www2.ohchr.org/english/issues/environment/environ/bp6.htm (accessed Nov. 15, 2010). The authors note that their review was based in part on a previous article by Adriana Fabra, *Enforcing the Right to a Healthy Environment in Latin America*, 3 Rev. Eur. Community & Int'l Envtl. L. 4 (1994).

[59] Following are the six cases cited (and quoted) in the Fabra-Arnal report, *supra* note 58:

Sub-Saharan Africa

A 1991 case in Tanzania appears to be the first African litigation to address the reach of a constitutional right-to-life provision in an environmental damage setting. In the case of *Joseph D. Kessy and Others v. Dar es Salaam City Council*,[60] residents of a Dar es Salaam suburb successfully enjoined the Dar es Salaam City Council from continuing to dump and burn waste in their area. The Court of Appeals of Tanzania forcefully admonished the City Council that its actions endangered the health and lives of the applicants and thus violated their constitutional right to life. In the words of Justice Lugakingira:

> I will say at once that I have never heard it anywhere for a public authority, or even an individual, to go to court and confidently seek for permission to pollute the environment and endanger people's lives, regardless of their

- In Argentina: (1) the 1986 case of *Bustos Miguel y Otros v. Dirección de Fábricas Militares*, Juzgado Federal de Primera Instancia No. 2. La Plata [JFPL] [Federal Court of First Impression], 30/12/1986 (right to life and health); (2) the 1993 case of Margarita v. Copetro S.A., Cámara Civil y Comercial de La Plata [CCC] [Civil and Commercial Court], 10/5/1993, *available at* www.elDial.com (accessed Nov. 28, 2010) (right to life affected by coal-burning cancerous pollutants); and (3) the 1995 and 1998 case of Almada Hugo N. v. Copetro and Others, Cámara De Apelaciones en lo Civil y Comercial de La Plata [CACC] [Civil and Commercial Court of Appeals], 9/9/1995, Suprema Corte de Justicia de la Ciudad de Buenos Aires [SCJBA] [Buenos Aires Supreme Court of Justice], 19/5/1998 (right to life and health affected by "environmental pollution");
- In *Chile*: (4) the case of Juan Pablo Orrego Silva et al. v. Empresa Eléctrica Pangue S.A., Corte Suprema [CS] [Supreme Court], 5 augusto 1993, (right to life of "communities" allegedly affected by water shortages and flooding resulting from dam construction);
- In *Colombia*: (5) the case of Organización Indígena de Antioquia v. Codechoco & Madarien, Juzgado Tercero Agrario del Círculo Judicial de Antioquia [JTA], 24 febrero 1993 (right to life of indigenous peoples affected logging operations); and
- In *Costa Rica*: (6) the case of Presidente de la sociedad MARLENE S.A. v. Municipalidad de Tibás Marlene, Sala Constitucional de la Corte Suprema de Justicia, Nov. 25, 1994 (right to life and health). Noteworthy in this case is the court's observation, as recounted by Fabra and Arnal, *supra*, "that the right to health and to a healthy environment emanate from the right to life and from the state's obligation, in that case, to protect nature. The court added that without recognition of the rights to health and to the environment the right to life would be severely limited."

The first two of the three Argentinian cases were decided before the Argentine Constitution recognized "the right to a healthy and balanced environment fit for human development," as it now does in Article 41. *See* Constitutión Nacional [Const. Nac.], available in English at http://www.servat.unibe.ch/icl/ar00000_.html (accessed Nov. 28, 2010). This constitutional provision and others like it, guaranteeing an autonomous right to a clean and healthy environment or its linguistic equivalent, are the subject of further discussion in *infra* § B(3), at 320–28.

[60] High Court of Tanzania, Dar es Salaam (Sept. 9, 1991), unreported, but recounted and partially extracted in 4 Int'l Envtl. L. Reps. 425 (2004).

number. Such wonders appear to be peculiarly Tanzanian, but I regret to say that it is not given to any court to grant such a prayer. Article 14 of our Constitution provides that [as] every person has a right to live and to protection of his life by the society it is therefore a contradiction in terms and a denial of this basic right deliberately to expose anyone's life to danger or, what is eminently monstrous, to enlist the assistance of the Court in this infringement.

Although reputedly unreported, the case and the admonition have been repeatedly cited and favorably quoted in Tanzanian and other African litigation.[61]

The *Kessy* judgment, it is clear, was not an isolated or unusual one. Three other sub-Saharan African cases bear witness: the 2005 Nigerian case of *Mr. Jonah Gbemre (for himself and as representing Iwherekan Community in Delta State, Nigeria) v. Shell Petroleum Development Company Nigeria Ltd. [Shell Nigeria], Nigerian National Petroleum Corporation [NNPC], & Attorney General of the Federation;*[62] the 2006 Kenyan case of *Peter K. Waweru v. Republic;*[63] and the 2007 Ghanian case of *Center for Public Interest Law and Another v. Tema Oil Refinery,*[64] a *locus standi* suit. As in *Kessy*, each case confirmed the environmental reach of the right to life.[65]

---

[61] For example, in a Complaint Relating to Violations of Fundamental Rights and Duties Arising from Forced Evictions of Artisanal Miners from Afrika Mashariki Gold Mine, Tarime, submitted to the Tanzania Commission for Human Rights in 2003, available at http://www.ecolex.org/start.php (search Ecolex for "Mashariki Gold Mine"; then follow hyperlink for first search result) (accessed Nov. 28, 2010). After quoting Justice Lugakingira in *Kessy*, *supra* note 60, it went on to quote Chief Justice Barnabas Samatta of Tanzania in a "welcoming address" opening a Judicial Symposium on Environmental Law in Arusha in June 2003:

> My Lords, as most of those present here very well know, the Constitution of this country recognizes the right to life. What are the ingredients of this right? Does the right mean merely the right to animal existence? If that is the correct meaning, then it follows that the right can scarcely be used by courts to protect the environment. If the fundamental right includes the right to a clean and wholesome environment and to a safe and clean air and water, then our courts will be able to play a significant role in the protection and improvement of natural environment, including forests, lakes, rivers and wildlife. Then they would be able to echo the words of Mr. Justice Holmes: "A river is more than [an] amenity; it is a treasure."

[62] Jonah Gbemre v. Shell Petroleum Dev. Co. Nigeria, Federal High Court of Nigeria in the Benin Judicial Division (Nigeria, Nov. 5, 2005), available at http://www.climatelaw.org/cases/case-documentsnigeria/ni-shell-nov05-judgment.pdf (accessed Nov. 28, 2010).

[63] Peter K. Waweru v. Republic, High Court of Kenya at Nairobi (Kenya, 2006), available at http://www.elaw.org/system/files/Kenya-Waweru.pdf (accessed Nov. 28, 2010).

[64] Ctr. for Pub. Interest Law v. Tema Oil Refinery, High Court of Justice at Tema (Ghana, Sept. 9, 2007), available at http://www.elaw.org/node/5353 (accessed Nov. 28, 2010).

[65] In *Jonah Gbemre, supra* note 62, responding to the polluting effects of "gas flaring" by Shell Nigeria and NNPC in the Niger Delta, and citing the 1981 Banjul Charter, *supra* note 10, the

South Asia

The unanimity of outlook evident in the Latin American and sub-Saharan case law, although quantitatively modest, prevails also in South Asia – more so, it seems, than anywhere else in the world. The decisions, however, are too numerous to report in full here. Brief explanatory citations of cases found

Nigerian Constitution, and Nigerian federal laws, the Federal High Court ruled that "these constitutionally guaranteed rights *inevitably* includes [sic] the rights to [a] clean, poison-free, pollution-free healthy environment," *id.* (emphasis added). Notwithstanding this pointed indictment, however, a subsequent court order for Shell Nigeria and the NNPC to cease and desist gas flaring, labeled a "gross violation" of the constitutionally guaranteed rights involved, was disregarded by the two companies, triggering contempt proceedings against them. The stakes were high. All the major multinational oil companies in Nigeria engaged in the practice of flaring gas (i.e., ExxonMobil, ChevronTexaco, Total, Fina, Elf, and Agip, as well as Shell), and the breadth of the ruling suggested that their flaring was illegal on human rights as well as other grounds also.

In *Waweru*, *supra* note 63, although ruling in favor of the applicants – sewage polluting property owners – on the grounds that they were victims of unlawful discrimination, the High Court of Kenya went on *sua sponte* to discuss the environmental implications of the applicants' behavior. Referencing the 1972 Stockholm Declaration, *supra* note 16; the 1992 Rio Declaration on Environment and Development, U.N. Doc. A/CONF.151/26 (1992) [hereinafter "Rio Declaration"], *reprinted in* 31 I.L.M. 874 (1992) *and* V Basic Documents, *supra* note 5, at V.B.18; the 1987 Report of the World Commission on Environment and Development (Our Common Future) [hereinafter the "Commission Report"]; the 1981 Banjul Charter, *supra* note 10; and a leading Pakistani decision, Shehla Zia v. WAPDA, Supreme Court of Pakistan (Pakistan, Sept. 27, 1992), available at http://www.elaw.org/node/1342 (accessed Sept. 30, 2011), *reprinted in* UNEP/UNDP, 1 Compendium of Judicial Decisions in Matters Related to Environment 323 (1998), available at http://www.unep.org/padelia/publications/Jud.Dec. Nat.pre.pdf (accessed Sept. 30, 2011) [hereinafter UNEP/UNDP Compendium]; it asserted that the constitutional right to life enshrined in Kenyan Constitution Section 71 includes the right to a clean and healthy environment and that in its view "the right to life is not just a matter of keeping body and soul together because in this modern age that right could be threatened by many things including the environment." The Court continued: "It is quite evident from perusing the most important international instruments on the environment that the word life and the environment are inseparable and the word life means much more than keeping body and soul together."

In *Center for Public Interest Law and Another*, the Superior Court of Judicature of the Ghanaian High Court of Justice responded favorably to the plaintiff's claim that a "negligent oil spill" by the defendant oil company into a lagoon, damaging its flora and fauna and causing the local inhabitants, predominately fishermen, to become destitute "due to the annihilation of all life forms in the . . . lagoon," was of sufficient public interest to have violated a constitutionally guaranteed right to life "and by implication the right to a clean and healthy environment." In so doing, lacking Ghanaian judicial precedent, but persuaded that "the courts must become proactive when handling cases involving environmental issues," it relied upon plaintiff's cited authorities, including the Article 24 guarantee of the 1981 Banjul Charter's, *supra* note 10, of "the right to a general satisfactory environment favourable to . . . development") and "the practices in other common law countries," especially India.

in Bangladesh,[66] India (which appears to have generated the most cases),[67]

[66] *See, e.g.,* Farooque v. Bangladesh, Supreme Court of Bangladesh, High Court Division (Bangladesh, 1996), available at http://www.elaw.org/node/3692 (accessed Sept. 27, 2011). Lacking a constitutional provision for the protection of the environment per se, the Supreme Court invoked the Bangladesh Constitution Articles 31 ("Right to Protection of Law") and 32 ("Right to Life and Personal Liberty"), identified the right to life as "a fundamental right," and ruled that it "encompasses within its ambit, the protection and preservation of environment, ecological balance free from pollution of air and water, sanitation without which life can hardly be enjoyed" such that "[a]ny act or omission contrary thereto will be violative of the said right to life." The decision is reprinted in UNEP/UNDP Compendium, *supra* note 65, at 37. For brief explanation of the prior unreported litigation see Y. K. Sabharwal (Chief Justice of India), *Human Rights and the Environment,* NLSEN LAW, available at http://www.nlsenlaw. org/environmental-protection/articles/human-rights-and-the-environment (accessed Nov. 28, 2010).

[67] India's many cases, often concerning air and noise pollution and access to clean water, typically affirm the right to a clean and healthy environment by invoking Article 21 of the Indian Constitution ("Life and Personal Liberty"), India Const., available at http://lawmin. nic.in/coi/coiason29july08.pdf (accessed Nov. 28, 2010). Early examples build on expanded constitutional interpretations in prior cases. *See, e.g.,* Mullin v. Union Territory of Delhi, Supreme Court of India (Jan. 13, 1981), available at http://www.indiankanoon.org/doc/78536/ (accessed Sept. 27, 2011). Notable are the 1988 case of Koolwal v. Rajasthan, High Court of Rajasthjan (Sept. 19, 1986), available at http://www.ielrc.org/content/e8601.pdf (accessed Sept. 27, 20110) and the famous 1990 case of Charan Lal Sahu v. Union Carbide (the so-called "Bhopal Disaster Case"), Supreme Court of India (India, Dec. 22, 1989), available at http://www.indiankanoon.org/doc/299215/ (accessed Sept. 27, 2011), *reprinted in* UNEP/UNDP Compendium, *supra* note 65, at 167, involving highly toxic Methyl Isocyanate (MIC) gas that, on Dec. 2, 1984, leaked from a storage tank at the Bhopal plant of Union Carbide (India) Ltd., killing some 3,000 people, injuring up to 30,000 people, and polluting the environment and its flora and fauna. The Supreme Court interpreted Article 21 to include "the right to [a] healthy environment free from hazardous pollutants." Later noteworthy holdings, substantively supportive even when sometimes rejecting petitions on procedural grounds, include the 1991 Supreme Court case of *Kumar v. Bihar,* Supreme Court of India (India, 1991), available at http://www.ielrc.org/content/e9108.pdf (accessed Sept. 30, 2011) ("[T]he right to live is a fundamental right under Art. 21 . . . and it includes the right of enjoyment of pollution free water and air for full enjoyment of life."), and the 1995 Supreme Court case of Gaur v. Haryana, Supreme Court of India (India, 1994), available at http://www.ielrc.org/content/e9407.pdf (accessed Sept. 30, 2011) ("[E]njoyment of . . . life and its attainment including [the] right to life with human dignity encompasses within its ambit, the protection and preservation of environment, ecological balance free from pollution of air and water, sanitation without which life cannot be enjoyed . . . [and a]ny contra acts should be regarded as amounting to violation of Article 21."); *see also* Thangal v. Union of India, Kerala High Court (India, 2002), available at http://www.elaw.org/node/2537 (accessed Nov. 28, 2010) ("There must be an effective and wholesome interdisciplinary interaction. At once, the administrative agency cannot be permitted to function in this manner as to make inroads, into the fundamental right under Art. 21. The right to life is much more than the right to an animal existence and its attributes are many fold, as life itself. A prioritization of human needs and a new value system has been recognized in these areas. The right to sweet water, and the right to free air, are attributes of the right to life, for, these are the basic elements which sustain life itself."). There are numerous others. *See, e.g.,* Ashram v. U.P., (1993) 2 S.C.C. 612; Mathur v. Union of India, (1996) 1 S.C.C. 119; Indian Council for Enviro-Legal Action v. Union

Nepal,[68] and Pakistan[69] must, for the most part, suffice. Especially noteworthy from an international law perspective, however, are two cases, one from Pakistan in 1994, the other from India in 2001.

In Pakistan, in the 1994 "public interest" litigation *Shehla Zia and Others v. WAPDA,*[70] the Supreme Court clarified that the right-to-life guarantee of the Pakistani Constitution (Article 9) includes "all such amenities and facilities which a person born in a free country is entitled to enjoy with dignity, legally and constitutionally."[71] Additionally, the Court cited Article 14(1) of

of India, (1996) 3 S.C.C. 212; Mehta v. Union of India, (1996) 4 S.C.C. 351; Jagannath v. Union of India, (1997) 2 S.C.C. 87; Mehta v. Union of India, (1999) 1 S.C.C. 413; *In re* Noise Pollution Restricting Use of Loudspeakers, Supreme Court of India (2005), available at http://www.indiankanoon.org/doc/1709298/ (accessed Sept. 30, 2011); Forum, Prevention of Envtl. & Sound Pollution v. Union of India, Supreme Court of India (2005), available at http://www.elaw.org/node/1515 (accessed Sept. 30, 2011); Krishnan v. Tamil Nadu, Madras High Court (2005), available at http://www.indiankanoon.org/doc/435772/ (accessed Sept. 30, 2011). A number of these cases and more may be found in UNEP/UNDP Compendium, *supra* note 65.

[68] *See,* for example, Dhungel v. Godawari Marble Indus., Supreme Court of Nepal (Oct. 31, 1995), available at http://www.elaw.org/node/1849 (accessed Sept. 30, 2011), wherein the Supreme Court, contemplating Article 11(1) of the then existing Nepalese Constitution (right to life), declared that "it is the legitimate right of an individual to be free from a polluted environment," that "protection of the environment is directly related with [the] life of [a] human being," and that, therefore, "this matter [of the right to a clean, healthy environment] is included in Article 11(1)." For the English language version of the Constitution of the Kingdom of Nepal extant at the time of this case, *see The Constitution of Nepal,* sambidhan.org, available at http://www.sambidhan.org/english%20verson/The%20Constitution%20of%20Nepal%202019%20En.pdf (accessed Nov. 28, 2010).

[69] *See, e.g., In re* Human Rights Case (Environment Pollution in Balochistan), Supreme Court of Pakistan (Sept. 27, 1992), *reprinted in* UNEP/UNDP COMPENDIUM, *supra* note 66, at 180. In this case, the Supreme Court noticed a news item in a daily newspaper reporting a private business plan to purchase a coastal area of Balochistan to create a dumping ground for nuclear and other waste material. After determining that no license had been issued for this purpose, the Court concluded that, if the plan succeeded, it would constitute an illegal clandestine act. It also stated that it would create an environmental hazard and pollution that would violate Article 9 of the Pakistani Constitution, providing that "[n]o person shall be deprived of life or liberty save in accordance with law." *See also* W. Pak. Salt Miners Labour Union (CBA) v. Indus. & Mineral Dev., Supreme Court of Pakistan (July 12, 1994), *reprinted in* UNEP/UNDP Compendium, *supra* note 65, at 282. In this case, fearing that continuing mining activities could cause a watercourse, reservoir, and pipeline to become contaminated, the petitioners sought enforcement of the local residents' right to have clean and unpolluted water. The Supreme Court observed that Article 9 of the Constitution guaranteed that "no person shall be deprived of life or liberty save in accordance with the law" and further clarified that the word "life" had "an extended meaning and cannot be restricted to vegetative life or mere animal existence." *Id.* It continued: "In hilly areas where access to water is scarce, difficult [or] limited, the right to have water free from pollution and contamination is a right to life itself." *Id.*

[70] *Shehla Zia, supra* note 65, at 323.

[71] *Id.,* para. 12.

the Constitution providing that "[t]he dignity of man and, subject to law, the privacy of home, shall be inviolable." Reading Articles 9 and 14(1) together, the Court observed, "[the] question will arise whether a person can be said to have dignity of man if his right to life is below bare necessity like without proper food, clothing, shelter, education, health care, clean atmosphere and unpolluted environment."[72] As a consequence, the Court held, "[a] person is entitled to protection of law from being exposed to hazards of electro-magnetic fields or any other such hazards which may be due to installation and construction of any grid station, any factory, power station or such like installations."[73] It therefore ordered an official inquiry into whether there is any likelihood of such hazard or adverse effect on the health of the residents of the locality. Significantly, the Court took note of the 1972 Stockholm and 1992 Rio declarations,[74] acknowledging their theoretically nonbinding status but at the same time accepting "the fact . . . that they have a persuasive value and command respect."[75] Additionally, and from similar perspective, it referenced the US Constitution and numerous judgments of the Indian Supreme Court, including several noted above.[76]

In India, in the 2001 case of *Andhra Pradesh Pollution Control Board-II v. Prof. M.V. Nayudu & Others*,[77] the Supreme Court relied on Article 21 of the Indian Constitution (right to life) and referenced the Resolution on Community Water Supply of the 1977 UN Water Conference ("All peoples, whatever their stage of development and their social and economic conditions, have the right to have access to drinking water in quantities and of a quality equal to their basic needs"),[78] the 1966 ICESCR and ICCPR,[79] the 1986 Declaration on the Right to Development,[80] and the 1992 Rio Declaration[81] as authority for interpolating a right of access to safe drinking water into the right to life guaranteed by Article 21. Indeed, further confirming the constant interplay of national and international law, it cited also the case law of the European

---

[72] *Id.*, para. 14.

[73] *Id.*, para. 12.

[74] *Supra* notes 16, 65.

[75] *Supra* note 66, para. 9.

[76] See *supra* note 67.

[77] Andhra Pradesh Pollution Control Bd. II v. Nayudu, Supreme Court of India (Dec. 1, 2000), available at http://www.ielrc.org/content/e0010.pdf (accessed Sept. 30, 2011).

[78] *See* Report of the United Nations Water Conference, Mar del Plata, Mar. 14–25, 1977, *Resolutions*, available at http://www.ielrc.org/content/e7701.pdf (accessed Nov. 28, 2010).

[79] *Supra* note 5.

[80] United Nations General Assembly Declaration on the Right to Development, Dec. 4, 1986, G.A. Res. 41/128, Annex, U.N. GAOR, 41st Sess., Supp. No. 53, U.N. Doc. A/41/53, at 186 (1987), *reprinted* in III Basic Documents, *supra* note 5, at III.R.2.

[81] *Supra* note 65.

Court of Justice, the European Court of Human Rights, and the IACHR, even decisions of national courts in Colombia, the Philippines, and South Africa. On the basis of Article 21 and these international and transnational sources – from which, it may be noted, it accepted and applied the precautionary principle – the Court allowed appeals that sought to prevent the establishment of industries potentially capable of polluting drinking water reservoirs.

———————

The foregoing Latin American, sub-Sahara African, and South Asian cases are not alone among national decisions affirming that environmental rights may be derived from the right to life, health, and respect for private and family life. There are others scattered elsewhere, sometimes in conjunction with a constitutionally mandated autonomous right to a clean and healthy environment.[82]

2. *The Environment and Other Recognized Substantive Human Rights*

Although the human rights to life, health, and respect for private and family life are the dominant entitlements through which protection from environmental harm has been given, they are not the only substantive human rights so utilized, at least not at the national level. Also invoked for this purpose in national fora, and generally with the same or similar logic, are the rights to habitat, livelihood, culture, dignity, equality and nondiscrimination, and sleep. Clearly, the spectrum of substantive human rights claimed as surrogates for protection from environmental harm or as a substitute for the autonomous right to a clean and healthy environment is a broad one. There are too many instances to detail here, and we therefore leave it to authoritative citations to substantiate the point.[83]

---

[82] *See, e.g.,* Özay v. Ministry of the Env't, Supreme Administrative Court of Turkey, Ref. No. 1996/5477, Ruling No. 1997.2312, 4 Int'l Envtl. L. Reps. 452 (1997); Oposa v. Factoran, G.R. No. 101083, 224 S.C.R.A. 792 (July 30, 1993) (Phil.), *reprinted in* 33 I.L.M. 173 (1994).

[83] *See, e.g.,* Juzgado Nacional de la Instancia en lo Contencioso Administrativo Federal. No. 2 [JNICAF] [National Administrative Court], 10/5/1983, "Kattan v. Nat'l Gov't," La Ley, 1983-D, 576 (Arg.) (habitat); Research Found. for Science v. Union of India, Supreme Court of India (Sept. 11, 2007), available at http://indiankanoon.org/doc/548962/ (accessed Sept. 30, 2011) (livelihood); Anderson v. Norwegian State, Supreme Court of Norway (Oct. 5, 2001), available at http://www.elaw.org/system/files/svartskogdommen.pdf (accessed Sept. 30, 2011) (culture); Irfan v. Lahore Dev. Auth., Lahore High Court (Pakistan, June 14, 2002), available at http://www.elaw.org/system/files/Paksistan –PLD2002Lahore555.doc (accessed Sept. 30, 2011) (dignity); Mossville Envtl. Action Now v. United States, 370 F.3d, 1232 (D.C. Cir. 2003) (equality and nondiscrimination); Forum, Prevention of Envtl. & Sound Pollution v. Union of India, Supreme Court of India (2005), available at http://www.elaw.org/node/1515 (accessed Sept. 30, 2011) (sleep).

B. THE HUMAN RIGHT TO A CLEAN AND HEALTHY ENVIRONMENT
AS AN AUTONOMOUS RIGHT

An autonomous human right is one that, separate unto itself, is not dependent on any other human right for its moral or legal recognition.[84] From a definitional standpoint, it matters not whether that recognition takes place on the global, regional, or national plane or all three.

1. *Recognition on the Global Plane*

The human right to a clean and healthy environment as an autonomous right appears to have emerged on the global plane in modern times first in Principle 1 of the 1972 Stockholm Declaration:[85]

> Man has the fundamental right to freedom, equality, and adequate conditions of life, in an environment of a quality that permits a life of dignity and well-being, and he bears a solemn responsibility to protect and improve the environment for present and future generations.[86]

As Luis Rodriguez-Rivera has observed, "the works of the Preparatory Committee of the United Nations Conference on the Human Environment reveal that the draft of the Stockholm Declaration 'was based on the recognition of

---

[84] *Accord* Sumudu Atapattu, *The Right to Life or the Right To Die Polluted: The Emergence of a Human Right to a Healthy Environment Under International Law*, 16 Tul. Envtl. L.J. 65, 70 (2002).

[85] *Supra* note 16; *see also supra* text accompanying notes 15–17. Principle 1 is reinforced by Principle 21, which provides that "States have, in accordance with the Charter of the United Nations and the principles of international law, the sovereign right to exploit their own resources pursuant to their own environmental policies, *and the responsibility to ensure that activities within their jurisdiction or control do not cause damage to the environment of other States or of areas beyond the limits of national jurisdiction*" (emphasis added).

[86] An historical curiosity may be found in the fact that, in the early presidency of Richard Nixon, the United States proposed an autonomous human right to a clean and healthy environment in the Stockholm Declaration, but, during the late presidency of Ronald Reagan, strongly opposed the inclusion of such a right in the Rio Declaration, *supra* note 65, twenty years later. *See* Dinah Shelton, *What Happened at Rio to Human Rights?*, 3 Y.B. Int'l Envtl. L. 75, 76–77 (1992). The US formulation for the Stockholm Declaration, which was rejected by the Stockholm Conference participants (from the developing countries in particular) for being too direct in favor of Principle 1, read as follows: "Every human being has a right to a healthful and safe environment, including air, water and earth, and to food and other material necessities, all of which should be sufficiently free of contamination and other elements which detract from the health or well-being of man." *See* Dinah Shelton, *Environmental Rights*, in *Peoples' Rights* 189, 194 (P. Alston ed., 2001).

the rights of individuals to an adequate environment,'"[87] thus refuting the claim, sometimes made, that the Declaration recognizes a right to a clean and healthy environment only as derived from other human rights.

In the years since Stockholm, the autonomous right to a clean and healthy environment has been reaffirmed both explicitly and implicitly in numerous international instruments of so-called soft law (which, in some cases, may be much harder than ordinarily presumed). A chronological account confirms this fact and demonstrates its historical evolution, beginning in earnest (and somewhat surprisingly) not until a full decade after Stockholm.

- In October 1982, in Resolution 37/7, the UN General Assembly adopted the World Charter for Nature, proclaiming twenty-four principles of conservation "by which all human conduct affecting nature is to be guided and judged," each based on the following general principles: (1) "nature shall be respected and its essential processes shall not be impaired"; (2) "genetic viability on the earth shall not be compromised"; (3) "[a]ll areas of the earth . . . shall be subject to these principles of conservation"; (4) "[e]cosystems and organisms, as well as the . . . resources utilized by man, shall be managed in such a way as [not] to endanger the integrity of . . . other ecosystems or species with which they coexist"; and (5) "[n]ature shall be secured against degradation caused by warfare or other hostile activities."[88]
- In June 1986, the Experts Group on Environmental Law of the World Conference on Environment and Development (WCED) adopted Legal Principles on Environmental Protection and Sustainable Development[89] which, later appended to the Brundtland Commission Report,[90] state that "[a]ll human beings have the fundamental right to an environment adequate for their health and well-being."
- In December 1986, in Resolution 41/128, the UN General Assembly adopted the Declaration on the Right to Development, Article 1(1) of

[87] Luis E. Rodriguez-Rivera, *Is the Human Right to Environment Recognized Under International Law? It Depends on the Source*, 12 Colo. J. Envtl. L. & Pol'y 1, 17 (2001) (citing Preparatory Committee for the United Nations Conference on the Human Environment, para. 77, U.N. Doc. A/Conf.48/PC/17 (1972)).

[88] U.N. General Assembly 37/7, Annex, U.N. GAOR, 37th Sess., Supp. No. 51, U.N. Doc. A/37/51, at 17 (1983), *reprinted in* 22 I.L.M. 455 (1983) *and* V Basic Documents, *supra* note 5, at V.B.12 (emphasis added). The World Charter was adopted 111–1-18, with 14 of the 18 abstentions being Latin American states and the sole vote against being that of the United States.

[89] U.N. Doc. WCED/86/23/Add.1 (June 18–20, 1986), *reprinted in* V Basic Documents, *supra* note 5, at V.B.13.

[90] *Supra* note 65.

which states that "[t]he human right to development also implies the full realization of the right of peoples to self-determination, which includes, subject to the relevant provisions of both International Covenants on Human Rights, the exercise of their inalienable right to full sovereignty over all their natural wealth and resources."[91]

- In March 1989, the Declaration of The Hague, adopted by twenty-four "Heads of State, Governments, or their Representatives,"[92] asserted that ozone depletion, climate change, and other forms of environmental degradation "involve not only the fundamental duty to preserve the ecosystem, but also the right to live in dignity in a viable global environment, and the consequent duty of the community of nations vis-à-vis present and future generations to do all that can be done to preserve the quality of the atmosphere."[93]

- In December 1990, in UN General Assembly Resolution 45/94, adopted without a recorded vote, the General Assembly recognized "that all individuals are entitled to live in an environment adequate for their health and well-being."[94]

- In June 1992, in Principle 1 of the Rio Declaration,[95] the United Nations Conference on Environment and Development, invoking the language of entitlement, asserted that "[h]uman beings are at the centre of concerns for sustainable development [and] are entitled to a healthy and productive life in harmony with nature."[96]

---

[91] *Supra* note 80.

[92] *I.e.*, Australia, Brazil, Canada, Côte d'Ivoire, Egypt, France, Germany (West), Hungary, India, Indonesia, Italy, Japan, Jordan, Kenya, Malta, Norway, New Zealand, Netherlands, Senegal, Spain, Sweden, Tunisia, Venezuela, and Zimbabwe.

[93] U.N. Doc. A/44/340, *reprinted in* 28 I.L.M. 1308 (1989) *and* V Basic Documents, *supra* note 5, at V.H.5.

[94] Resolution on the Need To Ensure a Healthy Environment for the Well Being of Individuals, G.A. Res. 45/94, U.N. GAOR, 45th Sess., Supp. No. 49, U.N. Doc. A/45/49, at 178 (1990), *reprinted in* V Basic Documents, *supra* note 5, at V.B.16.

[95] *Supra* note 65.

[96] While some have argued that this language constituted a retreat from the 1972 Stockholm Declaration (*e.g.*, Mariana T. Acevedo, *The Intersection of Human Rights and Environmental Protection in the European Court of Human Rights*, 8 N.Y.U. Envtl. L.J. 437, 451 (2000)), others contend, correctly in our view, that Rio Declaration Principle 1, "which was accepted without reservation by almost every nation, captures the ideals of a human right to a healthy environment, if not explicitly recognizing such a right." John Lee, *The Underlying Legal Theory To Support a Well-Defined Human Right to a Healthy Environment as a Principle of Customary International Law*, 25 Colum. J. Envtl. L. 283, 308 (2000). Lee continues:

> The language of Principle 1 of the Rio Declaration was reproduced *verbatim*, and accepted without reservation by 179 nations at the 1994 U.N. Conference on Population and Development; by 186 nations at the 1995 World Summit for Social Development;

- In July 1994, the UN Sub-Commission on Prevention of Discrimination and Protection of Minorities[97] issued the Final Report of its Special Rapporteur on Human Rights and the Environment[98] in which the Special Rapporteur (Ms. Fatma Zohra Ksentini), in addition to urging the greater recognition and implementation of procedural environmental rights, stated that "it is generally accepted" that Article 28 of the UDHR[99] – which entitles everyone to "a social and international order in which the rights and freedoms set forth in this Declaration can be fully realized" – "covers the environmental concerns of this day and age,"[100] and that, by virtue of "the indivisibility and interdependence of all human rights" as well as the UN General Assembly's Declaration on the Right to Development,[101] "it is impossible to separate the claim to the right to a healthy and balanced environment from the claim to the right to 'sustainable' development."[102]

---

by 175 nations at the 1996 Second Conference on Human Settlements (Habitat II); and by 17 nations at the OAS-sponsored 1997 Hemispheric Summit on Sustainable Development. For the purposes of customary international law, this reaffirmation of the language agreed upon in Principle 1 of the Rio Declaration is significant. While each of these reaffirmations is legally non-binding, the fact that almost every nation made this reaffirmation without reservation–at least three times–is evidence of a widespread and consistent state practice. Such practice can contribute to the creation of a right to a healthy environment as a principle of customary international law.

Id. at 308–09 (footnotes omitted).

"At the same time," observes Professor Lynda Collins, although herself supportive of Lee's thesis, "it will no doubt be argued that had the signatories to Rio intended to recognize a human *right* to environment, they would have been plain about it." Lynda M. Collins, *Are We There Yet? The Right to Environment in International and European Law*, McGill Int'l J. Sustainable Dev. L. & Pol'y 119, 133 (2007).

[97] Renamed the Sub-Commission on the Promotion and Protection of Human Rights in 1999, in turn replaced by the Human Rights Council Advisory Committee in 2008 to serve as a "think tank" for the Council and work under its direction.

[98] *Review of Further Developments in the Fields with Which the Sub-Commission Has Been Concerned, Human Rights and the Environment: Final Report Prepared by Ms. Fatma Zohra Ksentini, Special Rapporteur*, Annex I, U.N. EXCOR, 46th Sess., U.N. Doc. E/CN.4/Sub.2/1994/9 [hereinafter "Ksentini Report"].

[99] *Supra* note 7.

[100] Ksentini Report, *supra* note 98, para. 34.

[101] *Supra* note 80.

[102] Ksentini Report, *supra* note 98, para. 49. Also noteworthy is a Draft Declaration of Principles on Human Rights and the Environment that was appended to the Ksentini Report, Principle 2 of which provided that "[a]ll persons have the right to a secure, healthy and ecologically sound environment," adding that "[t]his right and other human rights, including civil, cultural, economic, political and social rigts, are universal, interdependent and indivisible...." The outcome of a meeting of international environmental law and human rights experts in Geneva in May 1994, the Draft Declaration, although never adopted by any international body, foretold

- In September 1997, the Institute of International Law declared in its Strasbourg session that "[e]very human being has the right to live in a healthy environment."[103]
- In February 1999, an International Seminar of Experts on the Right to the Environment, convened by the UN Educational, Scientific and Cultural Organization (UNESCO) and the UN High Commissioner for Human Rights in Bilbao, issued the Bizkaia Declaration on the Right to Environment, Article 1 of which affirmed that "[e]veryone has the right, individually or in association with others, to enjoy a healthy, ecologically balanced environment" and that "[t]he right to the environment may be exercised before public bodies and private entities, whatever their legal status under national and international law."[104]
- In January 2002, in a meeting convened by the OHCHR and the UNEP at the invitation of the United Nations Commission on Human Rights, a Seminar of Experts on the Right to the Environment recommended, among other things and within the context of a then forthcoming World Summit on Sustainable Development, that support be given to "the growing recognition of a right to a secure, healthy and ecologically sound environment, either as a constitutionally guaranteed entitlement/right or as a guiding principle of national and international law."[105]
- In June 2002, pursuant to Decision 2002/105 of the UN Commission on Human Rights and Resolution 2001/2 of the Sub-Commission on Prevention of Discrimination and Protection of Minorities, Special Rapporteur El Hadji Guissé published a preliminary report on the "relationship

the tripartite approach to the right to a clean and healthy environment under consideration here. *See* Collins, *supra* note 96, at 134 (citing Karrie Wolfe, *Greening the International Human Rights Sphere? Environmental Rights and the Draft Declaration of Principles on Human Rights and the Environment*, 9 *Appeal* 45, 48 (2003)); Neil Popovic, *In Pursuit of Environmental Human Rights: Commentary on the Draft Declaration of Principles on Human Rights and the Environment*, 27 Colum. Hum. Rts. L. Rev. 487 (1996).

[103] Institute of International Law, Resolution on the Environment, Session of Strasbourg, art. 2 (1997), available at http://www.idi-iil.orgo/idiE/resolutionsE/1997_str_02_en.PDF (accessed Nov. 28, 2010). Article 1 defines "environment" to include (a) "abiotic and biotic natural resources, in particular air, water, soil, fauna and flora, as well as the interaction between these factors" and (b) "the characteristic features of the landscape." *Id.*

[104] Declaration of Bizkaia on the Right to Environment, United Nations Educational, Scientific and Cultural Organization, 30th Sess., Doc. 30C/INF.11 (1999). Also noteworthy in this declaration is its preambulatory emphasis that "the right to environment is inherent to the dignity of all persons and is necessarily linked to the guaranteeing of other human rights including in particular the right to development."

[105] Available on the website of the Office of the United Nations High Commissioner for Human Rights, UNHCHR, available at http://www2.ohchr.org/english/issues/environment/environ/index.htm (accessed Nov. 28, 2010).

between the enjoyment of economic, social and cultural rights and the promotion of the realization of the right to drinking water supply and sanitation," and therein concluded that the right in question is not only a human right but one that necessarily implicates the "right to a healthy environment" – by implication, already in existence.[106]

- In September 2007, by a vote of 143–4-11, the UN General Assembly adopted the UN Declaration on the Rights of Indigenous Peoples in which it proclaimed, in Article 26(1), that "[i]ndigenous peoples have the right to the conservation and protection of the environment and the productive capacity of their lands or territories and resources."[107]
- In November 2007, the Alliance of Small Island States (AOSIS) adopted the Male' Declaration on the Human Dimension of Climate Change, which recognizes, among other things, "the fundamental right to an environment capable of supporting human society and the full enjoyment of human rights."[108]
- In September 2010, the UN Human Rights Council issued a Report of its Special Rapporteur on the Adverse Effects of the Movement and Dumping of Toxic and Dangerous Products and Wastes on the Enjoyment of Human Rights,[109] in which Special Rapporteur Okechukwu Ibeanu, following a mission to India and commenting on an Indian Supreme Court decision, stated that he "notes with satisfaction that the Supreme Court has on a number of occasions recognized the right to a safe and healthy environment as being implicit in the fundamental right to life."[110]

In combination, these and other instances of explicit and implicit recognition, too numerous to recount in full, give weight to the proposition that the right to a clean and healthy environment exists already in customary international law on the global plane or that it is well on its way to such validation. This proposition is the more persuasive when one makes room for the widely accepted logic that there can be no right without a countervailing duty (a

---

[106] *See* U.N. Doc. E/CN.4/Sub.2/2002/10 (2002) (accessed Nov. 28, 2010).

[107] *Supra* note 43. The four votes against were cast by Australia, Canada, New Zealand, and the United States, each countries with significant indigenous populations. The eleven abstentions were by Azerbaijan, Bangladesh, Bhutan, Burundi, Colombia, Georgia, Kenya, Nigeria, Russia, Samoa, and Ukraine.

[108] Available on the website of the Center for International Environmental Law (CIEL), available at http://www.ciel.org/Publications/Male_Declaration_Nov07.pdf (accessed Nov. 28, 2010).

[109] Report of the Special Rapporteur (Mission to India), U.N. General Assembly Human Rights Council, Agenda Item 3 (Promotion and Protection of All Human Rights, Civil, Political, Economic, Social and Cultural Rights, Including the Right to Development), Doc. A/HRC/15/22/Add.3, add. (Sept. 2, 2010).

[110] *Id.*, para. 87.

variant of the "right"–"remedy" equation). Accordingly, by reverse reasoning, this proposition infers a right to a clean and healthy environment when the duty to protect and preserve the same is spelled out but the right is not, as is often the case. It is all the more persuasive, too, when one takes into account the growing number of instances in which a right subsumed within the right to a clean and healthy environment (e.g., the right to water, habitat, or a standard of living adequate for health and well-being) is declared recognized, or when a particular environmental threat (e.g., pesticides or liquid hydrocarbons) is targeted for remedial legal action for the express or implied purpose of achieving a clean and healthy environment.

It is in this light, for example, that one may view the November 2002 decision of the UN CESCR, referencing Articles 11 and 12 of the ICESCR,[111] to adopt General Comment No. 15 on the right to water, stating, *inter alia*, that "[t]he human right to water is indispensable for leading a life in human dignity" and that "[i]t is a prerequisite for the realization of other human rights."[112] Even better, one might cite the July 2009 UN General Assembly Resolution 64/292, recognizing "the right to safe and clean drinking water and sanitation as a human right that is essential for the full enjoyment of life and all human rights."[113] It is in this light, too, that one may accept the adoption in January 2002 by the Basel Convention's Technical Working Group of technical guidelines designed "to promote the environmentally sound management of plastic wastes."[114] Singly and together, these and many other like actions in recent decades signal a legal presumption of obligation to a clean and healthy environment that is commonly viewed as a fundamental human right even if left unstated. To quote Rodriguez-Rivera once again:

---

[111] *Supra* note 11.

[112] Committee on Economic, Social and Cultural Rights, 29th Sess., Nov. 11–29, 2002, Agenda Item 3, Substantive Issues Arising in the Implementation of the International Covenant on Economic, Social and Cultural Rights, 29th Sess., Geneva, Nov. 11–29, 2002, Agenda Item 3, Substantive Issues Arising in the Implementation of the International Covenant on Economic, Social and Cultural Rights, General Comment No. 15 (2002), E/C.12/2002/11, para. 1, Jan. 20, 2003, available at http://www.unhchr.ch/tbs/doc.nsf/o/a5458 d1d1bbd713fc1256cc400389e94/$FILE/G0340229.pdf (accessed Nov. 28, 2010).

[113] G.A. Res. 64/292, U.N. GAOR 64th Sess., Supp. 49, (Vol. III), U.N. Doc. A/6449, at 45, (July 28, 2010) *reprinted in* III Basic Documents, *supra* note 5, at III.S.8.

[114] *See* Press Release, U.N. Env't Programme, New Guidelines Will Reduce Hazards Posed by Plastic Wastes (Jan. 18, 2002), available at http://www.basel.int/press/pr1–02%20basel%20tech%20legal%20wgs%20conclusions.pdf (accessed Nov. 28, 2010). The Basel Convention on the Control of Transboundary Movements of Hazardous Wastes and Their Disposal, Mar. 22, 1989, may be found at 1673 U.N.T.S. 57, *reprinted in* 28 I.L.M. 657 (1989) *and* V Basic Documents, *supra* note 5, at V.M.4.

[T]he proliferation of international environmental law instruments during the last [several] decades must be explained by something more than a mere assertion that states' participation in this process has been motivated by economic or political self-interest. Most international environmental law instruments do not offer states obvious economic or political gains. On the contrary, most of these instruments impose economic and political liabilities, which are the inevitable trade-offs associated with global environmental protection. States are not in the practice of entering into international legal instruments that limit their sovereignty in the absence of recognized legal or moral duties to do so.[115]

Therefore, Rodriguez-Rivera concludes, "the exponential growth of international environmental law instruments, *in and of itself*, evinces the existence of the expansive [i.e., autonomous] right to environment."[116]

At the same time, it must be borne clearly in mind that, at this writing, there exists no global treaty – only two on the regional plane – that proclaims the right to a clean and healthy environment as an autonomous right. Nor has any treaty body or other authorized decision-maker on the global plane ever ruled in this way as yet. At the global level, the human right to a clean and healthy environment as an autonomous right exists, if at all, in customary international law informed mostly by soft law communications (i.e., communications that tend to be more aspirational than justiciable in character, especially where powerful market economies are involved). The precise legal status of this right as a governing *global* norm of international law is, thus, ambiguous.

2. Recognition on the Regional Plane

On the regional plane, the autonomous right to a clean and healthy environment is more clearly recognized, thanks in part to two treaty endorsements. In 1981, the former Organization of African States (now the African Union) adopted the Charter on Human and Peoples' Rights (or Banjul Charter),[117] Article 24 of which provides that "[a]ll peoples shall have the right to a general satisfactory environment favorable to their development."[118] In 1988, the States Parties to the 1969 American Convention on Human Rights[119] adopted the Additional Protocol to the American Convention on Human Rights in the

---

[115] Rodriguez-Rivera, *supra* note 87, at 27.
[116] *Id.* (emphasis added).
[117] *Supra* note 10.
[118] The Banjul Charter did not enter into force until 1986, and of course applies only to the states party to it, fifty-three states at this writing.
[119] *Supra* note 11.

Area of Economic, Social and Cultural Rights,[120] Article 11 of which provides that "[e]veryone shall have the right to live in a healthy environment...." and that "the States Parties shall promote the protection, preservation, and improvement of the environment."[121]

Recognition of the right to environment on the regional plane extends beyond these two treaties, however. For example, at the 12th annual meeting of the Advisory Council of Jurists (ACJ) of the Asia Pacific Forum (APF) in September 2007, the ACJ explored several key questions regarding the inter-relation of the environment and human rights and analyzed existing international law doctrines, principles, and rules bearing on the subject. It thereafter advocated that a healthy environment should no longer be viewed as simply an "add-on" to the right to life or health, but should be understood as a stand-alone human right and be protected as such.[122] Instances such as this are many.[123]

It is, however, within the legal framework of the European Union (EU) where the existence of an autonomous right to a clean and healthy environment is most pronounced – beginning, it appears, with the 1998 Aarhus Convention.[124] An initiative of the UN Economic Commission for Europe signed and ratified by thirty-nine European and Central Asian states plus the European Community within ten years, its preamble records unequivocally that its States parties recognize "that adequate protection of the environment is essential to human well-being and the enjoyment of basic human rights, including the right to life itself." It also declares "that every person has the right

---

[120] *Supra* note 11 (also known as the "Protocol of San Salvador").

[121] The Additional Protocol did not enter into force until 1999, and of course applies only to the states party to it, sixteen states at this writing.

[122] Asia Pacific Forum, *Human Rights and the Environment: Final Report and Recommendations* 33 (2007), available at http://www.asiapacificforum.net/support/issues/acj/references/right-to-environment/listing_content/downloads/environment/final_report_recommendations.doc (accessed Sept. 30, 2011) ("The [Advisory Council of Jurist's] primary recommendation therefore is that [National Human Rights Institutions] advocate the adoption and implementation of a specific right to an environment conducive to the realisation of fundamental human rights.").

[123] *See* Earthjustice, *Environmental Rights Report 2008: Human Rights and the Environment* (2008), available at http://earthjustice.org/sites/default/files/library/reports/2008-environmental-rights-report.pdf (accessed Sept. 30, 2011) (detailing measures protecting environmental rights by international, regional, and domestic institutions) [hereinafter "EJ Report 2008"]. Similar reports from previous years, detailing past environmental-rights-protection measures, may be accessed at *Human Rights and the Environment*, Earthjustice, available at http://earthjustice.org/features/human-rights-and-the-environment (accessed Sept. 30, 2011).

[124] Convention on Access to Information, Public Participation in Decision-Making and Access to Justice in Environmental Matters, June 25, 1998, 2161 U.N.T.S 447, *reprinted in* 38 I.L.M. 517 (1999) *and* V Basic Documents, *supra* note 5, at V.B.20 [hereinafter the 1998 Aarhus Convention].

to live in an environment adequate to his or her health and well-being, and the duty, both individually and in association with others, to protect and improve the environment for the benefit of present and future generations. . . ."

After the conclusion of the Aarhus Convention, the presidents of the European Parliament, the Council, and the Commission of the European Council quickly adopted the EU's Charter of Fundamental Rights.[125] This charter was initially proclaimed on Dec. 7, 2001, and again (with minor changes not relevant here) on Dec. 12, 2007, in anticipation of the Dec. 13, 2007, Treaty of Lisbon amending the Treaty on European Union and the Treaty establishing the European Community[126] (following the debacle of the previously proposed EU constitution). Pertinent is Charter Article 37 ("Environmental Protection") providing that "[a] high level of environmental protection and the improvement of the quality of the environment must be integrated into the policies of the Union *and ensured in accordance with the principle of sustainable development*."[127] That language is embraced by Article 6(1)(1) of the Lisbon Treaty, which, in turn, provides that the EU "recognizes the rights, freedoms and principles set out in the Charter of Fundamental Rights . . . as adapted at Strasbourg on 12 Dec. 2007, *which shall have the same legal value as the Treaties*"[128] (a reference to the Maastricht and Rome treaties). Whereas Charter Article 37 speaks of duty rather than right, it is not unreasonable to assume, in the wake of the Aarhus Convention especially, that the drafters had in mind a fully autonomous right to environment as opposed to merely a derivative one. This is no small matter considering that, by virtue of Lisbon Treaty Article 6(1)(1), Charter Article 37 acquired legally binding and arguably constitutional status and potentially greater flexibility for not having been incorporated into the Treaty of Lisbon.[129] It is not

---

[125] Charter of Fundamental Rights of the European Union, Dec. 12, 2007, 2007 O.J. (C 303/1).

[126] 2007 O.J. (C 306/01), *reprinted in* I Basic Documents, *supra* note 5, at I.B.13(g); *see also* Treaty on European Union (a/k/a "the Treaty of Maastricht"), 1992 O.J.E.C. C191, *reprinted in* 31 I.L.M. 253 (1992) *and* I Basic Documents, at I.B.13a; Treaty Establishing the European Community (Consolidated Version, a/k/a "the Treaty of Rome"), 1992 O.J. (C 340), *reprinted in* 37 I.L.M. 56, 79 (1998) and I Basic Documents, at I.B.13(d). The Rome Treaty was renamed the Treaty on the Functioning of the European Union, 2008 O.J. (C 115/47), *reprinted in* I Basic Documents, at I.B.13h.

[127] Emphasis added.

[128] Emphasis added.

[129] An informed observer explains: "This new approach deliberately avoids the appearance of a Constitution. . . . [I]t avoids the very odd situation of including two preambles in one Treaty. . . . Instead, the reference . . . to the Charter as a separate constitutional document gives the Charter an independent existence and may even allow other Organisations or States to refer to it as a binding instrument. As Article 6, para. 1, clause 1 . . . expressly gives the Charter 'the same legal value as the Treaties,' all its merits as a Constitutional document for the EU, thus, are

unreasonable to assume either that, as Lynda Collins has astutely discerned, "the ambiguity as to the rights aspect of this provision would presumably allow courts to adopt either an anthropocentric or an eco-centric approach, since the provision does not specify the source of the duty,"[130] particularly in light of the Pachamama (Earth Goddess or Mother Earth) Movement now emerging in Latin America.[131] As of this writing, however, we find no legislative or judicial evidence that an eco-centric right to environmental protection and preservation has taken hold in EU jurisprudence.

At the same time, we do find important developments that support an autonomous right-to-environment interpretation of Charter Article 37. In June 2003, the Council of Europe's Parliamentary Assembly, said to be "one of the most powerful legislatures in the world,"[132] recommended first, to the governments of the Council's member states, that they "recognise a human right to a healthy, viable and decent environment which includes the objective obligation for states to protect the environment, in national laws, preferably at constitutional level";[133] and, second, to the Council's Committee of Ministers (the Council's decision-making body), that it "draw up an additional protocol to the European Convention on Human Rights concerning the recognition of individual procedural rights intended to enhance environmental protection, as set out in the Aarhus Convention..."[134] Additionally, in a case involving criminal sanctions for environmental offenses, the highest court in the EU, the Luxembourg-based European Court of Justice, took pains to underscore that "it is common ground that protection of the environment constitutes one of the essential objectives of the Community."[135] Also noteworthy in this case,

---

preserved, and its independent existence even allows it to be used as a more general reference for fundamental rights." Ingolf Pernice, *The Treaty of Lisbon and Fundamental Rights*, in *The Lisbon Treaty: EU Constitutionalism without a Constitutional Treaty?* (Stefan Griller & Jaques Ziller eds., 2008), available at http://www.judicialstudies.unr.edu/JSSummer09/JSPWeek 1/Pernice%20Fundamental%20Rights.pdf (Walter Hallstein-Institut Paper 7/08) (accessed Nov. 28, 2010).

[130] Collins, *supra* note 96, at 143.

[131] *See* Cormac Cullinan, *Wildlaw: Protecting Biological and Cultural Diversity* 183–9 (2d ed. 2011) (discussing the rise of the Pachamama movement in Latin America).

[132] Statement of Professor David Farrell, Head of the School of Social Sciences at The University of Manchester, available athttp://www.europarl.europa.eu/sides/getDoc.do?language= EN&type=IM-PRESS&reference=20070615IPR07837 (accessed Nov. 28, 2010).

[133] Council of Europe Parliamentary Assembly Recommendation 1614 (2003), *Environment and Human Rights*, available at http://assembly.coe.int/Main.asp?link=/Documents/AdoptedText/ ta03/EREC1614.htm (accessed Nov. 28, 2010).

[134] *Id.*

[135] Case C-176/03, Comm'n of the European Communities v. Council of the European Union (Sept. 13, 2005), para. 41, available at http://eur-lex.europa.eu/LexUriServ/LexUriServ.do?uri= CELEX: 62003J0176:EN:HTML (accessed Nov. 28, 2010).

arguably even more so, is a section of the Opinion of Advocate General Ruiz-Jarabo Colomer entitled, "The right to an acceptable environment and public responsibility for its preservation." The essence of this section is strong affirmation of the existence of an autonomous collective right to a clean and healthy environment consistent with the principle of sustainable development.[136] Although not specifically referenced by the Court of Justice, the Advocate General's Opinion is instructive as well as informative.

Most important in the European context, it appears, is the opinion of the European Court of Human Rights in *Taskin and Others v. Turkey*, a previously cited case dismissed on procedural grounds. The case demonstrated the

---

[136] *Id.* Stated the Advocate General, in part:

> 66. The concepts "sustainable development" and "quality of life" used in the EC Treaty (i.e., the Maastricht Treaty, *supra* note 190) occur closely linked with that of the "environment," alluding to a human dimension which cannot be overlooked when mention is made of protecting and improving the environment. In the geophysical medium which our natural surroundings represent, quality of life asserts itself as a citizenship right emanating from various factors, some of them physical (the rational use of resources and sustainable development) and some more intellectual (progress and cultural development). It is a matter of attaining dignity of life in qualitative terms, once the quantitative threshold sufficient for subsistence has been passed.
>
> 67. There thus emerges a right to enjoy an acceptable environment, not so much on the part of the individual as such, but as a member of a group, in which the individual shares common social interests [e.g., class action suits]. A number of constitutions of Member States of the Community at the time the contested Framework Decision was approved recognise that right....
>
> 68. Supplementing that right are the correlative duties on public authorities [as stipulated in the basic laws or constitutions of, e.g., Finland (art. 20), Germany (art. 20(a)), Greece (art. 24.1), Italy (art. 9.2) Netherlands (art. 21), Portugal (art. 9(e)), and Spain (art. 45.2)]....
>
> 69. The human dimension of that environmental concern is implicitly enshrined in the European Union, whose Charter of Fundamental Rights, of 7 December 2000, after declaring in the preamble that the Union is founded on the indivisible, universal values of human dignity, freedom, equality and solidarity, includes, in the Chapter devoted to the latter, alongside employment and welfare rights, a provision explaining that its policies include and ensure a high level of environmental protection and the improvement of the quality of the environment, in accordance with the principle of sustainable development (Article 37)....
>
> 70. I do not want to conclude the present section without emphasising that, irrespective of how the notion of the right to enjoy an appropriate natural environment is couched, *it is easy to discern its link with the content of certain fundamental rights.*

Id. (emphasis added). To corroborate his point, the Advocate General referenced the previously noted cases decided by the European Court of Human Rights: López Ostra v. Spain, *supra* note 33, and Guerra v. Italy, *supra* note 34.

legitimacy of the right to respect for family life and privacy as a basis for deriving protection from environmental harm.[137] In addition to accepting seemingly without question the propriety of the complainants asserting as well their "right to live in a healthy, balanced environment" per Article 56 of the Turkish Constitution,[138] the Court relied on the rulings of Turkish courts upholding that constitutional right. In so doing, the Court rendered no small influence in the shaping of international human rights decision-making unto national constitutions and domestic court decisions similarly articulated.[139] Also significant is a section of the Court's opinion entitled, "Relevant international texts on the right to a healthy environment,"[140] in which the Court discusses and quotes favorably the 1992 Rio Declaration,[141] the Aarhus Convention,[142] and the June 2003 Parliamentary Assembly of the Council of Europe Recommendation 1614 on environment and human rights.[143] The latter includes the Assembly's recommendation to the Council's Member States that they "recognise a human right to a healthy, viable and decent environment which includes the objective obligation for states to protect the environment, in national laws, preferably at constitutional level." As we observe in the next subsection, this recommendation has not gone unnoticed.

3. Recognition on the National Plane

As implied, the story on the national plane confirms the propensity of policy-making and decision-making on the regional plane to recognize an autonomous right to a clean and healthy environment and well beyond what so far has transpired on the global plane. Although not yet universally recognized, the right to a clean and healthy environment appears to have established itself as an autonomous right in the constitutions, laws, and judicial decisions of many countries worldwide.

A convenient if somewhat dated overview of the constitutional state of affairs is found in a 2005 "Environmental Rights Report" of Earthjustice, a leading

---

[137] *See supra* note 34 and accompanying text.
[138] *See infra* note 173.
[139] For extended discussion about constitutional provisions guaranteeing an autonomous right to environment, *see infra* Subsection 2.
[140] Taskin, *supra* note 34, at paras. 98–100.
[141] *Supra* note 65.
[142] *Supra* note 124.
[143] *Supra* note 133.

nonprofit public interest law firm based in California dedicated to protecting the earth "and to defending the right of all people to a healthy environment."[144] The report summarizes:

> Of the approximately 193 countries of the world, there are now 117 whose national constitutions mention the protection of the environment or natural resources.[145] One hundred and nine of them recognize the right to a clean and healthy environment and/or the state's obligation to prevent environmental harm.[146] Of these, 56 constitutions explicitly recognize the right to a clean and healthy environment,[147] and 97

---

[144] Earthjustice, *Environmental Rights Report: Human Rights and the Environment*, available at http://www.earth-justice.org/sites/default/files/library/references/2005ENVIRON-MENTALRIGHTSREPORTrev.pdf (accessed Nov. 28, 2010) [hereinafter "EJ Report 2005"] (Materials for the 61st Session of the United Nations Commission on Human Rights, Geneva, Mar. 14–Apr. 22, 2005).

[145] The Report references its Appendix I listing the 117 countries (together with brief descriptions of relevant constitutional provisions): Afghanistan, Albania, Algeria, Andorra, Angola, Argentina, Armenia, Austria, Azerbaijan, Bahrain, Belarus, Belgium, Benin, Bolivia, Brazil, Bulgaria, Burkina Faso, Burundi, Cambodia, Cameroon, Cape Verde, Chad, Chechnya, Chile, China, Colombia, Comoros, Congo (Brazzaville), Congo (Kinshasa), Costa Rica, Croatia, Cuba, Czech Republic, East Timor, Ecuador, El Salvador, Equatorial Guinea, Eritrea (draft), Estonia, Ethiopia, Finland, France, Georgia, Germany, Ghana, Greece, Guatemala, Guyana, Haiti, Honduras, Hungary, India, Iran, Kazakhstan, Kuwait, Kyrghyzstan, Laos, Latvia, Lithuania, Macedonia, Madagascar, Malawi, Mali, Malta, Mexico, Micronesia, Moldova, Mongolia, Mozambique, Namibia, Nepal, Netherlands, Nicaragua, Niger, North Korea, Norway, Palau, Palestine, Panama, Papua New Guinea, Paraguay, Peru, Philippines, Poland, Portugal, Qatar, Romania, Russia, Säo Tomé/Principe, Saudi Arabia, Seychelles, Slovakia, Slovenia, South Africa, South Korea, Spain, Sri Lanka, Sudan, Suriname, Switzerland, Taiwan, Tajikistan, Tanzania, Thailand, Togo, Turkey, Turkmenistan, Uganda, Ukraine, United Arab Emirates, Uruguay, Uzbekistan, Vanuatu, Venezuela, Vietnam, Yugoslavia (Serbia/Montenegro), and Zambia.

[146] The Report lists the following 109 countries: Afghanistan, Andorra, Angola, Argentina, Armenia, Austria, Azerbaijan, Bahrain, Belarus, Belgium, Benin, Bolivia, Brazil, Bulgaria, Burkina Faso, Cambodia, Cameroon, Cape Verde, Chad, Chechnya, Chile, China, Colombia, Congo (Brazzaville), Congo (Kinshasa), Costa Rica, Croatia, Cuba, Czech Republic, Ecuador, El Salvador, Equatorial Guinea, Eritrea (draft), Estonia, Ethiopia, Finland, France, Georgia, Germany, Ghana, Greece, Guatemala, Guyana, Haiti, Honduras, Hungary, India, Iran, Kazakhstan, Kuwait, Kyrghyzstan, Laos, Latvia, Lithuania, Macedonia, Madagascar, Malawi, Mali, Malta, Mexico, Micronesia, Moldova, Mongolia, Mozambique, Namibia, Nepal, Netherlands, Nicaragua, Niger, North Korea, Norway, Palau, Palestine, Panama, Papua New Guinea, Paraguay, Peru, Philippines, Poland, Portugal, Qatar, Romania, Russia, Säo Tomé/Principe, Saudi Arabia, Seychelles, Slovakia, Slovenia, South Africa, South Korea, Spain, Sri Lanka, Suriname, Switzerland, Taiwan, Tajikistan, Tanzania, Thailand, Togo, Turkey, Turkmenistan, Uganda, Ukraine, Uruguay, Uzbekistan, Venezuela, Vietnam, Yugoslavia (Serbia/Montenegro), and Zambia.

[147] The Report actually lists only fifty-three countries fitting this identification: Angola, Argentina, Azerbaijan, Belarus, Belgium, Benin, Brazil, Bulgaria, Burkina Faso, Cameroon, Cape Verde,

constitutions make it the duty of the national government to prevent harm to the environment.[148]

Earthjustice appears not to have issued comparable summaries since 2005. However, comparing the foregoing 2005 summary with similar Earthjustice summaries in 2003 and 2004,[149] and reviewing its reports from 2007 and

Chad, Chechnya, Chile, Colombia, Congo (Brazzaville), Congo (Kinshasa), Costa Rica, Czech Republic, Ecuador, Ethiopia, Finland, France, Georgia, Hungary, Kyrghyzstan, Latvia, Macedonia, Mali, Moldova, Mongolia, Mozambique, Nicaragua, Niger, Norway, Paraguay, Philippines, Portugal, Romania, Russia, São Tomé/Principe, Seychelles, Slovakia, Slovenia, South Africa, South Korea, Spain, Sudan, Togo, Turkey, Ukraine, Venezuela, and Yugoslavia (Serbia/Montenegro). However, as Serbia and Montenegro are now separately independent states with constitutions that warrant their inclusion here, and as Thailand's new 2007 constitution now makes explicit what previously was implicit (*see infra* note 153), the actual total at this writing is fifty-five.

[148] The Report lists the following ninety-seven countries: Afghanistan, Andorra, Angola, Argentina, Armenia, Austria, Bahrain, Belarus, Benin, Bolivia, Brazil, Bulgaria, Cambodia, Cameroon, Cape Verde, Chad, Chechnya, Chile, China, Colombia, Congo (Brazzaville), Congo (Kinshasa), Costa Rica, Croatia, Cuba, Czech Republic, Ecuador, El Salvador, Equatorial Guinea, Eritrea (draft), Finland, Georgia, Germany, Ghana, Greece, Guatemala, Guyana, Haiti, Honduras, Hungary, India, Iran, Kazakhstan, Kuwait, Laos, Latvia, Lithuania, Macedonia, Madagascar, Malawi, Mali, Malta, Mexico, Micronesia, Mongolia, Mozambique, Namibia, Nepal, Netherlands, Nicaragua, Niger, North Korea, Palau, Palestine, Panama, Papua New Guinea, Paraguay, Peru, Philippines, Poland, Portugal, Romania, Russia, São Tomé/Principe, Saudi Arabia, Seychelles, Slovakia, Slovenia, South Africa, South Korea, Spain, Sri Lanka, Suriname, Switzerland, Taiwan, Tajikistan, Tanzania, Thailand, Togo, Turkey, Turkmenistan, Uganda, Ukraine, Uzbekistan, Venezuela, Vietnam, Yugoslavia (Serbia/Montenegro), and Zambia.

[149] The Report actually lists only fifty-three countries fitting this identification: Angola, Argentina, Azerbaijan, Belarus, Belgium, Benin, Brazil, Bulgaria, Burkina Faso, Cameroon, Cape Verde, Chad, Chechnya, Chile, Colombia, Congo (Brazzaville), Congo (Kinshasa), Costa Rica, Czech Republic, Ecuador, Ethiopia, Finland, France, Georgia, Hungary, Kyrghyzstan, Latvia, Macedonia, Mali, Moldova, Mongolia, Mozambique, Nicaragua, Niger, Norway, Paraguay, Philippines, Portugal, Romania, Russia, São Tomé/Principe, Seychelles, Slovakia, Slovenia, South Africa, South Korea, Spain, Sudan, Togo, Turkey, Ukraine, Venezuela, and Yugoslavia (Serbia/Montenegro). However, as Serbia and Montenegro are now separately independent states with constitutions that warrant their inclusion here, and as Thailand's new 2007 constitution now makes explicit what previously was implicit (*see infra* note 153), the actual total at this writing is fifty-five.

The Report lists the following ninety-seven countries: Afghanistan, Andorra, Angola, Argentina, Armenia, Austria, Bahrain, Belarus, Benin, Bolivia, Brazil, Bulgaria, Cambodia, Cameroon, Cape Verde, Chad, Chechnya, Chile, China, Colombia, Congo (Brazzaville), Congo (Kinshasa), Costa Rica, Croatia, Cuba, Czech Republic, Ecuador, El Salvador, Equatorial Guinea, Eritrea (draft), Finland, Georgia, Germany, Ghana, Greece, Guatemala, Guyana, Haiti, Honduras, Hungary, India, Iran, Kazakhstan, Kuwait, Laos, Latvia, Lithuania, Macedonia, Madagascar, Malawi, Mali, Malta, Mexico, Micronesia, Mongolia, Mozambique, Namibia, Nepal, Netherlands, Nicaragua, Niger, North Korea, Palau, Palestine, Panama, Papua New Guinea, Paraguay, Peru, Philippines, Poland, Portugal, Romania, Russia, São

2008[150] that are otherwise replete with helpful information, it is clear that the trend is toward greater and more widespread constitutional recognition of the human right to a clean and healthy environment as an autonomous right.[151]

Substantiating this viewpoint are the countries listed in EJ Report 2005,[152] plus at least one other in 2007,[153] that have explicitly recognized an autonomous right to a clean and healthy environment in their constitutive instruments. Noteworthy among them are twenty-one countries in Europe: Belgium,[154]

Tomé/Principe, Saudi Arabia, Seychelles, Slovakia, Slovenia, South Africa, South Korea, Spain, Sri Lanka, Suriname, Switzerland, Taiwan, Tajikistan, Tanzania, Thailand, Togo, Turkey, Turkmenistan, Uganda, Ukraine, Uzbekistan, Venezuela, Vietnam, Yugoslavia (Serbia/Montenegro), and Zambia.

Earthjustice, *Issue Paper: Human Rights and the Environment* (2003), available at http://www.earthjustice.org/sites/default /files/library/references/HRE-Report-2003.pdf (accessed Nov. 28, 2010) (Materials for the 59th Session of the United Nations Commission on Human Rights, Geneva, Mar. 17–Apr. 25, 2003); Earthjustice, Issue Paper: Human Rights and the Environment (2004), available at http://www.earthjustice.org/msites/default/files/library/references/2004UNreport.pdf (accessed Nov. 28, 2010) (Materials for the 60th Session of the United Nations Commission on Human Rights, Geneva, Mar. 15–Apr. 23, 2004).

[150] Earthjustice, *Environmental Rights Report 2007: Human Rights and the Environment* (2007), available at http://www.earthjustice.org/sites/default/files/library/references/2007-environmental-rights-report.pdf (accessed Nov. 28, 2010); EJ Report 2008, *supra* note 123.

[151] In a press release announcing its 2008 Report, for example, Earthjustice called particular attention to "developments that illustrate how governments and international institutions are working to establish the human right to a healthy environment" (including 119 countries whose national constitutions mention the protection of the environment or natural resources as compared to a reported 109 in 2003). Press Release, Earthjustice, Earthjustice Presents 2008 "Environmental Rights Report" to U.N., available at http://earthjustice.org/news/press/2008/earthjustice-presents- 2008-environmental-rights-report-to-un (accessed Nov. 28, 2010). Additionally, in language implicitly accepting that the human right to a clean and healthy environment exists already autonomously, it counseled international, regional, and domestic governing bodies to work in cooperation "to ensure that the right to a clean and healthy environment is protected." *Id.*

[152] *See supra* note 144.

[153] *See* Part 12 (Community Rights) of the new 2007 Constitution of Thailand, asianlii.org, available at http://www.asianlii.org/th/legis/const/2007/1.html#C03 P03 (accessed Nov. 28, 2010), in particular Section 66, which provides: "Persons assembling as to be a community, local community or traditional local community shall have the right to conserve or restore their customs, local wisdom, arts or good culture of their community and of the nation and participate in the management, maintenance and exploitation of natural resources, the environment and biological diversity in a balanced and sustainable fashion." *Id.*

[154] Article 23(4) of the 1994 Belgian Constitution declares that "[e]veryone has ... the right to enjoy the protection of a healthy environment." *See* Const. art. 23(4) (Belg.), available at http://www.servat.unibe.ch/icl/be00000_.html (accessed Nov. 28, 2010); EJ Report 2008, *supra* note 123, at 92.

Bulgaria,[155] the Czech Republic,[156] Finland,[157] France,[158] Georgia,[159] Hungary,[160] Latvia,[161] Macedonia,[162] Moldova,[163] Montenegro,[164]

[155] Article 55 of the 1991 Bulgarian Constitution provides that "[e]veryone shall have the right to a healthy and favorable environment corresponding to established standards and norms. . . ." *See Bulgaria – Constitution*, ICL, available at http://www.servat.unibe.ch/icl/bu00000_.html (accessed Nov. 28, 2010); EJ Report 2008, *supra* note 123, at 93.

[156] Article 35(1) of the 1998 Charter of Fundamental Rights and Freedoms amending the 1992 Czech Republic Constitution stipulates that "[e]veryone has the right to a favorable environment." *See* 1998 Charter of Fundamental Rights and Freedoms [Constitution of the Czech Republic], available at http://spcp.prf.cuni.cz/aj/2–93en.htm (accessed Nov. 28, 2010); EJ Report 2008, *supra* note 123, at 96.

[157] Section 20(2) of the 1919 Finnish Constitution commands that "[t]he public authorities shall endeavour to guarantee for everyone the right to a healthy environment. . . ." *See Finland – Constitution*, ICL, available at http://www.servat.unibe.ch/icl/fi00000_.html (accessed Nov. 28, 2010); EJ Report 2008, *supra* note 123, at 98.

[158] After acknowledging that "[t]he environment is the common heritage of all human beings," a 2004 amendment to the 1958 French Constitution (titled the "Charter for the Environment") proclaims in its Article 1 that "[e]ach person has the right to live in a balanced environment which shows due respect for health." *See* 1958 Const., available at http://www.assemblee-nationale.fr/english/8ab.asp (accessed Nov. 28, 2010); EJ Report 2008, *supra* note 123, at 98.

[159] Article 37(3) of the 1995 Georgian Constitution as amended recognizes that "[e]veryone shall have the right to live in healthy environment and enjoy natural and cultural surroundings. . . ." *See Constitution of the Republic of Georgia*, European Comm'n for Democracy Through Law, available at http://www.venice.coe.int/docs/2004/CDL(2004)041-e.pdf (accessed Nov. 28, 2010); EJ Report 2008, *supra* note 123, at 98.

[160] Article 18 of the 1949 Hungarian Constitution declares that "[t]he Republic of Hungary recognizes and shall implement the individual's right to a healthy environment." *See* A Magyar Köztársaság Alkotmánya [Constitution of the Republic of Hungary], available at http://www.servat.unibe.ch/icl/hu00000_.html#A018_ (accessed Nov. 28, 2010); EJ Report 2008, *supra* note 123, at 100.

[161] Article 115 of the 1922 Latvian Constitution charges that "[t]he state protects everyone's right to live within a favorable environment. . . ." *See Constitution of the Republic of Latvia*, Humanrights.lv, available at http://www.humanrights.lv/doc/latlik/satver~1.htm (accessed Nov. 28, 2010); EJ Report 2008, *supra* note 123, at 101 (but misquoted).

[162] Article 43 of the 1991 Macedonian Constitution provides that "[e]veryone has the right to a healthy environment to live in." *See Constitution of Macedonia*, ICL, available at http://www.servat.unibe.ch/icl/mk00000_.html (accessed Nov. 28, 2010); EJ Report 2008, *supra* note 1234, at 101.

[163] Article 37(1) of the 1994 Moldovan Constitution stipulates that "[e]very human being has the right to live in an environment that is ecologically safe for life and health. . . ." *See Constitution of the Republic of Moldova*, Parliament of Thailand, available at http://web.parliament.go.th/parcy/sapa_db/cons_doc/constitutions/data/Moldova/Constitution%20of%20Moldova.htm (accessed Nov. 28, 2010); EJ Report 2008, *supra* note 123, at 102.

[164] Article 23 of the Montenegro Constitution proclaims that "[e]veryone shall have the right to a sound environment." *See Constitution of Montenegro*, UNHCR, available at http://www.unhcr.org/refworld/country,,,LEGISLATION,MNE,4562d8b62,47e11b0c2,0.html (accessed Nov. 28, 2010).

Norway,[165] Portugal,[166] Romania,[167] Russia,[168] Serbia,[169] Slovakia,[170] Slovenia,[171] Spain,[172] Turkey,[173] and Ukraine.[174] In contrast to most of the remaining thirty-four countries (i.e., excepting Argentina, Brazil, Chile, South Africa, South Korea, and Venezuela), all possess industrially developed or developing market economies. This is a remarkable fact considering

---

[165] Article 110b(1) of the 1814 Norwegian Constitution recognizes that "[e]very person has a right to an environment that is conducive to health and to natural surroundings whose productivity and diversity are preserved...." *See Constitution of Norway*, ICL, available at http://www.servat.unibe.ch/icl/no00000_.html (accessed Nov. 28, 2010); EJ Report 2008, *supra* note 123, at 104.

[166] Article 66(1) of the 1976 Portuguese Constitution pronounces that "[e]veryone has the right to a healthy and ecologically balanced human environment...." *See Constitution of Portugal*, ICL, available at http://www.servat.unibe.ch/icl/po00000_.html (accessed Nov. 28, 2010); EJ Report 2008, *supra* note 123, at 106.

[167] Article 35(1) of the 1991 Romanian Constitution as amended by Constitutional Revision Law No. 429/2003 commands that "[t]he State shall acknowledge the right of every person to a healthy, well preserved and balanced environment." *See Constitution of Romania*, ACE Electoral Knowledge Network, available at http://aceproject.org/ero-en/regions/europe/RO/constitution-of-romania-amended-in-october-2003–1/view (accessed Nov. 28, 2010); EJ Report 2008, *supra* note 123, at 106.

[168] Article 42 of the 1993 Russian Constitution pronounces that "[e]veryone has the right to a favorable environment...." *See* Konstitutsiia Rossiiskoi Federatsii [Konst. RF] [Constitution], available at http://www.servat.unibe.ch/icl/rs00000_.html (accessed Nov. 28, 2010); EJ Report 2008, *supra* note 123, at 106.

[169] Article 74 of the 2006 Serbian Constitution declares that "[e]veryone shall have the right to [a] healthy environment...." *See Constitution of the Republic of Serbia*, Serbian Gov't, available at http://www.srbija.gov.rs/cinjenice_o_srbiji/ustav.php?change_lang=en (accessed Nov. 28, 2010).

[170] Article 44(1) of the 1992 Slovak Constitution provides that "[e]veryone has the right to an auspicious environment." *See Constitution of Slovakia*, ICL, available at http://www.servat.unibe.ch/icl/lo00000_.html (accessed Nov. 28, 2010); EJ Report 2008, *supra* note 123, at 107 (but misquoted).

[171] Article 72(1) of the 1991 Slovene Constitution stipulates that "[e]veryone has the right in accordance with the law to a healthy living environment." *See Constitution of Slovenia*, ICL, available at http://www.servat.unibe.ch/icl/si00000_.html (accessed Nov. 28, 2010); EJ Report 2008, *supra* note 123, at 107 (but misquoted).

[172] Article 45(1) of the 1978 Spanish Constitution declares that [e]veryone has the right to enjoy an environment suitable for the development of the person...." *See* C.E., B.O.E. n. 311, Dec. 29, 1978, available at http://www.servat.unibe.ch/icl/sp00000_.html (accessed Nov. 28, 2010); EJ Report 2008, *supra* note 123, at 108.

[173] Article 56 of the 1982 Turkish Constitution provides that [e]veryone has the right to live in a healthy, balanced environment." *See Constitution of Turkey*, ICL, available at http://www.servat.unibe.ch/icl/tu00000_.html (accessed Nov. 28, 2010); EJ Report 2008, *supra* note 123, at 110.

[174] Article 50 of the 1996 Ukrainian Constitution stipulates that "[e]veryone has the right to an environment that is safe for life and health...." *See Constitution of Ukraine*, Verkhovha Rada of Ukraine, available at http://gska2.rada.gov.ua/site/const_eng/constitution_eng.htm (accessed Nov. 28, 2010); EJ Report 2008, *supra* note 123, at 110.

that, historically, market-based economies have not put a high premium on environmental values. Indeed, giving voice to the truism that there can be no right without a counterbalancing duty, these countries' constitutional endorsements of an autonomous right to a clean and healthy environment are typically coupled with constitutional provisions underwriting the duty of the state to protect, preserve, and enhance the environment; to pay damages when there is environmental negligence; and to otherwise honor procedural environmental rights such as the right to environmental information and decisional participation.[175]

In contrast, it must be acknowledged that, of the twenty-one European countries explicitly honoring an autonomous right to environment, only six are of long-standing capitalist tradition of some sort (most are former Soviet socialist republics); and among them are not to be found, except for France, any Western European industrial power that enjoys G-20 membership.[176] Indeed, of the entire group of fifty-five countries, only seven G-20 members are listed (Argentina, Brazil, France, Russia, South Africa, South Korea, and Turkey). Not to be found are Australia, Canada, China, the EU, Germany, India, Indonesia, Italy, Japan, Mexico, Saudi Arabia, the United Kingdom, and the United States, as are sixteen additional countries that are, at this writing, among the world's top thirty-three economies, as determined by the International Monetary Fund (IMF):[177] Austria, Cyprus, Denmark, Greece, Hong Kong SAR, Iceland, Ireland, Israel, Luxembourg, Malta, the Netherlands, New Zealand, Singapore, Sweden, Switzerland, and Taiwan. Noticeably absent as well are the oil-rich exporting states of the Middle East, Africa, and Southeast Asia (in contrast to oil-rich but economically diverse Norway, Russia, and Venezuela). This is not to infer that all these countries are unfriendly toward the environment.[178] Indeed, those that are members of the EU can claim commitment to an autonomous right to environment by virtue of the

---

[175] Regarding procedural environmental rights, *see infra* § C, at 328–36.

[176] Norway, one of the largest contributors to United Nations and World Bank development programs, has never been invited to become a member of the G-20.

[177] *See World Economic Outlook Database*, Int'l Monetary Fund, available at http://www.imf.org/external/pubs/ft/weo/2012/01/weodata/index.aspx (accessed Oct. 6, 2012).

[178] For example, according to the 2010 Environmental Performance Index each year authored by Yale University's Center for Environmental Law & Policy and Columbia University's Center for International Earth Science Information Network in collaboration with the World Economic Forum and the Joint Research Centre of the European Commission, Switzerland, Latvia, Norway, Luxembourg, and Costa Rica are, at this writing, the top five environmentally friendly countries in the world. *See EPI Rankings*, Envtl. Performance Index, available at http://epi.yale.edu/epi2012/rankings (accessed June 14, 2012). The authors explain: "The Environmental Performance Index (EPI) ranks countries on performance indicators tracked across policy categories that cover both environmental public health and ecosystem

previously noted favorable EU jurisprudence that has evolved in this regard in recent years.[179] It is, however, to suggest a possible explanation for resistance to an autonomous human right. Such countries may have a disinclination to establish a preemptive if not absolute norm that can be understood potentially to redefine significantly an economy's relationship to the natural world.

Elsewhere in the world, constitutional support for an autonomous right to environment appears to be on the rise, particularly in Africa, Eastern Europe, and Latin America (in that order), The support has much the same alacrity we noted earlier in the national judicial decisions that have lent support to environmental claims derived from already recognized human rights such as the rights to life, to health, and to respect for private and family life.[180] Indeed, as stated above, national decisions that focus exclusively on any specific substantive right or cluster of such rights are now giving way to a trend that, encouraged by constitutional amendments and revisions, favors more an autonomous than a derivative right to a clean and healthy environment.[181]

Of course, a trend is not necessarily law, and constitutional provisions explicitly proclaiming an autonomous right to environment do not of themselves guarantee their implementation in practice. No pedant's footnote is required to substantiate that the formal law and the operational law are not always the same. Yet, as we have noted already in passing,[182] and as the Earthjustice reports make abundantly clear,[183] the vast majority of countries that have proclaimed an autonomous right to environment in their constitutive instruments have in fact worked hard if not always successfully to ensure its effective operation – in their authorized statutes, regulations, judicial decisions, and so on. In so doing, they have contributed to the building of a general principle of law recognized by international law jurists everywhere as a legitimate "source of law" for the rendering of international environmental law decisions which, in turn, can contribute to the state practice and *opinio juris* that makes for customary international law, binding on all states.

Still, one must take care not to exaggerate the support that exists for an autonomous right to environment on the national plane. Many national

---

vitality. These indicators provide a gauge at a national government scale of how close countries are to established environmental policy goals." Envtl. Performance Index, available at http://epi.yale.edu/(accessed June 14, 2012).

[179] See *supra* text at notes 124–125.

[180] See *supra* text at notes 58–82.

[181] See *supra* Subsection III.B.2; *see also* texts accompanying notes 57, 116–22, and 145.

[182] See *supra* text at note 148.

[183] See *supra* notes 144, 149, and 150.

constitutions mention the protection of the environment or natural resources and even assert a state's obligation to prevent environmental harm, including in countries with advanced economies, but the majority of countries that have recognized the autonomous right to environment in their constitutions and, subsequently, in their statutes, regulations, and judicial decisions are not, as noted above, from the world of advanced market economies. They are found, instead, primarily in the developing world (particularly in South Asia, sub-Saharan Africa, and South America) and among the countries of Eastern Europe (formerly republics of the Soviet Union). In a highly decentralized and essentially voluntarist international legal order, this is not a recipe for juridical recognition in the most widespread sense. At the same time, insofar as regional international law creation is possible, neither should it be dismissed, as indeed we have seen in the European regional context.

C. THE HUMAN RIGHT TO PROCEDURAL ENVIRONMENTAL RIGHTS

Arguably the most widely recognized and entrenched of environmental rights are what have come to be known as "procedural environmental rights," sometimes referred to as "procedural and participatory rights."[184] Dinah Shelton sums them up nicely: "(1) a right to prior knowledge of [potential environmental harm], with a corresponding state duty to inform; (2) a right to participate in decision-making; and (3) a right to recourse before competent administrative and judicial organs."[185] She adds: "Implicit in the duty to inform [is] the state's duty to acquire and study for dissemination all relevant information on the environmental impact of planned actions."[186]

It is, of course, easy to imagine that these three pillars of procedural rights (and the duties that correspond to them) derive from specific provisions of the UDHR and/or the ICCPR and its regional offspring,[187] and in an important sense they do. Each of these instruments provides for a fair trial and other due process guarantees that can be applied to environmental disputes. However,

---

[184] *See, e.g.,* Jonas Ebbesson, *Participatory and Procedural Rights in Environmental Matters: State of Play* (unpublished draft paper to the UNEP-OHCHR High-Level Meeting on the New Future of Human Rights and Environment: Moving the Global Agenda Forward, Nov. 30–Dec. 1, 2009), available at http://www.unep.org/environmental governance/LinkClick.aspx?fileticket=vZU4Z-S4Vo%3D&tabid=2046&language=en-US (accessed Nov. 28, 2010). For convenience, we use the more succinct phrase in lieu of the longer one.

[185] Dinah Shelton, *Human Rights, Environmental Rights, and the Right to Environment,* 28 Stan. J. Int'l L. 103, 117 (1991).

[186] *Id.*

[187] *Supra* notes 5 and 7.

unlike the substantive human rights pressed into environmental service as discussed in Subsection A, this linkage has seldom been invoked in environmental law practice explicitly. Indeed, as Jonas Ebbesson has observed, "with few exceptions, the term 'right' hardly occurs in international environmental agreements, not even when providing for access to information and public participation."[188] It is more accurate, therefore, to think of these procedural rights as human rights drawn not specifically from some preexisting international human rights instrument, but, rather, implicitly from the great sweep of human experience from local to global and back again. They are not "derived" in the sense that we have used this term earlier. Instead, as Shelton explains, they "[refer] to the reformulation and expansion of existing human rights and duties in the context of environmental protection."[189]

In any event, the catalogue of international legal instruments confirming the existence of procedural environmental rights is impressive. Among them are at least the following two so-called soft law instruments that arguably are contributing to the development of customary international law:

- The 1982 World Charter for Nature,[190] Principle 23: "All persons, in accordance with their national legislation, shall have the opportunity to participate, individually or with others, in the formulation of decisions of direct concern to their environment, and shall have access to means of redress when their environment has suffered damage or degradation"; and
- The 1992 Rio Declaration,[191] Principle 10: "Environmental issues are best handled with participation of all concerned citizens, at the relevant level. At the national level, each individual shall have appropriate access to information concerning the environment that is held by public authorities, including information on hazardous materials and activities in their communities, and the opportunity to participate in decision-making processes. States shall facilitate and encourage public awareness and participation by making information widely available. Effective access to judicial and administrative proceedings, including redress and remedy, shall be provided."

[188] Ebbesson, *supra* note 184, at 2.
[189] Shelton, *supra* note 185, at 117. For helpful example within the United Nations system, *see* Linda A. Malone & Scott Pasternack, *Exercising Environmental Human Rights and Remedies in the United Nations System*, 27 Wm. & Mary Envtl. L. & Pol'y Rev. 365 (2002).
[190] *Supra* note 15.
[191] *Supra* note 65.

Principle 10 was reaffirmed, it should be noted, by the 2002 Johannesburg Plan of Implementation adopted at the 2002 World Summit on Sustainable Development,[192] suggesting a consensus or building of normative expectations that translates into a general principle of customary international law.

In a similar but arguably more persuasive vein may be understood the UN International Law Commission's (ILC's) Draft Preamble and Articles on Prevention of Transboundary Harm from Hazardous Activities adopted in May 2001.[193] Not a treaty, it is nonetheless, like most of the ILC's hard fought work, juridically persuasive for having been crafted by "persons of recognized competence in international law,"[194] and it is from this perspective, commanding respect, that its Article 13 ("Information to the Public") should be received:

> States concerned shall, by such means as are appropriate, provide the public likely to be affected by an activity within the scope of the present articles with relevant information relating to that activity, the risk involved and the harm which might result and ascertain their views.

The principle that the public must have access to relevant environmental information and be somehow consulted appears thus to be firmly entrenched in the minds of expert international law jurists.

This conclusion is confirmed, we believe, in the numerous, mostly multilateral treaties that address particular environmental concerns with provisions granting, in diverse language and scope, one or more of the three pillars of procedural rights just noted. For example, as Ebbesson points out,[195] Article 6 of the 1992 UN Framework Convention on Climate Change (UNFCCC);[196] Article 5(d) of the 1994 UN Convention to Combat Desertification in those Countries Experiencing Serious Drought and/or Desertification, Particularly in Africa (UNCCD);[197] Article 10(e) of the 1997 Kyoto Protocol to the

---

[192] World Summit on Sustainable Development, Aug. 26-Sept. 4, 2002, Johannesburg Plan of Implementation, U.N. Doc. A/Conf.199/L.1.

[193] Report of the International Law Commission on the Work of its Fifty-third Session, May 11, 2001, U.N. GAOR, 56th Sess., Supp. No. 10, U.N. Doc. A/56/10, at 370 & Corr. 1; G.A. Res 62/68, Annex, U.N. GAOR, 62nd Sess., Supp. No. 49, (Vol. I), U.N. Doc. A/62/49, at 512 (2008), *reprinted in* V Basic Documents, *supra* note 5, at V.B.22.

[194] Statute of the International Law Commission, art. 2(1), Nov. 21, 1947, G.A. Res 174, U.N. GAOR, 2d Sess., U.N. Doc. A/519, at 105.

[195] *Supra* note 184.

[196] May 9, 1992, 1771 U.N.T.S. 107, *reprinted in* 31 I.L.M. 849 (1992) *and* V Basic Documents, *supra* note 5, at V.H.8. The UNFCCC boasts 195 states parties at this writing.

[197] June 17, 1994, 1954 U.N.T.S. 3, *reprinted in* 33 I.L.M. 1328 (1994) *and* V Basic Documents, *supra* note 5, at V.L.3. The UNCCD boasts 195 states parties at this writing.

UNFCCC;[198] and Article 10 of the 2001 Stockholm Convention on Persistent Organic Pollutants[199] all call on their States parties to facilitate citizen access to information about, and to engage and facilitate citizen participation in, the efforts to combat the environmental hazards to which each is specialized. These commitments to information and participation, set forth in a general way, are seen too, but with greater specificity, in the 1992 Convention on Biological Diversity (CBD),[200] the 1998 Rotterdam Convention on the Prior Informed Consent Procedure for Certain Hazardous Chemicals and Pesticides in International Trade,[201] and the 2000 Cartagena Protocol on Biosafety to the CBD.[202] Additionally, access to information, albeit limited for security reasons to what is needed for protection against radiological emergency, is required by the 1994 International Atomic Energy Agency (IAEA) Convention on Nuclear Safety[203] and the 1997 IAEA Joint Convention on the Safety of Spent Fuel Management and on the Safety of Radioactive Waste Management.[204]

All the foregoing instruments are global in scope. To these and for like purpose may be added numerous environmental treaties on the regional plane, providing public access to information, participation in decision-making, and access to review procedures in varying combination and priority, sometimes without reference to the idea or language of rights.[205] For example, Article 3(8)

---

[198] Kyoto Protocol to the United Nations Framework Convention on Climate Change, Dec. 10, 1997, FCCC/CP/1997/7/Add.1, *reprinted in* 37 I.L.M. 32 (1998) *and* V Basic Documents, *supra* note 5, at V.H.20(a). The Kyoto Protocol boasts 192 states parties at this writing.

[199] Stockholm, Swed., May 22–23, 2001, Final Act, U.N. Doc. UNEP/POPS/CONF/4 (June 5, 2001), available at http://chm.pops.int/Portals/0/download.aspx?d=UNEP-POPS-COP-CONVTEXT.En.pdf (accessed Sept. 30, 2011), *reprinted in* 40 I.L.M. 532 (2001) *and* V Basic Documents, *supra* note 5, at V.K.4.

[200] *Supra* note 45.

[201] Sept. 10, 1998, 2244 U.N.T.S. 337, *reprinted in* 38 I.L.M. 1 (1999) *and* V Basic Documents, *supra* note 5, at V.K.3.

[202] Jan. 20, 2000, 2226 U.N.T.S. 208, *reprinted in* V Basic Documents, *supra* note 5, at V.H.26.

[203] Sept. 20, 1994, 1963 U.N.T.S. 293, *reprinted in* 33 I.L.M. 1514 (1994) *and* V Basic Documents, *supra* note 5, at V.Q.10.

[204] Sept. 5, 1997, *reprinted in* 36 I.L.M. 1431 (1997).

[205] *See, e.g.*, ASEAN Agreement on the Conservation of Nature and Natural Resources, July 9, 1985 (not in force at this writing), 15 J. Envtl. L. & Pol'y 64, *reprinted in* V Basic Documents, *supra* note 5, at V.C.6; the Espoo Convention on Environmental Impact Assessment in a Transboundary Context, Feb. 25, 1991, 1989 U.N.T.S. 309, U.N. Doc. E.ECE.1250, *reprinted in* 30 I.L.M. 802 (1991) *and* V Basic Documents, at V.B.17 [hereinafter "the 1991 Espoo Convention]; Convention on Transboundary Effects of Industrial Accidents, Mar. 17, 1992, 2105 U.N.T.S. 457; Convention on the Protection and Use of Transboundary Watercourses and International Lakes, Mar. 17, 1992, 1936 U.N.T.S. 269, *reprinted in* 31 I.L.M. 1312 (1992) *and* V Basic Documents, *supra* note 5, at V.J.5; North American Agreement on Environmental Cooperation, Sept. 8–14, 1993, available from US Department of State, *reprinted in* 32 I.L.M. 1480 (1993) *and* V Basic Documents, at V.C.11; USA-Mexico Agreement Concerning the

of the 1991 Espoo Convention,[206] the purpose of which is "to prevent, reduce and control significant adverse transboundary environmental impact from proposed activities,"[207] requires the concerned States Parties to "ensure that the public of the affected Party in the areas likely to be affected be informed of, and be provided with possibilities for making comments or objections on, the proposed activity, and for the transmittal of these comments or objections to the competent authority of the Party of origin, either directly to this authority or, where appropriate, through the Party of origin." But counsels Ebbesson, "even when an agreement does not provide for a right [per se], it may nevertheless support rather than be neutral or opposing the *notion* of participatory and procedural rights in environmental matters."[208]

Among these regional environmental agreements, one in particular stands out as worthy of special notice, to wit, the previously mentioned 1998 Aarhus Convention on Access to Information, Public Participation in Decision-Making and Access to Justice in Environmental Matters.[209] As its name implies, the Convention is comprehensive, embracing each of the three pillars of procedural environmental rights, and in considerable detail: the right to receive timely environmental information held by public authorities, coupled with the duty of public authorities to collect and disseminate such information;[210] the right to participate meaningfully in environmental decision-making, including the opportunity to comment on environmental matters of significance;[211] and the right to contest environmental decisions, be they substantive or procedural, before a court of law or other independent and impartial body established by law.[212] What is more, it is couched in the language of rights, a point not lost on the Aarhus Compliance Convention Committee (ACCC) in its compliance reviews wherein it has repeatedly confirmed the Convention's rights-based approach.[213] Said former UN Secretary-General Kofi Annan of the Convention on its adoption, it is a "most impressive elaboration of principle 10 of

---

Establishment of a Border Environment Cooperation Commission and a North American Development Bank, Nov. 16, 1993, T.I.A.S. no. 12, 516, *reprinted in* 32 I.L.M. 1545 (1993); the 1998 Aarhus Convention, *supra* note 124; Revised African Convention on the Conservation of Nature and Natural Resources, July 11, 2003 (not in force at this writing), available from the *African Union at* www.africa-union.org, *reprinted in* V Basic Documents, at V.C.14.

[206] *Supra* note 205.
[207] *Id.*, art. 2(1).
[208] Ebbesson, *supra* note 184, at 2.
[209] *Supra* note 124.
[210] *Id.*, arts. 4–5.
[211] *Id.*, arts. 6–8.
[212] *Id.*, art. 9.
[213] *See* Ebbesson, *supra* note 184, at 12.

the [1992] Rio Declaration"[214] and "the most ambitious venture in the area of environmental democracy so far undertaken under the auspices of the United Nations."[215]

Significantly, the Aarhus Convention can boast considerable implementation among its present forty-three European and Central Asian States parties, due in part, as Lynda Collins notes, to the influence, ironically, of many of the former Soviet bloc countries.[216] She writes:

> Stephen Stec [Head of the Environmental Security Programme at Central European University in Budapest] notes that many former Soviet – block [sic] countries had already embraced the notion of "environmental democracy" prior to Aarhus as an aspect of transition to democracy more generally. Indeed, Stec argues that as a result of these transition-driven advances in Eastern European countries, "the Convention has had a comparatively bigger impact on the legislation of Western Europe than that of Eastern Europe."[217]

Professor Collins then helps to clarify what some of this "bigger impact" has been within the context of the EU:[218]

> The EU itself has already made substantial progress in amending its environmental legislation to accord with the Aarhus Convention. Article 6 of Directive 2 2003/4/EEC on public access to environmental information gives effect to Article 9(1) of the Aarhus Convention, requiring the establishment of a review process in cases of refusal to provide environmental information. Article 3 3(7) of Directive 2 2003/35/EC on providing for public participation in respect of the drawing up of certain plans and programmes relating to the environment, brings EU law into conformity with Article 9(2) of the Aarhus Convention concerning public participating in environmental decisions. The Proposed Directive on Access to Justice in Environmental Matters responds to Article 9(3) of the Aarhus Convention, regarding citizen enforcement of environmental laws. Finally, the Commission adopted a proposal for a regulation applying the Aarhus Convention to EU institutions, and the Ministers of Environment agreed to this proposal in December, 2004.

[214] For the text of Principle 10 of the 1992 Rio Declaration, see *supra* text at note 191.
[215] *Quoted at* UNECE, available at http://www.unece.org/env/pp/media.html (accessed Nov. 28, 2010).
[216] Collins, *supra* note 96, at 140.
[217] *Id.* (citing Stephen Stec, *"Aarhus Environmental Rights" in Eastern Europe*, 5 Y.B. Eur. ENVTL. L. 1, 9 (2005)).
[218] *Id.* at 140–41.

Thus, legislatively, the Aarhus Convention has had substantial influence in advancing procedural environmental rights – as a matter of human rights law, not hortatory policy.

This commitment to procedural environmental rights, it must be added, is found also in at least five decisions of the European Court of Human Rights, several of them cited earlier for other reasons. In *Öneryildiz v. Turkey*,[219] the Court held that the public's right to information in situations involving dangerous activities may be based on protection of the right to life. In *Guerra and Others v. Italy*,[220] wherein the applicants were denied information about the risks of a hazardous industrial activity to which they were exposed, the Court determined that the right to access to information is violated when a state violates the human right to respect for family life and privacy. In *Taskin and Others v. Turkey*,[221] the Court reasoned that, in cases involving "complex issues of environmental and economic policy," the failure to undertake appropriate studies, to evaluate the data explored, and to provide public access thereto would risk violating both the right to respect for family life and privacy and the right to environment (citing the Turkish Constitution). Referencing *Guerra* as well as other cases, the Court emphasized that "[t]he importance of public access to the conclusions of such studies and to information, which would enable members of the public to assess the danger to which they are exposed is beyond question."[222] It added that concerned individuals "must also be able to appeal to the courts against any decision, act or omission where they consider that their interests or their comments have not been given sufficient weight in the decision-making process."[223] In *Giacomelli v. Italy*,[224] the Court held that the right of individuals to appeal to courts regarding decisions, acts, or omissions detrimental to their environmental interests may be based on the right to respect for private and family life. Finally, *Zander v. Sweden*[225] involved the denial of an appeal to the Swedish government challenging an authorized raising of the permissible level of cyanide in a city's water supply. The European Court of Human Rights – finding that the applicants were unable to secure judicial review by the Swedish courts even though they

[219] 41 Eur. Ct. H.R. 20 (2004).

[220] 26 Eur. Ct. H.R. 357 (1998).

[221] 2004-X Eur. Ct. H.R. 621 (2004); *see also supra* text accompanying notes 137–43.

[222] *Id.*, para. 119.

[223] *Id.*

[224] 45 Eur. Ct. H.R. 38 (2006), available at http://cmiskp.echr.coe.int/tkp197/view.asp?item=1&portal=hbkm&action=html&highlight=Giacomelli%20|%20v.%20|%20Italy&sessionid=79314428&skin=hudoc-en (2006) (accessed Nov. 28, 2010).

[225] 279B Eur. Ct. H.R. (ser. A) (1993).

were entitled by Swedish law to seek precautionary measures against water pollution – held that the applicant's right of access to justice under ECHR Article 6 had been violated.

We come, then, to the following conclusion: procedural environmental rights appear to enjoy authoritative recognition and support applicable as a matter of law everywhere, although most prominently in Europe and Central Asia. Perhaps most salient of these rights is the right to receive timely environmental information held by public authorities, coupled with the duty of public authorities to collect and disseminate such information. Rachel Carson put it thus in *Silent Spring*:

> This is an era . . . dominated by industry, in which the right to make a dollar at whatever cost is seldom challenged. When the public protests, confronted with some obvious evidence of damaging [environmental] results, . . . it is fed little tranquilizing pills of half truth. We urgently need an end to these false assurances, to the sugar coating of unpalatable facts. It is the public that is being asked to assume the risks. . . . The public must decide whether it wishes to continue on the present road, and it can do so only when in full possession of the facts. In the words of Jean Rostand,[226] "The obligation to endure gives us the right to know."[227]

And the right to participate in decision-making and to challenge by legal means as well!

Of course, as the applicants' experience with the Swedish environmental authorities in *Zander* makes clear, and as Shelton, citing *Zander*, has cautioned, one must take care not to be "overly optimistic . . . that a fully-informed public with rights of participation in environmental decision-making, and access to remedies for environmental harm would ensure a high level of environmental protection."[228] Shelton continues, perceptively:

> Such a beneficial outcome may result, but it cannot always be assured. Democratic states as well as dictatorial regimes have adopted laws at different moments in history that have denied or restricted the enjoyment of human rights. In a democracy, such results can occur despite an informed public and an adherence to democratic process. In the environmental field, well-known

---

[226] French biologist and philosopher (1894–1977), son of playwright Edmond Rostand.

[227] Rachel Carson, Silent Spring 13 (1962). We are indebted to Professor Lynda Collins, *supra* note 96, for calling our attention to this passage.

[228] Dinah Shelton, *Human Rights and Environment: Past, Present and Future Linkages and the Value of a Declaration*, at 6 (Background Paper for the High Level Expert Meeting on the New Future of Human Rights and Environment: Moving the Global Agenda Forward, Co-organized by UNEP and OHCHR, Nov. 30–Dec. 1, 2009).

problems of achieving environmental protection in the face of short term economic costs, as well as scientific uncertainty or the perception thereof, make reliance on procedure alone insufficient to ensure a safe, healthy or ecologically-sound environment.[229]

Still, for all the reasons stated at the outset of this addendum, human rights law and policy, which "sets limits for majority rule in addition to providing guarantees against dictatorial repression,"[230] is the best option in an imperfect world, particularly when substantive and procedural rights work together.

D. SUMMARY

The foregoing review may be briefly summarized. All three of the described manifestations of the human right to environment, however robust in their particularized applications, are essentially limited in their legal recognition and jurisdictional reach. Juridically, the human right to environment is most strongly recognized in its derivative form, not its autonomous form. Also, it is found to exist principally in the developing nations of Africa, Asia, and Latin America, especially when framed autonomously. There is also a growing sentiment, so far at the regional level only, to recognize procedural environmental rights, especially in Europe, but at bottom, it seems, the human right to a clean and healthy environment is likely to remain largely a moral rather than a legal claim, juridically unacceptable to the principal power brokers of the present world order even while gaining such recognition, at present at least, in the developing world. Barring some cataclysmic event, huge economic and political forces seem likely to continue to resist this right for reasons that are deeply historical and philosophical.

[229] *Id.*
[230] *Id.*

Bibliography of Pertinent Books

Abbate, Janet. *Inventing the Internet* (Cambridge, MA: MIT Press, 2000)

Abrell, Elan, et al. *Natural Justice, Implementing a Traditional Knowledge Commons: Opportunities and Challenges* (Cape Town, South Africa: Developments following the Traditional Knowledge Commons Workshop, 2009), available at http://naturaljustice.org/wp-content/uploads/pdf/Implementing_a_TKC-2009.pdf (accessed July 20, 2012)

Ackerman, Frank, and Lisa Heinzerling. *Priceless: On Knowing the Price of Everything and the Value of Nothing* (New York: The New Press, 2004)

Albertson, Peter, and Margery Barnett (eds.). *Managing the Planet* (Englewood Cliffs, NJ: Prentice-Hall, Inc., 1972)

Alexander, Christopher, et al. *A Pattern Language: Towns, Buildings, Construction* (New York: Oxford University Press, 1997)

Alexander, Gregory S. *Commodity and Propriety: Competing Visions of Property in American Legal Thought, 1776–1970* (Chicago: University of Chicago Press, 1997)

Alperovitz, Gar. *America Beyond Capitalism: Reclaiming Our Wealth, Our Liberty, and Our Democracy* (Takoma Park, MD: Democracy Collaborative, 2d ed., 2011)

Alston, Philip H. (ed.). *People's Rights* (Oxford; New York: Oxford University Press, 2001)

Amend, Thora, et al. (eds.). *Protected Landscapes and Agrobiodiversity Values* (Heidelberg: Kasparek, published on behalf of GTZ and IUCN, 2008)

Anand, Ram Prakash Anand. *Origin and Development of the Law of the Sea* (The Hague; Boston: Martinus Nijhoff, 1982)

Anton, Donald K., et al. *International Environmental Law: Cases, Materials, Problems* (Newark, NJ: LexisNexis Matthew Bender, 2006)

Anton, Donald K., and Dinah L. Shelton. *Environmental Protection and Human Rights* (Cambridge; New York: Cambridge University Press, 2011)

Aoki, Keith. *Seed Wars: Controversies and Cases on Plant Genetic Resources and Intellectual Property* (Durham, NC: Carolina Academic Press, 2008)

Archibugi, Daniele. *The Global Commonwealth of Citizens: Toward Cosmopolitan Democracy* (Princeton: Princeton University Press, 2008)

Archibugi, Daniele, and David Held (eds.). *Cosmopolitan Democracy: An Agenda for a New World Order* (Cambridge, UK: Polity Press; Cambridge, MA: Basil Blackwell [distributor], 1995)

Arsanjani, Mahnoush H., et al. *Looking to the Future: Essays on International Law in Honor of W. Michael Reisman* (Leiden/Boston: Martinus Nihoff Publishers, 2011)

Arthur, Brian, et al. (eds.). *The Economy as an Evolving Complex System II* (Reading, MA: Addison-Wesley, 1997)

Axelrod, Robert M. *The Complexity of Cooperation: Agent-Based Models of Competition and Collaboration* (Princeton, NJ: Princeton University Press, 1997)

_____. *The Evolution of Cooperation* (New York: Basic Books, rev. ed., 2006)

Baker, Howard A. *Space Debris: Legal and Policy Implications* (Dordrecht; Boston: Nijhoff, 1988; Norwell, MA: Kluwer Academic Publishers [distributor], 1989)

Baland, Jean-Marie, and Jean-Philippe Platteau. *Halting Degradation of Natural Resources: Is There a Role for Rural Communities?* (New York: FAO; Oxford: Clarendon Press, 1996)

Barlow, Maude. *Blue Covenant: The Global Water Crisis and the Coming Battle for the Right to Water* (New York: New Press: W.W. Norton [distributor], 2007)

Barnes, Peter. *Capitalism 3.0: A Guide to Reclaiming the Commons* (San Francisco: Berrett-Koehler Publishers Inc., 2006)

_____. *Who Owns the Sky? Our Common Assets and the Future of Capitalism Commons* (Washington, DC: Island Press, 2001)

Baslar, Kemal. *The Concept of the Common Heritage of Mankind in International Law* (The Hague: Kluwer Law International, 1998)

Bean, Michael J., and Melanie J. Rowland. *The Evolution of National Wildlife Law* (Westport, CT: Praeger, 3d ed. 1997)

Beinhocker, Eric D. *The Origin of Wealth: Evolution, Complexity and the Radical Remaking of Economics* (Boston: Harvard Business School Press, 2006)

Benkler, Yochai. *The Penguin and the Leviathan: How Cooperation Triumphs over Self-Interest* (New York: Crown Business, 2011)

_____. *The Wealth of Networks: How Social Production Transforms Markets and Freedom* (New Haven, CT: Yale University Press, 2006)

Bennholdt-Thomsen, Veronika, and Mies, Maria. *The Subsistence Perspective: Beyond the Globalised Economy* (London: Zed Books, Ltd.; New York: St. Martin's Press [distributor], 1999)

Benyus, Janine M. *Biomimicry: Innovation Inspired by Nature* (New York: Perennial, 2002)

Fikret Berkes. *Sacred Ecology: Traditional Ecological Knowledge and Resource Management* (Philadelphia, PA: Taylor & Francis, 1999)

Birnie, Patricia W., and Alan E. Boyle. *International Law and the Environment* (Oxford; New York: Oxford University Press, 2d ed., 2002)

Birnie, Patricia W., Alan E. Boyle, and Catherine Redgwell. *International Law and the Environment* (Oxford; New York: Oxford University Press, 3d ed., 2009)

Blackshield, A.R. (ed.). *Legal Change: Essays in Honour of Julius Stone* (Sydney: Butterworths, 1983)

Bodansky, Daniel, Jutta Brunnée, and Ellen Hey (eds.). *The Oxford Handbook of International Environmental Law* (Oxford; New York: Oxford University Press, 2007)

Bollier, David. *Silent Theft: The Private Plunder of Our Common Wealth* (New York: Routledge, 2003)

———. *Viral Spiral: How the Commoners Built a Digital Republic of Their Own* (New York: The New Press, 2008)

———. *Work and Future Society: Where Are the Economy and Technology Taking Us?* (Washington, DC: The Aspen Institute, 1998)

Bollier, David, and Silke Helfrich (eds.). *The Wealth of the Commons: A World Beyond Market and State* (Amherst, MA: Levellers Press, 2012)

Borkowski, Andrew, and Paul du Plessis. *Textbook on Roman Law* (Oxford; New York: Oxford University Press, 2005)

Bothe, Michael (ed.). *Trends in Environmental: Policy and Law* (Berlin: E. Schmidt, 1980)

Botsman, Rachrel, and Roo Rogers. *What's Mine Is Yours: The Rise of Collaborative Consumption* (New York: Harper Business, 2010)

Bowles, Samuel, and Herbert Gintis. *A Cooperative Species: Human Reciprocity and Its Evolution* (Princeton, NJ: Princeton University Press, 2011)

Boyd, David R. *The Environmental Rights Revolution: A Global Study of Constitutions, Human Rights, and the Environment* (Vancouver, BC: UBC Press, 2012)

Boyle, Alan E., and Michael R. anderson (eds.). *Human Rights Approaches to Environmental Protection* (Oxford: Clarendon Press; Oxford; New York: Oxford University Press, 1996)

Brooks, Richard O., et al. *Law and Ecology: The rise of the Ecosystem Regime* (Aldershot, Hants, England: Ashgate Publishing Ltd., 2002 & Burlington, VT: Ashgate Publishing Co., 2002)

Brown, Brian Edward. Religion, Law, and the Land: Native Americans and the Judicial Interpretation of Sacred Land (Westport, CT: Greenwood Press, 1999)

Brown, Donald, et al. (eds.). *White Paper on the Ethical Dimensions of Climate Change* (University Park, PA: Pennsylvania State University, undated)

Brown, Lester R. *Eco-Economy: Building An Economy for the Earth* (New York: W.W. Norton & Co. Inc., 2001)

———. *Plan B 3.0: Mobilizing to Save Civilization* (New York: W.W. Norton and Co. Inc., 2008)

Brown, Peter, and Geoffrey Garver. *Right Relationship: Building a Whole Earth Economy* (San Francisco: Berrett-Koehler Publishers Inc., 2009)

Brown Weiss, Edith. *In Fairness to Future Generations: International Law, Common Patrimony, and Intergenerational Equity* (Tokyo: United Nations University Press, 1988; Dobbs Ferry, NY: Transnational Publishers, 1992)

Brown Weiss, Edith, et al. *International Environmental Law and Policy* (Aspen, CO: Publishers 2d ed. 2009)

Brown Weiss, Edith (ed.). *Environmental Change and International Law: New Challenges and Dimensions* (Tokyo: United Nations University Press, 1992)

Buck, Susan J. *The Global Commons: An Introduction* (Washington, DC: Island Press, 1998)

Burdon, Peter (ed.). *Exploring Wild Law: The Philosophy of Earth Jurisprudence* (Adelaide, South Australia: Wakefield Press, 2011)

Burgenthal, Thomas, Dinah Shelton, and David P. Stewart. *International Human Rights in a Nutshell* (St. Paul, West Group, 2002)

Burger, Joanna, Elinor Ostrom, Richard B. Norgaard, David Policansky, and Bernard D. Goldstein. *Protecting the Commons: A Framework for Resource Management in the Commons* (Washington, DC: Island Press, 2001)

Caldwell, Lynton K. *In Defense of Earth: International Protection of the Biosphere* (Bloomington, IN: Ind. University Press, 1972)

Chambers, W. Bradnee, and Jessica F. Green (eds.). *Reforming International Environmental Governance: From Institutional Limits to Innovative Reforms* (Tokyo; New York: United Nations University Press, 2005)

Carlson, Jonathan C., Sir Geoffrey W.R. Palmer, and Burns H. Weston. *International Environmental Law and World Order: A Problem-Oriented Coursebook* (St. Paul, MN, 3d ed., 2012)

Carson, Rachel L. *Silent Spring* (New York: Fawcett Crest, 1962)

———. *The Sea Around Us* (New York: Oxford University Press, 1952)

Cech, Thomas V. *Principles of Water Resources: History, Development, Management, and Policy* (Hoboken, NJ: John Wiley & Sons, 2d ed., 2005)

Chesborough, Henry. *Open Business Models: How to Thrive in the New Innovation Landscape* (Boston, MA: Harvard Business School Press, 2006)

Chichilnisky, Graciella (ed.). *The Economics of Climate Change* (Cheltenham, UK; Northampton, MA: Edward Elgar, 2010)

Chichilnisky, Graciella, and Geoffrey Heal. *The Evolving International Economy* (Cambridge, UK; New York: Cambridge University Press, 1986)

Chichilnisky, Graciella, and Geoffrey Heal (eds.). *Environmental Markets: Equity and Efficiency* (New York: Columbia University Press, 2000)

Chopra, Samir, and Scott D. Dexter. *Decoding Liberation: The Promise of Free and Open Source Software* (New York: Routledge, 2008)

Christian, David. *Maps of Time: An Introduction to Big History* (Berkeley, CA: University of California Press 2004)

Claude, Richard Pierre, and Burns H. Weston (eds. & contribs.). Human Rights in the World Community: Issues and Action (Philadelphia, PA: 3d ed., 2006)

Cleveland, Harlan. *The Global Commons: Policy for the Planet* (Queenstown, MD: Aspen Institute; Lanham, MD: University Press of America, 1990)

Clippinger, III, John H. *A Crowd of One: The Future of Individual Identity* (New York: Public Affairs, 2007)

———. *The Biology of Business: Decoding the Natural Laws of Enterprise* (San Francisco: Jossey-Bass Publishers, 1999)

Clover, Charles. *The End of the Line: How Overfishing Is Changing the World and What We Eat* (Berkeley, CA: University of California Press, 2008)

Coghill, Ken. *Charles Sampford and Tim Smith* (eds.) Fiduciary Duty and the Atmospheric Trust (Farnham, Surrey, UK; Burlington, VT: Ashgate, 2012)

Common. Michael, and Sigrid Stagl. *Ecological Economics: An Introduction* (Cambridge, UK; New York: Cambridge University Press, 2005)

Community Forest Collaborative, *Community Forests: A Community Investment Strategy* (2007), available at http://www.communitiescommittee.org/pdfs/Community_Forests_Report_web.pdf (accessed July 29, 2012)

Cornelius, Wayne A. Cornelius, and David Myhre (eds.), *The Transformation of Rural Mexico: Reforming the Ejido Sector* (La Jolla, CA: Center for U.S.-Mexican Studies, University of California at San Diego, 1998)

Costanza, Robert, et al. *An Introduction to Ecological Economics* (Boca Raton, FL: St. Lucie Press, Int'l Society for Ecological Economics, 1997)

Coyle, Diane. *The Economics of Enough: How to Run the Economy as If the Future Matters* (Princeton, NJ: Princeton University Press, 2011)

Crawford, Stanley G. *Mayordomo: Chronicle of an Acequia in Northern New Mexico* (Albuquerque, NM: University of New Mexico Press, 1988)

Creative Commons, *The Power of Open* (Creative Commons, 2011), available at http://thepowerofopen.org (accessed July 20, 2012)

Crouch, Colin. *The Strange Non-Death of Neoliberalism* (Malden, MA: Polity, 2011)

Cullinan, Cormac. *Wild Law: A Manifesto for Earth Justice* (White River Jct., VT: Chelsea Green Publishing, 2d ed., 2011)

Daly, Herman E. *Beyond Growth: The Economics of Sustainable Development* (Boston: Beacon Press, 1996)

Davey, Brian (ed.). *Sharing for Survival: Restoring the Climate, the Commons and Society* (Feasta, 2012), available at http://www.sharingforsurvival.org (accessed July 20, 2012)

D'Amato, Anthony, and Kirsten Engel (eds.). *International Environmental Law Anthology* (Cincinnati, OH: Anderson Publishing Co., 1996)

De Graff, John. *Affluenza, The All-Consuming Epidemic* (San Francisco, CA : Berrett-Koehler Publishers, 2005)

Diamond, Jared. *Collapse: How Societies Choose to Fail or Succeed* (New York: Viking, 2005)

Donnelly, Jack. *The Concept of Human Rights* (New York: St. Martin's Press, 1985)

_____. *Universal Human Rights in Theory and Practice* (Ithaca, NY: Cornell University Press, 2003)

Dow, Kirstin, and Thomas E. Downing, *The Atlas of Climate Change: Mapping the World's Greatest Challenge* (Berkeley, CA: University Calif. Press, 3d ed., 2011)

Dowie, Mark. *Conservation Refugees: The Hundred-Year Conflict Between Global Conservation and Native Peoples* (Cambridge, MA: MIT Press, 2009)

Drinan, Robert F. *The Mobilization of Shame: A World View of Human Rights* (New Haven, CT: Yale University Press, 2001)

Duménil, Gérard, and Dominique Lévy. *The Crisis of Neoliberalism* (Cambridge, MA: Harvard University Press, 2011)

Duval, Jared. *Next Generation Democracy: What the Open-Source Revolution Means for Power, Politics, and Change* (New York: Bloomsbury, 2010)

Dworkin, Ronald. *Taking Rights Seriously* (Cambridge, MA: Harvard University Press, 1977)

Eide, Asbjørn, and Jan Helgesen (eds.). *The Future of Human Rights Protection in a Changing World: Fifty Years Since the Four Freedoms Address, Essays in Honor of Torkel Opsahl* (Oslo: Norwegian University Press, 1991)

Eiseley, Loren. *The Immense Journey* (New York: Vintage Books, 1958)

_____. *The Unexpected Universe* (New York: Harcourt Brace Jovanovich, 1969)

Eliot, T.S. *The Idea of a Christian Society* (New York: Harcourt, Brace & CO., 1940)

European Commission. *The Common Fisheries Policy: A User's Guide* (2008), available at http://ec.europa.eu/fisheries/documentation/publications/pcp2008_en.pdf (accessed July 21, 2012)

Eversley, George Shaw-Lefevre Eversley. *Commons, Forests and Footpaths: The Story of the Battle During the Last Forty-five Years for Public Rights Over the Commons, Forests and Footpaths of England and Wales* (London, New York: Cassell & Co., rev. ed. 1910)

Falk, Richard A. *A Study of Future Worlds* (New York: Free Press, 1975)

———. *Achieving Human Rights* (New York; London: Routledge, 2009)

———. *Predatory Globalization: A Critique* (Cambridge, UK: Polity Press, 1999)

———. *This Endangered Planet: Prospects and Proposals for Human Survival* (New York: Random House, 1971)

———. *On Human Governance: toward a New Global Politics* (University Park, PA: State University Press, 1995)

Falk, Richard A., Samuel S. Kim, and Saul H. Mendlovitz (eds.). *The United Nations and a Just World Order* (Boulder, CO: Westview Press, 1991)

Farber, Daniel A., and Jim Chen. *Disasters and the Law: Katrina and Beyond* (New York: Aspen Publishers, 2006)

Federici, Silvia. *Caliban and the Witch: Women, the Body and Primitive Accumulation* (Brooklyn, NY: Autonomedia, 2004)

Fiorino, D.J. *The New Environmental Regulation* (Cambridge, MA: MIT Press, 2006)

Fischer, Frank. *Citizens, Experts and the Environment: The Politics of Local Knowledge* (Durham, NC: Duke University Press, 2000)

Flannery, Tim F. *The Weather Makers: How Man is Changing the Climate and What It Means for Life on Earth* (New York: Atlantic Monthly Press, 2005)

Fligstein, Neil. *The Architecture of Markets: An Economic Sociology of Twenty-First Century Capitalist Societies* (Princeton, NJ: Princeton University Press, 2001)

Flournoy, Alyson C. and David M. Driesen (eds. & contribs). *Beyond Environmental Law: Policy Proposals for a Better Environmental Future* (Cambridge; New York: Cambridge University Press, 2010)

Foundation for Ecological Security, *Vocabulary of the Commons* (Bangalore, India: Foundation for Ecological Security, 2011)

Franck, Thomas M. *The Power of Legitimacy Among Nations* (New York: Oxford University Press, 1990)

Freeman, Michael D.A. *Human Rights: An Interdisciplinary Approach* (Cambridge, UK; Malden, MA: Polity Press, 2d. ed., 2011)

Freyfogle, Eric T. *The Land We Share: Private Property and the Common Good* (Washington, DC: Island Press, 2003)

Friedman, Milton and Rose Friedman. *Free to Choose: A Personal Statement* (New York: Harcourt Brace Jovanovich, 1980)

Frischmann, Brett M. *Infrastructure: The Social Value of Shared Resources* (Oxford, England: Oxford University Press, 2012)

Fukuyama, Francis. *The End of History and the Last Man* (New York: Free Press; Toronto: Maxwell Macmillan Canada; New York: Maxwell Macmillan International, 1992)

Galtung, Johan. *The True Worlds: A Transnational Perspective* (New York: Free Press, 1980)

Gintis, Herbert, Samuel Bowles, Robert Boyd, and Ernst Fehr. *Moral Sentiments and Material Interests* (Cambridge, MA: MIT Press, 2005)

Gerrard, Michael B. (ed.). *Global Climate Change and US Law* (Chicago: American Bar Association, 2007)

Joshua Getzler. *A History of Water Rights at Common Law* (Oxford; New York: Oxford University Press, 2004)

Gewirth, Alan. *The Community of Rights* (Chicago: University of Chicago Press, 1996)

Ghosh, Rishab Aiyer. *CODE: Collaborative Ownership and the Digital Economy* (Cambridge, MA: MIT Press, 2005)

Godoy, Horacio H., and Gustavo Matus Lagos. *Revolution of Being: A Latin American View of the Future* (New York: Free Press, 1977)

Goldman, Jeffrey, et al. *Participatory Sensing: A Citizen-Powered Approach to Illuminating the Patterns That Share Our World* (Washington, DC: Woodrow Wilson International Center for Scholars, 2009), available at http://wilsoncenter.org/sites/default/files/ participatory_sensing.pdf (accessed July 27, 2012)

Goldman, Michael (ed.). *Privatizing Nature: Political Struggles for the Global Commons* (New Brunswick, NJ: Rutgers University Press, 1998)

Goodell, Jeff. *How to Cool the Planet: Geoengineering and the Audacious Quest to Fix the Earth's Climate* (Boston: Houghton Mifflin Harcourt, 2010)

Gore, Al. *An Inconvenient Truth* (Emmaus, PA: Rodale, 2006)

———. *Earth in the Balance: Ecology and the Human Spirit* (Boston: Houghton Mifflin Co. 1992)

———. *Our Choice: A Plan to Solve the Climate Crisis* (Emmaus, PA: Rodale, 2009)

Gormley, W. PaUL. *Human Rights and the Environment: The Need for International Cooperation* (1976)

Gosseries, Axel, and Lukas H. Meyer (eds.). *Intergenerational Justice* (Oxford; New York: Oxford University Press, 2009)

Goulet, Denis. *The Uncertain Promise: Value Conflicts in Technology Transfer* (New York: New Horizons Press, New ed., 1989)

Graeber, David. *Debt: The First 5,000 Years* (Brooklyn, NY: Melville House, 2011)

Grear, Anna (ed.). *Should Trees Have Standing? 40 Years On* (Cheltenham, UK: Edward Elgar, 2012)

Griller, Stefan, and Jacques Ziller (eds.). *The Lisbon Treaty: EU Constitutionalism without a Constitutional Treaty?* (Vienna; New York: Springer, 2008)

Grinlington, David, and Prue Taylor (eds.). *Property Rights and Sustainability: The Evolution of Property Rights to meet Ecological Challenges* (Boston, MA: Martinus Nijhoff Publishers, 2012)

Hagel III, John, John Seely Brown, and Lang Davison. *The Power of Pull: How Small Moves, Smartly Made, Can Set Big Things in Motion* (New York: Basic Books, 2010)

Hannum, Hurst (ed.). *Guide to International Human Rights Practice* (Ardsley, NY: Transnational Publishers, 4th ed. 2004)

Hansen, James. *Storms of My Grandchildren: The Truth About the Coming Climate Catastrophe and Our Last Chance to Save Humanity* (New York: Bloomsbury, 2009)

Hardt, Michael, and Antonio Negri. *Commonwealth* (Cambridge, MA; London: The Belknap Press of Harvard University, 2009)

Hargrove, John Lawrence (ed.). *Law, Institutions, and the Global Environment* (Leiden: Oceana Publications Inc./A.W. Sijthoff, 1972)

Harvey, David. *A Brief History of Neoliberalism* (New York: Oxford University Press, 2005)

Hawken, Paul. *Blessed Unrest: How the Largest Social movement in History Is Restoring Grace, Justice, and Beauty to the World* (New York: Viking, 2007)

Heinberg, Richard. *The End of Growth: Adapting to Our New Economic Reality* (Gabriola Island, BC, Canada: New Society Publishers, 2011)

Held David. *Cosmopolitanism: Ideals and Realities* (Cambridge, UK; Malden, MA: Polity Press, 2010)

————. *Democracy and the Global Order* (Stanford, CA: Stanford University Press, 1995)

Held, David, Angus Fane-Hervey, and Marika Theros (eds.). *The Governance of Climate Change: Science, Economics, Politics and Ethics* (Cambridge, UK: Polity, 2011)

Held, David, and Mathais [sic] Koenig-Archibugi (eds.). *Global Governance and Public Accountability* (Malden, MA: Blackwell, 2005)

Heller, Michael. *The Gridlock Economy: How too Much Ownership Wrecks Markets, Stops Innovation and Costs Lives* (New York: Basic Books, 2008)

Henkin, Louis. *The Age of Rights* (New York: Columbia University Press, 1996)

Hindley, Geoffrey. *A Brief History of the Magna Carta* (Philadelphia, PA: Running Press Book Publishers, 2008)

Hippel, Eric von. *Democratizing Innovation* (Cambridge, MA: MIT Press, 2005)

Hiskes, Richard P. *The Human Right to a Green Future: Environmental Rights and Intergenerational Justice* (Cambridge, UK; New York: Cambridge University Press, 2009)

Hoeschele, Wolfgang. *The Economics of Abundance: A Political Economy of Freedom, Equity, and Sustainability* (Farnham, Surrey, UK; Burlington, VT: Gower, 2010)

Holland, John H. *Hidden Order: How Adaptation Builds Complexity* (Reading, MA: Addison-Wesley, 1995)

————. *Emergence: From Chaos to Order* (Reading, MA: Addison-Wesley, 1998)

Hopkins, Rob. *The Transition Handbook: From Oil Dependency to Locl Resilience* (White River Jct., VT: Chelsea Green Publishing, 2008)

Humphreys, Stephen J. (ed.). *Human Rights and Climate Change* (Cambridge, UK: Cambridge University Press, 2010)

Hyde, Lewis. *Common as Air: Revolution, Imagination and Ownership* (New York: Farrar Straus and Giroux, 2010)

Illich, Ivan. *Deschooling Society* (New York: Harper & Row, 1971)

————. *Medical Nemesis* (New York: Pantheon Books, 2d ed., 1982)

————. *Tools for Conviviality* (New York: Harper and Row, 1973)

————. *Shadow Work* (Boston: Marion Boyars, 1981)

Jacoby, Karl. *Crimes Against Nature: Squatters, Poachers, Thieves and the Hidden History of American Conservation* (Berkeley: University of California Press, 1st paperback printing, 2003)

Jenkins, Jerry C. *Climate Change in the Adirondacks: The Path to Sustainability* (Ithaca, NY: Cornell University Press; Wildlife Conservation Society, 2010)

————. *The Adirondack Atlas: A Geographic Portrait of the Adirondack Park* (Syracuse, NY: Syracuse University Press: Adirondack Museum, 2004)

Johnson, Steven. *Emergence: The Connected lives of Ants, Brains, Cities and Software* (New York: Scribner, 2001)

Joyner, Christopher C. *Governing the Frozen Commons: The Antarctic Regime and Environmental Protection* (Columbia, SC: University S. Carolina Press, 1998)

Kaldor, Mary. *Global Civil Society: An Answer to War* (Cambridge, UK: Polity Press, 2003)

———. *Human Security: Reflections on Globalization and Intervention* (Cambridge, UK: Malden, MA: Polity Press, 2007)

———. *New and Old Wars: Organized Violence in a Global Era* (Stanford, CA: Stanford University Press, 1999)

Kauffman, Stuart. *Origins of Order: Self-Organization and Selection in Evolution* (New York: Oxford University Press, 1993)

Kaza, Stephanie. *Hooked! Buddhist Writings on Greed, Desire and the Urge To Consume* (Boston: Shambhala, 2005)

Kelty, Christopher M. *Two Bits: The Cultural Significance of Free Software* (Durham, NC: Duke University Press, 2008)

Kennedy, Robert F. Jr. *Crimes Against Nature: How George W. Bush and His Corporate Pals Are Plundering the Country and Hijacking Our Democracy* (New York: Harper Collins, 2004)

Kennett, Douglas J., and Bruce Winterhalder (eds.). *Behavioral Ecology and the Transition to Agriculture* (Berkeley, CA: University of California Press, 2006)

Keynes, John Maynard. *The General Theory of Employment, Interest and Money* (London: Macmillan, 1936)

Kintisch, Eli. *Hack the Planet: Science's Best Hope – Or Worst Nightmare – For Averting Climate Catastrophe* (Hoboken, NJ: John Wiley & Sons, 2010)

Kiss, Alexandre and Dinah Shelton. *Guide to International Environmental Law* (Boston: Martinus Nijhoff Publishers, 2007)

———. *International Environmental Law* (Ardsley, NY: Transnational Publishers, 2004)

———. *International Environmental Law: 1994 Supplement* (Ardsley, NY: Transnational Publishers, 1994)

Kolbert, Elizabeth. *Field Notes from a Catastrophe: Man, Nature, and Climate Change* (New York: Bloomsbury, 2006)

Korten, David C. *The Great Turning: From Empire to Earth Community* (San Francisco: Berrett-Koehler Publishers Inc., 2006)

Kothari, Rajni. *Footsteps Into the Future: Diagnosis of the Present and a Design for an Alternative* (New York: Free Press, 1975, c1974)

Kravchenko, Svitlana, and John E. Bonine (eds. and contribs.), *Human Rights and the Environment: Cases, Law, and Policy* (Durham, NC: Carolina Academic Press, 2008)

Larmuseau, Isabelle (ed.). *Constitutional Rights to an Ecologically Balanced Environment* (Ghent: Vlaamse Vereniging voor Omgevingsrecht, 2007)

Leopold, Aldo. *A Sand County Almanac: With Essays on Conservation from Round River* (New York: Oxford University Press, 1968)

Leib, Linda Hajjar. *Human Rights and the Environment: Philosophical, Theoretical and Legal Perspectives* (Leiden; Boston: Martinus Nijhoff Publishers, 2011)

Lessig, Lawrence. *Code and Other Laws of Cyberspace* (New York Basic Books, 1999)

Lietaer, Bernard A. *The Future of Money: Creating New Wealth, Work and a Wiser World* (London: Century, 2001)

Linebaugh, Peter. *The Magna Carta Manifesto: Liberties and Commons for All* (Berkeley, CA: University of California Press, 2008)

Logue, John J. (ed.). *The Fate of the Oceans* (Villanova, PA; Villanova University Press, 1972)

Lovelock, James. *The Revenge of Gaia: Why the Earth Is Fighting Back – and How We Can Still Save Humanity* (New York: Basic Books, 2006)

———. *The Vanishing Face of Gaia: A Final Warning* (New York: Basic Books, 2009)

Lynas, Mark. *Six Degrees: Our Future on a Hotter Planet* (Washington, DC: National Geographic Society, 2008)

Jones, Gareth Lovett, and Richard Mabey. *The Wildwood: The in Search of Britain's Ancient Forests* (London: Aurum Press, 1993)

Mahoney, Kathleen, and Paul Mahoney (eds.). *Human Rights in the Twenty-First Century: A Global Challenge* (Dordrecht; Boston: M. Nijhoff; Norwell, MA: Kluwer Academic Publishers [distributor], 1993)

Maeckelbergh, Marianne. *The Will of the Many: How the Alterglobalisation Movement Is Changing the Face of Democracy* (London; New York: Pluto Press; New York: Palgrave Macmillan [distributor], 2009)

Mäki, Uskali. *The Economic World View: Studies in the Ontology of Economics* (Cambridge, UK; New York: Cambridge University Press, 2001)

Marshall, Graham R. *Economics for Collaborative Environmental Management: Renegotiating the Commons* (Sterling, VA: Earthscan, 2005)

Martinez, Steve, et al. *Local Food Systems: Concepts, Impacts, and Issues* (Washington, DC: US Department of Agriculture, Economic Research Service, 2010)

Mastrantonio, J. Louise, and John K. Francis. *A Student Guide to Tropical Forest Conservation* (New Orleans, LA: US Department of Agriculture, Forest Service, Southern Forest Experiment Station 1997)

Mattei, Ugo, and Laura Nader. *Plunder: When the Rule of Law is Illegal* (Malden, MA; Oxford: Blackwell Publishing, 2008)

Mazrui, Ali A. *A World Federation of Cultures: An African Perspective* (New York: Free Press, 1976)

McDougal, Myres S., et al. *Studies in World Public Order* (New Haven, CT: New Haven Press; Dordrecht: M. Nijhoff, 1987)

McDougal, Myres S., and Florentino P. Feliciano. *The International Law of War* (New Haven, CT: New Haven Press; Dordrecht; Boston: M. Nijhoff; Norwell, MA: Kluwer Academic Publishers [distributor], 1994)

McDougal, Myres S., Harold D. Lasswell, and Lung-chu Chen. *Human Rights and World Public Order: The Basic Policies of an International Law of Human Dignity* (New Haven, CT: Yale University Press, 1980)

McGarity, Thomas O., Sidney Shapiro, and David Bollier. *Sophisticated Sabotage: The Intellectual Games Used To Subvert Responsible Regulation* (Washington, DC: Environmental Law Institute, 2004)

McHarg, Ian. *Design with Nature* (Garden City, NY: American Museum of Natural History, Natural History Press, 1969)

McKay, Bonnie J. and James M. Acheson (eds.). *The Question of the Commons: The Culture and Ecology of Communal Resources* (Tucson, AZ: University of Arizona Press, 1987)

McKibben, Bill. *Deep Economy: The Wealth of Communities and the Durable Future* (New York: Henry Holt & Co., 2007)
_____. *Eaarth: Making a Life on a Tough New Planet* (New York: Henry Holt and Co., 2010)
_____. *The End of Nature* (New York: Anchor Books, 2d ed., 1999)
_____. *Wandering Home: A Long Walk Across America's Most Hopeful Landscape: Vermont's Champlain Valley and New York's Adirondacks* (New York: Crown Journeys, 2005)
McLuckie, Craig W., and Aubrey McPhail. *Ken Saro Wiwa: Writer and Political Activist* (Boulder, CO: Lynne Rienner Publishers, 2000)
McNeill, J.R. *Something New Under the Sun: An Environmental History of the Twentieth-Century World* (New York: W.W. Norton & Co., 2000)
Meadows, Dennis L. (ed.). *Alternatives to Growth–I: A Search for Sustainable Futures* (Cambridge, MA: Ballinger Publishing Co., 1977)
Meadows, Dennis L., et al. (eds.). *Beyond Growth: Essays on Alternative Futures* (New Haven, CT: Yale University School of Forestry and Environmental Studies, 1975)
Meadows, Donella H. *Meadows, Thinking in Systems: A Primer* (White River Junction, VT: Chelsea Green Publishing, 2008)
Meadows, Donella H., Dennis L. Meadows, and Jørgen Randers. *The Limits to Growth: A Report for the Club of Rome's Project on the Predicament of Mankind* (New York: Universal Books, 1972)
Meadows, Donella H., Jørgen Randers, and Dennis L. Meadows. *The Limits to Growth: The 30-Year Update* (White River Junction, VT: Chelsea Green Publishing., 2004)
Mendlovitz, Saul H. (ed.). *On the Creation of a Just World Order: Preferred Worlds for the 1990s* (New York: The Free Press, 1975)
Mendlovitz, Saul H., and Burns H. Weston (eds. & contribs). *Preferred futures for the United Nations* (Irvington-on-Hudson, NY: Transnational Publishers, 1995)
Miller, John H. *Complex Adaptive Systems: An Introduction to Computational Models of Social Life* (Princeton, NJ: Princeton University Press, 2007)
Milun, Kathryn. *The Political Uncommons: The Cross-Cultural Logic of the Global Commons* (Farmham, Surrey, England; Burlington, VT: Ashgate Publishing Ltd.; Ashgate Publishing Co., 2011)
Minow, Martha. *Between Vengeance and Forgiveness: Facing History After Genocide and Mass Violence* (Boston: Beacon Press, 1998)
Moore, Kathleen Dean, and Michael P. Nelson (eds.). *Moral Ground: Ethical Action for a Planet in Peril* (San Antonio, TX: Trinity University Press, 2010)
Mortensen, Gretchen, and Joshua Rosner. *Reckless Endangerment: How Outsized Ambition, Greed and Corruption Led to Economic Armageddon* (New York: Times Books, 2011)
Moyn, Samuel. *The Last Utopia: Human Rights in History* (Cambridge, MA; London: The Belknap Press of Harvard University, 2010)
Myers, Nancy J., and Carolyn Raffensperger (eds.). *Precautionary Tools for Reshaping Environmental Policy* (Cambridge, MA: MIT. Press, 2006)
Nafziger, James A.R., and Robert Kirkwood Paterson. *Alison Dundes Renteln Cultural Law: International, Comparative, and Indigenous* (Cambridge, UK; New York: Cambridge University Press, 2010)

Nash, Roderick Frazier. *The Rights of Nature: A History of Environmental Ethics* (Madison, WI: University of Wisconsin Press, 1989)

National Research Council. *Committee on the Human Dimensions of Global Change: The Drama of the Commons*. (Washington, DC: National Academy Press, 2002)

Nonini, Donald K. (ed.) *The Global Idea of "The Commons"* (New York: Berghahn Books, 2007)

Norgaard, Kari Marie. *Living in Denial: Climate Change, Emotions, and Everyday Life* (Cambridge, MA: MIT Press, 2011)

Norton, Bryan G. *Sustainability: A Philosophy of Adaptive Ecosystem Management* (Chicago: University of Chicago Press, 2005)

Nowak, Martin A. (with Roger Highfield). *Super Cooperators: Altruism, Evolution and Why We Need Each Other to Succeed* (Edinburgh; New York: Canongate, 2011)

Nussbaum, Arthur. *A Concise History of the Law of Nations* (New York: MacMillan, rev. ed. 1954)

Nussbaum, Martha, and Amartya K. Sen (eds.). *The Quality of Life* (Oxford: Oxford University Press, 1993)

Olson, Mancur. *The Logic of Collective Action* (Cambridge, MA: Harvard University Press, 1971)

Olson, Mancur, and Hans H. Landsberg (eds.). *The No-Growth Society* (New York: W.W. Norton & Co., 1973)

O'Neil, Mathieu. *Cyber Chiefs: Autonomy and Authority in Online Tribes* (London; New York: Pluto Press; Palgrave Macmillan [distributor], 2009)

Orr, David W. *Down to the Wire: Confronting Climate Collapse* (Oxford, New York: Oxford University Press, 2009)

————. *Hope Is an Imperative: The Essential* (Washington, DC: Island Press, 2011)

Osborn, Fairfield. *Our Plundered Planet* (Boston: Little, Brown, 1948)

Ostrom, Elinor. *Governing the Commons: The Evolution of Institutions for Collective Action* (Cambridge, UK; New York: Cambridge University Press, 1990)

————. *Understanding Institutional Diversity* (Princeton, NJ: Princeton University Press, 2005)

Page, Edward A. *Climate Change, Justice and Future Generations* (Cheltenham, UK; Northampton, MA: Edward Elgar, 2006)

Patel, Raj. *The Value of Nothing: How to Reshape Market Society and Redefine Democracy* (New York: Picador, 2010, c2009)

Pauly, Daniel, and Jay Maclean. *In A Perfect Ocean: The State of Fisheries and Ecosystems in the North Atlantic Ocean* (Washington, DC: Island Press, 2003)

Peccei, Aurelio. *The Human Quality* (Oxford, New York: Pergamon Press, 1977)

Picolotti, Romina, and Jorge Daniel Taillant (eds.). *Linking Human Rights and the Environment* (Tucson, AZ: University of Arizona Press, 2003)

Pirages, Dennis C. (ed.). *The Sustainable Society: Implications for Limited Growth* (New York: Praeger Publishers Inc., 1977)

Pirages, Dennis C., and Theresa Manley DeGeest. *Ecological Security: An Evolutionary Perspective on Globalization* (Lanham, MD: Rowman and Littlefield, 2004)

Pirages, Dennis C., and Paul R. Ehrlich. *Ark II: Social Response to Environmental Imperatives* (W.H. Freeman and Co. 1974)

Pogge, Thomas Winfried Menko. *World Poverty and Human Rights: Cosmopolitan Responsibilities and Reforms* (Cambridge, UK; Malden, MA: Polity Press, 2d ed., 2008)

Polayni, Karl. *The Great Transformation: The Political and Economic Origins of Our Time* (Boston: Beacon Press, 1944/1957/2001)

Porter, Gareth, Janet Welsh Brown, and Pamela S. Chasek. *Global Environmental Politics* (Boulder, CO: Westview Press, 3d ed., 2000)

Poteete, Amy R., Marco A. Janssen, and Elinor Ostrom. *Working Together: Collective Action, the Commons, and Multiple Methods in Practice* (Princeton, NJ: Princeton University Press, 2010)

Price, Richard. *Rainforest Warriors: Human Rights on Trial* (Philadelphia: University of Pennsylvania Press, 2011)

Princen, Thomas. *The Logic of Sufficiency* (Cambridge, MA: MIT Press, 2005)

Rawls, John. *Theory of Justice* (Cambridge, MA; London: The Belknap Press of Harvard University, 1971)

Reisman, W. Michael. *Law in Brief Encounters* (New Haven, CT: Yale University Press, 1999)

Reisman, W. Michael, and Burns H. Weston (eds.). *Toward World Order and Human Dignity: Essays in Honor of Myres S. McDougal* (New York: The Free Press, 1976)

Renteln, Alison Dundes, and Alan Dundes (eds.). *Folk Law: Essays in the Theory and Practice of Lex Non Scripta* (New York: Garland Publishing., 1994)

Revkin, Andrew. *The Burning Season: The Murder of Chico Mendes and the Fight for the Amazon Rain Forest* (Washington, DC: Island Press, 2004)

Ridgeway, James. *It's All for Sale: The Control of Global Resources* (Durham, NC: Duke University Press, 2004)

Robertson, A.H., and J.G. Merrills. *Human Rights in the World: An Introduction to the Study of the International Protection of Human Rights* (Manchester, UK; New York: Manchester University Press, 3d ed., 1992)

Rockström, Johan, and Mattias Klum. *The Human Quest: Prospering within Planetary Boundaries* (Stockholm: Bokförlaget Langenskiöld, 2012)

Rodell, Fred. *Nine Men: A Political History of the Supreme Court from 1790 to 1955* (New York: Random House, 1955)

Rodriguez, Sylvia. *Acequia: Water Sharing, Sanctity and Place* (Santa Fe, NM: School for Advanced Research Press, 2006)

Rose, Carol M. *Property and Persuasion: Essays on the History, Theory and Rhetoric of Ownership* (Boulder, CO: Westview Press, 1994)

Rotberg, Robert I. and Dennis Thompson (eds.). *Truth and Justice: The Morality of Truth Commissions* (Princeton, NJ: Princeton University Press, 2000)

Royte, Elizabeth. *Bottlemania: Big Business, Local Springs and the Battle over America's Drinking Water* (New York: Bloomsbury, 2008)

Ruskin, John. *Unto This Last: Four Essays on the First Principles of Political Economy* (London: Smith, Elder & Co., 1862)

Sagoff, Mark. *The Economy of the Earth: Philosophy, Law, and the Environment* (Cambridge, UK; New York: Cambridge University Press, 1988)

Salingaros, Nikos A. *Twelve Lectures on Architecture: Algorithmic Sustainable Design* (Solingen, Germany: Umbau-Verlag, 2010)

Samuelson, Paul A., and William D. Nordhaus. *Economics* (New York: McGraw-Hill, 17th ed. 2001)

Sands, Philippe. *Principles of International Environmental Law* (Cambridge, UK: Cambridge University Press, 2d ed., 2003)

Schaefer, Paul. *Defending the Wilderness: The Adirondack Writings of Paul Schaefer* (Syracuse, NY: Syracuse University Press, 1989)

Schneider, Jan. *World Public Order of the Environment: Towards an International Ecological Law and Organization* (Toronto: University of Toronto Press, 1979)

Schor, Juliet B. *Plenitude: The New Economics of True Wealth* (New York: Penguin Press, 2010)

Schroyer, Trent. *Beyond Western Economics: Remembering Other Economic Cultures* (New York: Routledge, 2009)

Scruton, Roger. *How To Think Seriously about the Planet: The Case for Environmental Conservatism* (Oxford, New York: Oxford University Press, 2012)

Segger, Marie-Claire Cordonier, and C.G. Weeramantry (eds.). *Sustainable Justice: Reconciling Economic, Social and Environmental Law* (Leiden; Boston: M. Nijhoff, 2005)

Sen, Amarta K. *The Idea of Justice* (Cambridge, MA: Belknap Press of Harvard University Press, 2009)

_____. *The Standard of Living* (Cambridge, UK; New York: Cambridge University Press, 1987)

Sennett, Richard. *Together: The Rituals, Pleasures and Politics of Cooperation* (New Haven, CT: Yale University Press, 2012)

Shelton, Dinah, and Alexandre Kiss. *Judicial Handbook on Environmental Law* (Nairobi, Kenya: United Nations Environment Programme, 2005)

Shendler, Auden. *Getting Green Done: Hard Truths from the Front Lines of the Sustainability Revolution* (New York: Public Affairs, 2010)

Shirky, Clay. *Here Comes Everybody: The Power of Organizing Without Organizations* (New York: Penguin Press, 2008)

Shiva, Vandana. *Globalisation, Food Security, and War* (Port Louis, Mauritius: Ledikasyon pu travayer, 2002)

_____. *Protect or Plunder? Understanding Intellectual Property Rights* (London; New York: Zed Books, 2001)

_____. *The Corporate Control of Life (Die Kontrolle von Konzernen über das Leben)* (Ostfildern, Germany: Hatje Cantz, 2011)

_____. *Water Wars: Privatization, Pollution and Profit* (Toronto: Between the Lines, 2002)

Shoumatoff, Alex. *The World Is Burning: Murder in the Rain Forest* (Boston: Little, Brown, 1990)

Sigmund, Paul E. (ed.). *The Selected Political Writings of John Locke: Texts, Background Selections, Sources, Interpretations* (New York: W.W. Norton, 2005)

Symonides, Janusz (ed.). *Human Rights: New Dimensions and Challenges* (Aldershot; Brookfield, VT: Ashgate, 1998)

Smith, Yves. *ECONned: How Unenlightened Self-Interest Undermined Democracy and Corrupted Capitalism* (New York: Palgrave Macmillan, 2010)

Snitow, Alan, and Deborah Kaufman (with Michael Fox). *Thirst: Fighting the Corporate Theft of Our Water* (San Francisco: Jossey-Bass, 2007)

Sober, Elliot, and David Sloan Wilson. *Unto Others: The Evolution and Psychology of Unselfish Behavior* (Cambridge, MA: Harvard University Press, 1998)

Soto, Hernando de. *The Mystery of Capital: Why Capitalism Triumphs in the West and Fails Elsewhere* (New York: Carnegie Council on Ethics and International Affairs, 2002)

Specter, Michael. *Denialism: How Irrational Thinking Harms the Planet and Threatens Our Lives* (New York: Penguin Press, 2009)

Speth, James Gustave. *Red Sky at Morning: America and the Crisis of the Global Environment* (New Haven: Yale University Press, 2004)

_____. *The Bridge at the Edge of the World: Capitalism, the Environment, and Crossing from Crisis to Sustainability* (New Haven: Yale University Press, 2008)

Sprankling, John, Raymond R. Coletta and M.C. Mirow. *Global Issues in Property Law* (St. Paul, MN: Thomson/West, 2006)

Stager, Curt. *Deep Future: The Next 100,000 Years of Life on Earth* (New York: Thomas Dunne Books, St. Martin's Press, 2011)

Stern, Sir Nicholas. *The Economics of Climate Change: The Stern Review* (Cambridge, UK; New York: Cambridge University Press, 2007)

Stiglitz, Joseph E, and Carl E. Walsh. *Economics* (New York: W.W. Norton, 3d ed., 2002)

Stone, Christopher D. *Should Trees Have Standing?: Law, Morality, and the Environment* (Oxford, New York: Oxford University Press, 3d ed., 2010)

Swindler, William F. *Magna Carta: Legend and Legacy* (Indianapolis, IN: Bobbs-Merrill, 1966, c1965)

Talberth, John, et al. *Building a Resilient and Equitable Bay Area: Towards a Coordinated Strategy for Economic Localization* (San Francisco: Center for Sustainable Economy, 2006), available at www.sustainable-economy.org (accessed July 29, 2012)

Tapscott, Don and Anthony D. Williams. *Wikinomics: How Mass Collaboration Changes Everything* (New York: Portfolio, expanded ed., 2008)

Tarnas, Richard. *The Passion of the Western Mind: Understanding the Ideas That Have Shaped Our World View* (New York: Ballantine, 1993, c1991)

The Ecologist. *Whose Common Future? Reclaiming the Commons* (Philadelphia: New Society, 1993)

The Rights of Nature: The Case for a Universal Declaration of the Rights of Mother Earth (Ottawa, ON: Council of Canadians, Fundación Pachamama, and Global Exchange, 2011)

Titmuss, Richard M. *The Gift Relationship: From Human Blood to Social Policy* (New York: Pantheon Books, 1971)

Tremmel, Jörg Chet. *A Theory of Intergenerational Justice* (London; Sterling, VA: Earthscan, 2009)

Tremmel, Jörg Chet (ed.). *Handbook of Intergenerational Justice* (Cheltenham, UK; Northampton, MA: Edward Elgar, 2006)

Valaskakis, Kimon et al. *The Conserver Society: A Workable Alternative for the Future* (New York: Harper and Row, 1979)

Van der Ryn, Sim, and Stuart Cowan. *Ecological Design* (Washington, DC: Island Press, 10th anniversary ed., 2007)

Vasak, Karel (ed.). *The International Dimensions of Human Rights* (revised and edited for the English transl. by Philip Alston) (Westport, CT: Greenwood Press; Paris, France: UNESCO, 1982)

Vásquez Castillo, María Teresa. *Land Privatizaion in Mexico: Urbanization, Formation of Region and Globalization in Ejidos* (New York: Routledge, 2004)

Victor, David G. *Climate Change: Debating America's Policy Options* (New York: Council on Foreign Relations, 2004)

Wade, Robert. *Village Republics: Economic Conditions for Collective Action in South India* (Cambridge, UK; New York: Cambridge University Press, 1988)

Waldron, Jeremy. *Liberal Rights: Collected Papers 1981–1991* (Cambridge, UK: Cambridge University Press, 1993)

Waldrop, M. Mitchell. *Complexity: The Emerging Science at the Edge of Order and Chaos* (New York: Simon & Schuster, 1992)

Walker, Brian, and David Salt. *Resilience Thinking: Sustaining Ecosystems and People in a Changing World* (Washington: Island Press, 2006)

Ward, Barbara. *A New Creation? Reflections on the Environmental Issue* (Vatican City: Pontifical Commission Justice and Peace 1973)

Watson, J. Shand. *Theory and Reality in the International Protection of Human Rights* (Ardsley, NY: Transnational Publishers, 1999)

Weber, Steven., *The Success of Open Source* (Cambridge, MA: Harvard University Press, 2004)

──────. *Spaceship Earth* (New York: Columbia University Press, 1966)

Weston, Burns H. and Tracy Bach. *Recalibrating the Law of Humans with the Laws of Nature: Climate Change, Human Rights, and Intergenerational Justice* (South Royalton, VT: Vermont Law School and University of Iowa Climate Legacy Initiative, 2009)

Weston, Burns H. (ed.). *Child Labor and Human Rights: Making Children Matter* (Boulder, CO; London: Lynne Rienner Publishers, 2005)

Weston, Burns H., and Stephen P. Marks (eds. & contribs). *The Future of International Human Rights* (Ardsley, NY: Transnational Publishers, 1999)

Westra, Laura. *Environmental Justice and the Rights of Unborn and Future Generations: Law, Environmental Harm, and the Right to Health* (London; Sterling, VA: Earthscan, 2006)

──────. *Human Rights: The Commons and the Collective* (Vancouver, B.C.: UBC Press, 2011)

Wilson, Edward O. *The Diversity of Life* (Cambridge, MA; London: The Belknap Press of Harvard University, 1992)

──────. *The Future of Life* (New York: Vintage Books, 2002)

──────. *The Social Conquest of Earth* (New York: W.W. Norton and Co, 2012)

Wilson E. O. (ed.). *Biodiversity* (Washington, DC: National Academy Press, 1988)

Winner, Langdon. *The Whale and the Reactor: A Search for Limits in an Age of High Technology* (Chicago: University of Chicago Press, 1986)

Wood, Mary Christina. *Nature's Trust: Environmental Law for a New Ecological Age* (forthcoming from Cambridge University Press, 2013)

Woodin, Nick. *The Natural History of the Present* (Create Space, 2011)

Young, Oran R. *Governance for the Environment: New Perspectives Governance for the Environment: New Perspectives* (Cambridge, UK; New York: Cambridge University Press, 2009)

──────. *Institutional Dynamics: Emergent Patterns in International Environmental Governance* (Cambridge, MA: MIT Press, 2010)

———. *Limits to Privatization: How to Avoid Too Much of a Good Thing: A Report to the Club of Rome* (Cambridge, MA: MIT Press, 1999)

———. *The Effectiveness of International Environmental Regimes: Causal Connections and Behavioral Mechanisms* (London, Sterling, VA: Earthscan, 2005)

Zittrain, Jonathan. *The Future of the Internet and How to Stop It* (New Haven, CT: Yale University Press, 2008)

Zupko, Ronald Edward, and Robert A. Laures. *Straws in the Wind: Medieval Urban Environmental Law – The Case of Northern Italy* (Boulder, CO: Westview Press, 1996)

Index

CPSIA information can be obtained at www.ICGtesting.com
Printed in the USA
LVOW10s0651060414

380499LV00006B/58/P